ISBN 2-84707-110-5
«Formula 1 Yearbook 2006-07» is also published
in French language under the title «L'Année Formule 1 2006-07» (ISBN 2-84707-109-1),
in Spanish language under the title «El Año de la Formula 1 2006-07» (ISBN 2-84707-127-X)
in Romanian language under the title «Anul Formulei 1 2006-07» (ISBN 2-84707-126-1)

© November 2006, Chronosports S.A.

Jordils Park, Rue des Jordils 40, CH-1025 St-Sulpice, Suisse. Tél. : (+41 21) 694 24 44. Fax : (+41 21) 694 24 46.
E-mail: info@chronosports.com   Web: www.chronosports.com

Printed in France by Imprimerie Clerc s.a.s., F-18206 St-Amand Montrond, France.
Bound by Reliures Brun, F-45331 Malesherbes Cedex, France.

Mario Renzi thanks for their technical support Carré Couleur, Nikon France, Picto Lyon, as well as Fuji Film France.
Special thanks to Robert Rui, Nicolas Brunet, Bruno Paré and all the Clerc team.

FORMULA 1 YEARBOOK

2006-07

Photos
Thierry Gromik
Mario Renzi
Laurent Charniaux
Agence WRI
(WRI: Jean-François Galeron & Jad Sherif)

Editor in Chief and Grands Prix reports
Luc Domenjoz

Page layout
Loraine Lequint & Cyril Davillerd
Sétphane Buonamico, Alex Dal Pizzol, Patricia Soler

Results and statistics
Vicky Paradisgarten & Cyril Davillerd

Drawings of the 2006 cars
Pierre Ménard

Gaps and lap charts
Michele Merlino

Translated into English by
David Waldron

CHRONOSPORTS
E D I T E U R

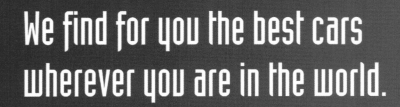

Contents

Foreword

2006 will remain a watershed year in the history of Ferrari. It is true that we did not achieve the objectives that we had set ourselves despite our nine victories and 201 points: namely, to bring the two titles back to Maranello. We missed opportunities to score precious points especially at the start of the season because of reliability was that was not optimal allied to a certain number of errors. These problems finally cost us dearly. But we have to accept the reality of the situation: our rivals were better than us; they made fewer mistakes.

A number of emotional events also marked the year – the difficulties at the start of the season, the fantastic comeback and then the final deception at the end. This year, though, will remain forever engraved in our memories, as it was the last of an exceptional driver and human being: Michael Schumacher. This was evident in the last race in Brazil in which Felipe Massa's magnificent victory was completely overshadowed by Michael's fabulous climb-back up through the field that will remain etched in the mind of motor sport lovers everywhere. The records that he holds – world titles, victories, pole positions, fastest laps, highest number of points – speak for themselves to those who want to find out what he has accomplished in his years in Formula 1. What these figures do not show is what will remain in our heart and in our mind at Ferrari, the man's value, his charisma and the affection that he has for his nearest and dearest and his team.

An extraordinary chapter in the history of Ferrari has just closed; all the more so as two other key members of this decade are also leaving us. Ross Brawn and Paolo Martinelli will not be at the start of the 2007 season.

So a new chapter is opening and we all hope that Ferrari will be a serious contender as has been the case over the past several years. We have a well-balanced duo of drivers including one who is young and talented, who has shown his ability to win races as he already has two victories to his name: Felipe Massa. The other, Kimi Raïkkönen, has demonstrated his capacity to achieve the ultimate objective. The restructuring of the organisation is based on the promotion of people trained inside Ferrari, who embody its values and working methods thus providing all the necessary guarantees for the continuity of our activities.

Everything is in place to open a new page in the history of Ferrari in a winning fashion. We know that we can again count on the permanent backing of our technical partners who have all played a crucial role in our successes.

We realise that we will face very strong rivals, especially considering the fact that all the major motor companies are now present in Formula 1. We are going to concentrate all our efforts in regaining the upper hand while counting on our Tifosi.

Our Tifosi who, on circuits throughout the world, drive us on with their warmth and passion.

Jean Todt
22nd November 2006

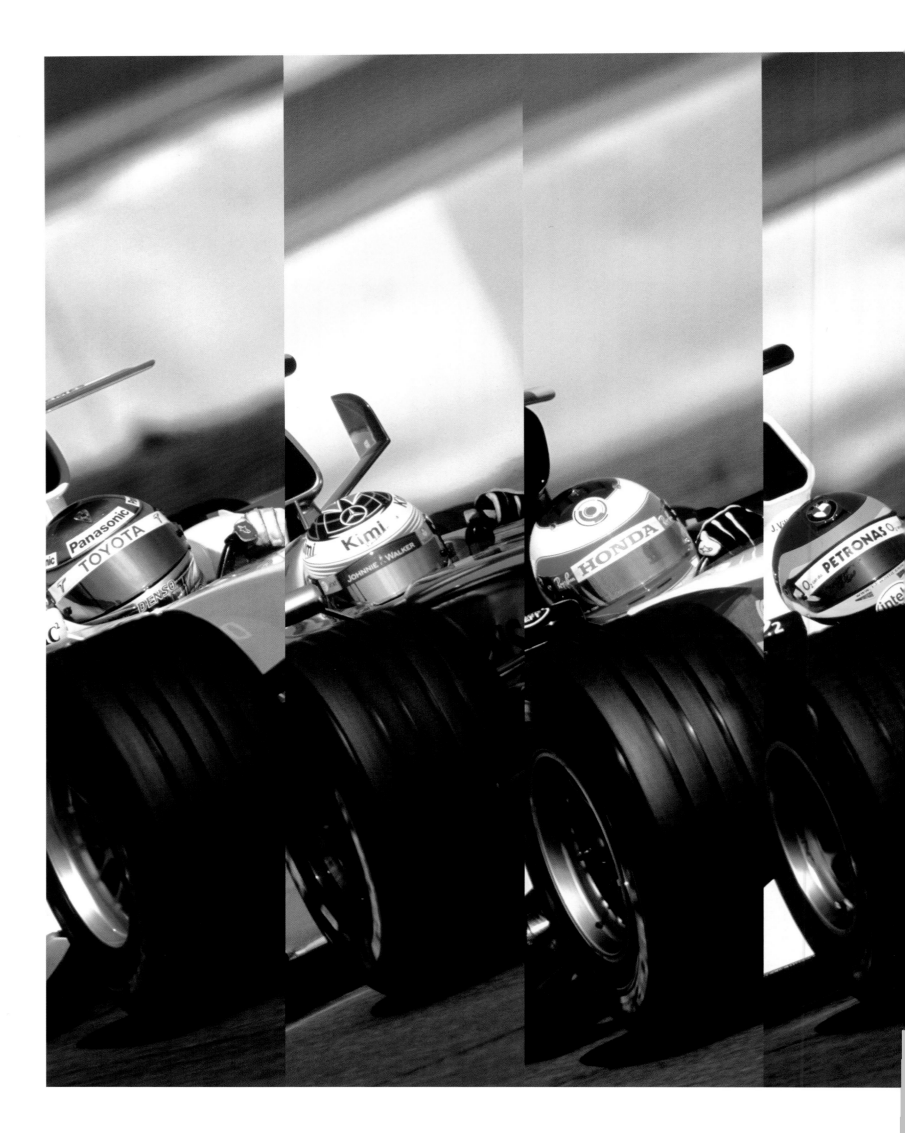

SEASON'S ANALYSIS

The fact that Fernando Alonso won his second title at the tender age of 25 shows, if it were necessary, just how talented he is.
The "little bull from the Asturias" was all the more impressive this season as he had to fight off Michael Schumacher in a Ferrari that was very quick especially in the latter half of the year.
The duel between them was extraordinary, breath-taking full of twists like in a good suspense novel.
The fact that Michael Schumacher lost and Alonso won is probably not the most important thing.
From beginning to end the 2006 season was fantastic and it was on the last lap of the year at Interlagos that Schumacher set the lap record on what was his last lap in a Grand Prix.

> The battle between the German and the Spaniard lasted the whole championship and its eighteen rounds. It was passionately exciting from beginning to end in what was Michael Schumacher's final season.

The five twists in the 2006 season

In thrillers the talent of the author keeps the reader guessing as to the outcome of his story. His skills use a mixture of twists and turns that upset the preconceived ideas of what is going to happen next.

The 2006 season, within certain limits, could have been born of the imagination of such an author. It had a complex scenario, several twists during the year and its conclusion was difficult to foresee two grand prix from the end.

As always during the winter there was a lot of speculation about the competitiveness of the different teams. The various test sessions on circuits like Barcelona and Jerez as well as Bahrain and Silverstone did not really give any clear-cut indications. The Scuderia Ferrari remained faithful to its habits and did not mix with the other teams when shaking down its 248 F1. It did go to Bahrain in February but waited until Honda had left before fitting its car with its final aerodynamics.

When the F1 teams arrived in Bahrain both Renault and McLaren were expected to be the yardsticks because of their 2005 successes. The

Ferrari 248 F1 was an unknown quantity. Not for long, though, as the 2 red cars set the fastest times in qualifying.

In the race Michael Schumacher was beaten to victory by a whisker by Fernando Alonso so the scene as set for the rest of the year. The Renault R26s and the Ferraris were the pick of the field. After this grand prix the season looked like being a very hotly-contested one with the battle for honours being fought out between the Renaults, Ferraris and McLarens as Kimi Räikkönen had finished third in Bahrain. The Williams too had been very quick and Nico Rosberg had set the fastest lap.

In Malaysia and Australia it all went south for Ferrari. At Sepang the cars suffered engine failure and lost 10 places on the grid while down under the team made the wrong tyre choice. When the teams returned to Europe from the overseas grands prix Michael Schumacher had fallen back to fourth place in the championship, and was already 17 points behind Alonso after only 3 races.

The season had just begun and yet it all seemed done and dusted as the Renaults – or rather Alonso – looked on course to win the 2006 championship without problems.

But that was all a bit premature and failed to

> Fernando Alonso refueling. Tricky operation that cost him dearly in Hungary...

take into account the capacity of both Ferrari and Bridgestone to react. The rule change concerning tyres proved a help to the Japanese make. In 2005, it had great difficulty in making rubber that lasted the full distance of a grand prix as required by the regs. It managed to have them changed for 2006 reintroducing tyre changes during the race.

On the Imola circuit the Ferraris were again slower than the Renaults but a cunning piece of driving by Michael Schumacher enabled him to win the race. Two weeks later at the Nürburgring the red cars were quicker than the Renaults for the first time in the 2006 title chase. Schumacher started behind Alosno but managed to overtake him during refuelling.

This second victory on the trot plus the fact that the Ferrari was now quicker than the R26 seemed to indicate that Michael Schumacher was going to win the championship. He was only 13 points behind Alonso with 13 races still to run.

Then came the Spanish Grand Prix on the Barcelona circuit, which is seen as a merciless test of chassis and Alonso proved unbeatable in front of thousands of fans. He then added three more wins to his tally: Monaco, Silverstone and Montreal. The Franco-Spanish car/driver combination seemed invincible.

After the Canadian Grand Prix Alonso's lead over Schumacher was 25 points. The German had done what he could to limit the damage.

In Monaco he was sent to the back of the grid for his faux pas in qualifying and in the other three events he finished in second place.

Nine races: six victories and three-second places;
The R26 was so quick that after nine races it was all over bar the shouting. Alonso had won six and finished the other three in second place. How could such consistency and performance leave Michael Schumacher any hope? He had beaten the Spaniard on only two occasions and at Imola he was slower.

And yet. Against all expectations and due to hard work Ferrari turned the tables on Renault, which slipped back. At Indianapolis the Michelin-shod

^
Lap 37 in the Japanese Grand Prix. It was the end of the dream for Michael Schumacher who retired when he was in the lead handing victory to Fernando Alonso.

^<
Felipe Massa on the Monza circuit. Alonso and Schumacher's team-mates both had a disappointing season and were completely overshadowed by their leaders. The little Brazilian managed to score a couple of victories compared to one for the Italian.

2006 Drivers Championship

	Driver	Team	Wins	Pts
1.	**F. Alonso**	Renault	7	134
2.	M. Schumacher	Ferrari	7	121
3.	F. Massa	Ferrari	2	80
4.	G. Fisichella	Renault	1	72
5.	K. Räikkönen	McLaren Mercedes		65
6.	J. Button	Honda	1	56
7.	R. Barrichello	Honda		30
8.	J. Montoya	McLaren Mercedes		26
9.	N. Heidfeld	BMW Sauber		23
10.	R. Schumacher	Toyota		20
11.	P. de la Rosa	McLaren Mercedes		19
12.	J. Trulli	Toyota		15
13.	D. Coulthard	Red Bull Ferrari		14
14.	M. Webber	Williams Cosworth		7
15.	J. Villeneuve	BMW Sauber		7
16.	R. Kubica	BMW Sauber		6
17.	N. Rosberg	Williams Cosworth		4
18.	C. Klien	Red Bull Ferrari		2
19.	V. Liuzzi	Toro Rosso Cosworth		1
20.	S. Speed	Toro Rosso Cosworth		0
21.	T. Monteiro	Spyker Midland Toyota		0
22.	C. Albers	Spyker Midland Toyota		0
23.	T. Sato	Super Aguri Honda		0
24.	R. Doornbos	Red Bull Ferrari		0
25.	Y. Ide	Super Aguri Honda		0
26.	S. Yamamoto	Super Aguri Honda		0
27.	F. Montagny	Super Aguri Honda		0

Constructors

	Team	Wins	Pts
1.	**Mild Seven Renault F1 Team**	8	206
2.	Scuderia Ferrari Marlboro	9	201
3.	Team McLaren Mercedes		110
4.	Lucky Strike Honda Racing F1 Team	1	86
5.	BMW Sauber F1 Team		72
6.	Panasonic Toyota Racing		35
7.	Red Bull Racing		16
8.	Williams F1 Team		11
9.	Scuderia Toro Rosso		1
10.	Spyker M F1 Team		0
11.	Super Aguri Formula 1		0

analysis

> Nico Rosberg has got what it takes to turn girls'heads as well as his Williams' steering wheel. He scored only 4 points this year, due to a car with poor aerodynamics, but he overshadowed his team-mate, Mark Webber.

> Rubens Barrichello left Ferrari to rebuild his reputation. He messed it up again! This year, he was completely eclipsed by his team-mate Jenson Button, who scored twice as many points as he did.

cars were expected to be slower to avoid a repeat of the previous year's fiasco but then came Magny-Cours. There Schumacher was unbeatable while Alonso finished second. After that it seemed that Lady Luck had chosen the 7-times world champion. At Hockenheim the FIA decided to ban the mass dampers, the anti-vibrations devices around which the R26 had been designed, with immediate effect even though they had been allowed for a year!! The R26 was outpaced on the German circuit and the best Alonso could do was fifth. In Budapest a few more unexpected twists were added to the novel. Alonso was given a 2-second penalty in practice and then a badly-fitted wheel nut put an end to his race when he was on his way to victory. Schumacher was unable to take advantage of the Spaniard's team's foul-up. At the wheel of a car whose tyres were completely shot he collided with Nick Heidfeld's BMW and lost points stupidly as the finish was in sight and all he had to do was to nurse his car home.

In Turkey the Scuderia won the race but victory went to Felipe Massa while Alonso managed to split the 2 Ferraris. It is difficult to understand why the Scuderia did not ask its two drivers to swap positions.

At Monza Alonso was again penalised for having baulked Massa in qualifying –a theoretical baulking given the evidence supplied by the FIA. In the race fate again hit the Renault who had to retire with a blown engine. Michael scored his sixth win of the season and closed the gap to the Spaniard to 2 points.

He got back on level pegging in China. Although the rain was supposed not favour the

---

The old F1 hands know that points lost at the start of the season are very difficult to pull back

---

Bridgestone tyres – Michael qualified sixth – he won the race from his rival. It was a remarkable victory by the German despite the fact that the race started on a wet track. After the Chinese Grand Prix the two drivers had the same number of points. Since Canada Renault had run into a number of problems. The Ferraris were back on the winning trail and it was difficult to see who could stop them. With just 2 grand prix left Alonso's chances of finishing in front of the 248 F1 looked very slim indeed especially as Schumacher was back at the very peak of his form.

And then for the fourth time this season the writer changed the script with another unexpected twist.

At Suzuka under the Japanese sun the race looked like ending in another victory for Michael Schumacher. The drivers' and constructors' titles were on their way back to Maranello until lap 37 when the V8 in Michael's car gave up the ghost in a cloud of white smoke handing victory to Fernando Alonso, who had never given up hope.

> Juan Pablo Montoya's career fizzled out. After making a great start in F1 in his early years at Williams, the Columbian was completely dominated by KR at MacLaren. He couldn't accept this and after a number of desperate manoeuvres to compensate, he was responsible for so many accidents that he ended up leaving F1 after a final crash. But what a beauty, the one at the start of the United States Grand Prix!

This time it looked like the game was up. Michael fought like a lion in the final grand prix of his career on the Interlagos circuit, but in vain. He finished fourth after another couple of twists of fate prevented him from helping Ferrari to the constructors' title. His fuel pump went on the blink in qualifying and he started the race from tenth place on the gird. He was then victim of a puncture in the early stages of the grand prix and he fell back to nineteenth and last place.

Thus, after a final upset the titles went to Fernando Alonso and Renault. But overall it had been a fantastic year full of twists and turns. Even if Michael Schumacher did not win his eighth title he bowed out with his head held high after one of the best races of his career. Although the season was over, one can still play the "what if" game! If Schumacher's engine had not failed with 16 laps to go in the Japanese Grand? If he had not collided with Heidfeld in the Hungarian Grand Prix? If he had not lost 15 points in 2 races at the start of the year? The 248 F1 was undoubtedly the quickest car from the US Grand Prix onwards. But the Scuderia lost too many points early on. The F1 old hands know that points lost at the start of the season are very difficult to pull back.

And the rest?

The duel between Ferando Alonso and Michael Schumacher and Ferrari and Renault overshadowed the rest of the field. Behind them were many disappointed championship hopefuls starting with Felipe Massa and Giancarlo Fisichella who were not up to the job asked of them. The first did not manage to take points away from Alonso by finishing just behind Schumacher (or by moving up a place like at Suzuka for example). The second committed more or less one gaffe per grand prix to such an extent that it kept everybody in a fever of anticipation until it happened! Rarely were we disappointed.

The Honda team was also a letdown. The Anglo-Japanese cars set some shattering times in winter testing and then fell back into anonymity until Hungary. From then on Jenson Button scored more points than the championship leaders but it was too late. Toyota had a disastrous season and fell back down the constructors' classification after its fourth place in 2005. McLaren had a very poor year. Juan Pablo Montoya was given the boot in mid-season while Kimi Räikkönen was only waiting for his transfer to Ferrari. Finally, Williams too had a very mediocre 2006 due to failed aerodynamics; Only on circuits like Bahrain, Melbourne and Monaco where the aerodynamic aspect is not all that important were Mark Webber and Nico Rosberg able to show their talent. Keke's young son looks to have an abundance of it.

The season finished. Michelin withdrew and the fact that Bridgestone is going to supply the whole field with an identical tyre – thus a slower one – will reshuffle the cards in 2007. It is the first post-Schumacher season. And maybe the dawning of the Räikkönen era?

Fernando Alonso: a second title, a second life

"*It's been a fantastic weekend. It's going to take me some time before what's happened sinks in. I'm only 25 and I'm world champion for the second time.*" When Fernando Alonso came down from the rostrum at Interlagos he was almost lost for words. The stress suddenly evaporated. "*I'm going to remember this day all my life,*" he went on. "*Winning the championship after such a duel goes beyond even my wildest dreams.*"
The Spaniard's race became a lot easier when Michael Schumacher suffered a puncture early on in the grand prix. "*When my team told me to reduce the engine revs it was the third lap after the safety car pulled off and I said to myself that it was a strange decision. A few minutes afterwards they told me that Michael was 18th. From then on I just had to remain concentrated. I knew we could win the championship; I always knew it and we deserve it.*"
The new world champion relaxed a little and a few hours later together with his girlfriend he went to the Café de la Musique, a switched-on nightspot that the Renault team had booked to celebrate the end of the season and the new world title.
Alonso got up on stage and spoke to the whole team: "*You've given me a fantastic car and I did my best to become world champion and battle for the constructors' title. We also have to thank the people from Michelin for all the work they've done over the past 3 years. Last year we beat McLaren and this year we've beaten Ferrari. It was all the more difficult as we had to fight both on the track and off it.*"

Not for a long time has a title battle been so indecisive as it went right down to the wire. Only in the last round were the outcomes of the 2006 championships decided. Fernando Alonso remained calm throughout the ups and downs of the season - the mass damper ban and the penalties in Budapest and at Monza. Almost serene as if the battle for the 2006 title had given him a new outlook.
Of course, the fact of having won the championship the previous year helped lessen the pressure that is on those wanting to win it for the first time. He did not hide the fact that part of it was down to the Renault team: "*You too have also taught me a lesson,*" he said during the 22nd October party in the Café de la Musique. "*It's fair play in everything that you do, not only in F1 but also in everyday life. I've learned a lot of things from a personal point of view. You will stay in my heart for ever.*"
In the past Alonso was haughty, disdainful even arrogant but as it went right down to the wire over the course of the 2006 season. Like the majority of drivers he remained fairly detached from his team that he criticised strongly before the Chinese Grand Prix accusing it of being more interested in the constructors' championship, and not wanting to help him to the drivers' title as he would bring the number 1 to McLaren.
This detachment is an integral part of Alonso's personality which is a complex one and difficult to grasp. Some days when he wins he really looks really down ion the mouth: especially at Silverstone this year at the post-race press conference (something that he does not like).

"*It's my way of showing I'm happy,*" he shot back when someone commented on his glum look.
It is necessary to go back to the Spaniard's origins, to his solitary childhood to understand his personality. He comes from a modest family in Oviedo (his father Jose works in the nearby explosives factory and his mother is a cashier in the local supermarket). He sat in a kart at the age of two-and-a-half and had his first race when he was three. Throughout his childhood he raced every weekend and became the Asturias' champion aged eight.
When he was 13 he went to Milan to become a works driver for a make of kart that paid his travel expenses. His schooling consisted of correspondence courses or a few days in Oviedo

"I've learned a lot from being with you. You'll always be in my heart."

What a sweet little boy!
4-year-old Fernando
Alonso sitting in his kart.
ᐯ

from time to time whenever he came home. Up to the age of 17 he lived alone in Italy. He missed his parents and they missed him. He never really had a proper adolescence. He sacrificed everything for motor racing; it was the only thing in his life. He is now the youngest ever back-to-back world champion at the age of twenty-five, and it is easy to understand that it is difficult for him to deal with such a situation.
His new outlook helps him to show greater outward serenity. In the recent past he was haughty and disdainful with his fans, but he is now coming to terms with his role as a star. Up to last year he refused to give autographs considering that it was a waste of time. This year he willingly signed them. After his title he went to Oviedo to salute his fans whereas in the past he ran away from them.
Alonso is beginning to take charge of his existence. Three weeks after the end of the season he left his home in Oxford and bought a house on the shores of Lake Leman in Switzerland. It is a simple little villa adjoining an identical one. When he was moving in he went to offer his neighbours a drink just like anybody else would have done.
After his goodbyes to Renault he is preparing for a new life at McLaren. It is another team, another ambience, and another challenge. Renault was a kind of family for him and he signed a contract with it back in 2000. The French team placed him at Minardi in 2001 and gave him the role of test driver in 2002 before making him a full-time driver in 2003.
McLaren will be a new adventure for the guy from Oviedo. Maybe he will win another title and forge another new outlook.

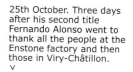

25th October. Three days after his second title Fernando Alonso went to thank all the people at the Enstone factory and then those in Viry-Châtillon.
ᐯ

homage

The career of the greatest driver of all times finished on a score of 7 world titles, 91 victories and 68 pole positions

> We will never see Michael Schumacher at the wheel of an F1 car again. It was a decision that he pondered from Indianapolis onwards and that he justified as follows in Brazil in his 249th Grand Prix. *"I feel that I won't have enough energy to fight at this level in the future. My batteries are flat! There's never a let-up in this business. The season has barely finished when you have to start testing for the next one. This year I felt that the drive was going be lacking if I continued for another season."*

Once upon a time there was a little boy who lived in Kerpen, a small town in the Cologne suburbs. His father, Rolf, built chimneys and his mother Elizabeth looked after a small refreshment stall at a karting track. His name was Michael and he was brought up in very modest surroundings.

When he was 4-years-old his father put together a kart for him and then scrimped and saved to allow him to fulfil his passion for karting. It was the start of the career of most-titled driver of all time, which finished on Sunday 22nd October 2006 after the Brazilian Grand Prix. A chapter in the history of motor sport was closed.

Michael Schumacher is worshipped in Germany but often disparaged elsewhere as he is seen as an arrogant, cold, calculating driver. However, even if his career, which is full of incredible exploits, has also been tainted by some contestable manoeuvres, he is anything but

"When you begin, you think that a good car will fulfil all your desires. But when you've got it, you realise that it doesn't fulfil anything at all."

arrogant. He is a discreet, simple human being who wants only traditional family happiness. It is as if his successes came from his love of driving and were never an end in themselves. After his 15 years in Formula 1 Michael has accumulated a huge fortune estimated at around 500 million euros. But he has always managed to keep his feet on the ground. He knows the price of a litre of milk and buys his digital camera in the supermarket where it is less expensive. He protects his private life and this is no reason to accuse him being full of self-importance.

"I know that not everybody likes me. Life's like that. You'll always find people who detest you," he says philosophically. *"In F1, you spend most of your time hiding quite simply because it's impossible to speak to everybody. And if you avoid people because you're too busy, they accuse you of being arrogant."*

Certainly, part of Michael Schumacher's reputation comes from the fact of the huge amounts of money he has demanded from Ferrari to drive for the team. *"For me that money represents security, nothing more. Perhaps independence too. I think I'm paid in relation to the work I do. I was happy enough with 450 marks when I was an apprentice mechanic. My salary has gone up bit by bit but it has never destabilised me. I hate waste. I never gamble in casinos and I'm very conservative about my investments. In fact, once you've reached a certain figure, money no longer has the same significance."*

Michael also spends to help others although he is very discreet about his philanthropic activities. He has given a commitment to UNESCO, which named him Children's Ambassador in 1996. He has already financed numerous projects including a school in Sarajevo. In 2002, he gave a million euros to help the victims of flooding in central Europe. His donation was even bigger for the 2004 Tsunami without him using this gesture as a way of generating publicity.

He says that he has not got luxury tastes. *"I'm not a complicated bloke. I like being at home with Corinna and the kids and eat a lunch that she's cooked. We haven't got staff in the house and we do our shopping ourselves. My favourite books are action novels and I like listening to Phil Collins or Michael Jackson."*

But he does buy himself the odd expensive toy like a private jet, a Challenger 601P worth over 15 million euros with a bedroom and bathroom. *"Obviously, it's a pretty costly luxury,"* he admits, *"especially as you have to pay two pilots full time. But it's essential for my work. At the French Grand Prix I did private testing in Italy up to 15h00. Three hours later I had to be at Magny-Cours for a Ferrari promotion. I couldn't live this life without my plane."*

Michael emphasizes his taste for simplicity and his love of nature: *"When you begin in motor sport you think that a good car will fulfil all your desires,"* he explains. *"In fact, what you've got it you realise that it fulfils nothing. It's nice to drive, that's all. Today my dreams have nothing to do with motor sport or another world title. I like sitting down at night contemplating the stars; Space fascinates me. I'm a deeply convinced believer. I think nature is the most remarkable thing on this earth."*

Michael and Corinna are the parents of two

children, Gina Maria and Mick Junior. Two children that fill him with happiness. *"I was present at Corinna's side when Gina Maria was born. It was a much more emotional moment than winning a world championship I can tell you. My real ambition has always been to have a family and raise children. You can't ask for anything more than to have children in good health and bring them up correctly. Doing that is much more important than winning any titles."*

These do not seem like the words of a cold, calculating driver.

Henceforth, he will have more time to devote to his family. It is not sure that he will attend all the grands prix in his role as Jean Todt's super assistant. He will probably watch the races on TV. And he says that he will not miss them at all.

Michael Schumacher has always known how to detach himself from Formula 1 and his retirement will allow him to put this philosophy into practice.

The most striking records held by Michael Schumacher

Number of world titles	7	Number of laps in the lead	5108
Number of victories	91	Number of kilometres in the lead	24130
Number of pole positions	68	Number of doubles with his team-mates	30
Number of fastest laps in a race	76	Number of hat tricks (pole, victory and fastest lap)	22
Number of points scored	1369	Nombre de victoires pour Ferrari	72
Number of rostrum finishes	154	Number of qualifications in front of his team-mate	214
Number of finishes in the points	191	Number of grands prix led in part at least	141
Number of points in a single season (2004)	148	Number of laps	13909
Number of victories in a single season (2004)	13	Number of kilometres	66176
Number of consecutive victories in a single season	7	Number of qualifications on the front row	115
Number of consecutive grand prix finishes on the rostrum	19	Average number of points scored per grand prix	5.50

Ross Brawn: *"Michael has been a source of inspiration. An example."*

Michael Schumacher will leave his mark on motor sport not only because of his records and his talent. Backstage in the shadow of the Ferrari pits he was also known for his ability to concentrate the energies of the team, motivate it and become an intrinsic part of it. Nobody is better placed than Ross Brawn, Ferrari's technical director, to describe Michael's working methods. The Englishman was already employed at Benetton in the 90s when the German made his F1 debut. When he joined Ferrari he suggested that the Italian team should hire Ross Brawn. This was done irrevocably linking the destinies of the two men.

"To win you have to assemble a group of talented people," explains the English engineer. *At Ferrari we were lucky enough to have an exceptional group of engineers whether for the chassis or the aerodynamics. But Michael played a key role in our success; he embodied such an example of devotion, of team spirit, that he managed to push us all to give even more of ourselves. He was not the type of guy who came to the factory and said 'you should do this, you should do that. No, he came to the factory and he began by thanking everybody for the work that they were doing for him. He then described how the car was behaving, and helped us to understand it better. He showed us just how devoted to Ferrari he was and it was a source of inspiration, a real example for us all. Obviously, when he came to speak to our engineers they were very pleased. Michael knew it and he was very gifted at playing this role to motivate all those around him. You could see that he loves Ferrari."*

Ross Brawn reckons that Michael's qualities are unique: *"Michael has incredible self-control. He never gets annoyed with the people who work with him. He has a strong character, it's indispensable in this job, but he always stays calm both in the car and out. And that is exceptional all the more so if you add to this his natural talent and his sheer speed;"*

For Patrick Head, the Williams' technical director, the German is a unique driver. *"Unfortunately, we never had the opportunity of working with Michael,"* says Patrick. *"This being said I think that he's a really exceptional guy. I realised this at the Japanese Grand Prix, which I was watching on TV at home. When Michael went to thank all the members of his team after he retired, I said to myself that we'd seen quite a few champions pass through the Williams team (Prost, Piquet, Mansell, Rosberg, Jones etc.) and none of them would have made such a gesture for their team. That was when I thought that Michael is someone really exceptional."*

The most striking records held by Michael Schumacher

1985. Karting debut in Kerpen

1988. Formula König

1988. Rostrum in Formula König

1991. Group C with Sauber-Mercedes

1991. First day in F1 with Jordan

1991. First start at Spa goes up in smoke!

1993. Adelaide. Prost retires from racing

1993. At Flavio Briatore's home in London

1994. With Ross Brawn, his engineer

1994. Demonstration at Bercy

1995. Marriage to Corinna

1995. Imola.

1997. European Grand Prix at the Nürburgring

1997. Jerez. The duel with Villeneuve

1998. Victory in Montreal

2001. Budapest. World Champion

2002. Magny-Cours. Champion already

2002. 1st victory at Hockenheim in a Ferrari

2005. FIA Prize Giving in Monaco

2006. Indianapolis. Back in front

2006. Monza. His last victory in front of the Tifosi

1989. Formula 3

1989. Winner in F1 at Nürburgring

1990. Group C with Mercedes-Benz

1991.Monza. Debut with Benetton

1992. Presentation of the season

1992. Spa. First F1 victory

1994. Imola. A tragic victory

1994. Adelaide. The title changes hands

1994. Adelaide. Celebrating his first title

1995. Second title on the Aïda circuit

1996. Team presentation at Fiorano

1996. First victory with Ferrari in Barcelona

1999. With Jean Todt and Eddie Irvine

2000. Duel between Ferrari and McLaren

2000. Ferrari wins the championship at last

2003. Victory in Montreall

2004. Melbourne; First GP, first victory

2005. Only victory of the season, Indy

2006. 91st and last victory; Shanghai

2006. Interlagos. Duel with Alonso

2006. Interlagos. Ferrari's homage

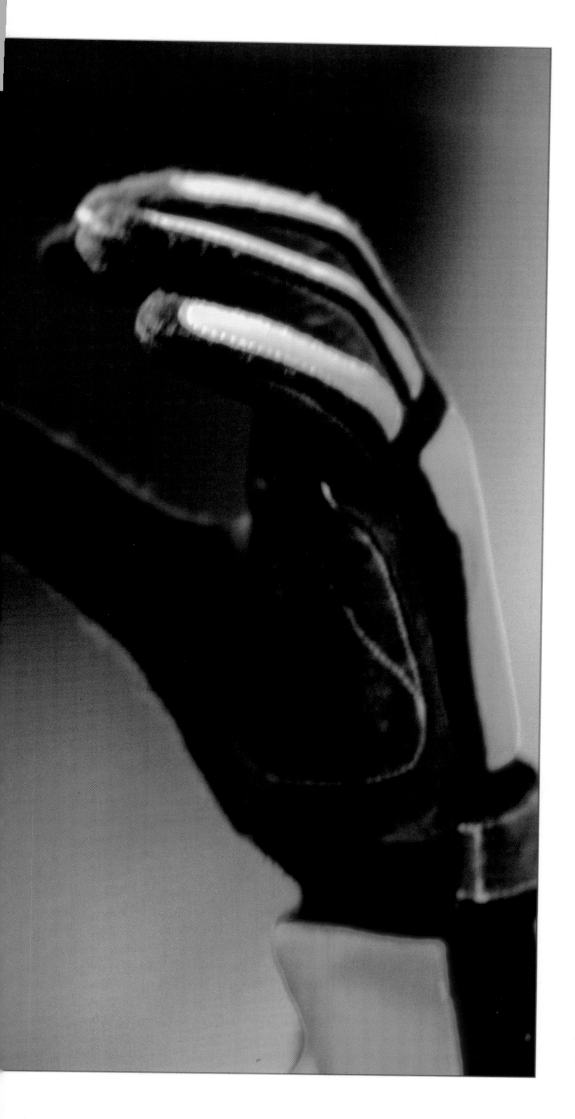

THE ACTORS

F1 drivers are not exactly normal people. They are worshipped, admired, criticised and provide the show on Sunday afternoons. They have exceptional reflexes and their skill at the wheel is equalled only by their physical strength. Even the slowest among them are still lords of the track. This does not prevent us from criticising them from time to time. But always with a certain affection.

Renault

1. Fernando ALONSO

DRIVER PROFILE

- Name — ALONSO DÍAZ
- Firstname — Fernando
- Nationality — Spanish
- Date of birth — 29th July 1981
- Place of birth — Oviedo (E)
- Lives in — Mont/Rolle (CH) & Oxford (GB)
- Marital status — engaged to Raquel del Rosario
- Kids — -
- Hobbies — sports on TV, movies, computers
- Favorite music — spanish groups
- Favorite meal — pasta
- Favorite drinks — mineral water
- Height — 171 cm
- Weight — 68 kg
- Web — www.fernandoalonso.com

STATISTICS

		PRIOR TO F1
Grands Prix	88	1984-98 Karting,
Starts	87	Champion Jr. (E) (93-94-95-96)
Wins	15	World Champion Jr. (96)
Pole positions	15	Champion Inter-A (E & I) (97)
Fastest laps	8	Champion Inter-A (E) (98)
Podiums	37	1999 Champion Euro-Open
Not qualified	0	Movistar Nissan
GPs in the lead	39	2000 F3000 (4th)
Laps in the lead	956	
Kms in the lead	4585	
Points scored	381	

F1 CAREER

2001	Minardi-European. 0 pt. 23rd of Championship.
2003	Renault. 55 pts. 6th of Championship.
2004	Renault. 59 pts. 4th of Championship.
2005	Renault. 133 pts. **World Champion.**
2006	Renault. 134 pts. **World Champion.**

2. Giancarlo FISICHELLA

DRIVER PROFILE

- Name — FISICHELLA
- Firstname — Giancarlo
- Nationality — Italian
- Date of birth — 14th January 1973
- Place of birth — Roma (I)
- Lives in — Roma (I) & Monaco (MC)
- Marital status — married to Luna
- Kids — daughter (Carlotta) & son (Cristofer)
- Hobbies — football, tennis, stream fishing, pool
- Favorite music — Elton John, Madonna, Robbie Williams
- Favorite meal — pasta "bucatini alla matriciana"
- Favorite drinks — Coca-Cola and orange juice
- Height — 172 cm
- Weight — 66 kg
- Web — www.giancarlofisichella.com

STATISTICS

		PRIOR TO F1
Grands Prix	179	1984-88 Karting
Starts	177	1989 World Championship of
Wins	3	Karting cat. 100 (4th)
Pole positions	3	1990 Championnat
Fastest laps	2	Intercontinental Karting (3rd)
Podiums	18	1991 Karting (EUR) (2nd),
Not qualified	0	F. Alfa Boxer
GPs in the lead	13	1992 F3 (I) (8th)
Laps in the lead	209	1993 F3 (I) (2nd)
Kms in the lead	1088	1994 Champion F3 (I)
Points scored	246	1995 DTM/ITC Alfa Romeo

F1 CAREER

1996	Minardi-Ford. 0 pt. 19th of Championship.
1997	Jordan-Peugeot. 20 pts. 8th of Championship.
1998	Benetton-Playlife. 16 pts. 9th of Championship.
1999	Benetton-Playlife. 13 pts. 9th of Championship.
2000	Benetton-Playlife. 18 pts. 6th of Championship.
2001	Benetton-Renault. 8 pts. 11th of Championship.
2002	Jordan-Honda. 7 pts. 11th of Championship.
2003	Jordan-Ford. 12 pts. 12th of Championship.
2004	Sauber-Petronas. 22 pts. 11th of Championship.
2005	Renault. 58 pts. 5th of Championship.
2006	Renault. 72 pts. 4th of Championship.

Did you know Alonso has now won back-to-back world championship titles? It may well have escaped your attention in Brazil, what with the hysteria surrounding Felipe Massa winning his home race and all the hype about Michael Schumacher's retirement. But maybe the Spaniard has only himself to blame as, speaking a few weeks after the final round, Bernie Ecclestone claimed Alonso was not yet a "great" because he had not been able to engage with his public. And there certainly won't be much "engaging" when he enters the ice cold environment at McLaren. But no matter, Fernando is still young and where it mattered – in the cockpit – he produced some brilliant if understated drives, in Spain and Japan for example. There are no obvious weaknesses in his package and although the pressure of having Schumi on his tail did show at times, with some strange outbursts in the Spanish media about not getting the full support of his team, once strapped into the cockpit he rediscovered his sang froid.

One of the big mysteries of the year was that before the summer was over, Giancarlo Fisichella already had a 2007 Renault contract in his pocket, or probably in his shrewd manager's briefcase. Hesitant would be the best word to describe the Roman's performance this year and there were days when his heart just did not seem to be in it. However, one has to take into account that no one has ever found it easy being a team-mate to a world champion. Even though all F1 drivers think they are world champion material, there obviously came a point when Fisichella would have admitted to himself that generally he did not have the pace to match his team-mate. There were flashes of the natural talent we know the Italian has by the bucket load and Malaysia, perhaps too long ago to mean much now, saw him produce a flawless pole to flag victory. But there were also signs of nerves, as when he threw himself off the track in Brazil, having spotted Schumacher in his mirrors. Now he will have to fend off the advances of another highly rated youngster in the shape of Finland's Heikki Kovalainen.

Flavio Briatore

Bob Bell

Rob White

Denis Chevrier

RENAULT R26
FERNANDO ALONSO
SPANISH GRAND PRIX

SPECIFICATIONS

- Chassis — Renault R26
- Type — Moulded carbon fibre and aluminium honeycomb composite monocoque
- Suspensions — Carbon fibre top and bottom wishbones operate an inboard rocker via a pushrod system. This is connected to a torsion bar and damper units which are mounted at the front of the monocoque (Front) / horizontally-mounted damper units mounted on the top of the gearbox casing (Rear)
- Engine — V8 Renault RS26 (90°)
- Displacement — 2400 cc
- Valves — 4 valves pneumatic distribution
- Electronic ignition — Magneti Marelli Step 11
- Transmission — 7-speed semi-automatic titanium + rev.
- Clutch — not revealed
- Radiators — Secan / Marston
- Fuel / oil — Elf / Elf
- Brakes (discs) — Hitco (carbon)
- Brakes (calipers) — AP Racing
- Spark plugs/Battery — Champion / Renault F1 Team
- Shock absorbers — not revealed
- Tyres — Michelin
- Wheels dimensions — 13"
- Wheels — O.Z. Racing
- Weight — 605 kg, driver + camera + ballast
- Wheelbase — 3100 mm
- Overall lenght — 4800 mm
- Overall width — 1800 mm
- Overall height — 950 mm
- Front track — 1450 mm
- Rear track — 1400 mm

TEAM PROFILE

- Addresses — Renault F1 UK / Whiteways Technical Centre, Enstone, Chipping Norton, Oxon OX7 4EE / Great Britain
  Renault F1 France / 1-15, avenue du Président Kennedy / 91177 Viry-Châtillon / France
- Telephone — +44 (0) 1608 678 000 / +33 (0) 1 69 12 58 00
- Fax — +44 (0) 1608 678 609 / +33 (0) 1 69 12 58 17
- Web — www.renaultf1.com
- Founded in — 1973
- First Grand Prix — Great Britain 1977
- Official name — Mild Seven Renault F1 Team
- President — Alain Dassas
- Managing Director — Flavio Briatore
- Technical Director — Bob Bell (Chassis)
- Executive Dir. of Engineering — Pat Symonds
- Deputy Managing Direc. — Rob White
- Engine Operations Manager — Denis Chevrier
- Chief Designer — Tim Densham
- Assistant Chief Designer — Martin Tolliday
- Engine Project Managers — Léon Taillieu, Axel Plasse
- Sporting Manager — Steve Nielsen
- Race Engineers (1) — Rod Nelson, Rémi Taffin
- Race Engineers (2) — Alan Permane, Fabrice Lom
- Number of employees — 500 (GB) / 250 (F)
- Partners — Mild Seven, Elf, Michelin, Hanjin, i-mode, Telefonica, Guru, Chronotech, Mutua Madrileña
- Official suppliers — 3D Systems, Altran, CD-Adapco, Champion, Charmilles, DMG, Elysium, Eutelsat, Jobs, Lancel, Magneti Marelli, Network Appliance, O.Z. Racing, Processia Solutions, Puma, Tecnomatix, Symantec, Xansa

STATISTICS

• Number of Grand Prix	210
• Number of victories	33
• Number of pole positions	50
• Number of fastest laps	27
• Number of podiums	89
• Number of drivers Championship	2
• Number of constructors Championship	2
• Total number of points scored	925

RENAULT F1 Team

POSITION IN CHAMPIONSHIP

1977	not classified	1984	5th – 34 pts
1978	12th – 3 pts	1985	7th – 16 pts
1979	6th – 26 pts	2002	4th – 23 pts
1980	4th – 38 pts	2003	4th – 88 pts
1981	3rd – 54 pts	2004	3rd – 105 pts
1982	3rd – 62 pts	2005	1st – 191 pts
1983	2nd – 79 pts	2006	1st – 206 pts

2006 TEST DRIVER

- Heikki KOVALAINEN (FIN)

SUCCESSION OF DRIVERS 2006

- Fernando ALONSO — all 18 Grands Prix
- Giancarlo FISICHELLA — all 18 Grands Prix

Heikki Kovalainen

"Va va voom!" says the advertisement for Renault cars, but on the race track this year, it was nearly va va bang! as the Anglo-French team, having apparently won the world championship by the mid-point of the season with seven race victories under its belt, nearly threw it all away and had to wait until the very last of the eighteen GPs to secure both Drivers' and Constructors' titles. As reigning champions, Renault had everything in place with a beautifully balanced R26 car, based on the previous year's model, Michelin tyres that still seemed to have an edge over their Japanese rivals and the perceived weakness of running a team with two operational bases – Viry and Enstone – now firmly consigned to the dustbin. But then came Indy and the well oiled machine faltered. It was partly down to tyres – thank goodness we go back to a single tyre supplier from 2007 – as the French rubber boys were not going to risk getting lynched by an angry American mob for a second year running. But the chief reason was that the Prancing Horse finally got into its stride. Back in Europe, the Red rout continued and eventually, with two races remaining, Michael Schumacher finally overhauled Fernando Alonso in the Drivers' classification. Why? Because of the dreaded Mass Damper. This insignificant component, which in very simple terms dials out vibration and allows the tyres to better do their job, had been a key element in the Renault package and indeed was also used less effectively by other teams. But it was deemed illegal just before the summer testing break which meant it took the Renault brains a while to cope with running without it. To add spice to the story, there were plenty of conspiracy theories flying around, implying the device had only been banned just to liven up the title battle. Now Renault showed its true strength as a team, standing toe to toe with Ferrari without losing its nerve, never faltering and being there to pick up the points when the Scuderia weakened. Without a ridiculous budget, with technology and team work their mantra and with a human face presented to the world, Renault is pretty much the ideal team of the moment

McLaren Mercedes

3. Kimi RÄIKKÖNEN

DRIVER PROFILE

- Name — *RÄIKKÖNEN*
- Firstname — *Kimi Matias*
- Nationality — *Finnish*
- Date of birth — *17th October 1979*
- Place of birth — *Espoo (FIN)*
- Lives in — *Pfäffikon (CH), Espoo (FIN)*
- Marital status — *married to Jenni*
- Kids — *-*
- Hobbies — *snowboard, skateboard, jogging*
- Favorite music — *U2, Darude, Bomfunk Mc, Eminem*
- Favorite meal — *pasta, chicken, finnish dish with reindeer*
- Favorite drinks — *pineapple juice, water and milk*
- Height — *175 cm*
- Weight — *71 kg*
- Web — *www.kimiraikkonen.com*

STATISTICS

		PRIOR TO F1
Grands Prix	105	1988-99 *Karting*
Starts	104	1998 *Champion karting*
Wins	9	*Formule A (SF & Nordic)*
Pole positions	11	1999 *Karting*
Fastest laps	19	*Formule A (SF) (2nd),*
Podiums	36	*championnat du monde*
Not qualified	0	*Formule Super A (10th)*
GPs in the lead	34	2000 *Champion*
Laps in the lead	638	*F. Renault (GB)*
Kms in the lead	3059	
Points scored	346	

F1 CAREER

2001 *Sauber-Petronas. 9 pts. 9th of Championship.*
2002 *McLaren-Mercedes. 24 pts. 6th of Championship.*
2003 *McLaren-Mercedes. 91 pts. 2nd of Championship.*
2004 *McLaren-Mercedes. 45 pts. 7th of Championship.*
2005 *McLaren-Mercedes. 112 pts. 2nd of Championship.*
2006 *McLaren-Mercedes. 65 pts. 5th of Championship.*

It is a sad reflection of Raikkonen's attitude to his job that the most famous image of him in 2006 was to be found on a video-clip web site, featuring him rather the worse for drink, falling on his head from the top deck of a yacht to the bottom deck. If people in the sport have criticised him for this sort of typical behaviour, it has not been out of a sense of Puritanism but rather a feeling that here is a great talent being wasted. The Kimster has probably got as much if not more raw speed than any of his rivals and a commitment to corners that few can match, but other than that, there's not much going on and these days, natural talent is not enough in F1. Kimi did produce some good drives – how can you fail when you have so much latent speed? For much of the season, McLaren insisted that no decision had been reached about Raikkonen's future, which was a strange decision, given the whole world knew he had signed for Ferrari early on in the year. The Scuderia is bound to be impressed with Kimi's lap times, but barring a miraculous personality change, it is unlikely that he will lead and motivate the team in the same way as the great Saint Michael. Unless he gets another bang on the head maybe?

Ron Dennis

Martin Whitmarsh

4. Juan Pablo MONTOYA

DRIVER PROFILE

- Name — *MONTOYA ROLDÁN*
- Firstname — *Juan Pablo*
- Nationality — *columbian*
- Date of birth — *20th September 1975*
- Place of birth — *Bogota (COL)*
- Lives in — *Monaco (MC)*
- Marital status — *married to Connie*
- Kids — *son & daughter (Sebastian & Paulina)*
- Hobbies — *water ski, video games*
- Favorite music — *rock, Shakira, Juanes et Carlos Vives*
- Favorite meal — *pasta*
- Favorite drinks — *orange juice*
- Height — *168 cm*
- Weight — *73.5 kg*
- Web — *www.jpmontoya.com*

STATISTICS

		PRIOR TO F1
Grands Prix	95	1981-91 *Karting (2 times*
Starts	94	*World Champion Jr)*
Wins	7	1992 *F. Renault (COL)*
Pole positions	13	1993 *Swift GTI (COL)*
Fastest laps	12	1994 *Karting-Sudam 125*
Podiums	30	*Champ. Barber Saab (3rd)*
Not qualified	0	1995 *F. Vauxhall (GB)*
GPs in the lead	32	1996 *F3 (GB)*
Laps in the lead	605	1997 *F3000 (2nd)*
Kms in the lead	2966	1998 *Champion F3000*
Points scored	307	1999 *Champion CART*
		2000 *CART (9th)*

F1 CAREER

2001 *Williams- BMW. 31 pts. 6th of Championship.*
2002 *Williams- BMW. 50 pts. 3rd of Championship.*
2003 *Williams- BMW. 82 pts. 3rd of Championship.*
2004 *Williams- BMW. 58 pts. 5th of Championship.*
2005 *McLaren-Mercedes. 60 pts. 4th of Championship.*
2006 *McLaren-Mercedes. 26 pts. 8th of Championship.*

In case you didn't know, Ron Dennis is a stickler for neatness and cleanliness. Armed with that information, imagine his sparkling glass paddock palace, The McLaren Communications Centre, littered with baby toys, babies, baby food, baby's mother, father and various other family members and friends. Every time Mr. Dennis looked down at this scene of Colombian families at play, he must have shivered. So, the relationship between him and "Monty" was never going to be great and it got worse as the year wore on: there was a disastrous Melbourne, when Montoya had to wait his turn for a pit stop behind his team-mate, then accidents in Montreal and in Indy, the latter running into the back of Raikkonen's car in a first corner multiple pile-up. So now, he has moved back to the USA, where he won't be considered a touch overweight and where his family entourage in the paddock motorhome will look no different to thousands of American families who live in trailers.

4. Pedro DE LA ROSA

DRIVER PROFILE

- Name — *MARTÍNEZ DE LA ROSA*
- Firstname — *Pedro*
- Nationality — *spanish*
- Date of birth — *24th february 1971*
- Place of birth — *Barcelona (E)*
- Lives in — *Barcelona (E)*
- Marital status — *married to Maria*
- Kids — *two daughters (Georgina and Olivia)*
- Hobbies — *helicopter modeling, reading*
- Favorite music — *pop rock, Bruce Springsteen*
- Favorite meal — *pasta and paëlla*
- Favorite drinks — *mineral water*
- Height — *177 cm*
- Weight — *74 kg*
- Web — *www.pedrodelarosa.com*

STATISTICS

		PRIOR TO F1
Grands Prix	84	1983-87 *2x Radio-controlled*
Starts	72	*cars Champion(EUR)*
Best result	1 x 2e	1988 *Karting (E)*
Best qualif.	1 x 4e	1989 *Champion F. Fiat (E)*
Fastest laps	1	1990 *Champion F. Ford 1600*
Podiums	1	*(E), F. Ford 1600 (GB)*
Not qualified	0	1991 *F. Renault (E) (4th)*
GPs in the lead	0	1992 *Champion F. Renault*
Laps in the lead	0	*(GB & EUR)*
Kms in the lead	0	1993 *F. Renault (6th)*
Points scored	29	1994 *F3 (GB)*
		1995 *Champion F3 (J)*
		1996 *F3000 & GT (J) (8th)*
		1997 *Champion F3000*
		& GT (J)

F1 CAREER

1999 *Arrows. 1 pt. 17th of Championship.*
2000 *Arrows-Supertec. 2 pts. 16th of Championship.*
2001 *Jaguar. 3 pts. 16th of Championship.*
2002 *Jaguar. 0 pt. 21st of Championship.*
2005 *McLaren-Mercedes. 4 pts. 20th of Championship.*
2006 *McLaren-Mercedes. 19 pts. 11th of Championship.*

Pedro de la Rosa's biggest crime is that he is Spanish. It means that despite the huge number of Iberian sponsors queuing up to give McLaren money for next season, it is hard to see the big money backers going with two Spanish drivers and when one of them is the current and double world champion, it seems very unlikely at the time of writing that Pedro will be racing again any time soon. A shame, as he is one of the "good guys."

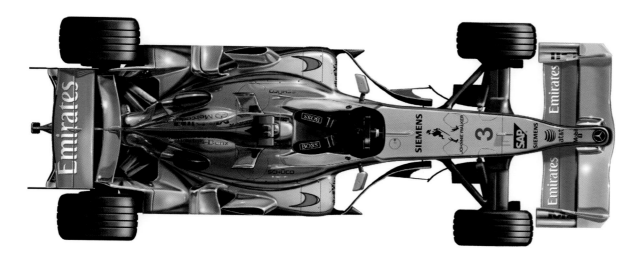

McLAREN MP4-21-MERCEDES
KIMI RÄIKKÖNEN
BRITISH GRAND PRIX

SPECIFICATIONS

- Chassis — McLaren MP4-21
- Type — McLaren moulded carbon fibre/aluminium honeycomb composite
- Suspensions — Inboard torsion bar/damper system operated by pushrod and bell crank with a double wishbone arrangement (F/R)
- Engine — V8 Mercedes-Benz FO 108S (90°)
- Displacement — 2398 cc
- Valves — 4 valves pneumatic distribution
- Electronic ignition — McLaren Electronic Systems
- Transmission — McLaren semi-automatic 7 speeds + reverse
- Clutch — AP Racing
- Radiators — McLaren / Calsonic / Marston
- Fuel / oil — Mobil 1 unleaded / Mobil 1
- Brakes (discs) — Hitco
- Brakes (calipers) — AP Racing
- Spark plugs/Battery — NGK / GS Yuasa Corporation
- Shock absorbers — McLaren
- Tyres — Michelin
- Wheels dimensions — 13"
- Wheels — Enkei
- Weight — 605 kg, driver + camera + ballast
- Wheel base — not revelated
- Overall lenght — not revelated
- Overall width — not revelated
- Overall height — not revelated
- Front track — not revelated
- Rear track — not revelated

TEAM PROFILE

- Address — McLaren Technology Centre Chertsey Road, Woking, Surrey GU21 5JY Great Britain
- Telephone — +44 (0) 1483 711 117
- Fax — +44 (0) 1483 711 119
- Web — www.mclaren.com
- Founded in — 1963
- First Grand Prix — Monaco 1966
- Official name — Team McLaren Mercedes
- Team Principal, Chairman and CEO, McLaren Group — Ron Dennis
- CEO F1, Team McLaren — Martin Whitmarsh
- Managing Director — Jonathan Neale
- Vice President Mercedes-Benz Motorsport — Norbert Haug
- Managing Director, Mercedes-Benz — Ola Kaellenius
- Engineering Director — Paddy Lowe
- Design and Development Director — Neil Oatley
- Chief Designer — Mike Coughlan
- Chiefs Engineer — Tim Goss/Pat Fry
- Chief Engineer (aero.) — Mark Williams
- Race Team Manager — Dave Ryan
- General Manager — Simon Roberts
- Chief Mechanic — Stephen Giles
- Race Engineer (3) — Mark Slade
- Race Engineer (4) — Phil Prew
- Number of employees — 520
- Partners (sponsors) Johnnie Walker, SAP, Emirates, Hugo Boss, AT&T, Hilton, Schüco, TAGHeuer, Direxiv • (tech.) Mobil 1, Siemens, Michelin, BAE Systems • (associate) Steinmetz, SSP • (official suppliers) Henkel, Nescafé XPress, Sonax, Eisenmann, Advanced Composites, Charmilles, Gs-Yuasa, Mazak, Targetti Lighting, Enkei, Sports Marketing Surveys, Kenwood, 3D Systems, Sparco, SGI

STATISTICS

- Number of Grand Prix — 613
- Number of victories — 148
- Number of pole positions — 125
- Number of fastest laps — 129
- Number of podiums — 394
- Number of drivers Championship — 11
- Number of constructors Championship — 8
- Total number of points scored — 3148,5 (3154,5)

POSITION IN CHAMPIONSHIP

Year		Year		Year		Year	
1966	7th – 2 *¹ pts	1977	3rd – 60 pts	1988	1st – 199 pts	1999	2nd – 124 pts
1967	8th – 3 pts	1978	8th – 15 pts	1989	1st – 141 pts	2000	2nd – 152 pts
1968	2nd – 49 *³ pts	1979	7th – 15 pts	1990	1st – 121 pts	2001	2nd – 102 pts
1969	4th – 38 (20) pts	1980	7th – 11 pts	1991	1st – 139 pts	2002	3rd – 65 pts
1970	4th – 35 pts	1981	6th – 28 pts	1992	2nd – 99 pts	2003	3rd – 142 pts
1971	6th – 10 pts	1982	2nd – 69 pts	1993	2nd – 84 pts	2004	5th – 69 pts
1972	3rd – 47 pts	1983	5th – 34 pts	1994	4th – 42 pts	2005	2nd – 182 pts
1973	3rd – 58 pts	1984	1st – 143,5 pts	1995	4th – 30 pts	2006	3rd – 110 pts
1974	1st – 73 pts	1985	1st – 90 pts	1996	4th – 49 pts		
1975	3rd – 53 pts	1986	2nd – 96 pts	1997	4th – 63 pts		
1976	2nd – 74 pts	1987	2nd – 76 pts	1998	1st – 156 pts		

2006 TEST DRIVERS

- Pedro DE LA ROSA (E)
- Gary PAFFETT (GB)

SUCCESSION OF DRIVERS 2006

- Kimi RÄIKKÖNEN — all 18 Grands Prix
- Juan Pablo MONTOYA — 10 Grands Prix (BRN > USA)
- Pedro DE LA ROSA — 8 Grands Prix (F > BR)

There was a cruel joke doing the rounds in the paddock this year that stated that Williams was "the new Tyrrell," as Sir Frank's team seemed to be slipping into a decline. But soon, another more cruel twist was added to this remark. "If Williams is the new Tyrrell, then McLaren is the new Williams." There is no mercy in this competitive sport! The team won ten races in 2005 and none in 2006, although Kimi Raikkonen came close at times. Indeed, the season did not start too badly as the Finn came home third and second in the two opening rounds. But silly and annoying reliability issues robbed them of the results the car was capable of in terms of performance. But once the Bridgestones came good, there was even less McLaren could do. This year's MP4/21 continued the previous year's trend of being very kind to its tyres, but this was pretty much a useless virtue now that race tyre changes were allowed once more. It has to be said there were plenty of other issues within the team that could not have helped and might even have found key players taking their eye off the ball. Even before the cars lined up on the grid in Bahrain, Alonso had already been signed up to drive for the Anglo-German squad as from 2007. McLaren management insisted that neither they nor Raikkonen had reached a decision for the future, even though the whole world knew the Finn had a nice red Ferrari contract sitting on top of his television at home. Then there was the mid-season departure of Montoya. McLaren chairman Ron Dennis has often maintained his team is good at giving its drivers the necessary pastoral care. Frankly this is something of a myth, if one cares to look back at the rivalry between Prost and Senna that nearly tore the team in half. Then there were other failures – Andretti, Magnussen, Mansell to name but three and now we had a very unhappy Colombian to add to the list. In a sport where everything has to run in harmony, these political problems may have had a disproportionately heavy effect on the team's overall performance. Next year, McLaren has a world champion on its books again, but as we saw from Michael Schumacher in 2005, even the best driver in the world cannot do much if the rest of the package is not up to scratch.

Ferrari

Do we really need to go through the statistics again? No. Suffice to say that Schumi came within a whisker of taking an unbelievable eighth world title in his final year as a driver. The season was not without its low points when the pressure seemed to get to him, such as his Rascasse "car park" move in Monaco and the very occasional driving error, but he left us all with a drive that has to stand as one of his best ever in Brazil. His passing move on Raikkonen going into the tricky Turn 1 said it all: "Kimi you're getting my car next year, but I'm still better than you!" And indeed, one has to say that the German does appear to have retired at the top of his game as his sheer speed and skill does not seem to have been diminished in any way. Why he is retiring? Maybe only he and his family know the real answer. The sport will get by just fine without him, as it did after the departure of Alain Prost and the death of Ayrton Senna, but next year's grid will be poorer without him. Those critics who say he is not the greatest, that he is a flawed character are deluding themselves. Perhaps it was just too hard to like a German with a big chin who drove for a team that often had an unbelievably arrogant attitude to the rest of the world, but in time, those of us who witnessed his 16 year F1 career will realise we had lived through something special. Apart from his personal achievements, he has to be credited with a great contribution to rebuilding the Ferrari team. Whoever wins the 2007 Drivers' crown should have one irritating fact niggling away at the back of their mind and that is they will have won the title knowing the best driver in the world is sitting at home in Switzerland.

5. Michael SCHUMACHER

DRIVER PROFILE

- Name — SCHUMACHER
- Firstname — Michael
- Nationality — German
- Date of birth — 3rd January 1969
- Place of birth — Hürth-Hermühlheim (D)
- Lives in — Vufflens-le-Château (CH)
- Marital status — married to Corinna
- Kids — daughter and son (Gina-Maria & Mick)
- Hobbies — karting, football, cycling, skiing
- Favorite music — rock
- Favorite meal — italian food, sushis
- Favorite drinks — sparkling apple juice
- Height — 174 cm
- Weight — 73 kg
- Web — www.michael-schumacher.de

STATISTICS

		PRIOR TO F1
Grands Prix	250	1984-85 Karting
Starts	249	Champion Junior (D)
Wins	91	1986 Karting 3rd (D & EUR)
Pole positions	68	1987 Karting
Fastest laps	76	Champion (D & EUR)
Podiums	154	1988 Champion F. Koenig,
Not qualified	0	F. Ford 1600 (EUR) (2nd),
GPs in the lead	141	F. Ford 1600 (D) (6th)
Laps in the lead	5108	1989 F3 (D) (3rd)
Kms in the lead	24130	1990 Champion F3 (D)
Points scored	1369	1990-91 Sport-prototypes
		Mercedes (5th & 9th)

F1 CAREER

1991	Jordan-Ford, Benetton-Ford. 4 pts. 12th of Championship.
1992	Benetton-Ford. 53 pts. 3rd of Championship.
1993	Benetton-Ford. 52 pts. 4th of Championship.
1994	Benetton-Ford. 92 pts. **World Champion.**
1995	Benetton-Renault. 102 pts. **World Champion.**
1996	Ferrari. 49 pts. 3rd of Championship.
1997	Ferrari. 78 pts. Exclu of Championship (2nd).
1998	Ferrari. 86 pts. 2nd of Championship.
1999	Ferrari. 44 pts. 5th of Championship.
2000	Ferrari. 108 pts. **World Champion.**
2001	Ferrari. 123 pts. **World Champion.**
2002	Ferrari. 144 pts. **World Champion.**
2003	Ferrari. 93 pts. **World Champion.**
2004	Ferrari. 148 pts. **World Champion.**
2005	Ferrari. 62 pts. 3rd of Championship.
2006	Ferrari. 121 pts. 2nd of Championship.

6. Felipe MASSA

DRIVER PROFILE

- Name — MASSA
- Firstname — Felipe
- Nationality — Bresilian
- Date of birth — 25th April 1981
- Place of birth — São Paulo (BR)
- Lives in — Hinwil (CH)
- Marital status — single
- Kids — -
- Hobbies — water, football, movies, music
- Favorite music — all, black music, hits
- Favorite meal — pasta, churrascaria
- Favorite drinks — champagne of the podiums!
- Height — 166 cm
- Weight — 59 kg
- Web — www.felipemassa.com

STATISTICS

		PRIOR TO F1
Grands Prix	71	1990-97 Karting
Starts	70	1998 F. Chevrolet (BR) (5th)
Wins	2	1999 Champion F. Chevrolet
Pole positions	3	(BR)
Fastest laps	2	2000 Champion F. Renault
Podiums	7	(EUR & I)
Not qualified	0	2001 Champion F3000
GPs in the lead	5	Euroseries (I)
Laps in the lead	156	
Kms in the lead	727	
Points scored	107	

F1 CAREER

2002	Sauber-Petronas. 4 points. 13th of Championship.
2004	Sauber-Petronas. 12 points. 12th of Championship.
2005	Sauber-Petronas. 11 points. 13th of Championship.
2006	Ferraru. 80 points. 3rd of Championship.

The accusations of nepotism were not even hidden behind a polite veil when it was announced that one Brazilian, Massa would replace another, Barrichello in the Ferrari camp. The fact that the ex-Sauber boy was managed by someone called Nicholas (yes, son of Jean) Todt was just the sort of juicy tid-bit of information that the gossips like to play with. On top of that, Massa had a reputation for being quick but erratic and too prone to crash. Surely family interests had triumphed over talent? While it was true that Felipe seemed to take a different line through every corner in his first stint as a grand prix driver, since those early headstrong days, he had been through the Ferrari test driver "school" and gone back to Sauber. And this year, he fully justified his promotion to the First Division. After a mid-season change of race engineer: he was given Englishman Rob Smedley to avoid the too volatile Latin driver – Latin engineer scenario, everything soon fell into place, with a first appearance on the podium, a first pole and then in Turkey, at the end of an inch-perfect weekend, his first win. This was followed up by a repeat performance at the end of the year, when he became the first Brazilian since Senna to win his home GP. Raikkonen could find him a difficult team-mate to deal with in 2007.

Jean Todt

Ross Brawn

Paolo Martinelli

Luca Badoer

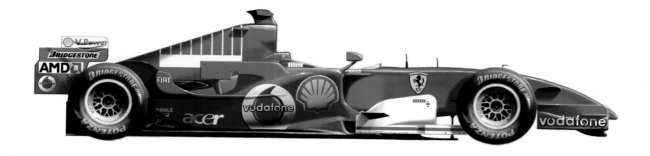

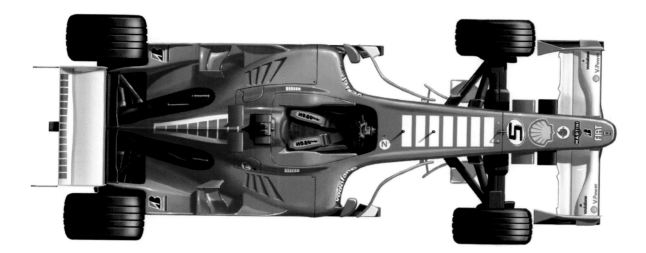

FERRARI 248 F1
MICHAEL SCHUMACHER
SAN MARINO GRAND PRIX

SPECIFICATIONS

- Chassis — *Ferrari 248 F1*
- Type — *Moulded carbon fibre monocoque/ aluminium composite honeycomb independent, push-rod activated torsion springs front and rear*
- Suspensions —
- Engine — *V8 Ferrari Type 056 (90°)*
- Displacement — *2398 cc*
- Maximum revs — *19,000 rpm*
- Valves — *4 valves, pneumatic distribution*
- Electronic ignition — *Magneti Marelli*
- Transmission — *Ferrari longitudinal, Ferrari longitudinal gearbox limited-slip differential / 7 + reverse*
- Clutch — *Sachs - AP*
- Radiators — *Secan*
- Fuel / oil — *Shell / Shell*
- Brakes (discs) — *Brembo (carbon)*
- Brakes (calipers) — *Brembo*
- Spark plugs — *NGK*
- Shock absorbers — *Sachs*
- Tyres — *Bridgestone Potenza*
- Wheels dimensions — *13"*
- Wheels — *BBS*
- Weight — *605 kg, driver + camera + ballast*
- Wheel base — *3050 mm*
- Overall lenght — *4545 mm*
- Overall width — *1796 mm*
- Overall height — *959 mm*
- Front track — *1470 mm*
- Rear track — *1405 mm*

TEAM PROFILE

- Address — *Ferrari SpA Via A. Ascari 55-57 41053 Maranello (MO) Italia*
- Telephone — *+ 39.536.949450*
- Fax — *+ 39.536.946049*
- Web — *www.ferrariworld.com*
- Founded in — *1929*
- First Grand Prix — *Monaco 1950*
- Official name — *Scuderia Ferrari Marlboro*
- General Director — *Jean Todt*
- Technical Director — *Ross Brawn*
- Engine Director — *Paolo Martinelli*
- Director F1 racing activities — *Stefano Domenicali*
- Chief Designer — *Rory Byrne, Aldo Costa*
- Race & Test Technical Manager — *Nigel Stepney*
- Race Engineer (5) — *Chris Dyer*
- Race Engineer (6) — *Gabrielle Delli Colli*
- Number of employees — *900*
- Sponsors — *Philip Morris (Marlboro), Vodafone, Shell, Bridgestone, Fiat, AMD, Martini, Olympus, Acer*
- Official suppliers — *Brembo, Magneti Marelli, Mahle, OMR, Puma, SKF, Beta Utensili, Europcar, Finmeccanica, Infineon, Iveco, NGK, Officine Panerai, Sanbittèr, Tata Consultancy Services, ZF Sachs*
- Associate suppliers — *BBS, Cima, Mecel, Poggipolini, Sabelt, Selex Communications, TRW, VeCa*

2006 TEST DRIVERS

- Luca BADOER (I)
- Marc GENÉ (E)

STATISTICS

- Number of Grand Prix — *741*
- Number of victories — *192*
- Number of pole positions — *186*
- Number of fastest laps — *193*
- Number of podiums — *582*
- Number of drivers Championship — *14*
- Number of constructors Championship — *14*
- Total number of points scored — *3600,5 (3647,5)*

POSITION IN CHAMPIONSHIP

1958	2ⁿᵈ – 40 (57) pts	1971	4ᵗʰ – 33 pts	1984	2ⁿᵈ – 57,5 pts	1997	2ⁿᵈ – 102 pts
1959	2ⁿᵈ – 32 (38) pts	1972	4ᵗʰ – 33 pts	1985	2ⁿᵈ – 82 pts	1998	2ⁿᵈ – 133 pts
1960	3ʳᵈ – 26 (27) pts	1973	6ᵗʰ – 12 pts	1986	4ᵗʰ – 37 pts	1999	1ˢᵗ – 128 pts
1961	1ˢᵗ – 40 (52) pts	1974	2ⁿᵈ – 65 pts	1987	4ᵗʰ – 53 pts	2000	1ˢᵗ – 170 pts
1962	5ᵗʰ – 18 pts	1975	1ˢᵗ – 72,5 pts	1988	2ⁿᵈ – 65 pts	2001	1ˢᵗ – 179 pts
1963	4ᵗʰ – 26 pts	1976	1ˢᵗ – 83 pts	1989	3ʳᵈ – 59 pts	2002	1ˢᵗ – 221 pts
1964	1ˢᵗ – 45 (49) pts	1977	1ˢᵗ – 95 (97) pts	1990	2ⁿᵈ – 110 pts	2003	1ˢᵗ – 158 pts
1965	4ᵗʰ – 26 (27) pts	1978	2ⁿᵈ – 58 pts	1991	3ʳᵈ – 55.5 pts	2004	1ˢᵗ - 262 pts
1966	2ⁿᵈ – 31 (32) pts	1979	1ˢᵗ – 113 pts	1992	4ᵗʰ – 21 pts	2005	3ʳᵈ – 100 pts
1967	4ᵗʰ – 20 pts	1980	10ᵗʰ – 8 pts	1993	4ᵗʰ – 28 pts	2006	2ⁿᵈ – 201 pts
1968	4ᵗʰ – 32 pts	1981	5ᵗʰ – 34 pts	1994	3ʳᵈ – 71 pts		
1969	5ᵗʰ – 7 pts	1982	1ˢᵗ – 74 pts	1995	3ʳᵈ – 73 pts		
1970	2ⁿᵈ – 52 (55) pts	1983	1ˢᵗ – 89 pts	1996	2ⁿᵈ – 70 pts		

SUCCESSION OF DRIVERS 2006

- Michael SCHUMACHER — *all 18 Grands Prix*
- Felipe MASSA — *all 18 Grands Prix*

The figures show that for the second consecutive year, Ferrari failed to win either titles. So, the Prancing Horse is in decline right? Absolutely wrong, because this year, the Italians fought back and actually won more races than Renault. But even this was a case of too little too late. The rule allowing tyre changing during the races again should have played to Ferrari's and Bridgestone's strengths, but it did not quite work like that in the early part of the season when a few clutch and engine difficulties did not help the situation either. In fact, unheard of, given the almost unbelievable reliability of Ferrari F1 engines over the years, it was engine troubles that would resurface in the closing stages of the season and prove to be the team's Achilles Heel. But the Scuderia was indefatigable in smoothing their rough edges and began mounting a strong challenge once the teams headed to North America in early summer. Development never stopped as the title battle hotted up and every race would see some new aero component, or progress with suspension and tyres to keep pushing Renault as hard as possible. A lot of testing, particularly on tyres, produced much needed development and relentlessly, they set about closing the gap to Renault. By the final quarter of the season there was little to choose between the only two teams who can claim to have done a really good job in 2006. They provided a thrilling climax, marred only by the fact we never got the two star drivers racing wheel to wheel in Brazil. Ferrari finished the year in good shape, but now a new regime will carry the torch: no Schumacher, no Brawn, no Martinelli, Todt taking on new responsibilities, the engineers of Ferrari's glorious recent past that broke all records with eleven world titles, are moving on. But the team is in good hands and Todt will still be at the helm. So, for a while anyway, the "flywheel effect" will continue and the momentum generated over the past decade should keep the Scuderia near the top of the pile for a couple more years at least.

Toyota

7. Ralf SCHUMACHER

DRIVER PROFILE

- Name — SCHUMACHER
- Firstname — Ralf
- Nationality — German
- Date of birth — 30th June 1975
- Place of birth — Hürth-Hermühlheim (D)
- Lives in — Hallwang (Salzburg) (A)
- Marital status — married to Cora
- Kids — one son (David)
- Hobbies — karting, tennis, horsing, backgammon
- Favorite music — soft rock
- Favorite meal — pasta
- Favorite drink — sparkling apple juice
- Height — 178 cm
- Weight — 73 kg
- Web — www.ralf-schumacher.de

STATISTICS

- Grands Prix — 165
- Starts — 163
- Wins — 6
- Pole positions — 6
- Fastest laps — 8
- Podiums — 27
- Not qualified — 0
- GPs in the lead — 21
- Laps in the lead — 401
- Kms in the lead — 1937
- Points scored — 324

PRIOR TO F1

- 1978-92 Karting
- 1993 F3 ADAC Jr. (2nd)
- 1994 F3 (D) (3rd)
- 1995 F3 (D) (2nd), F3 Macau Winner
- 1996 F3000 Champion (J)

F1 CAREER

1997	Jordan-Peugeot. 13 pts. 11th of Championship.
1998	Jordan-Mugen-Honda. 14 pts. 10th of Championship.
1999	Williams-Supertec. 35 pts. 6th of Championship.
2000	Williams-BMW. 24 pts. 5th of Championship.
2001	Williams-BMW. 49 pts. 4th of Championship.
2002	Williams-BMW. 42 pts. 4th of Championship.
2003	Williams-BMW. 58 pts. 5th of Championship.
2004	Williams-BMW. 24 pts. 9th of Championship.
2005	Toyota. 45 pts. 6th of Championship.
2006	Toyota. 20 pts. 10th of Championship.

8. Jarno TRULLI

DRIVER PROFILE

- Name — TRULLI
- Firstname — Jarno
- Nationality — Italian
- Date of birth — 13th July 1974
- Place of birth — Pescara (I)
- Lives in — Wokingham (GB)
- Marital status — married to Barbara
- Kids — two sons (Enzo et Marco)
- Hobbies — music, movie, karting, computers
- Favorite music — pop, rock, jazz, blues
- Favorite meal — pizza
- Favorite driks — Coca-Cola
- Height — 173 cm
- Weight — 60 kg
- Web — www.jarnotrulli.com

STATISTICS

- Grands Prix — 167
- Starts — 164
- Wins — 1
- Pole positions — 3
- Fastest laps — 0
- Podiums — 7
- Not qualified — 0
- GPs in the lead — 10
- Laps in the lead — 147
- Kms in the lead — 605
- Points scored — 175

PRIOR TO F1

- 1983-86 Karting
- 1988-90 Kart 100 Champion (I)
- 1991 Kart 100 FK World Champion
- 1992 Kart 125 FC (2nd)
- 1993 Kart 100 SA (2nd)
- 1994 Kart 125 FC World Champion & Kart 100 FSA Champion (EUR & North USA)
- 1995 Kart 100 FA Champion (I)
- 1996 F3 Champion (D)

F1 CAREER

1997	Minardi-Hart, Prost-Mugen Honda. 3 pts. 15th of Championship.
1998	Prost-Peugeot. 1 pt. 15th of Championship.
1999	Prost-Peugeot. 7 pts. 11th of Championship.
2000	Jordan-Mugen-Honda. 6 pts. 10th of Championship.
2001	Jordan-Honda. 12 pts. 9th of Championship.
2002	Renault. 9 pts. 8th of Championship.
2003	Renault. 33 pts. 8th of Championship.
2004	Renault, Toyota. 46 pts. 6th of Championship.
2005	Toyota. 43 pts. 7th of Championship.
2006	Toyota. 15 pts. 12th of Championship.

Seven race retirements and tenth in the world championship. Not a good year for Ralf, in a season where the highlights came at almost opposite ends of the series: a podium and third place in Australia and then, in Brazil, he knew he would no longer have to be referred to as "Michael's little brother" given that the seven times world champion was retiring. "Ralf has worked hard this year, but with no real results to show for his efforts," is what a school report might say. It is all too easy to dismiss performances like this but when the equipment is not up to the task involved what else can a driver do? In Ralf's case, look at his bank account and marvel at his huge pay cheques, keep appearing in Germany's dreadful tabloid newspapers and make the occasional rude remark about his brother. One could say that he allowed himself to be tempted by Toyota's over-generous offer and now he is having to live with that decision.

In 2005, the Italian picked up 43 points and finished seventh in the championship and had found his first season in the red and white of Toyota an encouraging start. Oh how much disappointment followed this year, as he just managed to beat David Coulthard to twelfth spot in the Drivers' classification, finishing a mere five times in the points. Trulli's talent was definitely being wasted thanks to the inadequacies of the team's technical package and a sniff of a podium in Monaco and Montreal were the only signs of what might have been. In simple terms, he was dogged by too many reliability problems and only occasionally did we see a glimmer of what Trulli can do. However, one wonder how much of an improvement can be expected, as Jarno is not the most forceful of characters and what Toyota really needs, in order to counter narrow minded officialdom back in their Japanese base, is a driver who can motivate the team, bang the table, shout a bit and get things moving. However, on the plus side, his vineyards are producing some excellent wine right now.

Tsutomu Tomita

John Howett

Pascal Vasselon

Luca Marmorini

TOYOTA TF106
RALF SCHUMACHER
AUSTRALIAN GRAND PRIX

SPECIFICATIONS

• Chassis	Toyota TF106 (BRN > E) & TF106B (MC > BR)
• Type	Moulded carbon fibre and honeycomb construction
• Suspensions	Carbon fibre double wishbone arrangement, with carbon fibre trackrod and pushrod. Pushrod activates rocker, torsion bar, damper and anti-roll bar assy (Front / Rear)
• Engine	V8 Toyota RVX-06 (90°)
• Displacement	2398 cc
• Power	≈ 740 bhp
• Maximum revs	≈ 19,000 rpm
• Valves	4 valves pneumatic distribution
• Electronic ignition	Toyota / Magneti Marelli
• Transmission	7-speed unit + reverse. Toyota-designed maincase with Toyota /Xtrac internals. Sequential electro-hydraulic actuation
• Clutch	Sachs
• Radiators	Denso
• Fuel / oil	Esso / Esso
• Brakes (discs)	Hitco (carbon)
• Brakes (calipers)	Brembo
• Spark plugs	Denso / Panasonic
• Shock absorbers	Penske
• Tyres	Bridgestone Potenza
• Wheels dimensions	13"
• Wheels	BBS Magnesium
• Weight	600 kg, driver + camera + ballast
• Wheel base	3090 mm
• Overall lenght	4530 mm
• Overall width	1800 mm
• Overall height	950 mm
• Front track	1425 mm
• Rear track	1411 mm

STATISTICS

• Number of Grand Prix	87
• Best result	2 x 2nd
• Number of pole positions	2
• Number of fastest laps	1
• Number of podiums	6
• Number of drivers Championship	0
• Number of constructors Championship	0
• Total number of points scored	150

POSITION IN CHAMPIONSHIP

2002	10th – 2 pts	2005	4th – 88 pts
2003	8th – 16 pts	2006	6th – 35 pts
2004	8th – 9 pts		

2006 TEST DRIVERS

• Ricardo ZONTA (BR) • Olivier PANIS (F)

SUCCESSION OF DRIVERS 2006

• Ralf SCHUMACHER all 18 Grands Prix
• Jarno TRULLI all 18 Grands Prix

TEAM PROFILE

• Address	Toyota Motorsport GmbH Toyota-Allee 7 50858 Köln Deutschland
• Telephone	+49 (0) 223 418 23 444
• Fax	+49 (0) 223 418 23 37
• Web	www.toyota-f1.com
• Founded in	1999
• First Grand Prix	Australia 2002
• Official name	Panasonic Toyota Racing
• Chairman and Team Principal	Tsutomu Tomita
• President	John Howett
• Excecutive Vice President	Yoshiaki Kinoshita
• Dir. Technical Co-ordination	Noritoshi Arai
• Senior General Manager	Pascal Vasselon (Chassis) Luca Marmorini (Engine)
• Team Manager	Richard Cregan
• Chief Engineer Race & Test	Dieter Gass
• Race Engineer (7)	Francesco Nenci
• Race Engineer (8)	Ossi Oikarinen
• Number of employees	580
• Partners	Panasonic, DENSO,BMC Software, Bridgestone, Dassault Systèmes, Ebbon-Dacs, EMC, Esso, Intel, Magneti Marelli, Alpinestar, Future Sport, KTC, MAN, EuroWind, Nautilus, Takata

Is it possible to feel sorry for a team owned by the biggest car company in the world? A company so rich, it is known back home as "The Bank of Japan." Can we have sympathy for an organisation that has a bigger budget than any other in the sport that has a six year one billion dollar plan and yet and yet....has never won a grand prix? Probably one can allow oneself to have some sympathy for the European side of the operation as most of Toyota's problems seem to stem from incompetence from their masters back home in Japan. One gets the impression that if Cologne was allowed to run its own show, take its own decisions and just get on with the job, things might really get better. Good people work for Toyota, or in the case of technical director Mike Gascoyne, used to work for Toyota. The sacking of the Englishman after the Melbourne race is just one example of how the "suits" in Tokyo ruled the roost in Germany. Their political influence got in the way of the racing, as with their decision to switch from Michelin to Bridgestone tyres. This delayed work on the new car so the cockpit that Schumacher and Trulli eased themselves into at the start of the season in Bahrain, was effectively the 2005 car with a few tweaks, and what should have been the new car only really appeared in Monaco. Technically, it was all a bit of a mess, the initial car running the TF105 keel but the new "zero keel" style of front suspension. This meant the car was losing out twice, having the old fashioned keel but with the limited range of adjustment on the new suspension. Given that the Bridgestone tyres always need to run with more camber than the Michelins, this suspension layout did not suit them at all. Problems extended to the new V8 engine, which although naturally shorter than the old V10, had not been shifted forward, in the way that every other team had done, which meant Toyota missed out on the aero advantage that the V8 should have offered. It is one long catalogue of cock-ups and it gets worse when you consider that, finally, the engine was not actually that powerful, maybe 30 to 45 horsepower down on a Ferrari for example. No, you cannot feel sorry for them can you.

Williams Cosworth

9. Mark WEBBER

DRIVER PROFILE

- Name — WEBBER
- Firstname — Mark Alan
- Nationality — australian
- Date of birth — 27th August 1976
- Place of birth — Queanbeyan (NSW, AUS)
- Lives in — Buckinghamshire (GB)
- Marital status — engaged to Ann
- Kids — -
- Hobbies — VTT, guided planes, Playstation2
- Favorite music — Dog Milo, Maroon 5, House music
- Favorite meal — pasta, pizza, chocolate, ice cream and desserts
- Favorite drink — apple juice, lemonade and mineral water
- Height — 184 cm
- Weight — 74 kg
- Web — www.markwebber.com

STATISTICS

- Grands Prix — 88
- Starts — 86
- Best result — 1 x 3rd
- Best qualification — 2 x 2nd
- Fastest laps — 0
- Podiums — 1
- Not qualified — 0
- GPs in the lead — 3
- Laps in the lead — 5
- Kms in the lead — 22
- Points scored — 69

PRIOR TO F1

- 1991-93 Karting, NSW and ACT Champion (92)
- 1994 F. Ford (AUS) (14th)
- 1995 F. Ford (AUS) (4th)
- 1996 F. Ford (GB) (2nd), F. Ford Festival Winner
- 1997 F3 (GB) (4th)
- 1998 FIA-GT Series (2nd)
- 2000 F3000 (3rd)
- 2001 F3000 (2nd)

F1 CAREER

2002 Minardi-Asiatech. 2 pts. 16th of the Championship.
2003 Jaguar. 17 pts. 10th of the Championship.
2004 Jaguar. 7 pts. 13th of the Championship.
2005 Williams-BMW. 36 pts. 10th of the Championship.
2006 Williams-Cosworth. 7 pts. 14th of the Championship.

10. Nico ROSBERG

DRIVER PROFILE

- Name — ROSBERG
- Firstname — Nico
- Nationality — german
- Date of birth — 27th June 1985
- Place of birth — Wiesbaden (D)
- Lives in — Monte-Carlo (F)
- Marital status — single
- Kids — -
- Hobbies — tennis, golf, motorbike, music, cinema
- Favorite music — everything, 3 Doors Down
- Favorite meal — pasta with vegetebles, chocolate cake
- Favorite drink — apple juice with, sparkling water
- Height — 178 cm
- Weight — 69 kg
- Web — www.nicorosberg.com

STATISTICS

- Grands Prix — 18
- Starts — 18
- Best result — 2 x 7th
- Best qualification — 1 x 3rd
- Fastest laps — 1
- Podiums — 0
- Not qualified — 0
- GPs in the lead — 0
- Laps in the lead — 0
- Kms in the lead — 0
- Points scored — 4

PRIOR TO F1

- 1996-97 mini-kart Champion(F)
- 1998 ICA Jr karting Champion (North America)
- 1999 Karting ICA Jr (I) (2nd), (EU) (4th)
- 2000 Formula A (EU) Karting (2nd)
- 2001 Super A Karting(World)
- 2002 F.BMW ADAC Champion (D), Test-F1 Williams
- 2003 Euro-Series F3 (8th), Test-F1 Williams
- 2004 F3 Euro-Series (4th), Test-F1 Williams
- 2005 GP2 series Champion , Williams F1 test driver

F1 CAREER

2006 Williams-Cosworth. 4 pts. 17th of the Championship.

The affable Aussie is in danger of watching his Formula 1 career go down the pan, which would be a great shame as he probably has the talent to do much better than his one meagre podium from 2005. After starting his career with Minardi and then Jaguar, the move to Williams in 2005 was supposed to see him finally blossom into a top ranking grand prix driver, but who could have foretold what a disaster area the English team would be. We occasionally saw flashes of what Mark can do this year and as usual his qualifying pace was his calling card, but results were just not an option this season and for the first time in his career, this most self-motivated of drivers seem to lose some of his spark. The switch to Red Bull Racing might reignite it and he should give new team-mate David Coulthard a hard time. But everything depends on what sort of car Adrian Newey has provided for him. It will be year six of Webber's F1 career and results must come now.

Coming off the back of a great year in GP2, the son of the 1982 world champion hit the ground running in Formula 1, finishing seventh and in the points in his debut race in Bahrain. Maybe that was not the best of starts, because it might have led to some over-confidence, as it was followed by several mistakes as he threw himself at the scenery and in the very last event of the year, he and his team-mate actually wiped themselves out of the race! Like all drivers new to the sport, the fact that the amount of free practice is so restricted, as teams struggle to conserve engines and tyres for the crucial qualifying and race, was his biggest handicap, especially at those tracks where he had never raced before. However, one thing is certain about the "Blonde Bombshell," apart from the fact he spends too much time brushing his hair, he is very quick and the experience will come with time. Williams certainly had no qualms about taking up their option on the youngster for 2007, when he will partner this year's tester, Alex Wurz.

Sir Frank Williams

Sam Michael

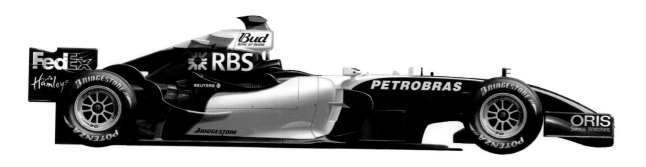

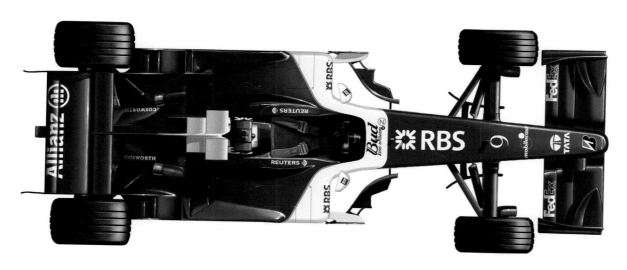

WILLIAMS FW28-COSWORTH
MARK WEBBER
MONACO GRAND PRIX

SPECIFICATIONS

- Chassis — Williams FW28
- Type — Monocoque construction fabricated from carbon aramid epoxy and honeycomb composite structure
- Suspensions — Carbon fibre double wishbone arrangement, with composite toelink and pushrod activated torsion springs (Front) and rockers (Rear)
- Engine — Cosworth CA 2006 V8 (90°)
- Displacement — 2398 cc
- Maximum revs — 20,000 rpm
- Valves — 4 valves per cylinder pneumatic distribution
- Electronic ignition — WilliamsF1 & Pi/Cosworth
- Transmission — WilliamsF1, 7-speed seamless sequential semi-automatic shift + reverse, gear selection electro-hydraulically actuated
- Clutch — Automotive Products
- Radiators — IMI Marston
- Fuel / oil — Petrobras / Castrol
- Brakes (discs) — Carbone Industrie
- Brakes (calipers) — AP Racing
- Spark plugs — Champion
- Shock absorbers — WilliamsF1
- Tyres — Bridgestone Potenza
- Wheels dimension — 13"
- Wheels diameter — 350 mm (Front) / 375 mm (Rear)
- Wheels — O.Z. Racing
- Weight — 605 kg, driver + camera + ballast
- Wheel base — 3100 mm
- Overall lenght — 4500 mm
- Overall width — 1800 mm
- Overall height — 950 mm

TEAM PROFILE

- Address — Williams F1 Grove, Wantage, Oxfordshire, OX12 0DQ - Great Britain
- Telephone — +44 (0) 1235 7777 00
- Fax — +44 (0) 1235 7777 39
- Web — www.bmw.williamsf1.com
- Founded in — 1969
- First Grand Prix — Argentina 1975 (ARG 1973, under ISO)
- Official name — Williams F1 Team
- Team Principal — Sir Frank Williams
- Director of Engineering — Patrick Head
- CEO Williams F1 — Chris Chapple
- Technical Director — Sam Michael
- Chief Operating Officer — Alex Burns
- Chief Aerodynamicist — Loïc Bigois
- Engineer (chassis) — Frank Dernie
- Race Team Manager — Tim Newton
- Chief mechanic — Carl Gaden
- Race Engineer (9) — Tony Ross
- Race Engineer (10) — Xevi Pujolar
- Number of employees — 400 (Williams)
- Partners — RBS, Accenture, Allianz, Battery, Bridgestone, Budweiser, FedEx, Hamleys,Mobilecast,ORIS, Petrobras,Philips,Qenetiq, Reuters Tata, Castrol, Dewalt,Fluent, MAN,O.Z.Racing,Puma,PPG Randsta

STATISTICS

- Number of Grand Prix — 532
- Number of victories — 113
- Number of pole positions — 125
- Number of fastest laps — 129
- Number of podiums — 293
- Number of drivers Championship — 7
- Number of constructors Championship — 9
- Total number of points scored — 2506,5

WILLIAMS F1 TEAM

POSITION IN CHAMPIONSHIP

1975	9th – 6 pts	1983	4th – 38 pts	1991	2nd – 125 pts	1999	5th – 35 pts
1976	not classified	1984	6th – 25,5 pts	1992	1st – 164 pts	2000	3rd – 36 pts
1977	not classified	1985	3rd – 71 pts	1993	1st – 168 pts	2001	3rd – 80 pts
1978	9th – 11 pts	1986	1st – 141 pts	1994	1st – 118 pts	2002	2nd – 92 pts
1979	2nd – 75 pts	1987	1st – 137 pts	1995	2nd – 112 pts	2003	2nd – 144 pts
1980	1st – 120 pts	1988	7th – 20 pts	1996	1st – 175 pts	2004	4th – 88 pts
1981	1st – 95 pts	1989	2nd – 77 pts	1997	1st – 123 pts	2005	5th – 66 pts
1982	4th – 58 pts	1990	4th – 57 pts	1998	3rd – 38 pts	2006	8th –11 pts

2006 TEST DRIVERS

- Alexander WURZ (A)
- Narain KARTHIKEYAN (IND)

SUCCESSION OF DRIVERS 2006

- Mark WEBBER — the 18 Grands Prix
- Nico ROSBERG — the 18 Grands Prix

A surprisingly good engine from the only truly independent engine supplier in the sport, Bridgestone tyres that, in the hands of others, won more races than its rivals, one experienced and competent driver and a young gun fresh from victory in the previous year's GP2 series. It should have been an annus mirabilis for Williams but it was a real case of annus horribilis, with eighth place in the championship and nothing better than a couple of sixth places. Sad to see that the only form of momentum that this once great team seems to be gathering at the moment, is the momentum that propels it downhill fast. In winter testing, it was clear that Cosworth had risen to the challenge of designing a powerful new generation version of their signature V8 configuration that had swept all before back in the glory days of Jim Clark and the Lotus 49, so there was cause for optimism in the Grove camp. Sure, an engine did let go in the Malaysian heat and for a few races after that, the team operated on a self-imposed rev restriction until the problem was sorted. However, the switch from Michelin to Bridgestone did not go quite as smoothly and it was evident that this was one area where the team was going to struggle. The FW28 did not like going into corners at speed and the way to solve that particular issue was to apply more aerodynamic downforce: an obvious solution but one that robbed the car of speed. But the biggest problem of all and one that is unforgivable as it reflects badly on the team's level of preparation and quality control, was that the cars were simply too fragile and unreliable and whenever a good result seemed within the team's grasp, the car would more often than not end up stranded at the side of the track. Hard to believe that a podium was on the cards for Webber in Monaco until a cracked exhaust wrecked the electrics. As a genuinely independent team, Williams really does need good results to pull in the sponsors to fund its racing and a portfolio of poor 2006 results does not make the task of its marketing department any easier. What seemed like a good move in making the switch from Cosworth to Toyota might not be as good as it appears on paper, given that the Toyota engine - at least in its 2006 incarnation - was well short of what the top V8 builders were producing in terms of horsepower. Another difficult year in 2007?

Honda

11. Rubens BARRICHELLO

DRIVER PROFILE

- Name · BARRICHELLO
- Firstname · Rubens Gonçalves
- Nationality · brasilian
- Date of birth · 23rd May 1972
- Place of birth · São Paulo (BR)
- Lives in · Monaco (MC)
- Marital status · married to Silvana
- Kids · two sons (Eduardo and Fernando)
- Hobbies · karting, bowling
- Favorite music · pop, rock, Biagio Antonacci
- Favorite meal · pasta
- Favorite drink · Red Bull
- Height · 172 cm
- Weight · 71 kg
- Web · www.barrichello.com.br

STATISTICS

- Grands Prix · 236
- Starts · 233
- Wins · 9
- Pole positions · 13
- Fastest laps · 15
- Podiums · 61
- Not qualified · 0
- GPs in the lead · 44
- Laps in the lead · 722
- Kms in the lead · 3487
- Points scored · 519

PRIOR TO F1

- 1981-88 Karting (5 times Brasil Champion)
- 1989 F. Ford 1600 (3rd)
- 1990 Opel Lotus Euroseries Champion, F. Vauxhall (11th)
- 1991 F3 Champion (GB)
- 1992 F3000 (3rd)

F1 CAREER

- 1993 Jordan-Hart. 2 pts. 17th of the Championship.
- 1994 Jordan-Hart. 19 pts. 6th of the Championship.
- 1995 Jordan-Peugeot. 11 pts. 11th of the Championship.
- 1996 Jordan-Peugeot. 14 pts. 8th of the Championship.
- 1997 Stewart-Ford. 6 pts. 13th of the Championship.
- 1998 Stewart-Ford. 4 pts. 12th of the Championship.
- 1999 Stewart-Ford. 21 pts. 7th of the Championship.
- 2000 Ferrari. 62 pts. 4th of the Championship.
- 2001 Ferrari. 56 pts. 3rd of the Championship.
- 2002 Ferrari. 77 pts. 2nd of the Championship.
- 2003 Ferrari. 65 pts. 4th of the Championship.
- 2004 Ferrari. 114 pts. 2nd of the Championship.
- 2005 Ferrari. 38 pts. 8th of the Championship.
- 2006 Honda. 30 pts. 7th of the Championship.

12. Jenson BUTTON

DRIVER PROFILE

- Name · BUTTON
- Firstname · Jenson
- Nationality · british
- Date of birth · 19th January 1980
- Place of birth · Frome, Somerset (GB)
- Lives in · Monaco (MC)
- Marital status · single
- Kids · -
- Hobbies · web surfing, video games, shopping
- Favorite music · Jamiroquai, Kool And The Gang, the 70'
- Favorite meal · curry, fish and pasta
- Favorite drink · water and orange juice
- Height · 183 cm
- Weight · 68.5 kg
- Web · www.jensonbutton.com

STATISTICS

- Grands Prix · 122
- Starts · 118
- Victoire · 1
- Pole positions · 3
- Fastest laps · 0
- Podiums · 15
- Not qualified · 0
- GPs in the lead · 13
- Laps in the lead · 104
- Kms in the lead · 522
- Points scored · 223

PRIOR TO F1

- 1989-95 Karting, Cadet Champion (GB) (90-91) / Open (GB) (91-92-93) / Jr. TKM (GB) (91-92) / Senior ICA (I) (95)
- 1996 Karting (3rd of the World cup and US Championship)
- 1997 Karting Champion Super A (EUR) and A. Senna cup Winner
- 1998 F. Ford and F. Ford Festival Champion (GB)
- 1999 F3 (GB) (3rd)

F1 CAREER

- 2000 Williams-BMW. 12 pts. 8th of the Championship.
- 2001 Benetton-Renault. 2 pts. 17th of the Championship.
- 2002 Renault. 14 pts. 7th of the Championship.
- 2003 B·A·R-Honda. 17 pts. 9th of the Championship.
- 2004 B·A·R-Honda. 85 pts. 3rd of the Championship.
- 2005 B·A·R-Honda. 37 pts. 6th of the Championship.
- 2006 Honda. 56 pts. 6th of the Championship.

They say that if you think the grass looks greener on the other side of the fence, it probably means you have not been cultivating and watering your own grass enough. The Brazilian's move from Ferrari was supposed to represent a freedom of sorts, an escape from the terrible burden of living in the shadow of Michael Schumacher, a move to a team where he would be treated as an equal to his team-mate, a move to a team run by fellow countryman and friend, Gil de Feran. But it did not quite work out like that and Rubens probably realised that things had not been so bad in Maranello and the Reds had actually been quite good at growing a nice lawn. Honda had plenty of its own problems to sort out and therefore getting the car to suit Barrichello's style was not an immediate priority. In short, Rubens had spent years driving Ferrari's very sophisticated traction control system that simply allowed him to hit the throttle hard coming out of a corner, allowing the control system to deal with any bad behaviour from the chassis. Honda's system did not work like that, which was not so much of a problem for Button's very smooth throttle control. By the time Rubens' problem was solved, the season was well underway. But the youngest veteran on the grid is still young enough to turn things around next year.

"This is going to be my year," is something that "Jense" and his followers have been too keen to trot out almost since his second year in Formula 1. It was beginning to become something of an embarrassment that the man the British media had wanted to christen the new Damon Hill, had yet to win a race. And the fact he had paid a fortune to buy his way out of his Williams contract also seemed like complete lunacy. But, by the end of the year, it looked as though, for once, he had made the right decision sticking with Honda. Finally the lack of wins was exorcised in Budapest. Seven consecutive points finishes rounded off the Englishman's best season and he finally seems to fitting the big pair of shoes his supporters had placed by his bed. All it needed was a decent car and Jenson's peerlessly smooth driving style; easy on the throttle, tyres, brakes and steering would do the rest. Now it is up to the team to keep moving forward when Jenson could really deliver for them in 2007.

Nick Fry

Yasuhiro Wada

Shuhei Nakamoto

Gil de Ferran

HONDA RA106
JENSON BUTTON
HUNGARIAN GRAND PRIX

SPECIFICATIONS

- Chassis — Honda RA106
- Type — Moulded carbon fibre and honeycomb composite structure
- Suspensions — Wishbone and pushrod-activated torsion springs and rockers, mechanical anti-roll bar (Front / Rear)
- Engine — V8 Honda RA0806E (90°)
- Displacement — 2400 cc
- Power — + 700 bhp
- Maximum revs — 19,000 rpm
- Valves — 4 valves per cylinder; pneumatic valve system
- Electronic ignition — Honda PGM-IG
- Transmission — Honda F1 Sequential, semi-automatic, hydraulic activation. 7-speed unit + reverse
- Clutch — AP Racing
- Fuel / oil — Elf / Nisseki
- Brakes (discs) — Alcon (carbon)
- Brakes (calipers) — AP Racing
- Spark plugs — NGK / 3Ah lead acid
- Shock absorbers — Showa
- Tyres — Michelin
- Wheels dimensions — 13" width 312 mm (Front) / 340 mm (Rear)
- Wheels — BBS
- Weight — 605 kg, driver + camera + ballast
- Wheel base — 3140 mm
- Overall lenght — 4675 mm
- Overall width — 1800 mm
- Overall height — 950 mm
- Front track — 1460 mm
- Rear track — 1420 mm

TEAM PROFILE

- Address — Honda Racing F1 Team Operations Centre, Brackley, Northants NN13 7BD Great Britain
- Telephone — +44 (0) 1280 84 40 00
- Fax — +44 (0) 1280 84 40 01
- Web — www.hondaracingf1.com
- Founded in — 1964
- First Grand Prix — Germany 1964
- Official name — Lucky Strike Honda Racing F1 Team
- Chief Executive Officer — Nick Fry
- President, Honda Racing Development Ltd. — Yasuhiro Wada
- Technical Director — Shuhei Nakamoto
- Sporting Director — Gil de Ferran
- Vice President, Honda Racing Development Ltd — Otmar Szafnauer
- Chief Engineer (Research) — Jacky Eckelaert
- Chief Engineer (Race) — Craig Wilson
- Chief Engineer (Vehicle perf.) — Mark Ellis
- Race Engineer (11) — Jock Clear
- Race Engineer (12) — Andy Shovlin
- Race Team Manager — Ron Meadows
- Number of employees — 360
- Partners — British American Tobacco, Celerant Consulting, ENEOS, Intercond, Michelin, NTN, Ray-Ban, Seiko, Asahi Soft Drinks
- Technical Partners — Alcon, Avaya, Haas, Automation, Matrix, NGK, Showa, UGS – The PLM Company
- Suppliers — AlpineStars, Autoglym, Cablefree Solutions Ltd, CIBER UK, Creative Print Group, CYTEC, Endless Advance Ltd, NCE, Glasurit Automotive Refinish, Pipex, Sandvik Coromant, Snap-on Tools, STL Communications Ltd, Takata, Tripp Luggage

STATISTICS

- Number of Grand Prix — 53
- Number of victories — 3
- Number of pole positions — 2
- Number of fastest laps — 2
- Number of podiums — 8
- Number of drivers Championship — 0
- Number of constructors Championship — 0
- Total number of points scored — 134

POSITION IN CHAMPIONSHIP

1964	not classified	1967	4th – 20 pts
1965	6th – 11 pts	1968	6th – 14 pts
1966	8th – 3 pts	2006	4th – 86 pts

2006 TEST DRIVER

- Anthony DAVIDSON (GB)

SUCCESSION OF DRIVERS 2006

- Rubens BARRICHELLO — all 18 Grands Prix
- Jenson BUTTON — all 18 Grands Prix

Anthony Davidson

As a result of the cigarette companies fleeing the sport - only Marlboro will be left with Ferrari in 2007 - Honda bought out British American Tobacco and BAR-Honda metamorphosed into plain Honda this year. Not since the Sixties had the sport's longest serving Japanese company stood on its own rather than be an engine supplier. The operation was still run out of Brackley, England as far as the chassis was concerned, but Honda's influence now extended far deeper into the boardroom and the psyche of the team. Would it work? It had to work. And in a small way it did, as the team and perhaps more importantly, Jenson Button finally secured his first F1 win at the dramatic Hungarian Grand Prix. Winter testing had gone well, but then how many times have we seen winter performance melt in the summer heat? That's exactly what happened for Honda, with rather too many embarrassing clouds of engine smoke punctuating the season. Inevitably heads had to roll, starting with that of technical director, Geoff Willis and Shuhei Nakamoto was brought in to hold the reins. Apart from reliability issues, the car would be quick in qualifying but lack race pace and even that latter attribute seemed to disappear during the season. But eventually, slowly, steadily, like a giant tanker on the ocean, the whole team was turned around and from Hockenheim onwards it scored points at every race to the end of the year and the historic Hungarian win was a natural morale booster for everyone.

Ending the year on an upward trend, the future is looking genuinely rosy for the upcoming season, as the team finally got its new wind tunnel up and running and the "frozen" 2007 engine specification was actually tried out before the end of the season with encouraging results in terms of performance. The superficial veneer of confidence that team boss Nick Fry tried valiantly to hide behind at the pre-season launch actually turned into the real thing come the season finale when Button was yet again on the podium in third place. In the battle between the Japanese, Toyota must be wondering why it bothers.

Red Bull Ferrari

14. David COULTHARD

DRIVER PROFILE

- Name — COULTHARD
- Firstname — David
- Nationality — scottish
- Date of birth — March 27th 1971
- Place of birth — Twynholm (Scotland, GB)
- Lives in — Monaco (MC)
- Marital status — engaged to Karine Minier
- Enfants — -
- Hobbies — Golf, swimming, cycling, cinema
- Favorite music — Maroon 5, Scissor Sisters
- Favorite meal — pasta, thai food
- Favorite drink — tea and mineral water
- Height — 182 cm
- Weight — 72.5 kg
- Web — www.davidcoulthard-f1.com

STATISTICS

		PRIOR TO F1
Grands Prix	212	1983-88 Karting (3 times Jr.
Starts	211	and Open Kart (Ecos.) Champion,
Wins	13	2 times Super Kart (GB) Champion)
Pole-positions	12	1989 F. Ford 1600 Champion (GB)
Fastest laps	18	1990 F. Vauxhall-Lotus (4th),
Podiums	61	GM Lotus Euroseries (5th)
Not qualified	0	1991 F3 (GB) (2nd), Winner of
GPs in the lead	60	F3 Macau and Marlboro Masters
Laps in the lead	896	1992 F3000 (9th)
Kms in the lead	4206	1993 F3000 (3rd)
Points scored	513	1994 F3000 (9th)

F1 CAREER

1994	Williams-Renault. 14 pts. 8th of the Championship.
1995	Williams-Renault. 49 pts. 3rd of the Championship.
1996	McLaren-Mercedes. 18 pts. 7th of the Championship.
1997	McLaren-Mercedes. 36 pts. 3rd of the Championship.
1998	McLaren-Mercedes. 56 pts. 3rd of the Championship.
1999	McLaren-Mercedes. 48 pts. 4th of the Championship.
2000	McLaren-Mercedes. 73 pts. 3rd of the Championship.
2001	McLaren-Mercedes. 65 pts. 2nd of the Championship.
2002	McLaren-Mercedes. 41 pts. 5th of the Championship.
2003	McLaren-Mercedes. 51 pts. 7th of the Championship.
2004	McLaren-Mercedes. 24 pts. 10th of the Championship.
2005	RBR-Cosworth. 24 pts. 12th of the Championship.
2006	RBR-Ferrari. 14 pts. 13th of the Championship.

Christian Horner

Adrian Newey

"DC" found it hard to hide his frustration in what he expected to be a follow-on season to the successes of 2005. Evidently aware that there are not too many years left in his F1 driver allowance, the Scotsman was keen to get back to the front part of the grid that had been his regular home in his Williams and McLaren days. With a few notable exceptions, it was not to be, so that actually getting through to the final third part of the qualifying session was in itself an achievement, albeit a rare one. The season had one major highpoint: a visit to the podium in third place in his "home" race at Monaco. It was a great performance on a track where driver ability and bravery has always counted for more than the sum of the technical elements of the car. Otherwise it was the usual Coulthard: capable of some very strong drives when everything went well, but often disheartened and apparently disinterested when the cause seemed hopeless. He is pinning everything on what he has worked on for two years with Red Bull, namely driving an Adrian Newey car again in 2007. Let's hope he's right.

15. Christian KLIEN

DRIVER PROFILE

- Name — KLIEN
- Firstname — Christian
- Nationality — austrian
- Date of birth — February 7th 1983
- Place of birth — Hohenems, Vorarlberg (A)
- Lives in — Hohenems (A)
- Marital status — single
- Enfants — -
- Hobbies — web, VTT, skiing
- Favorite music — Rythm'n Blues
- Favorite meal — italian food
- Favorite drink — apple juice and mineral water
- Height — 169 cm
- Weight — 68 kg
- Internet — www.christian-klien.com

STATISTICS

		PRIOR TO F1
Grands Prix	47	1996-98 Karting,
Starts	46	Champion (96) (CH)
Best result	1 x 5th	1999 F. BMW Jr. Cup (D) (4th)
Best qualification	1 x 4th	2000 F. BMW (D) (10th)
Fastest laps	0	2001 F. BMW (D) (3rd)
Podiums	0	2002 Champion F. Renault (D),
Not qualified	0	F. Renault Eurocup (5th)
GPs in the lead	0	2003 F3 Euro Series (2nd),
Laps in the lead	0	F3 Marlboro
Kms in the lead	0	Masters Zandvoort
Points scored	14	Winner

F1 CAREER

2004	Jaguar. 3 pts. 16th of the Championship.
2005	RBR-Cosworth. 9 pts. 15th of the Championship.
2006	RBR-Ferrari. 2 pts. 18th of the Championship.

It went unnoticed in all the brouhaha surrounding David Coulthard's third place in Monaco that, if he had not retired with mechanical bothers, it would have been Christian Klien standing on the podium wearing the Superman cape. But as soon as the team announced it had signed Mark Webber for 2007, the writing was on the wall for the Austrian. Although he had shown himself more than capable of producing a good race, there just was not enough about Christian to make him worth keeping if the team planned to step up a gear over the next couple of years. In some ways, this was a harsh judgment as it's fair to say Klien had possibly never recovered from coming into Formula 1 too quickly.

15. Robert DOORNBOS

DRIVER PROFILE

- Name — DOORNBOS
- Firstname — Robert Michael
- Nationality — Dutch
- Date of birth — September 23rd 1981
- Place of birth — Rotterdam (NL)
- Lives in — Viareggio (I), Monaco (MC)
- Marital status — single
- Kids — -
- Hobbies — snowboard, golf
- Favorite music — lounge and club
- Favorite meal — pasta, sushis
- Favorite drink — Red Bull
- Height — 182 cm
- Weight — 74 kg
- Web — www.robertdoornbos.com

STATISTICS

		PRIOR TO F1
Grands Prix	11	1999 Opel Lotus Winter
Starts	11	Series (GB) (2nd)
Best result	2 x 12th	2000 F. Ford (B) (2nd)
Best qualification	1 x 10th	2001 F3 (GB) (5th)
Fastest laps	0	2002 F3 (D) (11th)
Podiums	0	2003 F3 (EUR) (9th)
Not qualified	0	2004 F3000 (3rd),
Laps in the lead	0	Test-F1 Jordan
Kms in the lead	0	
Points scored	0	

F1 CAREER

2005	Minardi-Cosworth. 0 pt. 25th of the Championship.
2006	RBR-Ferrari. 0 pt. 24th of the Championship.

With Webber on the way for 2007 and Klien turning down a Red Bull-funded Champ car drive, it was the perfect opportunity for the team to assess its Friday test driver over a race weekend. Enter Robert Doornbos, who had gone through a similar scenario, stepping into a Minardi cockpit to finish off the 2005 season. The Dutch are very a la mode right now with all the fuss surrounding Spyker and clogs might soon be compulsory footwear in parts of the paddock next year. Doornbos has more media savvy than most of his fellow drivers, but now for the final part of the season he had to prove he could walk the walk as well as he could talk the talk. With the underperforming RB2 he was never going to shine, but he did a workmanlike job. Was it enough to secure him a full time race seat in '07? We will have to wait and see.

RBR RB2-FERRARI
DAVID COULTHARD
UNITED STATES GRAND PRIX

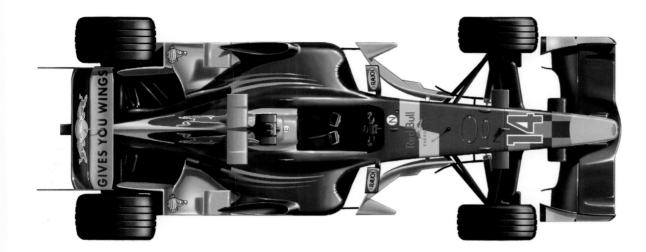

SPECIFICATIONS

- Chassis · *Red Bull RB2*
- Type · *Composite monocoque structure, designed and built in-house, carrying the Ferrari V8 engine as fully stressed member*
- Suspensions · *Aluminium alloy uprights, upper and lower carbon wishbones and pushrods, torsion bar springs and anti roll bars, Multimatic dampers (Front/Rear)*
- Engine · *V8 Ferrari type 056 (90°)*
- Displacement · *2398 cc*
- Maximum revs · *19,000 rpm*
- Valves · *32 valves pneumatic distribution*
- Electronic ignition · *Magneti Marelli*
- Transmission · *7-speed gearbox, longitudinally mounted with hydraulic system for power shift and clutch operation + reverse.*
- Embrayage · *AP Racing*
- Fuel / oil · *Shell*
- Brakes (discs) · *Hitco (carbone)*
- Brakes (calipers) · *Brembo*
- Shock absorbers · *Multimatic*
- Tyres · *Michelin*
- Wheels dimensions · *12.7"-13 (Front) / 13.4"-13 (Rear)*
- Wheels · *AVUS*
- Weight · *605 kg, driver + camera + ballast*
- Wheelbase · *not revealed*
- Total length · *not revealed*

STATISTICS

- Number of Grand Prix · 36
- Best result · 1 x 3rd
- Best qualification · 1 x 4th
- Number of fastest laps · 0
- Number of podiums · 1
- Number of drivers Championship · 0
- Number of constructors Championship · 0
- Nombre total de Points scored · 50

POSITION IN CHAMPIONSHIP

2005 7th – 34 pts
2006 7th – 16 pts

2006 TEST DRIVERS

- Robert DOORBNBOS (NL)
- Michael AMMERMULLER (D)

SUCCESSION OF DRIVERS 2006

- David COULTHARD · *the 18 Grands Prix*
- Christian KLIEN · *15 Grands Prix (BRN > I)*
- Robert DOORNBOS · *3 Grands Prix (CHI > BR)*

TEAM PROFILE

- Address · *Red Bull Racing Bradbourne Drive, Tilbrook, Milton Keynes, MK7 8BJ Great Britain*
- Telephone · *+44 (0) 1908 27 07 00*
- Fax · *+44 (0) 1908 27 97 11*
- Web · *www.redbullf1.com*
- Founded in · *2005*
- First Grand Prix · *Australia 2005*
- Official name · *Red Bull Racing*
- Chairman · *Dietrich Mateschitz*
- Sporting Director · *Christian Horner*
- Technical Director · *Adrian Newey*
- Chief engineer · *Mark Smith*
- Chief aerodynamistic · *Ben Agathangelou*
- Chief team · *Jonathan Wheatley*
- Chief development · *Anton Stipinovich*
- Head of R&D · *Andrew Green*
- Race engineer (14) · *Mark Hutcheson*
- Race engineer (15) · *Ciaron Pibleam*
- Number of employees · *300*
- Official partners · *Hangar-7, Rauch, UGS, Alpinestars, Michelin, Quehenberger, Michelin, Metro*

Everyone's darling in 2005, the honeymoon period well and truly came to an end in 2006 for Red Bull Racing. The previous year had seen plenty of points, plenty of talking points - the Energy Station hospitality unit and its open door policy, pretty girls imported for every race, unusual promotions and everyone-is-welcome parties. But 2006 started like a bad hangover. Ferrari engines should have been cause for elation, instead, an over aggressive cooling policy found the team struggling through winter testing with cooling problems. This meant that either engines were going bang or only a few laps at a time could be completed, thus curtailing the development programme on the rest of the car. The team arrived in Bahrain with no real mileage under its belt. Added to this specific technical problem, generally the team suffered with the standard "difficult second season syndrome" that historically has affected just about every team to try its hand at the harder-than-it-looks game of grand prix racing. Red Bull Racing had expanded massively from its Jaguar days, got rid of some dead wood and poached a variety of department heads from other teams. Of course, it is not the work of a moment for new people to stamp their mark on a department, change working methods and generally learn to operate as a single unit. Inevitably, a changed team, even if it might be better in the long term, operates at a lower level for a few months.

But it was the lack of winter testing that hit the team hardest with no less than seven retirements in the first half a dozen races. With no chance of doing very much at all, the decision was taken to freeze development of the 2006 car around German GP time and put every effort into the 2007 model that would represent Adrian Newey's first piece of handiwork for the energy drinks team, given he had only come on board in February. Red Bull Racing was not always popular with its peers, particularly as it was the only Michelin team to vote in favour of reinstating pit stops this season. And morale took a bit of a knock once development on RB2 dried up as it effectively meant that the Red Bull drivers found themselves constantly sharing starting rows with their cheeky little colleagues from the "trainer team" Scuderia Toro Rosso. So 2007 is an important year, as the Newey chassis gets mated (finally, as the politicking took for ever when it came to off-loading Ferrari power to Toro Rosso) to the championship winning Renault engine.

BMW Sauber

16. Nick HEIDFELD

DRIVER PROFILE

- Name — *HEIDFELD*
- Firstname — *Nick*
- Nationality — *german*
- Date of birth — *May 10th 1977*
- Place of birth — *Mönchengladbach Rheydt (D)*
- Lives in — *Stäfa (CH)*
- Marital status — *engaged to Patricia*
- Kids — *one daughter (Juni)*
- Hobbies — *tennis, golf, motoecycle, music, cinema*
- Favorite music — *the good hits*
- Favorite meal — *pasta, appetizers*
- Favorite drink — *apple juice with, sparkling water*
- Height — *165 cm*
- Weight — *59 kg*
- Web — *www.adrivo.com/nickheidfeld/*

STATISTICS

		PRIOR TO F1
Grands Prix	99	1986-92 *Karting*
Starts	97	1993 *Formule A Laval (F)*
Best result	2 x 2nd	1994 *Champion*
Pole positions	1	*F. Ford 1600 (D)*
Fastest laps	0	1995 *Champion F. Ford*
Podiums	4	*1800 (D), F. Ford (D) (2nd)*
Not qualified	0	1996 *F3 (D) (3rd)*
GPs in the lead	1	1997 *Champion F3 (D)*
Laps in the lead	1	1998 *F3000 (2nd)*
Kms in the lead	5	1999 *Champion F3000*
Points scored	56	

F1 CAREER

2000	*Prost-Peugeot. 0 pt. 20th of the Championship.*
2001	*Sauber-Petronas. 12 pts. 8th of the Championship.*
2002	*Sauber-Petronas. 7 pts. 10th of the Championship.*
2003	*Sauber-Petronas. 6 pts. 14th of the Championship.*
2004	*Jordan-Ford. 3 pts. 18th of the Championship.*
2005	*Williams-BMW. 28 pts. 11th of the Championship.*
2006	*BMW. 23 pts. 9th of the Championship.*

Mario Theissen

Willy Rampf

Peter Sauber

Longer hair, a bit of stubble; Nick was certainly trying an image shift to go with his team's makeover, but try as he might, he is still "little Nicky" to the rest of the paddock! On track, he had his usual workmanlike but anonymous season, although when Kubica arrived as a race driver, the German did wake himself up to finish on the podium in the lottery that was the Hungarian Grand Prix. BMW claims it is halfway through a rebuilding and regrouping period that is due to come to fruition in time to challenge the top teams starting with the 2008 season. Heidfeld may have to dig deep and pull a little extra out of the hat, if he wants to fight off the young pretenders who want his seat by then. At the moment though, he is very much part of the team and his contribution in taking the team from eighth to fifth in the Constructors' should not be underestimated.

17. Jacques VILLENEUVE

DRIVER PROFILE

- Name — *VILLENEUVE*
- Firstname — *Jacques*
- Nationality — *canadian*
- Date of birth — *April 9th 1971*
- Place of birth — *St-Jean-sur-Richelieu, Québec, (CDN)*
- Lives in — *Monaco (MC), Villars (CH), Montréal (CDN)*
- Marital status — *married to Ellie*
- Kids — *one son (Jules)*
- Hobbies — *skiing, playing the guitar, music, electronic*
- Favorite music — *acoustic pop/rock*
- Favorite meal — *pasta*
- Favorite drink — *milk and the "Root beer"*
- Height — *171 cm*
- Weight — *67 kg*
- Web — *www.jv-world.com*

STATISTICS

		PRIOR TO F1
Grands Prix	153	1986 *Jim Russel school*
Starts	151	1987 *piloting school*
Wins	11	*Spenard-David*
Pole-positions	13	1988 *F. Alfa (I)*
Fastest laps	9	1989-91 *F3 (I) (-, 14th, 6th)*
Podiums	23	1992 *F3 (J) (2nd)*
Not qualified	0	1993 *Formula Atlantique (3rd)*
GPs in the lead	20	1994 *IndyCar (6th)*
Laps in the lead	633	1995 *IndyCar Champion*
Kms in the lead	2965	
Points scored	228	

F1 CAREER

1996	*Williams-Renault. 78 pts. 2nd of the Championship.*
1997	*Williams-Renault. 81 pts. **World Champion**.*
1998	*Williams-Mecachrome. 21 pts. 5th of the Championship.*
1999	*B·A·R-Supertec. 0 point. 21st of the Championship.*
2000	*B·A·R-Honda. 17 pts. 7th of the Championship.*
2001	*B·A·R-Honda. 12 pts. 7th of the Championship.*
2002	*B·A·R-Honda. 4 pts. 12th of the Championship.*
2003	*B·A·R-Honda. 6 pts. 16th of the Championship.*
2004	*Renault. 0 pt. 21st of the Championship.*
2005	*Sauber-Petronas. 9 pts. 14th of the Championship.*
2006	*BMW. 7 pts. 15th of the Championship.*

Imagine you have bought a new house and when you finally move in, you discover that one of the previous residents still thinks he should live with you. That was the situation BMW reluctantly faced with Jacques Villeneuve, as the moody Canadian had a contract in place for 2006 with Sauber before the operation was bought out. Some of the new set-up's enthusiasm seemed to have rubbed off on the former world champion as he upped his game, contributed to the team's development and out-qualified Heidfeld 7 to 5 in the first part of the season. But, Villeneuve always seemed to be on borrowed time as he did not really fit the new BMW image. Then, at Hockenheim in the summer, the German team was presented with an easy way to dispense with his services. Jacques had a big crash and after the race weekend, he complained of headaches. It was just the excuse BMW had been looking for to blood their Friday tester Robert Kubica and Villeneuve found he had no alternative but to head down to the Job Centre. His departure meant that there were now only two champions on the F1 grid - Michael Schumacher and Fernando Alonso.

17. Robert KUBICA

DRIVER PROFILE

- Name — *KUBICA*
- Firstname — *Robert*
- Nationality — *polish*
- Date of birth — *December 7th 1984*
- Place of birth — *Cracovia (PL)*
- Lives in — *Varsovia (PL)*
- Marital status — *single*
- Kids — *-*
- Hobbies — *karting, bowling, video games*
- Favorite music — *pop/rock*
- Favorite meal — *italian pasta*
- Favorite drink — *soda*
- Height — *184 cm*
- Weight — *74 kg*
- Web — *www.kubica.pl*

STATISTICS

		PRIOR TO F1
Grands Prix	6	1998 *Karting Champion (I),*
Starts	6	*Winner (MC), (EU) (2nd)*
Best result	1 x 3rd	1999 *Karting Champion (I)*
Pole-positions	0	*(D), Winner (MC)*
Fastest laps	0	*Elf Master (F), (EU) (5th)*
Podiums	1	2000 *Karting (EU) (4th)*
Not qualified	0	*(Monde) (4th)*
GPs in the lead	1	2001 *Renault F2000 (EU) (I)*
Laps in the lead	5	2002 *Renault F2000*
Kms in the lead	29	*(EU), (I) (2nd)*
Points scored	6	2003 *F3 Euro Series (12th)*
		2004 *F3 Euro Series (7th)*
		2005 *World Series*
		by Renault Champion

F1 CAREER

2006	*BMW. 6 pts. 16th of the Championship.*

When you run an F1 team, having your very own Junior formula suddenly makes a lot of sense and the BMW junior drivers seem to be getting plenty of their share of the limelight at the moment. Kubica was a graduate of this school and, as BMW-Sauber's third driver, he made an immediate impact and he soon took over from Honda's third man, Anthony Davidson, as the driver most likely to top the Friday free practice time sheets. However, as we have seen before, being quick on a Friday, when there is no pressure, you can do as many laps as you like without worrying about tyres or engine life, is one thing, while actually putting together a whole race weekend, can be a completely different and much more daunting challenge. How good was the Kubica Kid? The answer came in his very first race in Budapest, where he picked up a couple of points before being disqualified for a technical fault on the car. And then, in only his third ever grand prix at Monza, something of a home track as he lived in Italy for five years, he made it to the podium in third place. A star? Maybe not yet, but a star of the future? Definitely.

BMW-SAUBER F1.06
NICK HEIDFELD
AUSTRALIAN GRAND PRIX

SPECIFICATIONS

- Chassis — BMW Sauber F1.06
- Type — Carbon fibre monococque, composite honeycomb strucutre
- Suspensions — Aluminium alloy uprights, upper and lower carbon wishbones and pushrods, torsion bar springs and anti roll bars + shock absorber (Front/Rear)
- Engine — V8 BMW P86 (90°)
- Displacement — 2400 cc
- Maximum revs — 19,000 rpm
- Valves — 4 valves per cylinder pneumatic distribution
- Electronic ignition — Magneti Marelli
- Transmission — BMW Sauber sequential longitudinal hydraulic semi-automatique, 7-speed + reverse
- Fuel / oil — Petronas / Petronas
- Brakes (discs) — Brembo, Carbone Industrie
- Brakes (calipers) — Brembo
- Shock absorbers — Sachs Race Engineering
- Tyres — Michelin
- Wheels dimensions — 27x66x13 (AV) - 32x66x13 (AR)
- Wheels — O.Z. Racing 12.5"-13 (AV) / 13.7"-13 (AR)
- Weight — 605 kg, driver + camera + ballast
- Wheel base — 3110 mm
- Overall lenght — 4610 mm
- Overall width — 1800 mm
- Overall height — 950 mm

TEAM PROFILE

- Address — BMW Motorsport - Sauber Wildbachstrasse 9 CH - 8340 Hinwil Switzerland
- Telephone — + 41 19 37 90 00
- Fax — + 41 19 37 90 01
- Web — www.bmw-sauber-f1.com
- Founded in — 1970 (Sauber)
- First Grand Prix — Barheïn 2006
- Official name — BMW Sauber F1 Team
- Chairman BMW Motorsport — Mario Theissen
- Technical Director (chassis) — Willy Rampf
- Technical Director (engine) — Heinz Paschen
- Head of engineering — Mike Krack
- Chief aerodynamistic — Willem Toet
- Team manager — Beat Zehnder
- Main Consultant — Peter Sauber
- Race engineer (16) — Andy Borme
- Race engineer (17) — Giampaolo Dall'Ara
- Chief mechanic — Urs Kuratle
- Number of employees — 670
- Main sponsors — Petronas, Intel, Crédit Suisse
- Partners — O2, Dell, Certina, Dalco, Dräxilmaier, Fluent, MAN, NGK, Puma, Walter Meier, WL gore, Würth, APC, Brütsch/Rüegger, Busin, DuPont, Egro, Gamatech, Klauke, LISTA, Mitsubishi, MTS, Oerlikon Balzers, Sun World, Winkler.

STATISTICS

- Number of Grand Prix — 18
- Best result — 2 x 3rd
- Best qualification — 1 x 3rd
- Number of fastest laps — 0
- Number of podiums — 2
- Number of drivers Championship — 0
- Number of constructors Championship — 0
- Total number of points scored — 36

POSITION IN CHAMPIONSHIP

2006   5th – 36 pts

2006 TEST DRIVERS

- Robert KUBICA (PL)
- Sebastian VETTEL (D)

SUCCESSION OF DRIVERS 2006

- Nick HEIDFELD — the 18 Grands Prix
- Jacques VILLENEUVE — 12 Grands Prix (BRN > D)
- Robert KUBICA — 6 Grands Prix (H > BR)

Sebastian Vettel

Well, who would have thought it? Here finally was a Swiss motor racing team that seemed to work as well as.....a Swiss watch. A brand new Swiss watch, albeit with a few internal mechanisms manufactured across the border in Munich. Actually, its previous incarnation, the plain old Sauber team, had always been a tidy timepiece except that while the rest of the world had moved on to quartz and digital, it was still an analogue operation. But BMW injected some modern thinking, some big company attitude and, of course, because this is Formula 1 after all, a healthy helping of money. But engines from Munich and cars from Hinwil? Years ago, Ferrari decided running a team from Italy and England was impossible and it took Renault a while to get Viry and Enstone to work in perfect harmony.

However, Mario Theissen, who has dreamed of heading an F1 team for some time now, was not about to get things wrong. In Hinwil, an extra 150 people were added to the workforce, while work on BMW's new V8 engine began as far back as November of 2004, with its staff of 250 people, the new power unit seeing the light of the day in the back of a Sauber chassis in November 2005. Willy Rampf was still the man in charge of technical matters, but former BAR man, Willem Toet was brought in to head up the aero work, using Sauber's state of the art wind tunnel. On the engine side, former Mercedes man, Markus Duesmann has been tempted to switch allegiance and will be a useful addition for 2007. There were some early season engine failures in Bahrain, Australia, Malaysia and Spain, but after that, things began to get better. This was an unheard of concept for the Sauber side of the operation. The Swiss team has traditionally shown well in the early part of the season, running a well sorted but not very developed car. Then, as all the other teams progressed, the Hinwillians would slide down the order. But this year, under BMW's guidance, the team actually had a development programme and made progress throughout the year. In fact, they were so adventurous, they twice got in trouble with the rule makers; once over the flexible rear wing and then with the "twin towers" aero attachments ahead of the cockpit that made a short lived appearance in Magny-Cours. In short, BMW-Sauber was the "nice" surprise of the season.

Spyker Midland Toyota

18. Tiago MONTEIRO

DRIVER PROFILE

- Name — *MONTEIRO*
- Firstname — *Tiago*
- Nationality — *portuguese*
- Date of birth — *July 24th 1976*
- Place of birth — *Oporto (P)*
- Lives in — *Oporto (P)*
- Marital status — *single*
- Kids — -
- Hobbies — *sport, cinema, reading, photography*
- Favorite music — *all sort*
- Favorite meal — *asian food*
- Favorite drink — *water*
- Height — *174 cm*
- Weight — *64 kg*
- Web — *www.tiagoracing.com*

STATISTICS

- Grands Prix — 37
- Starts — 37
- Best result — 1 x 3rd
- Best qualification — 1 x 11th
- Fastest laps — 0
- Podiums — 1
- Not qualified — 0
- GPs in the lead — 0
- Laps in the lead — 0
- Kms in the lead — 0
- Points scored — 7

PRIOR TO F1

- 1997 *B Champion , Porsche Cup(F)*
- 1998 *F3 (F) (12th)*
- 1999 *F3 (F) (6th), 24H Mans (17th), F. Renault (EUR)*
- 2000 *F3 (F) (2nd), F3 Int., Euro F3 (2nd), Lamborghini Super Trophy*
- 2001 *F3 (F) (2nd), GT (F), Andros Trophy*
- 2002 *F3000 (13rd), Test F1-Renault*
- 2003 *Champ Car (15th)*
- 2004 *World Series Nissan (2nd), Test F1-Minardi*

F1 CAREER

- 2005 *Jordan-Toyota. 7 pts. 16th of the Championship.*
- 2006 *Spyker Midland-Toyota. 0 pt. 21st of the Championship.*

19. Christijan ALBERS

DRIVER PROFILE

- Name — *ALBERS*
- Firstname — *Christijan*
- Nationality — *Dutch*
- Date of birth — *April 16th 1979*
- Place of birth — *Eindhoven (NL)*
- Lives in — *Laaren (NL)*
- Marital status — *single*
- Kids — -
- Hobbies — *walk, karting, squash*
- Favorite music — *hits*
- Favorite meal — *pizza*
- Favorite drink — *Coca-Cola light*
- Height — *176 cm*
- Weight — *68 kg*
- Web — *www.christijan.com*

STATISTICS

- Grands Prix — 37
- Starts — 37
- Best result — 1 x 5th
- Best qualification — 1 x 13th
- Fastest laps — 0
- Podiums — 0
- Not qualified — 0
- GPs in the lead — 0
- Laps in the lead — 0
- Kms in the lead — 0
- Points scored — 4

PRIOR TO F1

- 1997 *Champion: Karting ICA 100cc (NL), F. Ford 1800 (NL, B), Renault Megane Masters*
- 1998 *F3 (D) (5th)*
- 1999 *F3 Champion (D)*
- 2000 *F3000*
- 2001-02 *DTM, Test-F1, Minardi*
- 2003 *DTM (2nd)*
- 2004 *DTM, Test-F1, Minardi & Jordan*

F1 CAREER

- 2005 *Minardi-Cosworth. 4 pts. 19th of the Championship.*
- 2006 *Spyker Midland-Toyota. 0 pt. 22nd of the Championship.*

For the likeable Portuguese driver (journalists tend to say that because of his habit of handing out free T-shirts in the paddock!) this was a second year in Formula 1 and one where he did his best to get himself noticed, which is a tough act when you are down in the swamp at the back of the grid. Highlight was finishing ninth in Budapest and making it into the second part of qualifying on a couple of occasions. Articulate, intelligent and a hard worker, the only thing that is unclear, because of the quality, or lack of it, of his equipment, is whether or not he is a quick enough driver to make any progress in this level of the sport. But there were genuine signs of progress.

What is it about Dutch drivers? Robert Doornbos should be heading up a Public Relations company, so adept is he at blowing his own trumpet and Christijan Albers is also a dab hand at the self-publicity business, be it wearing Dutch wooden clogs painted to match his nationalistic helmet colours or simply by being loud and vociferous when it comes to extolling his own virtues. What is true is that in the early part of the season he out-paced his team-mate. He also made the headlines when Super Aguri's Ide drove into him during the San Marino Grand Prix, sending the Dutchman flying through the air, barrel rolling his Midland several times. Unsurprisingly, he has a contract to continue with Spyker in 2007.

Dr. Colin Kolles

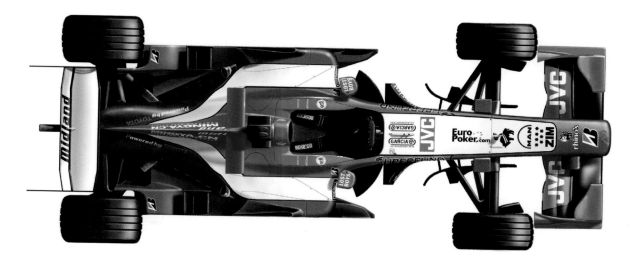

MIDLAND M16-TOYOTA
CHRISTIJAN ALBERS
SAN MARINO GRAND PRIX

SPECIFICATIONS

• Chassis	Midland M16
• Type	Full carbon fibre composite monocoque
• Suspensions	Composite pushrods activating chassis (Front) / Gearbox (Rear) mounted in-line dampers and torsion bars, unequal length composite aerodynamic wishbones, anti-roll bar (Front) and cast uprights (F/R)
• Engine	V8 Toyota RVX-06 (90°)
• Displacement	2398 cc
• Power	+ 700 bhp
• Maximum revs	≈ 20,000 rpm
• Valves	4 valves per cylinder pneumatic distribution
• Electronic ignition	Toyota / Magneti Marelli
• Transmission	MF1 Racing design. 7-speed + reverse longitudinal gearbox with electrohydraulic sequential gear change
• Clutch	AP Racing
• Radiators	Denso
• Fuel / oil	Esso / Liqui Moly
• Brakes (discs)	Carbone Industrie
• Brakes (calipers)	Brembo
• Spark plugs	Denso
• Shock absorbers	Penske
• Tyres	Bridgestone Potenza
• Wheels dimensions	13"
• Wheels	BBS
• Weight	605 kg, driver + camera + ballast
• Wheel base	+ 3000 mm
• Total lenght	5000 mm
• Total width	1800 mm
• Total height	950 mm
• Front track	1480 mm
• Rear track	1418 mm

TEAM PROFILE

• Address	Spyker F1 Team Ltd., Dadford Road, Silverstone, Northamptonshire, NN12 8TJ Great Britain
• Telephone	+44 (0) 1327 850 800
• Fax	+44 (0) 1327 857 993
• Web	www.midlandf1.com www.spykerf1.nl
• Founded in	1981 (Jordan)
• First Grand Prix	Bahrain 2006
• Official name	MF1 Racing > Spyker M F1 Team
• Owner	Alex Shnaider > Michiel Mol
• Team Principal	Dr. Colin Kolles
• Team Manager	Andy Stevenson
• Chief Race & Test Engineer	Dominic Harlow
• Technical Director	James Key
• Chief Designer	John McQuilliam
• Chief Aerodynamistic	Simon Phillips
• Chief Electronic	Mike Wroe
• Chief Mechanic	Andy Deeming
• Race Engineer (18)	Bradley Joyce
• Race Engineer (19)	Jody Egginton
• Number of employees	200
• Sponsors	JVC, LBi, Lease Plan, Eccky, Lost Boys, MAN, Rhino's, Scalable, Networks, Superfund, Zecco, Tekstor, ZIM, Dremel, F1Racing, Futurecom, Garcia, Midland, RotoZip, BBS, Bridgestone, Euro Poker, Fangadgets.com, Mingya, Portugal.
• Official suppliers	Eccky, Stops, Laurent-Perrier, Scalable, Scientio, STL, Rocket, Sparco, SuperGenco, Zecco, Touchpaper, UPS, Vandenberg, Argiva, Cesare Attolini, CMG, Samsung, Futurecom, Gr8, TAG, Metris, BBS, DDS Catia, Fangadgets, Mingya, Weigl.

STATISTICS

• Number of Grand Prix	18
• Best result	1 x 9th
• Best qualification	1 x 14th
• Number of fastest laps	0
• Number of podiums	0
• Number of drivers Championship	0
• Number of constructors Championship	0
• Total number of points scored	0

POSITION IN CHAMPIONSHIP

2006   10th – 0 pt

2006 TEST DRIVERS

- Giorgio MONDINI (CH)
- Markus WINKELHOCK(D)
- Adrian SUTIL (D)
- Alexandre PREMAT (F)
- Ernesto VITO (YV)
- Roman RUSINOV (RUS)

SUCCESSION OF DRIVERS 2006

• Tiago MONTEIRO	the 18 Grands Prix
• Christijan ALBERS	the 18 Grands Prix

Giorgio Mondini

There's an old joke about a group of market traders who keep buying and selling the same consignment of tinned sardines off one another. Eventually, driven by curiosity, one of the traders opens a tin and tastes the sardines. He rings the man he bought them from to complain they taste disgusting and is met with the reply: "But those sardines, they are not for eating, they are only for buying and selling." In the pit lane, it seemed that the old Jordan team had indeed turned into a consignment of sardines.

Jordan was taken over by Alex Schnaider's Midland Group right at the start of 2005 and it soon became clear, judging by the Russian-Canadian's very infrequent visits to a race track, that he was not particularly interested in his new acquisition. Colin Kolles was left to run the operation as best he could and in this he was undoubtedly helped by the loyalty of the former Jordan staff, with Andy Stevenson effectively running the ship at the track and Ian Phillips dealing with much of the politicking. One nice touch, which proved the new bosses realised they had an image problem, was the appointment of the ever-cheerful Johnny Herbert as their ambassador. Not much money was spent on development and although the car did make some progress, under the guidance of technical chief James Key, the relatively easy goal of beating the ancient Auguris was the best Midland could hope for and the second part of qualifying rarely featured one of the grey and red cars. Having a Toyota engine did not seem to be as much of a boost as it should have been - you have been warned Mr. Williams! - and indeed there were some embarrassing failures towards the end of the season. The team's attitude was reflected in their choice of Friday drivers, as the bottom line was to employ as many as possible who could pay as much as possible. But with the year's chequered flag in sight, hope came in the shape of yet another buy-out. Months of speculation ended with the announcement that Schnaider had sold his team to Spyker, a Dutch company that makes high-performance, exclusive road cars. And the first thing the new owners did was to negotiate a supply of Ferrari V8 engines for 2007. And former Toyota head technical man, Mike Gascoyne comes on board too.

Toro Rosso Cosworth

20. Vitantonio LIUZZI

DRIVER PROFILE

- Name — *LIUZZI*
- Firstname — *Vitantonio "Tonio"*
- Nationality — *Italian*
- Date of birth — *6th August 1981*
- Place of birth — *Locorotondo (BA) (I)*
- Lives in — *Pescara (I)*
- Marital status — *single*
- Kids — *-*
- Hobbies — *girls, music, football, karting*
- Favorite music — *Rythm'n Blues, pop*
- Favorite meal — *pizza and pasta*
- Favorite drink — *Coca-Cola, Red Bull*
- Height — *178 cm*
- Weight — *68 kg*
- Web — *www.liuzzi.com*

STATISTICS

- Grands Prix — 22
- Starts — 22
- Best result — *1 x 8th*
- Best qualification — *1 x 11th*
- Fastest laps — 0
- Podiums — 0
- Not qualified — 0
- GPs in the lead — 0
- Laps in the lead — 0
- Kms in the lead — 0
- Points scored — 2

PRIOR TO F1

1991-97 *Karting, Champion (I) (93 & 96), (EUR, 5th) (95), (World, 2nd) (95)*
1998 *Karting, (World, 7th), (EUR, 3rd), F. Super A*
1999 *Karting, (Wins Val d'Argenton & Trophée Senna), F. Palmer Audi*
2000 *Karting, (World, 6th), (World Cup, 2nd), (World 125cc, 3rd)*
2001 *Champion karting FIA-CIK, F. Renault (D) (2nd)*
2002 *F3 (9th)*
2003 *F3000 (4th)*
2004 *Champion F3000*

F1 CAREER

2005 *RBR-Cosworth. 1 pts. 24th Championship.*
2006 *STR-Cosworth. 1 pts. 19th Championship.*

21. Scott SPEED

DRIVER PROFILE

- Name — *SPEED*
- Firstname — *Scott*
- Nationality — *American*
- Date of birth — *24th January 1983*
- Place of birth — *Manteca, CA (USA)*
- Lives in — *Fuschl Am See (A)*
- Marital status — *single*
- Kids — *-*
- Hobbies — *bike, golf, ski*
- Favorite music — *U2*
- Favorite meal — *pasta*
- Favorite drink — *soda*
- Height — *177 cm*
- Weight — *67 kg*
- Web — *www.scottspeed.com*

STATISTICS

- Grands Prix — 18
- Starts — 18
- Best result — *1 x 9th*
- Best qualification — *1 x 11th*
- Fastest laps — 0
- Podiums — 0
- Not qualified — 0
- GPs in the lead — 0
- Laps in the lead — 0
- Kms in the lead — 0
- Points scored — 0

PRIOR TO F1

1993-2000 *Champion Karting (USA), several titles*
2001 *Champion F.Russell (USA)*
2002 *F.Mazda (USA) F. Barber Dodge (USA)*
2003 *F3 (GB) (23rd)*
2004 *Champion F.Renault (D), Champion F.Renault 2000 Europcup, IRL tests*
2005 *GP2 Series (3rd), RBR F1 test*

F1 CAREER

2006 *STR-Cosworth. 0 pt. 20th Championship.*

The most promising driver to emerge from the lower formula, the Italian had to make do with the role of Red Bull Racing third driver for most of 2005 and it actually seemed to take him a while to get in the groove when promoted to the full time race seat at Toro Rosso. But there were flashes of class now and again and it was finally rewarded with a single point for eighth place at Indianapolis. It is hard to really assess his performance, as he had to work in an environment that was growing and evolving around him, the V10 engine made his performances difficult to assess against anyone other than his even less experienced team-mate and testing sessions were few and far between with not much tyre evaluation time available. The talent was there, but it was mixed in with several spins and other signs of inexperience. Hopefully these are now a thing of the past, because away from the track, Tonio is a very colourful character, who fits the Red Bull way perfectly and livens up the rather staid atmosphere that is a modern era F1 weekend.

The Californian Kid has probably been brought into Formula 1 a year too early, making the switch from GP2. But, Toro Rosso was planned as a team designed to bring on members of Red Bull's Young Driver programme and, along with the fact he comes from the United States, a very important market for the team's owners, the bosses probably thought he was worth the gamble. And generally, it paid off. Despite his laidback West Coast image, Scott appeared to think clearly about the task he had in front of him and soon got to grips with the demands of F1, although occasionally he made some truly novice calls, such as being the first driver to try switching from rain tyres to dries in the Budapest race, when the conditions were patently far too slippery! He nearly got a point in only his third race, when he finished eighth in Melbourne, but he was stripped of the point when Coulthard pointed out the American had passed under yellow flags. It was the first test of the "brotherly love" between the two teams from the same family, as both men ended up in front of the Stewards. Bad language and blows were exchanged! He also drove a very strong season finale in Brazil, but these things are hard to spot when you are at the back of the grid.

Franz Tost

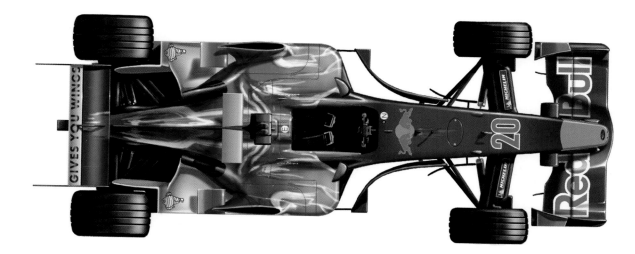

TORO ROSSO STR1-COSWORTH
VITANTONIO LIUZZI
UNITED STATES GRAND PRIX

SPECIFICATIONS

• Chassis	Toro Rosso STR1
• Type	Moulded carbon fibre monocoque/aluminium composite honeycomb
• Suspensions	Cast titanium uprights, upper and lower carbon wishbones and pushrods, torsion bar springs and anti roll bars
• Engine	V10 Cosworth Racing TJ 2006 (90°)
• Displacement	2998 cc
• Maximum revs	16,700 rpm (FIA rules)
• Valves	4 valves pneumatic distribution
• Electronic ignition	Pi Research, Magnetti Magnelli
• Transmission	7-speed gearbox, longitudinally mounted hydraulic system for power shift and clutch operation + reverse
• Clutch	AP Racing
• Radiators	Secan
• Fuel / oil	Shell
• Brakes (discs)	Hitco (carbon)
• Brakes (calipers)	AP Racing
• Shock absorbers	Koni
• Tyres	Michelin
• Wheels	AVUS Racing
• Wheels dimensions	12.7"-13 (Front) / 13.4"-13 (Rear)
• Weight	605 kg, driver + camera + ballast

TEAM PROFILE

• Address	Scuderia Toro Rosso Via Spallanzani 21 48018 Faenza (RA) Italie
• Telephone	+39 (0) 0546 696 111
• Fax	+39 (0) 0546 620 998
• Web	www.scuderiatororosso.com
• Founded in	2006
• First Grand Prix	Bahrain 2006
• Official name	Scuderia Toro Rosso
• Ower	Dietrich Mateschitz
• President	Franz Tost
• Co-ower	Gerhard Berger
• Technical Director	Gabriele Tredozi
• Director general	Gianfranco Fanuzzi
• Chief designer	Robert Taylor
• Team manager	Massimo Rivola
• Engineer	Laurent Mekies
• Race engineer (20)	Riccardo Adami
• Race engineer (21)	Graziano Michelacci
• Mechanical chief	Bruno Fagnocchi
• Number of employees	300
• Partners officials	Hangar-7, VolksWagen, Alpine, Michelin

Out of the ashes of Minardi rose Scuderia Toro Rosso. It was still seriously Italian, it was still a long way down the pit lane, but it had loads more money. It shared its paddock space with Red Bull Racing, but not its ideology. It was also the only team to take advantage of the FIA "special offer" which allowed them to run a V10 Cosworth with a restrictor. Other teams moaned, reckoning the restrictor rule had been introduced to help "poor" teams and Toro Rosso were no longer poor. But once it was seen that the V10 was no match for most V8s, the complaints died out. In fact, the V10 was allowed an extra 300 rpm for qualifying after the mid-point of the season. Another thing its rivals could complain about was that, contrary to current rules, but legal from 2008, they were perceived to be using a chassis built by another team, namely the previous year's Red Bull. But a convenient loophole saw FIA turn a blind eye. While the parent company threw money at Red Bull Racing, it was clear that Toro Rosso would get by on less, although to the employees kept on from its Minardi days, it still seemed like their first real budget in a long time. Former BMW logistics man, Franz Tost was put in charge of the team and applied his diligent Austrian mind to curbing some of the more Latin aspects of the operation and putting a bit more method into the melting pot. While Tost handled the day to day running of things, a more famous Austrian turned up as co-owner. Gerhard Berger added credibility to proceedings and would invariably prove useful in behind the scenes negotiations at the highest political level; close to Ecclestone, thick as thieves with Mosley and a direct line to Red Bull supremo, Mateschitz. Over the year, the team did better than expected and although slow, the cars were evidently well screwed together, as Toro Rosso was the fifth most successful squad in terms of races completed. However, 2007 will be a much tougher proposition as there will be no excuses when the team joins the V8 club courtesy of a Ferrari engine. At the end of the season, Cosworth's Alex Hitzinger was taken on as technical director.

STATISTICS

• Number of Grand Prix	18
• Best result	1 x 8th
• Best qualification	1 x 11th
• Number of fastest laps	0
• Number of podiums	0
• Number of drivers Championship	0
• Number of constructors Championship	0
• Total number of points scored	1

POSITION IN CHAMPIONSHIP

2006   9th – 1 pt

2006 TEST DRIVERS

• Neel JANI (CH)

SUCCESSION OF DRIVERS 2006

• Vitantonio LIUZZI	all 18 Grands Prix
• Scott SPEED	all 18 Grands Prix

Super Aguri Honda

22. Takuma SATO

DRIVER PROFILE

- Name   SATO
- Prénom   Takuma
- Nationality   Japanese
- Date of birth   28ᵗʰ January 1977
- Place of birth   Tokyo (J)
- Lives in   Monaco (MC)
- Marital status   single
- Kids   -
- Hobbies   bike, walks, to be with friends
- Favorite music   pop, some japanese groups
- Favorite meal   japanese food
- Favorite drink   fresh fruits juice
- Height   164 cm
- Weight   59 kg
- Web   www.takumasato.com

STATISTICS

		PRIOR TO F1
Grands Prix	70	1996 Champion Karting (J)
Starts	69	1997 Champion Karting (J),
Best result	1 x 3ʳᵈ	Ecole de pilotage Honda
Best qualification	1 x 2ⁿᵈ	1998 F. Vauxhall Jr. (GB)
Fastest laps	0	1999 F. Opel Euroseries (GB)
Podiums	1	(6ᵗʰ), F3 (GB)
Not qualified	0	2000 F3 (GB) (3ʳᵈ)
GPs in the lead	1	2001 Champion F3 (GB)
Laps in the lead	2	
Kms in the lead	10	
Points scored	40	

F1 CAREER

2002   Jordan-Honda. 2 pts. 15ᵗʰ Championship.
2003   B·A·R-Honda. 3 pts. 18ᵗʰ Championship.
2004   B·A·R-Honda. 34 pts. 8ᵗʰ Championship.
2005   B·A·R-Honda. 1 pt. 23ʳᵈ Championship.
2006   Super Aguri-Honda. 0 pt. 23ʳᵈ Championship.

After the first three races of the season, the former BAR driver, now finding himself in the role of team leader, seemed to have risen to the occasion and had actually completed more laps in the opening grands prix than any other driver. Of course, they were relatively slow laps. Until you go to Suzuka, or at least pick up a Japanese F1 magazine, it is hard to understand the hero status that "Taku san" commands in his native land. He was under a lot of pressure, but proved up to the task, getting involved with every aspect of the new team and outwardly at least showing his usual cheerful disposition. He matured during the year, as he was effectively the team leader as his team-mates changed several times during the season.

Aguri Suzuki

Daniel Audetto

23. Yuji IDE

DRIVER PROFILE

- Name   IDE
- Firstname   Yuji
- Nationality   Japanese
- Date of birth   21ˢᵗ January 1975
- Place of birth Saitama (J)
- Lives in   Japan
- Marital status single
- Kids   -
- Hobbies   football, jogging
- Height   177 cm
- Weight   65 kg
- Web   www.yuji-ide.com

STATISTICS

		PRIOR TO F1
Grands Prix	4	1992 Karting Series A1 (J) (2ⁿᵈ),
Starts	4	Champion GP SS stock class (J)
Best result	1 x 13ᵗʰ	1993 Karting (J), FA
Best qualification	1 x 18ᵗʰ	1994-1998 F3 (J)
Fastest laps	0	1999 GT300 (2ⁿᵈ), Champion
Podiums	0	F. Dream Series
Not qualifies	0	2000 F3 (J) (2ⁿᵈ), GT500 (J) (22ⁿᵈ)
GPs in the lead	0	2001 F3 (J) (5ᵗʰ), GT500 (J) (4ᵗʰ)
Laps in the lead	0	2002 F3 (J) (7ᵗʰ)
Kms in the lead	0	2003 F. Nippon (J) (7ᵗʰ),
Points scored	0	Super GT500 (J) (4ᵗʰ)
		2004 F. Nippon (J) (3ʳᵈ),
		Super GT500 (J) (11ᵗʰ),
		Champion Super Endurance
		Class 3

PRIOR TO F1

1991 Champion National   2005 F. Nippon (J) (2ⁿᵈ),
Kart (J)   Super GT500 (J) (11ᵗʰ)

F1 CAREER

2006   Super Aguri-Honda. 0 pt. 25ᵗʰ Championship.

The joke (which incidentally works much better in the French language) was that Mr. Ide had no Idea about driving an F1 car. It was sad but true, but in mitigation, one has to explain he was thrown in at the deepest of deep ends, with no F1 experience, virtually no winter testing and so little command of English that his team boss had to act as interpreter between driver and engineers. After some scary spins and a serious crash with Christijan Albers, the FIA withdrew his Superlicense. He was replaced by Franck Montagny, who had been fulfilling Friday driver duties, having previously had the same role with Renault. The Frenchman did what he could, but of course it was at the back of the field. Super Aguri was always supposed to be as much of a Japanese team as possible and so, as from the German GP, Montagny was stood down to allow Sakon Yamamoto to make his Formula 1 debut for the rest of the year. The highlight of the rookie's year was finishing the last three races in 16, 17 and 16th places respectively.

23. Sakon YAMAMOTO

DRIVER PROFILE

- Name   YAMAMOTO
- Prénom   Sakon
- Nationality   Japanese
- Date of birth   9ᵗʰ July 1982
- Place of birth Toyohashi (J)
- Lives in   Japan (I)
- Marital status single
- Kids   -
- Hobbies   music, football
- Height   172 cm
- Weight   63 kg
- Web   www.sakon-yamamoto.com

STATISTICS

		PRIOR TO F1
Grands Prix	7	1994-1999 Suzuka Karting
Starts	7	2000 Karting Series (J) (3ʳᵈ)
Best result	1 x 16ᵗʰ	2001 F3 Series (J) (4ᵗʰ)
Best qualifications	2 x 19ᵗʰ	2002 F3 (D) (11ᵗʰ)
Fastest laps	0	2003 F3 (EUR)
Podiums	0	2004 F3 (J)
Not qualified	0	2005 F Nippon (2ⁿᵈ),
GPs in the lead	0	Super GT500
Laps in the lead	0	
Kms in the lead	0	
Points scored	0	

F1 CAREER

2006   Super Aguri-Honda. 0 pt. 26ᵗʰ Championship.

23. Franck MONTAGNY

DRIVER PROFILE

- Name   MONTAGNY
- Firstname   Franck
- Nationality   French
- Date of birth   5ᵗʰ January 1978
- Place of birth Feurs (French)
- Lives in   Oxford (GB),
                  Barcelona (E)
- Marital status single
- Kids   -
- Hobbies   music, jet skiing
- Height   183 cm
- Weight   73 kg
- Web   www.fmontagny.com

STATISTICS

		PRIOR TO F1
Grands Prix	7	1992-1994 Champion
Starts	7	Karting (F)
Best result	1 x 16ᵗʰ	1995 F. Renault (F) (4ᵗʰ)
Best qualification	1 x 19ᵗʰ	1997 F3 (F) (4ᵗʰ)
Fastest laps	0	1998 F3 (F) (2ⁿᵈ)
Podiums	0	1999 F3000, Le Mans 24h,
Not qualified	0	Winner Masters
GPs in the lead	0	Karting (F)
Laps in the lead	0	2000 F3000 (9ᵗʰ), Le Mans 24h
Kms in the lead	0	2001 Champion Le Mans 24h
Points scored	0	2002 World Series (2ⁿᵈ),
		24h du Mans (6ᵗʰ)
		2003 Champion World
		Series, Test F1-Renault
		2004 F1-Renault 3ʳᵈ pilote
		2005 F1-Renault 3ʳᵈ pilote,
		24h du Mans (9ᵗʰ)

F1 CAREER

2006   Super Aguri. 0 pt. 27ᵗʰ Championship.

The only Frenchman to appear on a grand prix grid in 2005 was Franck Montagny. Formerly Renault's Friday driver, when this team lost the right to run three cars on the first day of practice, Montagny took on the same role for the fledgling Super Aguri squad. Hard to make an impression when you are driving an "antique" but he did the best he could and impressed the team enough to race in seven grands prix when Ide was thrown on the scrap heap. The team did not have the resources to treat both its drivers equally, but they were honest about this and Montagny knew he was running 8 to 10 kilos heavier than Sato. He did a reasonable job and the team kept him as third driver when they were obliged to try Yamamoto in the race seat. A solid year paid off as Montagny, given plenty of warning by Aguri that he would not have a race seat in 2007, was able to do a quick deal and he has now replaced Zonta as Toyota's tester.

The team's attempt to replace Ide with another Japanese driver hardly caused a ripple on the Formula 1 pond. Yamamoto raced in seven grands prix, starting in Germany, but did not actually finish one until the circus arrived in Shanghai. China actually proved that even his fellow drivers were not sure who he was. On the penultimate lap of the grand prix, Nick Heidfeld was involved in an incident caused by Takuma Sato and the little German was furious as he got out of the car. In the paddock, Yamamoto was preening himself at having recorded his first F1 finish, when Heidfeld came along and tried to strangle him, thinking he was Sato! Next year, there will be none of this confusion as Super Aguri has decided not to waste any more time trying to find a Japanese driver to partner Sato, instead giving the drive to Anthony Davidson, the Englishman thus getting his first fulltime F1 drive, after testing for Honda.

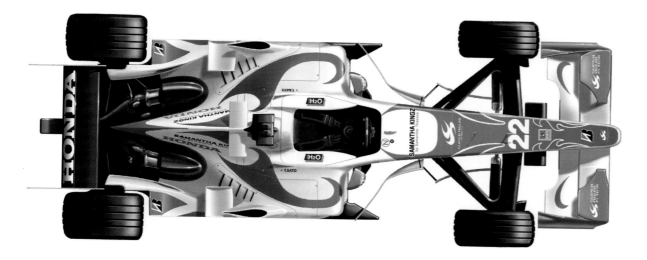

SUPER AGURI SA06-HONDA
TAKUMA SATO
GRAND PRIX GERMANY

SPECIFICATIONS

- Chassis — Super Aguri SA05 (BRN > F) & Super Aguri SA06 (D > BR)
- Type — Moulded carbon fibre monocoque/ aluminium composite honeycomb
- Suspensions — Wishbones, pushrod operated torsion bars and dampers. Mechanical anti-roll bar (Front and Rear).
- Engine — V8 Honda RA806E (90°)
- Displacement — 2400 cc
- Power — + 700 bhp
- Maximum revs — 19000 rpm
- Valves — 4 valves per cylinder, pneumatically operated
- Electronic ignition — Honda PGM-IG
- Transmission — SAF1 Aluminium maincase. 7 speed semi automatic electro hydraulically controlled + reverse
- Clutch — Sachs
- Fuel / oil — Elf / Nisseki
- Brakes (discs) — AP Racing
- Brakes (calipers) — Hitco
- Spark plugs / battery — NGK / 2.5 Ah lead acid
- Shock absorbers — Ohlins
- Tyres — Bridgestone
- Wheels dimensions — 13" x 12.75" (Front) / 13" x 13.7" (Rear)
- Wheels — BBS
- Weight — 605 kg, driver + camera + ballast
- Wheel base — 3,100 mm
- Total lenght — 4,666 mm
- Total width — 1,800 mm
- Total height — 950 mm
- Front track — 1,472 mm
- Rear track — 1,422 mm

TEAM PROFILE

- Address — Super Aguri F1 Limited Leafiel Technical Centre Langley, Witney, Oxfordshire OX 29 9 EF Great Britain
- Telephone — +44 1993 87 1600
- Fax — +44 1993 87 1702
- Web — www.saf1.co.jp
- Founded in — 2006
- First Grand Prix — Bahrain 2006
- Official name — Super Aguri Formula 1
- President Director General — Aguri Suzuki
- Director General — Daniel Audetto
- Technical Director — Mark Preston
- Chief designer — Peter McCool
- Aerodynamicist — Ben Wood
- Operations chief — Kevin Lee
- Team manager — Mick Ainsley-Cowlishau
- Engineer and chief race — Graham Taylor
- Mechanical chief — Phil Spencer
- Race engineer (22) — Gerry Huges
- Race engineer (23) — Antonio Cuquerella
- Number of employees — 85
- Partners — Honda, Samantha Kingz, Bridgestone, Lifecard, Aderans, Asahisolar, Taisei Shoko, Hisamitsu Pharmaceutical, ECC, Autobacs Seven, Seiko, Asahi Soft Drinks (H2O), All Nippon Airways, Greenstar, Nippon Oil Corporation (ENEOS), NGK, Takata, Rodac, AXA, Nissin Food Products (Cup Noodle), BEAMS

STATISTICS

- Number of Grand Prix — 18
- Best results — 1 x 10th
- Best qualification — 1 x 17th
- Number of fastest laps — 0
- Number of podiums — 0
- Number of drivers Championship — 0
- Number of constructors Championship — 0
- Total number of points scored — 0

POSITION IN CHAMPIONSHIP

2006   11th – 0 pt

Mark Preston

2006 TEST DRIVERS

- Franck MONTAGNY (F)

SUCCESSION OF DRIVERS 2006

- Takuma SATO — all 18 Grands Prix
- Yuji IDE — 4 Grands Prix (BRN > RSM)
- Franck MONTAGNY — 7 Grands Prix (E > F)
- Sakon YAMAMOTO — 7 Grands Prix (D > BR)

At the start of 2006 it was very easy to dismiss the sport's newest team as a joke, a publicity stunt, an indulgence on the part of Honda, stung into the preposterous act of creating a team simply to keep Takuma Sato on the grid, after an outcry in Japan when he was dropped by BAR-Honda. By the end of the season, Aguri Suzuki and his crew had achieved something of a miracle.

The only Japanese driver to have ever stood on an F1 podium, Suzuki had plenty of experience successfully running teams at all levels and when plans to buy into BAR or Jordan fell through, Honda backed his plan to set up his own team by supplying engines. The old Arrows factory was available when he went to have a look back in September 2005. So were the 2002 (yes they were four years out of date!) Arrows chassis. A team was hurriedly put together; a difficult task as there was a gentlemen's agreement the new team would not poach staff from other teams. This meant there were quite a few old faces among the new recruits and the green light finally came after Suzuki had stumped up the necessary 48 million Euro entry fee. Al this only happened in January, so merely getting to Bahrain was an incredible achievement, even if the cars were hopelessly off the pace. Effectively, they were testing at races and the team was basically waiting for the new car, which eventually saw the light of day in Hockenheim, although despite being perceived as a Honda satellite team, they only got two engine upgrades during the course of the year. The new car was a big improvement – how could it be anything else? It featured a purpose-built gearbox, specifically designed to mate with the Honda V8, new suspension to suit the modern tyres and a big weight saving, which actually allowed the team to run with ballast, while the aerodynamics on the new car resulted in a significant increase in downforce. This was truly a remarkable achievement with no other Formula 1 team in the modern era ever having been put together so quickly. But of course there is a dark side and that consists of trying to progress from simply making up the numbers on the grid, to moving up the order in 2007.

INSIGHTS

There are enough incidents in an F1 seaon to fill an encyclopedia several times over. As always the F1 Yearbook brings you the insights of five of the best known journalists to tell you how the season was perceived in their respective countries.
From an historical point of view we took advantage of the French Grand Prix's Centenary to go back over the story of this famous race.

2006: a British point of view

Williams: a hell of a season

Nigel Roebuck
Autosport

No question about it, the 2006 season was a disastrous one for WilliamsF1. Eighth in the constructors' championship: 11 points from 18 races, and not a single podium all season long. This from a team with nine championship victories, a team which was dominant a decade ago. At the final race, in Brazil, the two Williams-Cosworths had a coming-together on the very first lap, and both were out on the spot. As a metaphor for the season as a whole, it could hardly have been more poignant. Increasingly it has been said that maybe Williams might be going the way of Tyrrell, who had years of glory and World Championship success, and then gradually faded away to nothing. And certainly it's a fact that the last few seasons have been very difficult for Frank's team. The last Grand Prix win came at Interlagos in 2004, Juan Pablo Montoya's final drive for Williams before leaving for McLaren, and although Williams has had flurries of success in the 21st century – as in mid-2003, when Ralf Schumacher won at the Nurburgring and Magny-Cours, and Montoya at Hockenheim) – it is nine years since a Williams driver – Jacques Villeneuve – won the World Championship. A variety of things went wrong over time, notably the relationship between Williams and BMW, which began in 2000, and ended – a year earlier than expected – at the conclusion of the '05 season. For quite a while the relationship had been deteriorating, with BMW increasingly critical of Williams's contribution to the partnership, and Williams less than delighted by both the gradual decline in performance of the BMW V10, and the autocratic behaviour of the company hierarchy. Patrick Head and Mario Theissen had what may be termed 'a

difficult relationship', and in the end both parties were glad to separate. Except in one respect, that is. BMW's engines may no longer have been as dominant, as in the early days of the partnership with Williams, but they did have the abiding virtue of being free. Once the decision had been taken to part, there was no immediate opportunity for Frank to do a deal with another manufacturer, and thus his only option for 2006 was to use the new Cosworth V8 – which could not be free, of course. It is true that the price of a year's supply of

engines from Cosworth was a steal, compared, for example, with what Red Bull were paying Ferrari, but it was still a huge chunk of money for a team accustomed to free motors – and, what was more, feeling the chill of greatly reduced sponsorship, notably with the departure of Hewlett-Packard at the end of 2005. At the time Williams were fortunate that Jenson Button, having decided to stay with Honda, after all, was obliged to pay Frank a great deal of compensation. Probably, it paid the Cosworth bill.

Nigel Roebuck
58-year-old Nigel Roebuck decided to leave his job in industry at the age of 24 to begin a career as a journalist. In 1971, he worked for the American magazine Car & Driver before joining the British weekly Autosport in 1976. He has covered F1 for it since then while also writing for the Sunday Times, Auto Week and the Japanese magazine Racing On.

In fact, the team began the '06 season in what appeared to be fine shape – indeed, Mark Webber has said that if the opening races had been in January, rather March, he believes a Williams-Cosworth would have been absolutely the quickest car. Despite working with a budget minute by comparison with those of the major manufacturers, Cosworth worked wonders with their V8, and initially had a power advantage over all the rest. The Williams FW28, too, looked the most effective car the company had produced in a long time. At the first race of the season, Bahrain, F1 debutant Nico Rosberg turned in a storming drive, and rocked the establishment by setting the fastest lap.

At Melbourne Webber found himself briefly in the lead of his home race, a heady experience for him. "*It felt tremendous,*" he said, "*but then the transmission failed, and that was that, which was a shame, because third place was a good possibility. We wouldn't have beaten Alonso and Raikkonen, but otherwise we were right there. With the budget they had available, Cosworth were doing a ridiculously good job.*"

"The Cosworth attitude was very positive," agreed Head. "*There was a high level of respect between engineers on both sides. Cosworth did phenomenally well, in terms of what they produced for the buck paid. It put some of the manufacturers to shame, quite honestly.*" As the season progressed, though, it became more and more apparent that the FW28 lacked the aerodynamic grip of some of its rivals. At Monaco, where (itals) mechanical (end itals) grip is of paramount importance, Webber was a strong contender for victory (until his almost inevitable retirement), but elsewhere the cars increasingly struggled. As Head predicted before the season, too, the competitiveness of the Cosworth, began to slip a little, simply because, as other engines came on ever stronger, there wasn't the money available to develop it. For all that, though, Head had nothing but praise for Cosworth. After a problem early in the season, it was necessary to run with reduced revs for a whole, but the problem was overcome, and Patrick stressed that invariably it was the Williams half of the equation was that at fault. "*The car was simply short of grip – particularly at the rear, and it was especially apparent on corner entry. Because of that, we had to run more rear wing than we wanted – and that, of course, cost us straightline speed…*"

"We changed from Michelin to Bridgestone for '06, and that brought difficulties, too – not, I hasten to say, because Bridgestone weren't making good tyres, but simply because they were new to us, and there was a lot to learn. It was clear from what Ferrari were doing that there wasn't anything wrong with Bridgestone."

Compared with times past, too, the team was struggling financially, which perhaps explained in part a reliability record which can only be described as lamentable. When an outfit of Williams's pedigree is eighth in a points table of 11 teams, there is something very amiss somewhere. "*Our reliability was awful,*" said Head. "*Unacceptable. Sometimes the problem was a fault in design, sometimes it was quality control – and sometimes, in the search for performance, we probably took risks, too.*"

It was time for a period of intense self-examination, and the team has acted on it. Many would suggest that, for the all that Williams now have two state-of-the-art wind-tunnels, aerodynamics have been a fundamental weakness ever since Adrian Newey left for McLaren, 10 years ago. There have been major changes among the technical staff, with Jon Tomlinson, formerly Renault's deputy head of aerodynamics, coming in to head the aero department, where he will be joined by Amit Chakraborty, previously with McLaren.

Some compare Williams to Jordan as the team fades into the twilight. It is a ridiculous comparison.

The team's new chief designer, Ed Wood, arrived in the late spring of 2006, and working with him will be John Russell, who previously worked at Williams before moving to Jaguar Racing. As well as that, the signs are that Head himself, having reduced his day-to-day involvement in the team over the last few years, will revert to a more 'hands on' role. Technical director Sam Michael has his supporters, and his detractors, but Frank and Patrick have always stressed their faith in him. It's a fact, though, that a complete reappraisal of the technical staff was necessary if Williams are ever to return to anything like their glory years. A major change for 2007 is that the team will use Toyota engines – sad in a way, for it spells the end for the Cosworth motor, which has not been taken up by any other team. Although Toyota have spent a massive amount of money to relatively little effect in F1 thus far, from the outset it was clear there was very little wrong with their engines, and that should be a big plus point for Williams. It will also save Frank a great deal of money.

As well as that, there is a new, very substantial, sponsor on board. With the arrival at McLaren of Vodafone, as title sponsor, the American telecommunications giant AT&T, if it wished to stay in F1, was obliged to look elsewhere for 2007 and beyond. The company will in future be the title sponsor at Williams, and the deal is believed to be worth $50m a year. At the same time Williams is fortunate in not having a huge driver bill to pay. Webber has left for Red

Bull, and the failure of team and driver to gel properly was a great surprise to everyone: when the contract was signed, two years ago, most thought Mark and Williams were made for each other.

Although the high point of young Rosberg's season was his very first race, Williams and Head remain convinced of his potential in F1. "*Nico drove a quite brilliant race in Bahrain,*" said Head, "*and set a standard that inevitably couldn't be maintained. He made a mess of one or two races, but at others he was outstanding, even if the results didn't show it. I have to say that he – and Mark, too – did a perfectly good job for us, and we let them down with cars that were neither quick nor reliable enough. We have great faith in Nico for the future.*" Partnering Rosberg in the race team will be '06 test driver Alex Wurz, and although he hasn't raced regularly for some six years, he has a big point to make, and many believe could well spring a surprise or two. In many ways, Williams looks like a team which has lost its way in recent years, but some have made fatuous comparisons with Jordan, suggesting that Frank's team was going the way of Eddie's, sliding into oblivion. To compare Williams with Jordan – in (itals) any (end itals) way – is absurd. To finance that second-wind tunnel, Frank parted with his private jet, and that tells you everything about where his priorities lie, and have always lain. "*Patrick and I have always agreed,*" he said, "*that the only thing that really speaks is performance on the track, right? We finished third in the constructors' points in 2000 and '01, our first couple of seasons with BMW, then second for a couple of years, then we fell from grace, with fourth in '04, fifth in '05 – and eighth this year. If that negative progress continues much longer, then the people writing us off are probably right to do so. But we don't intend that to happen.*"

^
The full Williams team on the morning of the Japanese Grand Prix. Next year will see a lot of changes.

<
Mark Webber finished 14th in the drivers' championship with a total of only 7 points. He was not very happy about this and has gone to Red Bull for 2007.

A little goodbye ceremony for Cosworth at the Brazilian Grand Prix with Nico Rosberg and Patrick Head (behind the cake).
∨

Schumacher's shadow hangs over F1

Anno Hecker
Frankfurter Allgemeine Zeitung

2006 aus deutscher Sicht

The experts are at loggerheads. Is Michael Schumacher the greatest driver of all time? *"Yes,"* says Niki Lauda. *"No,"* shoots back Sir Jackie Stewart. Yesterday's drivers contradict one another and throw figures in each other's face to back up their arguments. These include the highest number of titles, the highest number of voluntary accidents (2), and without doubt the highest number of dangerous manoeuvres ever carried out on a track by a world champion. However, once a few generations have passed by the chicaneries of the driver who has dominated F1 over the last 15 years will no longer be relevant. His results will earn the respect of the drivers of tomorrow. In 2006, Michael Schumacher was way ahead of the 21 other drivers in the paddock: 7 titles to 2 and 91 victories to 59 (the total of all his rivals added together). His average is 1 victory per 2.7 grands prix. For the drivers of the future their only question will be: how did he do it? Michael was a bit sceptical to begin with: *"I never thought I'd be capable of getting to the next stage,"* explained the German. *"It was only when I found myself at Spa (on his 1991 F1 debut) that I realised I still had room for improvement. That day it became obvious that I could make it. In fact, it was almost the same in all the formulas in which I raced."*

Obviously, Michael had enormous talent. He also had the odd bit of luck but he shared that with his rivals. On the other hand, no driver before him had ever worked so hard to be able to maintain qualifying speeds over a whole race or indeed a whole season - even 15 years! Where are the drivers who went up against Michael Schumacher? Jacques Villeneuve? Pettifogging, completely out of it. Heinz-Harald Frentzen? Overestimated, eliminated. Mika Häkkinen? Erratic, left behind. Juan Pablo Montoya? Destroyed by his team-mate, fled to the United States. Fernando Alonso fought and won against his elder rival (by 12 years) and was crowned world champion. But the Spaniard deployed so much energy to achieve this feat that he will never beat Michael's records. *"To do that I'll have to continue driving up 2019,"* Alonso joked. *"I'll certainly never do such a thing."* Consistency has always been the German's key to success allied to a life style that is reminiscent of that of Frank Williams: live Formula 1 twenty-four hours a day. For 6 years Michael ate the same müsli!

Sometimes his urge to party proves that he is a true Prussian. For 2 decades his body has been honed to perfection from a muscular point of view. His dedicated professionalism, which he keeps up 24 hours out of 24, has only one aim: to serve Michael Schumacher. He never wanted to lose concentration during the final laps of a difficult race.

The Schumacher method not only crushed half the paddock; it also profoundly modified his team's whole environment. For example, he rang up the sub-contractor making the dampers to find out about the development of a new model. When he was not on the list for private testing, as was the case just before the last grand prix in 2006, he phoned Jaramillo and asked politely but firmly if he had not been forgotten! His whole talent lay in his capacity to improve the car step by step. *"Don't you want to solve the problem today?"* Michael asked his helmet specialist one day. The man felt a shiver run down his spine. Two hours later the modified helmet was in its box – just in time for the start of practice.

When he was with Benetton the German had already learned how to save time off the track. *"He was capable of describing how the car was reacting whether it was due to the chassis or the engine,"* said Vincent Gaillardot, his former engineer. *"With Michael the technical meetings were intense for about ten minutes. With others things weren't clear even after more than an hour-and-a-half's discussion."*

One thing is certain: nobody wants to let him down.

His raw speed also engendered respect. *"It's not exactly true that Michael helped us design the cars,"* declared Ross Brawn, the Ferrari technical director, about the German driver's influence. *"One thing, though, is certain, nobody wanted to let him down."* Who would have believed that? While his team designed cars with computers and its directors praised his absence of emotion, Michael was able to motivate the people surrounding him by his feelings making them give the very best of themselves for him. If this had not been the case he would never have stayed at Ferrari for 10 years. Michael never bit the hand that fed him; he never openly criticised his team; not even after the 1996 season that was peppered by breakdowns or the failed crash test because of the fatigue of certain materials; and even less after he crashed in England in 1999 breaking his leg because the brakes on the rear wheels failed.

On the other hand, the Scuderia pardoned him doubtful manoeuvres like Jerez in 1997 against Jacques Villeneuve or in 2006 in Monaco when the master of opposite lock blocked the track during qualifying killing any hopes his rivals might have had of improving their times. The world of motor sport saw red that day except Jean Todt, the Ferrari general manager. Who saw a brighter shade of pink! Only Michael Schumacher's most controversial actions have triggered a reaction as proved by the

decision of the GPDA not take sanction against the Monaco manoeuvre. The watchword: don't do anything against Schumi! Success, the poison that eventually destroys all the teams that win, never affected his sense of team spirit. All the members of the Scuderia met up every Thursday before a grand prix for a game of football, Michael's other passion. "We work hard at maintaining our cohesion," he said. *"Thanks to football you see each person's character and you know how to relate to him. It's something you can't learn at work."* When the ball was being kicked around, he was everywhere he was needed: he compensated. And he worked exactly like he played. Finding the perfect balance of a single-seater is so difficult to determine and to maintain; it is like a kind of tightrope walk. It is a delicate harmony, a form of alchemy distilled with the team.

Cars are like men; there is blood running inside. A lot of tears flowed after Michael Schumacher's final test on the Jerez de la Frontera circuit. Johnny Herbert, Eddie Irvine and Rubens Barrichello were all right. Michael Schumacher was the no.1 at Ferrari and Benetton although the German never needed to see that clause in writing.

Anno Hecker
41-year-old Anno Hecker first worked as a gymnastics professor before deciding on a career as a journalist. He followed a training course in a Bonn press agency as a political correspondent. He then joined the "Frankfurter Allgeimeine Zeitung" in 1991 as motor sports editor. He is a specialist in subjects which combine sport and politics.

Even if his boss did not acknowledge his role automatically the German soon imposed himself. Herbert, Irvine, Barrichello as well as Schumacher's ten or so team-mates during his career never had the strength to set up such a system. It fell apart - very quickly.

"After a race is before the next one," said Michael Schumacher after the last lap of his last race in São Paolo just before going into his final technical debriefing. When he came out he was speechless for a moment. "What does it feel like to be retired?" "Are you going to go back on your decision?" "What will you miss most?" Only to the last question did he give an answer: *"These are questions that you just can't answer."*

He'll have no problem watching the grands prix on TV, unless he's got something more urgent to do.

He was also asked what he was going to do in the future. "And now, Mr. Schumacher, what next? " A shrug of his shoulders. The best plan is not to have one. *"After my retirement I'd like to have a while during which I can empty my mind,"* he had already said for several years. *"And then I'll see what I'll do after having had a good think."* That was all.

A lot of people are digging their brains to guess what role Michael Schumacher will have in the future. They think that his quest for speed is not satisfied. They think that it's not over; it's lasted for 30 years, ever since he drove a kart. *"He'll*

drive again," was Mika Häkkinen's opinion. *"He can't stay still for more than six months"*, predicted Willy Weber, his manager.
Michael, though, saw no problem in watching the opening grands prix of the 2007 season on TV. Unless he had something more urgent to do: *"If my son, Mick, is playing in an ice hockey match at the same time, then it'll be more important than a grand prix."*
But he will not come back. That is why such work no longer has a place in his life. He is too logical to change his mind. From now on he can turn down press conferences and the demands of his sponsors. But that does not mean that F1 will not play a role in his life. Ferrari would be foolish not to call upon his services. *"I think he can still give a lot more to Ferrari,'* stated Ross Brawn, the Scuderia's technical director. *"But I'm not sure it'll be a role linked to driving in any capacity."*
An office job like Jean Todt is excluded for Schumacher who is a pragmatic hands-on guy. "You can forget that," he said.
What is left is a consultant's role for the more delicate aspects of coordination. This is the kind of work that would appeal to Schumacher's meticulous approach as he has already done it: go to grands prix, wrong-foot the opposition and work with the engineers. *"He has often helped us by his technical knowledge,"* Ross Brawn admitted. Thus, the Scuderia Ferrari will do its best to tempt its hero back. And hope that one day it will see him leave the pits at the wheel of a car!
For the moment it appears that Schumacher, passionate driver that he is, wants nothing more than a quiet family life. After an average of 224 days spent away from home per season

for the past 15 years, it seems normal for him to want to find his marks. This hyperactive bloke has enough money to play football, go for rides on motorbike or on horseback.

In this concept of retirement, his wife, who is a great fan of Westerns, does not really play a part. Because *"everything he starts,"* she says jokingly, *"he does it very quickly and better than me."*
Perhaps Corinna holds the key to Ferrari's wish. Is Mrs Schumacher going to send him back to work so as not to have him under her feet at home?

Michael Schumacher indulging in his favourite hobby: football. From now on he'll be able to devote more time to it. Unless… v

A vintage year

Another two world titles for Renault and a French driver back in an F1 car. It was a year to whet the appetites of French F1 lovers everywhere and they enjoyed a vintage season in 2006

2006 vu de France

Frédéric Ferret
L'Equipe

Fernando Alonso's first words were in French. As soon as he crossed the finishing line of the last grand prix of the season, the final straight of the year on the Interlagos circuit before the Senna Esses Alonso, whose second place in the final round gave him the 2006 title, did not forget the car that had helped him to the second world championship in his career.

The man from the Asturias' first words were in French: "*Merci, merci à tous pour ces années.*" (Thank you, thank you for all these years). This delighted all Alonso's and Renault's French fans who were delighted with the present he had given them before his departure for McLaren. And there were a lot of them if the record figure of over 13 million viewers on the TF1 channel on Sunday 22nd October is to be believed.

It has to be said that the season had all the ingredients to whet the enthusiasts' appetite and it got off to a flying start. Fernando Alonso, the youngest-ever champion in the history of F1, was back to defend his title in the opening round in Bahrain. He won the first race from Michael Schumacher and Kimi Raïkkönen. A Renault ahead of a Ferrari and a McLaren promised a brilliant start to the season and so it turned out. But the tension evaporated rapidly. And whose fault was it? The French team's which was particularly well prepared for the opening rounds. Three grands prix, three victories and five rostrum finishes for the two R26 drivers. France triumphed but when the teams came back to European soil and more particularly Imola, Alonso was beaten by

Schumacher in a replay of their 2005 duel. Michael's Ferrari was not as quick as the Renault and he held up the Spaniard fighting off all his attacks to score his first victory of the season. He was back in the title hunt and two weeks later on the Nürburgring he won again. It all added a bit of spice to the championship battle. Later on in early summer the German won on Renault's home turf as Alonso was never in a position to threaten him. The day after France's defeat in the Football World Cup the Scuderia rubbed salt into the wound after having dominated at Indianapolis. Schumacher's

chief mechanic Michele Guintoli came to the rostrum to receive the winner's champagne clad in Materazzi's jersey. Talk about barefaced cheek! More spice was added to the mix in Hungary (home of paprika) where Renault was deprived of its mass damper, one of its major assets. It was introduced in F1 by the French company at the 2005 Italian Grand Prix and integrated into the R26 last winter. It consisted of a form of ballast made up of a mass element between two springs which allowed the parasitical movements of the chassis on bumps, over kerbs and under braking to

Frédéric Ferret
38-years-old. He made his journalistic debut in the Associated Press Agency. He joined L'Equipe in 1992 and has stayed there ever since covering F1 since 2003.

be reduced thus improving the car's grip. It was then copied by several teams with varying degrees of success. Suddenly the FIA declared the system illegal and while awaiting the final verdict it hit Alonso with a shower of penalties, which deprived him of the pole shoot-out and sent him back down the grid. France was up in arms. Fortunately, a similar penalty sanctioned the German. In Hungary, both men fought a titanic battle that they both lost victims of a poorly fastened wheel nut in one cars and pride in the other. Finally, victory fell to Brit Jenson Button after an excellent drive. The race excited French enthusiasm, all the more so as Laure Manadou was winning all before her in the European Championships in Budapest.

Beaten but not defeated Alonso was back in Turkey deprived of a vital weapon in his championship struggle. The FIA handed down its judgement after the summer break. Mass dampers were now banned. End of story!

Wine is like F1.
It's the earth but also the men.

The engineers went into maximum attack mode while on the track the drivers did the same. The former had to revise their cars especially Renault. On the other hand at Ferrari, the mass dampers had been grafted on so they were easier to remove. Bridgestone was out to put one over on its French rival, Michelin, which although on the point of withdrawing from F1, was after the miraculous compound.

As for the spectators they were licking their lips, as they were not very much au courant with the backstage technical war. All that interested them was the marvellous battle unfolding on the track in the final stages of the championship.

Despite a car that was not as quick Alonso managed to fend off the attacks of Schumacher in their battle. In addition, it was rumoured that the German was going to retire. He announced his decision fifteen days later at Monza in front of a packed house. The Scuderia's scenario was well rehearsed, above all for the Tifosi. Michael won the Italian Grand Prix in front of packed grandstands, announced his retirement at the end of the year and took advantage of the Spaniard's car's first engine failure to reduce his championship lead to a mere two points. Italy was in ecstasy while in Viry-Châtillon the engineers rolled up their sleeves and the test beds were running at full speed to provide a fast and reliable engine for the last three rounds. In China, it was the tyres that let the Spaniard down and the 7-times world champion scored a magnificent victory. On a drying track the Michelins on the Renault got glued to the surface while the German's Bridgestones worked wonders on the Shanghai asphalt. Fisichella gifted the German his first place and he was back on level pegging with Alonso.

The effect of this on the Renault team can only be imagined. Rumours about a break-up between Alonso and his squad abounded in the French and Spanish press. His chances of resisting the man from Kerpen looked slimmer and slimmer. Everybody thought that Suzuka would see the German victorious sounding the death knell of Alonso's hopes. And then Michael's engine blew in the middle of a grand prix that he was leading comfortably, and his hopes of an eighth title went up in a cloud of white smoke. Suddenly the Spaniard's second championship was a certainty. Two weeks later in Sao Paulo the "little bull from the Asturias" was duly crowned thanks to his second place.

<

Giancarlo Fisichella and Fernando Alonso helped Renault to its second constructors' title on the trot.

The French, though, had a bitter taste in their mouths despite Renault's triumph. Michelin was quitting the F1 scene albeit with two more titles leaving the field open to its Japanese rival, Bridgestone, which, in 2006, had snatched first place from the Clérmont-Ferrand make as the world no.1 tyre manufacturer. The French firm left F1 after 216 grands prix split up into two periods, from 1977 to 1984 and then 2001 to 2006 with a score of 102 victories and 9 world championship titles (5 drivers' and 4 constructors').

The French bigmouths were probably complaining (as is their wont!) about the triumph of a Spaniard at the wheel of a French car. It was a good vintage but not an excellent one. Wine is like F1. It is the soil but also the men. There were no French drivers at the start of the 2006 season so looked like it would be a choice between drinking thin wine from Spain or an eighth stein of beer from Germany. But instead, they had the right to a young vintage full of promise.

Hope was back albeit slight. The 2006 season looked like it would be as dry and dusty as the previous one. Sébastien Bourdais, ignored by the little world of F1, continued his successful career on the other side of the Atlantic and Franck Montagny, the former Renault test driver, did not have a seat. He found a place in the little Super Aguri team that he was obliged to leave on the eve of the Malaysian Grand Prix. But luck and Yuji Ide, the no.2 in the Japanese team whose lack of skills at that level were soon apparent, would allow Montagny back into the F1 fold. It was the end of the French drought in F1 after a 2-year period. Olivier Panis started his last race in Japan at Suzuka in 2004 finishing fourteenth after a 10-year career. Montagny began his on another mythic circuit, the Nürburgring. It was not an easy debut as he was at the wheel of the aged Arrows revised and baptised the SA05, which was around 6 seconds off the pace. For Franck it was a childhood dream come true as he finished the legendary Monaco Grand Prix before quitting the F1 scene on home turf under the applause of his fellow-countrymen in the French Grand Prix at Magny-Cours.

But things were about to improve. On the Shanghai circuit in China on Friday there were two French drivers' names on the time sheets. Alexandre Prémat was given a drive by Spyker and Montagny was back in his role of test driver for the Super Aguri team. Prémat, third in the GP2 Championship, was even briefly in front of Michael Schumacher.

Hope sprang afresh in French breasts. Alas, not for long as there will be no French driver at the start of the 2007 season. A pity as they will still have the championship winning car thanks to Alonso so at least the Marseillaise will ring out over the circuits.

Go the whole hog

Kunio Shibata
Autosport Japon

2006 wo hurikaeru

I n 2006, a new Japanese team called Super Aguri F1 was born. Soon afterwards BAR was completely bought out by Honda. By adding Toyota to these two Japan now had three teams out of the eleven in the world championship making it the richest country in terms of team numbers.

Is it a good thing? Probably better than nothing, but given the poor results achieved this year (one victory for the three) it is not yet time for celebration.

"Gascoyne is only a symbol"

Flavio Briatore said the following in Monaco: *"All these people who talk about technology have never won in F1, or not for the last ten years anyway. They've got no right to talk about it."*

This comment concerned the cost reduction in F1 and the people Briatore was aiming at were apparently the two Japanese giants. But so bad were their results up to the halfway mark that neither of them dared to contradict the Italian. Honda was on the rostrum in Malaysia and so was Toyota in Australia. Then nothing. Neither in qualifying nor in the race were the cars quick enough. The gap between them and the leading teams just grew wider and wider. Toyota was as disappointed as Honda and was the first to react. Just after its one and only rostrum finish in 2006 in Melbourne it fired Mike Gascoyne, its technical director. It seems that the decision had been taken well beforehand. One of the directors said to me in Bahrain the day before the grand prix, *"Mike is only a symbol. His time with us is up."* Until the end of last year anyway Gascoyne was the key man for Toyota.

Before he joined the Japanese giant the team already had enough means and personnel but lacked a chief co-ordinator. Gascoyne filled this role beautifully. He restructured the team and put people where they were needed. Fourth place in the 2005 championship was the reward for his efforts. However, the English engineer has a

strong personality and a very independent character like most of his fellow-boffins in the milieu. Toyota has always privileged harmony in its organisation and did not want to let him exercise too much influence that was contradictory to the team's principles. In addition, the management felt that Gascoyne had done his job as the team was now working like clockwork, so the poor start to the season provided the ideal excuse to get rid of him. Pascal Vasselon, who was given the job of technical director, is a hard-working honest man. But was he good enough to replace Gascoyne? The management thought that the answer was yes. The unfolding of the season seemed to prove otherwise. The team did not score any points between the San Marino and Spanish Grands Prix. In Monaco the B spec version of the T106 was launched with modified front suspension and the best that Ralf Schumacher could do was a lowly eighth place. The cars' lack of reliability was another major stumbling block this season. In almost all the races they ran into problems with engines, brakes, hydraulic systems, the electronics, steering etc. In the end Toyota could do no better than sixth in the Constructors' Championship.

"Don't be afraid to make mistakes"

Honda did not really shine either. It too fired its technical director as if in imitation of Toyota. Where Honda differed from its Japanese rival was that it replaced Geoff Willis with Shuhei Nakamoto. This 49-year-old Japanese engineer had been with Honda for twenty-five years looking after motorbike and car racing, something that is extremely rare in Japanese motor sporting culture. But Nakamoto had never designed a racing car in his life; he was very much a nuts and bolts man. Thus, it was normal that the former BAR engineers were a bit worried about how they were going to develop a car under his direction.

Nakamoto, on the other hand, didn't seem too over-awed about the situation. He said: *"Contrary to what people might think my experience in the area of development gives me additional strength as everybody believes we're going to fail. So I can ask my men to present me with original or daring ideas unlike my predecessor. Even if they don't work it'll be my fault, not theirs. Thus, they have much greater freedom to develop their ideas."*

At Honda it seemed that people who made mistakes were not criticised. *"You can always*

Kunio Shibata
48-year-old Kunio Shibata left Japan and his job as a journalist in 1982 to come and live in Paris and study at the Science Po. He then became a free-lance director for Japanese television. He has always been interested in motor sport and began following the grands prix for a Press Agency when Satoru Nakajima arrived in F1 in 1987. He has been collaborating with the specialised Japanese magazine Grand Prix Xpress since 1991.

learn from these mistakes," continued Nakamoto. "But it was difficult to get English people to understand this philosophy. They were scared of making mistakes. They were used to hesitating before taking a step forward. That kind of stodgy mentality had to be changed."

He said that his reform was only halfway through when in Hungary, the fourth race since he had taken over the technical direction, Jenson Button won his first race.

"It was a kind of a present," Nakamoto acknowledged. "Since Canada we've kept improving the car in aerodynamics, the engine and the weight distribution. The car's been progressing all the time. Even so, if Alonso had

---

One of the four Arrows of the Super Aguri team held pride of place in the Melbourne airport's duty free shop!

---

not had a problem with a wheel nut we wouldn't have won."

Button continued to rack up the results right to the end of the season and Honda finished the year in fourth place. During the traditional end-of-season party the Englishman said to Nakamoto: "If we'd had this pace of development since the start of the year the final result would've been very different." Button was certainly right. Ferrari was uncatachable right to the end in part because of the Bridgestone tyres' supremacy. Among the Michelin runners Honda reached a level where it could have beaten Renault provided that everything functioned correctly.

Hero despite himself
What is the best way of describing the Super Aguri team's first F1 season? It did not score any points and finished eleventh and last in the Constructors' Championship. On the basis of this result it was a setback. What I would prefer to emphasize is the unremitting effort, which they showed all year.
Aguri Suzuki, a former F1 driver, always wanted to set up his own team in the top category. He tried to buy BAR but as Honda had already taken that decision, he had to start from zero. He launched the project in November 2005 only four months before the start of the 2006 season. He had no means, no people except his

faithful friend Daniel Audetto and the technical/financial back-up of Honda. Aguri and Daniel first tried to buy the intellectual property rights to Honda, in other words the BAR-Honda 007 know-how. The FIA forbade this and so they had to fall back on the Arrows A23 that dated from 2002. Among the four cars that they bought one was one display in Melbourne airport duty free shop!
They rented a factory in England, recruited personnel and looked for sponsors but in vain. In the meantime their first entry had been refused by the FIA; officially because the dossier was incomplete. The truth was apparently that this decision was made to force them to sign the new Concorde Agreement, which Honda was totally against. Aguri said he had no choice:
"I almost gave up on several occasions. I was completely desperate asking myself how I was going to come up with the 48 million dollars guarantee and the find the 100 million necessary to run the team. But I knew that my men were working night and day to get two cars on the grid in Bahrain so I had to make the impossible happen!"
To make it to the first race was a miracle in itself but in addition Super Aguri finished the first three grand prix. It was not only due to the efforts of the personnel directed by Mark Preston, but also by the big contribution made by Takuma Sato.
The Japanese driver had left BAR at the end of the 2005 season and Aguri asked him to come and join him immediately. Takuma accepted but he must have thought long and hard before saying yes.
"I was delighted by this offer," he laughed. "But it was a completely new team with a small budget and not that many experienced people. In addition, I had to drive an old up-dated car. I was sure to race at the very back of the field." However, the unexpected happened on several occasions. In Malaysia Taku managed to keep a Midland behind him for ten laps and in the final corner he slipped past a Toro Rosso powered by a 3-litre engine in a chassis that came directly from Red Bull. "I'd had enough of driving carefully. I wanted to race and fight with the others."
In the suffocating heat he had no drinks bottle or power assisted steering. His face and his hands looked like they had been boiled but he

was happier than ever. His contribution was not only on the track. Every Thursday before the grand prix he walked the circuit with his engineers explaining to them the layout, the state of the surface and the races he had done. "Right from the start I felt that his involvement was 100%," stated Aguri. "He wants to do everything with the team and grow with it." Seven months later in Brazil Taku received the chequered flag in tenth place. During the race the Super Aguri was consistently quicker than the Toro Rossos, the Spykers and even Red Bull.
The famous F1 daily "The Red Bulletin" chose Taku as the uinknown hero of the year. The magazine appreciated the way in which the driver had overcome the frustration and indifference and that he carried the team by his enthusiasm and unflagging motivation.

Super Aguri brought a breath of fresh air into the stuffy world of F1. Now the team is recognised by its rivals but its financial situation is still precarious. At present the name of Anthony Davidson, the Honda third driver is being touted as Taku's team-mate. Does that imply much bigger backing from the Japanese manufacturer? There is also a rumour going round that Aguri will become the future Honda F1 boss.
Toyota has signed an agreement with Williams not only as an engine supplier but with financial backing as well. In return it will receive the English team's know-how and will also have its say in the choice of drivers.
The Japanese teams have an original approach to the question of surviving in, or vanishing from the "Piranha Pond!"

insights

Tomorrow's coming men with their fresh, innocent faces

2006 vu du Canada

Dominic Fugère
Le Journal de Montréal

Two of the F1 drivers of American origin were shown the door this season. Juan Pablo Montoya and Jacques Villeneuve have both gone and F1 has lost a couple of hard-chargers as well as two men who were not afraid to say what they thought when faced with a microphone, camera or notebook.

If Montoya gave the impression that he had chosen to quit McLaren-Mercedes of his own free will, everybody knew what happened to Villeneuve. Mario Thiessen, the BMW boss, never wanted to have anything to do with Jacques and as soon as he found the right opportunity he sent the man from Quebec back to his log cabin in Canada.

This opportunity presented itself after the German Grand Prix during which Villeneuve hit the wall in a car that was understeering like crazy with which he had been battling for half the race. The reason for the understeer was because Jacques had to have the BMW's nose changed as he had thumped his team-mate up the rear in the first corners.

Super Mario went ballistic and brought in Robert Kubica the young Pole who had recorded some shattering times since the start of the season in the third BMW in the Friday sessions.

BMW tried to justify Villeneuve's replacement by saying that he was suffered from the sequels of his accident in Germany. A quick phone call to the Canadian soon exposed the subterfuge. "*I'm not dying,*" he exclaimed. "*I just need to rest at home. I've been better but I've also been worse.*"

The true story came out later. Thiessen wanted to use the injury as a pretext to test Kubica whom he regarded as his discovery. He then wanted to arrange a play-off to see who would have the drive. Villeneuve saw that as a lack of confidence in him, and it was also as a slap in the face for the former world champion. "After ten years in F1, after having won races and the championship even if it's a long time ago, I wasn't ready to sit at home and wait while a young driver attempted to prove himself. Had I accepted that I don't see how I could have been motivated and 100% dedicated to the team," he said to Autosport. He refused to accept the offer and that gave Thiessen the argument he needed to convince the BMW Board of Directors to fork out the millions of dollars necessary to break the Canadian's watertight contract.

Dominic Fugère, 33-year-old Dominique Fugère worked for the family grocery in his remote little Canadian village while racing 4X4s and doing motocross. He then worked as a press officer for Formula Ford and Formula Atlantic. After university he took up journalism and found a job at "Le Journal de Montréal" in 2000. After general and economic journalism he joined the sports department in 2003 and has been covering F1 since 2005

But up to his Hockenheim accident Villeneuve's 2006 season was much better than the previous year. He ser the quickest times in several test sessions; he was fast but opportunities did not present themselves. His team-mate Nick Heidfeld was not much quicker but managed to score more points. In Canada, Villeneuve was stuck behind his

team-mate (and Ralf Schumacher) due to a blunder by his team in the pits. Schumacher took him off on lap 59 when he was in seventh place. In the USA he was also in seventh place and lapping quicker than the 3 drivers in front of him when his BMW-P86 engine went bang.

Overall, Jacques had done what it took to keep his place but he needed another name on his fan club list: Mario Thiessen!

It was impossible for Jacques to stay in the team without the backing of the German who was fighting for his own survival as the results were not coming in, and the BMW Board of Directors was not very happy about this. Kubica's stunning performance was the final nail if the Canadian's coffin.

Rumours went about saying hat he was going to join up with his former manager Craig Pollock who is always is n the centre of them when they are about buying a team. Villeneuve, though, was far too occupied by his personal life to be tempted by a drive at the back of the field.

Love had struck the man from Quebec just at the moment he launched himself on a new career, that of a singer. When he was in Paris to record his first disc during the 2005-2006 inter-season he fell hook line and sinker for the beautiful Johanna Martinez, the daughter of a friend of Jacques Laffite's.

Villeneuve has wanted a family for the past few years and he took the bull by

VIEW FROM CANADA — INSIGHTS

54

< (opposite): Jacques Villeneuve seen at the wheel of an F1 car for the last time in the German Grand Prix.

Silverstone: Jacques Villeneuve's first Grand Prix as a married man. Love's beautiful face!

the horns and asked Johanna to marry him. The civil ceremony was held in Switzerland and the religious one in Paris. Already a little Villeneuve was on the way and at the time of writing these lines Mrs Villeneuve is on the point of giving birth in Quebec.

In less than a year he has found a new love who became his wife and with his first child on the way it is easy to understand that racing is no longer his first priority. His career as a singer is not taking off as quickly as he would like and he has brought out just one single called "Accepteras-tu" plus an improvised performance with his friend Garou at the Hot Air Balloon festival. In any case his role of husband and father is keeping him busy full time. "I think that at the moment he's pretty well occupied with his wife who's just about to have a baby and motor racing is far from his thoughts," said Craig Pollock, his manager.

In Canada the loss of a driver in a major series makes itself felt. F1 coverage is falling off in the media. The end of the Champ Car adventure on the Gilles Villeneuve circuit and the announcement of the arrival of a round of the Busch and NASCAR Championships encourages journalists to change their focus, all the more so as Villenevue is trying to find a drive in NASCAR.

He is perhaps better fitted for changing nappies than tyres but this has not prevented him from testing the waters in the big stock car series that is much more popular than F1 in the land of Uncle Sam!

Juan Pablo Montoya already announced that he was going back to the States, and Villeneuve said that if he drove elsewhere it would be in NASCAR. The enforced liberty given to him by Mario Thiessen allows him to explore this avenue.

He has had contacts with some of the Ford teams. Roush Racing the Blue Oval's no.1 outfit has offered him a contract in the Busch Series and in the Craftsman Truck championship, but the former

---

He is more preoccupied with changing nappies than changing tyres.

---

champion wants nothing to do with them. It's the Nextel Cup or nothing. Thus for the moment no decisions have been taken. However, if he wants to make a few concessions or if a sponsor appears who wants to join up with the first driver to win the Indy car, F1 and NASCAR championships, or if a team decides to put its trust in a driver who has shown his speed in single-seaters but whose stock car talents remain an unknown quantity, Father Jacques might have the odd drive between two bottles!

If Villeneuve goes to NASCAR he can thank Montoya.

The Colombian sent a shock wave through motor sport when he announced after the USA Grand Prix that he was going to drive a stock car for Chip Ganassi, the team owner with whom he won the CART series and the Indy 500. He is now the yardstick to see how a single-seater driver will adapt to the Chevrolet Monte Carlos, Dodges and Fords in the American Stock Car Championship. "*You can't pas anybody in F1; it's not racing any more,*" Montoya complained.

The agreement between Ganassi and Montoya is good news for Ron Dennis, the McLaren-Mercedes team boss who had had a bellyful of the Colombian. As soon as Montoya announced that he was going to NASCAR in 2007 Dennis found a replacement for him alongside Raïkkönen.

He made Ganassi wait and asked him for a 5 million dollar cheque to allow Montoya to begin his preparation for the 2007 Nextel Cup season at the wheel of the no.42 Texaco Havoline Big/Red Dodge Charger.

Montoya who has an innate sense of car control and is not afraid of speed was immediately at home in these big saloons that weight 1600 kilos. He finished third on his first outing in a stock race in the ARCA Championship (the Stock Car GP2) on the mythic Talladega oval where the cars hit 320 km./h. A communications error with his spotter (a team

member perched on the roof of the stands and equipped with a radio) sent him into the wall in his second ARCA race. He rejoined after a long stop for repairs and the speed that he kept up without a bonnet, wings and bumpers showed that he has what it takes to cut out a career in NASCAR for himself.

He found it a bit more difficult in the Busch Series the following week. In his first race he qualified ninth on the Memphis oval, but a collision with J-J Yeley and a self-inflicted spin sent him tumbling down to the rear of the 43-car field. He fought his way back up to eleventh place.

The following weekend in Texas Montoya could not get his car sorted to his liking. He qualified in tenth place but had to start from the rear of the pack because his crew chief (the NASCAR equivalent of race engineer) Brad Parrott made him pit during the warm-up laps to straighten a bumper. Juan Pablo had problems with the traffic and came home in twenty-eighth place.

"*It was a good opportunity to learn and that's what he did,*" explained Parrott. "*He learned how to drive a car that wasn't good, how to change the car during stops in the pits and how to cut his way up through the field;*"

In Phoenix he again kissed the wall and spun finishing in twentieth position.

This being said all the practice, all the laps that

Montoya has done in stock cars are training for his 2007 season in the NASCAR Nextel Cup. His performances will be watched by everybody to see if single-seater drivers can adapt to the big NASCAR saloons.

A.J Almendinger, 5-times Champ car race winner found a seat with Red Bull NASCAR and Roger Penske put his trust in his IRL star Sam Hornish Jr to try and find him a seat in stock car racing.

Montoya's pioneering work even before his first race in the top NASCAR category has already opened the way for his single-seater colleagues. It remains to be seen if they will be able to cut the mustard with Dale Earnhardt Jr, Tony Stewart, Jeff Gordon, Jimmie Johnson and other aces in their big saloons in the premier racing series in the USA.

Montoya made a big splash on his NASCAR debut. It is the way to go for Jacques Villeneuve
∨

The french Grands Prix: The men and the cars

Jacques Vassal, «Automobile historique»

> Charade: 27/06/65. Pole setter and future winner Jim Clark (Lotus-Climax 33) hits the front. Behind him comes the other Scot "Wee" Jackie Stewart (V8 BRM) and then Italian Lorenzo Bandini and Brit John Surtees (Ferrari 158s).

Jacques Vassal is a journalist, writer and translator. Since the 80s he has written for the main French motor sporting magazines: Le Fanauto, Auto-Passion, Automobile Historique, Rétroviseur, Gentlemen Drivers plus the British mag azine Octane. He is the co-author with Pierre Ménard of the Formula 1 Legends Collection published by Chronosport. In 2006, he wrote the "Livre d'Or" for the FFSA covering the French Grands Prix for the Centenary. He is also well know for his writings on popular, folk and country and blues music as well as on French and world blues and songs (in magazines from Rock & Folk to Chorus).

On 16th July 2006, the Centenary of the first ACF Grand Prix was celebrated at Magny-Cours. The event in question was also the first international grand prix in the history of motor racing. The following article retraces the evolution of the cars, the technology and the circuits in the space of 100 years of French grand prix racing.

The first A.C.F Grand Prix was held on a circuit near Le Mans. Between 1906 and 1967 the circuits changed and a great many improvements were made. Since 1968 and the first French (as opposed to AC.F) Formula 1 Grand Prix the whole technical, sporting and human aspects as well as the tracks have undergone a sea change. This centenary marks the fact that since the first race in 1906 53 ACF Grands Prix were held up to 1967, and since 1968 another 39 French ones have been organised. Before the 1914-1918 war there was no talk of a world or even European championship for cars or drivers, but the urge for international racing was already present. In fact, as soon as the car was able to exceed the speed of a horse and cover a distance that was more than a lap round the backyard, the idea of organising competitions to enable manufacturers to do battle for advertising

reasons, and between nations for prestige and economic purposes had already been sown. This led to the birth of the Gordon Bennett Cup launched by the American press magnate of the same name (owner of the International Tribune) who lived in France. He convinced the Automobile Club de France, of which he was one of the founder members, to organise the race for the cup that he was putting up. It was to go to the winning nation whose task was to hold the following year's race on home territory. Three cars chosen after elimination heats represented each country. The event was created in 1900 and received entries from France, which had the highest number of manufacturers at the time, Great Britain, Belgium, Germany, Italy and America. The French won the 1900 and 1901 races easily thanks to the Panhard-Levassors and in 1902 victory went to Britain and Francis Edge's Napier. However, the 1903 event was held in Ireland as it was forbidden to race cars in England. Camille Jenatzy from Belgium at the wheel of a Mercedes won so the Germans had the honour of organising the 1904 event at Taunus. First home was Frenchman, Léon Thiry in his Brasier, which was a bit of a slap in the face for the Germans. For the 1905

and last Gordon Bennett Cup a 137-km circuit was laid out in the Clérmont-Ferrand region home of the Michelin tyre company. The Cup was already under threat from a movement among the French manufacturers who reckoned that the rule limiting the number of entries to three per country was grossly unfair as they were far more numerous than the Belgians or Germans for example. Again victory went to Léon Thiry in (or maybe on!) his Brasier.

The circuit' war

So a new chapter was about to open in 1906 even if in February 1901 the "Sud Ouest circuit" race in Pau was called "Grand Prix Automobile" (a designation inspired by horse racing). The ACF, however, was the first to use this term in an international context. It is now part of history that the Automobile Club de la Sarthe (the future Automobile Club de l'Ouest) was chosen to hold the race in its region. On 26/27th June 1906 32 cars representing 12 makes from 3 different nations set off on a 103-km circuit for a distance of 1238 kilometres spread out over two days with 6 laps per day. The cars were placed in parc fermé during the night of Saturday/Sunday. Ferenc Szisz, a Frenchman of Hungarian origin won the race in his Renault at a speed of over 101 km/h! The cars whose cubic capacities varied from 7.4 to 18 litres already exceeded 150 km/h on the long straights. The road surface of the era was precarious to say the least (gravel and small stones leading to frequent punctures). Tarring was tried specially for the occasion and on certain portions wooden railway sleepers were also laid down. The next two races were held on a very fast 77-km circuit near Dieppe. It was triangular and speed and power were even more important that at Le Mans. The 12-litre FIATS were hitting 160 km/h on the straights and the average of the winner, Felice Nazzaro, exceeded 113 km/h over 770 kms. In 1908, it was Christian Lautenschlager's turn to triumph in his Mercedes.

Then the regulations changed and the French manufacturers once again disagreed with the ACF and boycotted the event imitated by the foreign constructors. The newspaper L'Auto organised a Coupe des Voiturettes in the Bois de Boulogne for cars with a limited bore which saw the emergence of new manufacturers like Hispano and Delage, but also led to a huge increase in the stroke of the engine. In 1911, a Formula Libre French Grand Prix (including a Coupe des Voiturettes) was held at Le Mans on a 54,600 km circuit which already included the Pontlieue hairpin and Les Hunaudières that would become famous ten years later. The ACF Grand Prix for big cars was revived in 1912 at Dieppe on the same circuit as in 1907-1908 that had to be covered 20 times without a break giving a distance of 1539 kms, the longest grand prix in the history of the sport. The winner, Georges Boillot in his 7.6-litre Peugeot, crossed the finishing line after a titanic duel with American Bruce-Brown in his FIAT after 13h 58m racing! On the Amiens circuit in 1913 Boillot triumphed again but this time in a 5.6-litre Peugeot – the formula had changed in the meantime – becoming the first back-to-back winner of the ACF Grand Prix. The Grand Prix Peugeots designed by the engineer of Swiss origin, Victor Henry and his team nicknamed the "Charlatans" were the first cars to be fitted with a hemispherical cylinder head and four valves per cylinder plus double overhead camshafts. The 1914 ACF Grand Prix was eagerly awaited. Cubic capacity was now limited to 4.5 litres and the 37,6 km circuit near Lyon had to be covered 20 times. The big favourites were Peugeot and Delage (which had just won the Indy 500). Tyres and poor strategy were to decide otherwise. Boillot drive a superb race before retiring and Mercedes, the best-organised team, saw its star driver Christian Lautenschlager win the race becoming the second double victor of the event. War broke out a few weeks afterwards and not until seven years and millions of dead later was the ACF Grand Prix held again.

Le Mans: 2/7/67. The Bugatti circuit hosted the last ACF Grand Prix. Graham Hill and Jim Clark in their Lotus 49s both ran into mechanical trouble. The Repco-Brabhams of Jack Brabham and Denny Hulme scored a double in that order

The revival

The revival took place at Le Mans. This time, though, the circuit was completely different. It was near the town and measured 17,262 kms and with its Pontlieue hairpin, the long Les Hunaudières straight and the Mulsanne and Arnage corners it gave a foretaste of the famous Le Mans 24-Hours layout where the first 24-Hours race took place in 1923. The ACF Grand Prix remained faithful to its peripatetic tradition and was held in various different regions and towns, which, like the tradition of the Tour de France for bicycles, wanted a slice of the financial cake generated by the event. It brought in a lot of money to the region and to its shopkeepers, innkeepers and hotels thanks to the hundreds of thousands of spectators who came on foot, on horseback, by car, by bicycle, motorbike or in buses. In 1922, it went to Strasbourg, which was a way of underlying the fact that Alsace was French once again after the Armistice. German manufacturers were not welcome, strangely enough!

In 1921, victory went to American Jimmy Murphy in his 3-litre Dusenberg. In 1922 with the cubic capacity reduced to 2 litres into first place came the 1907 grand prix winning combination, Nazzaro in his FIAT. The Strasbourg circuit measured 13,380 kms and was very quick. Pietro Bordino set the fastest lap at over 140 km/h. In 1923, the grand prix moved to Tours and the 22,830 km layout consisted mainly of long straights. Once again the men in charge privileged outright speed over road holding even though in that era the 200 km/h barrier was a real challenge for manufacturers, engineers and drivers. Sunbeam and FIAT looked the best placed to win. The Italian drivers took too much out of their cars and victory went to the great Henry Seagrave, who was to become the world land speed record holder later on, in his Sunbeam at a speed of 121 km/h. Bordino again set the fastest lap in his FIAT at 147 km/h. The French, though, made a dog's breakfast of the race. Bugatti and Voisin designed streamlined bodies based around the profile of an aircraft wing, which

^
Rouen-Les-Essarts: 7/7/68. Jacky Ickx (Ferrari 312 F1) scored his first F1 grand prix victory in pouring rain in a race that was marred by Jo Schlesser's fatal accident.

was supposed to be more conducive to maximum speed even with unsupercharged engines. It was a disastrous choice given the lack of proper aerodynamic studies. Not only were the cars slower than their rivals, they were also less reliable. They lagged behind and then retired one after another.

In 1924, the grand prix was back in the Lyon region on a shorter circuit (23 kms) that used around half of the famous 1914 layout. It was here that the legendary Type 35 Bugattis made their debut but they suffered from thrown tyre treads or punctures; and in any case their 2-litre unsupercharged engines were no match for their rivals. Victory went to the fabulous 2-litre 8-cylinder supercharged P2 Alfa Romeo designed by Vittorio Jano. Antonio Ascari, the initial leader, had to retire and amateur opera singer Guiseppe Campari won the rca. Delages driven by Divo and Benoist filled second and third places.

From Montlhery to Reims

In 1925, a new era began with the opening of Linas-Montlhéry which included a banked oval and a road circuit (total length: 12.500 kms) like the ones in Britain (Brooklands), Italy (Monza) and Germany (AVUS). As Montlhéry was only 25 kilometres to the south of Paris it was hoped that it would attract big crowds. In addition, the spectators would see the cars passing 80 times. Unfortunately, the huge traffic jams (that would become notorious!) prevented enthusiasts from arriving on time. Then there was the problem of leaving the circuit afterwards. The race, which, on paper anyway, looked like being a very exciting one turned out to be a disappointment first of all and then a tragedy. There were only 14 cars at the start: 3 Alfas, 3 Delages, 3 Sunbeams and 5 Bugattis. Alfa Romeo was far too strong and the P2 drivers got involved in a personal battle in particular between Campari and Ascari who were great friends. Ascari overdid it and went off. One of the wheels of his car got caught in the wire on the side of the track and it overturned. He was fatally injured and died on his way to

>
Charade: 5/7/70. The race saw a fierce duel between Jackie Ickx (Ferrari 312 B) and Jean-Pierre Beltoise (Matra MS 120). The Belgian and the Frenchman retired with mechanical problems and victory went to Jochen Rindt (Lotus 72-Cosworth) from Austria.

hospital. Alfa Romeo withdrew its other two cars as a sign of respect and Delage scored a hollow victory thanks to Albert Divo who had taken over from Robert Benoist. Immediately after the race the latter went to the spot where Ascari had had his accident where he laid his wreath of flowers. In 1927, Benoist and Delage won the Manufacturers' World Championship and the ACF Grand Prix on the Montlhéry circuit.

Montlhéry was home to the ACF Grands Prix on several more occasions. In 1931, still on the oval plus road circuit it was run over 10 hours and the car were driven by two drivers like in the Le Mans 24 Hours. Then in 1934, Montlhéry was the scene of an historic first, that of the first race abroad of the Mercedes-Benz and Auto Unions. They fell victim to various mechanical problems and accidents and victory went to Louis Chiron's Alfa Romeo. It was just a hiccup in the Germans' triumphant march and their cars dominated grand prix racing up till 1939. In 1935, the Bugattis were beaten into a cocked hat and the Mercedes-Benz W25s scored a crushing victory. They also won in Monaco, Tripoli, Belgium, Switzerland and Spain with Auto Union coming first in Czechoslovakia and Italy. Such was the German stranglehold that the A.C.F decided to accept only sports cars for its grand prix as it was an area in which France did not have any serious rivals. Bugatti won in 1936 and Talbot the following year (both races at Montlhéry). In

the meantime French journalists and officials were hoping that the country would be tempted back into grand prix racing by the new formula coming into force in 1938 (4.5 lites unsupercharged and 3 litres supercharged). As the equivalence was not very favourable for unsupercharged cars Mercedes-Benz and Auto Union continued to dominate. Delahaye brought out a rather ungainly offset 4.5-litre singe-seater in which René Dreyfus triumphed on the twisty Pau circuit: Elsewhere the car was far too slow. Neither Talbot with its 4-litre engine nor Bugatti with a 3-litre supercharged power unit did much better. The final two grands prix of the period just before WWII were held on the ultra-fast 7,82 km Reims circuit. It was first used by the ACF in 1932 and its main characteristics were its long straights favourable to high speeds and slip-streaming leading to frequent lead changes and exciting races much loved by the spectators. In 1932, the winner Tazio Nuvolari in his P3 Alfa Romeo set the fastest lap at a speed of 156 km/h. In 1938, Lang's Mercedes-Benz raised this figure to 170 km/h and the following year he increased it to almost 185 km/h. Reims became a kind of high-speed roller-coaster rivalling Monza and Spa-Francorchamps for the title of the fastest circuit in Europe. This battle for prestige would continue for a long time after the end of WWII.

Champagne and tears

The International Racing Formula no.1 was drawn up by the FIA in Paris in October 1946. Even if the World Championship for Drivers was not officially inaugurated until 1950 most grands prix were organised in compliance with these regulations from 1947 onwards. That year the ACF Grand Prix was back in Lyon but the Parilly layout had nothing in common with the previous ones used in 1914 and in 1924. Victory went to Louis Chiron in his Talbot, a feat that he repeated two years later for the same make in the French Grand Prix on the Reims circuit. The ACF Grand Prix was back in the champagne-growing region where the 1.5-litre supercharged Alfettas won three times (1948,50 and 51). From 1952 onwards the race alternated between Reims and the dauting Rouen-les-Essarts circuit. The Norman layout measured 5,100 kms and included a series of natural difficulties- traps might be a better word – which made it similar to the Nürburgring but on a reduced scale. It was lined with trees and ravines and was very dangerous in the case of an accident. Thus, it was not down to chance that the drivers who won there combined both calm and bravery. In 1952, it was Ascari, then Fangio in 1957, Dan Gurney in 1962 and Jackie Ickx in 1968. In 1955, the length of the Norman circuit was increased to 6,542 kms thanks to the addition of two quick corners (Le Grésil and la Scierie) that only increased its difficulty. Reims too was extended to 8,347 km/h making it even quicker. The crossing of the Gueux village was by-passed and the Garenne sector abandoned by adding the Muizon section that increased the length of the straight leading down to the village of Thillois. This gave rise to the mythic duel between Fangio and Hawthorn in 1953 as well as some memorable slip-streamers like in 1956 with the battle between the Lancia-Ferraris of Fangio, Collins and Castellotti and Harry Schell's Vanwall. The track was also the scene of breathtaking finishes as in 1953

(Hawthorn victorious) and 1961 when the debutant Giancarlo Baghetti held of the much more experienced Dan Gurney in his Porsche to win the race by 2/10s after passing the American not far from the finish. Reims regained its status as the fastest circuit in Europe under the reign of the picturesque Raymond "Toto" Roche who offered 50 bottles of champagne to every driver beating the lap record during practice. Fangio, who was a past master in this aspect of racing, used to beat it by just tenths of a second and one year he came away with 200 bottles of the precious liquid! Unfortunately, the chase after the fastest lap and victory (the winner received a cash prize of several million francs, a huge sum for the era) led to a few dramas. In 1958, Luigi Musso in his Ferrari went off in the fast Gueux curve and was killed in the ensuing accident. A year earlier, Annie Bousquet had met her death in

the same place in a sports car race. Despite these mishaps Reims hosted the ACF Grand Prix again in 1963 and 1966. Jim Clark in his Lotus was victorious in 1963 and the last grand prix on the Champagne circuit fell to Jack Brabham in his eponymous car. One year later the Le Mans Bugatti circuit hosted the last ACF Grand Prix and again Brabham was the winner.

Charade's hour of glory
In 1968, the grand prix changed hands and was henceforth organised under the banner of the French Motor Sporting Federation. It was held in pouring rain on the Rouen-les-Essarts circuit and the victor was the rising young Belgian star, Jackie Ickx, who showed amazing sang froid in the diabolical conditions. It was also the last F1 grand prix held on the Norman circuit as an accident in

^
Dijon-Prenois: 7/7/74. Austrian Niki Lauda (Ferrari 312 B 3) hassled by Ronnie Peterson (Lotus-Cosworth 72). The Swede went on to victory.

<
Dijon-Prenois: 5/7/81. Alain Prost (Renault RE 30) scored his first win helped by the weather and a wise tyre choice at the just the right moment when the race was interrupted

Le Castellet: 3/7/88. Alain Prost (McLaren MP4/4-Honda) takes the lead from Gerhard Berger (Ferrari F1 87/88C) and Ayrton Senna (McLaren MP4/4-Hnoda). The Frenchman won his home grand prix by 31.752s from the Brazilan. Berger finished fourth behind his team-mate the late Michele Alboreto.

the opening laps cost the life of Jo Schlesser. It was on the day of his 40th birthday and he had at last fulfilled his dream of taking part in a world championship grand prix. His Honda RA 302 was far from being fully sorted and most of its chassis was in magnesium. It went off on the run down to the Nouveau Monde hairpin, caught fire and Schlesser had no chance of survival.

Even before Reims and Rouen were condemned as they were obsolete and did not meet modern safety requirements, the ACF was looking for another circuit. Its first choice fell on the Charade layout in the Auvergne, a very twisty 8,055 km circuit with a lot of corners and ups and downs. The drivers said it was good at sorting the men from the boys but was as dangerous as the circuits it replaced. The stones thrown up caused punctures on a regular basis and also injured drivers. Austrian Helmut Marko almost lost an eye there in 1972. The rocky walls in many places plus the narrow verges could turn a seemingly harmless off-course excursion into a tragedy. In 1959, Ivor Bueb, the double Le Mans 24 Hours winner, went off and lost his life in an F2 race after having set the lap record in the inaugural event in 1958. He was the only car driver to be killed at Charade. In 1962, Frenchman Marcellin Herranz met with a fatal accident in a motorcycle race. Four F1 grands prix were held there.

In 1965, the last year of the 1500 cc formula victory fell to Jim Clark in his Lotus from another Scot (and future triple world champion) Jackie Stewart. In 1966, the cubic capacity was raised to 3 litres and even with the huge power increases it implied drivers and teams returned to the Auvergne for a further 3 F1 grands prix in 1969,1970 and 1972. They were 3 memorable races with victory going to Steward in the first one at the wheel of a Matra-Ford entered by Ken Tyrrell while

the Scot's French team-mate Jean-Pierre Beltoise fought like a lion to snatched 2nd by 2/10s from Belgian Jackie Ickx in a Brabham. The following year Beltoise, this time at the wheel of the V12-engined version of the Matra, dominated the opening part of the race, but a slow puncture that required an extra pit stop plus a fuel feed problem deprived him, the constructor and the home crowd of a French victory. The race was won by Austrian Jochen Rindt who suffered from serious stomach cramps on the Auvergne roller coaster where he averaged over 158 km/h. In 1972, Jackie Stewart won again in his Tyrrell-Ford and his new team-mate was that shooting star on the world F1 scene, the very talented François Cevert. The final grand prix saw the debut of a young local lad from Clérmont-Ferrand, former motorcycle rider Patrick Depailler, who was destined for a successful career that also ended in death.

Le Castellet/Dijon: end of the alternation

Charade was also condemned to disappear like Rouen and Reims as there was now a new circuit in the Var, Le Castellet, that hosted the French Grand Prix for the first time in 1971. It was designed with the help of some well-known drivers (Jean-Pierre Beltoise and Jean-Pierre Jabouille) and was know as the "Paul Ricard" circuit after the name of its founder, the eponymous drinks magnate. It soon became the yardstick thanks to its ultra-modern installations and its exceptional safety. Its geographical location meant good weather and that attracted both French and foreign teams which set up shop there for private testing especially during the winter months. The only drawback was the gusty Mistral that swept the track from time to time. Overall Le Castellet was the theatre of 14 French Grands Prix, the last of which was held in 1990. It saw some marvellous battles

between the 3-litre F1 cars with Fittipaldi, Lauda Hunt, Andretti etc and then the fabulous era of the 1500 cc turbocharged racers in the hands of Prost, Piquet, Rosberg and Mansell with some fantastic scraps between the Brazilian and the Englishman in the Williams-Hondas and Prost in the McLaren-TAG Porsche in 1986 and 1987. Then came the return of the 3.5-litre normally aspirated cars in 1989 and the Frenchman's thrilling victory in 1990. 1982 will always be remembered for René Arnoux's runaway win in his Renault when he refused to obey team orders and hand victory to his team-mate Alain Prost. Tragedy struck in 1986 when Italian Elio de Angelis was killed after his Brabham went off at 280 km/h in the La Verrerie left-hander and caught fire.

In the same period the event also went to the Dijon-Prenois track. Grands Prix had also been held in Burgundy capital before and after WWII. In 1974, the F1 grand prix took place on a permanent circuit laid out in hilly countryside beside an aerodrome. The winner was Ronnie Peterson in his Lotus 72. But the circuit had one drawback; it was too short measuring only 3,289 kms giving a lap time of around 1 minute, and was neither selective nor technically much of a challenge. This defect was partially remedied in 1977 with the addition of a new section that increased the length to 3,8 kms. It consisted of two short portions, one going upwards and the other slanting downwards. The Dijon-Prenois circuit was the scene of a few firsts like the victory in 1979 of the turbocharged Renault in the hands of that excellent test driver Jean-Pierre Jabouille, which was also his own first success in a race counting for the F1 World Championship. Alain Prost also scored his first win on this circuit in his Renault in 1981. He beat John Watson from Northern Ireland thanks to his sense of strategy and race skills that were to be the hallmarks of his very successful career. However, the outstanding memory left by the Burgundy circuit was the famous battle between René Arnoux in his Renault and Gilles Villeneuve's Ferrari in1979. It was a real mano à mano and finally victory (but not in the race) went to the little Canadian. Dijon-Prenois was a much-appreciated circuit that frequently provided very exciting races and was also appreciated by the Swiss whose border was not far away. Circuit racing has been forbidden there since 1955 and in1982 a Swiss Grand Prix counting for the F1 World Championship was held on the French circuit on which that year's world champion Keke Rosberg scored his only victory.

Magny-Cours

In turn Dijon Prenois was abandoned by the F1 circus, more for financial reasons than for technical or sporting ones. It was becoming more and more complicated to attract enough people to pay for the modernisation of the installations as well as the increasingly exorbitant cost of the F1 field. In 1984, François Chambelland the director threw in the towel the same year that the last grand prix was held there. Since then Dijon, where several 1000-km events for sports car also took place, has survived thanks to national championships (Touring Cars, Promotion Formulas) and the Burgundy Historic Grand Prix. After the closure of Montlhéry in 2004 it now

hosts the famous "Grands Prix de l'Age d'Or."
The Paul Ricard circuit renamed the "Circuit de Castellet" had to face up to the escalation in costs as well as the political and federal attacks. This was especially true under the reign of President François Mitterand who, with the blessing of the local council, wanted the grand prix moved to the Nièvre department of which he was the member of parliament for a long time. Since 1991, it has been the unique home of the French Grand Prix. However, this former kart track turned into a club circuit for cars and bikes, which also housed a branch of the Jim Russell Driving School as well as a few workshops like that of the legendary Tico Martini, did not at first glance appear to be the ideal site for a grand prix circuit. Drivers like René Arnoux, Didier Pironi and Jacques Laffite had learned their trade there in the promotional formulas like F3 and F2, F. or F. Renault, but the track was too short and too old to be able to hold a candle to Le Castellet or Dijon-Prenois. This was without taking into account the wishes of the socialist president who, aided and abetted by his friends Pierre Bergeron, the mayor of Nevers and minister of the interior, and Guy Ligier whose factory was within a stone's throw of the track in what was to become the Technopole, gave the green light for the modernisation of Magny-Cours. It was said the friendship between Ligier and Mitterand went back to the seventies when the latter was first secretary of the socialist party (and losing candidate in

the presidential elections against Valéry Giscard d'Estaing in 1974). It appeared that Mitterand was driven at high speed from the Nièvre to Paris by the former racing driver who had became a constructor.
The new circuit was inaugurated with great pomp and ceremony in 1991 in the presence of the President of the Republic who got onto the rostrum to present the prizes to the first three (Mansell, Prost and Senna). All the great names of the modern era have won there including Michael Schumacher a record 8 times as well as championship teams like Benetton, McLaren, Williams, Renault and Ferrari. It has been the scene of the odd unexpected success like in 1999 when Heinz-Harald Frentzen gave the Irish team Jordan a surprise victory in the wet. In 2002, young Finn Kimi Raïkkönen almost pipped Schumacher but went off on oil in the final laps. However, its layout which is interesting for drivers and engineers, tends to give rise to rather boring, monotonous races where most of the overtaking happens in the pits! Despite modifications and the big crowds Magny-Cours is but a pale imitation of the great circuits that have been mentioned in this article. Since 2004, the FFSA (French Motor Sporting Federation) has taken over the organisation of the race and has invested a lot of time and energy into it . In 2006, it put on an historic grand prix plus a parade to celebrate the Centenary to keep the flame of motor sport alive in the country in which it saw the light of day over one hundred years ago.

< Magny-Cours: 2/7/02. Michael Schumacher (Ferrari F 2002) took advantage of young Finn Kimi Raîkkönen's slide in his McLaren MP4/17-Mercedes-Benz and overtook him under yellow flags. This victory gave the German the 2002 drivers (and his fifth) title by mid-season.

Aged 75 he still runs Formula 1 in his own very personal way. In his battle against the major manufacturers and their attempts to run a parallel championship he again came out on top after years of furious combat.

Bernie Ecclestone: the monopoly man

> *"I'm going to make the major manufacturers eat their passes!"* After years of negotiations, discussions, betrayals and upsets Bernie Ecclestone succeeded in quelling the major manufacturers' attempt to create their own championship.

Bernie Ecclestone looks like a nice guy when you meet him casually. He is always smiling, affable and gives you the odd slap on the back. But don't be misled. Charles Bernard Ecclestone known as Bernie or Mr. X directs F1 with an iron fist. He is far-sighted, brilliant and often sarcastic and you quickly realise that it is better not to have him among your enemies.
Not a lot is known about his past. He was born on 28th October 1930 into a modest family of fishermen. He was an amateur racing driver and then began selling second-hand motorbikes before he bought the Brabham team in 1971 for the sum of 25 000 pounds sterling. He quickly realised that the teams did not know how to sell themselves – at the time F1 was not really shown a lot on TV. After years of hard work he has made it into a worldwide show. F1 owes him everything and sometimes forgets it.
At the end of 2005 Bernie sold his company shares to an investment fund CVC Capital. It now holds the commercial rights of F1 up to 2099. Bernie is now their manager. But on the spot it has done nothing to curb his power. At the start of May 2006 he won another victory by convincing the major manufacturers involved in F1 (BMW, Honda, Mercedes-Benz, Toyota and Renault)) to extend their contract with him for an additional 5 years –up to 2012 – while for 6 years the manufacturers in question had threatened to leave him and set up a pirate championship.
To sum up, they wanted more from Bernie who was accused of giving the teams only a tiny part of the advertising rights. It was a very complex political war and Bernie emerged victorious – as always!
Interview.

- *Why have you sold your company to CVC Capital? And why did they buy it?*

- "In fact, I sold my family company a long time ago to a firm that was bought up by the Kirsch Media Group and then sold on to CVC Capital. It's all a bit complicated but through the procedure I held on to 25% of the company. That's what I sold recently. I suppose they bought it because they reckon it's a good investment."

- *They're talking about improving the show. How are you going to do that?*

- "To be frank I probably haven't done all I could for the sport. I've spent most of my time battling against the others (the major manufacturers). They wanted more money; they weren't satisfied with what they had signed for. It's always the same old story. Many people would prefer to have 90% of 100 million than 50% of 500 million. It's the usual human stupidity! Now that everything's done and dusted I'm going to do a lot to improve the show. We've already settled the qualifying problem and we didn't do it alone. But I've got a lot of other ideas and there are quite a few out there who're willing to follow me."

- *Which ones?*

- (Sly grin) "Don't count on me to let the cat out of the bag!"

- *Do you like today's F1?*

- "Of course, I like it and I like this job. I don't have to do what I do to earn a living. If I'm here it's because I like it. I haven't got any hobbies. Outside my work I devote myself to my family above all, to my wife and my two children. This being said and to answer your question. Of course today's Formula 1 is not the same as 30 years ago. The paddock isn't as much fun; there used to be more ambience, more girls. But what can I do about it?

- *When you watch a race on TV do you like the show?*

-"Well yes and no; what we have to do and quickly is to produce all the programmes ourselves. Today we only do a bit, but we have to have the same producer everywhere who knows F1 like the back of his hand. Sometimes the direction isn't great."

- *How do you see F1 in 10 or 20 years?*

- "I haven't got the slightest idea! Had you asked the same question 10 years ago I'd have been incapable of telling you what it would be like today. I just try and improve things, each detail one after another. I don't think there'll be a revolution."

- *The aim of the conflict with the manufacturers that has just finished was to replace you. What are your relations like with the team bosses that led the putsch, Flavio Briatore, for example?*

- "Flavio's OK; he doesn't criticise me too much."

- *Really! He said you were too old and that you should go...*

- "(He laughs) "That's nothing. Flavio and I are good friends."

- *The team bosses who criticise you owe you a lot, though.*

(on the right) >> Slavica and Bernie Ecclestone. Slavia is the real F1 commercial rights holder; these are grouped in the SLEC (Slavica Ecclestone) Holding company.

(above) Bernie Ecclestone owned the Brabham team before going on to look after the FOM (Formula One Management).
(above): Bernie with his driver Niki Lauda on the grid at the 1978 Argentinean Grand Prix.
(below): With Nelson Piquet at the 1984 Dutch Grand Prix. The Brazilian won the world championship twice at the wheel of a Brabham.

- "Yes, the F1 millionaires. I made every damn one of 'em."

- *Speaking of grand prix organisers, they all lose money except you. When you organise a race you make money, when they do the same they lose money. How do you explain this?*

- "How do I know? They probably spend too much money and they spend it badly. Maybe they don't set the right prices for the tickets. It must an accumulation of small details. It's

> ## *"The F1 millionaires? I made every damn one of 'em."*

also a question of experience. The people from Barcelona came to see me and asked what prices they should charge for their tickets. They showed me what they wanted to do and I said that it wasn't going to work. They listened to me and then they came and thanked me for giving them good advice. The people from Bahrain did the same. But some of those who've been there for a long time don't realise that the world has changed."

- *Take the case of Canada, for example. Is its long-term future assured?*

- "Hmm, truthfully Montreal is one of the circuits that's starting to show its age. The press centre is an antique, as you know. They're trying to stay in the game by

improving their circuit little by little each year. But what we're maybe going to have to do is to force them to make a big step forward and align themselves with the present standards."

- *Apparently the contract with Normand Legault runs until 2011 but it is not stated that the Canadian Grand Prix must take place in Montreal.*

- "That's right."

- *Legualt says he pays one of the lowest fees that you've ever accepted. Why does he pay less than the others for F1?*

- "It's one of the races on which we make the least money. I try and draw up a grand prix season that's strategically important for the manufacturers, the sponsors or for any other good reason. Canada is a valuable country for us. That's why I want to have a grand prix there. And it's for that reason that I accept a lower price."

- *Have you any projects to hold a grand prix elsewhere like Toronto or Vancouver?*

- "How should I know? You'll have to ask Normand the question. It's his problem not mine!"

- *And the United Sates? We keep hearing rumours about a grand prix in Las Vegas for example.*

- "Oh yes, Las Vegas. I've seen a whole string of projects since the last grand prix there in 1982. The big problem with the Americans is

that they want a guarantee that they'll make a profit. It's their point of views and it doesn't cause me any problems. We've got a product and we sell it. If they reckon they can't make money out of it, what can I do? You know, the United Sates is a funny country. The income from the ticket sales is lowerthan in Europe. In fact, it's one of the lowest in the world. The sponsors pay much less than in other parts of the globe, here for example. They've got all kinds of racing over there. Their market is about the same as in Europe but they're there in their own world. Their races can be fantastic but we get more people watching the German Grand Prix, for example, than their best TV audience of the season. We've got more people for everyone of our events. I don't know, I really don't know. The United States is really a difficult country to understand.

- *Everybody wonders what will happen when you depart. Have you prepared your succession?*

- "Hmm (he hesitates) I don't think anyone is going to replace me and do what I do. I started from nothing and I built up the system bit by bit creating several companies. I presume there'll be several people in charge of these companies who'll come along with their own ideas. And maybe they'll do better than me. Who knows?"

> ^
> "*Hello!*" Often considered the most brilliant man in the paddock by a long chalk Bernie Ecclestone has managed to make F1 into an international show over the years. Without ever losing his acerbic British sense of humour!

> The world champion's rear tyre in the Brazilian Grand Prix: that black doughnut the object of so much desire!

The tyre, that mysterious doughnut that makes and breaks world champions

In the duel between Michael Schumacher and Fernando Alonso this year the slightest detail assumed critical importance. The tiniest incident could have a major impact. Ross Brawn and Pat Symonds, the technical directors of Ferrari and Renault respectively, estimated that the 248 F1 and the R26 were very close to each other in terms of performance. They did not maker any attempt to hide the fact that this year's title owed a great deal to the tyres.

How can these rubber doughnuts have such importance? While months of research are necessary to gain a second a lap by improving the chassis, the same result can be obtained immediately by putting on a softer tyre. It is easy to understand why tyres are the object of such desire.

Of course, they are not all that easy to make. An F1 tyre is the work of many scientists. It is made of a mixture of rubber on a metal carcass that puts the rubber on the track and copes with the aerodynamic load of the car (up to a ton in certain corners because of the downforce generated by the wings).

A question of the mixture

The rubber is made up of a mixture of several synthetic polymers (natural rubber is no longer used). Some of them are necessary for their rigidity and others for their grip. The whole secret consists of determining the right mixture according to the characteristics sought. Michelin tests over 300 different mixtures

> A summit meeting in the Barcelona circuit paddock during the Spanish Grand Prix: Jacques Jordan, the Michelin Group communications officer (left) talking to Nick Shamrock, the make's F1 director, Frédéric Henry-Biabaud, the Michelin competitions manager and Séverine Ray, the make's super press attaché who was awaiting a new arrival the following month!

during a grand prix season and almost fifty architectures. Everything is done to optimise the contact between the rubber and the asphalt that lasts 2/1000th of a second!

Two thousandths that seduces

The above is the duration that a part of the rubber is in contact with the track at 300 km/h and this concerns only around 15 cms of the tread at any one time.

Slow-motion image: When the surface is in contact with the asphalt it must stay there despite the centrifugal forces that push it outwards. Two thousandths of a second later as the wheel continues to turn the rubber leaves the asphalt and waits for the next revolution. Its contact with the track has lasted for two thousandths of a second a process repeated 40 times a second.

How does it work? The main phenomenon of grip is called indentation: the flexibility of the rubber mixture that enables it to marry the shapes of the rough patches of the surface and to stick to it, which is contrary to the way the car wants to slide. Another phenomenon takes place at the same time: the grip. In a flash the molecules in the rubber and those on the asphalt bond at the microscopic level (around a hundredth of a micron

Zigzag to heat up the tyres

For these two phenomena to work properly a tyre has to be hot as maximum grip can only be obtained if its surface is between 100 and 140 degrees. This is difficult to obtain in cool conditions and when the field is running behind the safety car. This is why there are "offs" in these circumstances and why the drivers zigzag to maintain their tyres' temperature.

This grip phenomenon is little understood by the scientists. A tyre is a bit of chemistry, a lot of alchemy and more black magic than mathematics.

Unlike touring car rubber which has to be able to go anywhere whatever the temperatures the same is not the case for an F1 tyre. "*Several factors are taken into account when designing a tyre,*" says Nick Shorrock, the Michelin F1 boss. "*The most important is the circuit layout. One with long, fast corners does not impose the same restrictions as a slow one. The extremes are Montreal where we bring along very soft*

rubber and Silverstone. There the fast sections destroy the tyres very quickly and we have to use the hardest compounds."

The following are taken into account when it comes to choosing the tyres for a circuit: the granulometry (the microscopic structure of the track), the temperatures forecast, the chassis characteristics and the team's' strategies (short or long stints).

This explains the number of tyres brought to each circuit; up to 10 different types for the five teams supplied by Bridgestone. Multiply this figure by 2 cars per team and 7 sets per weekend per car plus the wet weather tyres and you get a figure of around 1000 to 2000 tyres per grand prix per manufacturer- around ten transporters. During a grand prix weekend the drivers must choose the compounds they want to use for the race on Saturday at midday. Then it's up to them

In a flash the molecules of the rubber and those of the surface bond

to do the work. "*According to the driver we see very different wear on the tyres with the same chassis,*" states Nick Shorrock. "*Last year at Sauber Felipe Massa, who has a very aggressive driving style, wore them very quickly and he was forced to choose harder compounds. His team-mate of the time, Jacques Villeneuve, had a very flowing style and it was the opposite for him. Sometimes he had problems getting his tyres up to temperature and he had to use very soft rubber.*"

The manufacturer's best work can be destroyed by numerous problems. The tyre can blister (it overheats and blisters form on its surface). Then it is necessary to opt for a harder compound or a different architecture, which transmits less heat to the tyre. The tyre can also suffer from graining (it picks up the rubber deposited on the track and little balls start to appear) which makes the car slide.

In 2007, the danger of seeing a manufacturer putting its partners in danger will no longer exist. Michelin has withdrawn and Bridgestone will become the sole supplier giving teams and chassis a single tyre. Which may not adapt to every one or to the different driving styles. The doughnut saga is far from over!

The FIA opts for a single tyre supplier

When you see an F1 car on a circuit it is difficult to believe that it is a (very) distant cousin of the car you drive to the office every day. Sometimes the average punter reproduces the very situations that are a real headache for the F1 team engineers. In a car park on smooth concrete you can make your tyres scream, which, without you knowing it, reproduces exactly the same phenomenon at a microscopic level as that of an F1 car cornering on the very limits of grip. The scream of the tyres on the concrete is that of the rubber entering into resonance with the surface like that of a tyre losing and regaining grip at its limit. In a car park this phenomenon takes place at a low speed. It would be impossible to hold a grand prix on such a surface as it totally lacks grip. In F1 grip is the key to victory and it is all engineers think about. The aerodynamicists spend their days in the wind tunnel for it sacrificing their free time on the altar of grip. Nowadays, the these grip levels are so high that an F1 could run on a ceiling upside down from 240 km/h upwards. But as we have already said (see opposite) the easiest way to increase grip is to make better tyres.

This year in F1 the war between Bridgestone and Michelin was so intense that all other technical considerations were of almost secondary importance. Between each grand prix the teams spent their time testing the compounds that would be used in the following race. The manufacturers were caught up in this crazy spiral and sometimes brought along more than 10 compounds to be tested in each session. In 2006, the tyres were the determining performance factor.

The FIA decided that enough was enough and to stop this costly and futile war chose a single supplier from 2007 onwards. Michelin did not even tender for the role as it is against the make's sporting instinct and tradition and withdrew at the end of the 2006 season. "*We were present in F1 for 4 main reasons,*" explained Frédéric Henry-Biabaud, the Michelin competitions boss. "*For internal motivation, for the make's visibility – even though Michelin has an 80% recognition factor which is huge – to develop partnerships with manufacturers and the technical development driven by F1.From now on we'll continue to work in endurance. F1 is expensive unless we win. 2006 will certainly have earned us money.*"

As the FIA had opted for the single supplier Michelin had no choice but to withdraw otherwise it would have been thrown out at the end of 2006 with its titles in its pocket.

^
A Michelin family photo in Australia (above) and in Brazil (below) the make's last F1 grand prix.

Why are rain tyres so difficult to manufacture?

At Ferrari the alarm bells began to ring during the Hungarian Grand Prix. In the opening stages Michael Schumacher was losing around 7 seconds a lap to Fernando Alonso. Despite his reputation as a wet-weather ace his Bridgestone tyres would have led to his humiliation had the rain not stopped and the track begun to dry. In Shanghai he could only manage the sixth quickest time on the gird because of the wet.

The Bridgestone tyres were not up to the same standards as the Michelins. "*The problem with rain tyres is that their development is very expense compared with their infrequent use,*" explains Nick Shorrock. "*Last year we only used them in Belgium. So we did not really want to spend huge amounts of cash on them. In addition they're not easy to test. Most of the teams do their testing in Spain and we have to wet the track with special lorries to try out rain tyres. It's so complicated that we don't do it very often.*"

Technically speaking manufacturing rain tyres is a tricky operation. The cold water requires soft rubber and the grooves need a hard compound so as not to degrade too quickly. So producing a good tyre depends on a compromise between these two factors.

This year Bridgestone obviously did not do a lot of work on rain tyres. The manufacturer reckoned it was too far behind with its dry rubber (after a disastrous 2005 season) and all its energy was concentrated on remedying this problem. As the latter had undergone a considerable evolution its rain tyres came from a very different family.

When Michael Schumacher put on his dry rubber in China a couple of mechanics drastically modified the angle of attack of the front wing with around 11 turns of the screw. At Renault the same change to dry tyres required only a couple. It was proof that the Bridgestone rain tyres belonged to another generation and they tried to adjust them by modifying the front wing angles. The 2006 Ferrari with a different chassis was completely unsuited to them as it was designed with a new tyre architecture in mind. Hence the 7-second difference in Budapest. It was not only a tyre problem but also that of a chassis that was not adapted to the rubber.

Jacques Villeneuve, the ejected champion who could not lie

Hockenheim: end of July. A few hours before the accident that would cost Jacques Villeneuve his F1 career. The F1 summer was running its course calmly helped by the heat wave that had gripped Europe. Nothing was happening in the Hockenheim paddock simmering in the 37° heat in the shade. The German Grand Prix was one that generally was generally a pivotal moment for a certain number of contracts but nothing was moving.

It was trying Jacques Villeneuve's patience. He was hoping to stay on in the BMW Sauber team. He had contacted several others but they were not exactly beating a path to his door. "*Nothing new,*" he confirmed. "*Nothing's changed since Magny-Cours. I've had no serious contacts.*" It was not a case of nature abhorring a vacuum. "*If there were five teams trying to sign me for next season, things would be settled very quickly. It's completely calm and it's a pity. I hope to stay on at BMW because everybody here is very happy with me.*"

The man from Quebec's problem seemed to boil down to one of persuasion. "*This year everybody can see that I'm driving well so I say to myself that things should work out. In 2004, when I was completely alone it was much tougher. I called Sir Frank Williams and he decided to suggest to Peter Sauber that he should take me on. Without Frank's putting in a word for me I'd have had no chance. This year I've made all the contacts myself and it's not very good for my image. For example, I was invited to the gala dinner to celebrate Jean Alesi's Legion d'Honneur. I was sat beside Ron Dennis and I talked to him all evening. It was not the right solution. I approach people too personally and it's not very positive for my image. It even reduces my value.*" Villeneuve's past successes did nothing to help his future "*The fact of having been world champion is no use. It's like I won nothing afterwards; it's negative even. Also I don't know how to sell myself. To do that you have to able to lie and I don't know how to do that.*"

Ten years ago, reality was more important. Nowadays all people see is the image. Team bosses speak only about young drivers. They all want to discover the new Alonso. It's discouraging and above all I'm not expensive. I shouldn't say that! It lowers my value even more."

- But you have a huge amount of experience. That counts for a team. Frank Williams says that it's the most important thing.

"He says that but when it comes to signing a contract he doesn't take it into account. Unfortunately, it seems that experience no longer counts in the eyes of team bosses. I find it incomprehensible; It's not even a question of money. Some of the older drivers are very cheap. Much more so that some of the youngsters who have never won a grand prix. I think that quality/pricewise I'm very well placed. I'm not at all expensive for what I'm worth."

- So why is it so complicated?

"Some team managers also want to be drivers' managers. They all thing they've ferreted out the next super star. The next Alonso or Raïkkönen and they think that this guy is going to drive for them for almost nothing. It may work with one driver but they don't see that it doesn't with twenty others. Guys like Mark Webber don't achieve anything."

- How much more time will you give yourself to find a drive?

- "I don't really know. A few more weeks until I've had enough. The longer I wait the less chance I've got of finding a good contract. It's becoming more and more difficult. There are still a few good ones left but I'm not going to stay in F1 at any price. I won't go to Super Aguri, for example. If things don't work out I'll look after my family or I'll do something else. It'd be a pity because I feel I've still got a lot to offer F1."

- You've spoken a bit about NASCAR recently. Would you be tempted like Montoya?

- "Why not? If I can't stay in F1 it's a possibility. It would not be a backward step, rather a completely different path. Going to IRL or Champ Car would be a backward step. It's another style of driving but I'm not afraid of trying something new. I like that kind of thing. It's a bit like a mathematical problem. If I'm half-a-second off the best, it's up to me to find out why and close the gap. It's a challenge."

- Yes but it need a total change lifestyle. No more chalets in Villars, for example.

- "That's for sure. We'd have to move to the USA and that's a difficult choice. It was easier for Juan Pablo as he lives in Florida."

- You've said to us that being a racing driver is incompatible with being a father. How are you going to combine the two?

- He smiles. "Yes. I said that because up till then I had never gone out with a girl who was ready to drop everything. As soon as I met Johanna, she stopped working. She made a huge sacrifice and after that everything's possible. She can follow me everywhere on the circuits. We've live well in my motorhome so it's no problem. We can build our own little nest and nobody can bother us. To succeed in that kind of life and make my job compatible with having children, you've got to have an old-fashioned wife who accepts the situation and is ready to devote her time to looking after the children. And when I say old-fashioned I'm not being pejorative. I'm very lucky to have found Johanna."

Jacques Villeneuve did not know it at the time but this interview that he gave on the Friday before practice for the German Grand Prix was the last he would give in an F1 paddock. On Sunday, he crashed and hurt himself. He was replaced for the rest of the season by Robert Kubica, and his 11-year long career ended "not with a bang but with a whimper."

> Jacques Villeneuve felt very isolated in the BMW Sauber team that didn't want him and was looking for the slightest reason to get rid of him. The accident at Hockenheim was just the pretext it needed. He never set foot in an F1 paddock after this.

"We're reaching the limits of what we can bear"

Between the sporting authorities and the engineers the on-going battle never stops. The former keep changing the regulations to slow down the cars and the latter do everything in their power to make them go quicker. The cat and mouse game between them has existed since the dawn of motor racing.

This year the FIA decided to reduce the engine's cubic capacity from 3 litre 10 cylinder power units to 2.4 litre V8s. The idea was that the 200 bhp drop in power would lead to lower corner speeds. They got it wrong (again one is tempted to say)! The smaller engines have enabled the airflow around the car to be improved thus increasing the aerodynamic grip. This, in turn, has led to higher cornering speeds.

At the same time the FIA modified the tyre regulations bring back changes during the race. Thus, the manufacturers were able to use softer compounds that were quicker.

T soon became obvious that the changes were not going to slow down the cars even if it took the engineers a little time to find the most effective solutions to get round the new regs.

It was done by Imola. The previous week the teams had a 4-day test session at Silverstone during which the times fell in, a spectacular manner. The 2006 F1s were lapping as quickly as the 2005 3-litre cars even if they had 200 bhp less.

"It was incredible,' said a delighted Jacques Villeneuve when he arrived in the Nürburgring paddock on Thursday. "These are the best F1s I've ever driven. Their cornering speeds are higher than ever and they're very stable. That means that we can drive in a more aggressive fashion. Brake later, slide the car more and keep it on the track. If you were a bit too aggressive last year and made a mistake you spun immediately. This year you feel that you can do whatever you like with the car. It's great."

Of course, the cars are slower in a straight line but this doesn't change anything for Villeneuve. "You feel it's less powerful and we lose around 15 km/h on the straight but that doesn't make any difference. You make up what you lose on the straights in the corners. It's mind-boggling. Silverstone is a circuit where sheer grunt is very important. It's an engine circuit. Yet we were as quick as lat year. The first corner is taken flat out. The impression of speed is fabulous; we absorb more G forces than on an oval in an Indycar."

Jacques likes speed. It's his job but this time he felt he was near his limits. "The quicker it is the better I like it but sometimes I come into a corner and I say to myself, "My God, any quicker and I won't be able to make it. In certain corners my liver hurts and my eyes are pushed back into my head. It's a bizarre sensation."

His team-mate Nick Heidfeld had to call an early halt to his Silverstone session. A nerve in his hip got pinched and he suffered from cramps. In fact, three drivers had to stop early.

This season the drivers are subjected to 5 Gs (up to 5 times their weight) in certain corners. "It's very difficult to concentrate with such forces," said Villeneuve. *"Physically I train harder than ever but that doesn't help a great deal. We are now reaching the limit of what we can bear."*

The engineers are certainly going to find new ways of making the cars even quicker and the lawmakers will be trying to slow them down. The game between the cat and the mouse is not over yet!

Jacques Villeneuve did not know it at the time but this interview that he gave on the Friday before practice for the German Grand Prix was the last he would give in an F1 paddock. On Sunday, he crashed and hurt himself. He was replaced for the rest of the season by Robert Kubica, and his 11-year long career ended "not with a bang but with a whimper."

^
They were not yet married but it was not far off. Johanna and Jacques were obviously very much in love with each other at the Australian Grand Prix.

A child is the most important thing

Jacques Villeneuve has never been very forthcoming about his private life. While he maintained that he was only able to think of nothing but driving during the summer, he also had another project in mind. *"In this business you can't make 5-year plans because you know that three months later they'll be turned upside down. Of course I'd like to have children. After all, what are we here for? It's the most important thing in the world. But it's not very compatible with the job of* an F1 driver. Going off every couple of days and leaving a kid at home is no good even if my wife doesn't work."

Children, work; future, fiancée: since the beginning of the season the once-insouciant Jacques Villeneuve has been replaced by the family man, the farsighted individual that he never was before. He is a new man and that is probably down to the fact that he is about to become a father.

AMBIENCES

Apart from the duel between Fernando Alonso and Michael Schumacher, the 2006 season was full of other emotions and other events. A season is also a symphony of colours, movement, fleeting close-ups and flashes that the photographers manage to give life to.

Fleeting beauties

What would Formula 1 be with the models prancing around between the motor homes? These lovely ladies are invited just for the weekend and cross the F1 firmament like so many shooting stars leaving behind a fleeting image like a mirage. Luckily, the most beautiful sometimes find work in F1 and stay.

Quantum mechanics

F1 single-seaters are not just aerodynamics and suspension. A chassis consists of around 5000 parts most of which are made by the teams themselves. They provide the photographers with a wide variety of unusual images.

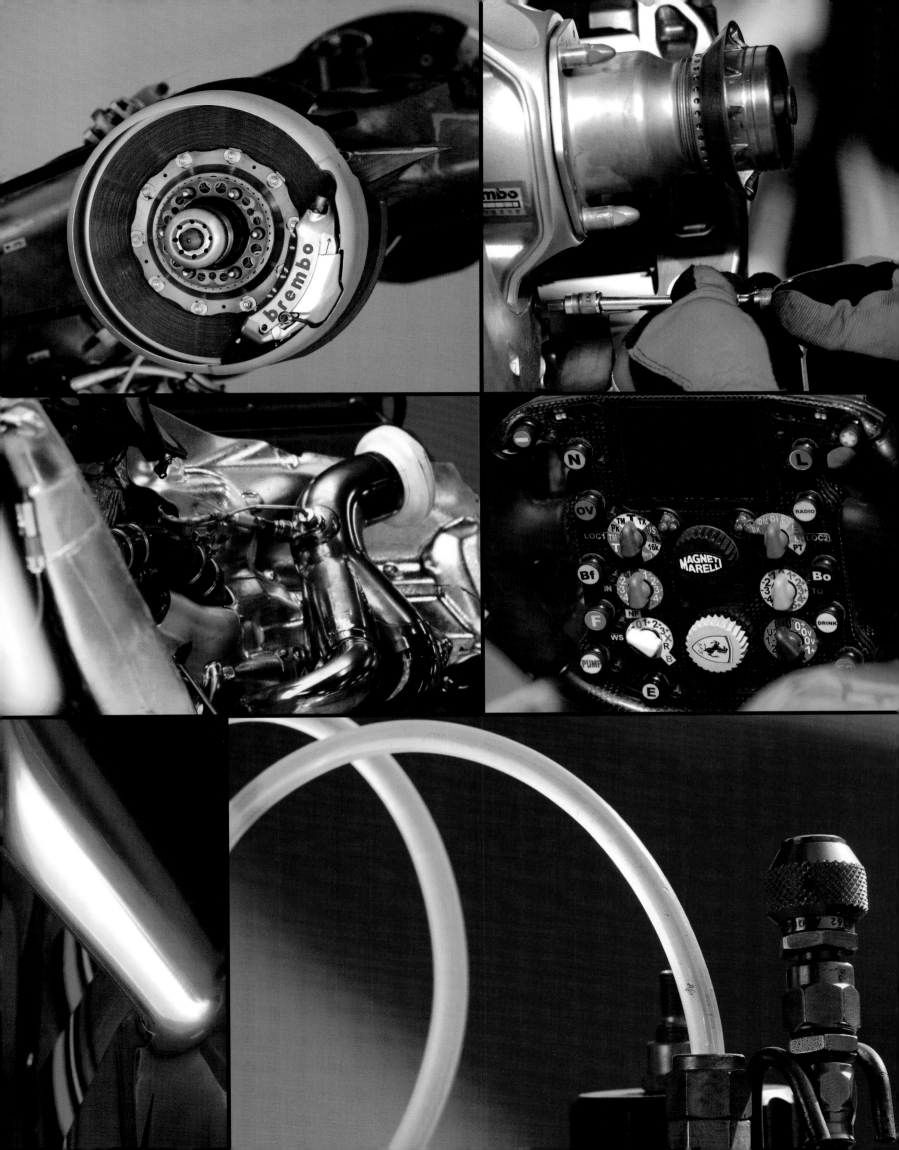

Kaléidoscope

There is so much to tell. A Formula 1 season cannot be summed up in a 224-pgae annual no matter how complete.

As a photo is worth a thousand words here are some fleeting snapshots stolen during the year to add to your memory bank.

Champions' regards

Their helmet is their home from home.
When the driver pulls down his visor he is in his own little world isolated from the noise, the photographers – in a state of complete concentration.
Can you recognise them? Some of them practice only on Friday and are locked in a kind of anonymity that makes them difficult to identify.

From left to right and from bottom to top: Scott Speed, Tiago Monteiro, Adrian Sutil, Vitantonio Liuzzi, Sakon Yamamoto, Kimi Raïkkönen, Jarno Trulli, Takuma Sato, Christian Klien, Felipe Massa, Markus Winkelhock, Jenson Button, Franck Montagny, Pedro de la Rosa and Alexander Wurtz.

THE 18 GRANDS PRIX

Few jobs allow one to roam the world every year from Australia to Japan by way of Brazil and the United States. For drivers, mechanics, engineers and journalists the wide range of countries visited counts for a lot in the magic that F1 exercises on all those who have come into contact with it. For them the race on Sunday afternoon is but a small part of the whole grand prix weekend.

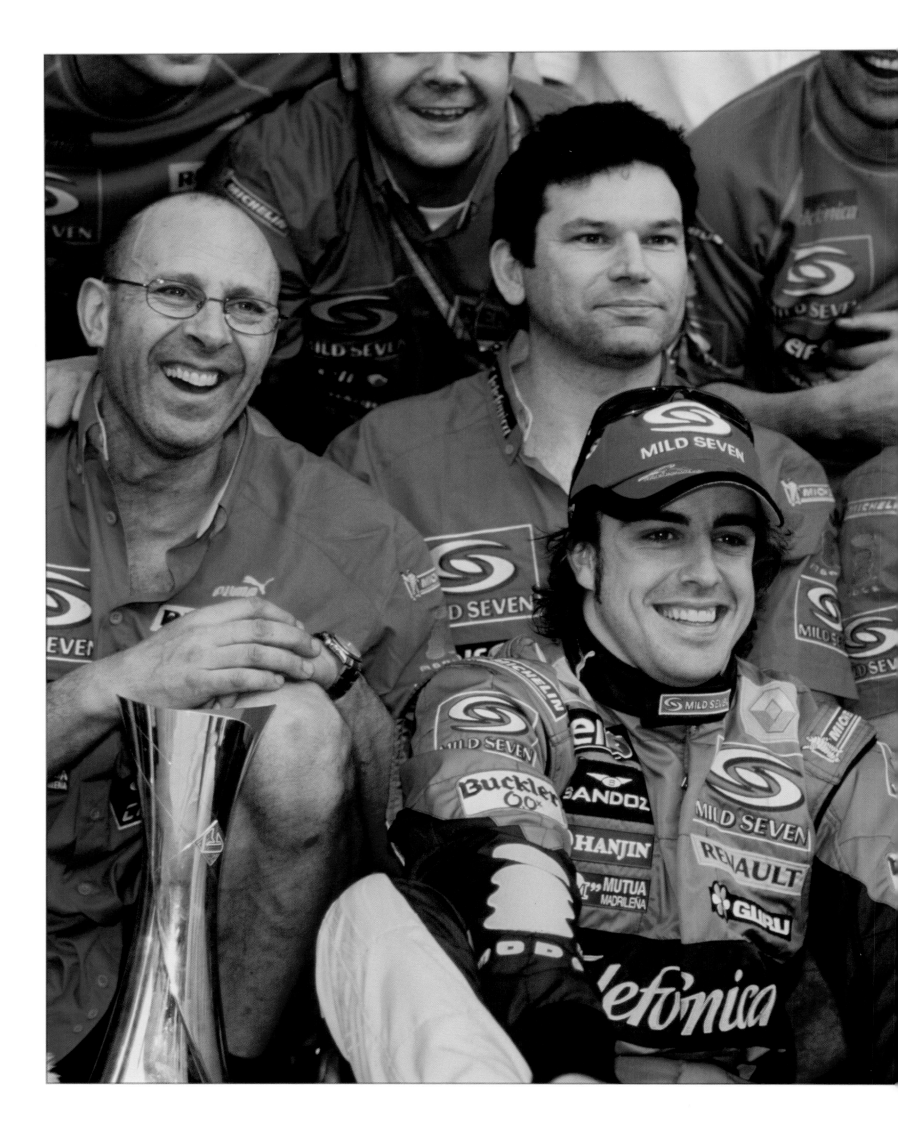

ALONSO GETS OFF TO A FLYING START!

A cracking race! The first grand prix of the season lived up to expectations with overtaking all through the field and teams fighting neck-and-neck with each other. It looked like the battle for honours would be fought out between Renault, Ferrari, McLaren and Honda. Victory in the Bahrain Grand Prix finally went to the reigning world champion, Fernando Alonso, after a race-long battle with Michael Schumacher's Ferrari, which set pole. The Spaniard managed to snatch the lead by a few hundredths of a second during his second refuelling stop.

The real star of the race was Kimi Raïkkönen who finished third. He started last after a problem in qualifying and used his talent and an audacious one-stop strategy to finish on the rostrum.

Michael back on top!

Michael Schumacher was all smiles. Usually he is a bit reserved but he was as happy as a sand boy at the end of qualifying. After a disastrous 2005 season in which he set only one pole he tackled the 2006 season with revenge uppermost in his mind.

And he made a great start. "*It's true, I've had to wait a long time to be back at the top again,*" he confirmed. "*Everybody in the team worked day and night to help us make our comeback. I really feel it. It's a long time since I've had such a sensation. Too long…*"

It was the 65th pole of his career.

The German also said he was surprised, "*given the way practice went on Friday, I didn't think we'd be so well placed,*" he went on. "*It's a really great surprise especially if you remember where we were at the end of last season. Frankly, what happened in 2005 really hurt us; it forced us to react. We've had so much success in the past that it was normal that we'd have a bad patch one day. When that happens, it's very difficult to turn things around. But we've managed finally.*"

Was the 2005 bad patch forgotten? Probably, "*We've got good reasons to think that we'll have a great season. All you've got to do is to look at Felipe's time (Massa, his team-mate). This being said I knew he was quick and Ferrari was right to pick him.*"

The little Brazilian qualified only 47/1000ths behind the German. And he was even a bit disappointed when he got out of his car. "*I'm happy. It's fantastic for sure,*" said the former Sauber driver. "*But Giancarlo deprived me of pole. I was quicker in my final lap and he baulked me.*"

The performance of the two Ferrari set tongues wagging. Several technical directors suspected that the rear wing of the 248 F1 bent under the aerodynamic load to give less drag.

Such a system is considered a moveable aerodynamic device and is forbidden. The FIA scrutineers examined the Ferrari wings closely on Saturday morning and declared that they were legal. End of story. For the moment.

Michael's Bahrain pole enabled him to equal one of the records that had so far escaped him. With 65 poles the German equalled Ayrton Senna's record and he set his first pole in the 1994 Monaco Grand Prix, the event that followed the Brazilian's death.

A title dream and Honda's first let-down

On Friday morning a wind from the desert (where else as the circuit is surrounded by it) swept the Sakhir circuit.

It covered the track with a fine coat of sand that slowed the cars by around two to three seconds a lap. The top drivers stayed prudently in their garages while they let the others get on with the job of road sweeping!

Not until the end of the session did the times start to come down. If one forgets the demonstrations of the Friday drivers (of no real significance) the two Ferraris set the fastest times with Michael leading Massa. It was a good start for the Scuderia.

The Renaults too looked impressive while the McLarens' speed augured ill for the rest of the year. Kimi Raïkkönen had his engine blow in the afternoon session. Was it starting all over again? "*In fact, we don't yet know what's happened. We hope it's just an electrical problem and that we won't have to change the engine,*" said Norbert Haug, the Mercedes-Benz competitions director. It was yet another setback that

looked like pushing the Finn into Ferrari's waiting arms as rumour had it.

In the Honda camp Jenson Button was optimistic about setting pole after being quickest in the Saturday morning practice.

Finally, he ended up third on the grid. "*The wind made qualifying very tricky,*" he stated. *We'll see in the race. I'm sure that our strategy will show that we're the quickest.*"

The Hondas had been very rapid in winter testing and Button was hoping for victory and the world title in 2006. "*We did several days' testing in Bahrain,*" the Brit said. "*The car is fantastic. I paid a fortune to Frank Williams to get out of my contract and I think I made the right decision.*"

All the more so as the Honda team seemed stronger and more motivated than ever. "*Honda doesn't come into F1 to sell cars like some of the others,*" he clarified. "*It's the opposite; they sell cars to do F1. You just can't imagine how enthusiastic they are about motor racing. It's marvellous.*"

Starting grid

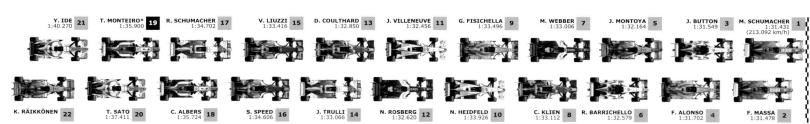

Y. IDE 21 1:40.270	T. MONTEIRO* 19 1:35.900	R. SCHUMACHER 17 1:34.702	V. LIUZZI 15 1:33.416	D. COULTHARD 13 1:32.850	J. VILLENEUVE 11 1:32.456	G. FISICHELLA 9 1:33.496	M. WEBBER 7 1:33.006	J. MONTOYA 5 1:32.164	J. BUTTON 3 1:31.549	M. SCHUMACHER 1 1:31.431 (213.092 km/h)
K. RAÏKKÖNEN 22 1:37.411	T. SATO 20	C. ALBERS 18 1:35.724	S. SPEED 16 1:34.606	J. TRULLI 14 1:33.066	N. ROSBERG 12 1:32.620	N. HEIDFELD 10 1:33.926	C. KLIEN 8 1:33.112	R. BARRICHELLO 6 1:32.579	F. ALONSO 4 1:31.702	F. MASSA 2 1:31.478

* T. MONTEIRO starts from the pit lane.

Fernando wins. Kimi stars

The 22 drivers and hundreds of engineers were awaiting the first grand prix of the 2006 season with eager anticipation. After working flat out during the winter on the new cars, after covering thousands of kilometres in private testing and after designing new V8s the first race was the moment of truth when the results of all that hard toil would be known.

The first thing that was obvious was the fact that Ferrari was back at the front after a very difficult 2005 season. Honda too was looking strong while Toyota's first outing with the new T106 was a disaster after the team's promising 2005 season. McLaren seemed to have come up with a good car if Raïkkönen's performance in the race after his suspension breakage was anything to go by.

He was incredibly quick in a car that was loaded with fuel as he was on a one-stop strategy. He quickly dispatched all the drivers who were with him at the back of the grid and at the end of the first lap he was up in thirteenth place. By lap 24 Kimi was third: an awesome performance. It was a very encouraging drive for the Anglo-German team whose testing in January and February had been anything but promising what with unreliability, lack of pace etc. Now the McLarens made people sit up and take notice. *"We've made a big step forward in the past few weeks,"* Raïkkönen confirmed.*"After all the things people said about us it's very encouraging for the whole team. The guys have worked very hard."*

Technically speaking it was confirmed after the race. *"A close examination of the stopwatches showed that Kimi was the most consistently quick driver in the grand prix,"* explained one of the McLaren engineers. *"The Ferraris were very fast in practice but we were better in the race in terms of tyre wear and sheer pace. Even when the car was full of petrol it did not wear its tyres as much as the Renaults. Without his suspension problem the Finn would've won the grand prix in a canter."* This analysis seemed to confirm that Kimi would be the man to beat in 2006. Juan Pablo Montoya who came home in a modest fourth place in Bahrain could already start looking for another job!

<
Victory! Fernando Alonso crosses the finishing line at the end of the first grand prix of the 2006 season. He just managed to get out on the track in front of Michael Schumacher after his second refuelling stop (below).
v

Flashes

> Nico Rosberg did the family name proud by setting the fastest lap in the race and finishing in the points in his first grand prix – a rare exploit and one that generally indicates real talent. In the past Kimi Raïkkönen, Jean Alesi and Alain Prost also scored points in their very first grand prix.
Nico's seventh-place finish came after a tough battle as he was last at the end of lap 1 after a coming together with Nick Heidfeld obliged him to stop at his pit.

> Jacques Villeneuve had had a very anonymous 2005 season but in Bahrain he showed a few flashes of his old talent and held on to sixth place for a long time until his engine went up in smoke on lap 30. He did not stay on for the end of the race and left the circuit hand-in-hand with his fiancée Joanna from Paris.

> It was the first grand prix of the season but the last for Patrick Faure, the president of the Renault team, who had reached retirement age, as he would be sixty in June. The man who had helped Renault to the world titles the previous year was to be replaced by Alain Dassas up till then the Renault financial director and a mere stripling aged 58! Youth was all the rage in the French company!

> Felipe Massa had a rather eventful race. He made an excellent start but let Alonso pass him after which he made a mistake under braking at the end of the straight. The young Brazilian finished ninth just outside the points.

> David Coulthard did not score any points

after flat-spotting his tyres at the start of the race. *"The vibrations were so strong that I couldn't see anything. My eyes were being shaken up in my head. It was like I was in a washing machine."* In order to transfer some oil as requested by his engineer David had to ask him what colour the button in question was. Not very serious.

<
It was the first start in 2006 and Michael Schumacher was determined to beat his rivals. Behind him Nick Heidfeld has forgotten his gloves and goes back to his pit.

Nico Rosberg grabbed the limelight

Nico was in twelfth place on the grid and finished his first F1 grand prix in the points in seventh place as well as setting the fastest lap.

Dispute over a lap that probably cost Ferrari victory

The very abstruse 2006 qualifying regulations allowed the cars taking part in the third qualifying session on Saturday afternoon to add fuel for every lap covered at a speed at least equal to 110% of their fastest lap. This system prevented them from being penalised in fuel for qualifying; and the 110% rule meant that they couldn't crawl round saving fuel to be able to add more that they used.

In Bahrain the amount of fuel allocated by the FIA for each qualifying lap was 2.75 kilos. In Michael Schumacher's case the FIA contested one of his laps (7th) arguing that he was 110.9% off his quickest time. Thus, the German's 248 F1 started the race with less fuel on board than calculated and he had to refuel a lap earlier than planned. This probably made the difference at the moment Fernando Alonso passed him.

"It's really a pity that the FIA refused us that lap," regretted Jean Todt after the race. "That little drop of fuel would probably have allowed us to stay in the lead. We had all the right ingredients to win today; we just lacked a little luck."
The Bahrain Grand Prix confirmed that in 2006 the difference between victory and defeat would probably boil down to small details as was to be the case in the races to come.

> "Close your eyes and go to sleep:" Gil de Ferran the Honda team manager looks like he's trying to hypnotise Nick Shorrock the Michelin F1 boss. To have better tyres no doubt!

Schumacher brimming with confidence

The Michael of old was back. After a disastrous season in 2005 – just one victory in very special conditions at Indianapolis – the German reckoned that the new Ferrari 248 F1 would bring him back to the top.
The stopwatch did not back up his optimism. During the winter the Scuderia had tested on different circuits to those used by its rivals. When it did run on the same tracks it bluffed its opponents by using last year's aerodynamics or waited until it was the only team left like in Bahrain in February. In the week before the first grand prix the Ferraris went to Mugello near Florence for a final shakedown, which was cut short by pouring rain. "It's true," said Schumacher. "Even if we didn't manage to cover as many kilometres as we'd have liked because of the weather, I'm very confident. Even if we can't win all the opening grands prix, we got a pretty good idea of how we're going to improve the car during the season, and that's vital. But I'd still like to score a few points on Sunday. We're very motivated and I'm convinced that our 248 F1 has what it takes to win the world title." The German reckoned that the main opposition would come from the reigning world champions: "I think that the Renaults are the ones to beat at the moment as they're just in front of the Hondas, McLarens and Ferraris. It's going to be a very tight battle and that's not a bad thing. It really boosts our motivation."
And that was something he lacked a little in 2005. "In the conditions in which I found myself, it's true that I didn't always give 100%," he admitted. "But how do you manage to find the will to fight when you're a lap off the quickest and everything's going wrong."

Weekend news

> 2 billion 6 hundred thousand million; that's the number of tins that Red Bull sold in 2005 throughout the world. Its price has a good built-in profit margin, enough to pay for its extravagancies like the huge party held on Thursday evening in Bahrain. The brand invited some 2000 people to a private island to celebrate the start of the season with the presentation of its cars, sumptuous buffets and a whole host of pretty young girls.

> Before the start of the season it was generally reckoned that the Super Aguris would be around 6 seconds off the pace and practice on Friday confirmed it. Takuma Sato and Yuji Ide were at the very back of the field over 6 seconds off the quickest time. "As we couldn't practice before this grand prix, it was a kind of shakedown test for us. And it went pretty well," said the optimistic team boss, Aguri Suzuki.

> Not for 25 grands prix had the Ferraris locked out the front row. The Italian team's long period in the wilderness was over.

> "It all went so quickly that I had no time to be nervous." So spoke the Super Aguri driver Yuji Ide who set the slowest time on Saturday. Because of Kimi Raïkkönen's problem he was not the last on the grid.

> The rumours concerning the transfer of Raïkkönen to Ferrari became much more insistent on Saturday afternoon following the Finn's technical problem. "Does Kimi want to come to us? Maybe. It's up to him to see," quipped Michael Schumacher.

> Prince Albert from Monaco was at Sakhir on Saturday in the Toro Rosso pit. The Prince is a great mate of Gerhard Berger's and he left his girlfriend at the hotel. "There are far too many photographers in the paddock to bring her here," he justified.

> Surprise! Surprise! David Coulthard had a new girlfriend. Gone was Simone Abdelnour, the beautiful Brazilian, and in her place was Karen Milner, the former TF1 F1 host (who was entrusted with the staring grid interviews two years ago).

> While the manufacturers only had a couple of weeks to enter for the 2008 championship those united under the GPMA banner (Grand Prix Manufacturers' Association made up of Renault, Honda, Toyota, BMW and Mercedes-Benz) seemed to want to join up with Bernie Ecclestone rather than putting their 3-year-old threat of a parallel championship into effect.

> "If he's free and we need him than I'd like to have Kimi. He's very gifted and he never complains," said Jean Todt. "As for Valentino Rossi, we've taken our decision but I've got nothing to say for the moment." This comment came from the Frenchman on Saturday afternoon after Michael Schumacher had thought it 'improbable' that the motorbike superstar would be driving alongside him in 2007.

> Juan Pablo Montoya on the grid before what was a bad race for the Colombian. While Kimi Raïkkönen's was full of fireworks, anonymous is probably the best adjective to describe Juan Pablo's. Was he already thinking of leaving?

> "Do you recognise me?" Jacques Villeneuve came to Bahrain with his new girlfriend, Johanna Martinez, whom he married on 30th May

Practice

All the time trials

N° Driver	Nat.	N° Chassis - Engine [Nbr. GP]	Pos. Free 1 Friday	Laps	Pos. Free 2 Friday	Laps	Pos. Free 3 Saturday	Laps	Pos. Q1 Saturday	Laps	Pos. Q2 Saturday	Laps	Pos. Super Pole Saturday	Laps
1. Fernando Alonso	E	Renault R26 02 [1]	19.	2	5. 1:32.538	13	3. 1:31.975	11	1. 1:32.433	3	1. 1:31.215	3	**4. 1:31.702**	14
2. Giancarlo Fisichella	I	Renault R26 03 [1]	20.	2	8. 1:33.215	14	4. 1:32.050	12	3. 1:32.934	3	3. 1:31.831	3	**9. 1:33.496**	14
3. Kimi Räikkönen	FIN	McLaren MP4-21 02 - Mercedes [1]	3. 1:33.388	6	12. 1:33.577	11	8. 1:33.262	12	**22. DNF**	2				
4. Juan Pablo Montoya	CO	McLaren MP4-21 03 - Mercedes [1]	7. 1:34.887	6	13. 1:33.726	15	15. 1:34.406	11	5. 1:33.233	5	2. 1:31.487	3	**5. 1:32.164**	12
5. Michael Schumacher	D	Ferrari 248 F1 253 [1]	4. 1:33.469	5	2. 1:31.751	15	2. 1:31.868	8	6. 1:33.310	5	6. 1:32.025	3	**1. 1:31.431**	12
6. Felipe Massa	BR	Ferrari 248 F1 252 [1]	8. 1:34.925	6	4. 1:32.175	13	5. 1:32.826	6	9. 1:33.579	5	5. 1:32.014	3	**2. 1:31.478**	12
7. Ralf Schumacher	D	Toyota TF106/05 [1]	22.	1	22. 1:35.170	18	9. 1:33.523	14	**17. 1:34.702**	7				
8. Jarno Trulli	I	Toyota TF106/04 [1]	21.	2	24. 1:35.898	11	7. 1:33.038	16	13. 1:33.987	7	**14. 1:33.066**	4		
9. Mark Webber	AUS	Williams FW28 03 - Cosworth [1]			17. 1:34.333	5	10. 1:33.876	11	8. 1:33.454	5	9. 1:32.309	3	**7. 1:33.006**	12
10. Nico Rosberg	D	Williams FW28 04 - Cosworth [1]			21. 1:34.953	5	16. 1:34.434	11	4. 1:32.945	5	**12. 1:32.620**	5		
11. Rubens Barrichello	BR	Honda RA106-03 [1]			18. 1:34.384	9	12. 1:34.009	15	12. 1:33.922	7	10. 1:32.322	7	**6. 1:32.579**	12
12. Jenson Button	GB	Honda RA106-04 [1]			9. 1:33.226	12	1. 1:31.857	16	2. 1:32.603	4	7. 1:32.025	6	**3. 1:31.549**	13
14. David Coulthard	GB	Red Bull RB2 3 - Ferrari [1]	9. 1:35.017	4	19. 1:34.432	7	14. 1:34.142	16	10. 1:33.678	6	**13. 1:32.850**	6		
15. Christian Klien	A	Red Bull RB2 2 - Ferrari [1]	5. 1:34.800	6	11. 1:33.557	8	11. 1:33.944	14	15. 1:34.308	6	8. 1:32.106	6	**8. 1:33.112**	13
16. Nick Heidfeld	D	BMW Sauber F1.06-04 [1]	23.	1	14. 1:33.848	9	13. 1:34.094	11	7. 1:33.374	5	4. 1:31.958	7	**10. 1:33.926**	12
17. Jacques Villeneuve	CDN	BMW Sauber F1.06-03 [1]	24.	1	25. 1:36.264	8	6. 1:32.913	14	11. 1:33.882	4	**11. 1:32.456**	7		
18. Tiago Monteiro	P	Midland M16-03 - Toyota [1]	13. 1:36.542	9	20. 1:34.459	14	18. 1:35.026	14	**19. 1:35.900**	4				
19. Christijan Albers	NL	Midland M16-02 - Toyota [1]	14. 1:36.930	9	26. 1:36.314	16	17. 1:34.541	14	**18. 1:35.724**	6				
20. Vitantonio Liuzzi	I	Toro Rosso STR01 03 - Cosworth [1]	10. 1:35.083	8	6. 1:32.703	24	19. 1:35.351	13	16. 1:34.439	6	**15. 1:33.416**	7		
21. Scott Speed	USA	Toro Rosso STR01 02 - Cosworth [1]	12. 1:35.371	7	16. 1:34.284	22	20. 1:35.532	13	14. 1:33.995	6	**16. 1:34.606**	4		
22. Takuma Sato	J	Super Aguri SA05-02 - Honda [1]	16. 1:38.190	15	27. 1:37.588	19	21. 1:36.994	15	**20. 1:37.411**	6				
23. Yuji Ide	J	Super Aguri SA05-03 - Honda [1]	17. 1:40.782	15	28. 1:39.021	21	22. 1:41.889	10	**21. 1:40.270**	6				
35. Alexander Wurz	A	Williams FW28 01 - Cosworth	2. 1:32.184	18	3. 1:31.764	27								
36. Anthony Davidson	GB	Honda RA106-01	18.	2	1. 1:31.353	28								
37. Robert Doornbos	MC	Red Bull RB2 1 - Ferrari	11. 1:35.203	15	7. 1:32.926	24								
38. Robert Kubica	PL	BMW Sauber F1.06-02	1. 1:32.170	20	10. 1:33.244	26								
39. Markus Winkelhock	D	Midland M16-01 - Toyota	15. 1:37.918	16	23. 1:35.686	24								
40. Neel Jani	CH	Toro Rosso STR01 01 - Cosworth	6. 1:34.831	15	15. 1:33.900	24								

Fastest lap overall
F. Alonso 1:31.215 (211,280 km/h)

Maximum speed

N° Driver	S1 Qualifs	Pos.	S1 Race	Pos.	S2 Qualifs	Pos.	S2 Race	Pos.	Finish Qualifs	Pos.	Finish Race	Pos.	Radar Qualifs	Pos.	Radar Race	Pos.
1. F. Alonso	247,1	1	243,2	2	277,7	2	276,0	5	281,9	3	282,4	7	305,0	1	308,3	4
2. G. Fisichella	245,5	5	235,4	20	276,8	5	266,2	19	281,5	4	273,6	21	302,9	5	297,3	20
3. K. Räikkönen	243,8	9	242,3	7	265,7	20	275,7	7	280,3	12	285,1	2	298,4	11	308,2	5
4. J. Montoya	246,2	2	243,6	1	277,6	3	278,4	2	284,4	1	282,3	8	303,4	4	303,4	12
5. M. Schumacher	242,5	14	242,0	9	278,4	1	279,6	1	280,8	9	283,0	5	304,8	2	308,4	3
6. F. Massa	244,6	7	242,9	3	277,0	4	278,2	3	281,2	7	287,7	1	299,5	8	311,6	1
7. R. Schumacher	240,6	18	237,8	16	268,8	18	270,5	16	280,7	10	275,9	17	297,9	14	303,0	14
8. J. Trulli	242,3	16	236,4	19	270,2	17	267,3	18	274,8	18	274,7	20	293,0	20	301,3	18
9. M. Webber	244,3	8	242,6	5	276,1	8	274,1	10	282,5	2	284,2	4	298,9	10	306,9	9
10. N. Rosberg	245,7	4	242,5	6	275,5	11	275,4	8	281,1	8	285,1	3	298,4	12	304,9	11
11. R. Barrichello	246,0	3	242,2	8	275,7	10	272,7	12	278,3	13	277,9	14	297,8	15	302,1	17
12. J. Button	244,8	6	242,8	4	276,1	9	276,2	4	281,3	6	281,4	10	300,1	7	307,0	8
14. D. Coulthard	242,3	15	238,9	14	274,0	14	273,6	11	276,3	16	275,2	19	295,4	17	302,9	15
15. C. Klien	243,8	10	240,5	10	274,7	13	275,2	9	276,0	17	280,6	12	297,0	16	303,0	13
16. N. Heidfeld	242,9	13	238,0	15	276,2	7	271,4	15	278,3	14	280,0	13	299,5	9	309,7	2
17. J. Villeneuve	242,9	12	239,3	12	274,9	12	272,5	14	281,3	5	281,3	11	303,7	3	306,6	10
18. T. Monteiro	236,2	20	235,3	21	271,6	16	267,9	17	272,8	20	277,7	15	293,8	19	302,5	16
19. C. Albers	236,8	19			267,7	19			273,2	19			294,8	18		
20. V. Liuzzi	243,3	11	240,4	11	271,9	15	272,5	13	280,6	11	281,4	9	300,3	6	307,8	6
21. S. Speed	241,8	17	239,0	13	276,7	6	275,8	6	277,0	15	282,7	6	298,0	13	307,5	7
22. T. Sato	233,7	22	236,6	18	256,6	22	258,5	21	267,3	22	275,8	18	283,5	22	299,7	19
23. Y. Ide	234,8	21	236,7	17	258,9	21	258,9	20	267,7	21	277,0	16	284,2	21	294,4	21

Race

Classification & Retirements

Pos.	Driver	Constructor	Tyres	Laps	Time	Average	
1.	F. Alonso	Renault	M	57	1:29:46.205	206,018 km/h	
2.	M. Schumacher	Ferrari	B	57	+1.246	205,970 km/h	
3.	K. Räikkönen	McLaren Mercedes	M	57	+19.360	205,280 km/h	
4.	J. Button	Honda	M	57	+19.992	205,256 km/h	
5.	J. Montoya	McLaren Mercedes	M	57	+37.048	204,610 km/h	
6.	M. Webber	Williams Cosworth	B	57	+41.932	204,426 km/h	
7.	N. Rosberg	Williams Cosworth	B	57	+1:03.043	203,634 km/h	
8.	C. Klien	RBR Ferrari	M	57	+1:06.771	203,495 km/h	
9.	F. Massa	Ferrari	B	57	+1:09.907	203,378 km/h	
10.	D. Coulthard	RBR Ferrari	M	57	+1:15.541	203,168 km/h	Engine (cooling-off lap)
11.	V. Liuzzi	STR Cosworth	M	57	+1:25.997	202,780 km/h	
12.	N. Heidfeld	BMW	M	56	1 lap	202,021 km/h	
13.	S. Speed	STR Cosworth	M	56	1 lap	201,815 km/h	
14.	R. Schumacher	Toyota	B	56	1 lap	200,971 km/h	
15.	R. Barrichello	Honda	M	56	1 lap	200,304 km/h	
16.	J. Trulli	Toyota	B	56	1 lap	199,978 km/h	
17.	T. Monteiro	MF1 Toyota (T-Car)	B	55	2 laps	197,703 km/h	
18.	T. Sato	Aguri Honda	B	53	4 laps	188,489 km/h	

Driver	Constructor	Tyres	Laps	Reason
Y. Ide	Aguri Honda	B	35	Fuel rig complications
J. Villeneuve	BMW	M	29	Engine failure
G. Fisichella	Renault	M	21	Loss of power on the engine, Hydraulic leak
C. Albers	MF1 Toyota	B	0	Driveshaft failure

Fastest laps

	Driver	Time	Laps	Average
1.	N. Rosberg	1:32.408	42	210,838 km/h
2.	M. Schumacher	1:32.523	38	210,576 km/h
3.	F. Alonso	1:32.534	21	210,551 km/h
4.	M. Webber	1:32.660	25	210,265 km/h
5.	J. Button	1:32.729	39	210,109 km/h
6.	F. Massa	1:32.739	28	210,086 km/h
7.	J. Montoya	1:32.771	21	210,013 km/h
8.	K. Räikkönen	1:32.864	29	209,803 km/h
9.	S. Speed	1:33.108	45	209,253 km/h
10.	C. Klien	1:33.212	40	209,020 km/h
11.	D. Coulthard	1:33.376	26	208,653 km/h
12.	V. Liuzzi	1:33.480	26	208,421 km/h
13.	J. Villeneuve	1:33.694	20	207,945 km/h
14.	N. Heidfeld	1:33.772	26	207,772 km/h
15.	R. Barrichello	1:33.840	14	207,621 km/h
16.	R. Schumacher	1:34.112	25	207,021 km/h
17.	G. Fisichella	1:34.320	15	206,564 km/h
18.	J. Trulli	1:34.852	24	205,406 km/h
19.	T. Monteiro	1:35.940	41	203,076 km/h
20.	T. Sato	1:37.104	17	200,642 km/h
21.	Y. Ide	1:38.302	11	198,197 km/h

Pit stops

	Driver	Laps	Duration	Stop	Total
1.	N. Rosberg	1	38.477	1	38.477
2.	Y. Ide	7	15.797	•1•	15.797
3.	F. Massa	8	1:05.526	1	1:05.526
4.	R. Schumacher	12	25.853	1	25.853
5.	M. Schumacher	15	27.009	1	27.009
6.	Y. Ide	14	33.196	2	48.993
7.	R. Barrichello	16	27.177	1	27.177
8.	G. Fisichella	16	27.474	1	27.474
9.	N. Heidfeld	17	27.416	1	27.416
10.	J. Button	18	27.658	1	27.658
11.	T. Monteiro	18	27.481	1	27.481
12.	Y. Ide	17	10:45.296	3	11:34.289
13.	T. Sato	18	15.302	1	15.302
14.	F. Alonso	19	26.602	1	26.602
15.	T. Sato	19	1:14.871	2	1:30.173
16.	T. Sato	20	40.992	3	2:11.165
17.	C. Klien	22	27.937	1	27.937
18.	V. Liuzzi	22	27.441	1	27.441
19.	J. Trulli	22	25.885	1	25.885
20.	J. Montoya	23	27.492	1	27.492
21.	M. Webber	23	26.208	1	26.208
22.	J. Villeneuve	23	27.041	1	27.041
23.	T. Sato	22	33.459	4	2:44.624
24.	S. Speed	25	27.579	1	27.579
25.	R. Schumacher	26	25.781	2	51.634
26.	N. Rosberg	27	25.849	2	1:04.326
27.	T. Sato	25	35.539	5	3:20.163
28.	K. Räikkönen	30	29.638	1	29.638
29.	D. Coulthard	30	29.271	1	29.271
30.	F. Massa	32	28.245	2	1:33.771
31.	N. Heidfeld	35	26.846	2	54.262
32.	M. Schumacher	36	27.374	2	54.383
33.	T. Monteiro	37	27.136	2	54.617
34.	F. Alonso	39	26.220	2	52.822
35.	R. Barrichello	38	25.935	2	53.112
36.	M. Webber	39	26.605	2	52.813
37.	V. Liuzzi	39	28.244	2	55.685
38.	J. Trulli	39	25.637	2	51.522
39.	J. Button	40	25.424	2	53.082
40.	C. Klien	41	26.075	2	54.012
41.	R. Schumacher	41	25.497	3	1:17.131
42.	T. Sato	39	30.916	6	3:51.079
43.	N. Rosberg	43	26.178	3	1:30.504
44.	S. Speed	43	27.118	2	54.697
45.	J. Montoya	44	25.369	2	52.861

•• Drive-through penalty: Ide. Because his team remained on the grid beyond the permited time limit.

Race Leader

Driver	Laps in the lead	Nbr of Laps
M. Schumacher	1 > 15	15
F. Alonso	16 > 19	4
J. Montoya	20 > 23	4
M. Schumacher	24 > 35	12
F. Alonso	36 > 39	4
J. Button	40	1
F. Alonso	41 > 57	17

Driver	Laps in the lead	Kilometers
M. Schumacher	27	145,878 km
F. Alonso	25	135,300 km
J. Montoya	4	21,648 km
J. Button	1	5,412 km

Lap chart

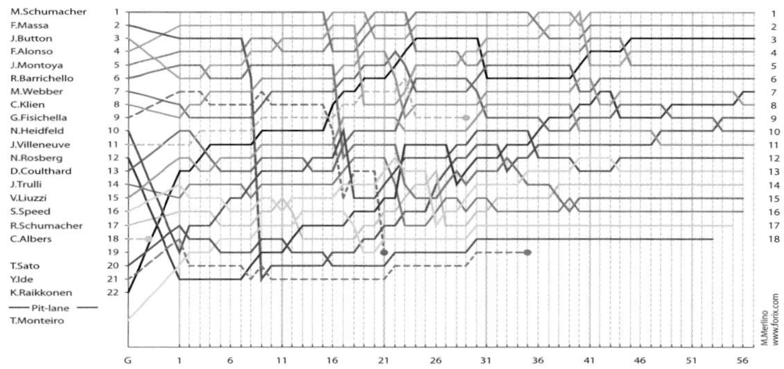

Gaps on the leader board

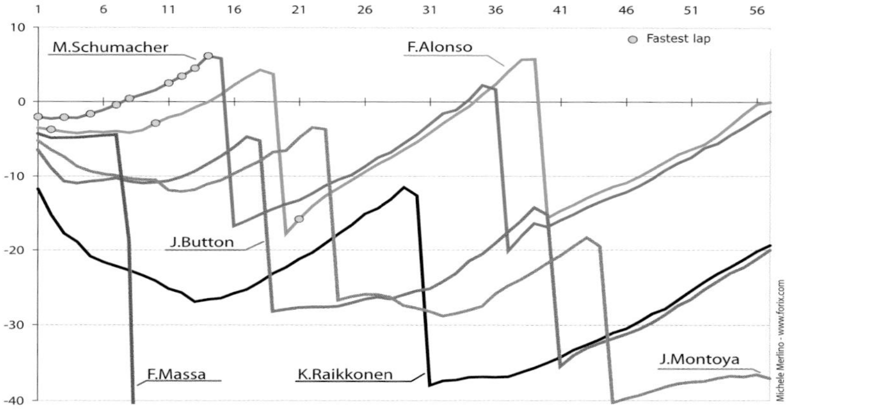

The table "Leading Gaps" is base on the lap by lap information, but only for some selected drivers (for ease of understanding). It adds-in the gaps between these drivers. The line marked "0" represents the winner's average speed. In general, this starts at a slower speed than its eventual average speed, because of the weight of fuel carried on board the car. Then, it goes above the average, before dropping again during the refueling pit stops. This graph therefore allows one to see at any given time the number of seconds (vertically) seperating the drivers on every lap (horizontally).

Championships 1/18

Drivers

1. F. Alonso ....Renault ....1 🏆....10
2. M. Schumacher .....Ferrari 8
3. K. Räikkönen ....McLaren Mercedes...............6
4. J. Button ....Honda 5
5. J. Montoya ....McLaren Mercedes...............4
6. M. Webber............Williams Cosworth...............3
7. N. Rosberg ....Williams Cosworth...............2
8. C. Klien................RBR Ferrari 1
9. F. Massa...............Ferrari 0
10. D. Coulthard ....RBR Ferrari 0
11. V. Liuzzi ....STR Cosworth......................0
12. N. Heidfeld ....BMW 0
13. S. Speed ....STR Cosworth......................0
14. R. Schumacher .....Toyota 0
15. R. Barrichello ....Honda 0
16. J. Trulli.................Toyota 0
17. T. Monteiro ....MF1 Toyota 0
18. T. Sato ....Aguri Honda 0

Y. Ide...................Aguri Honda ....-
J. Villeneuve ....BMW...................................-
G. Fisichella..........Renault ....-
C. Albers ....MF1 Toyota ....-

Constructors

1. Mild Seven Renault F1 Team ....1 🏆....10
2. Team McLaren Mercedes 10
3. Scuderia Ferrari Marlboro..........................8
4. Lucky Strike Honda Racing F1 Team 5
5. Williams F1 Team.......................................5
6. Red Bull Racing 1
7. Scuderia Toro Rosso 0
8. BMW Sauber F1 Team.................................0
9. Panasonic Toyota Racing 0
10. MF1 Racing 0
11. Super Aguri F1 0

The circuit

Name	Bahrain International Circuit, Sakhir; Manama	Weather	Sunny and warm
		Air temperature	23-24°c
Lenght	5412 m	Track tempature	36-40°c
Distance	57 laps, 308,238 km	Humidity	43-45%
Date	March 12, 2006	Wind speed	1.0 m/s

S1: at corner
S2: 48m before corner
Radar: 144m before corner

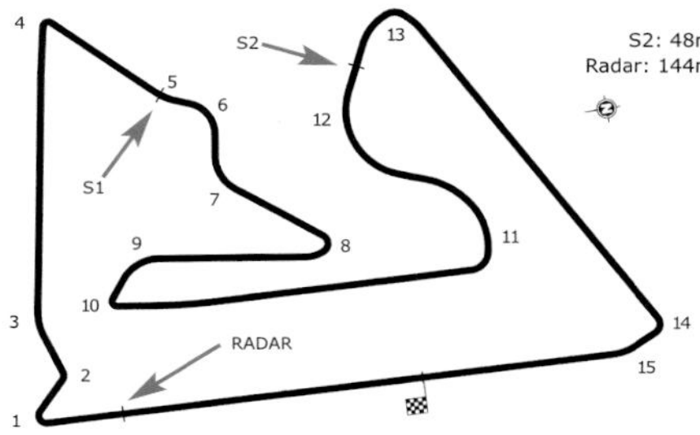

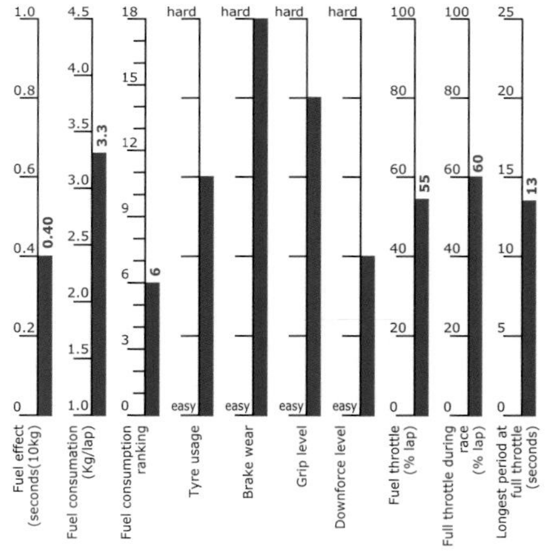

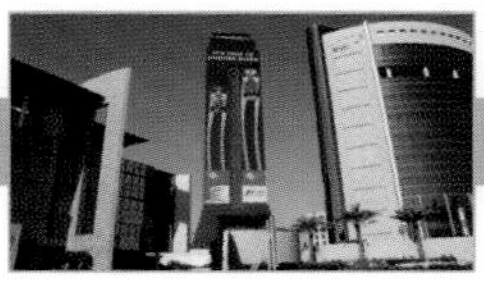

FISI SPARKLES!

The outcome of the battle for victory between Giancarlo Fisichella and Fernando Alonso was decided in qualifying. The Spaniard had a small problem with his fuel tank and could do no better than eighth while the Italian set pole. In the race he dominated his rivals while Alonso charged back up the field to see the flag in second place. Behind the Renault pair Jenson Button scored his (and Honda's) first rostrum finish of the season.

practice

Seven engine failures in practice. And as many unknown factors on the grid

Jenson Button qualified on the front row and finished the race in third place. But he wasn't all that happy. "Coming third is a disappointment," he groaned.

As the French say: why make it simple when you can make it complex? It took a large number of meetings between team representatives to come with the qualifying session in three parts which gives spectators a thrill on Saturday afternoons. Contested, appreciated, praised this system at least has the merit of keeping the cars on the track for almost the full hour's practice. It guarantees the spectacle for the people sitting in the grandstands, and requires a high level of concentration for those who try to keep abreast of what is happening.

One of the consequences of the new system that was not really expected was the fact that it sowed mayhem among the V8s. In the very hot Malaysian conditions the engines obliged by the regulations to last for two grand prix were not always able to cope with the additional laps imposed by the new qualifying format.

Thus, on Saturday 7 V8s had to be changed dropping their drivers back ten places on the grid. In Massa's case he was the victim of a double whammy and he had to go back twenty positions! So he did not come out at all for qualifying.

Snippets

> "I'm ready for the challenge. It'll be fun," said Fernando Alonso about the challenge put to him by Valentino Rossi. To see which of the two was the quickest the MotoGP rider proposed that the two world champions should drive an F1, a WRC rally car and a MotoGP bike and then add up the times.

Mike Gascoyne with Richard Cregan, the Toyota F1 operations boss. Gascoyne's salary, some 8 million dollars, set tongues wagging both inside and outside the Japanese team.

> "A lot of people underestimated the work required to change from a V10 revving at 18 000 rpm and a V8 revving at 20 000 rpm. It's a huge jump," declared Norbert Haug the Mercedes-Benz competitions director to explain the number of blown engines.

On Saturday evening in the FIA offices there was lot of blood, sweat but not too many tears! Michael Schumacher was first of all given place no.14 on the grid (4th time +10) but then the German moved up to eleventh because of his brother's, David Coulthard's and Ruben Barrichello's relegation. Then it was thirteenth! So it was only a few hours before the start on Sunday morning that the final gird was published.

Gascoyne defends himself and accuses the tyres

In F1 the good old days can be very recent like for Toyota, for example. They went back to 2005 when the team finished the world championship in fourth place only twelve points behind Ferrari.

Thus, the Japanese squad was expected even better things in 2006. In Bahrain the dream began to crumble. The Toyotas suffered from poor road holding and were but a pale shadow of what they had been the previous year; Mike Gascoyne quickly jumped to his own defence! On Monday, he put the responsibility for the disaster squarely on the fact that the Bridgestone tyres did not work properly (the previous year the Toyotas were on Michelins) blaming Pascal Vaselon, the new Toyota

development manager, also a former Michelin engineer and as such a tyre specialist.

Mike Gascoyne receives a huge salary - around 8 million dollars annually if gossip was to be believed - so he had to find a scapegoat quickly. He was not very happy about Vaselon's rapid rise to prominence in the company so he did his best to shoot him down. All the more so as it seemed that the tyres really were the problem. "We can't manage to heat up our rubber," Jarno Trulli confirmed. "At present we're unable put our finger on the problem. Everything's OK for the first two laps and then the tyres deteriorate and the car slides around all over the place."

Starting grid

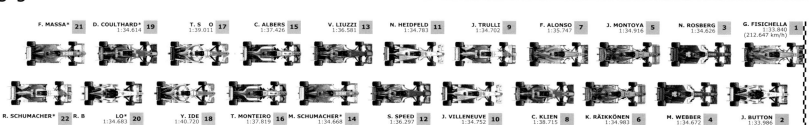

* M. SCHUMACHER, D. COULTHARD, R.BARRICHELLO et R. SCHUMACHER penalty for an engine exchange (-10 pos.).

F. MASSA penalty for a double engine exchange (2 x -10 pos.).

Pos	Driver	Time
21	F. MASSA*	1:34.614
19	D. COULTHARD*	
17	T. S O	1:39.011
15	C. ALBERS	1:37.426
13	V. LIUZZI	1:36.581
11	N. HEIDFELD	1:34.783
9	J. TRULLI	1:34.702
7	F. ALONSO	1:35.747
5	J. MONTOYA	1:34.916
3	N. ROSBERG	1:34.626
1	G. FISICHELLA	1:33.840 (212.647 km/h)
22	R. SCHUMACHER*	
20	R. B LO*	1:34.683
18	Y. IDE	1:40.720
16	T. MONTEIRO	1:37.819
14	M. SCHUMACHER*	1:34.668
12	S. SPEED	1:36.297
10	J. VILLENEUVE	1:34.752
8	C. KLIEN	1:38.715
6	K. RÄIKKÖNEN	1:34.983
4	M. WEBBER	1:34.672
2	J. BUTTON	1:33.986

Fisichella: an undervalued winner

Suzuka 2005. Last lap. Giancarlo Fisichella in the lead folded under the first attack from Kimi Raïkkönen and lost the grand prix. There were long faces in the Renault camp. "*In our team we've got a genius and a dead loss,*" said one of the engineers with a dismissive gesture.

It was a setback that summed up a poor season for the Roman. After winning the first round in Australia, Fisichella spent the rest of the year in Alonso's shadow. The Renault management stated openly that the only reason it had kept him on in 2006 was because he had a contract that could not be broken. "*At least this grand prix shows that Giancarlo can up his game,*" joked Briatore after the Malaysian Grand Prix reminding everybody that he had no contract for 2007 and that he had to work well if he wanted to stay at Renault.

At least he got 2006 off to a good start. He had retired in Bahrain due to an electrical problem but on the Sepang circuit he was unbeatable. "*It's the exact opposite of last year. I hope that my bad luck ended last week and that I'm going to tot up the points from now,*" smiled Fisichella. He did not sound very convincing. Even his own team-mate did not take him seriously.

"*This race was important for me as neither of my two main rivals Michael Schumacher and Kimi Raïkkönen scored points,*" was Alonso's comment on his second place. He then twisted the knife a little, "*if I hadn't had a problem in qualifying I'd have set pole and won easily!*" He obviously did not count Fisichella among his rivals. "*I don't give a monkey's uncle if Fernando doesn't consider me a rival,*" shot back the winner. "*I can live with it. I'm just going to try and change his mind.*"

Renault: a winning system

Kimi in his silver arrow could not be ignored at the start of the season. He was unlucky again at Sepang as he was punted off into retirement by Christian Klien's Red Bull on the first lap. It was, however, obvious that the Renaults were a cut above their rivals and looked like the ones to beat in 2006. The perfectly balanced R26s had bullet-proof reliability, as the French V8 was the only one not to have any problems in Malaysia. Fisichella's win from Alonso was proof of this.

"*Fernando won in Bahrain but we were very disappointed by Giancarlo's retirement,*" admitted Denis Chevrier, the Renault engineering director. "*We'll have to do better here. This 2006 season is very hard on the engines. The chassis are better, the tyres have progressed by several seconds per lap and the V8s are less powerful. We're flat out more often and the engines are subjected to much more stress than last year.*" Renault had gained an advantage by working differently. "*I think that we're better prepared than some of our rivals,*" continued Chevrier. "*We didn't work like the others. Some people found it strange that we didn't test a provisional V8 from July onwards like everybody else. We didn't waste time. We concentrated on the definitive version of the engine and we installed it in the car for the first time in January. And it worked. Others probably scattered their energies too much.*"

It was the Renault team's first double since that of René Arnoux and Alain Prost in the 1982 French Grand Prix. But the company confirmed that it would not take another generation for it to happen again.

^
A very happy Giancarlo Fisichella savours his moment of triumph on the rostrum. And so he should. It was to be his first and last time on the topmost step! He had a problem-free race losing the leadership only during refuelling stops.

<
"*Well done, lads!*" Flavio Briatore congratulates his two drivers in the Malaysian Grand Prix parc fermé.

<
Juan Pablo Montoya refuels. The Colombian started fifth and finished fourth for the second time on the trot. "*I suffered during the first stint but after changing tyres, my rhythm was the same as Jenson's. It's very encouraging,*" was how he summed it up.

> Nico Rosberg qualified on the second row after his points-scoring finish in Bahrain. He retired in the race with an engine problem. Yet another in the Malaysian cauldron.

Giorgio Mondini drove his first day in F1 with a virgin white helmet. "*In fact, my helmet man came up with a super new design,*" he explained. "*But there was a problem and my helmet caught fire in its bag! We had to get a new one in a hurry and we didn't have the time to paint it!*"
∨

Giorgio's dream

Friday 18h00: Cap jammed down on his head Giorgio Mondini was still a bit shattered after his day. And he had every reason to be. That very morning the Swiss had experienced the lot: his team Midland, the circuit, the car in which he had only done a handful of laps on the Silverstone circuit in the snow! His task looked tricky if not mission impossible! At 11h00 the pit lane opened and he set off for his reconnaissance lap. He came back to his pit, the car was checked and this time he went out for real. 1m 49s, 1m 46s, 1m 43s, 1m 41s his times came down and he ended the day in 1m 38.256s.

> Jean Alesi came to Sepang as bronzed and determined as ever to talk business and put his new team on the F1 landscape. The project was cancelled a few months later as the Japanese Dirivex Group was nothing but a hollow shell.

He made good progress as practice unfolded and for a first timer it was a pretty impressive performance. In 42 laps the man from Geneva proved that he deserved his place in F1. "*I'm really happy. I took about ten laps to find the limit. It's great. Today I can say that I've fulfilled my boyhood dream,*" he laughed. "*This afternoon I went out behind Michael Schumacher. I followed him for a lap - or at least I tried. Wonderful.*"

Ferrari in the news

Felipe Massa finished in fifth place with Michael Schumacher in sixth. Even if the German was still second in the world championship the performance of the red cars in Malaysia left the Tifosi unsatisfied. "*Our engine's lack of reliability prevented us from doing any better,*" said Jean Todt. "*But we still don't know why they failed.*"

> "*I don't know, but the steering is a bit rubbery.*" Christian Klien tries to bring his Red Bull back to its pit after colliding with Kimi Raïkkönen on the first lap. He rejoined after a long stop for repairs to rack up the kilometres. His team-mate "Uncle" David Coulthard went out with hydraulic failure which blocked the power assisted steering and left the car stuck in sixth gear

In the meantime eight of the eleven teams sent an open letter to the FIA at the end of the race contesting the legality of the Ferraris' front wings. The governing body did not want to spoil the start of the season with a scandal so it asked the Scuderia to change them for the next race, the Australian Grand Prix.

Alesi back in the role of team boss

Jean Alesi had not changed. Looking as bronzed as always he was in top form and still driving - he was still at the wheel of a Mercedes-Benz in the DTM (German Touring Car Championship).

He is still as enthusiastic as ever and adulated in Japan helped no doubt by his wife Kumiko. He had just been named motor sports director by Direxiv, a Japanese company specialising in luxury products and services in the land of the rising sun.

This season the company has decided to invest heavily in motor racing sponsoring a GP2 team as well as a Porsche in the Super GT series and the Formula Nippon single-seaters.

Dirivex's main project was the creation of a kind of McLaren Junior team in 2007. A few weeks earlier it had all seemed a bit far-fetched but it was now taking shape in England. The brand was already one of the McLaren team sponsors.

Jean Alesi, the future boss of the team, wore a big smile in the Sepang paddock. "*Everything's being put into place,*" he declared in his inimitable south-of-France accent. "*We've already got the factory; it's the old McLaren one. We've got our engine; it's the Mercedes V8. We're designing the car.*"

On the F1 time scale 2007 is tomorrow. To found a new team means taking on hundreds of people, dealing with huge problems but this did not seem to frighten the former Ferrari driver. "*We'll be ready; we've got the cash and it won't cost Mercedes a lot extra to build a few more engines.*"

The Daimler-Benz bean counters must have appreciated this comment!

Even though the Frenchman quit F1 in October 2001 after a career spanning some 201 grands prix he had not forgotten its ambience. "*When you start in the DTM it's nice, but once you've done F1 it's all you think about,*" he admitted.

Practice

All the time trials

N° Driver	Nat.	N° Chassis - Engine [Nbr. GP]	Pos. Free 1 Friday	Laps	Pos. Free 2 Friday	Laps	Pos. Free 3 Saturday	Laps	Pos. Q1 Saturday	Laps	Pos. Q2 Saturday	Laps	Pos. Super Pole Saturday	Laps
1. Fernando Alonso	E	Renault R26 02 [2]	21.	2	3. 1:35.806	14	2. 1:34.180	13	12. 1:35.514	3	3. 1:33.997	6	**8. 1:35.747**	13
2. Giancarlo Fisichella	I	Renault R26 03 [1]	22.	2	6. 1:36.182	14	3. 1:34.585	13	11. 1:35.488	3	2. 1:33.623	6	**1. 1:33.840**	13
3. Kimi Räikkönen	FIN	McLaren MP4-21 02 - Mercedes [2]	20.	1	5. 1:36.132	15	6. 1:34.854	10	2. 1:34.667	3	5. 1:34.351	3	**7. 1:34.983**	12
4. Juan Pablo Montoya	CO	McLaren MP4-21 03 - Mercedes [2]	4. 1:36.709	4	14. 1:37.463	12	16. 1:37.053	8	1. 1:34.536	3	8. 1:34.568	3	**6. 1:34.916**	12
5. Michael Schumacher	D	Ferrari 248 F1 253 [2->1]	6. 1:37.043	4	7. 1:36.617	17	1. 1:34.126	16	16. 1:35.810	5	9. 1:34.574	5	**4. 1:34.668**	13
6. Felipe Massa	BR	Ferrari 248 F1 252 [2->1]	7. 1:37.557	18	4. 1:35.924	22	17. 1:37.148	21	5. 1:35.091	3	**16.**			
7. Ralf Schumacher	D	Toyota TF106/05 [2->1]	9. 1:37.826	9	17. 1:37.695	20	7. 1:35.040	7	8. 1:35.214	7	10. 1:34.586	3	**10.**	
8. Jarno Trulli	I	Toyota TF106/04 [2]	12. 1:38.837	8	11. 1:37.317	23	10. 1:35.690	19	13. 1:35.517	6	**13. 1:34.702**	6		
9. Mark Webber	AUS	Williams FW28 03 - Cosworth [2]			20. 1:38.081	5	11. 1:35.700	11	9. 1:35.252	3	4. 1:34.279	3	**5. 1:34.672**	12
10. Nico Rosberg	D	Williams FW28 04 - Cosworth [2]			21. 1:38.205	6	8. 1:35.242	14	6. 1:35.105	4	7. 1:34.563	3	**3. 1:34.626**	12
11. Rubens Barrichello	BR	Honda RA106-03 [2->1]			10. 1:37.270	13	15. 1:36.655	13	14. 1:35.526	6	**12. 1:34.683**	8		
12. Jenson Button	GB	Honda RA106-04 [2]			8. 1:36.661	12	4. 1:34.616	20	4. 1:35.023	3	1. 1:33.527	3	**2. 1:33.986**	13
14. David Coulthard	GB	Red Bull RB2 3 - Ferrari [2->1]	5. 1:37.042	7	16. 1:37.603	8	9. 1:35.639	14	3. 1:34.839	6	**11. 1:34.614**	6		
15. Christian Klien	A	Red Bull RB2 2 - Ferrari [2]	10. 1:38.448	5	23. 1:38.644	10	5. 1:34.815	12	7. 1:35.171	6	6. 1:34.537	6	**9. 1:38.715**	4
16. Nick Heidfeld	D	BMW Sauber F1.06-04 [2]	24.	1	12. 1:37.418	7	13. 1:36.505	13	15. 1:35.588	4	**15. 1:34.783**	6		
17. Jacques Villeneuve	CDN	BMW Sauber F1.06-03 [1]	23.	1	9. 1:37.045	9	12. 1:36.144	9	10. 1:35.391	4	**14. 1:34.752**	6		
18. Tiago Monteiro	P	Midland M16-03 - Toyota [2]	14. 1:39.899	8	26. 1:39.416	20	20. 1:37.900	17	**20. 1:37.819**	6				
19. Christijan Albers	NL	Midland M16-02 - Toyota [2]	17. 1:40.608	12	24. 1:38.918	20	18. 1:37.232	18	**19. 1:37.426**	7				
20. Vitantonio Liuzzi	I	Toro Rosso STR01 03 - Cosworth [2]	16. 1:40.123	8	15. 1:37.590	22	14. 1:36.549	15	**18. 1:36.581**	7				
21. Scott Speed	USA	Toro Rosso STR01 02 - Cosworth [2]	13. 1:39.599	14	19. 1:37.926	21	19. 1:37.437	19	**17. 1:36.297**	6				
22. Takuma Sato	J	Super Aguri SA05-02 - Honda [2]	18. 1:41.072	18	27. 1:41.549	22	21. 1:38.821	15	**21. 1:39.011**	6				
23. Yuji Ide	J	Super Aguri SA05-01 - Honda [2]	19. 1:43.449	19	28. 1:43.164	16	22. 1:40.542	18	**22. 1:40.720**	6				
35. Alexander Wurz	A	Williams FW28 01 - Cosworth	1. 1:34.946	19	2. 1:35.388	30								
36. Anthony Davidson	GB	Honda RA106-01	3. 1:35.997	25	1. 1:35.041	14								
37. Robert Doornbos	MC	Red Bull RB2 1 - Ferrari	8. 1:37.604	18	25. 1:39.105	28								
38. Robert Kubica	PL	BMW Sauber F1.06-02	2. 1:35.733	22	13. 1:37.457	28								
39. Giorgio Mondini	CH	Midland M16-04 - Toyota	15. 1:40.092	22	20. 1:38.256	20								
40. Neel Jani	CH	Toro Rosso STR01 01 - Cosworth	11. 1:38.668	21	18. 1:37.831	23								

Fastest lap overall
J. Button 1:33.527 (213,358 km/h)

Maximum speed

N° Driver	S1 Qualifs	Pos.	S1 Race	Pos.	S2 Qualifs	Pos.	S2 Race	Pos.	Finish Qualifs	Pos.	Finish Race	Pos.	Radar Qualifs	Pos.	Radar Race	Pos.
1. F. Alonso	282,6	14	286,0	8	156,7	4	157,4	2	259,0	14	260,4	6	291,6	8	294,5	12
2. G. Fisichella	284,5	9	285,7	9	158,3	1	156,6	4	261,7	7	261,3	4	293,2	6	297,1	5
3. K. Räikkönen	287,1	1	282,1	16	154,0	11			262,8	4			293,9	3		
4. J. Montoya	286,8	3	292,2	1	155,5	10	155,0	6	265,4	1	263,9	1	296,1	1	297,6	4
5. M. Schumacher	286,5	4	289,6	3	157,5	2	155,0	7	262,9	3	262,5	3	293,4	5	297,9	3
6. F. Massa	287,0	2	291,4	2	157,4	3	157,6	1	264,0	2	263,5	2	291,4	9	300,0	1
7. R. Schumacher	278,8	20	282,4	15	153,6	12	152,6	11	257,6	15	256,9	15	284,8	19	290,9	16
8. J. Trulli	279,2	18	281,6	18	152,7	15	149,5	18	256,7	16	254,6	17	286,3	16	289,0	20
9. M. Webber	284,6	8	285,7	10	156,2	6	153,8	9	262,3	6	260,1	7	290,0	14	295,4	9
10. N. Rosberg	283,9	11	284,8	12	156,2	7	152,3	13	260,7	8	259,1	10	292,2	7	295,7	7
11. R. Barrichello	283,3	13	284,7	13	153,4	13	152,4	12	260,3	10	259,5	8	290,2	13	295,4	8
12. J. Button	283,6	12	286,1	7	153,3	14	152,2	14	260,6	9	260,6	5	290,5	12	294,6	11
14. D. Coulthard	286,1	6	289,5	4	156,1	9	149,3	20	262,4	5	258,4	12	293,7	4	295,9	6
15. C. Klien	284,4	10	287,7	5	152,5	16	151,0	16	259,6	11	259,4	9	291,0	11	298,0	2
16. N. Heidfeld	286,4	5	285,6	11	156,5	5	157,1	3	259,6	12	258,8	11	295,3	2	294,9	10
17. J. Villeneuve	284,7	7	286,7	6	156,1	8	155,7	5	259,2	13	258,3	13	291,1	10	294,4	13
18. T. Monteiro	274,7	22	279,0	22	148,9	21	152,7	10	251,7	22	252,2	20	282,5	21	290,4	17
19. C. Albers	279,5	16	279,1	21	152,4	17	149,5	19	254,7	19	252,5	19	285,4	18	289,0	19
20. V. Liuzzi	277,7	21	283,3	14	152,4	18	151,6	15	254,0	21	253,8	18	281,1	22	294,2	14
21. S. Speed	279,3	17	280,3	20	151,9	19	154,2	8	254,2	20	252,1	21	286,5	15	289,0	18
22. T. Sato	279,0	19	282,0	17	151,0	20	150,6	17	256,4	17	257,1	14	285,7	17	293,5	15
23. Y. Ide	280,9	15	281,1	19	142,6	22	143,7	21	255,0	18	254,6	16	284,5	20	288,9	21

Race

Classification & Retirements

Pos.	Driver	Constructor	Tyres	Laps	Time	Average
1.	G. Fisichella	Renault	M	56	1:30:40.529	205,397 km/h
2.	F. Alonso	Renault	M	56	+ 4.585	205,224 km/h
3.	J. Button	Honda	M	56	+ 9.631	205,034 km/h
4.	J. Montoya	McLaren Mercedes	M	56	+ 39.351	203,922 km/h
5.	F. Massa	Ferrari	B	56	+ 43.254	203,776 km/h
6.	M. Schumacher	Ferrari	B	56	+ 43.854	203,754 km/h
7.	J. Villeneuve	BMW	M	56	+ 1:20.461	202,403 km/h
8.	R. Schumacher	Toyota	B	56	+ 1:21.288	202,373 km/h
9.	J. Trulli	Toyota	B	55	1 lap	201,669 km/h
10.	R. Barrichello	Honda	M	55	1 lap	201,259 km/h
11.	V. Liuzzi	STR Cosworth	M	54	2 laps	197,150 km/h
12.	C. Albers	MF1 Toyota	B	54	2 laps	196,914 km/h
13.	T. Monteiro	MF1 Toyota	B	54	2 laps	194,566 km/h
14.	T. Sato	Aguri Honda	B	53	3 laps	193,819 km/h

Driver	Constructor	Tyres	Laps	Reason
N. Heidfeld	BMW	M	48	Engine failure
S. Speed	STR Cosworth	M	41	Failure with the clutch lever on the steering wheel
Y. Ide	Aguri Honda	B	33	Mechanical problem
C. Klien	RBR Ferrari	M	26	Hydraulics failure
M. Webber	Williams Cosworth	B	15	Hydraulics leak
D. Coulthard	RBR Ferrari	M	10	Hydraulics failure
N. Rosberg	Williams Cosworth	B	6	Engine failure
K. Räikkönen	McLaren Mercedes	M	0	Hit by Klien... Rear suspension broken, off

Fastest laps

	Driver	Time	Laps	Average
1.	F. Alonso	1:34.803	45	210,487 km/h
2.	G. Fisichella	1:35.294	16	209,402 km/h
3.	J. Montoya	1:35.566	39	208,806 km/h
4.	J. Button	1:35.604	35	208,723 km/h
5.	M. Schumacher	1:35.647	44	208,629 km/h
6.	R. Schumacher	1:35.686	34	208,544 km/h
7.	N. Heidfeld	1:35.751	41	208,403 km/h
8.	F. Massa	1:35.954	51	207,962 km/h
9.	J. Villeneuve	1:36.002	43	207,858 km/h
10.	R. Barrichello	1:36.188	54	207,456 km/h
11.	J. Trulli	1:36.380	52	207,042 km/h
12.	M. Webber	1:36.771	12	206,206 km/h
13.	C. Klien	1:36.867	14	206,002 km/h
14.	S. Speed	1:37.313	25	205,057 km/h
15.	N. Rosberg	1:37.366	6	204,946 km/h
16.	V. Liuzzi	1:37.387	40	204,902 km/h
17.	D. Coulthard	1:38.078	4	203,458 km/h
18.	C. Albers	1:38.198	34	203,209 km/h
19.	T. Monteiro	1:39.510	39	200,530 km/h
20.	T. Sato	1:40.199	14	199,151 km/h
21.	Y. Ide	1:42.833	18	194,050 km/h

Pit stops

	Driver	Laps	Duration	Stop	Total
1.	V. Liuzzi	1	34.193	1	34.193
2.	C. Klien	1	9:34.749	1	9:34.749
3.	C. Klien	4	4:08.631	2	13:43.380
4.	T. Monteiro	12	28.625	1	28.625
5.	R. Schumacher	13	27.796	1	27.796
6.	M. Webber	14	26.486	1	26.486
7.	G. Fisichella	17	29.126	1	29.126
8.	Y. Ide	16	30.339	1	30.339
9.	J. Button	19	26.023	1	26.023
10.	C. Albers	19	26.871	1	26.871
11.	T. Sato	19	28.588	1	28.588
12.	V. Liuzzi	19	34.239	2	1:08.432
13.	J. Trulli	20	25.511	1	25.511
14.	S. Speed	22	29.904	1	29.904
15.	R. Schumacher	22	28.675	2	56.471
16.	J. Montoya	23	26.518	1	26.518
17.	M. Schumacher	23	30.135	1	30.135
18.	J. Villeneuve	23	27.015	1	27.015
19.	N. Heidfeld	24	25.701	1	25.701
20.	F. Alonso	26	25.455	1	25.455
21.	F. Massa	29	28.412	1	28.412
22.	R. Barrichello	31	30.540	1	30.540
23.	J. Trulli	36	30.312	2	55.823
24.	R. Barrichello	•36•	30.219	2	1:00.759
25.	G. Fisichella	38	25.473	2	54.599
26.	J. Button	38	26.325	2	52.348
27.	T. Monteiro	36	28.686	2	57.311
28.	C. Albers	37	28.201	2	55.072
29.	V. Liuzzi	37	28.073	3	1:36.505
30.	R. Schumacher	38	28.431	3	1:24.902
31.	T. Sato	39	28.241	2	56.829
32.	J. Villeneuve	41	25.341	2	52.356
33.	J. Montoya	42	25.467	2	51.985
34.	N. Heidfeld	42	24.971	2	50.672
35.	F. Alonso	43	24.441	2	49.896
36.	M. Schumacher	45	25.614	2	55.749

•• Stop-go penalty (10 sec.): Barrichello. Speeding in pit lane.

Race leader

Driver	Laps in the lead	Nbr of Laps	Driver	Laps in the lead	Nbr of Laps	Driver	Nbr of Laps	Kilometers
G. Fisichella	1 > 17	17	G. Fisichella	27 > 38	12	G. Fisichella	42	232,806 km
J. Button	18 > 19	2	F. Alonso	39 > 43	5	F. Alonso	12	66,516 km
F. Alonso	20 > 26	7	G. Fisichella	44 > 56	13	J. Button	2	11,086 km

Gaps on the leader board

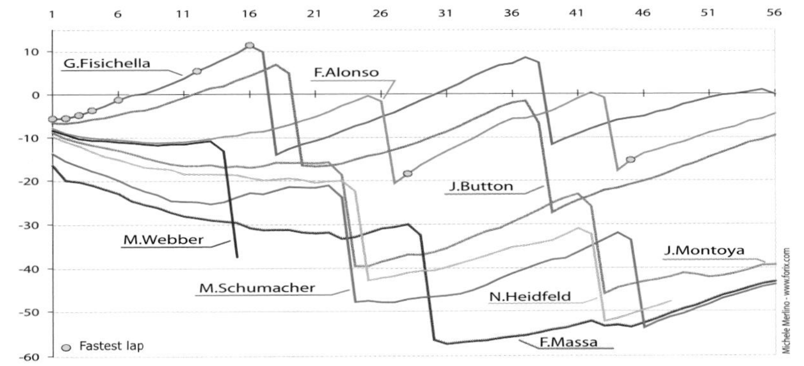

Lap chart

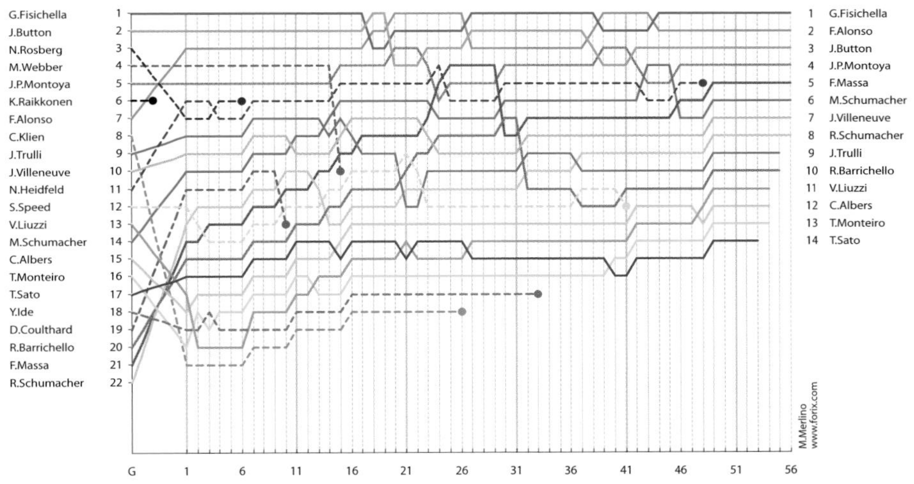

Championships 2/18

Drivers

1. F. Alonso ....Renault ....1 🏆....18
2. M. Schumacher .....Ferrari 11
3. J. Button ....Honda 11
4. G. Fisichella..........Renault ....1 🏆....10
5. J. Montoya ....McLaren Mercedes...............9
6. K. Räikkönen ....McLaren Mercedes...............6
7. F. Massa..............Ferrari 4
8. M. Webber............Williams Cosworth...............3
9. N. Rosberg ....Williams Cosworth...............2
10. J. Villeneuve ....BMW 2
11. R. Schumacher .....Toyota 1
12. C. Klien................RBR Ferrari 1
13. J. Trulli.................Toyota 0
14. R. Barrichello........Honda 0
15. D. Coulthard ....RBR Ferrari 0
16. V. Liuzzi ....STR Cosworth.......................0
17. N. Heidfeld ....BMW 0
18. C. Albers..............MF1 Toyota 0
19. T. Monteiro ....MF1 Toyota 0
20. S. Speed ....STR Cosworth.......................0
21. T. Sato.................Aguri Honda 0

Y. Ide..................Aguri Honda ....-

Constructors

1. Mild Seven Renault F1 Team ....2 🏆....28
2. Scuderia Ferrari Marlboro 15
3. Team McLaren Mercedes 15
4. Lucky Strike Honda Racing F1 Team 11
5. Williams F1 Team.......................................5
6. BMW Sauber F1 Team..................................2
7. Panasonic Toyota Racing 1
8. Red Bull Racing 1
9. Scuderia Toro Rosso 0
10. MF1 Racing 0
11. Super Aguri Formula 1................................0

The circuit

Name	Sepang Circuit; Kuala Lumpur	Weather	Cloudy, warm
		Air temperature	33-34°c
Lenght	5543 m	Track temperature	36-39°c
Distance	56 laps, 310,408 km	Humidity	57%
Date	March 19, 2006	Wind speed	0.7 m/s

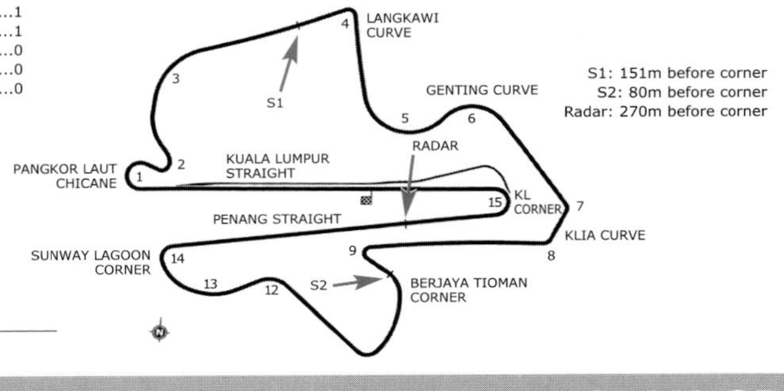

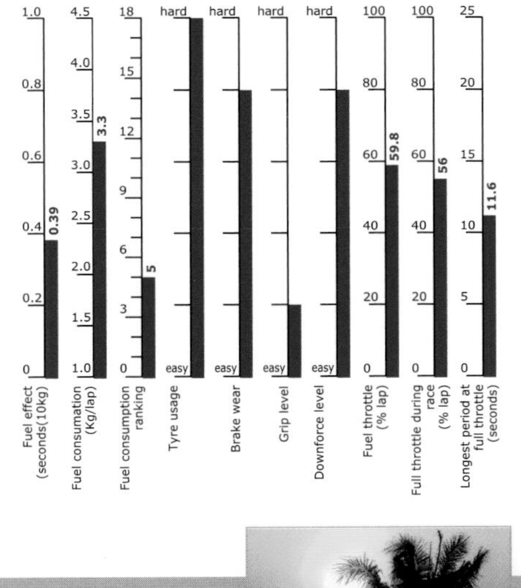

All results : © 2006 Formula One Administration Ltd, 6 Princes Gate, London, SW7 1QJ, England

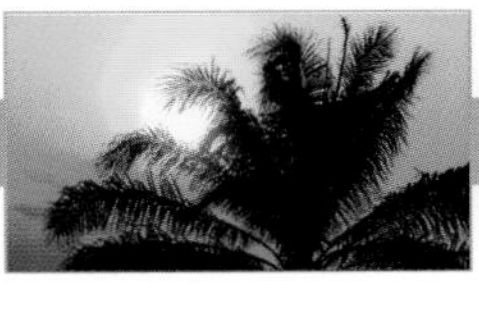

FROM POLE TO BROKE

Jenson Button had said it loud and clear. 2006 would be Honda's year and he was not surprised when he set pole in Melbourne.
When Sunday came things did not go according to plan in the Japanese camp and he bowed out in flames a few metres from the finish
The Ferraris were never in the hunt all weekend and Fernando Alonso took advantage of the situation to score his second win of the year.

Ferrari bends before the FIA

> Jenson Button was on pole. Rain as well as a couple of red flags upset the qualifying session for the Australian Grand Prix. It was a very confused one and the Brit took advantage of this to put his Honda on pole for the first time this season and the third in his career. Giancarlo Fisichella carried on where he left off in Malaysia. There he won the race and in Melbourne he was on the front row ahead of his team-mate Alonso. Michael Schumacher could do no better than eleventh having not taken part in the final shoot-out. "*The main problem is that w we're just not quick enough,*" the Ferrari driver grumbled.

The McLarens, Saubers and above all the Ferraris had complied with the FIA recommendations and modified the controversial wings used in the first two grands prix of the season. "*In this milieu, you know, you never conclude an agreement with your rivals. It's a principle.*" The Malaysian Grand Prix had finished a few hours earlier and Jean Todt, the Scuderia boss, was categorical. The Ferraris' front wing was perfectly legal. "*Had our cars been illegal they'd have been banned,*" he went on. "*And if our rivals thought they were illegal they could've protested. If they didn't do it it's not because we negotiated; it's because they're not sure.*"

That evening in Sepang there was no formal protest but 8 out of the 11 teams (everybody except Red Bull and Toro Rosso) signed an open letter to the FIA asking it to ban the Ferraris' front wing. The controversy had begun a week earlier in Bahrain where the Scuderia had entered a car whose wing was said to deform on the straight to cut drag and give the 248 F1 a higher top speed. "*I'm not at all happy with what I see on the Ferrari,*" raged Pat Symonds, the Renault technical director. He was immediately backed up by Geoff Willis, the man in the same position at Honda. "*It's a point we've discussed at the FIA Technical Commission and it's quite clear that it is banned,*" underlined Willis. "*I don't understand why Ferrari has tried to use such a system. The FIA should sanction them.*"

In fact, the Scuderia decided to play it softly – not always the case. Like the situation at the start of the 2005 season when Renault had attempted to use flexi-wings (!) the FIA asked Ferrari as well as the other teams under suspicion to fit normal ones under pain of severe sanctions.

It was a way of avoiding disqualification, which always has a rather bad smell about it. It worked

and Ferrari arrived in Australia with wings that did not bend. "*It's not a question of the regulations,*" stated Luca Ciolajanni, the team's spokesman. "*We've fitted these new wings to improve performance.*" It was a lie that the people

in charge of Soviet propaganda during the Cold War would have been proud of!

Ferrari was not the only team to have modified its wings as McLaren and Sauber had done the same and turned up down under with new equipment.

> Magnificent Melbourne. The capital of the state of Victoria and its 3500 restaurants is for many their favourite halt on the world championship trail. In the background is the Albert Park circuit seen from the town centre.

> Ferrari's new revised front wing after the complaints from the teams.

Takuma Sato in his Super Aguri qualified in 21st place some 4 seconds ahead of his team-mate, Yuji Ide.
∨

Starting grid

Pos	Driver	Time
21	T. SATO	1:32.279
19	J. VILLENEUVE*	1:29.239
17	C. ALBERS	1:30.226
15	F. MASSA	
13	C. KLIEN	1:27.591
11	D. COULTHARD	1:27.023
9	J. TRULLI	
7	M. WEBBER	1:26.937
5	J. MONTOYA	1:25.976
3	F. ALONSO	1:25.778
1	J. BUTTON	1:25.229 (223.994 km/h)

Pos	Driver	Time
22	Y. IDE	1:36.164
20	T. MONTEIRO	1:30.709
18	S. SPEED	1:30.426
16	R. BARRICHELLO	1:29.943
14	N. ROSBERG	1:29.422
12	V. LIUZZI	1:27.219
10	M. SCHUMACHER	1:26.718
8	N. HEIDFELD	1:27.579
6	R. SCHUMACHER	1:26.612
4	K. RÄIKKÖNEN	1:25.822
2	G. FISICHELLA*	1:25.635

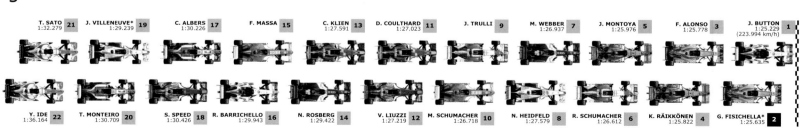

Alonso racks up another victory. A host of retirements.

Fernando Alonso who started from third on the grid scored a relatively easy victory while behind him retirements fell thick and fast. The concrete walls are never too far way on the Albert Park circuit. As their openings are few and far between unlike Monaco where there is a crane every 300 metres accidents lead to the race being neutralised behind the safety car until the track is cleared. This year race control had to intervene four times causing the Renault team's collective heartbeat to go off the radar. Each time Alonso's lead was reduced to nought.

While both Ferraris caused a neutralisation period the spectacular accidents that befell Christian Klien's Red Bull (tyres too cold) and Viantonio Liuzzi's Toro Rosso pushed off by Jacques Villeneuve also brought out the safety car.

Later on Juan Pablo Montoya's McLaren did a bit of a dance and came to a halt. The Colombian bounced it off a kerb and the circuit breaker cut out his engine while he was still airborne so he stalled on landing!

The last bit of suspense came on the final lap. Jenson, Button was in fifth place far away from his pole hotly pursued by Fisichella's Renault. With only 2 corners to go before the finish the Honda's engine suddenly began to smoke before bursting into flames. In order to have a new one for the next race without losing 10 places the Brit braked just before the finishing line.

Giancarlo stalled, suffered wheel spin and finished fifth. Sepang was but a distant memory.

Nobody contested Alonso's superiority over his team-mate Giancarlo Fisichella (except perhaps, the Italian himself and even then...). Sometimes one had the impression that they were from a different planet. Before Australia there were signs that the Roman had managed to up his game to match that of the Spaniard. He qualified on the front row while the "little bull from the Asturias" was behind. Before the start Giancarlo showed what his real level was, that of a good driver but not a super-gifted star

like Alonso. At the end of the formation lap the Italian stalled like somebody taking a driving test! "*The start procedure of an F1 is quite complex,*" explained one of the team's engineers. "*The drivers have to push a series of buttons for it to work. The programme tries to anticipate any uncatered for situations but Giancarlo got himself into one that was not foreseen and he stalled.*"

Genius driver that he is Fernando knows how his car works like the back of his hand. Such a thing would

not happen to him. "*Our programme will have to be more intelligent to take into account the competence or lack of same of our drivers,*" concluded the engineer almost tearing his hair out!

So Giancarlo's race was compromised right from the start. He was far behind and his speed was not enough to warm up his tyres. To bring up their temperature the Roman gave them a hammering by sliding the car around in a brutal manner. This only served to damage them and diminished their grip even further as well as cooling them down: a vicious circle.

A few laps before the end a sensor signalled that the Italian's clutch had broken. But the finish was near so his engineers asked him to bypass the sensor's function. Fisico said he didn't know how to do this on the steering wheel. Faced with such incompetence they buried their heads in their hands!

Finally, he came home in fifth place thanks to blazing Button's retirement. In two hours' racing he lost the reputation he had just built up with such aplomb.

A flat spot for 2 seconds

Just when the safety car unleashed the pack on lap 10 Kimi Raïkkönen pulled a magnificent passing move on Jenson Button with his wheels locked up. It flat-spotted a tyre. The resulting vibrations were so strong that a winglet fell off his McLaren, which lost 2% of its efficiency. It was enough to destroy the car's balance, its front tyres and cost him over a second a lap. Today's F1 cars are very sensitive beasts.

^
Kimi Raïkkönen had an eventful race in Melbourne. Despite his off here plus a vibration problem he finished on the second step of the rostrum pocketing the fastest lap into the bargain.

<
Nick Heidfeld caught in a beautifully controlled slide. The German came home fourth scoring his first points of the year. His team-mate Jacques Villeneuve added to BMW's joy with a sixth-place finish and three points.

paddock

Michael Schumacher's retirement. Ferrari's hopes at a low ebb

The Scuderia's engineers were not a very happy bunch when they left the circuit. In three days the team had been the victim of three accidents and had not scored a single point. Michael Schumacher was down in fourth place in the championship ratings and the horizon looked dark.

During Saturday's qualification session Massa went a bit wide, ran over a kerb and hit the wall. Result: the little Brazilian ended up on 15th place on the grid right in the middle of the wild things! At the start he was attacked from the right, found himself caught up in a sandwich and did not get any further than the first corner ending up with a badly damaged car.

This left just Michael Schumacher to defend the Maranello colours; He was in eighth place in the first part of the race struggling with his tyres which he was unable to bring up to a working temperature because of the laps behind the safety car. He stopped in lap 25 to change them and his Ferrari's road holding improved. An all-fired up German closed the gap to Button's Honda. Just when he was about to attack the Brit he went off in the last corner and slammed into the wall.

In 33 laps Ferrari had lost both cars. In Malaysia two weeks earlier the rout had been attributed to the engines. In Melbourne it was the road holding. "We're too slow," groaned Schumacher. "The tyres

> The wreck of Michael Schumacher's Ferrari. After finishing sixth in Malaysia the German failed to score in Melbourne.

> Scott Speed, the F1 equivalent of the Louisville lip, did not exactly enhance his reputation in Melbourne. He finished 9th and was hit with a 5000 dollar fine for using "foul language" in front of the stewards after the race. He was asked to explain why he had passed David Coulthard under yellow flags and the feisty American gave the Scot a mouthful for having denounced him!...

"You'll be back to see us, won't you?" These lovely ladies are just a part of the charm of the Aussi Grand Prix.

"Where's the circuit?" Ralf Schumacher sets off any which way. The younger Schumacher came home third in the race itself.

are not getting up the right working temperature. This causes you to lock them up under braking and after a few laps they're dead. We're going to have to work to solve this problem."

Work and more work: this was the comment that was heard most frequently on Sunday evening. In 2005, Ferrari had had a dreadful season but during the winter it looked like things had taken a turn for the better. Now it did not seem to be the case. Naturally, the Scuderia did not stand there with its arms folded. On Saturday in Melbourne, it announced the arrival of a new car for Imola, the

following race. "Our deceptions this weekend haven't modified our objectives but they just make them harder to achieve," stated Jean Todt, the Scuderia boss. "We've got what it takes to make it back to the top, but we've got to get our act together."

Ferrari was certainly hoping to avoid another season like 2005 but the future did not look very bright. The points lost early on in the year compared with those racked up by an on-form Fernando Alonso would cost the Scuderia both titles at the end of the championship.

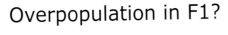

Overpopulation in F1?

Success, success! Just at the moment when the world economy was faltering Formula 1 was in scintillating form. The major manufacturers involved wanted to stay in and poured huge sums of dosh into the sport while more and more sponsors jostled for places on the cars' gleaming bodywork.

It looked like the world economy had no influence on the grand prix world. But cost cutting was on the menu when it came to drawing up the 2008 regulations. The latter were not yet finalised and Max Mosley the FIA president was out to reduce the costs in F1 to a quarter of their present level. He was aiming for a maximum ceiling of 100 million euros for a complete season for a team. It was a sum outside the reach of the ordinary punter but it seemed to attract a swarm of candidates. They had up to the Friday evening before the Australian Grand Prix to send in their entry for the 2008 championship and a total of 22 reached the FIA.

It was a huge success that surprised everybody in the Melbourne paddock. There were even some who thought it was all a bit of a hoax!

The list of teams refused (the maximum number of the world championship is fixed at 12) was not published until 28th April (but some did not wait until then to announce their candidature). These included the current 11 teams and Prodrive entered in the Rally World Championship plus Dirivex, the Japanese brand whose racing activities were looked after by Jean Alesi. Several GP2 teams also decided to try their luck in this "bargain" F1. Friday's deadline had upset the gentlemen of the GPMA (the association made up of 5 major manufacturers Renault, BMW, Mercedes-Benz, Honda and Toyota), which had threatened to set up a parallel championship in 2008 if its members did not get a larger slice of the TV rights cake. The GPMA members all entered for the 2008 championship and the spectre of a rogue series vanished like a ghost at dawn!

Practice

All the time trials

N° Driver	Nat.	N° Chassis - Engine [Nbr GP]	Pos. Free 1 Friday	Laps	Pos. Free 2 Friday	Laps	Pos. Free 3 Saturday	Laps	Pos. Q1 Saturday	Laps	Pos. Q2 Saturday	Laps	Pos. Super Pole Saturday	Laps
1. Fernando Alonso	E	Renault R26 02 [1]	19.	2	5. 1:27.443	14	17. 1:39.654	11	13. 1:28.569	6	1. 1:25.729	3	3. **1:25.778**	15
2. Giancarlo Fisichella	I	Renault R26 03 [2]	20.	2	11. 1:28.280	11	4. 1:36.414	13	5. 1:27.765	5	6. 1:26.196	4	2. **1:25.635**	14
3. Kimi Räikkönen	FIN	McLaren MP4-21 02 - Mercedes [1]	4. 1:28.713	5	7. 1:27.773	16	21. 1:48.284	3	2. 1:27.193	5	5. 1:26.161	3	4. **1:25.822**	14
4. Juan Pablo Montoya	CO	McLaren MP4-21 03 - Mercedes [1]	22.	1	9. 1:28.200	15	20. 1:44.350	3	1. 1:27.079	5	2. 1:25.902	3	5. **1:25.976**	14
5. Michael Schumacher	D	Ferrari 248 F1 253 [2]	6. 1:29.041	5	6. 1:27.658	16	7. 1:37.332	10	9. 1:28.228	5	11. **1:26.718**	6		
6. Felipe Massa	BR	Ferrari 248 F1 252 [2]	5. 1:29.025	7	10. 1:28.227	17	6. 1:36.506	11	15. 1:28.868	6	16. **DNF**	2		
7. Ralf Schumacher	D	Toyota TF106/05 [2]	7. 1:29.411	5	18. 1:29.379	16	5. 1:36.445	10	7. 1:28.007	7	9. 1:26.596	7	6. **1:26.612**	14
8. Jarno Trulli	I	Toyota TF106/04 [1]	21.	2	16. 1:29.138	20	9. 1:37.492	10	4. 1:27.748	7	7. 1:26.327	7	10.	
9. Mark Webber	AUS	Williams FW28 03 - Cosworth [1]			14. 1:28.860	10	12. 1:38.036	7	3. 1:27.669	5	4. 1:26.075	5	7. **1:26.937**	12
10. Nico Rosberg	D	Williams FW28 04 - Cosworth [1]			22. 1:29.933	11	15. 1:39.401	11	10. 1:28.351	4	15. **1:29.422**	7		
11. Rubens Barrichello	BR	Honda RA106-03 [2]	24.	1	8. 1:28.075	20	8. 1:37.481	15	17. **1:29.943**	6				
12. Jenson Button	GB	Honda RA106-04 [1]			4. 1:27.213	12	13. 1:38.505	11	8. 1:28.081	7	8. 1:26.337	4	1. **1:25.229**	14
14. David Coulthard	GB	Red Bull RB2 3 - Ferrari [2]	11. 1:29.676	9	13. 1:28.531	18	14. 1:38.683	15	11. 1:28.408	5	12. **1:27.023**	6		
15. Christian Klien	A	Red Bull RB2 2 - Ferrari [1]	10. 1:29.601	7	21. 1:29.879	9	11. 1:37.947	12	14. 1:28.757	7	14. **1:27.591**	7		
16. Nick Heidfeld	D	BMW Sauber F1.06-04 [1]	23.	1	15. 1:29.053	5	1. 1:35.335	10	6. 1:27.796	7	3. 1:26.014	9	8. **1:27.579**	14
17. Jacques Villeneuve	CDN	BMW Sauber F1.06-03 [2->1]	3. 1:28.595	16	12. 1:28.440	22	2. 1:36.281	16	12. 1:28.460	6	10. 1:26.714	8	9. **1:29.239**	5
18. Tiago Monteiro	P	Midland M16-03 - Toyota [1]	14. 1:31.812	10	19. 1:29.713	21	16. 1:39.515	7	20. **1:30.709**	7				
19. Christijan Albers	NL	Midland M16-02 - Toyota [1]	13. 1:31.039	9	25. 1:30.830	18	22.	3	18. **1:30.226**	8				
20. Vitantonio Liuzzi	I	Toro Rosso STR01 03 - Cosworth [1]	25.	2	24. 1:30.734	14	3. 1:36.373	10	16. 1:28.999	9	13. **1:27.219**	9		
21. Scott Speed	USA	Toro Rosso STR01 02 - Cosworth [1]	12. 1:31.017	8	17. 1:29.196	18	10. 1:37.852	11	19. **1:30.426**	9				
22. Takuma Sato	J	Super Aguri SA05-02 - Honda [1]	15. 1:34.036	9	27. 1:32.556	27	19. 1:41.448	5	21. **1:32.279**	7				
23. Yuji Ide	J	Super Aguri SA05-03 - Honda [1]	16. 1:36.684	19	28. 1:34.224	22	18. 1:40.261	18	22. **1:36.164**	7				
35. Alexander Wurz	A	Williams FW28 02 - Cosworth	8. 1:29.461	19	2. 1:26.832	27								
36. Anthony Davidson	GB	Honda RA106-01	1. 1:28.259	26	1. 1:26.822	28								
37. Robert Doornbos	NL	Red Bull RB2 1 - Ferrari	2. 1:28.559	19	20. 1:29.876	32								
38. Robert Kubica	PL	BMW Sauber F1.06-02	9. 1:29.576	13	3. 1:27.200	25								
39. Marcus Winkelhock	D	Midland M16-04 - Toyota	17. 1:36.859	17	26. 1:31.260	25								
40. Neel Jani	CH	Toro Rosso STR01 01 - Cosworth	18. 1:40.818	4	23. 1:30.686	26								

Fastest lap overall
F. Alonso 1:25.729 (222,687 km/h)

Maximum speed

N° Driver	S1 Qualifs	Pos.	S1 Race	Pos.	S2 Qualifs	Pos.	S2 Race	Pos.	Finish Qualifs	Pos.	Finish Race	Pos.	Radar Qualifs	Pos.	Radar Race	Pos.
1. F. Alonso	280,3	8	278,7	5	287,0	5	288,1	11	290,2	6	286,3	8	303,4	2	297,5	12
2. G. Fisichella	278,3	14	278,1	8	285,1	10	296,3	1	285,8	15	286,7	6	297,4	16	297,4	13
3. K. Räikkönen	284,8	1	281,1	3	285,9	6	291,4	4	292,7	2	289,6	2	302,0	6	302,7	3
4. J. Montoya	284,2	2	281,8	1	287,6	4	294,4	2	292,3	3	290,5	1	303,2	3	303,5	2
5. M. Schumacher	282,8	4	281,6	2	289,3	1	293,3	3	291,4	4	289,5	3	302,1	4	304,0	1
6. F. Massa	282,3	5			287,6	3			290,4	5			301,9	8	239,4	21
7. R. Schumacher	275,7	18	272,7	14	278,9	21	284,8	16	284,8	18	282,8	14	297,9	15	294,7	16
8. J. Trulli	276,4	17	251,3	20	278,9	20			284,2	19			295,0	19	247,7	20
9. M. Webber	281,6	6	276,2	13	284,9	12	288,2	10	290,1	8	286,0	10	302,0	7	300,4	7
10. N. Rosberg	278,1	16	180,1	21	283,6	14	225,9	20	295,5	1			298,6	14	229,3	22
11. R. Barrichello	278,2	15	278,4	7	281,7	17	287,7	12	284,8	17	285,2	13	295,3	18	299,1	10
12. J. Button	283,8	3	278,7	4	285,4	9	286,9	13	290,2	7	286,5	7	300,6	10	298,2	11
14. D. Coulthard	280,3	9	278,5	6	283,9	13	291,1	5	287,0	13	287,4	4	299,5	13	301,6	6
15. C. Klien	279,5	11	261,1	19	285,7	7	278,6	19	287,3	12	282,0	16	301,0	9	284,2	19
16. N. Heidfeld	279,6	10	276,4	12	283,5	15	288,6	9	288,2	11	286,0	11	302,0	5	301,7	5
17. J. Villeneuve	280,7	7	276,9	11	288,3	2	289,7	8	289,1	9	287,0	5	303,4	1	302,5	4
18. T. Monteiro	273,7	20	268,8	17	277,8	22	282,5	18	281,1	22	280,0	19	292,9	22	292,6	18
19. C. Albers	275,1	19	272,5	15	279,4	19	286,0	14	281,4	20	282,2	15	293,3	21	295,8	15
20. V. Liuzzi	279,1	13	277,7	9	285,6	8	289,8	7	289,0	10	285,4	12	300,0	12	300,2	8
21. S. Speed	279,2	12	277,2	10	284,9	11	290,0	6	286,5	14	286,0	9	300,2	11	300,0	9
22. T. Sato	268,3	21	270,8	16	281,9	16	285,6	15	285,0	16	281,9	17	295,4	17	294,3	17
23. Y. Ide	263,8	22	263,6	18	281,1	18	284,6	17	281,3	21	280,3	18	294,1	20	296,2	14

Race

Classification & Retirements

Pos.	Driver	Constructor	Tyres	Laps	Time	Average	
1.	F. Alonso	Renault	M	57	1:34:27.870	191,990 km/h	
2.	K. Räikkönen	McLaren Mercedes	M	57	+ 1.829	191,928 km/h	
3.	R. Schumacher	Toyota	B	57	+ 24.824	191,153 km/h	
4.	N. Heidfeld	BMW	M	57	+ 31.032	190,944 km/h	
5.	G. Fisichella	Renault	M	57	+ 38.421	190,697 km/h	
6.	J. Villeneuve	BMW	M	57	+ 49.554	190,326 km/h	
7.	R. Barrichello	Honda	M	57	+ 51.904	190,248 km/h	
8.	D. Coulthard	RBR Ferrari	M	57	+ 53.983	190,178 km/h	
9.	S. Speed	STR Cosworth	M	57	+ *1:18.817	189,357 km/h	*53.817+25.0 penalty ○
10.	J. Button	Honda	M	56	1 lap	190,379 km/h	Engine blows
11.	C. Albers	MF1 Toyota	B	56	1 lap	186,232 km/h	
12.	T. Sato	Aguri Honda	B	55	2 laps	182,713 km/h	
13.	Y. Ide	Aguri Honda	B	54	3 laps	179,648 km/h	

Driver	Constructor	Tyres	Laps	Reason
J. Montoya	McLaren Mercedes	M	46	Hit a kerb, the impact activated a default system which switched off the engine
T. Monteiro	MF1 Toyota	B	39	Mechanical failure
V. Liuzzi	STR Cosworth	M	37	Off into the wall
M. Schumacher	Ferrari	B	32	Clipping a kerb and ended up in the wall
M. Webber	Williams Cosworth	B	22	Transmission
C. Klien	RBR Ferrari	M	4	Off into the wall
J. Trulli	Toyota	B	0	Rear suspension broken after a clash with Coulthard
N. Rosberg	Williams Cosworth	B	0	Hit by Massa. Rear wing off and radiators too damaged
F. Massa	Ferrari	B	0	Collision with Klien and Rosberg

Fastest laps

	Driver	Time	Laps	Average
1.	K. Räikkönen	1:26.045	57	221,869 km/h
2.	F. Alonso	1:26.189	49	221,499 km/h
3.	M. Schumacher	1:27.180	27	218,981 km/h
4.	J. Montoya	1:27.464	45	218,270 km/h
5.	G. Fisichella	1:27.561	53	218,028 km/h
6.	R. Barrichello	1:27.690	32	217,707 km/h
7.	N. Heidfeld	1:27.700	49	217,683 km/h
8.	J. Button	1:27.799	17	217,437 km/h
9.	M. Webber	1:27.800	19	217,435 km/h
10.	R. Schumacher	1:27.810	45	217,410 km/h
11.	V. Liuzzi	1:27.988	25	216,970 km/h
12.	D. Coulthard	1:28.250	32	216,326 km/h
13.	J. Villeneuve	1:28.321	56	216,152 km/h
14.	S. Speed	1:28.367	26	216,039 km/h
15.	C. Albers	1:29.238	53	213,931 km/h
16.	T. Monteiro	1:29.687	31	212,860 km/h
17.	T. Sato	1:30.574	54	210,775 km/h
18.	Y. Ide	1:33.737	49	203,663 km/h
19.	C. Klien	1:41.351	4	188,363 km/h

Pit stops

	Driver	Laps	Duration	Stop	Total
1.	T. Monteiro	8	22.093	1	22.093
2.	J. Montoya	18	22.924	1	22.924
3.	J. Button	19	21.287	1	21.287
4.	R. Schumacher	19	20.878	1	20.878
5.	G. Fisichella	19	23.327	1	23.327
6.	F. Alonso	20	23.013	1	23.013
7.	K. Räikkönen	21	23.199	1	23.199
8.	Y. Ide	20	23.592	1	23.592
9.	C. Albers	22	22.226	1	22.226
10.	V. Liuzzi	23	22.449	1	22.449
11.	R. Schumacher	•23•	10.164	2	31.042
12.	T. Sato	23	22.059	1	22.059
13.	S. Speed	24	22.871	1	22.871
14.	Y. Ide	23	22.445	2	46.037
15.	N. Heidfeld	25	20.800	1	20.800
16.	M. Schumacher	25	21.260	1	21.260
17.	D. Coulthard	29	20.525	1	20.525
18.	R. Barrichello	30	19.667	1	19.667
19.	J. Villeneuve	33	22.901	1	22.901
20.	S. Speed	33	40.915	2	1:03.786
21.	T. Monteiro	33	37.932	2	1:00.025
22.	F. Alonso	34	20.934	2	43.947
23.	C. Albers	33	30.698	2	52.924
24.	K. Räikkönen	34	29.926	2	53.125
25.	J. Montoya	34	36.160	2	59.084
26.	N. Heidfeld	34	20.160	2	40.960
27.	T. Sato	33	22.983	2	45.042
28.	J. Button	34	21.479	2	42.766
29.	R. Schumacher	34	20.822	3	51.864
30.	V. Liuzzi	34	22.848	2	45.297
31.	G. Fisichella	34	19.612	2	42.939
32.	Y. Ide	33	40.486	3	1:26.523
33.	R. Barrichello	38	20.396	2	40.063
34.	D. Coulthard	38	19.899	2	40.424
35.	T. Sato	47	19.486	3	1:04.528

•• Drive-through penalty: R. Schumacher. Speeding in pit lane.

Race leader

Driver	Laps in the lead	Nbr of Laps
J. Button	1 > 3	3
F. Alonso	4 > 19	16
K. Räikkönen	20	1
M. Webber	21 > 22	2
F. Alonso	23 > 57	35

Driver	Nbr of Laps	Kilometers
F. Alonso	51	270,453 km
J. Button	3	15,909 km
M. Webber	2	10,606 km
K. Räikkönen	1	5,303 km

Gaps on the leader board

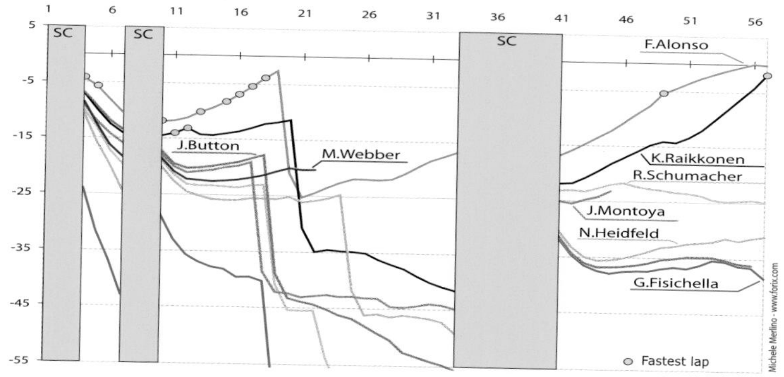

Lap chart

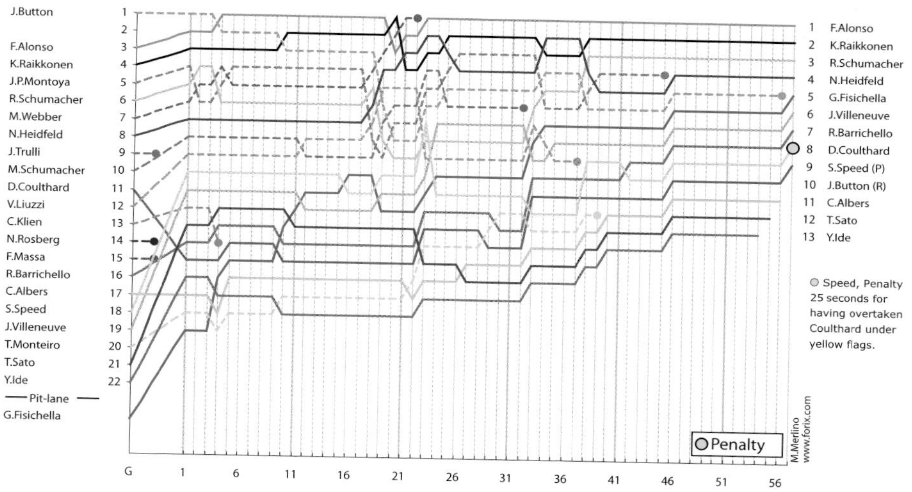

Championships 3/18

Drivers

1. F. Alonso ....Renault ....2 🏆....28
2. G. Fisichella..........Renault ....1 🏆....14
3. K. Räikkönen ....McLaren Mercedes.............14
4. M. Schumacher .....Ferrari 11
5. J. Button ....Honda 11
6. J. Montoya ....McLaren Mercedes...............9
7. R. Schumacher .....Toyota 7
8. N. Heidfeld ....BMW 5
9. J. Villeneuve ....BMW 5
10. F. Massa...............Ferrari 4
11. M. Webber............Williams Cosworth...............3
12. R. Barrichello........Honda 2
13. N. Rosberg ....Williams Cosworth...............2
14. D. Coulthard ....RBR Ferrari 1
15. C. Klien.................RBR Ferrari 1
16. S. Speed ....STR Cosworth......................0
17. J. Trulli.................Toyota 0
18. V. Liuzzi ....STR Cosworth......................0
19. C. Albers ....MF1 Toyota 0
20. T. Sato.................Aguri Honda 0
21. T. Monteiro ....MF1 Toyota 0
22. Y. Ide...................Aguri Honda 0

Constructors

1. Mild Seven Renault F1 Team ....3 🏆....42
2. Team McLaren Mercedes 23
3. Scuderia Ferrari Marlboro 15
4. Lucky Strike Honda Racing F1 Team 13
5. BMW Sauber F1 Team..............................10
6. Panasonic Toyota Racing 7
7. Williams F1 Team.....................................5
8. Red Bull Racing 2
9. Scuderia Toro Rosso.................................0
10. MF1 Racing 0
11. Super Aguri Formula 1..............................0

The circuit

Name	Albert Park Grand Prix Circuit; Melbourne	Weather	overcast
Lenght	5303 m	Air temperature	16-19°c
Distance	58 laps, 57 cover for 302,271 km	Track temperature	22-25°c
Date	April 2, 2006	Humidity	50%
		Wind speed	0.9 m/s

S1: 147m before corner
S2: 143m before corner
Radar: 123m before corner

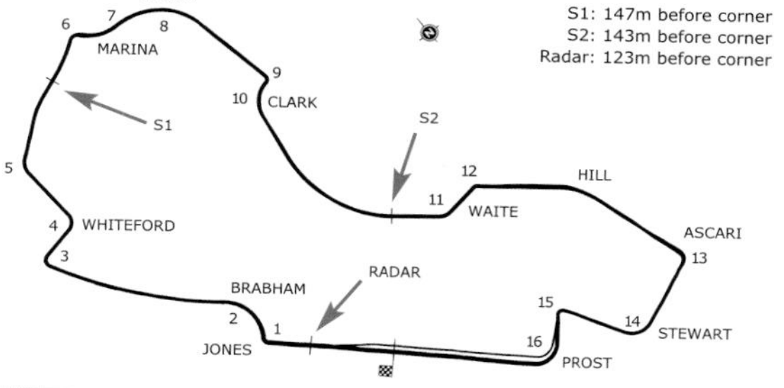

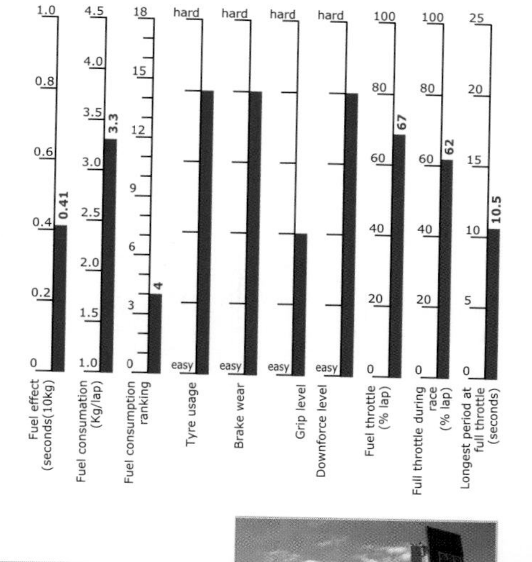

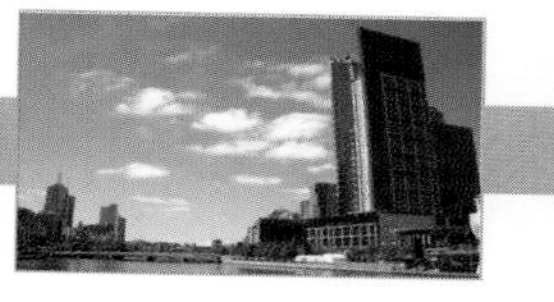

FERRARI PULLS THE WOOL OVER RENAULT'S EYES!

What a crafty trick! Michael Schumacher was much slower than Fernando Alonso in the race but he managed to stay in front of the Spaniard during the refuelling stops thanks to a cunning ploy by Ross Brawn, the Scuderia's technical director.

It worked perfectly. Renault fell into the trap and called Alonso in first losing the race, as all he had to do was to wait for Michael to come in for fuel and then stroll on to victory.

Michael Schumacher's pole, a blessing for Imola!

"I don't like the new qualifying system. It's too confused. In the car you don't know what's going on." Jacques Villeneuve said out loud what several drivers were thinking. *"You just keep on lapping and you don't go for an outright performance. Maybe it's more exciting for the spectators but for us it's a mess."*

> A little off for Felipe Massa who qualified fourth at Imola while his team-mate snatched pole.

And he was right. This year the staring grid was decided by three sessions the last of which was the pole shoot-out. It lasted 20 minutes and focalised everybody's attention.

The cars were then locked up in the parc fermé and the amount of fuel they were carrying depended on the morrow's strategy. Like in 2005, the grid did not necessarily reflect the true potential of each one. At Imola Ferrari took advantage of the possibilities offered by the system. Here on what is almost home territory it is traditional to see the red cars well placed to pull in the Tifosi for the race. So any ploy was good enough to achieve this. The Ferraris probably qualified with an almost-empty tank and they could be expected to refuel early on in the race – around lap 15 – which corresponded to the amount of fuel put into their tanks on Sunday morning. Michael Schumacher denied any form of skulduggery. *"I haven't stopped repeating that we're on the ball this weekend. And we've proved it,"* he said. *"Our car has made a big leap forward since Australia."*

Thanks to a similar strategy the 2 Hondas of Jenson Button and Rubens Barrichello had also jumped up to the front of the grid. They were well ahead of the McLarens and Renaults. *"It's thought-provoking,"* admitted the Englishman, *"they must be stopping very late or else they've made a mistake."*

Thus the key to the outcome of the San Marino Grand Prix was in the bottom of the Renault's and McLaren's fuel tanks. They were full which explained their drivers' poor showing in qualifying but augured well for the race.
As Jacques Villeneuve said with the new qualifying format nobody really knew what was going on.

Jacques Villeneuve: just the wrong side of the stop watch

Jacques Villeneuve really believed that his moment had come on Saturday afternoon. He was going to score points, soon rack up a win and he was convinced of the potential of the BMW F1 06. Since the start of the Imola weekend he kept on repeating to all and sundry that rostrum finishes were well within his grasp this season. While he did not say so out loud he was hoping to achieve this feat in the San Marino Grand Prix.
But he looked like he'd missed the boat. He had already explained that he did not like the new system

> Nico Rosberg ended up 13th on the grid. The German made a couple of mistakes in qualifying.

> On Friday, Anthony Davidson covered 58 laps before being stopped by a fire. Nonetheless he set the fourth quickest time.

and what happened on Saturday was not destined to make him change his mind. While he got though the first part of qualifying without problems he was eliminated in he second by 128/1000s! A wink of an eye. "I'm really very, very disappointed," he groaned. "A bloody tenth of a second, do you realise? It's nothing. Of course everybody always says that. But when it's so close it's difficult to accept. I'm just on the wrong side of the tenth!"
The results of the second session could not have been tighter. Had Villeneuve progressed by 2/10s he would have been fifth, 3/10ths and he was third behind Michael Schumacher and Raïkkönen. While "ifs" do not win grands prix the man from Quebec's disappointment was understandable. "Especially as the car was quick enough to do it," he continued. "I went out with enough fuel for 2 laps but I was delayed by yellow flags on my second flying lap. Everything becomes critical at this stage. Had I a lap less in the tank it would've given me that tenth that was missing. Thus, I'd have been in the first ten and I could've gone for fourth or fifth place on the grid, good enough for a rostrum finish. That tenth had an enormous effect."
Nick Heidfeld did not make it onto the top ten either. He went straight on in the Ravazza double left-hander and ended up 15th on the grid with the time he set on the previous lap. This counter performance at least gave both drivers free reign to choose their strategy as only the first ten went into parc fermé. Jacques was still dreaming about the points he was going to score, his victory and so on.

Starting grid

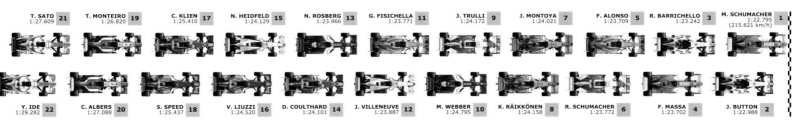

Pos	Driver	Time	Pos	Driver	Time
21	T. SATO	1:27.609	22	Y. IDE	1:29.282
19	T. MONTEIRO	1:26.820	20	C. ALBERS	1:27.088
17	C. KLIEN	1:25.410	18	S. SPEED	1:25.437
15	N. HEIDFELD	1:24.129	16	V. LIUZZI	1:24.520
13	N. ROSBERG	1:23.966	14	D. COULTHARD	1:24.101
11	G. FISICHELLA	1:23.771	12	J. VILLENEUVE	1:23.887
9	J. TRULLI	1:24.172	10	M. WEBBER	1:24.795
7	J. MONTOYA	1:24.021	8	K. RÄIKKÖNEN	1:24.158
5	F. ALONSO	1:23.709	6	R. SCHUMACHER	1:23.772
3	R. BARRICHELLO	1:23.242	4	F. MASSA	1:23.702
1	M. SCHUMACHER	1:22.795 (215.621 km/h)	2	J. BUTTON	1:22.988

Ferrari pulls the wool over Renault's eyes!

Michael Schumacher was not the quickest drive on the track, but he still won at Imola. This was thanks to several factors: a strategy that tripped up Renault, a circuit on which overtaking is impossible and a fault-free drive by the German. It was the Scuderia's first victory since Indianapolis in 2005.

Lap 35: Things were not going well in the cockpit of the no.5 Ferrari. The car's road holding had deteriorated and Michael's lead had gone from 11 seconds to zero in a few laps. The air temperature was 29°, a lot hotter than forecast, and the tyres were graining. There was nothing he could do except wait to change them. The problem was that Fernando Alonso, now stuck to the Ferrari's gearbox, was a full second quicker. All he was waiting for was Michael's refuelling stop and he could then waltz off into the distance. Ross Brawn,

the Ferrari strategist, decided to try and pull the wool over Renault's eyes. He asked the German to do reduce his speed by around a second a lap. Imola is the only place where such a gamble is feasible as overtaking is impossible.

On the pit wall Flavio Briatore and Pat Symonds, the two Renault brains, fell into the trap. They reckoned that Fernando Alonso could lap 2 seconds quicker if he were not stuck behind Schumacher who, they thought, had problems. So they brought in the Spaniard on lap 41 to give him a clear track.

That was exactly what Ross Brawn was waiting for. He told Michael to go flat out before coming in for fuel next time round. He did so and rejoined in front. "*If Renault hadn't acted as we'd hoped I don't know how the race would've ended,*" admitted Ross with a smile on his lips, as he'd just

put one over on his rival. If Michael had to refuel first the Renault would certainly have gone into the lead.

But it wasn't the kind of stroke that Ferrari could pull every Sunday. Contrary to appearances the team's victory at Imola did not mean that the Scuderia was back on the championship-winning trail. The San Marino victory could have been a one-off.

That's what Fernando Alonso felt: "*I'm not sure that Michael's my toughest rival this season,*" he analysed. "*I fear McLaren more or even Giancarlo. Last year we saw that the Ferraris were quicker here than anywhere else.*"

Two weeks later the Nürburging followed by Barcelona would give a clearer picture. It was not certain that the red cars would shine as brightly there as at Imola.

∧
Fernando Alonso was the quickest driver on the track but he was unable to find the flaw in Michael Schumacher's armour. He lost the race in qualifying in which he finished fifth.

Alonso stuck to Schumacher's gearbox sums up the San Marino Grand Prix. The German's win was celebrated on the rostrum. And how!
∨<

"*We're back in contention,*" Jean Todt

Jean Todt swept away all the doubts expressed about the competitiveness of the Ferraris at Imola by his rivals. The Frenchman firmly believed that

the Scuderia would be battling for the title. "*It's wrong to say that we always go particularly well at Imola. We had engine problems in Malaysia and our tyre choice in Australia didn't work out, as the rubber was too hard for the cool conditions. Today they were a little too soft for the heat. It's pretty difficult to forecast the weather and to choose the right rubber.*" Jean reckoned that the race was lost when he saw Alonso close the gap to Schumacher. "*I thought Fernando was going to overtake Michael during the second round of refuelling stops. When I saw Renault stopping him I knew we were in with a chance. They made a mistake but, you know, when you're on the pit wall you're really under pressure. Sometimes you take the right decisions, and sometimes you get it wrong.*"

<
The race is just about to start and Jenson Button is on the front row for the third race on the trot.

The Flying Dutchman: 2006 version!

Christijan Albers had a narrow escape. On the first lap he was punted into a barrel roll by Yuji Ide. He was unhurt: "the Super Aguri drivers are too aggressive," he complained. "They take too many risk and look what happens." The FIA reacted immediately and withdrew Ide's super licence.

Formula 1 and delusions of grandeur!

Economic crisis? You must be joking! If the rise in oil prices gave the stock markets the shivers and

^
The new Red Bull Motor Home did not stand out because of its discretion. It was 31 metres long with three floors and it took 25 trailers to transport it. It was both mind-boggling and outlandish at the same time! (Above, the first assembly a week before the San Marino Grand Prix; below; the second floor with bars and living spaces). .

frightened off investors, the little world of Formula 1 seems to live in a paradise where resources are unlimited.

After three overseas grands prix Formula 1 was back on European soil where it could use the traditional motor homes, these increasingly luxurious travelling offices and restaurants. Long gone are the camping cars of the 80s as in F1 competition is not limited to the track alone. Behind the scenes the team are on a race of Brobdingingian proportions in keeping with the over-inflated egos of their bosses.

This year the winner was Red Bull. Who else? Since the company absorbed Minardi it now had the space in the paddock generally allotted to two teams. It took advantage of this to design a building that can be dismantled called the Energy Station. It is 31 metres long, 14 wide and has three floors.

This steel and glass monster requires 50 people to put it up in three days and 25 trailers to move it from circuit to circuit. "*It has to said that our motor home is a bit like the Great Wall of China. The astronauts can see it from outer space,*" joked Christian Horner, the team boss.

Everybody could take advantage of this 'amusement park' because unlike Williams or McLaren for example, Red Bull welcomed anybody who passed by with open arms. To do this 8 chefs and 15 waiters beavered away in the kitchens to serve up to 500 people at the same time!

Any excuse for a party is good enough for Red Bull. To celebrate the beginning of the European season the second floor was turned into a discotheque while a competition between engineers from all the teams was held on a huge Scalectrix circuit. The rise in petrol prices obviously had no effect on the sales on energy drinks!

Weekend chatter

> When Ferrari is home ground Luca di Montezemola, the feisty Ferrari president, usually holds a little press conference on Sunday morning. In the end he got fed up with it, as there were so many questions about singing Kimi Raïkkönen and the arrival of Valentino Rossi. "*We need a little touch of the romantic in F1,*" he said as he finished the conference. "*We'll have two new drivers in 2007, Jean Alesi and Gerhard Berger. Michael's going to set up his own team and Felipe is off to Renault to replace the two current drivers. That way they'll save money!*"

> Jacques Villeneuve lost 15 seconds during his first refuelling stop: two wheel bolts jammed and slowed down the tyre changes. It dropped the Canadian from 7th to 13th place.

> This time it was all done and dusted. The five major manufacturers make up the GPDA (Grand Prix Manufacturers' Association) were about to sign an agreement with Bernie Ecclestone (the F1 commercial rights holder) rather than set up a parallel championship as they had threatened to do for the past 3 years. "*What Bernie's offering suits me,*" grinned Flavio Briatore in the name of Renault. "*I'm going to sign, but I've left my pen at home!*" Bernie was playing the doubting game: "*Even if someone tells me he's paid a bill I don't believe it till I see the money in the bank!*"

> The Maserati dealers in Strasbourg gave the four Red Bull drivers a Maserati Gransport each. David Coulthard chose silver, Christian Klien black, Vitantonio Liuzzi dark blue and Scott Speed bright red.

Prodrive chosen as the 12th team

The decision was taken without any warning. At the start of the year the FIA announced that those teams wanting to take part in the 2008 F1 World Championship had to send in their entry between 24th and 31st March. It was a very narrow window and its aim was to force the hand of the people who still wanted to set up a pirate series.

No fewer than 22 teams sent in entries. The procedure was very open as the form was available on the FIA Internet site. Which led to a few doubtful dossiers!

As all 11 teams currently entered in the championship sent in their forms and 12 is the maximum number allowed there would be only one lucky candidate. This limit was set to avoid too much traffic on the track as well as taking into account the size of modern paddocks calculated to house 12 F1 teams. Max Mosley, the FIA President, who attended the Imola race, stated that it was very unlikely that the regulations would change in the future to increase this number.

The success of this phase of the entry procedure was due above all to the 2008 regulations. Although they had not yet been published they made provision for people to enter chassis built by other teams, something that has been forbidden up to the present and is very difficult to control. Combined with measures destined to limit the use of electronics this should enable teams to reduce their annual budget to around 100 million euros (as against four times that amount at present for the richest outfits).

After a fax vote by the FIA members the governing body decided to accept Prodrive's candidature as the 12th team to be allowed in in 2008. "Prodrive sent in the best dossier in terms of its financial soundness and its experience in motor sport. We know this team very well because of its involvement in the Rally World Championship," stated Max Mosley. "The fact that its boss has already run an F1 team was an additional card in its favour."

>
Juan Pablo Montoya in maximum attack mode. He was seventh on the grid and finished third.

Practice

All the time trials

Nº Pilote	Nat.	Nº Chassis - Engine [Nbr GP]	Pos. Free 1 Friday	Laps	Pos. Free 2 Friday	Laps	Pos. Free 3 Saturday	Laps	Pos. Q1 Saturday	Laps	Pos. Q2 Saturday	Laps	Pos. Super Pole Saturday	Laps
1. Fernando Alonso	E	Renault R26 02 [2]	19.	3	1. 1:25.043	15	2. 1:24.068	15	1. 1:23.536	3	7. 1:23.743	3	5. **1:23.709**	15
2. Giancarlo Fisichella	I	Renault R26 04 [1]	21.	2	6. 1:25.991	15	3. 1:24.377	21	4. 1:24.434	3	11. **1:23.771**	3		
3. Kimi Räikkönen	FIN	McLaren MP4-21 02 - Mercedes [2]	9. 1:26.938	5	12. 1:26.500	16	5. 1:24.626	12	2. 1:24.259	3	2. 1:23.190	3	8. **1:24.158**	15
4. Juan Pablo Montoya	CO	McLaren MP4-21 05 - Mercedes [2]	22.	1	9. 1:26.334	15	22.	1	13. 1:24.960	3	10. 1:23.760	6	7. **1:24.021**	15
5. Michael Schumacher	D	Ferrari 248 F1 254 [1]	1. 1:24.751	4	2. 1:25.371	13	1. 1:23.787	14	8. 1:24.598	5	1. 1:22.579	3	1. **1:22.795**	14
6. Felipe Massa	BR	Ferrari 248 F1 250 [1]	7. 1:26.596	4	5. 1:25.879	16	4. 1:24.383	17	12. 1:24.884	5	4. 1:23.595	3	4. **1:23.702**	14
7. Ralf Schumacher	D	Toyota TF106/05 [1]	20.	1	22. 1:27.639	5	6. 1:24.667	21	3. 1:24.370	6	3. 1:23.565	6	6. **1:23.772**	14
8. Jarno Trulli	I	Toyota TF106/04 [2]	5. 1:26.417	7	7. 1:26.029	24	17. 1:25.806	15	5. 1:24.446	7	6. 1:23.727	6	9. **1:24.172**	14
9. Mark Webber	AUS	Williams FW28 05 - Cosworth [1]			19. 1:27.157	6	12. 1:25.205	14	14. 1:24.992	4	5. 1:23.718	3	10. **1:24.795**	14
10. Nico Rosberg	D	Williams FW28 06 & 04 - Cosworth [1]			17. 1:26.989	10	19. 1:27.019	11	7. 1:24.495	6	13. **1:23.966**	3		
11. Rubens Barrichello	BR	Honda RA106-01 [1]	25.	1	13. 1:26.653	19	11. 1:25.041	20	9. 1:24.727	3	9. 1:23.760	3	3. **1:23.242**	14
12. Jenson Button	GB	Honda RA106-04 [1]			11. 1:26.427	12	7. 1:24.850	23	6. 1:24.480	3	8. 1:23.749	3	2. **1:22.988**	14
14. David Coulthard	GB	Red Bull RB2 3 - Ferrari [1]	8. 1:26.678	7	20. 1:27.503	12	13. 1:25.575	15	10. 1:24.849	6	14. **1:24.101**	6		
15. Christian Klien	A	Red Bull RB2 2 - Ferrari [1]	13. 1:29.106	6	24. 1:27.990	12	9. 1:24.984	13	17. **1:25.410**	6				
16. Nick Heidfeld	D	BMW Sauber F1.06-03 [2]	23.	1	10. 1:26.387	7	15. 1:25.701	9	16. 1:25.410	3	15. **1:24.129**	7		
17. Jacques Villeneuve	CDN	BMW Sauber F1.06-02 [2]	24.	1	15. 1:26.797	13	8. 1:24.916	13	15. 1:25.081	3	12. **1:23.887**	6		
18. Tiago Monteiro	P	Midland M16-03 - Toyota [2]	15. 1:29.697	13	21. 1:27.544	20	18. 1:26.476	18	19. **1:26.820**	6				
19. Christijan Albers	NL	Midland M16-02 - Toyota [2]	10. 1:28.048	13	14. 1:26.783	24	16. 1:25.803	22	20. **1:27.088**	6				
20. Vitantonio Liuzzi	I	Toro Rosso STR01 03 - Cosworth [1]	16. 1:30.348	6	18. 1:27.128	24	10. 1:24.994	15	11. 1:24.879	8	16. **1:24.520**	8		
21. Scott Speed	USA	Toro Rosso STR01 02 - Cosworth [2]	11. 1:28.498	6	23. 1:27.719	25	14. 1:25.662	19	18. **1:25.437**	8				
22. Takuma Sato	J	Super Aguri SA05-02 - Honda [2]	17. 1:31.217	17	27. 1:29.870	23	20. 1:28.267	18	21. **1:27.609**	6				
23. Yuji Ide	J	Super Aguri SA05-03 - Honda [2]	18. 1:31.482	17	28. 1:31.042	20	21. 1:29.330	20	22. **1:29.282**	8				
35. Alexander Wurz	A	Williams FW28 04 - Cosworth	2. 1:25.132	19	8. 1:26.328	31								
36. Anthony Davidson	GB	Honda RA106-03	4. 1:26.012	27	4. 1:25.699	31								
37. Robert Doornbos	NL	Red Bull RB2 1 - Ferrari	6. 1:26.498	18	16. 1:26.917	27								
38. Robert Kubica	PL	BMW Sauber F1.06-04	3. 1:25.942	24	3. 1:25.421	31								
39. Giorgio Mondini	CH	Midland M16-04 - Toyota	12. 1:28.969	20	26. 1:28.833	27								
40. Neel Jani	CH	Toro Rosso STR01 01 - Cosworth	14. 1:29.695	13	25. 1:28.361	21								

Fastest lap overall
M. Schumacher 1:22.579 (216,185 km/h)

Maximum speed

Nº Driver	S1 Qualifs	Pos.	S1 Race	Pos.	S2 Qualifs	Pos.	S2 Race	Pos.	Finish Qualifs	Pos.	Finish Race	Pos.	Radar Qualifs	Pos.	Radar Race	Pos.
1. F. Alonso	225,0	9	220,8	5	255,1	5	254,5	7	183,0	3	179,5	2	291,2	4	294,9	5
2. G. Fisichella	222,8	15	218,3	10	253,3	10	255,0	5	178,3	14	176,7	7	288,2	8	295,8	4
3. K. Räikkönen	224,9	10	219,4	6	254,7	6	255,5	4	180,1	10	172,7	15	287,0	11	294,5	6
4. J. Montoya	226,7	2	223,0	1	256,5	3	256,5	3	180,8	7	176,1	9	291,8	3	295,9	3
5. M. Schumacher	228,3	1	221,3	3	258,6	1	257,5	2	184,0	1	180,2	1	295,1	1	297,6	1
6. F. Massa	226,4	4	221,4	2	258,5	2	258,0	1	182,3	5	177,2	6	294,0	2	296,5	2
7. R. Schumacher	223,2	13	216,2	16	252,5	14	250,9	17	177,1	18	171,7	17	286,8	12	289,8	11
8. J. Trulli	223,4	12	211,6	20	251,4	17	250,1	19	180,7	8	172,5	16	284,8	16	289,1	16
9. M. Webber	224,8	11	218,5	9	254,2	9	253,8	9	182,3	4	175,5	13	285,8	13	289,6	12
10. N. Rosberg	223,2	14	218,0	11	254,4	8	254,4	8	176,2	19	177,7	4	288,3	6	291,7	9
11. R. Barrichello	225,1	6	219,2	7	254,7	7	252,8	11	183,5	2	177,8	3	285,6	14	289,6	14
12. J. Button	226,6	3	220,9	4	253,2	11	252,9	10	181,9	6	176,7	8	283,3	18	288,1	18
14. D. Coulthard	225,1	7	215,3	17	253,1	13	250,8	18	180,2	9	175,7	11	288,1	10	287,6	19
15. C. Klien	219,2	18	216,8	15	251,3	18	252,2	13	178,5	13	175,5	12	282,4	20	289,6	15
16. N. Heidfeld	225,0	8	218,7	8	252,3	15	251,1	16	180,1	11	177,6	5	288,2	7	290,7	10
17. J. Villeneuve	225,9	5	217,3	14	255,2	4	252,6	12	179,6	12	175,8	10	290,3	5	289,0	17
18. T. Monteiro	211,5	21	213,8	18	247,3	21	248,1	21	173,8	21	170,8	20	280,1	22	282,6	21
19. C. Albers	214,2	20			246,7	22			176,1	20			280,5	21		
20. V. Liuzzi	220,8	16	217,3	13	253,1	12	254,6	6	177,8	15	174,7	14	288,1	9	293,3	7
21. S. Speed	220,0	17	217,9	12	250,0	20	251,6	14	177,5	17	171,4	19	283,2	19	289,6	13
22. T. Sato	216,3	19	212,0	19	251,9	16	251,6	15	177,8	16	171,6	18	284,4	17	291,9	8
23. Y. Ide	209,5	22	204,0	21	251,2	19	249,1	20	168,5	22	170,5	21	284,8	15	285,7	20

Race

Classification & Retirements

Pos.	Driver	Constructor	Tyres	Laps	Time	Average
1.	M. Schumacher	Ferrari	B	62	1:31:06.486	202,322 km/h
2.	F. Alonso	Renault	M	62	+ 2.096	202,245 km/h
3.	J. Montoya	McLaren Mercedes	M	62	+ 15.868	201,737 km/h
4.	F. Massa	Ferrari	B	62	+ 17.096	201,692 km/h
5.	K. Räikkönen	McLaren Mercedes	M	62	+ 17.524	201,676 km/h
6.	M. Webber	Williams Cosworth	B	62	+ 37.739	200,935 km/h
7.	J. Button	Honda	M	62	+ 39.635	200,866 km/h
8.	G. Fisichella	Renault	M	62	+ 40.200	200,845 km/h
9.	R. Schumacher	Toyota	B	62	+ 45.511	200,652 km/h
10.	R. Barrichello	Honda	M	62	+ 1:17.851	199,482 km/h
11.	N. Rosberg	Williams Cosworth	B	62	+ 1:19.675	199,416 km/h
12.	J. Villeneuve	BMW	M	62	+ 1:22.370	199,319 km/h
13.	N. Heidfeld	BMW	M	61	1 lap	198,761 km/h
14.	V. Liuzzi	STR Cosworth	M	61	1 lap	198,706 km/h
15.	S. Speed	STR Cosworth	M	61	1 lap	198,649 km/h
16.	T. Monteiro	MF1 Toyota	B	60	2 laps	193,736 km/h

Driver	Constructor	Tyres	Laps	Reason
D. Coulthard	RBR Ferrari	M	47	Drive shaft broken
T. Sato	Aguri Honda	B	44	Spin
C. Klien	RBR Ferrari	M	40	Hydraulic problem
Y. Ide	Aguri Honda	B	23	Rear suspension problem
J. Trulli	Toyota	B	5	Problem with his steering column
C. Albers	MF1 Toyota	B	0	Ide tips Christijan into a spectacular roll

Fastest laps

	Driver	Time	Laps	Average
1.	F. Alonso	1:24.569	23	211,098 km/h
2.	M. Schumacher	1:24.624	19	210,961 km/h
3.	K. Räikkönen	1:25.027	49	209,961 km/h
4.	J. Montoya	1:25.096	22	209,791 km/h
5.	R. Schumacher	1:25.316	45	209,250 km/h
6.	J. Button	1:25.347	29	209,174 km/h
7.	G. Fisichella	1:25.353	43	209,159 km/h
8.	J. Villeneuve	1:25.438	53	208,951 km/h
9.	M. Webber	1:25.488	39	208,829 km/h
10.	F. Massa	1:25.528	12	208,731 km/h
11.	V. Liuzzi	1:25.679	43	208,363 km/h
12.	N. Heidfeld	1:25.996	53	207,595 km/h
13.	R. Barrichello	1:26.129	12	207,275 km/h
14.	S. Speed	1:26.248	57	206,989 km/h
15.	N. Rosberg	1:26.418	30	206,581 km/h
16.	C. Klien	1:26.759	30	205,770 km/h
17.	D. Coulthard	1:26.855	41	205,542 km/h
18.	T. Monteiro	1:27.160	53	204,823 km/h
19.	J. Trulli	1:28.039	4	202,778 km/h
20.	T. Sato	1:29.100	40	200,363 km/h
21.	Y. Ide	1:31.032	15	196,111 km/h

Pit stops

	Driver	Laps	Duration	Stop	Total
1.	Y. Ide	1	1:19.951	1	1:19.951
2.	Y. Ide	2	11:55.326	2	13:15.277
3.	R. Barrichello	14	32.618	1	32.618
4.	J. Button	15	26.651	1	26.651
5.	R. Schumacher	16	23.342	1	23.342
6.	T. Monteiro	17	25.767	1	25.767
7.	F. Massa	19	25.381	1	25.381
8.	M. Schumacher	20	25.502	1	25.502
9.	K. Räikkönen	22	25.185	1	25.185
10.	J. Montoya	23	24.292	1	24.292
11.	M. Webber	23	24.469	1	24.469
12.	S. Speed	24	26.539	1	26.539
13.	F. Alonso	25	26.041	1	26.041
14.	T. Sato	24	26.350	1	26.350
15.	V. Liuzzi	25	25.272	1	25.272
16.	J. Villeneuve	27	41.869	1	41.869
17.	N. Rosberg	27	27.538	1	27.538
18.	D. Coulthard	27	24.743	1	24.743
19.	N. Heidfeld	28	25.749	1	25.749
20.	C. Klien	28	26.000	1	26.000
21.	G. Fisichella	29	23.905	1	23.905
22.	J. Button	30	38.792	2	1:05.443
23.	R. Schumacher	32	23.150	2	46.492
24.	R. Barrichello	34	26.958	2	59.576
25.	T. Monteiro	37	25.957	2	51.724
26.	F. Alonso	41	23.310	2	49.351
27.	F. Massa	41	24.531	2	49.912
28.	M. Schumacher	42	23.936	2	49.438
29.	M. Webber	42	25.456	2	49.925
30.	S. Speed	42	27.964	2	54.503
31.	J. Montoya	44	23.999	2	48.291
32.	T. Sato	42	25.322	2	51.672
33.	J. Button	44	24.110	3	1:29.553
34.	V. Liuzzi	44	25.228	2	50.500
35.	R. Schumacher	46	23.432	3	1:09.924
36.	D. Coulthard	46	25.055	2	49.798
37.	K. Räikkönen	47	22.918	2	48.103
38.	G. Fisichella	48	22.856	2	46.761
39.	N. Rosberg	48	24.163	2	51.701
40.	J. Villeneuve	48	25.103	2	1:06.972
41.	N. Heidfeld	51	23.759	2	49.508

Race leader

Driver	Laps in the lead	Nbr of Laps
M. Schumacher	1 > 20	20
F. Alonso	21 > 25	5
M. Schumacher	26 > 42	17
J. Montoya	43 > 44	2
M. Schumacher	45 > 62	18

Driver	Nbr of Laps	Kilometers
M. Schumacher	55	272,508 km
F. Alonso	5	24,795 km
J. Montoya	2	9,918 km

Gaps on the leader board

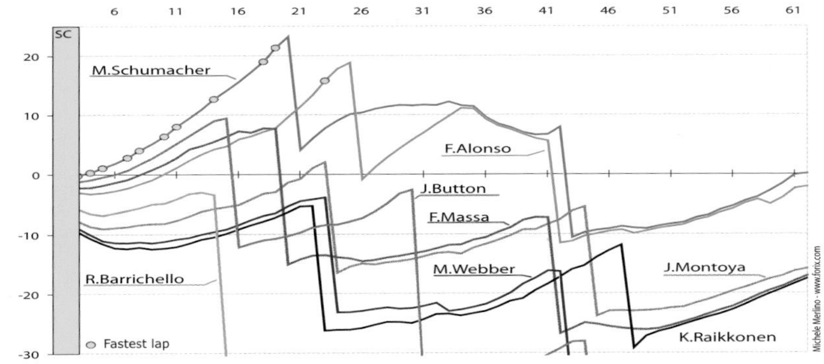

Lap chart

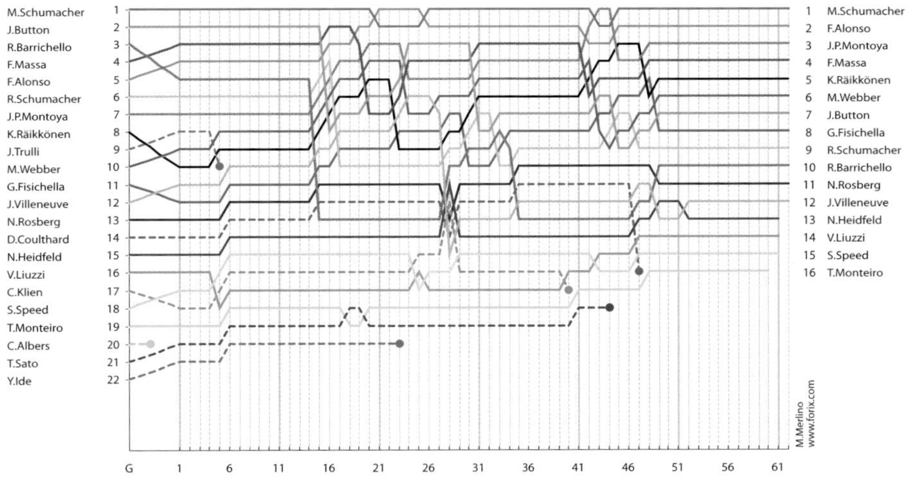

Championships 4/18

Drivers

1. F. Alonso ....Renault ....2 🏆....36
2. M. Schumacher .....Ferrari.....................1 🏆....21
3. K. Räikkönen ....McLaren Mercedes.............18
4. G. Fisichella..........Renault ....1 🏆....15
5. J. Montoya ....McLaren Mercedes.............15
6. J. Button ....Honda 13
7. F. Massa..............Ferrari 9
8. R. Schumacher .....Toyota 7
9. M. Webber............Williams Cosworth................6
10. N. Heidfeld ....BMW 5
11. J. Villeneuve ....BMW 5
12. R. Barrichello ....Honda 2
13. N. Rosberg ....Williams Cosworth................2
14. D. Coulthard ....RBR Ferrari 1
15. C. Klien................RBR Ferrari 1
16. S. Speed ....STR Cosworth.......................0
17. J. Trulli.................Toyota 0
18. V. Liuzzi ....STR Cosworth.......................0
19. C. Albers ....MF1 Toyota 0
20. T. Sato.................Aguri Honda 0
21. T. Monteiro ....MF1 Toyota 0
22. Y. Ide...................Aguri Honda 0

Constructors

1. Mild Seven Renault F1 Team ....3 🏆....51
2. Team McLaren Mercedes 33
3. Scuderia Ferrari Marlboro ....1 🏆....30
4. Lucky Strike Honda Racing F1 Team 15
5. BMW Sauber F1 Team.............................10
6. Williams F1 Team.....................................8
7. Panasonic Toyota Racing 7
8. Red Bull Racing 2
9. Scuderia Toro Rosso 0
10. MF1 Racing 0
11. Super Aguri Formula 1..............................0

The circuit

Name	Autodromo International 'Enzo e Dino Ferrari'; Imola	Weather	Sunny and warm
		Air temperature	26-29°c
Lenght	4959 m	Track temperature	43-33°c
Distance	62 laps, 307,221 km	Humidity	25-22%
Date	April 23, 2006	Wind speed	1.7 m/s

S1: 120m before corner
S2: 195m before corner
Radar: 170m before corner

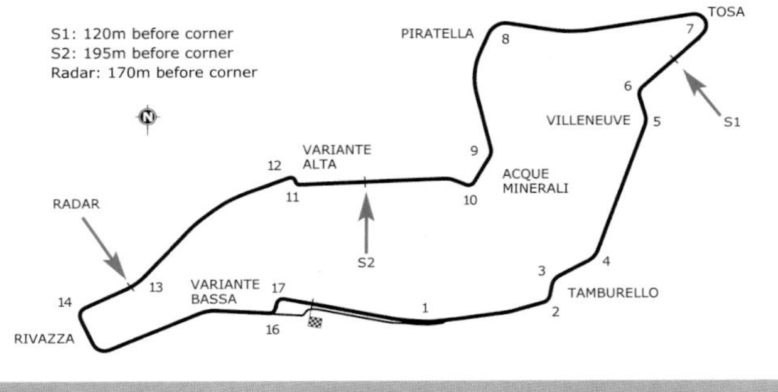

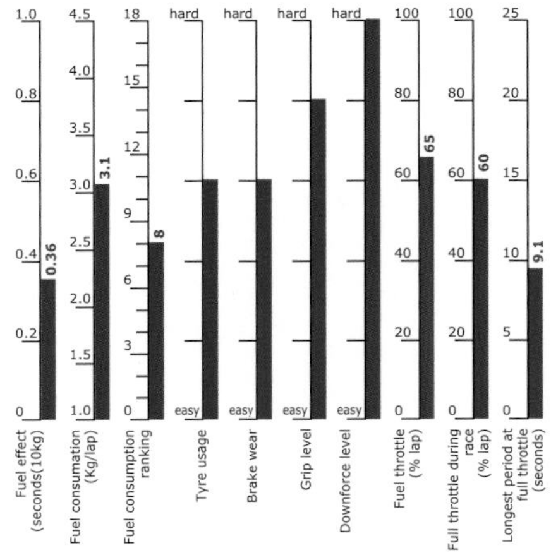

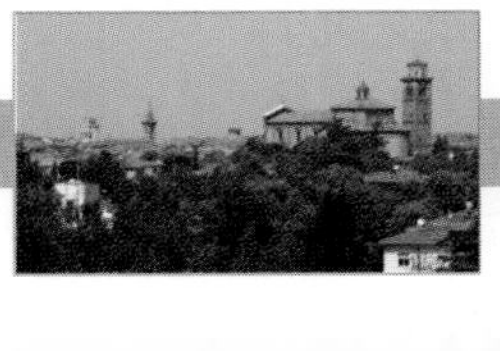

FERRARI BACK IN THE HUNT

The Nürburgring was the theatre of another no-holds-barred battle between Michael Schumacher and Fernando Alonso with the German coming out on top.
The F248 F1 was quicker than the Renault at the 'Ring and Felipe Massa took advantage of this to score his first rostrum finish.
In the world championship the gap between Schumacher and Alonso was down to 13 points and the Ferrari driver was back in the title hunt.

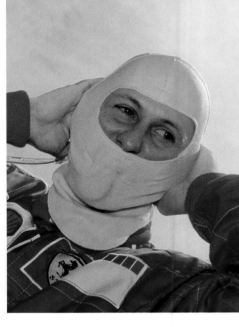

The Schumacher/Alonso duel back on again!

In Germany, Fernando Alonso was on pole for the first time in the 2006 season. His best place on the grid before that was third. As the temperature rose the whole Renault team expected to see him behind the Ferraris but the Spaniard was not giving up and made pole his own with bravura lap. *"So far we haven't had an easy weekend,"* admitted Fernando. *"The car's balance was not very good but we made a few last-minute adjustments and it worked fine in qualifying. This year I've always had problems during the third part of the timed session but not today. No traffic, no mistakes and that's the result!"*

Michael Schumacher, who was second on the grid, was as confident as his no.1 rival. His chances of victory looked pretty good because the Scuderia reckoned that it had found out why the cars were so slow during the San Marino Grand Prix. *"I'm persuaded that we'll be on top form,"* smiled the 7-times world champion. *"Now I think we'll be competitive whatever the type of circuit."* On Saturday morning during the final untimed session the German was over a second quicker than Alonso so pole looked on the cards. But the Spaniard snatched it by a few tenths. *"It doesn't really surprise me,"* said Michael. *"Fernando's been on the job all the time so it's not surprising that he's quick I ran into a little traffic during my two flying laps. In the race, we should be good. We know what we need to do to win."*

The fact that Felipe Massa was on the second row was an added help for the German. *"The perfect scenario would be for Felipe to hold up Alonso; we can always dream,"* laughed Michael. After Imola a race that Renault should never have lost, it looked like the Nürburgring would be the scene of a bitter battle between the 2 teams.

Jacques Villeneuve in the first ten before being penalised

On Friday it was better to give Jacques Villeneuve a wide berth. The Canadian was down in 24th place after a day in which everything that could go wrong did. *"I'm not at all happy,»* he snarled. *"I've got no grip. The car's sliding everywhere. It's a nightmare. I don't know whether the problem comes from the tyres, the settings or the suspension. Really a crap day."*

The subtlety (!) of this analysis enabled his engineers to find a solution to the problem. He gained 20 places and ended free practice in 4th spot and first of the Michelin runners. In qualifying he got into the last ten for the first time in 2006 and finished the pole shoot-out in eighth place.

15h30: With his driving suit still knotted around his hips Jacques Villeneuve planted a little kiss on his girl-friend's forehead before following Beat Zehnder, the BMW team manager. He was off to the stewards' room in the control tower for a bout of verbal fisticuffs with Giancarlo Fisichella the result of which would not be know for 6 hours. Overall, Villeneuve's qualifying session was a rather hectic one. A time-keeping breakdown interrupted the first 15 minutes and the red flag came out for a few seconds just when he was on the track. He was first of all among the six drivers eliminated but when the time keeping started to work again his time was re-instated. *"I know that this problem got everybody's knickers in a twist. But for me it's a non-event. I didn't see anything. My engineer told me over the radio that I was among the drivers who had qualified. End of story."*

Then came the second incident of the day in the second part of the session. According to Fisichella Villeneuve baulked him when the Canadian was rejoining the track. The furious Roman was eliminated from the pole shoot-out and told Jacques what he thought of him in no uncertain terms.

But even venting his spleen did not calm down the pugnacious Fisi! He was wound up like a clock. *"I didn't realise that I baulked him,"* said a surprised Villeneuve. *"If I did, it was not on purpose. There was plenty of room between us. But then Giancarlo arrived shouting 'one day you'll pay for that.' Unbelievable!"*

Race control too was a bit flummoxed by the incident and it took six hours to decide that the Canadian deserved to be penalised. At 21h00, after a long video session the stewards decided that the times set by the BMW driver in the third part of qualifying would be cancelled and he would start from 10th place. As Mark Webber was relegated because his Cosworth had to be changed Jacques finally lined up ninth on the grid. *"Baulking another driver is an infringement of article 116 b of the sporting regulations,"* droned the stewards adding that the Canadian could have acted unintentionally. He lost just one place and the sanction could have been much heavier. For Jacques it was still his best qualifying performance of the season so far. *"The race'll be another story,"* concluded Villeneuve. *"With my qualifying set-up it'll be very difficult. I'll have to fight."* This was nothing new for the man from Quebec!

Starting grid

Driver	Time	Pos
F. MONTAGNY	1:46.505	21
M. WEBBER*	1:33.405	19
S. SPEED	1:32.992	17
C. KLIEN	1:32.901	15
N. HEIDFELD	1:31.422	13
G. FISICHELLA	1:31.197	11
J. VILLENEUVE*	1:36.998	9
J. TRULLI	1:31.419	7
K. RÄIKKÖNEN	1:30.933	5
F. MASSA	1:30.407	3
F. ALONSO	1:29.819 (206.334 km/h)	1
N. ROSBERG*	1:31.194	22
T. SATO	1:35.239	20
T. MONTEIRO	1:33.658	18
C. ALBERS	1:32.936	16
V. LIUZZI	1:31.728	14
D. COULTHARD	1:31.227	12
R. SCHUMACHER	1:30.944	10
J. MONTOYA	1:31.880	8
J. BUTTON	1:30.940	6
R. BARRICHELLO	1:30.754	4
M. SCHUMACHER	1:30.028	2

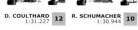

<
Michael Schumacher
receives the chequered
flag to win the European
Grand Prix from Fernando
Alonso. It was the second
time on the trot he had
beaten the Spaniard.

Scuderia Ferrari 2 - Renault 0

The circumstances were very different but the final outcome was the same: victory for Ferrari. At Imola Alonso was much quicker than Schumacher and the Maranello grand masters of strategy had to put in their thinking caps to help their driver win. They had much less difficulty in obtained the same result at the Nürburgring. In terms of sheer performance the 248 F1 was unbeatable on the Eifel circuit. No matter how the Renault team approached the problem it was unable to keep Fernando in front of his German rival as proved by Michael's fastest lap which 4/10ths quicker than the Spaniard's best. Felipe Massa's third place confirmed the superiority of the Ferrari/Bridgestone combination on the Nürburgring.

Such domination came as a surprise given that Fernando had set pole on Saturday. After the race the Spaniard was a bit baffled by the way things had turned out. "*Given the unfolding of the grand prix, I don't understand how I could've been so quick in Saturday qualifying. This weekend we were well off the Ferraris' pace.*"
Alonso shot into the lead and was still there after the first round of refuelling stops. But not after the second. "*We realised it was all over around lap 35,*" stated Denis Chevrier, the Renault chief engineer. "*Fernando needed a 2-second lead before coming in to be able to stay in front. He did everything he could but each time he upped the pace Michael did the same.*"
The Ferrari stopped 3 laps after the Renault.

The German banged in three very quick times before refuelling and emerged in front. It was all over bar the shouting.
"*The performances of the Ferraris and Renaults are very close this year,*" summed up Chevrier. "*We needed an extra tenth per lap to win. Multiply one tenth by twenty and you get the 2 seconds we wanted before stopping.*"
That represents around 3 litres of fuel in the tank: an extra lap before stopping, and shows the crucial importance of the strategy decided on Saturday when the amount of fuel on board for qualifying is calculated. Thus, the world championship that looked like Alonso's for the taking was now under threat from his German rival.

Jacques Villeneuve, victim of the 'Banana Republic'!

With the constructors' title hanging in the balance Renault had to be able to count on its two drivers. Everything was done so that Fisichella felt protected, backed up, cosseted. Two weeks earlier at Imola the Italian had been excluded from the pole shoot out as the French team had underestimated the speed of its rivals. At the Nürburgring the qualifying session had been meticulously planned so that this misadventure would not happen again. Durng the second part Fisichella had the right to a reconnaissance lap before putting on new tyres for a flyer. Unfortunately, the Italian found himself just behind Jacques Villeneuve who baulked him accidentally. A furious Fisi put all the blame on the

BMW driver for his not making it into the last ten. In order to support its own driver Renault lodged a protest.
It did not seem to have much chance of succeeding, as it is the very nature of qualifying to lead to the odd bit of pushing and shoving. This time Flavio Briatore pulled all his rabbits out of his hat to have Villenuve sanctioned. After trying to convince the German stewards, Flav phoned Max Mosley, the FIA President in London. His call

bore fruit and the BMW driver's times were cancelled.
"*We've got to show our support for Fisichella to make him believe that we back him 100%,*" whispered one of the Renault managers. "*But we're not going to shout it from the rooftops!*"
In other words the sanction was totally unjustified and decided for the psychological health of the Italian. Occasionally F1 looks like a Banana Republic!

<
Juan Pablo Montoya was
eighth on the grid and
retired with engine failure
when he was about to
score the point for eighth
place. "*I seemed to spend
all the race in traffic,*"
sighed the Colombian.

<<
Fernando Alonso was a bit
worried. He still had a
good lead in the
championship but the
Ferraris were becoming
more and more of a
threat

< Nick Heidfeld was dominated by his team-mate throughout the European Grand Prix. It was a very odd weekend for Villeneuve. He had his times cancelled on Saturday, finished in the points on Sunday and was then rubbished by his boss.

One point made no difference. Mario Thiessen had had his fill of Jacques Villeneuve

Mario Thiessen is no joker. He is German down to his fingertips and does not like having others' choices imposed on him. He is the BMW competitions boss and over the years he has managed to get rid of his enemies and persuade the Munich manufacturer to set up its own F1 team.

Mario has his own ideas about the way it should be run and the way its drivers should be selected. First of all, Nick Heidfeld, his young protégé, was exactly what he wanted. Then his choice fell upon Frenchman Sébastien Bourdais to add an international touch to his team. Mario did not want Villeneuve, his impertinence and his wild side. But despite all his attempts he was unable to get rid of the man from Quebec who had a watertight contract.

That Mario did not like. At the Nürburgring Jacques drove a great race and eclipsed his team-mate Heidfeld throughout the weekend. And Thiessen had to admit it even if getting him to compliment Villeneuve was like getting blood out of a stone! "*Jacques was very good this weekend,*" he grudgingly conceded. "*He did not make any big blunders; he wasn't too bad. Unfortunately, we were too slow and we also lost a place during refuelling. We're going to have to see what happened.*"

The Canadian started from 9th place on the grid and rarely had he driven such a hard-charging race. He refuelled twice, fought a merciless duel with his weekend "enemy," Fisichella, and scored a point for eighth place in a car that had no grip. "*It was bloody tough,*" he said afterwards. "*Fisichella was very close and with the car he had I thought that he'd pass me more easily. A good scrap!*" Not until the second round of refuelling stops did the Roman manage to get past the BMW.

In the championship the Canadian was in 11th place one point ahead of his team-mate. Was this enough to make Mario Thiessen think about giving him a drive in 2007. "*Not at all. It does nothing to make me take him into account,*" he replied curtly. "*It just persuades me to keep him on for the next grand prix.*" And with that comment Mario strode away. It took him another 2 months to get rid of the "Quebecois".

> It was Felipe Massa's first rostrum finish after 57 grands prix. "*Everything went off marvellously this weekend: we had good tyres and the car was perfect,*" he warbled afterwards.

At the very limits of human endurance

The sporting authorities keep modifying the regulations to slow down the cars while the engineers spend their lives trying to make them quicker. This cat and mouse game has been going on since the dawn of racing. This year the FIA decided to reduce cubic capacity and drop the power output by around 200 bhp hoping it would result in slower lap times. Parallel to this it also modified the tyre regulations by bringing back changes during the race, which enabled the manufacturers to use softer compounds. Thus, it soon became apparent that the FIA's changes had had the opposite effect to the one intended: the cars were quicker not slower! This had happened the previous weekend at Silverstone. "They're the best F1 cars I've ever driven," enthused Jacques Villeneuve. "They're very stable and their cornering speeds are mind-boggling. Sometimes I come into a corner and I say to myself 'my God, any quicker and I won't be able to cope!' In some bends my liver hurts and my eyes feel like they're being pushed into my head. A strange sensation..."

Practice

All the time trials

N° Driver	Nat.	N° Chassis - Engine [Nbr GP]	Pos.	Free 1 Friday	Laps	Pos.	Free 2 Friday	Laps	Pos.	Free 3 Saturday	Laps	Pos.	Q1 Saturday	Laps	Pos.	Q2 Saturday	Laps	Pos.	Super Pole Saturday	Laps
1. Fernando Alonso	E	Renault R26 02 [1]	17.		2	2.	1:33.579	14	6.	1:31.807	14	1.	1:31.138	3	3.	1:30.336	3	1.	**1:29.819**	14
2. Giancarlo Fisichella	I	Renault R26 04 [2]	18.		2	9.	1:34.030	19	5.	1:31.584	12	8.	1:31.754	3	13.	**1:31.197**	6			
3. Kimi Räikkönen	FIN	McLaren MP4-21 02 - Mercedes [1]	8.	1:34.402	5	13.	1:34.536	13	10.	1:32.320	11	3.	1:31.263	3	2.	1:30.203	3	5.	**1:30.933**	14
4. Juan Pablo Montoya	CO	McLaren MP4-21 05 - Mercedes [1]	20.		1	17.	1:34.968	14	17.	1:32.989	12	12.	1:31.774	3	5.	1:30.671	6	9.	**1:31.880**	13
5. Michael Schumacher	D	Ferrari 248 F1 254 [2]	4.	1:32.858	4	3.	1:33.619	14	1.	1:30.788	12	2.	1:31.235	3	1.	1:30.013	3	2.	**1:30.028**	13
6. Felipe Massa	BR	Ferrari 248 F1 250 [2]				14.	1:34.546	18	2.	1:31.093	10	14.	1:31.921	4	6.	1:30.732	4	3.	**1:30.407**	13
7. Ralf Schumacher	D	Toyota TF106/05 [2]	9.	1:34.995	6	6.	1:33.883	19	3.	1:31.395	21	6.	1:31.470	6	11.	**1:30.944**	7			
8. Jarno Trulli	I	Toyota TF106/04 [1]	19.		1	28.		5	18.	1:33.120	24	13.	1:31.809	6	7.	1:30.733	6	7.	**1:31.419**	14
9. Mark Webber	AUS	Williams FW28 04 - Cosworth [2->1]				16.	1:34.825	14	14.	1:32.711	16	10.	1:31.712	4	10.	1:30.892	3	10.	**1:33.405**	13
10. Nico Rosberg	D	Williams FW28 06 - Cosworth [2->1]				11.	1:34.215	19	11.	1:32.459	15	15.	1:32.053	4	12.	**1:31.194**	3			
11. Rubens Barrichello	BR	Honda RA106-01 [2]	7.	1:34.213	6	15.	1:34.631	11	13.	1:32.534	18	9.	1:31.671	4	4.	1:30.469	3	4.	**1:30.754**	13
12. Jenson Button	GB	Honda RA106-04 [2]	6.	1:33.635	7	7.	1:33.920	12	7.	1:32.104	16	4.	1:31.420	4	8.	1:30.755	6	6.	**1:30.940**	13
14. David Coulthard	GB	Red Bull RB2 3 - Ferrari [2]	22.		1	19.	1:35.241	14	16.	1:32.779	15	11.	1:31.742	7	14.	**1:31.227**	6			
15. Christian Klien	A	Red Bull RB2 2 - Ferrari [2]	21.		1	18.	1:35.066	19	8.	1:32.197	13	17.	**1:32.901**	7						
16. Nick Heidfeld	D	BMW Sauber F1.06-03 [1]				20.	1:35.308	12	15.	1:32.773	16	5.	1:31.457	3	15.	**1:31.422**	6			
17. Jacques Villeneuve	CDN	BMW Sauber F1.06-02 [1]				24.	1:35.688	12	4.	1:31.531	13	7.	1:31.545	3	9.	1:30.865	6	8.	**1:31.542**	13
18. Tiago Monteiro	P	Midland M16-03 - Toyota [1]	14.	1:36.062	10	25.	1:35.902	18	19.	1:33.744	19	20.	**1:33.658**	6						
19. Christijan Albers	NL	Midland M16-04 - Toyota [1]	13.	1:35.985	8	12.	1:34.472	23	20.	1:34.469	21	18.	**1:32.936**	5						
20. Vitantonio Liuzzi	I	Toro Rosso STR01 03 - Cosworth [2]	23.		2	21.	1:35.406	19	9.	1:32.290	17	16.	1:32.621	6	16.	**1:31.728**	6			
21. Scott Speed	USA	Toro Rosso STR01 02 - Cosworth [1]	12.	1:35.612	8	23.	1:35.669	21	12.	1:32.505	18	19.	**1:32.992**	7						
22. Takuma Sato	J	Super Aguri SA05-05 - Honda [1]	15.	1:37.817	20	26.	1:36.255	25	22.	1:36.082	15	21.	**1:35.239**	4						
23. Franck Montagny	F	Super Aguri SA05-02 - Honda [1]	16.	1:37.933	16	27.	1:36.665	16	21.	1:35.706	20	22.	**1:46.505**	4						
35. Alexander Wurz	A	Williams FW28 05 - Cosworth	1.	1:32.079	20	1.	1:32.675	27												
36. Anthony Davidson	GB	Honda RA106-03	2.	1:32.399	29	5.	1:33.870	29												
37. Robert Doornbos	NL	Red Bull RB2 1 - Ferrari	5.	1:32.944	19	4.	1:33.799	25												
38. Robert Kubica	PL	BMW Sauber F1.06-04	3.	1:32.852	22	8.	1:33.991	30												
39. Adrian Sutil	D	Midland M16-02 - Toyota	10.	1:35.332	21	10.	1:34.179	23												
40. Neel Jani	CH	Toro Rosso STR01 01 - Cosworth	11.	1:35.365	19	22.	1:35.479	26												

Fastest lap overall
F. Alonso 1:29.819 (206,334 km/h)

Maximum speed

N° Driver	S1 Qualifs	Pos.	S1 Race	Pos.	S2 Qualifs	Pos.	S2 Race	Pos.	Finish Qualifs	Pos.	Finish Race	Pos.	Radar Qualifs	Pos.	Radar Race	Pos.
1. F. Alonso	263,7	8	262,1	7	229,5	5	225,7	7	247,1	5	242,7	8	293,7	4	289,1	9
2. G. Fisichella	264,3	6	264,8	4	230,5	3	226,5	4	246,0	6	244,3	4	295,4	2	295,1	2
3. K. Räikkönen	267,4	3	266,6	1	232,4	1	228,3	1	248,8	2	245,5	2	289,3	6	295,3	1
4. J. Montoya	263,6	9	263,6	5	227,5	8	226,4	5	248,7	3	243,6	6	287,9	8	290,2	7
5. M. Schumacher	268,7	1	266,1	2	230,6	2	227,5	2	250,1	1	245,6	1	295,6	1	293,8	4
6. F. Massa	267,7	2	265,5	3	229,2	6	226,5	3	247,9	4	244,7	3	294,4	3	294,6	3
7. R. Schumacher	260,5	15	261,1	10	225,8	12	221,3	14	244,6	13	241,9	11	285,4	12	287,4	11
8. J. Trulli	264,4	5	259,5	15	225,0	14	221,3	13	243,9	15	239,8	15	287,0	9	285,5	14
9. M. Webber	259,8	16	258,9	17	225,9	11	219,6	16	244,9	11	238,6	17	285,7	11	284,8	15
10. N. Rosberg	261,8	11	262,1	8	223,9	17	222,9	10	242,1	18	241,8	12	287,0	10	292,4	5
11. R. Barrichello	262,7	10	260,1	13	229,8	4	226,2	6	245,7	7	243,9	5	285,2	13	284,1	16
12. J. Button	261,4	14	260,6	11	229,2	7	224,2	8	245,7	8	241,6	14	283,9	14	281,9	19
14. D. Coulthard	261,7	12	250,5	21	225,1	13	210,2	21	244,6	12			281,6	18	269,0	21
15. C. Klien	257,0	20	259,2	16	224,2	16	223,4	9	244,3	14	242,7	7	276,1	22	285,8	13
16. N. Heidfeld	263,8	7	261,3	9	226,8	10	222,8	11	245,5	10	242,3	9	292,2	5	290,3	6
17. J. Villeneuve	265,0	4	262,7	6	227,4	9	221,1	15	245,6	9	242,2	10	288,9	7	290,2	8
18. T. Monteiro	256,6	21	257,0	20	216,0	21	217,7	19	240,5	20	236,6	19	279,7	20	281,9	18
19. C. Albers	258,6	17	259,8	14	214,0	22	217,9	17	239,4	21	237,1	18	278,7	21	283,6	17
20. V. Liuzzi	258,5	19	154,5	22	224,5	15			242,5	16			280,3	19		
21. S. Speed	261,5	13	260,4	12	223,2	18	221,8	12	242,2	17	241,7	13	282,2	15	287,8	10
22. T. Sato	258,6	18	257,6	19	220,1	20	217,9	18	240,7	19	238,9	16	281,9	17	281,6	20
23. F. Montagny	255,7	22	257,6	18	221,4	19	214,6	20	238,5	22	236,2	20	281,9	16	286,9	12

Race

Classification & Retirements

Pos.	Driver	Constructor	Tyres	Laps	Time	Average
1.	M. Schumacher	Ferrari	B	60	1:35:58.765	193,080 km/h
2.	F. Alonso	Renault	M	60	+ 3.751	192,955 km/h
3.	F. Massa	Ferrari	B	60	+ 4.447	192,931 km/h
4.	K. Räikkönen	McLaren Mercedes	M	60	+ 4.879	192,917 km/h
5.	R. Barrichello	Honda	M	60	+ 1:12.586	190,677 km/h
6.	G. Fisichella	Renault	M	60	+ 1:14.116	190,627 km/h
7.	N. Rosberg	Williams Cosworth	B	60	+ 1:14.565	190,612 km/h
8.	J. Villeneuve	BMW	M	60	+ 1:29.364	190,130 km/h
9.	J. Trulli	Toyota	B	59	1 lap	189,789 km/h
10.	N. Heidfeld	BMW	M	59	1 lap	189,552 km/h
11.	S. Speed	STR Cosworth	M	59	1 lap	189,513 km/h
12.	T. Monteiro	MF1 Toyota	B	59	1 lap	187,025 km/h
13.	C. Albers	MF1 Toyota	B	59	1 lap	186,948 km/h

Driver	Constructor	Tyres	Laps	Reason
R. Schumacher	Toyota	B	52	Engine failure
J. Montoya	McLaren Mercedes	M	52	Engine failure
T. Sato	Aguri Honda	B	45	Hydraulic problem
F. Montagny	Aguri Honda	B	29	Hydraulic problem
J. Button	Honda	M	28	Engine failure
C. Klien	RBR Ferrari	M	28	Transmission/Gearbox problem
M. Webber	Williams Cosworth	B	12	Loss of hydraulic fluid
D. Coulthard	RBR Ferrari	M	2	Damaged car further to the collision between RSC-LIU
V. Liuzzi	STR Cosworth	M	0	1st corner: Hit by Ralf Schumacher, collision Coulthard, right rear tyre punctured, spin

Fastest laps

	Driver	Time	Laps	Average
1.	M. Schumacher	1:32.099	39	201,226 km/h
2.	K. Räikkönen	1:32.472	43	200,415 km/h
3.	F. Alonso	1:32.532	37	200,285 km/h
4.	G. Fisichella	1:32.964	46	199,354 km/h
5.	F. Massa	1:33.099	19	199,065 km/h
6.	J. Montoya	1:33.571	47	198,061 km/h
7.	N. Rosberg	1:33.579	48	198,044 km/h
8.	R. Schumacher	1:33.607	27	197,985 km/h
9.	R. Barrichello	1:33.952	59	197,258 km/h
10.	J. Trulli	1:33.953	58	197,256 km/h
11.	N. Heidfeld	1:34.035	47	197,084 km/h
12.	J. Villeneuve	1:34.037	38	197,079 km/h
13.	J. Button	1:34.042	9	197,069 km/h
14.	S. Speed	1:34.091	57	196,966 km/h
15.	C. Klien	1:34.553	16	196,004 km/h
16.	M. Webber	1:35.415	11	194,233 km/h
17.	C. Albers	1:35.428	35	194,207 km/h
18.	T. Monteiro	1:35.504	41	194,052 km/h
19.	T. Sato	1:36.706	26	191,640 km/h
20.	F. Montagny	1:37.214	21	190,639 km/h
21.	D. Coulthard	2:24.500	2	128,254 km/h

Pit stops

	Driver	Laps	Duration	Stop	Total
1.	D. Coulthard	1	39.531	1	39.531
2.	D. COulthard	2	39.601	2	1:19.132
3.	F. Alonso	17	24.330	1	24.330
4.	F. Massa	17	25.076	1	25.076
5.	M. Schumacher	18	24.781	1	24.781
6.	R. Barrichello	20	25.431	1	25.431
7.	J. Button	21	25.270	1	25.270
8.	J. Villeneuve	21	25.070	1	25.070
9.	C. Klien	21	24.301	1	24.301
10.	N. Heidfeld	22	24.623	1	24.623
11.	C. Albers	22	25.996	1	25.996
12.	K. Räikkönen	23	24.882	1	24.882
13.	F. Montagny	22	25.514	1	25.514
14.	S. Speed	23	25.866	1	25.866
15.	T. Monteiro	24	24.615	1	24.615
16.	T. Sato	24	24.213	1	24.213
17.	J. Trulli	25	23.624	1	23.624
18.	G. Fisichella	26	24.415	1	24.415
19.	J. Montoya	27	25.691	1	25.691
20.	R. Schumacher	28	23.261	1	23.261
21.	N. Rosberg	33	23.501	1	23.501
22.	F. Alonso	38	25.225	2	49.555
23.	F. Massa	40	24.185	2	49.261
24.	M. Schumacher	41	23.754	2	48.535
25.	C. Albers	41	24.766	2	50.762
26.	T. Sato	41	25.605	2	49.818
27.	T. Monteiro	42	25.123	2	49.738
28.	J. Trulli	43	23.755	2	47.379
29.	S. Speed	43	25.255	2	51.121
30.	K. Räikkönen	44	23.542	2	48.424
31.	R. Barrichello	44	23.129	2	48.560
32.	R. Schumacher	44	22.771	2	46.032
33.	J. Villeneuve	44	24.100	2	49.170
34.	G. Fisichella	44	23.098	2	47.513
35.	N. Heidfeld	45	23.546	2	48.169
36.	J. Montoya	48	24.857	2	50.548
37.	N. Rosberg	49	23.175	2	46.676

Race leader

Driver	Laps in the lead	Nbr of Laps
F. Alonso	1 > 16	16
M. Schumacher	17 > 18	2
K. Räikkönen	19 > 23	5
F. Alonso	24 > 37	14
M. Schumacher	38 > 41	4
K. Räikkönen	42 > 44	3
M. Schumacher	45 > 60	16

Driver	Nbr of Laps	Kilometers
F. Alonso	30	154,423 km
M. Schumacher	22	113,256 km
K. Räikkönen	8	41,184 km

Lap chart

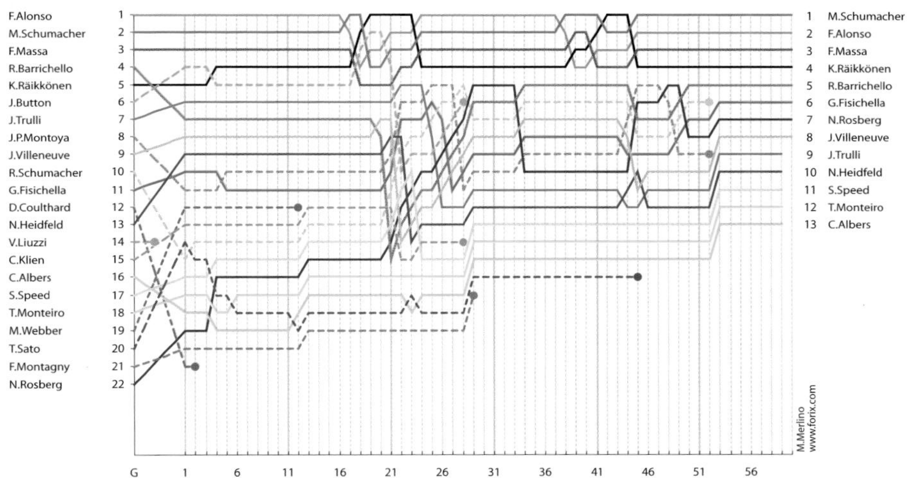

Gaps on the lead board

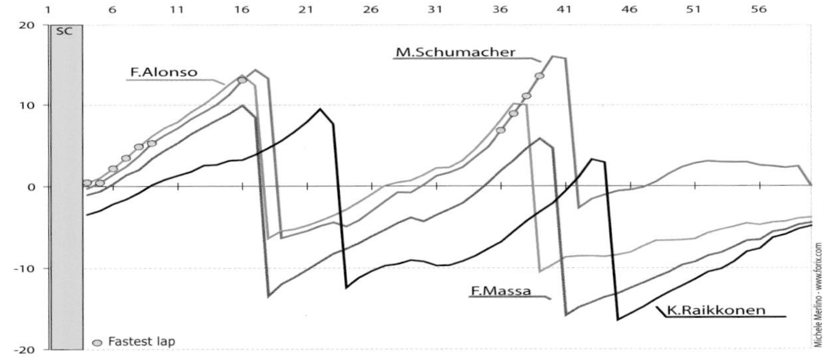

Championships 5/18

Drivers

1. F. Alonso ....Renault ....2 🏆....44
2. M. Schumacher .....Ferrari.....................2 🏆....31
3. K. Räikkönen ....McLaren Mercedes.............23
4. G. Fisichella..........Renault ....1 🏆....18
5. F. Massa..............Ferrari 15
6. J. Montoya ....McLaren Mercedes.............15
7. J. Button ....Honda 13
8. R. Schumacher .....Toyota 7
9. R. Barrichello........Honda 6
10. M. Webber...........Williams Cosworth................6
11. J. Villeneuve ....BMW 6
12. N. Heidfeld ....BMW 5
13. N. Rosberg ....Williams Cosworth................4
14. D. Coulthard.........RBR Ferrari 1
15. C. Klien...............RBR Ferrari 1
16. J. Trulli................Toyota 0
17. S. Speed ....STR Cosworth......................0
18. V. Liuzzi ....STR Cosworth......................0
19. C. Albers.............MF1 Toyota 0
20. T. Monteiro ....MF1 Toyota 0
21. T. Sato................Aguri Honda 0
22. Y. Ide..................Aguri Honda 0

F. Montagny.........Aguri Honda ....-

Constructors

1. Mild Seven Renault F1 Team ....3 🏆....62
2. Scuderia Ferrari Marlboro ....2 🏆....46
3. Team McLaren Mercedes 38
4. Lucky Strike Honda Racing F1 Team 19
5. BMW Sauber F1 Team.............................11
6. Williams F1 Team 10
7. Panasonic Toyota Racing 7
8. Red Bull Racing 2
9. Scuderia Toro Rosso 0
10. MF1 Racing 0
11. Super Aguri Formula 1.............................0

The circuit

Name	Nürburgring; Nürburg	Weather	Sunny and warm
Lenght	5148 m	Air temperature	19-21°c
Distance	60 laps, 308,863 km	Track temperature	34-40°c
Date	May 7, 2006	Humidity	32%
		Wind speed	2.2 m/s

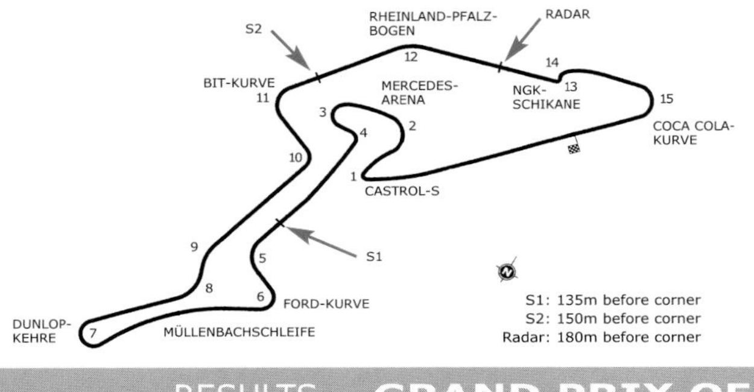

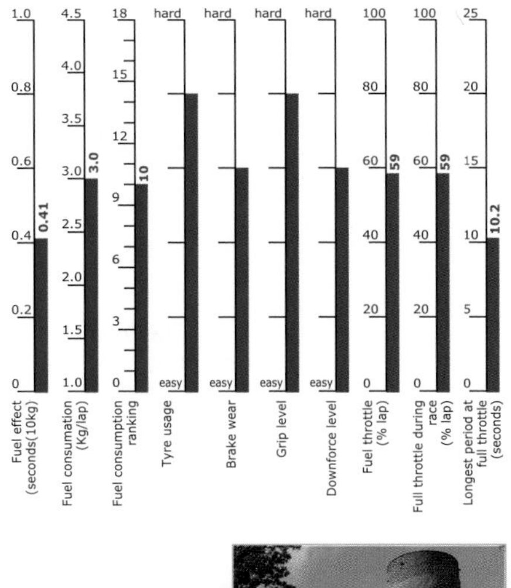

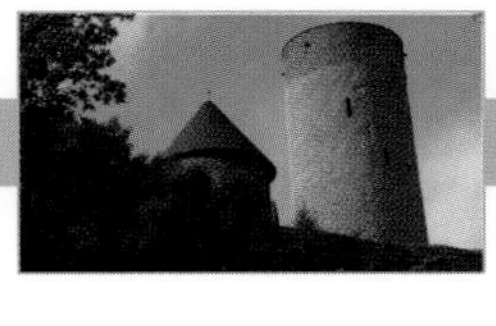

OLÉ FERNANDO !

What a triumph! Fernando Alonso grabbed pole on Saturday afternoon and then went on to win his home grand prix on the Barcelona circuit in front of 130,000 spectators who were all rooting for their hero. Michael Schumacher finished second but was never in a position to threaten the little Spaniard; he lost the two points he had pulled back the weekend before.

First blood to Renault

Fernando Alonso snapped on the Barcelona circuit on his way to his second pole of the season.

The performance differences between the Ferraris and Renaults were so minimal that the slightest little thing made a difference. The French cars locked out the front row on the Barcelona circuit, which seemed to strike a decisive blow, as passing is very difficult there. The glum faces in the Scuderia camp bore eloquent testimony to the size of the deception. The men from Maranello knew that Renault would do everything in its power to put its no.1 driver on pole in front of his home crowd. All he had to do was to qualify with a small amount of fuel in his tank. At the end of the session Fernando was 3/10s ahead of Schumacher, which represented some 10 kilos of fuel or around 4 laps in the race. Or at least that's what Ferrari thought. They were not too unhappy about this situation, as all Michael Schumacher had to do was to wait calmly for the Spaniard to stop before upping the pace and passing him in the pits. The spanner in the Scuderia's works was called

Friday: Robert Kubica flat out in the third BMW-Sauber.

Giancarlo Fisichella. For once the Italian filled his role of team-mate perfectly and joined Alonso on the front row. He was probably very light and was maybe going for a 3-stopper so his quick time in qualifying was down to a barely filled tank.
Ferrari feared that Fisi would hold up Schumacher. *"If Fisichella slows Michael and he loses around a second a lap to Alonso before refuelling, the race'll be lost,"* analysed one of the team's strategists. The only option to avoid this was for the German to barrel his way past Fisichella before the first corner. Which looked pretty difficult in relation to a light Renault that was also just about the quickest car off the grid.
Thus, the Spanish Grand Prix looked like turning into another tactical battle between Michael Schumacher and Fernando Alonso. This time, after their Imola and Nürburgring setbacks, the blue and yellow men were out to gain the upper hand.

Flashes

> Jacques Villeneuve lost 20 places on the Spanish Grand Prix grid. A transport problem between the Nürburgring and Barcelona led to the first engine replacement on Thursday, and on Saturday the BMW squad decided to change the man from Quebec's V8 a second time.

> As Michael Schumacher had decided to put off any announcement concerning his future till the end of the season Flavio Briatore had no choice but to offer Kimi Raïkkönen a golden shoe- in at Renault estimated at 143 million dollars for 3 years. The Finn declined the offer, as it seemed that he had already signed with Ferrari.

Starting grid

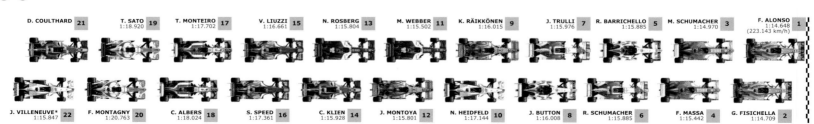

* J. VILLENEUVE penalty for an engine exchange (-10 pos.).

Position	Driver	Time
21	D. COULTHARD	1:18.920
19	T. SATO	1:17.702
17	T. MONTEIRO	1:16.661
15	V. LIUZZI	1:15.804
13	N. ROSBERG	1:15.502
11	M. WEBBER	1:16.015
9	K. RÄIKKÖNEN	1:15.976
7	J. TRULLI	1:15.885
5	R. BARRICHELLO	1:14.970
3	M. SCHUMACHER	1:14.648 (223.143 km/h)
1	F. ALONSO	
22	J. VILLENEUVE*	1:15.847
20	F. MONTAGNY	1:20.763
18	C. ALBERS	1:18.024
16	S. SPEED	1:17.361
14	C. KLIEN	1:15.928
12	J. MONTOYA	1:15.801
10	N. HEIDFELD	1:17.144
8	J. BUTTON	1:16.008
6	R. SCHUMACHER	1:15.885
4	F. MASSA	1:15.442
2	G. FISICHELLA	1:14.709

Renault back in front of Ferrari without knowing exactly why

This was not a bright red Sunday afternoon, rather a blue and yellow one. The previous weekend Schumacher's Ferrari had dominated in the Eifel but in Barcelona Fernando thrilled his home crowd with a telling victory. Only seven days had elapsed between the two races but once again the balance of power seemed to have swung in Renault's favour. The Ferrari strategists were hoping their drivers would pass the R26s during refuelling but they were quite simply uncatchable. At the start of the race Alonso opened up a gap of 12.8s before coming in to refuel and it was impossible for the reds to close it. "*We were very surprised by his pace,*" explained one of the Ferrari boffins. "*In practice, we were very close to the Renaults. But in the race they simply walked away and it's difficult to say why.*" In the opening laps Alonso was pulling away from Schumacher at over a second a lap. This was

due in part to the fact that the German had more fuel on board but also because the Renault was far quicker on the Barcelona circuit.
"*At the 'Ring we were beaten by a car that was faster,*" smiled Denis Chevrier. "*We could do nothing. Here it's the opposite. Maybe because of the nature of the track or because of the new Michelin tyres. I really don't know.*"
Flat-out Fernando had obviously helped. "*He was awesome at the start of the race,*" acknowledged Chevrier. "*In the same car he was pulling away from Fisichella at over half-a-second a lap which is enormous. He really wanted this win so much; he was on another planet. To lose would've been terrible for him.*"
In Spain Renault also showed flexibility in its strategy that was new for the French team. At the start neither driver knew whether he was on two or

three-stoppers. "*We took the decision, and it was the right one to stop twice after around 15 laps just before Fernando came in for the first time;*" Chevrier went on. "*We took into account the performance of the Ferraris, the tyre wear on our cars and their consumption. We just added some more juice to the refuelling rig.*"
The Scuderia won at the Nürburgring, Renault triumphed in Spain. It looked like victory could pass from one camp to the other for the tiniest of reasons at each race. "*The gap between Ferrari and ourselves is very small,*" smiled Denis. "*Maybe one or two tenths. It's nothing. Two tenths is the equivalent of a new engine spec like the ones we bring in several times each season. Don't be surprised if the advantage see-saws back and forth between Ferrari and Renault several times this year.*"

^
Fernando Alonso on the grid for the Spanish Grand Prix. Les than 2 hours later the Renault driver won his home race for the first time.

Before the grand prix Alonso did a lap of the circuit in the company of the King of Spain Juan Carlos in a Renault Megane. The "little Bull from the Asturias' with the King must have fired the emotions of all the spectators massed around the circuit.
v

Michael Schumacher blocks the transfer market

> ^
> 130,000 spectators were massed around the Barcelona with their eyes riveted on one driver Fernando Alonso. Who repaid their adulation in the best possible way.

Ferrari was playing with strategy with mastery unequalled in the history of F1.

On the track Michael Schumacher had just won two grands prix (Imola and the Nürburgring) thanks to the tactical genius of the Scuderia. On Thursday in the Barcelona paddock Ferrari decided to push its formidable tactical sense beyond the confines of racing itself. The German announced that he was putting off his decision about retirement (that he had promised to announce in mid-June) until the end of the season: "*I haven't made up my mind and I haven't the slightest idea about my future. At present I'm just concentrating on 2006. I can take the decision about stopping or not later on. Ferrari has told me that I can wait until the end of the season. So I'll decide then.*"

Although it seemed like a fairly harmless remark, it was of capital importance for the other teams as a large number of important decisions depended on Schumacher's. If he were to quit F1 his departure left a plum seat at Ferrari open – apparently promised to Kimi Raïkkönen. Were he to continue then the Finn could go to Renault or to yet another team sparking off a kind of domino series of transfers.

Ferrari too had to cope with the Valentino Rossi factor. Up till then the motorcycle champion let on that he had been offered a seat in the Scuderia for

2007. And that he would decide whether or not to accept it in June.

While his fans dreamed of seeing him on four wheels nobody really believed that he was serious. Many years of practice are necessary to get the best out of an F1 car. In fact, during the numerous days of testing for Ferrari he was well off the pace. So the Scuderia was trying to pull the wool over everybody's eyes by saying that it was waiting for

Messrs Schumacher's and Rossi's decisions. But nobody was fooled. A team of its stature could not take that kind of risk.

Michael's decision to put off his decision was a red herring that was part and parcel of the Scuderia's stategy. All the crucial choices had obviously already been made. By hiding the reality Ferrari effectively blocked the transfer market and gave several team bosses a few sleepless nights.

The GPMA is dead. Bernie's won again

It was the end of a long saga. It was also a relief after several years of disagreement during which the major manufacturers involved in Formula 1 threatened to leave it and set up their own championship.

In Barcelona on race morning the GPMA (Grand Prix Manufacturers' Association made up of BMW, DaimlerChrysler, Renault, Honda and Toyota) agreed to sign a commercial contract with the FOA (Formula One Administration), Bernie Ecclestone's company that manages the F1 commercial rights. "*The GPMA has signed an agreement that'll keep them in F1 up to 2012,*" said Xander Heijnen, the group's spokesman. This signature also put an end to the doubt surrounding Renault's future involvement in F1 - unless of course the French company decides to sell its team. Alain Dassas its new boss explained that it was vital to attract a top-line driver for 2007 to replace the departing Fernando Alonso.

The agreement signed in Barcelona was the fruit of months of hard work by a battery of lawyers as it consisted of a wide range of measures giving the teams more money.

Up till then they had to share 42% of the TV rights the rest going to Bernie Ecclestone who also pocketed all the income from on-circuit advertising and the sale of the Paddock Club Hospitality suites.

Henceforth all this income would be taken into account and the teams would receive between 50 and 60%.

With the future of F1 assured it would be much easier when it came to fishing for sponsors. "*We were negotiating this agreement for years without making any real headway,*" explained Ron Dennis, the boss of McLaren-Mercedes-Benz, a GPMA member with DaimlerChrysler. "*It was beginning to undermine our credibility. We met in Jersey at the start of the week to find a solution to the 15 outstanding litigious points. It has to be understood that the letter of intention on which we were working is a fairly complex document. It lays down the basis of the future Concorde Agreement (the contract linking the teams to the FOA) as well as the technical and sporting regulations that will come into force in 2008. We still have a lot more to do but it was not easy to get everyone to agree. As we were finally in phase about most things we speeded the whole process up over the last 2 days to announce the contract here. Our lawyers have been working on it night and day in a hotel in Barcelona.*"

Reason finally won out. And wily old Bernie too. And that, my friends, was no surprise!

> >
> Michael Schumacher relaxed with a bit of football on the Thursday evening before the race. That afternoon he announced that he would not take a decision about 2007 until later.

> >
> Bernie Ecclestone and Flavio Briatore locked in discussion. Bernie had managed to kill the decision of the major manufacturers to go their own way and Flavio had been a great help

Practice

All the time trials

N° Driver	Nat.	N° Chassis - Engine [Nbr GP]	Pos. Free 1 Friday	Laps	Pos. Free 2 Friday	Laps	Pos. Free 3 Saturday	Laps	Pos. Q1 Saturday	Laps	Pos. Q2 Saturday	Laps	Pos. Super Pole Saturday	Laps
Tr.														
1. Fernando Alonso	E	Renault R26 02 [2]	26.	2	3. 1:16.860	16	8. 1:16.595	10	1. 1:15.816	3	4. 1:15.124	3	1. **1:14.648**	16
2. Giancarlo Fisichella	I	Renault R26 04 [1]	27.	2	7. 1:17.291	17	2. 1:15.707	14	2. 1:16.046	3	2. 1:14.766	6	2. **1:14.709**	16
3. Kimi Räikkönen	FIN	McLaren MP4-21 02 - Mercedes [2]			15. 1:17.933	4	10. 1:16.705	9	12. 1:16.613	3	9. 1:15.422	3	9. **1:16.015**	16
4. Juan Pablo Montoya	CO	McLaren MP4-21 05 - Mercedes [1]	21.	1	18. 1:18.261	5	9. 1:16.660	9	7. 1:16.195	4	12. **1:15.801**	7		
5. Michael Schumacher	D	Ferrari 248 F1 254 [1]	2. 1:16.099	4	6. 1:17.100	21	1. 1:15.658	14	3. 1:16.049	5	1. 1:14.637	3	3. **1:14.970**	16
6. Felipe Massa	BR	Ferrari 248 F1 250 [1]	1. 1:15.796	4	17. 1:18.223	19	7. 1:16.410	15	11. 1:16.359	4	7. 1:15.245	3	4. **1:15.442**	15
7. Ralf Schumacher	D	Toyota TF106/05 [1]	17.	1	10. 1:17.506	25	13. 1:17.199	19	8. 1:16.234	6	6. 1:15.164	6	6. **1:15.885**	16
8. Jarno Trulli	I	Toyota TF106/04 [2]	13.	1	11. 1:17.610	30	18. 1:18.411	18	6. 1:16.174	6	3. 1:15.068	6	7. **1:15.976**	16
9. Mark Webber	AUS	Williams FW28 03 - Cosworth [2]	12.	1	14. 1:17.908	14	16. 1:17.743	14	14. 1:16.685	3	11. **1:15.502**	6		
10. Nico Rosberg	D	Williams FW28 06 - Cosworth [2]	15.	1	19. 1:18.283	18	15. 1:17.645	14	16. 1:17.213	3	13. **1:15.804**	6		
11. Rubens Barrichello	BR	Honda RA106-01 [1]	25.	1	9. 1:17.417	16	6. 1:16.399	16	9. 1:16.266	5	8. 1:15.258	3	5. **1:15.885**	15
12. Jenson Button	GB	Honda RA106-04 [1]	18.	1	8. 1:17.414	12	11. 1:16.999	18	4. 1:16.054	5	5. 1:15.150	3	8. **1:16.008**	16
14. David Coulthard	GB	Red Bull RB2 3 - Ferrari [1]	23.	1	20. 1:18.410	6	5. 1:16.352	16	22.	2				
15. Christian Klien	A	Red Bull RB2 2 - Ferrari [1]	24.	1	5. 1:17.086	10	4. 1:16.277	12	13. 1:16.627	6	15. **1:15.928**	6		
16. Nick Heidfeld	D	BMW Sauber F1.06-02 [2]	20.	1	12. 1:17.622	18	3. 1:16.057	13	10. 1:16.322	3	10. 1:15.468	6	10. **1:17.144**	16
17. Jacques Villeneuve	CDN	BMW Sauber F1.06-03 [2->1]	22.	2	16. 1:18.007	13	17. 1:17.924	16	5. 1:16.066	3	14. **1:15.847**	6		
18. Tiago Monteiro	P	Midland M16-03 - Toyota [2]	16.	1	27. 1:20.311	19	19. 1:18.747	22	18. **1:17.702**	6				
19. Christijan Albers	NL	Midland M16-04 - Toyota [2]	14.	1	25. 1:19.358	15	21. 1:19.587	19	19. **1:18.024**	7				
20. Vitantonio Liuzzi	I	Toro Rosso STR01 03 - Cosworth [1]	19.	1	24. 1:19.334	18	14. 1:17.240	19	15. 1:17.105	7	16. **1:16.661**	7		
21. Scott Speed	USA	Toro Rosso STR01 02 - Cosworth [2]	11.	3	23. 1:19.257	22	12. 1:17.004	13	17. **1:17.361**	8				
22. Takuma Sato	J	Super Aguri SA05-05 - Honda [2]	9. 1:20.744	9	26. 1:19.616	30	20. 1:18.857	20	20. **1:18.920**	6				
23. Franck Montagny	F	Super Aguri SA05-02 - Honda [2]	10.	3	28. 1:22.222	21	22. 1:20.031	24	21. **1:20.763**	6				
35. Alexander Wurz	A	Williams FW28 04 - Cosworth	3. 1:16.125	21	4. 1:17.075	30								
36. Anthony Davidson	GB	Honda RA106-03	5. 1:16.961	24	1. 1:16.533	38								
37. Robert Doornbos	NL	Red Bull RB2 1 - Ferrari	6. 1:17.424	20	2. 1:16.824	29								
38. Robert Kubica	PL	BMW Sauber F1.06-05	4. 1:16.628	21	13. 1:17.844	34								
39. Giorgio Mondini	CH	Midland M16-02 - Toyota	8. 1:20.708	21	22. 1:18.910	22								
40. Neel Jani	CH	Toro Rosso STR01 01 - Cosworth	7. 1:19.720	20	21. 1:18.774	32								

Fastest lap overall
M. Schumacher 1:14.637 (223,176 km/h)

Maximum speed

N° Driver	S1 Qualifs	Pos.	S1 Race	Pos.	S2 Qualifs	Pos.	S2 Race	Pos.	Finish Qualifs	Pos.	Finish Race	Pos.	Radar Qualifs	Pos.	Radar Race	Pos.
1. F. Alonso	288,0	6	286,5	3	285,3	5	278,4	12	285,8	3	283,8	3	304,8	9	307,3	9
2. G. Fisichella	288,8	5	284,7	6	279,2	14	276,2	15	285,0	7	281,3	4	311,2	3	305,6	13
3. K. Räikkönen	286,7	9	287,4	2	282,6	11	283,1	2	283,0	13	280,0	6	303,7	12	305,6	14
4. J. Montoya	284,6	13	279,5	17	281,9	12	271,9	21	285,5	5	275,6	17	302,8	14	308,3	7
5. M. Schumacher	292,6	1	290,2	1	284,2	6	283,5	1	290,0	1	287,3	1	314,1	2	314,4	2
6. F. Massa	289,8	2	282,8	13	287,0	2	280,9	4	289,6	2	284,9	2	319,7	1	317,1	1
7. R. Schumacher	289,6	3	285,0	5	290,7	1	280,6	7	283,3	12	279,7	7	307,6	7	311,1	4
8. J. Trulli	289,0	4	278,4	19	285,8	4	275,8	16	282,8	14	276,0	16	307,5	8	306,5	10
9. M. Webber	284,5	14	283,2	12	283,0	8	280,6	9	283,4	11	279,0	9	301,6	15	304,5	17
10. N. Rosberg	285,1	12	283,9	10	283,3	7	280,6	8	283,5	10	278,3	12	303,1	13	307,4	8
11. R. Barrichello	286,3	10	285,2	4	277,2	16	278,9	11	285,4	6	278,8	10	308,2	6	304,3	18
12. J. Button	283,8	16	283,2	11	278,7	15	276,7	14	284,5	9	280,5	5	301,5	16	304,9	15
14. D. Coulthard	262,6	22	284,0	9	263,4	22	280,9	5			277,3	14	256,8	22	306,3	11
15. C. Klien	286,3	11	281,0	15	286,7	3	281,0	3	280,8	15	278,3	13	303,8	11	308,9	6
16. N. Heidfeld	287,3	8	284,4	7	283,0	10	277,9	13	285,5	4	279,6	8	308,5	5	309,8	5
17. J. Villeneuve	287,9	7	280,7	16	274,2	18	275,5	17	284,9	8	278,4	11	308,7	4	313,0	3
18. T. Monteiro	276,8	19	278,5	18	268,5	20	272,3	20	276,2	18	270,2	20	295,6	19	295,9	20
19. C. Albers	278,3	18	276,9	20	275,6	17	274,5	18	274,8	20	269,1	21	291,4	20	294,1	22
20. V. Liuzzi	283,4	17	281,6	14	281,6	13	280,7	6	279,5	16	275,4	18	300,5	18	303,7	19
21. S. Speed	284,0	15	284,2	8	283,0	9	280,3	10	278,9	17	276,4	15	304,4	10	306,2	12
22. T. Sato	275,5	21	275,0	21	270,7	19	272,5	19	275,3	19	272,5	19	301,4	17	304,7	16
23. F. Montagny	275,7	20	268,3	22	267,1	21	266,6	22	271,0	21	266,9	22	289,7	21	295,1	21

Race

Classification & Retirements

Pos.	Driver	Constructor	Tyres	Laps	Time	Average	
1.	F. Alonso	Renault	M	66	1:26:21.759	212,074 km/h	
2.	M. Schumacher	Ferrari	B	66	+ 18.502	211,320 km/h	
3.	G. Fisichella	Renault	M	66	+ 23.951	211,099 km/h	
4.	F. Massa	Ferrari	B	66	+ 29.859	210,859 km/h	
5.	K. Räikkönen	McLaren Mercedes	M	66	+ 56.875	209,772 km/h	
6.	J. Button	Honda	M	66	+ 58.347	209,713 km/h	
7.	R. Barrichello	Honda	M	65	1 lap	208,358 km/h	
8.	N. Heidfeld	BMW	M	65	1 lap	208,087 km/h	
9.	M. Webber	Williams Cosworth	B	65	1 lap	208,032 km/h	
10.	J. Trulli	Toyota	B	65	1 lap	207,123 km/h	
11.	N. Rosberg	Williams Cosworth	B	65	1 lap	207,102 km/h	
12.	J. Villeneuve	BMW	M	65	1 lap	207,056 km/h	
13.	C. Klien	RBR Ferrari	M	65	1 lap	206,443 km/h	
14.	D. Coulthard	RBR Ferrari	M	65	1 lap	206,263 km/h	
15.	V. Liuzzi	STR Cosworth	M	63	3 laps	206,132 km/h	Hydraulic pb. / steering
16.	T. Monteiro	MF1 Toyota	B	63	3 laps	201,839 km/h	
17.	T. Sato	Aguri Honda	B	62	4 laps	198,929 km/h	

Driver	Constructor	Tyre	Laps	Reason
C. Albers	MF1 Toyota	B	48	Front wing broke and destroyed other parts, car undriveable
S. Speed	STR Cosworth	M	47	Engine failure
R. Schumacher	Toyota	B	31	Electronics problem
J. Montoya	McLaren Mercedes	M	17	Spun and got stuck on the kerb
F. Montagny	Aguri Honda	B	10	Drive shaft failure

Fastest laps

	Driver	Time	Laps	Average
1.	F. Massa	1:16.648	42	217,320 km/h
2.	F. Alonso	1:16.723	39	217,108 km/h
3.	M. Schumacher	1:16.922	43	216,546 km/h
4.	G. Fisichella	1:17.083	38	216,094 km/h
5.	K. Räikkönen	1:17.357	40	215,328 km/h
6.	J. Button	1:17.367	40	215,301 km/h
7.	R. Barrichello	1:17.399	40	215,212 km/h
8.	N. Rosberg	1:17.861	51	213,935 km/h
9.	D. Coulthard	1:17.862	55	213,932 km/h
10.	N. Heidfeld	1:17.869	49	213,913 km/h
11.	M. Webber	1:17.900	61	213,827 km/h
12.	J. Villeneuve	1:18.050	62	213,417 km/h
13.	J. Trulli	1:18.465	42	212,288 km/h
14.	V. Liuzzi	1:18.488	52	212,226 km/h
15.	C. Klien	1:18.516	59	212,150 km/h
16.	S. Speed	1:18.541	41	212,082 km/h
17.	R. Schumacher	1:18.621	24	211,867 km/h
18.	T. Monteiro	1:19.265	28	210,145 km/h
19.	J. Montoya	1:19.482	17	209,571 km/h
20.	C. Albers	1:19.532	28	209,440 km/h
21.	T. Sato	1:20.411	42	207,150 km/h
22.	F. Montagny	1:22.389	9	202,177 km/h

Pit stops

	Driver	Laps	Duration	Stop	Total
1.	T. Sato	10	23.684	1	23.684
2.	R. Schumacher	16	26.230	1	26.230
3.	F. Alonso	17	23.741	1	23.741
4.	G. Fisichella	18	23.001	1	23.001
5.	F. Massa	19	23.173	1	23.173
6.	K. Räikkönen	22	23.299	1	23.299
7.	M. Schumacher	23	23.347	1	23.347
8.	R. Barrichello	24	23.299	1	23.299
9.	J. Button	25	23.026	1	23.026
10.	S. Speed	26	24.393	1	24.393
11.	T. Monteiro	26	22.441	1	22.441
12.	J. Trulli	27	22.432	1	22.432
13.	N. Rosberg	27	23.540	1	23.540
14.	V. Liuzzi	27	23.418	1	23.418
15.	D. Coulthard	27	23.672	1	23.672
16.	M. Webber	28	23.809	1	23.809
17.	C. Klien	28	23.625	1	23.625
18.	N. Heidfeld	29	23.157	1	23.157
19.	C. Albers	29	43.051	1	43.051
20.	T. Sato	31	23.635	2	47.319
21.	C. Albers	37	29.272	2	1:12.323
22.	F. Alonso	40	23.407	2	47.148
23.	J. Villeneuve	40	24.559	1	24.559
24.	C. Albers	38	4:08.136	3	5:20.459
25.	G. Fisichella	41	23.285	2	46.286
26.	R. Barrichello	41	24.032	2	47.331
27.	F. Massa	43	23.422	2	46.595
28.	J. Button	44	22.770	2	45.796
29.	T. Sato	43	22.956	3	1:10.275
30.	M. Schumacher	46	22.630	2	45.977
31.	K. Räikkönen	46	22.848	2	46.147
32.	J. Trulli	46	22.242	2	44.674
33.	T. Monteiro	45	24.584	2	47.025
34.	M. Webber	47	22.398	2	46.207
35.	N. Rosberg	49	25.740	2	49.280
36.	V. Liuzzi	49	22.318	2	45.736
37.	N. Heidfeld	50	21.449	2	44.606
38.	C. Klien	50	22.288	2	45.913
39.	D. Coulthard	53	21.187	2	44.859

Race leader

Driver	Laps in the lead	Nbr of Laps
F. Alonso	1 > 17	17
G. Fisichella	18	1
M. Schumacher	19 > 23	5
F. Alonso	24 > 40	17
M. Schumacher	41 > 46	6
F. Alonso	47 > 66	20

Driver	Nbr of Laps	Kilometers
F. Alonso	54	249,732 km
M. Schumacher	11	50,897 km
G. Fisichella	1	4,627 km

Lap chart

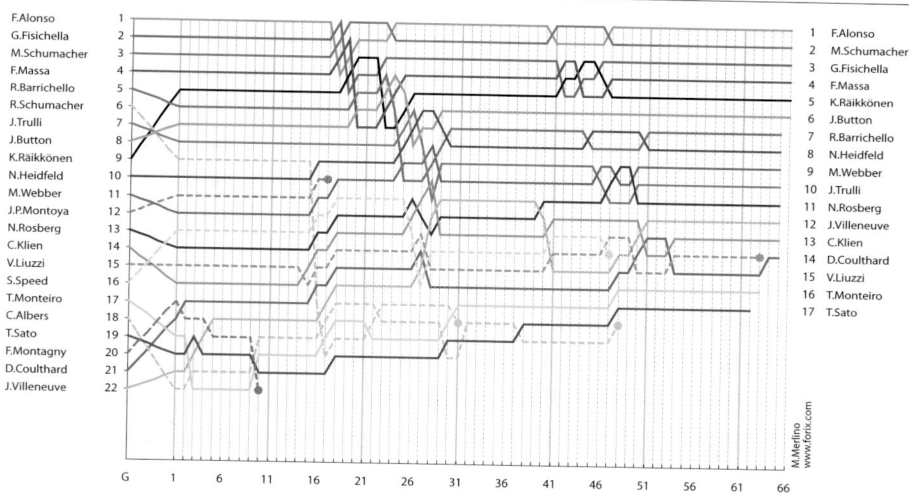

F.Alonso
G.Fisichella
M.Schumacher
F.Massa
R.Barrichello
R.Schumacher
J.Trulli
J.Button
K.Räikkönen
N.Heidfeld
M.Webber
J.P.Montoya
N.Rosberg
C.Klien
V.Liuzzi
S.Speed
T.Monteiro
C.Albers
T.Sato
F.Montagny
D.Coulthard
J.Villeneuve
1 F.Alonso
2 M.Schumacher
3 G.Fisichella
4 F.Massa
5 K.Räikkönen
6 J.Button
7 R.Barrichello
8 N.Heidfeld
9 M.Webber
10 J.Trulli
11 N.Rosberg
12 J.Villeneuve
13 C.Klien
14 D.Coulthard
15 V.Liuzzi
16 T.Monteiro
17 T.Sato
G 1 6 11 16 21 26 31 36 41 46 51 56 61 66
M.Merlino
www.forix.com

Gaps in the lead board

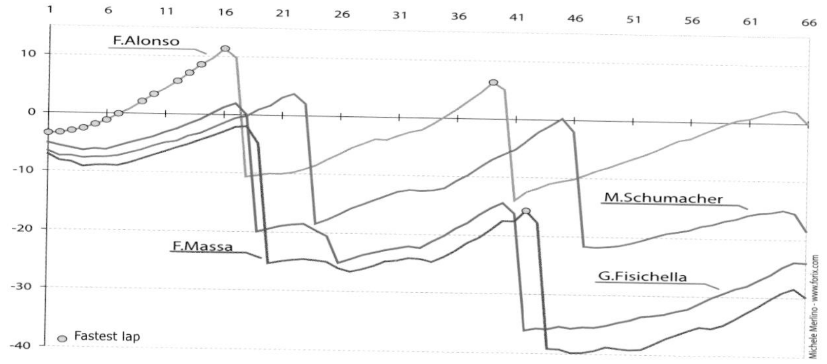

1 6 11 16 21 26 31 36 41 46 51 56 61 66
10
0
-10
-20
-30
-40
F.Alonso
M.Schumacher
F.Massa
G.Fisichella
Fastest lap
Michele Merlino - www.forix.com

Championships 6/18

Drivers

1. F. Alonso ....Renault ....3 🏆....54
2. M. Schumacher .....Ferrari......................2 🏆....39
3. K. Räikkönen ....McLaren Mercedes.............27
4. G. Fisichella..........Renault ....1 🏆....24
5. F. Massa...............Ferrari 20
6. J. Button ....Honda 16
7. J. Montoya ....McLaren Mercedes.............15
8. R. Barrichello........Honda 8
9. R. Schumacher .....Toyota 7
10. N. Heidfeld ....BMW 6
11. M. Webber............Williams Cosworth...............6
12. J. Villeneuve ....BMW 6
13. N. Rosberg ....Williams Cosworth...............4
14. D. Coulthard ....RBR Ferrari 1
15. C. Klien.................RBR Ferrari 1
16. J. Trulli.................Toyota 0
17. S. Speed ....STR Cosworth.......................0
18. V. Liuzzi ....STR Cosworth.......................0
19. C. Albers..............MF1 Toyota 0
20. T. Monteiro ....MF1 Toyota 0
21. T. Sato.................Aguri Honda 0
22. Y. Ide...................Aguri Honda 0

F. Montagny..........Aguri Honda ....-

Constructors

1. Mild Seven Renault F1 Team ....4 🏆....78
2. Scuderia Ferrari Marlboro ....2 🏆....59
3. Team McLaren Mercedes 42
4. Lucky Strike Honda Racing F1 Team 24
5. BMW Sauber F1 Team.............................12
6. Williams F1 Team 10
7. Panasonic Toyota Racing 7
8. Red Bull Racing 2
9. Scuderia Toro Rosso 0
10. MF1 Racing 0
11. Super Aguri Formula 1..............................0

The circuit

Name	Circuit de Catalunya; Montmelò, Barcelona	Weather	Sunny and warm
Lenght	4627 m	Air temperature	26-28°c
Distance	66 laps, 305,256 km	Track temperature	36-42°c
Date	May 14, 2006	Humidity	38%
		Wind speed	0.6 m/s

S1: 60m before corner
S2: 85m before corner
Radar: 250m before corner

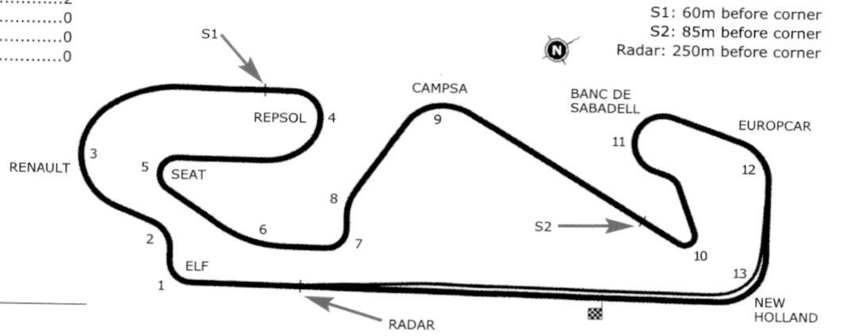

S1
REPSOL
4
CAMPSA
9
BANC DE SABADELL
11
EUROPCAR
12
RENAULT
3
5
SEAT
8
6
7
2
S2
10
13
1
ELF
RADAR
NEW HOLLAND
N

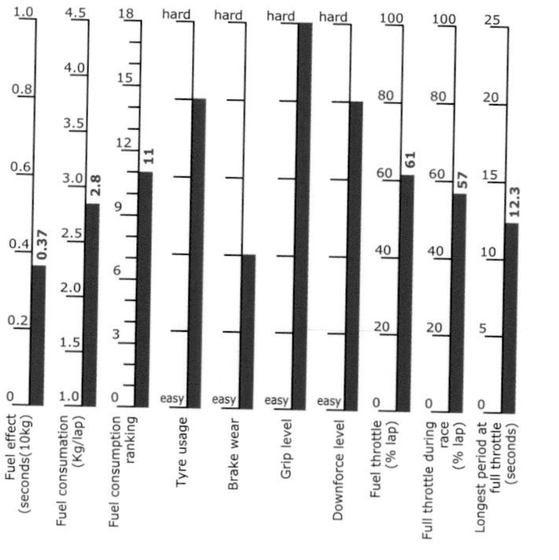

0.37
2.8
11
61
57
12.3
hard
easy
Fuel effect (seconds(10kg)
Fuel consumation (Kg/lap)
Fuel consumption ranking
Tyre usage
Brake wear
Grip level
Downforce level
Fuel throttle (% lap)
Full throttle during race (% lap)
Longest period at full throttle (seconds)

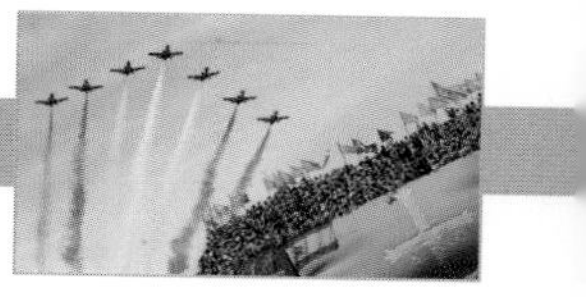

MONTOYA IN CRACKING FORM

Fernando Alonso blitzed his rivals in Monaco with pole position and victory. He increased his lead over Michael Schumacher who started from last place on the grid after blocking the track during qualifying – one of the most serious offences of his career.
Juan Pablo Montoya was back on cracking form for once and finished second.

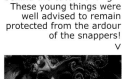

Kimi Raïkkönen qualified third in Monaco. He reckoned that without the traffic he could have snatched pole.

Michael Schumacher disqualified for deliberately blocking the track and stopping qualifying

"Don't touch Mario, you're behind the catch fencing:" These young things were well advised to remain protected from the ardour of the snappers!

> *"I think there's a photographer over there."* For some people the Monaco Grand Prix is more an occasion to be seen then to see.

The qualifying session in the Monaco sun promised to be a humdinger with McLaren, Ferrari and Renault going head-to-head for that all-important pole position crucial for victory in the Principality. The battle lasted until the final minutes of the session. At that precise moment Michael had the fastest time a mere 64/1000s ahead of Alonso. The two drivers came in, put on fresh rubber and rejoined for a final joust to decide pole. They were only a few seconds behind each other. The first split time gave Alonso a slight advantage and Schumacher began to run into minor difficulties around the swimming pool. He then got the Rascasse all wrong and his car blocked the track right on the line for the corner. For all those coming behind it was the end of their hopes of trying to improve their times. But it was also the start of a major row.

The session was barely over when comments were flying round the paddock and pressroom. The stewards decided to carry out an in-depth investigation about what had happened. Michael Schumacher kept repeating that his manoeuvre was not deliberate: *"I braked too hard, I locked up my front wheel and I went straight on,"* was how he justified the incident. *" I tried to put the car into reverse and the engine stalled. I couldn't do anything else."*

To those who said to him that his manoeuvre was too blatant to be anything other than deliberate he replied without batting an eyelid:*"If I'd done it on purpose, it'd be shameful."* But, he added, *"your enemies believe one thing and the people who support you another. Our sport's like that."* Michael made himself a host of enemies in this

affair. The video was so damning that not one driver supported the German's action.

After long discussions the Stewards of the Meeting decided to cancel Schumacher's times at 23h00 on Saturday evening. It was a logical decision based on in-depth analysis of all the parameters including the various pieces of camera footage.

"The stewards have analysed the telemetry and time keeping read-outs supplied by the Ferrari team and the FIA," stated the decision.

"By comparing the data of the lap on which the driver stopped with those of his previous ones, the stewards saw that he arrived in corner no. 18 (the Rascasse hairpin) at a speed that was similar to that of his previous laps, and braked so hard that his front wheels locked up. He managed to control his car in such a way as to avoid hitting the barriers. The car's engine then stalled and it partially blocked the track. By analysing the telemetry readouts the stewards see no reason why the driver should have braked so hard and

with such excessive force in that spot. They are left with no choice other than to conclude that he deliberately stopped his car on the circuit at the moment when he had the fastest time which is a breach of article 116 of the sporting regulations."

This article states that in such a case the driver's times must be cancelled, and this was done sending Michael Schumacher to the back of the grid.

A few years ago the Ferrari driver's action would probably have gone unpunished. Today, thanks to the telemetry, which records all possible parameters from the driver's pressure on the pedals to the engine revs as well as the angle of the steering wheel, such things cannot be hidden.

Felipe Massa joined his team-mate on the last row as he had not been able to do a flying lap after going off. In the past the Scuderia had often got away with such actions so the decision taken in Monaco marked an end to what many considered a kind of favouritism.

Starting grid

| * G. FISICHELLA was relegated for blocking Coulthard. His three fastest times were cancelled. | M. SCHUMACHER* 22 | F. MONTAGNY 20 1:17.502 | S. SPEED 18 1:16.236 | C. ALBERS 16 1:15.598 | J. VILLENEUVE 14 1:15.052 | V. LIUZZI 12 1:14.969 | R. SCHUMACHER 10 1:14.398 | N. ROSBERG 8 1:16.636 | J. TRULLI 6 1:15.857 | J. MONTOYA 4 1:14.664 | M. WEBBER 2 1:14.082 |

F. MASSA penalty for an engine change.

M. SCHUMACHER was penalised for deliberately stopping his car in the middle of the track. The team changed his engine and he started from the pit lane.

| F. MASSA* 21 1:17.276 | T. SATO 19 1:15.993 | T. MONTEIRO 17 1:15.137 | N. HEIDFELD 15 1:14.982 | J. BUTTON 13 1:14.747 | C. KLIEN 11 1:17.260 | G. FISICHELLA* 9 1:16.426 | D. COULTHARD 7 1:15.804 | R. BARRICHELLO 5 1:14.140 | K. RAÏKKÖNEN 3 1:13.962 (162.710 km/h) | F. ALONSO 1 |

Reactions: "I hope he did it on purpose!"

The reactions in the paddock after qualifying were highly critical of the German's manoeuvre.
"*As we're not in Snow White and the seven Dwarves, I think that his behaviour is anti-sporting,*" roared Flavio Briatore, the Renault team boss.
"*Was it a mistake? I'm not so sure,*" said Juan Pablo Montoya.
"*To make a balls-up like that he must have hidden his on-board camera with his left hand,*" remarked Kimi Raïkkönen.
"*I hope it was deliberate,*" stated Jacques Villeneuve. "*Because if that really was a mistake he should not even have a super licence! If you make*

a blunder like that and you do not do it on purpose you shouldn't even be allowed to drive a racing car. I hope he'll end up by admitting he did it on purpose because it's impossible to make a such a mistake."
The Canadian was outraged by Schumacher's action as it reminded him of the various doubtful manoeuvres committed by the 7-times world champion throughout his career. It has to be said that in terms of contestable exploits and dirty tricks it was not the first time the German had been caught red-handed. Many people still remembered his attempt to punt Villeneuve off the track in the 1997 European Grand Prix.

"*You can only have the benefit of the doubt on a limited number of occasions,*" Villeneuve went on. "*And at that moment, you understand, that when it happened there was always a good reason. It's rubbish, a guy like Michael doesn't need that. He's won seven titles; he holds the record for the number of victories and pole positions. Why does he bring discredit on himself? I just don't understand especially as he knew that the whole world was watching him. He could at least have turned in sooner and hit the wall or scraped along the guardrail - I don't know - do something a bit more credible: He didn't even slide. We're going to have it out at the GPDA.*"

^
Robert Doornbos in the tunnel. On Friday the Dutchman ended practice in fifth place in his Red Bull.

Two Swiss drivers practised on Friday: Neel Jani (left) and Giorgio Mondino (below). The former was once again quicker than his team-mate Scott Speed in the same car, while the latter got his Midland up into 14th place despite missing his braking in Mirabeau.
v<

They're off! Fernando Alonso keeps his pole position advantage and fends off Mark Webber.

Victory: Alonso falls into the arms of his mechanics.

Giancarlo Fisichella in kamikaze mode as he attacks David Coulthard. He started 9th and finished 6th.

It does not look like it but we can assure you that Carlos Ghosn, the Renault boss, really enjoyed himself in Monaco!

Alonso: a cut above the rest

Was Lady Luck Spanish? This was what Fernando Alonso's rivals could have asked themselves at the end of the Monaco Grand Prix. Things got off to a great start for the reigning world champion on Saturday evening with the news that Michael Schumacher's times had been cancelled, and he had been sent to the back of the gird (he started from the pit lane). This put Fernando on pole. But the race was not won yet as right on his heels was Kimi Raïkkönen in his McLaren who gave the Spaniard a run for his money with the evident intention of launching an attack during the second round of refuelling stops. Mark Webber's breakdown that required the intervention of the safety car effectively dashed the Finn's hopes. It was Lady Luck's second gift to Alonso.
A couple of laps later Kimi was out stopping his car on the side of the track; it had overheated behind the safety car. When Juan Pablo Montoya inherited second place his chances of attacking the Renault were reduced to nil by back-markers.
Alonso would probably have found it difficult to beat Michael Schumacher if the latter had started from pole. Fernando did not give a damn! "*I've got no idea and it doesn't interest me,*" he grinned. "*He wasn't on pole and I don't usually analyse the race of those who start from the back of the grid! I know that Michael set*

the fastest lap but all I was worried about was nursing my tyres and keeping an eye on my nearest rivals."
It was Fernando's first Monaco victory. Taking into account his win in Barcelona two weeks earlier he was now 21 points in front of Schumacher.
Another title looked on the cards as the McLarens' season had been plagued by problems and the Ferraris had had a series of ups and downs. "*Kimi didn't score today and Michael bagged only four,*" concluded Alonso. "*With the current system you can't gain a lot but you can lose a lot. And that's what's happened to them. I'm beginning to open out a gap slowly but steadily so that things are easier at the end of the year.*"
While the Spaniard's second title was now in the realms of the probable rather than the possible, there was a big question mark hanging over the ofuture beyond 2006. In December 2005, he had signed with McLaren at a moment when he thought the English team would be the one to beat. And now it Renault that was winning everything.
So was Fernando asking himself if he had not made a mistake. "*It's sure 2007 will be a big challenge,*" he admitted. "*I'm certain that I can fight for the title again.*" Provided Lady Luck continues to grant her favours to the Spaniard!

In brief

> "*I suggested he should wash. When you're going to photographed in the buff, you should make sure you look your best!*" quipped David Coulthard who finished third about his boss Christian Horner.
The latter had said he would bathe in the nude in the swimming pool beside the Red Bull Motorhome if one of his cars finished on the rostrum. It did and he did!

> As all three teams that finished on the rostrum were Michelin shod they did not spray the champagne in homage to Edouard Michelin.

> In Monaco the McLarens had a special steering wheel to commemorate the Woking firm's partnership with the Steinmetz Company and to celebrate the team's 40th anniversary as it had made its debut in the Principality on 22nd May 1966. In the centre was a Mercedes-Benz star set with several white diamonds: Beautiful but useless!

> "Bad boy" Fernando Alonso refused to attend the Gala dinner closing the grand prix weekend during which the winner sits beside the Prince.
The Renault management found itself in a very embarrassing position and had to say that their driver had suddenly fallen ill to justify his absence.

Ferrari: disappointment and frustration

A new chapter in the history of motor sport was opened on Saturday by Brit Tony Scott Andrews, Joaquin Verdegay from Spain and Monegasque Christian Calmes, the three Monaco Grand Prix Stewards of the Meeting.

They decided to cancel the times set by Michael Schumacher during qualifying and sanctioned the driver for what they estimated was a deliberate driving error –which the German said was involuntary.

On Sunday once the images had been seen over and over again, the verdict was unanimous: *"It's the ugliest thing I've ever seen in F1. Michael should retire and not come back,"* thundered Keke Rosberg, the 1982 world champion, former Williams driver and Nico's father.

"It was puerile. In his time Senna also did a few strange things but he at least seemed to be right," added Mark Webber.

The man in question said it was a driving error and pleaded not guilty. *"This business is really horrible for us,"* said Luca Colajanni, the Ferrari PR man. *"Michael admits having braked too hard and making a mistake, but not a deliberate one. He reckoned he could improve his time in the final sector and there was no way he could've know Fernando's split time behind as he's been accused of."* This was true as the Stewards listened

to the radio conversations between the Ferrari driver and his pit. There was no mention of Alonso. *"We tried everything to convince them of our good faith,"* said Colajanni. *"But when somebody decides your car is green when it's red, there's nothing that can change his mind!"*

On Sunday evening the Ferrari personnel were not exactly jumping for joy. *"We feel very alone"*, moaned Jean Todt, the Scuderia boss. *"We like being alone but we'll leave Monaco in a very disappointed state of mind. We thought we could win."*

What added to the team's frustration was the

fact that the stewards had invoked one of the few articles against which no appeal is possible. Would this incident influence Michael Schumacher who was soon to take a decision concerning his future? He was booed in the pressroom, criticised by his fellow- drivers so one can imagine that the Monaco Grand Prix might lead Michael to reconsider his presence in F1. *"I don't think Michael will take this incident into account in making his decision,"* Jean Todt declared; *"It's not very important. We're not giving up; we're still in with a chance of winning the championship."*

Chances that were growing slimmer race by race.

Bad hair day for Jacques Villeneuve

While the F1 paddock has a population of engineers per square metre that would send any university into paroxysms of jealously, motor racing is not an exact science. Despite the most carefully studied calculations there is always the odd gremlin that disrupts the machine. So many hit Jacques Villeneuve in Monaco that he could well have imagined he was starring in the film of the same name!

In qualifying he had no grip and finished 14th on the grid. In such conditions a miracle was necessary for him to score points. And Monaco isn't Lourdes! He spent most of the race stuck behind Vitantonio Liuzzi and his only refuelling stop on lap 44 changed nothing. He was about to finish 11th when he received a penalty for overtaking Nico Rosberg during a safety car period. He finished where he started: 14th.

^
Juan Pablo Montoya had a good race in the Principality. "I lost too much time in traffic to be able to catch Fernando," he explained after his second place. Little did the Colombian know that it would be his best result of the season.

In Monaco the Red Bull team was again decked out in eye-catching colours. This time the theme was Superman and David Coulthard chose just the right moment for his only rostrum appearance of the year.
∨<

Rubens Barrichello had a good race in Monaco. He started from 5th and finished 4th. His team-mate Jenson Button started from 13th spot and came home eleventh.
∨

In maximum attack mode

The Williams were lightning fast in Monaco. Mark Webber qualified on the front row for the only time in 2006. Nico Rosberg (photo) started from 8th but went out in the race with a blocked accelerator that sent him cannoning into the guardrail.

^
Jacques Villeneuve flat out in the Portier corner. He qualified 14th and finished 14th! He was penalised for having overtaken behind the safety car which he vehemently denied: "What's the use of protesting; we're outside the points anyway," he said philosophically.

Jacques Villeneuve flat out in the Portier corner. He qualified 14th and finished 14th! He was penalised for having overtaken behind the safety car which he vehemently denied: "What's the use of protesting; we're outside the points anyway," he said philosophically.

Rossi-Ferrari: the end of the suspense!

The birth was stillborn. For nine months Valentino Rossi and the Scuderia Ferrari had been making eyes at one another during a love affair in which the Italian motorcycle championship had been shilly-shallying. F1 or MotoGP in 2007? His bride was all in red and was one of the most coveted one in the whole field in which all drivers dream of sitting one day. Valentino hesitated; he wondered what it was hiding under its dress! He did a lot of practising on the Fiorano circuit, at Mugello and Valencia.

He took his time over his decision. On Thursday in Monaco he announced that he would remain faithful to 2 wheels. "*I've still got a lot to achieve in bike racing,*" he explained. "*I won't think about F1 for a few years yet.*"

Nobody in the Monaco paddock was really very surprised by the Italian's decision. Rossi had not practised with the Scuderia since 2nd February. He wanted to take a break in his F1 apprenticeship. An omen..?

Michael Schumacher was not amazed by the Italian's decision. "*I'm a bit sad that Valentino won't be joining us, but I fully understand his decision. Motorcycle racing is his universe while F1 is unknown territory. He didn't really know what he was going to find and how he would adapt. He's got enormous talent and I'm sure that he could drive in it. F1 is more than that. The environment*

is so complex beyond the driving itself.*"
Jean Todt said he respected the Italian's decision. "*All of us were struck by his ability to adapt to F1, by his talent and by his courtesy,*" added the Scuderia's boss.

For other drivers Rossi's choice was a purely pragmatic one. "*In his last tests he was over a second off Michael Schumacher's pace,*" quipped Jarno Trulli. "*It's very difficulty to find that extra second and I don't think he'd have made it.*"
There were others who were delighted that

Valentino was staying in the motorbike world. "*It's good that Valentino's staying with bikes,*"said Alonso. "*That way there'll be no more talk about him. I've been asked questions about him for 4 months and I hope it's over!*"
A few weeks earlier the Spaniard had turned down a challenge that Rossi had put to him saying that he (Rossi) was wasting his time at Ferrari. Maybe not everybody in the F1 milieu was friendly towards the Italian. An additional reason to justify his choice.

Edouard Michelin lost at sea

The news was announced in the Monaco paddock at 20h00 on Friday: the body of Edouard Michelin, who has gone fishing in Brittany, had been found in the afternoon.

It was a huge blow to the 45 employees present in Monaco. "*I joined Michelin 27 years ago,*" said Frédéric Henri-Biabaud, the competitions boss. "*It's the kind of news that tugs your heartstrings. I feel very sad. But we'll cope with out emotions and tomorrow morning we'll be at the circuit to make sure the weekend goes off well and we'll win the Monaco Grand Prix. That's our job.*"
Bernie Ecclestone had already left the circuit. Contacted by phone he said how sorry he was about the death of a man he called a real gentleman. Pierre Dupasquier was also contacted by phone and the former competitions manager who had followed Edouard Michelin's career since he was a child was speechless. "*Edouard was a man who took risks at*

several moments in his existence,*" he recalled. "*He was a very responsible guy but he did not want that to stop him from living life to the full. He's part of a long line of Michelin family members who've been killed in accidents.*"
The loss of its co-chairman was a big blow to the group. "*It's a tragedy for everybody but above all for his wife and his six young kids,*" Dupasquier went on. "*This being said Edouard managed to instil a certain dynamic in the group that'll continue. He started from a family company that he's tuned into a well-managed multinational. He'd already finished this job.*"
Edouard Michelin had decided to withdraw his company from F1 at the end of 2006 despite its long sporting tradition. Michel Rollier was designated as his successor less than an hour after his death. He had never attended a grand prix but this was put right at Interlagos in the last race of the season.

Nothing broken - yet. Valentino Rossi tested a Ferrari for the last time on the Valencia circuit. He went off after 300 metres! It's no easy job changing from 2 wheels to 4.
v

results

Practice

All the time trials

N° Driver	Nat.	N° Chassis - Engine [Nbr. GP]	Pos. Free 1 Friday	Laps.	Pos. Free 2 Friday	Laps	Pos. Free 3 Saturday	Laps	Pos. Q1 Saturday	Laps	Pos. Q2 Saturday	Laps	Pos. Super Pole Saturday	Laps
1. Fernando Alonso	E	Renault R26 02 [1]	1. 1:16.712	13	4. 1:16.221	18	1. 1:13.823	19	2. 1:14.232	6	2. 1:13.622	3	2. **1:13.962**	16
2. Giancarlo Fisichella	I	Renault R26 04 [2]	3. 1:16.888	12	7. 1:16.721	23	3. 1:14.056	20	7. 1:14.614	7	3. 1:13.647	3	5. **1:14.396**	16
3. Kimi Räikkönen	FIN	McLaren MP4-21 02 - Mercedes [1]	28.	3	6. 1:16.707	18	10. 1:15.124	17	1. 1:13.887	7	1. 1:13.532	3	4. **1:14.140**	16
4. Juan Pablo Montoya	CO	McLaren MP4-21 05 - Mercedes [2]	5. 1:17.458	7	3. 1:16.138	24	6. 1:14.785	21	5. 1:14.483	7	9. 1:14.295	10	6. **1:14.664**	15
5. Michael Schumacher	D	Ferrari 248 F1 254 [2->1]	4. 1:16.973	8	15. 1:17.603	25	2. 1:14.031	20	13. 1:15.118	5	5. 1:13.709	3	1. **1:13.898**	15
6. Felipe Massa	BR	Ferrari 248 F1 250 [2->1]	14. 1:18.695	15	10. 1:17.251	25	8. 1:14.842	24	22.	2				
7. Ralf Schumacher	D	Toyota TF106/07B [1]	16. 1:19.021	14	18. 1:17.793	26	21. 1:17.860	21	4. 1:14.412	7	11. **1:14.398**	7		
8. Jarno Trulli	I	Toyota TF106/08B [1]	15. 1:18.703	11	11. 1:17.325	25	19. 1:16.456	24	9. 1:14.883	4	8. 1:14.211	6	8. **1:15.857**	14
9. Mark Webber	AUS	Williams FW28 03 - Cosworth [1]	13. 1:18.571	17	17. 1:17.744	19	7. 1:14.804	16	3. 1:14.305	9	6. 1:13.728	8	3. **1:14.082**	14
10. Nico Rosberg	D	Williams FW28 06 - Cosworth [1]	12. 1:18.480	15	19. 1:17.845	15	5. 1:14.623	17	10. 1:14.888	10	7. 1:13.909	8	10. **1:16.636**	15
11. Rubens Barrichello	BR	Honda RA106-01 [2]	10. 1:18.406	12	13. 1:17.456	24	11. 1:15.283	20	8. 1:14.766	9	10. 1:14.312	7	7. **1:15.804**	15
12. Jenson Button	GB	Honda RA106-04 [2]	8. 1:18.329	12	9. 1:16.903	20	9. 1:15.020	21	11. 1:15.085	7	14. **1:14.982**	10		
14. David Coulthard	GB	Red Bull RB2 3 - Ferrari [2]	11. 1:18.447	10	8. 1:16.870	19	4. 1:14.550	19	12. 1:15.090	7	4. 1:13.687	7	9. **1:16.246**	16
15. Christian Klien	A	Red Bull RB2 2 - Ferrari [2]	18. 1:19.543	10	21. 1:18.123	22	12. 1:15.476	19	6. 1:14.489	7	12. **1:14.747**	5		
16. Nick Heidfeld	D	BMW Sauber F1.06-02 [1]	27.	1	22. 1:18.257	10	13. 1:15.591	20	16. 1:15.324	11	16. **1:15.137**	9		
17. Jacques Villeneuve	CDN	BMW Sauber F1.06-03 [2]	17. 1:19.246	16	20. 1:17.874	13	18. 1:16.285	27	15. 1:15.316	8	15. **1:15.052**	8		
18. Tiago Monteiro	P	Midland M16-03 - Toyota [1]	21. 1:19.730	17	12. 1:17.439	30	14. 1:15.809	26	18. **1:15.993**	8				
19. Christijan Albers	NL	Midland M16-04 - Toyota [1]	24. 1:20.552	17	24. 1:18.430	24	15. 1:16.066	26	17. **1:15.598**	8				
20. Vitantonio Liuzzi	I	Toro Rosso STR01 03 - Cosworth [1]	22. 1:19.857	16	16. 1:17.638	31	16. 1:16.147	27	14. 1:15.314	10	13. **1:14.969**	10		
21. Scott Speed	USA	Toro Rosso STR01 02 - Cosworth [1]	23. 1:20.137	13	23. 1:18.420	29	17. 1:16.201	21	19. **1:16.236**	7				
22. Takuma Sato	J	Super Aguri SA05-05 - Honda [1]	25. 1:21.144	23	28. 1:19.803	31	20. 1:17.148	24	20. **1:17.276**	6				
23. Franck Montagny	F	Super Aguri SA05-02 - Honda [1]	26. 1:21.594	21	25. 1:18.731	19	22. 1:17.934	21	21. **1:17.502**	7				
35. Alexander Wurz	A	Williams FW28 04 - Cosworth	7. 1:17.949	28	1. 1:15.907	27								
36. Anthony Davidson	GB	Honda RA106-03	2. 1:16.872	31	2. 1:16.075	15								
37. Robert Doornbos	NL	Red Bull RB2 5 - Ferrari	9. 1:18.394	23	5. 1:16.292	36								
38. Robert Kubica	PL	BMW Sauber F1.06-05	6. 1:17.869	19	26. 1:19.273	12								
39. Giorgio Mondini	CH	Midland M16-02 - Toyota	20. 1:19.669	29	14. 1:17.497	30								
40. Neel Jani	CH	Toro Rosso STR01 01 - Cosworth	19. 1:19.651	25	27. 1:19.445	27								

Fastest lap overall
K. Räikkönen 1:13.532 (163,520 km/h)

Maximum speed

N° Driver	S1 Qualifs	Pos.	S1 Race	Pos.	S2 Qualifs	Pos.	S2 Race	Pos.	Finish Qualifs	Pos.	Finish Race	Pos.	Radar Qualifs	Pos.	Radar Race	Pos.
1. F. Alonso	212,4	1	207,6	1	233,9	5	226,9	4	257,8	4	256,5	5	284,8	3	284,9	4
2. G. Fisichella	212,0	2	207,6	2	237,1	1	225,9	5	259,3	2	260,3	3	285,2	2	286,0	3
3. K. Räikkönen	208,1	13	203,1	6	235,6	3	232,9	1	258,5	3	257,8	4	284,8	4	284,9	5
4. J. Montoya	209,3	10	206,6	3	234,1	4	229,4	3	256,2	6	253,5	12	281,1	13	284,2	6
5. M. Schumacher	211,5	3	206,5	4	237,1	2	231,0	2	259,8	1	260,8	2	288,1	1	289,3	1
6. F. Massa	192,0	22	202,8	7	160,0	22	220,2	9	257,8	5	262,7	1	283,1	5	286,6	2
7. R. Schumacher	210,1	6	199,3	16	221,2	19	210,5	22	255,5	10	253,8	9	281,9	7	278,4	19
8. J. Trulli	211,3	4	196,6	20	227,1	14	212,9	21	255,8	9	253,6	10	281,6	9	279,3	16
9. M. Webber	208,8	12	203,9	5	226,4	15	220,3	8	255,4	11	253,2	13	283,0	6	282,7	8
10. N. Rosberg	209,9	8	201,3	12	232,6	6	217,2	16	255,0	14	252,9	14	281,8	8	282,1	9
11. R. Barrichello	209,3	11	200,3	15	228,2	13	219,6	10	254,4	17	255,4	6	277,5	20	282,1	10
12. J. Button	205,6	17	194,6	22	230,4	9	221,2	7	256,1	7	254,8	7	278,2	19	281,0	12
14. D. Coulthard	210,8	5	201,5	11	229,8	11	217,6	15	255,8	8	253,6	11	280,3	16	283,8	7
15. C. Klien	209,9	7	202,7	8	226,4	16	218,5	14	255,1	12	250,6	19	280,8	14	280,4	13
16. N. Heidfeld	208,0	14	202,0	10	230,1	10	218,8	12	254,8	15	252,6	15	280,7	15	279,6	14
17. J. Villeneuve	209,4	9	200,5	14	231,5	8	219,0	11	253,8	18	254,6	8	281,3	11	281,6	11
18. T. Monteiro	202,2	19	197,8	18	221,3	18	213,0	20	251,1	22	249,2	21	277,0	21	274,8	22
19. C. Albers	206,8	16	196,0	21	228,7	12	218,6	13	251,9	21	251,2	17	276,5	22	277,4	21
20. V. Liuzzi	206,9	15	202,5	9	232,6	7	216,4	17	255,0	13	252,6	16	281,2	12	279,6	15
21. S. Speed	205,1	18	200,8	13	225,8	17	225,0	6	254,8	16	250,5	20	280,3	17	278,7	18
22. T. Sato	201,5	20	198,1	17	213,4	20	213,6	19	253,6	19	249,0	22	279,1	18	277,6	20
23. F. Montagny	196,5	21	197,6	19	212,7	21	213,7	18	253,2	20	251,1	18	281,3	10	278,8	17

Race

Classification & Retirements

Pos.	Driver	Constructor	Tyres	Laps	Time	Average	
1.	F. Alonso	Renault	M	78	1:43:43.116	150,707 km/h	
2.	J. Montoya	McLaren Mercedes	M	78	+ 14.567	150,355 km/h	
3.	D. Coulthard	RBR Ferrari	M	78	+ 52.298	149,451 km/h	
4.	R. Barrichello	Honda	M	78	+ 53.337	149,427 km/h	
5.	M. Schumacher	Ferrari	B	78	+ 53.830	149,415 km/h	
6.	G. Fisichella	Renault	M	78	+ 1:02.072	149,219 km/h	
7.	N. Heidfeld	BMW	M	77	1 tour	147,792 km/h	
8.	R. Schumacher	Toyota	B	77	1 tour	147,757 km/h	
9.	F. Massa	Ferrari	B	77	1 tour	147,745 km/h	
10.	V. Liuzzi	STR Cosworth	M	77	1 tour	147,684 km/h	
11.	J. Button	Honda	M	77	1 tour	147,469 km/h	
12.	C. Albers	MF1 Toyota	B	77	1 tour	147,175 km/h	
13.	S. Speed	STR Cosworth	M	77	1 tour	147,142 km/h	
14.	J. Villeneuve	BMW	M	77	1 tour	146,988 km/h	
15.	T. Monteiro	MF1 Toyota	B	76	2 tours	146,005 km/h	
16.	F. Montagny	Aguri Honda	B	75	3 tours	144,674 km/h	
17.	J. Trulli	Toyota	B	72	6 tours	149,209 km/h	Hydraulic problem

Driver	Constructor	Tyres	Laps	Reason
C. Klien	RBR Ferrari	M	56	Loss of drive, Transmission
N. Rosberg	Williams Cosworth	B	51	Throttle sticking open, pushed it into the barriers
K. Räikkönen	McLaren Mercedes	M	50	Excessive heat burnt a wiring loom
M. Webber	Williams Cosworth	B	48	Exhaust failure
T. Sato	Aguri Honda	B	46	Electrical problem

Fastest laps

	Driver	Time	Laps	Average
1.	M. Schumacher	1:15.143	74	160,014 km/h
2.	K. Räikkönen	1:15.325	19	159,628 km/h
3.	F. Alonso	1:16.671	11	158,898 km/h
4.	M. Webber	1:15.680	23	158,879 km/h
5.	G. Fisichella	1:15.919	58	158,379 km/h
6.	J. Montoya	1:16.008	20	158,193 km/h
7.	F. Massa	1:16.612	40	156,946 km/h
8.	J. Trulli	1:17.180	30	155,791 km/h
9.	N. Rosberg	1:17.227	43	155,696 km/h
10.	J. Button	1:17.300	59	155,549 km/h
11.	N. Heidfeld	1:17.319	72	155,511 km/h
12.	R. Barrichello	1:17.320	67	155,509 km/h
13.	T. Monteiro	1:17.329	71	155,491 km/h
14.	S. Speed	1:17.481	77	155,186 km/h
15.	R. Schumacher	1:17.540	72	155,068 km/h
16.	C. Albers	1:17.603	77	154,942 km/h
17.	V. Liuzzi	1:17.660	75	154,828 km/h
18.	J. Villeneuve	1:17.767	74	154,615 km/h
19.	D. Coulthard	1:17.849	45	154,452 km/h
20.	C. Klien	1:17.930	19	154,292 km/h
21.	T. Sato	1:18.793	39	152,602 km/h
22.	F. Montagny	1:19.104	72	152,002 km/h

Pit spots

	Driver	Laps	Duration	Stop	Total
1.	T. Monteiro	1	29.002	1	29.002
2.	C. Albers	•18•	14.781	1	14.781
3.	J. Montoya	21	26.513	1	26.513
4.	K. Räikkönen	22	26.739	1	26.739
5.	N. Rosberg	23	28.155	1	28.155
6.	F. Alonso	24	24.857	1	24.857
7.	M. Webber	25	27.378	1	27.378
8.	G. Fisichella	27	27.419	1	27.419
9.	D. Coulthard	29	29.227	1	29.227
10.	M. Schumacher	36	25.331	1	25.331
11.	F. Massa	37	29.217	1	29.217
12.	R. Schumacher	39	28.923	1	28.923
13.	N. Heidfeld	40	25.857	1	25.857
14.	C. Albers	40	28.604	2	43.385
15.	C. Klien	41	26.222	1	26.222
16.	J. Button	41	25.337	1	25.337
17.	J. Villeneuve	44	24.670	1	24.670
18.	R. Barrichello	45	25.702	1	25.702
19.	J. Trulli	45	25.997	1	25.997
20.	T. Sato	46	29.380	1	29.380
21.	F. Alonso	49	23.553	2	48.410
22.	K. Räikkönen	49	23.555	2	50.294
23.	F. Montagny	47	26.176	1	26.176
24.	T. Monteiro	47	26.110	2	55.112
25.	G. Fisichella	48	24.510	2	51.929
26.	J. Montoya	49	26.060	2	52.573
27.	V. Liuzzi	48	26.521	1	26.521
28.	N. Rosberg	48	26.630	2	54.785
29.	S. Speed	48	36.640	1	36.640
30.	J. Villeneuve	•58•	14.733	2	39.403
31.	R. Barrichello	•63•	14.686	2	40.388

•• Drive-through penalty:
> Albers. To have to cause an avoidable collision with Monteiro at the start.
> Villeneuve. To have to exceed under the mode of the safety car.
> Barrichello. Excessive speed in the stands.

Race Leader

Driver	Laps in the lead	Nbr of Laps
F. Alonso	1 > 23	23
M. Webber	24	1
F. Alonso	25 > 78	54

Driver	Laps in the lead	Kilometers
F. Alonso	77	257,180 km
M. Webber	1	3,340 km

Gaps on the leader board

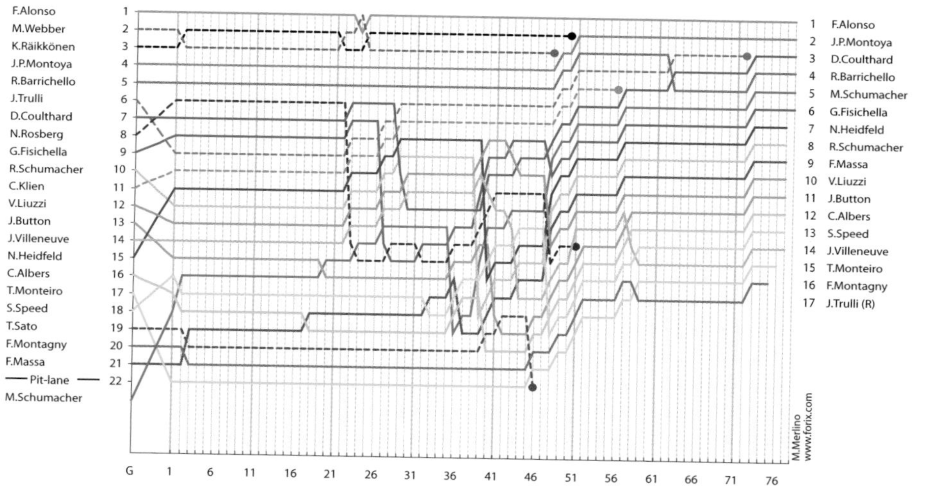

Lap chart

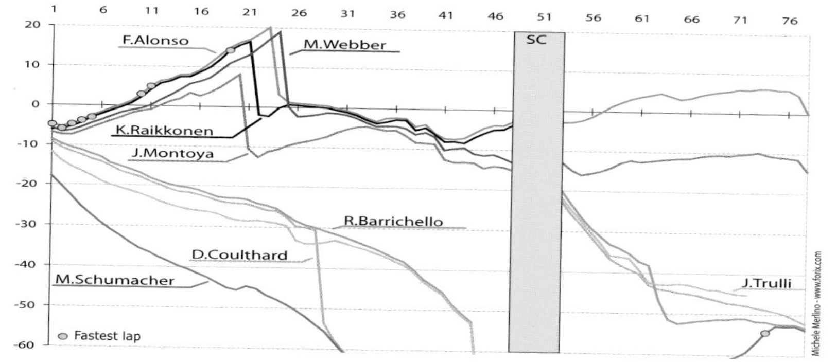

Championships 7/18

Drivers

1. F. Alonso ....Renault ....4 🏆....64
2. M. Schumacher .....Ferrari.......................2 🏆....43
3. G. Fisichella..........Renault ....1 🏆....27
4. K. Räikkönen ....McLaren Mercedes..............27
5. J. Montoya ....McLaren Mercedes..............23
6. F. Massa...............Ferrari 20
7. J. Button ....Honda 16
8. R. Barrichello........Honda 13
9. R. Schumacher .....Toyota 8
10. N. Heidfeld ....BMW 8
11. D. Coulthard ....RBR Ferrari 7
12. M. Webber............Williams Cosworth................6
13. J. Villeneuve ....BMW 6
14. N. Rosberg ....Williams Cosworth................4
15. C. Klien................RBR Ferrari 1
16. J. Trulli.................Toyota 0
17. S. Speed ....STR Cosworth......................0
18. V. Liuzzi ....STR Cosworth......................0
19. C. Albers ....MF1 Toyota 0
20. T. Monteiro ....MF1 Toyota 0
21. T. Sato.................Aguri Honda 0
22. Y. Ide...................Aguri Honda 0
23. F. Montagny..........Aguri Honda 0

Constructors

1. Mild Seven Renault F1 Team ....5 🏆....91
2. Scuderia Ferrari Marlboro ....2 🏆....63
3. Team McLaren Mercedes 50
4. Lucky Strike Honda Racing F1 Team 29
5. BMW Sauber F1 Team..............................14
6. Williams F1 Team 10
7. Panasonic Toyota Racing 8
8. Red Bull Racing 8
9. Scuderia Toro Rosso 0
10. MF1 Racing 0
11. Super Aguri Formula 1...............................0

The circuit

Name	Circuit de Monaco; Monte-Carlo	Weather	Sunny and warm
Lenght	3340 m	Air temperature	24-26°c
Distance	78 tours soit 260,520 km	Track tempature	27-39°c
Date	May 28, 2006	Humidity	64%
		Wind speed	0.1 m/s

S1: 70m before corner
S2: 80m before corner
Radar: 145m before corner

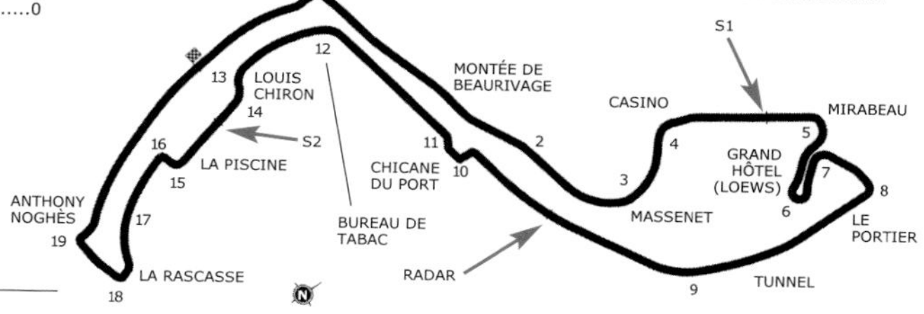

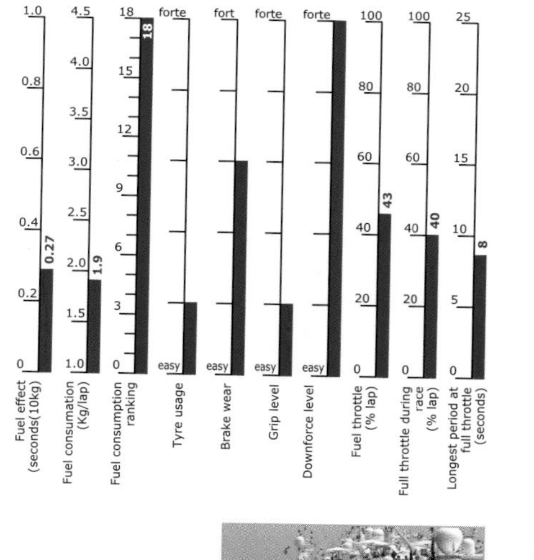

All results : © 2006 Formula One Administration Ltd, 6 Princes Gate, London, SW7 1QJ, England

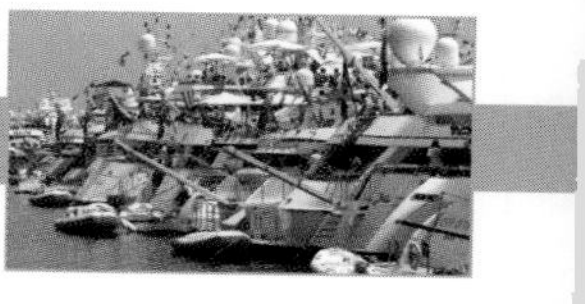

ALONSO'S CLEAN SWEEP

Pole position, victory and fastest lap. The Spaniard showed who was boss at Silverstone. He finished in front of Michael Schumacher and increased his lead in the world championship.

Fernando on top

The qualifying session looked like being a pretty exciting one. In the morning's free practice Michael Schumacher had blitzed his opponents with a lap that over half-a-second quicker than his nearest rival and almost 1 second better than Alonso. It looked like nobody could catch the German in his Ferrari, which had a very high top speed because of a controversial rear wing. But that was without counting on the talent and obstinacy of Alonso. With just 3 minutes to go to the end of qualifying the drivers came in to put on fresh tyres good enough to gain a full second per lap in relation to worn rubber. Michael set the fastest time from the Spaniard by just a fraction of a second. The cars use around 3 kilos of fuel per lap, which, at Silverstone, represents around 1/10s. So the final lap is always the quickest.

As scheduled both drivers stopped to fit another set of fresh rubber and to everybody's surprise Alonso snatched pole while Kimi Raïkkönen also managed to nip past Schumacher. "*I knew that I had a chance on that last lap provided I didn't make any mistakes,*" smiled Alonso. *And I did it! Four poles on the trot, it's bloody marvellous.*"

It was a big blow to the Scuderia, which had hoped to put both its cars on the front row. "*I'm very disappointed; it's normal,*" remarked Michael Schumacher. "*But all isn't lost as we'll have to see what the strategies are in the race. It's not been an easy weekend so far. The circuit is very tricky and we're finding it difficult to get the right set-up.*"

The major surprise came from the McLaren team. On Friday, both cars were way off the pace but on Saturday Kimi managed to get to within a tenth of a second of Alonso; "*We've really made a lot of progress since yesterday,*" said a jubilant Finn. "*In fact, I'm a little bit miffed not to be on pole. We're so close.*"

Johanna said "Yes!" Villeneuve is now wedded!

Jacques Villeneuve was no longer an eligible bachelor since the Monday following the Monaco Grand Prix. And he was also soon to become a father.

It was in the air for a few weeks and a look at Johanna's spectacular wedding ring was proof enough. On the Monday after the Monaco Grand Prix Jacques Villeneuve tied the knot with Johanna Martinez at 16h30 in the Aigle registry office. People who live in Villars-sur-Orne, Jacques' home, have to go to Aigle to get married as the town hall of the little seaside resort is not big enough for such ceremonies.

The discrete ceremony lasted only 20 minutes and was attended by around 30 people made up of family and friends of the couple.

The guests went on to celebrate the marriage in "La Renadière" a magnificent restaurant in Villars-sur-Orne where the man from Quebec has a chalet like his friend David Coulthard and his manager Craig Pollock who were among the guests. Johanna was the first to actually get Jacques to commit himself as during his career the Canadian has had quite a few girl-friends but without ever being led to the altar.

In fact, he had only met Johanna during the ceremony in the winter when Jean Alesi was awarded the Légion d'Honneur.

The fact that she was pregnant may have persuaded Jacques to hurry things up, as he has never hid the fact that a family and children are among his priorities. "*It's obvious that I'd like to have children,*" he confided a few weeks earlier. His words indicated a new direction in his life.

"*After all continuing the species is what we're here for. It's the most important thing in the world. But it's not necessarily compatible with driving racing cars. Frankly leaving every few days with a baby at home is no good even if my girlfriend doesn't work,*" he concluded.

Johanna Martinez is from Paris and a close friend of a friend of Jacques Laffite's. She is 21-years-old, 14 younger than her husband, and worked in the music business before going to join Jacques in Switzerland. The couple celebrated the religious marriage in Paris the weekend before the British Grand Prix in a catholic church. "*Jacques and Johanna are a lovely couple; he's been literally transformed since he met her,*» commented Sylvain Kohli, Jacques' former skiing instructor and friend who was present at the ceremony. "*She's a really nice, bright girl and she hasn't got a big head.*"

Starting grid

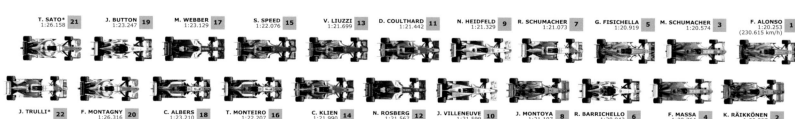

Position	Driver	Time
21	T. SATO*	1:26.158
19	J. BUTTON	1:23.247
17	M. WEBBER	1:23.129
15	S. SPEED	1:22.076
13	V. LIUZZI	1:21.699
11	D. COULTHARD	1:21.442
9	N. HEIDFELD	1:21.329
7	R. SCHUMACHER	1:21.073
5	G. FISICHELLA	1:20.919
3	M. SCHUMACHER	1:20.574
1	F. ALONSO	1:20.253 (230.615 km/h)
22	J. TRULLI*	1:26.316
20	F. MONTAGNY	1:23.210
18	C. ALBERS	1:22.207
16	T. MONTEIRO	1:21.990
14	C. KLIEN	1:21.567
12	N. ROSBERG	1:21.599
10	J. VILLENEUVE	1:21.107
8	J. MONTOYA	1:20.943
6	R. BARRICHELLO	1:20.764
4	F. MASSA	1:20.397
2	K. RÄIKKÖNEN	

the race

Fernando takes another step towards the title

Three days previously the Ferraris had had a brilliant private test session on the Barcelona circuit that indicated a leap forward in competitiveness. The Tifosi had every right to think that the incredible top speed of the 248 F1s would enable them to dominate the British Grand Prix. That was also Fernando's opinion when he arrived at the circuit.

When it came to assessing the results of the weekend Ferrari's hopes were dashed. It turned out in the race that the Spaniard had set pole with more fuel in his car than Michael Schumacher – 10 kilos or 4 laps – a huge difference. Alonso was never threatened by his rivals throughout the 60-lap race and he was able to slow a little towards the end to nurse his tyres.

So the Ferraris were just not quick enough and despite the enormous effort made by the team they were not able to close the gap to the Renaults. Which had also progressed. "*We brought along new aerodynamic and suspension parts,*" confirmed Pat Symonds, the French team's technical director. "*They're very big changes and they've helped the car to show a big improvement.*"

This quantum leap forward finally got to the Scuderia's morale. On Sunday evening one look at team boss Jean Todt's grim face was enough to confirm the extent of the damage. The Frenchman had probably just realised that the 2006 championships were virtually lost. "*We're up*

against very tough opposition," he said glumly. "*When you're after victory and you finish second then obviously you're disappointed. But we're going to fight back to the best of our ability with the help of our partners especially Bridgestone.*" It was a small dig at the Japanese manufacturer, which had not supplied sufficiently competitive rubber at Silverstone.

In the meantime Alonso continued to rack up the points. With eight grands prix run he had 74 points from 5 victories and 3 second places. It was a dream score obtained at the wheel of a dream car. It looked like nothing could stop the Spaniard from winning his second title.

^
A deliriously happy Alonso on the rostrum was accompanied by Rémy Taffin, his race engineer in the Renault team.

A wing that was too flexible to be true!

Since moveable aerodynamic devices were banned some 30 years ago engineers have been trying every trick in the book to get round this rule. An aerodynamicist's dream would be to have very steeply angled wings in corners to keep the car glued to the track and then almost flat ones on the straight to give a very high top speed. As mobile wings are banned the engineers are always trying to find the right balance between top speed and drag.

A few months earlier some teams had been accused of using flexi-wings whose angle was very acute at low velocity and then resumed their normal shape when the speed increased. It was a very difficult phenomenon to check when the cars were stopped. Thus, the scrutineers at the grands prix decided to apply weights to the wings to simulate the aerodynamic load generated by cornering speeds.

Thus cheating was supposed to be impossible. Except at Ferrari, which seemed to have found a loophole. In private practice on the Barcelona circuit a week earlier the 248 F1 suddenly gained around 20 km/h on the straight compared with its top speed in the Spanish Grand Prix two weeks earlier. It represented a huge advantage for the red cars, which nobody could catch or overtake on the straight.

The Scuderia's rivals noticed that the Italian team's mechanics manipulated the cars' rear wings with incredible care and did not use them to push the 248 F1s. "*We think that Ferrari has found a solution whereby their wings are rigid when the scrutineers measure them and flexible between these two points,*" grumbled the technical director of a rival team.

At Silverstone Schumacher and Massa confirmed

the top speed of their cars and only BMW test driver Robert Kubica was quicker, but with an empty tank as they set the quickest times in the first section of the circuit where top speed is crucial.

Was it cheating or not? It looked like a new row was about to break out. In the race itself the red cars' advantage did not seem to be so pronounced so their opponents decided not to bring the affair to the FIA's notice. For the time being anyway.

Jenson Button did not shine in front of his home crowd. He started from 19th position on the grid after being eliminated in the first session and went out on lap 9 with an oil leak.
∨<

Fanck Montagny had no chance of upsetting the F1 apple cart at Silverstone. He qualified 20th for the third grand prix in succession.
∨

Nick Heidfeld and Jacques Villeneuve probably both went across the grass (photo) but they finished in the points. It was the first time they had managed to do so when none of the Ferraris, Renaults or McLarens retired.

Copse Corner: the most spectacular bend of the season

There are stories that are told and retold among motor sporting aficionados on special occasions like Christmas Eve for example to get away from the boring routine of family chatter.

Among them is the one that Alain Prost never tires of telling about Nigel Mansell, his team-mate for a year in 1990 when they both drove Ferraris. While Prost as was his wont did a lot of work in close collaboration with his engineers to make his car quicker Mansell was content to drive what he was given. Which did not allow him to beat his team-mate. Except on the Silverstone circuit where "Il Leone' as the Italians named him was unbeatable in front of his home crowd. In certain respects this race was more important for him than the whole championship. "*Nigel had something special at Silverstone,*" said the Frenchman. "*He went through Copse flat out. I tried but couldn't do it. I found it difficult to believe and I studied his telemetry read-outs. It was true. He didn't even lift off. I still don't know how he did it; it was impossible.*"

Since then and especially since Senna's fatal accident the FIA has tried to lower cornering speeds by legal means. Narrower tyres, then sculpted ones, flat bottoms, smaller wings, almost each year it brings in measures to limit the cars' performances.

Except this year. The FIA's decision to bring back tyre changes enabled the manufacturers to come up with softer compounds thus quicker rubber. With the help of aerodynamic progress (the V8s are smaller than the V10s) the cars are cornering much quicker than last year: quicker in fact than ever in F1 history.

You didn't have to be called Nigel to go through Copse flat out this year. Most drivers did but few people expected it. "*We tested here a few weeks ago,*" said Juan Pablo Montoya, "*and I couldn't believe it. We were going through Copse flat out. It's become the most awesome corner of the season.*"

It's all the more important as it dictates the speed in a series of mind-boggling curves

–Maggots and Beckets – where the cars are thrown from left to right before coming onto Hangar straight, the longest on the circuit. At the end of this there is no room for improvement. The first third of the circuit dictates the speed over the rest of the lap. Time lost here cannot be made up. "*We've designed tyres to go thought Copse without lifting,*" explained a Michelin engineer. "*This corner is very important for the rhythm of the sequence that follows. But for the tyres it's terrible as they are subjected to extreme forces in this spot.*" This year anyway, it was vital to go through Copse flat out to qualify at the top of the time sheets. It was not without its risks. "*I'd hate to think what would happed if we suffered mechanical failure in this corner,*" declared Mark Webber.

Maybe for some drivers the thrill of going through Copse flat-out will be a memory that they'll want to recall when they are old and grey and sitting by the fireside!

The starting grid for the British Grand Prix. That moment when everything is still, the calm before the storm, and one of the few times when emotion can be experienced during a grandprix weekend

Jacques Villeneuve walks out on the GPDA

It was the Jacques Villeneuve of old. The scruffy guy with his shirt sticking out of his pants who made fun of the efforts of his fellow-drivers in the GPDA (The Grand Prix Drivers' Association) whose aim was to put forward the drivers' point of view to help improve circuit safety. When he arrived F1 in 1996 he refused to join the Association. He was the only one not to support a group that was trying to look after his interests. As he was away from the circuits in 2004 he decided to make an effort when he came back so he joined the GPDA and attended their meetings on a regular basis.

But now it was all over. He went back to his role as the lone gunslinger as he quit the GPDA. At Silverstone he wanted Michael Schumacher to resign from his post as GPDA chairman after his Monaco gesture. The German did nothing. Villeneuve was disappointed by the passivity of the other members who confirmed Schumacher in his role of chairman and said he wanted out. "*Jacques wanted excuses on the part of Michael or for him to be stripped of his role as chairman,*" explained his friends. The GPDA noted his action, which Jarno Trulli said he understood.

Michael Schumacher also went off line slightly. He qualified third and finished second. "*I really didn't have any particular problems with my car,*" he confessed. "*We just weren't quick enough.*"

results

Practice

All the time trials

N° Driver	Nat.	N° Chassis - Engine [Nbr GP]	Pos.	Free 1 Friday	Laps	Pos.	Free 2 Friday	Laps	Pos.	Free 3 Saturday	Laps	Pos.	Q1 Saturday	Laps	Pos.	Q2 Saturday	Laps	Pos.	Super Pole Saturday	Laps
1. Fernando Alonso	E	Renault R26 02 [2]	18.		1	7.	1:22.603	13	6.	1:21.870	13	1.	1:21.018	6	1.	1:20.271	3	1.	**1:20.253**	15
2. Giancarlo Fisichella	I	Renault R26 04 [1]	19.		1	2.	1:22.294	3	5.	1:21.859	12	8.	1:22.411	3	3.	1:20.594	3	5.	**1:20.919**	15
3. Kimi Räikkönen	FIN	McLaren MP4-21 06 - Mercedes [2]	22.		1	21.	1:23.915	4	4.	1:21.771	12	4.	1:21.648	6	2.	1:20.497	3	2.	**1:20.397**	15
4. Juan Pablo Montoya	CO	McLaren MP4-21 05 - Mercedes [1]	23.		1	14.	1:23.199	10	15.	1:23.412	7	7.	1:22.169	3	7.	1:20.816	5	8.	**1:21.107**	15
5. Michael Schumacher	D	Ferrari 248 F1 254 [2]	5.	1:22.925	3	8.	1:22.825	14	1.	1:20.919	13	6.	1:22.096	4	5.	1:20.659	3	3.	**1:20.574**	15
6. Felipe Massa	BR	Ferrari 248 F1 250 [2]	8.	1:23.816	4	6.	1:22.476	19	3.	1:21.633	15	3.	1:21.647	3	8.	1:20.846	3	4.	**1:20.764**	15
7. Ralf Schumacher	D	Toyota TF106/07B [2]	17.		2	11.	1:23.114	22	19.	1:24.386	12	14.	1:22.886	7	10.	1:21.043	6	7.	**1:21.073**	15
8. Jarno Trulli	I	Toyota TF106/08B [2->1]	4.	1:22.877	7	5.	1:22.437	17	16.	1:23.459	13	22.		2						
9. Mark Webber	AUS	Williams FW28 03 - Cosworth [2]				9.	1:23.099	15	17.	1:23.964	12	17.	**1:23.129**	3						
10. Nico Rosberg	D	Williams FW28 06 - Cosworth [2]				19.	1:23.816	16	18.	1:24.010	11	16.	1:23.083	3	12.	**1:21.567**	6			
11. Rubens Barrichello	BR	Honda RA106-01 [1]	6.	1:23.128	5	10.	1:23.104	17	7.	1:22.023	12	15.	1:22.965	3	9.	1:20.929	6	6.	**1:20.943**	15
12. Jenson Button	GB	Honda RA106-04 [1]	7.	1:23.415	6	17.	1:23.707	18	11.	1:22.596	15	19.	**1:23.247**	3						
14. David Coulthard	GB	Red Bull RB2 3 - Ferrari [1]	21.		1	25.	1:24.392	13	12.	1:22.681	15	9.	1:22.424	6	11.	**1:21.442**	6			
15. Christian Klien	A	Red Bull RB2 2 - Ferrari [1]	20.		1	23.	1:24.158	12	14.	1:22.921	14	12.	1:22.773	6	14.	**1:21.990**	6			
16. Nick Heidfeld	D	BMW Sauber F1.06-06 [2]	26.		1	20.	1:23.895	14	2.	1:21.361	13	5.	1:21.670	7	4.	1:20.629	6	9.	**1:21.329**	15
17. Jacques Villeneuve	CDN	BMW Sauber F1.06-08 [1]	25.		1	18.	1:23.750	13	8.	1:22.229	14	2.	1:21.637	3	6.	1:20.672	3	10.	**1:21.599**	15
18. Tiago Monteiro	P	Midland M16-03 - Toyota [2]	10.	1:24.070	6	13.	1:23.194	23	13.	1:22.812	19	13.	1:22.860	7	16.	**1:22.207**	3			
19. Christijan Albers	NL	Midland M16-04 & 02 - Toyota [2]	9.	1:24.019	6	15.	1:23.499	14	22.		3	18.	**1:23.210**	7						
20. Vitantonio Liuzzi	I	Toro Rosso STR01 03 - Cosworth [2]	27.		1	22.	1:24.012	19	9.	1:22.456	18	11.	1:22.685	7	13.	**1:21.699**	6			
21. Scott Speed	USA	Toro Rosso STR01 02 - Cosworth [2]	24.		1	24.	1:24.167	19	10.	1:22.532	14	10.	1:22.541	7	15.	**1:22.076**	4			
22. Takuma Sato	J	Super Aguri SA05-05 - Honda [2->1]	13.	1:27.724	10	27.	1:25.870	26	21.	1:27.525	12	20.	**1:26.158**	6						
23. Franck Montagny	F	Super Aguri SA05-02 - Honda [2]	16.		3	28.	1:26.248	22	20.	1:27.229	10	21.	**1:26.316**	6						
35. Alexander Wurz	A	Williams FW28 04 - Cosworth	1.	1:21.946	26	3.	1:22.300	30												
36. Anthony Davidson	GB	Honda RA106-03	2.	1:22.003	31	4.	1:22.310	34												
37. Robert Doornbos	NL	Red Bull RB2 5 - Ferrari	15.		9	12.	1:23.140	25												
38. Robert Kubica	PL	BMW Sauber F1.06-04	3.	1:22.365	30	1.	1:21.082	29												
39. Giorgio Mondini	CH	Midland M16-02 - Toyota	11.	1:24.087	19	16.	1:23.529	25												
40. Neel Jani	CH	Toro Rosso STR01 01 - Cosworth	12.	1:24.145	22	26.	1:24.666	22												
41. Sakon Yamamoto	J	Super Aguri SA05-01 - Honda	14.	1:29.678	22	29.	1:27.908	27												

Fastest lap overall
F. Alonso 1:20.253 (230,615 km/h)

Maximum speed

N° Driver	S1 Qualifs	Pos.	S1 Race	Pos.	S2 Qualifs	Pos.	S2 Race	Pos.	Finish Qualifs	Pos.	Finish Race	Pos.	Radar Qualifs	Pos.	Radar Race	Pos.
1. F. Alonso	296,6	3	294,7	7	271,2	2	270,5	1	280,0	3	285,4	3	289,3	3	292,2	4
2. G. Fisichella	295,3	5	294,9	6	270,8	3	269,0	2	279,9	4	283,9	4	287,3	6	291,9	5
3. K. Räikkönen	292,1	10	294,2	8	269,6	7	265,6	4	278,7	7	282,4	6	286,5	7	289,8	10
4. J. Montoya	291,5	11	291,7	14	270,2	6	265,0	6	278,0	9	279,8	13	285,0	12	287,9	13
5. M. Schumacher	299,7	1	298,0	2	270,3	5	264,4	7	281,8	2	286,8	2	293,6	1	294,4	1
6. F. Massa	299,4	2	299,9	1	270,4	4	265,4	5	282,4	1	287,2	1	291,9	2	294,3	2
7. R. Schumacher	292,6	8			264,5	15			278,9	6			284,9	13		
8. J. Trulli	290,3	14	295,0	5	250,5	21	261,3	11	272,8	15	282,2	7	282,2	14	292,2	3
9. M. Webber	290,2	15			265,8	13			274,9	14			279,0	18		
10. N. Rosberg	293,3	7	295,0	4	267,5	10	265,8	3	276,5	10	281,1	11	285,9	9	290,3	7
11. R. Barrichello	292,3	9	293,9	10	271,6	1	260,3	13	279,7	5	283,7	5	285,9	10	289,6	11
12. J. Button	290,0	17	294,1	9	255,3	20	248,6	19	272,1	17	281,8	8	282,0	15	282,2	17
14. D. Coulthard	290,0	16	293,0	11	266,9	11	257,4	15	276,3	12	281,6	9	286,3	8	288,6	12
15. C. Klien	290,4	13	289,6	16	266,4	12	262,0	10	276,2	13	281,1	10	285,1	11	291,4	6
16. N. Heidfeld	295,4	4	292,1	13	267,5	9	264,3	8	278,6	8	279,6	14	288,4	5	289,8	9
17. J. Villeneuve	294,8	6	292,3	12	267,9	8	262,9	9	276,4	11	281,0	12	288,8	4	290,0	8
18. T. Monteiro	288,0	19	289,0	18	260,5	18	255,9	16	271,6	19	273,7	19	279,7	17	284,0	16
19. C. Albers	288,6	18	290,2	15	261,3	17	259,3	14	270,1	21	278,2	15	278,9	20	285,0	14
20. V. Liuzzi	287,3	20	289,5	17	264,2	16	260,8	12	271,0	20	275,3	16	277,1	22	284,1	15
21. S. Speed	290,7	12	269,1	20	265,0	14	172,8	20	271,9	18			280,0	16	184,9	20
22. T. Sato	285,3	21	295,8	3	247,1	22	248,7	17	269,5	22	274,5	18	277,1	21	281,4	19
23. F. Montagny	285,0	22	287,8	19	256,8	19	248,7	18	272,3	16	274,8	17	279,0	19	281,9	18

Race

Classification & Retirements

Pos.	Driver	Constructor	Tyres	Laps	Time	Average
1.	F. Alonso	Renault	M	60	1:25:51.927	215,468 km/h
2.	M. Schumacher	Ferrari	B	60	+ 13.951	214,886 km/h
3.	K. Räikkönen	McLaren Mercedes	M	60	+ 18.672	214,690 km/h
4.	G. Fisichella	Renault	M	60	+ 19.976	214,636 km/h
5.	F. Massa	Ferrari	B	60	+ 31.559	214,156 km/h
6.	J. Montoya	McLaren Mercedes	M	60	+ 1:04.769	212,793 km/h
7.	N. Heidfeld	BMW	M	60	+ 1:11.594	212,515 km/h
8.	J. Villeneuve	BMW	M	60	+ 1:18.299	212,242 km/h
9.	N. Rosberg	Williams Cosworth	B	60	+ 1:19.008	212,214 km/h
10.	R. Barrichello	Honda	M	59	1 lap	211,238 km/h
11.	J. Trulli	Toyota	B	59	1 lap	210,912 km/h
12.	D. Coulthard	RBR Ferrari	M	59	1 lap	210,091 km/h
13.	V. Liuzzi	STR Cosworth	M	59	1 lap	209,658 km/h
14.	C. Klien	RBR Ferrari	M	59	1 lap	209,445 km/h
15.	C. Albers	MF1 Toyota	B	59	1 lap	208,893 km/h
16.	T. Monteiro	MF1 Toyota	B	58	2 laps	207,622 km/h
17.	T. Sato	Aguri Honda	B	57	3 laps	202,900 km/h
18.	F. Montagny	Aguri Honda	B	57	3 laps	201,898 km/h

Driver	Constructor	Tyres	Laps	Reason
J. Button	Honda	M	8	Engine oil leak, spins off
S. Speed	STR Cosworth	M	1	Damaged car after collision with R. Schumacher
R. Schumacher	Toyota	B	0	Hit by Speed, spin, collision with Webber
M. Webber	Williams Cosworth	B	0	Collision with R. Schumacher

Fastest laps

	Driver	Time	Laps	Average
1.	F. Alonso	1:21.599	21	226,811 km/h
2.	M. Schumacher	1:21.934	53	225,884 km/h
3.	G. Fisichella	1:22.238	42	225,049 km/h
4.	F. Massa	1:22.371	43	224,685 km/h
5.	K. Räikkönen	1:22.461	15	224,440 km/h
6.	N. Heidfeld	1:22.706	43	223,775 km/h
7.	J. Trulli	1:22.744	19	223,673 km/h
8.	J. Montoya	1:22.780	38	223,575 km/h
9.	N. Rosberg	1:22.916	47	223,209 km/h
10.	J. Villeneuve	1:22.921	46	223,195 km/h
11.	R. Barrichello	1:23.224	38	222,382 km/h
12.	C. Klien	1:23.712	30	221,086 km/h
13.	C. Albers	1:23.977	27	220,388 km/h
14.	D. Coulthard	1:23.995	42	220,341 km/h
15.	V. Liuzzi	1:24.221	25	219,750 km/h
16.	T. Monteiro	1:24.636	25	218,672 km/h
17.	J. Button	1:25.207	8	217,207 km/h
18.	T. Sato	1:26.520	23	213,911 km/h
19.	F. Montagny	1:27.167	26	212,323 km/h

Pit stops

	Driver	Laps	Duration	Stop	Total
1.	J. Trulli	17	23.169	1	23.169
2.	M. Schumacher	18	23.736	1	23.736
3.	K. Räikkönen	19	24.124	1	24.124
4.	F. Massa	19	23.932	1	23.932
5.	R. Barrichello	19	23.590	1	23.590
6.	J. Montoya	20	25.329	1	25.329
7.	G. Fisichella	21	23.516	1	23.516
8.	F. Alonso	22	23.020	1	23.020
9.	T. Sato	21	25.122	1	25.122
10.	T. Monteiro	22	22.832	1	22.832
11.	F. Montagny	23	22.793	1	22.793
12.	N. Heidfeld	25	31.398	1	31.398
13.	N. Rosberg	25	23.534	1	23.534
14.	D. Coulthard	25	23.717	1	23.717
15.	C. Albers	25	22.072	1	22.072
16.	J. Villeneuve	27	25.422	1	25.422
17.	V. Liuzzi	27	27.091	1	27.091
18.	C. Klien	27	21.822	1	21.822
19.	J. Trulli	37	23.435	2	46.604
20.	M. Schumacher	41	21.708	2	45.444
21.	T. Monteiro	40	25.684	2	48.516
22.	C. Klien	41	23.377	2	45.199
23.	K. Räikkönen	42	22.969	2	47.093
24.	T. Sato	40	23.100	2	48.222
25.	R. Barrichello	42	21.895	2	45.485
26.	C. Albers	42	25.542	2	47.614
27.	F. Montagny	41	23.545	2	46.338
28.	F. Alonso	44	21.967	2	44.987
29.	G. Fisichella	45	21.687	2	45.203
30.	F. Massa	45	21.301	2	45.233
31.	J. Montoya	45	21.529	2	46.858
32.	N. Rosberg	45	23.877	2	47.411
33.	D. Coulthard	45	21.904	2	45.621
34.	N. Heidfeld	46	23.404	2	54.802
35.	J. Villeneuve	48	21.047	2	46.469

Race leader

Driver	Laps in the lead	Nbr of Laps
F. Alonso	1 > 44	44
G. Fisichella	45	1
F. Alonso	46 > 60	15

Driver	Nbr of Laps	Kilometers
F. Alonso	59	303,214 km
G. Fisichella	1	5,141 km

Gaps in the lead board

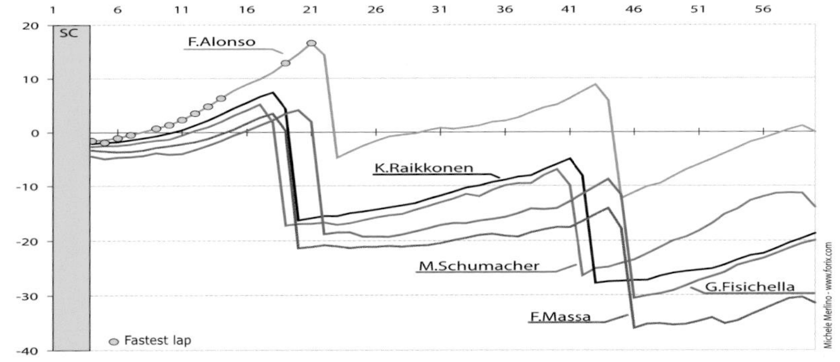

Lap chart

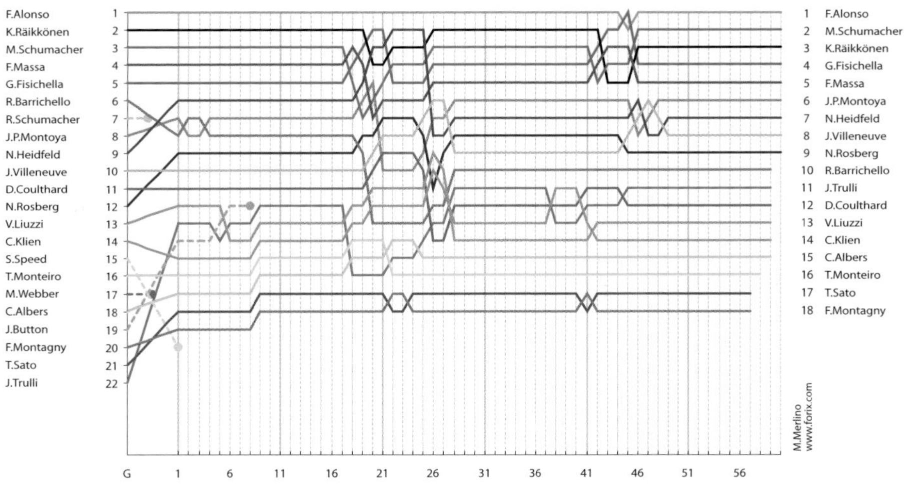

Championships 8/18

Drivers

1. F. Alonso ....Renault ....5 🏆....74
2. M. Schumacher .....Ferrari.....................2 🏆....51
3. K. Räikkönen ....McLaren Mercedes.............33
4. G. Fisichella..........Renault ....1 🏆....32
5. J. Montoya ....McLaren Mercedes.............26
6. F. Massa..............Ferrari 24
7. J. Button ....Honda 16
8. R. Barrichello........Honda 13
9. N. Heidfeld ....BMW 10
10. R. Schumacher .....Toyota 8
11. D. Coulthard ....RBR Ferrari 7
12. J. Villeneuve ....BMW 7
13. M. Webber...........Williams Cosworth................6
14. N. Rosberg ....Williams Cosworth................4
15. C. Klien................RBR Ferrari 1
16. J. Trulli................Toyota 0
17. S. Speed ....STR Cosworth.......................0
18. V. Liuzzi ....STR Cosworth.......................0
19. C. Albers ....MF1 Toyota 0
20. T. Monteiro ....MF1 Toyota 0
21. T. Sato................Aguri Honda 0
22. Y. Ide..................Aguri Honda 0
23. F. Montagny.........Aguri Honda 0

Constructors

1. Mild Seven Renault F1 Team ....6 🏆....106
2. Scuderia Ferrari Marlboro ....2 🏆 75
3. Team McLaren Mercedes 59
4. Lucky Strike Honda Racing F1 Team 29
5. BMW Sauber F1 Team...............................17
6. Williams F1 Team....................................10
7. Panasonic Toyota Racing.............................8
8. Red Bull Racing 8
9. Scuderia Toro Rosso...................................0
10. MF1 Racing..0
11. Super Aguri Formula 1 0

The circuit

Name	Silverstone Circuit; Silverstone	Weather	Warm and sunny
Lenght	5141 m	Air temperature	24-26°c
Distance	60 laps, 308,355 km	Track temperature	27-39°c
Date	June 11, 2006	Humidity	64%
		Wind speed	0.1 m/s

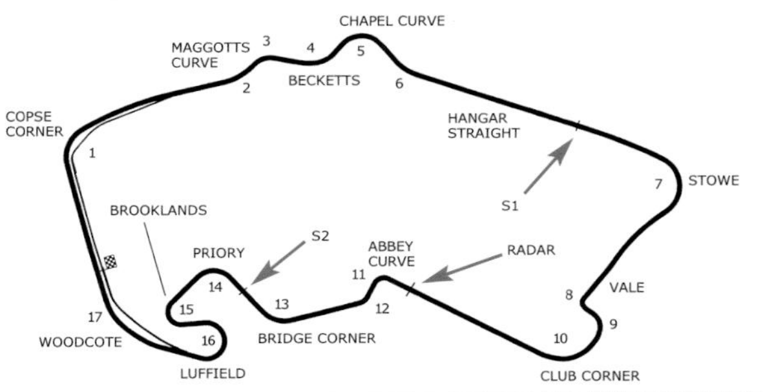

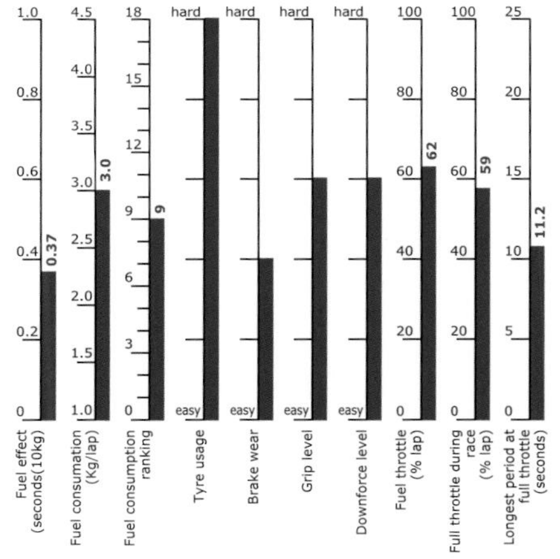

Al results : © 2006 Formula One Administration Ltd, 6 Princes Gate, London, SW7 1QJ, England

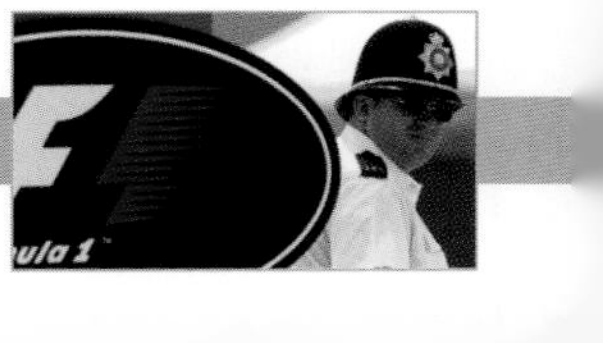

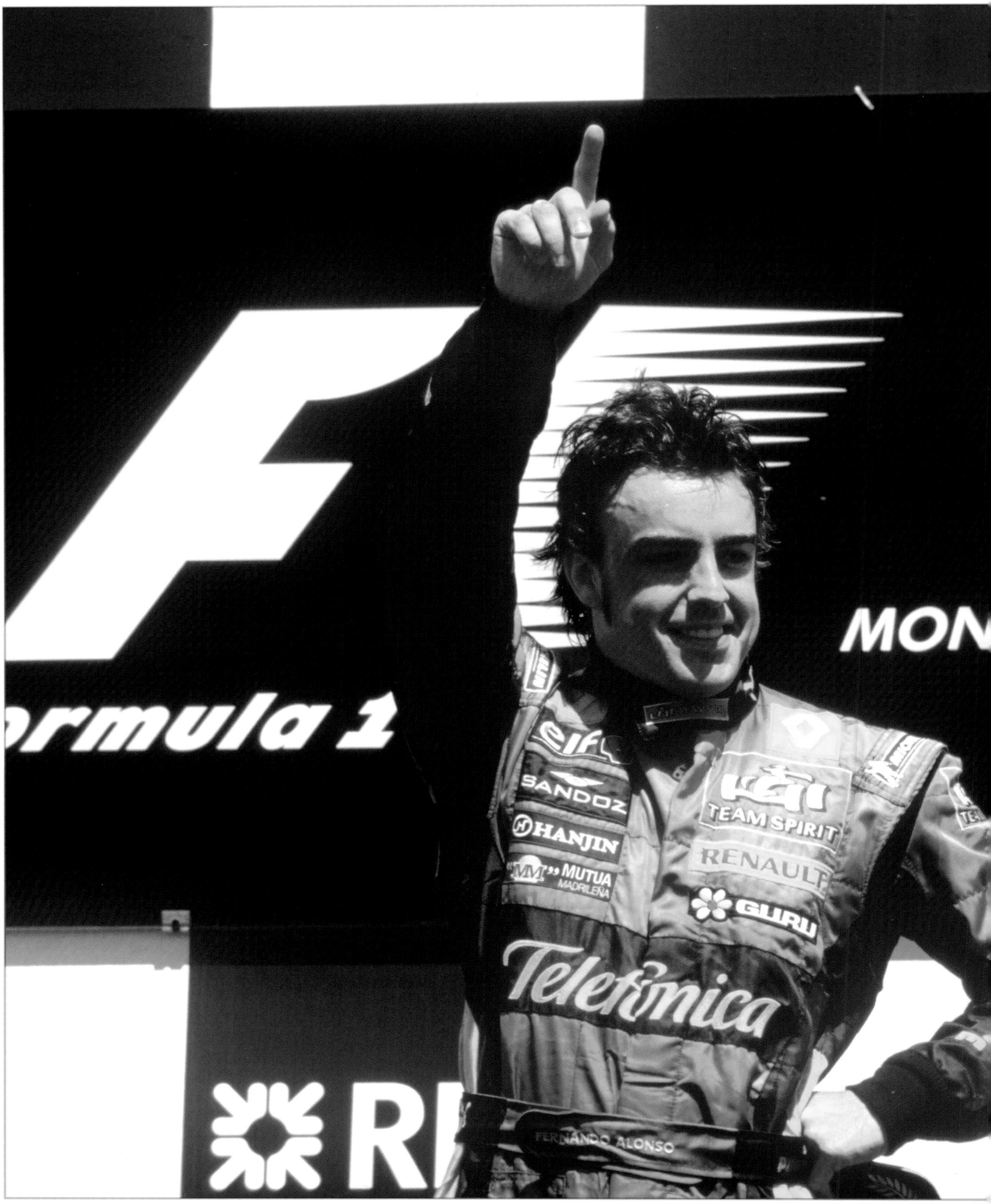

SANDOZ
HANJIN
MUTUA
MADRILEÑA
TEAM SPIRIT
RENAULT
GURU
Telefónica
FERNANDO ALONSO

FERNANDO RACKS UP NO.6

As the Sundays rolled by Fernando Alonso got closer and closer to his second consecutive world championship title.
He scored his sixth win in 9 races in Montréal. His other 3 results were all second places. Awesome! Although he did not know it that was the day that his domination came to an end.
The Canadian Grand Prix marked a turning point in the season.

> Scott Speed snapped in the pit lane on Friday. The American qualified 17th on the grid. "*Driving on this circuit is pretty exciting,*' he said. "*You've got to jump over the kerbs; the car slides around a bit; it's great. And the Toro Rosso is very much at home in such conditions.*"

Between the BMW Pit Lane Park and downtown Montréal Jacques Villeneuve had a busy time with the local media. In addition, the Canadian had just brought out his first single "Accepteras-tu?" This allowed Michael Schumacher to take a dig at him: "*It looks like Jacques is preparing a career as a singer. Maybe he'll be a bit more competitive there..!*"
>∨

Quebec is a place full of many and varied charms some of which are difficult to resist!
∨

It shaped up as a Ferrari/McLaren shoot-out until Renault put a spanner in their works.

It looked like the qualifying battle for the Canadian Grand Prix would between Ferrari and McLaren. But once again Renault trumped its rivals and the unstoppable Alonso racked up his fifth pole on the trot! Whatever the circuit layout, the twists and turns of Monaco, the long curves at Silverstone or the Montréal straights the Spaniard was the quickest driver.
But the Gilles Villeneuve track is not like any other on the calendar. It consists of long straights split up by chicanes with no quick curves and is not very demanding on the chassis. What it

needs above all is engines with plenty of grunt low down to enable the cars to accelerate quickly away from the chicanes.
Traditionally, the Ferraris have been very difficult to beat on this circuit. This year again the pundits reckoned that they would play a major role in the grand prix despite the rule banning their flexible wings. On Friday they were nowhere. The next day they were a bit quicker but still not on the pace. Finally, Michael Schumacher qualified in fifth place and Felipe Massa in tenth. It was a surprise for Alonso. "*I really thought the Ferraris would be more

competitive here; Friday, they were not quick, today it's a bit better so tomorrow they'll be even faster. If they do improve I hope we'll still be in front.*"
While the Renault drivers were both delighted with their qualifying performances the Scuderia management could only count on the top speed of their cars to hope to achieve a good result in the race. On Saturday the 248 F1s were credited with a speed of 320,6 km/h at the end of the main straight as compared to Alonso's 313,3 km/h, a bit slow to hope to overtake his main rivals in the race should the need arise.

Starting grid

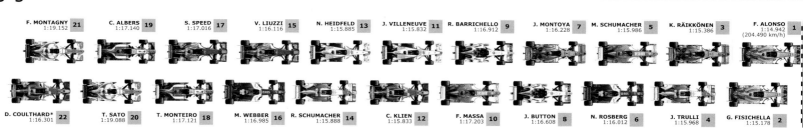

* D. COULTHARD penalty for an engine exchange. (-10 pos.)	F. MONTAGNY 21 1:19.152	C. ALBERS 19 1:17.140	S. SPEED 17 1:17.016	V. LIUZZI 15 1:16.116	N. HEIDFELD 13 1:15.885	J. VILLENEUVE 11 1:15.832	R. BARRICHELLO 9 1:16.912	J. MONTOYA 7 1:16.228	M. SCHUMACHER 5 1:15.986	K. RÄIKKÖNEN 3 1:15.386	F. ALONSO 1 1:14.942 (204.490 km/h)
	D. COULTHARD* 22 1:16.301	T. SATO 20 1:19.088	T. MONTEIRO 18 1:17.121	M. WEBBER 16 1:16.985	R. SCHUMACHER 14 1:15.888	C. KLIEN 12 1:15.833	F. MASSA 10 1:17.203	J. BUTTON 8 1:16.608	N. ROSBERG 6 1:16.012	J. TRULLI 4 1:15.968	G. FISICHELLA 2 1:15.178

Fernando homing in on the title

The grands prix followed each other and whether in the wide open spaces of Silverstone or the tight chicanes in Montréal the same trio filled the first 3 places: victory for Fernando Alonso followed by Michael Schumacher and Kimi Raïkkönen. This seemed to indicate that at this stage of the season nobody could beat the Spaniard but it also highlighted the fact that the team-mates of the 3 stars were not up to their jobs. On the Gilles Villeneuve circuit Fisichella jumped the start, Felipe Massa was nowhere and Juan Pablo Montoya had 2 accidents!

Once Alonso had his team-mate out of the way as the Italian was penalised for jumping the start a wide-open road to his sixth victory in 2006 lay before him even if the first few laps were a bit tense. "*Kimi gave me a few headaches at the start of the race,*" said the reigning world champion. "*On some laps he was quicker than me while the opposite was the case on others. I don't really know why as I was flat out all the time.*"

While his race looked easy to an outside observer, it was a different story in the Renault's cockpit. "*The track was very slippery today. If you went off line just a little it was like a skating rink. I scared myself on three or four occasions because when you're in the lead it's not always easy to remain concentrated.*"

Kimi Raïkkönen in his McLaren-Mercedes-Benz posed a threat to the Spaniard until he began to lose ground at the end of the race – especially after running into problems during his 2 refuelling stops. "*Early on I was able to follow Fernando very closely, but not enough to get past him,*" explained the Finn. "*I was very quick in the first stint but at the end of the race my performance dropped away and I don't know why. In any case we weren't good enough to win today. But I can't really complain; I'm not in the running for the championship. Whether I'm second or third doesn't really make any difference,*" he shrugged

Montréal was the halfway mark in the championship and Fernando Alonso had a 25-point lead over Michael Schumacher. That was to be the biggest gap between the two. From the following week onwards the Ferrari driver began to eat into the Spaniard's lead.

Michael still believes in his chances

As the 2006 season unfolded Michael's chances of becoming world champion for the eighth time looked slimmer and slimmer.

Montréal did not help. On Friday his 248 F1 was completely out-paced. On Saturday his engineers had turned the situation around and the German qualified in fifth place. The car was even better on Sunday and he finished on the second step of the rostrum.

He was lucky. While the gap between himself and Alonso was only 2 seconds it was because the Spaniard had lifted off. In addition, the safety car period had cancelled out the lead (almost 23 seconds) Fernando had built up over his pursuers. In terms of pure speed the Ferraris were well behind the Renaults.

Michael's race got off to a bad start. He was stuck behind Jarno Trulli for 25 laps; "*I was beginning to get a little hot around the collar,*" admitted the German. "*To make our strategy work, I had to pass him and I couldn't.*" He finally sliced past the Italian and also overtook Raïkkönen on the second-last lap in what was a good damage-limitation exercise.

Kimi Räikkönen did not come out of the Canadian Grand Prix too badly. He finished third after making a small error in the hairpin that allowed Michael Schumacher to slip past.

Week end chatter

> A complex lease affair opposed the Montréal mayor and the Canadian Grand Prix organiser, Norman Legault, who had exclusive rights to hold 2 races a year on the Gilles Villeneuve circuit. During the weekend the mayor announced that he would renew the lease for another 5 years with Legault so the future of the grand prix was assured until 2011 at least.

> An end was put to the controversy surrounding Ferrari's flexible wings in Montréal. Charlie Whiting, the FIA race director, decided at the start of the week with immediate effect that 5 cm slot-gap separators had to be fitted stabilising the gap between the two planes of the rear wing, which prevented any form of deformation on the straight.

> Jacques Villeneuve has never met with much success in his home race. His only points finish was in 1996 the year of his grand prix year debut when he saw the flag in second place. This year he looked like he was going to make into the points again but he went off with only 11 laps to go. It was a huge disappointment for the spectators massed around the track.

> Jarno Trulli confirmed that he had renewed his contract with Toyota until 2009, an additional 3 years.

The Italian had joined the Japanese team in 2005 when he was in his tenth season in Formula 1.

> Jacques Villeneuve's walkout on the GPDA, the F1 drivers' association, was still causing a few waves. He had resigned in England as a sign of protest against Michael Schumacher, the chairman. Jacques had accused the German over the Monaco incident where he blocked the track to hang on to pole. Alexander Wurtz, one of the most active GPDA members, wanted the Canadian to come back, "*Jacques has got some good ideas,*

clear ones and we need people like him in the GPDA."

> When the safety car went in at the British Grand Prix Fernando Alonso had braked in front of Kimi Räikkönen on several occasions to prevent the Finn from passing him when they crossed the line. In Montréal Charlie Whiting gave the reigning world champion a good bollocking about his attitude that could have caused an accident. The dispute lasted 15 minutes during the Drivers' briefing as some defended the Spaniard while other condemned him.

> It was a very emotional weekend for Michelin as it announced that it had no intention of replying to the tender to become the sole F1 tyre manufacturer in 2007. On Sunday the company racked up its 100th F1 victory.

The magnificent Ile de Notre Dame circuit in Montréal with the famous city in the background – an unforgettable sight.

results

Practice

All the time trials

N° Driver	Nat.	N° Châssis - Engine [Nbr. GP]	Pos. Free 1 Friday	Laps	Pos. Free 2 Fridayi	Laps Tr.	Pos. Free 3 Saturday	Laps	Pos. Q1 Saturday	Laps	Pos. Q2 Saturday	Laps	Pos. Super Pole Saturday	Laps
1. Fernando Alonso	E	Renault R26 02 [1]	19.	2	2. 1:17.095	15	1. 1:15.455	20	1. 1:15.350	4	1. 1:14.726	3	1. **1:14.942**	16
2. Giancarlo Fisichella	I	Renault R26 04 [2]	20.	1	6. 1:17.805	21	2. 1:15.521	19	5. 1:15.917	3	6. 1:15.295	3	2. **1:15.178**	16
3. Kimi Räikkönen	FIN	McLaren MP4-21 03 - Mercedes [1]			4. 1:17.490	10	5. 1:15.902	12	2. 1:15.376	7	5. 1:15.273	8	3. **1:15.386**	15
4. Juan Pablo Montoya	CO	McLaren MP4-21 05 - Mercedes [2]			17. 1:18.761	14	7. 1:15.975	12	6. 1:16.251	4	3. 1:15.253	6	7. **1:16.228**	16
5. Michael Schumacher	D	Ferrari 248 F1 254 [1]	4. 1:18.994	5	15. 1:18.549	17	6. 1:15.959	13	3. 1:15.716	4	2. 1:15.139	4	5. **1:15.986**	16
6. Felipe Massa	BR	Ferrari 248 F1 250 [1]	16. 1:23.179	5	22. 1:19.099	15	9. 1:16.348	18	7. 1:16.259	4	8. 1:15.555	4	10. **1:17.209**	16
7. Ralf Schumacher	D	Toyota TF106/07B [1]	12. 1:20.861	6	16. 1:18.614	23	19. 1:18.212	18	15. 1:16.702	6	14. **1:15.888**	6		
8. Jarno Trulli	I	Toyota TF106/08B [2]	17. 1:24.029	7	19. 1:18.868	17	17. 1:17.503	24	9. 1:16.455	6	7. 1:15.506	7	4. **1:15.968**	16
9. Mark Webber	AUS	Williams FW28 03 - Cosworth [1]			7. 1:17.848	13	13. 1:16.710	13	17. **1:16.985**	7				
10. Nico Rosberg	D	Williams FW28 06 - Cosworth [1]			21. 1:19.048	10	15. 1:16.829	19	8. 1:16.404	7	4. 1:15.269	6	6. **1:16.012**	15
11. Rubens Barrichello	BR	Honda RA106-01 [2]	5. 1:19.070	6	12. 1:18.279	16	8. 1:16.334	17	16. 1:16.735	9	9. 1:15.601	6	9. **1:16.912**	16
12. Jenson Button	GB	Honda RA106-05 [1]	6. 1:19.165	6	13. 1:18.429	18	12. 1:16.673	15	14. 1:16.594	8	10. 1:15.814	6	8. **1:16.608**	16
14. David Coulthard	GB	Red Bull RB2 3 - Ferrari [2->1]	24.	1	24. 1:19.313	15	14. 1:16.765	11	11. 1:16.514	5	16. **1:16.301**	6		
15. Christian Klien	A	Red Bull RB2 2 - Ferrari [2]	21.	1	18. 1:18.865	15	11. 1:16.660	17	13. 1:16.585	6	12. **1:15.833**	6		
16. Nick Heidfeld	D	BMW Sauber F1.06-04 [1]	25.	1	9. 1:18.015	13	4. 1:15.616	12	4. 1:15.906	5	13. **1:15.885**	6		
17. Jacques Villeneuve	CDN	BMW Sauber F1.06-08 [2]	23.	1	10. 1:18.035	14	3. 1:15.554	13	10. 1:16.493	4	11. **1:15.832**	6		
18. Tiago Monteiro	P	Midland M16-04 - Toyota [1]	11. 1:20.799	8	28. 1:20.262	18	18. 1:17.747	18	19. **1:17.121**	8				
19. Christijan Albers	NL	Midland M16-02 - Toyota [1]	10. 1:20.646	9	14. 1:18.503	20	22. 1:19.531	16	20. **1:17.140**	7				
20. Vitantonio Liuzzi	I	Toro Rosso STR01 03 - Cosworth [1]	9. 1:20.154	7	8. 1:18.009	18	16. 1:16.928	19	12. 1:16.581	8	15. **1:16.116**	8		
21. Scott Speed	USA	Toro Rosso STR01 02 - Cosworth [1]	22.	1	20. 1:18.907	21	10. 1:16.493	18	18. **1:17.016**	7				
22. Takuma Sato	J	Super Aguri SA05-05 - Honda [2]	14. 1:21.891	20	26. 1:19.624	22	20. 1:18.926	18	21. **1:19.088**	6				
23. Franck Montagny	F	Super Aguri SA05-02 - Honda [1]	13. 1:21.783	17	29. 1:21.434	22	21. 1:19.160	19	22. **1:19.152**	7				
35. Alexander Wurz	A	Williams FW28 04 - Cosworth	3. 1:18.941	23	3. 1:17.337	21								
36. Anthony Davidson	GB	Honda RA106-03	2. 1:18.306	26	5. 1:17.627	32								
37. Robert Doornbos	NL	Red Bull RB2 5 - Ferrari	8. 1:19.681	20	11. 1:18.201	32								
38. Robert Kubica	PL	BMW Sauber F1.06-03	1. 1:16.390	30	1. 1:16.965	33								
39. Giorgio Mondini	CH	Midland M16-01 - Toyota	18.	2	23. 1:19.138	24								
40. Neel Jani	CH	Toro Rosso STR01 01 - Cosworth	7. 1:19.258	24	25. 1:19.541	28								
41. Sakon Yamamoto	J	Super Aguri SA05-01 - Honda	15. 1:23.159	29	27. 1:20.197	26								

Fastest lap overall
F. Alonso 1:14.726 (210,095 km/h)

Maximum speed

N° Driver	S1 Qualifs	Pos.	S1 Race	Pos.	S2 Qualifs	Pos.	S2 Race	Pos.	Finish Qualifs	Pos.	Finish Race	Pos.	Radar Qualifs	Pos.	Radar Race	Pos.
1. F. Alonso	261,8	9	261,2	4	287,1	10	289,1	5	284,2	11	285,1	7	313,3	11	319,9	9
2. G. Fisichella	261,5	10	260,2	6	289,1	5	290,1	3	284,4	8	284,9	8	315,2	5	321,3	7
3. K. Räikkönen	264,3	2	263,2	2	292,6	1	290,4	1	286,7	3	288,1	3	314,3	6	319,8	10
4. J. Montoya	263,5	4	254,1	14	288,3	7	285,4	14	284,3	10	280,1	16	310,6	15	322,2	4
5. M. Schumacher	264,1	3	263,3	1	291,1	3	289,5	4	287,8	1	288,7	2	320,6	2	326,3	1
6. F. Massa	264,8	1	262,6	3	291,5	2	290,3	2	286,7	2	289,0	1	320,6	1	324,7	2
7. R. Schumacher	257,6	19	252,2	16	287,3	9	281,1	19	282,5	15	279,1	19	309,9	17	318,1	14
8. J. Trulli	259,1	17	255,8	13	285,8	17	283,9	16	281,7	18	281,1	14	312,3	14	312,5	20
9. M. Webber	261,8	8	253,4	15	286,0	16	287,6	7	286,3	4	280,8	15	313,5	9	318,6	13
10. N. Rosberg	263,0	6	239,4	20	286,4	14	282,1	17	283,0	13	276,2	20	313,5	10	316,9	15
11. R. Barrichello	262,7	7	257,2	12	289,3	4	284,3	15	285,0	5	282,1	13	314,0	7	314,3	19
12. J. Button	263,2	5	259,8	7	289,1	6	288,7	6	284,4	9	286,0	5	313,3	12	316,5	17
14. D. Coulthard	260,5	12	258,0	10	286,3	15	287,0	9	282,3	16	283,2	11	310,1	16	319,6	12
15. C. Klien	260,5	13	258,4	8	285,2	18	286,0	12	281,8	17	283,1	12	309,3	19	316,8	16
16. N. Heidfeld	259,4	16	260,3	5	286,5	13	286,7	11	282,8	14	283,9	9	312,7	13	319,7	11
17. J. Villeneuve	261,4	11	258,0	9	288,1	8	286,9	10	284,5	7	285,5	6	315,2	4	321,4	6
18. T. Monteiro	255,0	21	246,4	19	281,3	20	281,6	18	277,6	20	279,7	17	309,4	18	320,2	8
19. C. Albers	259,8	15	197,1	22	282,5	19	280,8	20	279,1	19			309,2	20		
20. V. Liuzzi	260,2	14	251,9	18	286,9	11	285,4	13	284,9	6	283,4	10	313,5	8	321,6	5
21. S. Speed	258,2	18	257,9	11	286,8	12	287,4	8	283,9	12	287,4	4	316,8	3	324,0	3
22. T. Sato	255,2	20	252,1	17	277,9	22	280,0	21	276,7	21	279,6	18	305,6	21	315,0	18
23. F. Montagny	253,9	22	213,9	21	279,7	21	271,2	22	275,0	22	266,7	21	304,9	22	303,0	21

Race

Classification & Retirements

Pos.	Driver	Constructor	Tyres	Laps	Time	Average
1.	F. Alonso	Renault	M	70	1:34:37.308	193,572 km/h
2.	M. Schumacher	Ferrari	B	70	+ 2.111	193,500 km/h
3.	K. Räikkönen	McLaren Mercedes	M	70	+ 8.813	193,272 km/h
4.	G. Fisichella	Renault	M	70	+ 15.679	193,039 km/h
5.	F. Massa	Ferrari	B	70	+ 25.172	192,718 km/h
6.	J. Trulli	Toyota	B	69	1 lap	190,419 km/h
7.	N. Heidfeld	BMW	M	69	1 lap	190,371 km/h
8.	D. Coulthard	RBR Ferrari	M	69	1 lap	190,174 km/h
9.	J. Button	Honda	M	69	1 lap	190,103 km/h
10.	S. Speed	STR Cosworth	M	69	1 lap	190,089 km/h
11.	C. Klien	RBR Ferrari	M	69	1 lap	189,948 km/h
12.	M. Webber	Williams Cosworth	B	69	1 lap	189,752 km/h
13.	V. Liuzzi	STR Cosworth	M	68	2 laps	186,759 km/h
14.	T. Monteiro	MF1 Toyota	B	66	4 laps	181,067 km/h
15.	T. Sato	Aguri Honda	B	64	6 laps	180,803 km/h

Driver	Constructor	Tyres	Laps	Reason
J. Villeneuve	BMW	M	58	Accident
R. Schumacher	Toyota	B	58	Road-holding wheel failure
J. Montoya	McLaren Mercedes	M	13	Damaged car
R. Barrichello	Honda	M	11	Engine
F. Montagny	Aguri Honda	B	2	Engine failure
N. Rosberg	Williams Cosworth	B	1	Collision with Montoya
C. Albers	MF1 Toyota	B	0	Collision with Monteiro

Fastest laps

	Driver	Time	Laps	Average
1.	K. Räikkönen	1:15.841	22	207,006 km/h
2.	F. Alonso	1:15.911	22	206,815 km/h
3.	M. Schumacher	1:15.993	68	206,592 km/h
4.	G. Fisichella	1:16.669	49	204,771 km/h
5.	F. Massa	1:17.308	31	203,078 km/h
6.	J. Villeneuve	1:17.394	29	202,852 km/h
7.	N. Heidfeld	1:17.454	52	202,695 km/h
8.	J. Trulli	1:17.503	15	202,567 km/h
9.	C. Klien	1:17.576	55	202,377 km/h
10.	D. Coulthard	1:17.619	39	202,264 km/h
11.	M. Webber	1:17.705	17	202,041 km/h
12.	S. Speed	1:17.720	52	202,002 km/h
13.	J. Button	1:18.001	21	201,274 km/h
14.	V. Liuzzi	1:18.078	50	201,075 km/h
15.	J. Montoya	1:18.493	5	200,012 km/h
16.	R. Schumacher	1:18.793	19	199,251 km/h
17.	R. Barrichello	1:19.286	10	198,012 km/h
18.	T. Monteiro	1:19.291	5	197,999 km/h
19.	T. Sato	1:20.490	40	195,050 km/h
20.	F. Montagny	2:07.709	2	122,932 km/h

Pit stops

	Driver	Laps	Duration	Stop	Total
1.	T. Monteiro	1	1:39.447	1	1:39.447
2.	J. Montoya	2	44.391	1	44.391
3.	F. Montagny	2	27.564	1	27.564
4.	T. Sato	4	53.249	1	53.249
5.	G. Fisichella	•7•	14.488	1	14.488
6.	V. Liuzzi	14	44.285	1	44.285
7.	M. Webber	15	25.510	1	25.510
8.	F. Alonso	23	26.036	1	26.036
9.	T. Sato	22	27.054	2	27.054
10.	K. Räikkönen	25	30.270	1	30.270
11.	R. Schumacher	24	16.391	1	16.391
12.	J. Trulli	25	29.515	1	29.515
13.	G. Fisichella	25	25.686	2	40.174
14.	R. Schumacher	25	30.199	2	46.590
15.	V. Liuzzi	26	25.778	2	1:10.063
16.	J. Button	27	26.357	1	26.357
17.	S. Speed	28	27.047	1	27.047
18.	C. Klien	29	25.973	1	25.973
19.	R. Schumacher	28	14.627	3	1:01.217
20.	M. Schumacher	32	25.706	1	25.706
21.	J. Villeneuve	33	24.922	1	24.922
22.	N. Heidfeld	34	27.326	1	27.326
23.	D. Coulthard	34	25.360	1	25.360
24.	F. Massa	36	28.589	1	28.589
25.	T. Monteiro	34	27.977	2	2:07.424
26.	M. Webber	44	27.227	2	52.737
27.	T. Sato	43	26.896	3	1:47.199
28.	J. Trulli	48	24.812	2	54.327
29.	F. Alonso	50	24.574	2	50.610
30.	V. Liuzzi	48	27.300	3	1:37.363
31.	S. Speed	50	25.985	2	53.032
32.	G. Fisichella	52	24.283	3	1:04.457
33.	K. Räikkönen	53	32.505	2	1:02.775
34.	J. Button	52	24.823	2	51.180
35.	C. Klien	53	27.033	2	53.006
36.	R. Schumacher	51	24.674	4	1:25.891
37.	N. Heidfeld	54	24.293	2	51.619
38.	J. Villeneuve	55	25.632	2	50.554
39.	D. Coulthard	56	24.815	2	50.175
40.	M. Schumacher	57	23.639	2	49.345
41.	T. Monteiro	57	24.518	3	2:31.942
42.	R. Schumacher	57	25.708	5	1:51.599

•• Drive-through penalty: Fisichella
Speeding in pit lane.

Race leader

Driver	Laps in the lead	Nbr of Laps
F. Alonso	1 > 22	22
K. Räikkönen	23 > 24	2
F. Alonso	25 > 49	25
K. Räikkönen	50 > 52	3
F. Alonso	53 > 70	18

Driver	Nbr of Laps	Kilometers
F. Alonso	65	283,465 km
K. Räikkönen	5	21,805 km

Gaps on the leader board

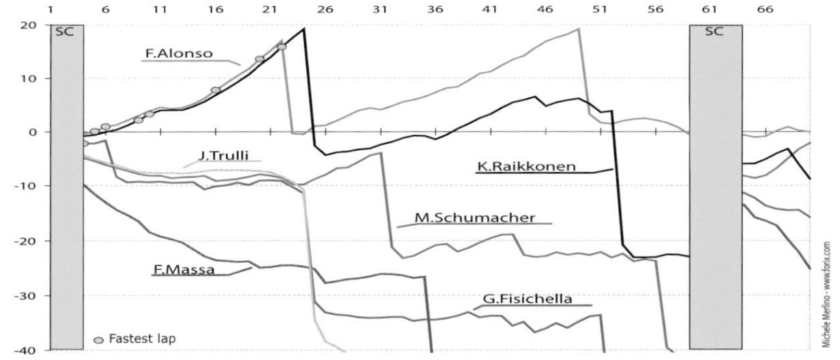

Lap chart

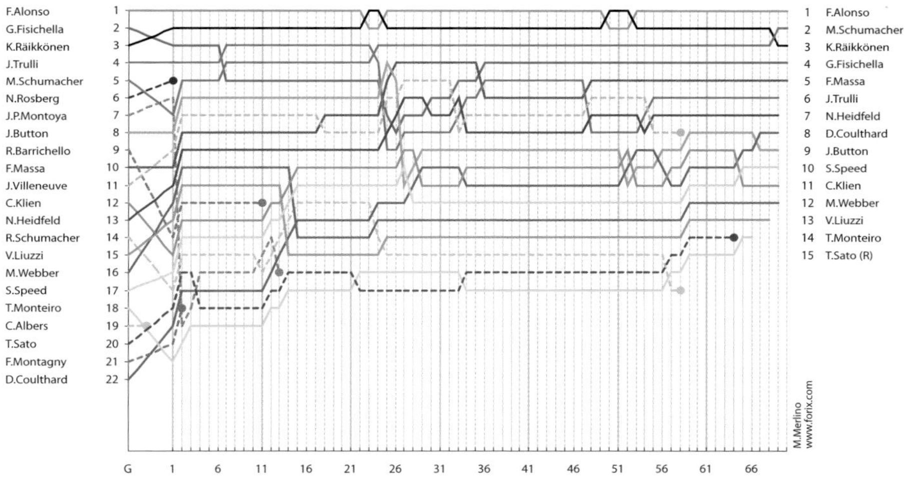

Championships 9/18

Drivers

1. F. Alonso ....Renault ....6 ♀....84
2. M. Schumacher .....Ferrari......................2 ♀....59
3. K. Räikkönen ....McLaren Mercedes.............39
4. G. Fisichella..........Renault ....1 ♀....37
5. F. Massa..............Ferrari 28
6. J. Montoya ....McLaren Mercedes.............26
7. J. Button ....Honda 16
8. R. Barrichello........Honda 13
9. N. Heidfeld ....BMW 12
10. R. Schumacher .....Toyota 8
11. D. Coulthard ....RBR Ferrari 8
12. J. Villeneuve ....BMW 7
13. M. Webber...........Williams Cosworth................6
14. N. Rosberg ....Williams Cosworth................4
15. J. Trulli................Toyota 3
16. C. Klien...............RBR Ferrari 1
17. S. Speed ....STR Cosworth.......................0
18. V. Liuzzi ....STR Cosworth.......................0
19. C. Albers ....MF1 Toyota 0
20. T. Monteiro ....MF1 Toyota 0
21. T. Sato................Aguri Honda 0
22. Y. Ide..................Aguri Honda 0
23. F. Montagny.........Aguri Honda 0

Constructors

1. Mild Seven Renault F1 Team ....7 ♀....121
2. Scuderia Ferrari Marlboro ....2 ♀ 87
3. Team McLaren Mercedes 65
4. Lucky Strike Honda Racing F1 Team 29
5. BMW Sauber F1 Team.................................19
6. Panasonic Toyota Racing 11
7. Williams F1 Team......................................10
8. Red Bull Racing 9
9. Scuderia Toro Rosso....................................0
10. MF1 Racing...0
11. Super Aguri Formula 1 0

The circuit

Name	Gilles-Villeneuve; Ile Notre-Dame, Montreal	Weather	Cloudy, warm
Lenght	4361 m	Air temperature	29-32°c
Distance	70 laps, 305,270 km	Track temperature	47-48°c
Date	June 25, 2006	Humidity	30-32%
		Wind speed	1.1 m/s

S1: 165m before corner
S2: 220m before corner
Radar: 255m before corner

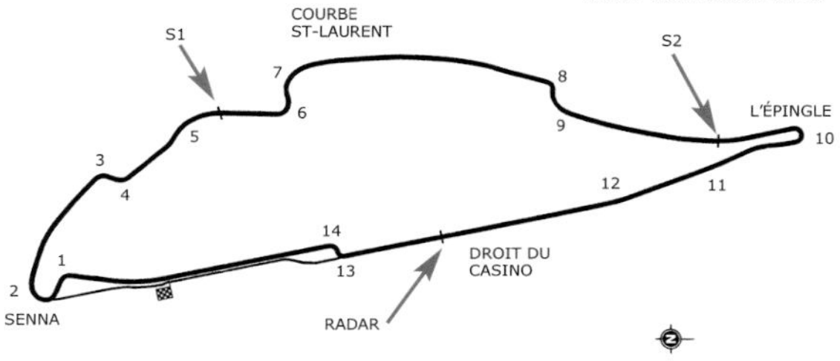

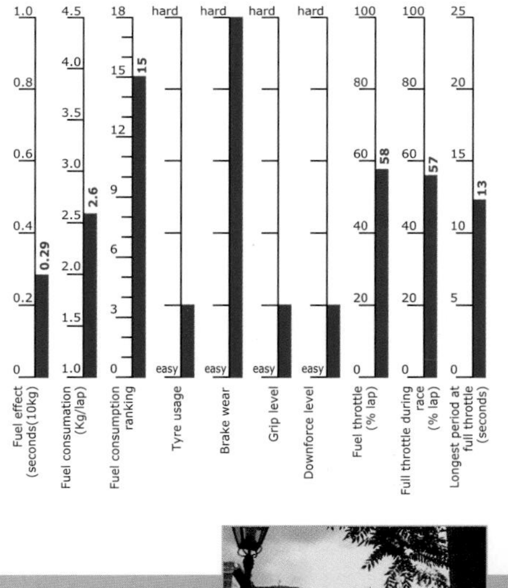

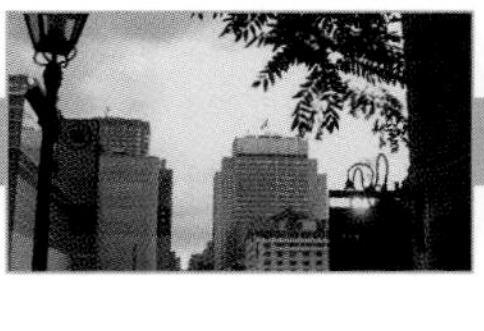

FERRARI TURNS THE TIDE

Michael Schumacher can never be written off. Those who reckoned that Fernando Alonso was going to stroll home to his second world title had to have a rethink.
In Indianapolis the Scuderia Ferrari dominated while the Spanish driver could do no better than fifth.
Ferrari was back with a bang!

The first all-red front row since Bahrain

^ Ferrari was back on form on the legendary Indy Speedway.

In 2005, the grand prix had turned into a fiasco with the problems that hit Michelin. All the teams shod by the French manufacturer had to withdraw from the USA race and victory went to Schumacher's Ferrari on Bridgestone tyres. This year everybody was wondering how the Michelins were going to cope with the no.13 banked turn on the Indianapolis Speedway. The Clérmont-Ferrand manufacturer obviously went for safety to avoid a repeat of the 2005 disaster. So far it had dominated Bridgestone but its advance on the Japanese company was not enough to compensate for its conservative approach. The drivers on Bridgestone rubber had the advantage during the weekend as Ross Brawn

the Scuderia's technical director confirmed: "*We haven't changed anything on the car since the Canadian race last week. If we're in front today we owe it to the Bridgestone tyres. They give us an advantage here.*"
And a big one at that. On Saturday Michael Schumacher qualified over a second faster than Giancarlo Fisichella. It was a huge gap in the context and none was more surprised than Michael himself. "*I'm not all that surprised to be in front as we've been quicker all weekend. What does amaze me is the gap between myself and the others. I'd like to stock a little in my reserves for the next grands prix! A second is a lot and shows that we're very strong when we don't run*

into problems which has not been the case over the previous weeks."
In the Renault camp Alonso adopted a philosophical approach. "*We knew it'd be our worst grand prix of the season. I did my best but the car was understeering a lot. In fact, I was afraid we'd do even worse here.*"

In brief

> "*We build the most expensive cars in the world to put on the most boring show on earth.*" Such were the words of Flavio Briatore who was very critical of the discussions about the future cubic capacity of the engines, and did not include any suggestions on how to improve the F1 spectacle.

> Michael Schumacher concentrated most of his attention on the German football team

> Scott Speed was pretty happy to be on home turf. He qualified in 13th place his best since Malaysia (12th).

on Friday when the Mannschaft qualified between the two sessions. Luckily for him the penalty shoot-outs ended just before the start of the second untimed practice.

> Some manufacturers (Honda and Toyota included) wanted more flexibility built into the 2008 regulations. Max Mosley explained at Indianapolis that he could not change anything. "*We're not going to ask the teams to spend a fortune,*" said the FIA President.

Starting grid

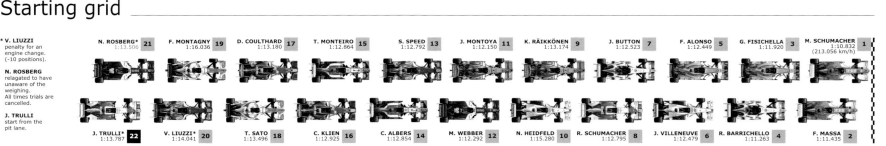

Position	Driver	Time	No.
	N. ROSBERG*	1:13.506	21
	F. MONTAGNY	1:16.036	19
	D. COULTHARD	1:13.180	17
	T. MONTEIRO	1:12.864	15
	S. SPEED	1:12.792	13
	J. MONTOYA	1:12.150	11
	K. RÄIKKÖNEN	1:13.174	9
	J. BUTTON	1:12.523	7
	F. ALONSO	1:12.449	5
	G. FISICHELLA	1:11.920	3
	M. SCHUMACHER	1:10.832 (213.056 km/h)	1
	J. TRULLI*	1:13.787	22
	V. LIUZZI*	1:14.041	20
	T. SATO	1:13.496	18
	C. KLIEN	1:12.925	16
	C. ALBERS	1:12.854	14
	M. WEBBER	1:12.292	12
	N. HEIDFELD	1:15.280	10
	R. SCHUMACHER	1:12.795	8
	J. VILLENEUVE	1:12.479	6
	R. BARRICHELLO	1:11.263	4
	F. MASSA	1:11.435	2

< "Bravo Michael, bravo Felipe. All the members of the Scuderia accompanied by their boss Jean Todt congratulated their drivers as they went into the parc fermé at the end of the USA Grand Prix.

One of Michael Schumacher's famous victory leaps. It was probably a bit higher than usual after his US win.
v

A good car and a good weekend for the reds

Things got off to a bad start for Renault at Indianapolis. Right from the first day of practice the drivers were complaining of excessive understeer. In the Ferrari camp it was the opposite and 248 F1s were flying on the famous oval.
In the race these tendencies were confirmed. The two Ferraris hit the front in the first corner and were never threatened going on to score their first double of the season. Giancarlo Fisichella finished in 3rd place some 16 seconds in arrears and was never in the hunt for victory.
It was Michael Schumacher's 3rd victory of the season and for Felipe Massa his 2nd place was his best-ever result in F1. "*It's been a great weekend for us,*" exulted Michael. "*We had a great car and Germany won their quarter final so it's been a marvellous weekend for the whole country. In fact, when we have no problems we're difficult to beat. In Canada, I had a few small setbacks during practice. In the race I was very quick but it was too late. Here everything went perfectly.*"

The tyres were, of course, one of the main factors that helped Ferrari to victory. Michelin was very careful so as not to have a repeat of the 2005 fiasco.

It cost Fernando Alonso dearly. With eight races to go his lead over Michael Schumacher had shrunk to 19 points.

Juan Pablo Montoya's gaffe gave him his F1 exit visa.

First corner. Montoya came in from the exterior and hit his team-mate Kimi Raïkkönen's car in the rear sending him into Jenson Button's Honda which then struck Nick Heidfeld's BMW launching the latter into a series of 5 barrel rolls.
When the smoke cleared seven cars were already out while Jenson Button and Christijan Albers went back to their pit. Apart from the 2 McLarens and the BMW Mark Webber, Scott Speed, Christian Klien and Franck Montagny were all eliminated in the accident, which obliged race control to bring out the safety car for 5 laps. " *I really don't know what happened,*" was how Montoya tried to justify

himself when he got back to his pit. "*Kimi braked in front of me and I couldn't avoid him. It was just a simple racing accident.*"
But not quite as simple as that. All the drivers involved in the crash were convened by the stewards after the race to explain what happened. They decided not to sanction anybody but in the McLaren camp the discussions were stormy to say the least. Ron Dennis was absolutely hopping mad about the elimination of both his cars. Juan Pablo decided there and then to quit F1 and go to NASCAR. His last F1 grand prix was a fiasco.

< Fernando Alonso came home in 5th place. It was the end of a series of 15 consecutive rostrum finishes and it could have been worse for him if the 2 McLaren drivers had not been elimination in the pile up in the first corner. "*Fifth was the best I could hope for here,*" explained the Spaniard. We were not competitive right from the start of the weekend so it wasn't going to get any better in the race.

Big scare in the first corner

For what was to be his last F1 appearance
(even though he did not know it) Juan Pablo Montoya
went out in style!
The previous weekend in Canada he had punted off
Nico Rosberg on the first lap by trying to pass him
where it was impossible. At Indy he caused
the biggest pile-up of the season in which 9 cars
were involved.
Nick Heidfeld in his BMW had the narrowest escape
of all and literally took off. His immediate reflex
as he left the ground was to let go of his steering
wheel to hold his helmet. It was a miraculous survival.

^
Fernando Alonso did not want Michelin to adopt a conservative approach at Indianapolis but the Clérmont-Ferrand manufacturer probably did so. And how can one blame it.

BMW-Sauber's bad patch continues

The pessimists and his detractors would say that Villeneuve retired for the second time on the trot after the Canadian Grand Prix while the optimists would argue that never had the BMW–Sauber gone so well before being eliminated. Jacques qualified on the third row and while his team-mate got all tangled up in the first-corner accident the "Quebecois" was in 7th place at the end of the first lap. He made a good start but was overtaken by Ralf

Schumacher's Toyota in the first bend. But it was not too important; there was still a long way to go and Jacques was waiting for the first round of refuelling stops to pick up a few places. But he never got that far. On lap 24 his BMW came to a halt in a cloud of white smoke and Villeneuve parked it on the grass. "It's really very disappointing," he growled when he came back to the paddock.

"It was this engine's first race. Something must have gone radically wrong because normally it lasts two events." BMW too was baffled. "Up to then everything was going fine," went on Villeneuve. "I was quicker than the three cars in front of me and I was waiting for them to refuel. The BMW was really very fast in the race which makes it all the more discouraging."

Michelin sure of its tyres after the 2005 disaster

"We wanted to take part in the grand prix without scoring any points to satisfy the spectators and TV viewers. But there was one team that didn't agree with this solution." Fernando Alonso the leader of the championship recalled the unfortunate events in 2005 which had led to all the teams with Michelin rubber going into the pits at the end of the formation lap leaving Ferrari, Jordan and Minardi alone on the grid.
On Friday and Saturday Michelin realised that their tyres would not last longer than 10 laps due to the exceptional load engendered by the banked corner on the straight which is taken flat out.
The teams involved had proposed installing a chicane in the middle of the banking so that they could take part in the race without scoring points. Ferrari was against and racked up a double in the grand prix.
"I remember the formation lap," said Alonso. "Kimi was in front of me and he began to heat up his tyres. I said to myself, 'if he starts, I will too.' But then he went into his pit and I followed him." A year later the Spaniard was back at the scene of the crime. "I'm 100% sure that this time the Michelin tyres will be able to cope. They know what happened and they'll avoid the problem."

The French manufacturer stated the its tyres were able to cope with the loads generated by this very special circuit. It was rumoured in the paddock that the Clérmont-Ferrand firm had made a very conservative choice to avoid any problems. Alonso denied this:
"Conservative? We don't have a big enough lead over our rivals to do that. Last year there was a very precise problem that we don't have now; I want to come first here. It's the only grand prix that I haven't won. This being said I'm remaining

cautious. We've never been very good here." However, when Sunday dawned it seemed that Michelin had gone the conservative route. Its highest-placed driver was Giancarlo Fisichella who finished third well behind the two Ferraris. "We had two aims here," declared Nick Shorrock, the Michelin F1 boss on the evening of the race. "We wanted tyres that would last and that were quick. While we achieved the first, we missed out on the second."

>
"Bibendum mon Amour!" After the 2005 disaster 2006 went off without a hitch.

Practice

All the time trials

Nº Driver	Nat.	Nº Chassis - Engine [Nbr. GP]	Pos.	Free 1 Friday	Laps	Pos.	Free 2 Friday	Laps	Pos.	Free 3 Saturday	Laps	Pos.	Q1 Saturday	Laps	Pos.	Q2 Saturday	Laps	Pos.	Super Pole Saturday	Laps
1. Fernando Alonso	E	Renault R26 03 [2]	20.		1	9.	1:13.474	14	6.	1:12.202	15	9.	1:12.416	3	9.	1:11.877	6	5.	**1:12.449**	17
2. Giancarlo Fisichella	I	Renault R26 05 [1]	19.		3	3.	1:12.933	14	3.	1:11.940	15	8.	1:12.287	4	3.	1:11.200	6	3.	**1:11.920**	17
3. Kimi Räikkönen	FIN	McLaren MP4-21 03 - Mercedes [2]	22.		1	10.	1:13.554	9	9.	1:12.569	13	14.	1:12.777	7	10.	1:12.135	8	9.	**1:13.174**	16
4. Juan Pablo Montoya	CO	McLaren MP4-21 05 - Mercedes [1]	24.		1	15.	1:13.825	10	10.	1:12.592	10	10.	1:12.477	3	11.	**1:12.150**	9			
5. Michael Schumacher	D	Ferrari 248 F1 254 [2]	2.	1:12.458	3	6.	1:13.346	18	1.	1:10.760	15	2.	1:11.588	3	1.	1:10.636	3	1.	**1:10.832**	16
6. Felipe Massa	BR	Ferrari 248 F1 252 [2]	27.		0	4.	1:13.264	26	2.	1:11.039	8	1.	1:11.088	3	2.	1:11.146	3	2.	**1:11.435**	17
7. Ralf Schumacher	D	Toyota TF106/07B [1]	18.		2	27.	1:15.063	10	15.	1:13.101	19	3.	1:11.879	6	5.	1:11.673	6	8.	**1:12.795**	17
8. Jarno Trulli	I	Toyota TF106/08B [1]	17.		2	23.	1:14.449	16	14.	1:13.091	21	20.	**1:13.787**							
9. Mark Webber	AUS	Williams FW28 03 - Cosworth [2]	28.		0	12.	1:13.691	15	12.	1:12.904	15	15.	1:12.935	7	12.	**1:12.292**	6			
10. Nico Rosberg	D	Williams FW28 04 - Cosworth [1]	29.		0	24.	1:14.562	17	19.	1:13.230	12	19.	**1:13.506**	7						
11. Rubens Barrichello	BR	Honda RA106-01 [1]	4.	1:13.090	5	18.	1:14.011	20	5.	1:12.149	13	6.	1:12.156	7	4.	1:11.263	6	4.	**1:12.109**	16
12. Jenson Button	GB	Honda RA106-05 [2]	5.	1:13.189	6	8.	1:13.397	16	7.	1:12.269	18	7.	1:12.238	7	8.	1:11.865	6	7.	**1:12.523**	16
14. David Coulthard	GB	Red Bull RB2 3 - Ferrari [2]	23.		1	25.	1:14.676	18	20.	1:13.364	17	17.	**1:13.180**	6						
15. Christian Klien	A	Red Bull RB2 2 - Ferrari [1]	21.		1	20.	1:14.084	15	17.	1:13.113	15	13.	1:12.773	6	16.	**1:12.925**	6			
16. Nick Heidfeld	D	BMW Sauber F1.06-06 [2]	25.		1	13.	1:13.725	14	4.	1:12.049	18	4.	1:11.891	7	6.	1:11.718	3	10.	**1:15.280**	6
17. Jacques Villeneuve	CDN	BMW Sauber F1.06-08 [1]	26.		2	16.	1:13.857	17	8.	1:12.327	13	5.	1:12.114	3	7.	1:11.724	6	6.	**1:12.479**	17
18. Tiago Monteiro	P	Midland M16-04 - Toyota [2]	11.	1:15.091	8	7.	1:13.387	21	13.	1:12.913	18	11.	1:12.627	6	15.	**1:12.864**	3			
19. Christijan Albers	NL	Midland M16-02 - Toyota [2]	13.	1:15.647	10	21.	1:14.169	19	18.	1:13.172	19	12.	1:12.711	6	14.	**1:12.854**	3			
20. Vitantonio Liuzzi	I	Toro Rosso STR01 03 - Cosworth [2]	12.	1:15.532	8	14.	1:13.735	24	11.	1:12.675	18	21.	**1:14.041**	10						
21. Scott Speed	USA	Toro Rosso STR01 02 - Cosworth [2]	9.	1:14.791	8	11.	1:13.688	26	16.	1:13.103	17	16.	1:13.167	7	13.	**1:12.792**	7			
22. Takuma Sato	J	Super Aguri SA05-05 - Honda [1]	14.	1:15.971	17	22.	1:14.391	24	21.	1:13.806	16	18.	**1:13.496**	6						
23. Franck Montagny	F	Super Aguri SA05-02 - Honda [1]	16.	1:16.489	17	29.		2	22.	1:14.454	10	22.	**1:16.036**	4						
35. Alexander Wurz	A	Williams FW28 06 - Cosworth	8.	1:14.745	38	19.	1:14.050	39												
36. Anthony Davidson	GB	Honda RA106-03	1.	1:12.083	27	1.	1:12.013	38												
37. Robert Doornbos	NL	Red Bull RB2 5 - Ferrari	10.	1:15.018	22	26.	1:14.839	13												
38. Robert Kubica	PL	BMW Sauber F1.06-04	3.	1:13.008	31	2.	1:12.809	39												
39. Giorgio Mondini	CH	Midland M16-01 - Toyota	7.	1:14.654	33	5.	1:13.327	33												
40. Neel Jani	CH	Toro Rosso STR01 01 - Cosworth	6.	1:13.710	24	17.	1:13.946	31												
41. Sakon Yamamoto	J	Super Aguri SA05-01 - Honda	15.	1:16.116	31	28.	1:15.120	33												

Fastest lap overall
Michael Schumacher 1:10.636 (213,647 km/h)

Maximum speed

Nº	Driver	S1 Qualifs	Pos.	S1 Race	Pos.	S2 Qualifs	Pos.	S2 Race	Pos.	Finish Qualifs	Pos.	Finish Race	Pos.	Radar Qualifs	Pos.	Radar Race	Pos.
1.	F. Alonso	253,6	10	253,0	3	173,3	8	170,5	4	321,6	6	324,5	6	330,6	5	333,1	2
2.	G. Fisichella	255,8	3	252,6	5	177,1	1	172,3	2	324,5	4	327,9	2	331,7	3	335,8	1
3.	K. Räikkönen	253,4	11			171,0	15			323,0	5			329,1	7	282,4	19
4.	J. Montoya	254,9	6			175,0	3			319,4	12			326,4	10	287,4	16
5.	M. Schumacher	255,3	5	253,5	1	173,2	9	173,9	1	325,3	3	325,6	4	333,6	2	332,8	3
6.	F. Massa	257,6	1	253,3	2	175,7	2	171,4	3	327,9	1	326,9	3	334,3	1	330,8	6
7.	R. Schumacher	255,6	4	252,6	4	172,7	10	168,6	8	319,6	11	322,8	9	327,9	8	330,2	7
8.	J. Trulli	254,6	7	252,5	6	167,1	21	168,9	6	316,6	15	329,1	1	323,4	14	332,4	4
9.	M. Webber	254,4	8			174,7	4			320,4	9			326,2	12	263,9	18
10.	N. Rosberg	248,9	21	246,8	11	167,8	20	166,5	12	311,7	21	317,9	13	315,0	22	327,5	10
11.	R. Barrichello	256,0	2	252,2	7	173,9	5	170,2	5	320,9	8	318,3	12	326,8	9	324,4	13
12.	J. Button	252,8	13	217,9	15	172,2	12	148,5	15	326,7	2	173,5	15	326,4	11	278,4	21
14.	D. Coulthard	252,3	14	249,8	9	169,2	17	168,3	10	315,8	17	322,3	10	321,5	17	326,7	11
15.	C. Klien	251,7	16			173,3	7			319,4	13			325,6	13	295,1	15
16.	N. Heidfeld	253,6	9			172,6	11			317,6	14			331,2	4	267,1	22
17.	J. Villeneuve	252,9	12	248,6	10	172,1	13	168,0	11	321,3	7	321,9	11	329,4	6	332,0	5
18.	T. Monteiro	247,5	22	238,0	13	168,0	19	160,2	14	313,4	20	312,7	14	319,5	20	321,1	14
19.	C. Albers	251,1	19	244,5	12	173,5	6	168,4	9	316,1	16	323,6	8	323,3	15	324,8	12
20.	V. Liuzzi	251,2	18	251,4	8	169,3	16	168,6	7	315,1	18	325,1	5	319,7	19	327,6	9
21.	S. Speed	251,2	17			171,7	14			315,1	19			320,8	18	279,2	20
22.	T. Sato	252,2	15	236,1	14	168,0	18	160,5	13	320,2	10	323,7	7	322,5	16	327,9	8
23.	F. Montagny	249,0	20			164,9	22			310,4	22			316,9	21	287,0	17

Race

Classification & Retirements

Pos.	Driver	Constructor	Tyres	Laps	Time	Average
1.	M. Schumacher	Ferrari	B	73	1:34:35.199	194,117 km/h
2.	F. Massa	Ferrari	B	73	+ 7.984	193,845 km/h
3.	G. Fisichella	Renault	M	73	+ 16.595	193,551 km/h
4.	J. Trulli	Toyota	B	73	+ 23.604	193,313 km/h
5.	F. Alonso	Renault	M	73	+ 28.410	193,150 km/h
6.	R. Barrichello	Honda	M	73	+ 36.516	192,876 km/h
7.	D. Coulthard	RBR Ferrari	M	72	1 lap	190,658 km/h
8.	V. Liuzzi	STR Cosworth	M	72	1 lap	190,446 km/h
9.	N. Rosberg	Williams Cosworth	B	72	1 lap	190,320 km/h

Driver	Constructor	Tyres	Laps	Reason
R. Schumacher	Toyota	B	62	Left front wheel bearing failure
C. Albers	MF1 Toyota	B	37	Transmission problem
J. Villeneuve	BMW	M	23	Engine failure
T. Monteiro	MF1 Toyota	B	9	Shunt with Sato, extensive sidepod damage
T. Sato	Aguri Honda	B	6	Collision with Monteiro
J. Button	Honda	M	3	Damaged car following the start collision
K. Räikkönen	McLaren Mercedes	M	0	Collision with Montoya
N. Heidfeld	BMW	M	0	Roll on Button's wheel
J. Montoya	McLaren Mercedes	M	0	Collision with Räikkönen, Button then Speed
M. Webber	Williams Cosworth	B	0	Hit by Klien
S. Speed	STR Cosworth	M	0	Collision with Montoya
C. Klien	RBR Ferrari	M	0	Spun into Webber and Montagny
F. Montagny	Aguri Honda	B	0	Hit by Klien

Fastest laps

	Driver	Time	Laps	Average
1.	M. Schumacher	1:12.719	56	207,527 km/h
2.	F. Massa	1:12.954	29	206,859 km/h
3.	G. Fisichella	1:13.131	28	206,358 km/h
4.	R. Schumacher	1:13.225	29	206,093 km/h
5.	J. Trulli	1:13.269	37	205,969 km/h
6.	F. Alonso	1:13.316	72	205,837 km/h
7.	R. Barrichello	1:13.611	47	205,012 km/h
8.	J. Villeneuve	1:13.934	19	204,117 km/h
9.	V. Liuzzi	1:14.286	41	203,149 km/h
10.	N. Rosberg	1:14.707	42	202,005 km/h
11.	D. Coulthard	1:14.730	33	201,942 km/h
12.	C. Albers	1:14.731	34	201,940 km/h
13.	T. Monteiro	1:22.036	9	183,958 km/h
14.	T. Sato	1:43.802	6	145,384 km/h
15.	J. Button	2:04.692	2	121,027 km/h

Pit stops

	Driver	Laps	Duration	Stop	Total
1.	C. Albers	1	28.941	1	28.941
2.	J. Button	3	25.800	1	25.800
3.	T. Monteiro	8	33.704	1	33.704
4.	R. Barrichello	24	23.705	1	23.705
5.	C. Albers	28	23.808	2	52.749
6.	M. Schumacher	29	24.283	1	24.283
7.	G. Fisichella	29	23.334	1	23.334
8.	F. Massa	30	24.272	1	24.272
9.	R. Schumacher	30	23.019	1	23.019
10.	F. Alonso	31	23.147	1	23.147
11.	C. Albers	32	24.936	3	1:17.685
12.	J. Trulli	39	25.314	1	25.314
13.	V. Liuzzi	39	25.070	1	25.070
14.	N. Rosberg	43	26.597	1	26.597
15.	D. Coulthard	47	23.712	1	23.712
16.	R. Barrichello	49	23.101	2	46.806
17.	F. Massa	52	22.732	2	47.004
18.	G. Fisichella	53	21.784	2	45.118
19.	R. Schumacher	53	22.160	2	45.179
20.	M. Schumacher	54	22.901	2	47.184
21.	F. Alonso	55	24.784	2	47.931

Race leader

Driver	Laps in the lead	Nbr of Laps
F. Massa	1 > 29	29
F. Alonso	30	1
M. Schumacher	31 > 73	43

Driver	Nbr of Laps	Kilometers
M. Schumacher	43	180,256 km
F. Massa	29	121,568 km
F. Alonso	1	4,192 km

Gaps on the leader board

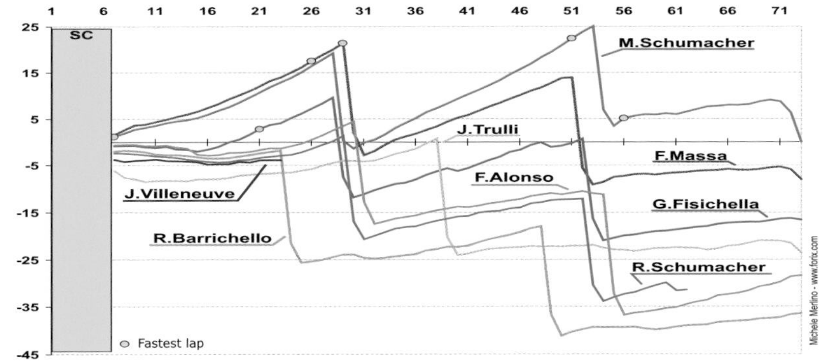

Lap chart

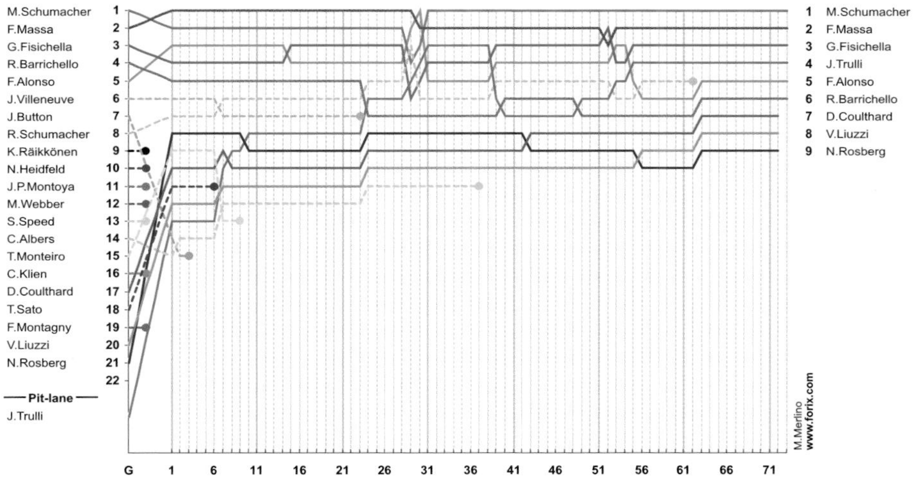

Championships 10/18

Drivers

1. F. Alonso ....Renault ....6 🏆....88
2. M. Schumacher .....Ferrari.....................3 🏆....69
3. G. Fisichella..........Renault ....1 🏆....43
4. K. Räikkönen ....McLaren Mercedes.............39
5. F. Massa..............Ferrari 36
6. J. Montoya ....McLaren Mercedes.............26
7. J. Button ....Honda 16
8. R. Barrichello........Honda 16
9. N. Heidfeld ....BMW 12
10. D. Coulthard ....RBR Ferrari.......................10
11. R. Schumacher .....Toyota 8
12. J. Trulli.................Toyota 8
13. J. Villeneuve ....BMW 7
14. M. Webber............Williams Cosworth................6
15. N. Rosberg ....Williams Cosworth................4
16. V. Liuzzi ....STR Cosworth.......................1
17. C. Klien................RBR Ferrari 1
18. S. Speed ....STR Cosworth.......................0
19. C. Albers.............MF1 Toyota 0
20. T. Monteiro ....MF1 Toyota 0
21. T. Sato................Aguri Honda 0
22. Y. Ide..................Aguri Honda 0
23. F. Montagny..........Aguri Honda 0

Constructors

1. Mild Seven Renault F1 Team ....7 🏆....131
2. Scuderia Ferrari Marlboro ....3 🏆....105
3. Team McLaren Mercedes 65
4. Lucky Strike Honda Racing F1 Team 32
5. BMW Sauber F1 Team...............................19
6. Panasonic Toyota Racing 16
7. Red Bull Racing 11
8. Williams F1 Team....................................10
9. Scuderia Toro Rosso.................................1
10. MF1 Racing..0
11. Super Aguri Formula 1 0

The circuit

Name	Indiana Motor Speedway; Indianapolis	Weather	Sunny and warm
		Air temperature	36-37°c
Lenght	4192 m	Track temperature	50-55°c
Distance	73 laps, 306,016 km	Humidity	38%
Date	July 2, 2006	Wind speed	1.2 m/s

S1: 50m before corner
S2: 85m before corner
Radar: 200m before corner

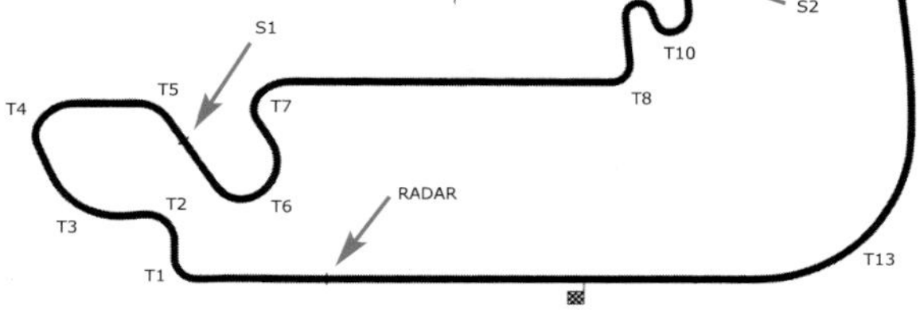

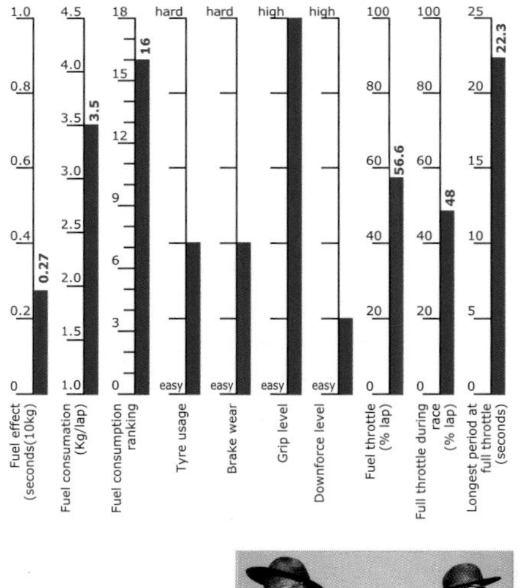

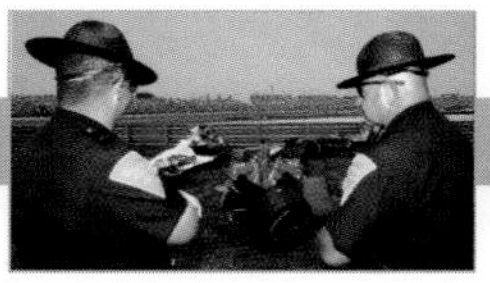

FERRARI FAVOURITE

Indianapolis had been an exception. Michelin had been too conservative and the Ferraris won. End of story.

That was the explanation put forward by the Renault strategists to explain their American stumble. Finding a way to justify the Mangy-Cours setback was a lot more difficult. The Ferraris again dominated the race and victory in the summer grands prix looked like theirs for the taking. It was the turning point of the season.

> Michael Schumacher set his second pole on the trot and his fourth of the year.

An all-red front row at Magny-Cours

The duel between Ferrari and Renault was extremely close. In the constructors' championship the gap between them was 26 points and in the drivers' Alonso had 19 points in hand over his German rival. It seemed a lot and yet...

Especially as the Ferraris were on a roll in the middle of the season. Two weeks earlier the Scuderia had scored a double on the Indy circuit without Renault ever posing the slightest threat to the Italian cars. Italy beat France in the final of the Football World Cup and many spectators at Magny-Cours were hoping that Renault would revenge this insult to national pride. As the circuit was supposed to favour the R26's chassis victory looked well within Alonso's grasp.

Friday's practice confirmed that the Renaults were back on form but on Saturday the situation was reversed. The Ferraris were on another planet right from the start of qualifying. "*We soon understood that we could not fight for pole,*" groaned Fernando Alonso. "*Third was the best I could do. But at least I'm back at the front of the field; it's much better than at Indianapolis. Even if we're not on the front row, I'm sure we'll be competitive in the race. Our tyres are very consistent and I'm very confident.*"

The Scuderia drivers were just a teeny bit surprised to be on the front row. "*We began qualifying without any real reference points,'* said Michael Schumacher. "*I did not run this morning after my car caught fire (see caption). We were slightly worried but then we realised that nobody was capable of matching our pace. It's great to have a repeat of the Indy front row. Now we're after another double.*"

The French Grand Prix marked a turning point between Ferrari and Renault in the 2006 season. The Magny-Cours circuit with its high downforce requirements and fast curves was similar to the remaining tracks on the calendar. A Ferrari victory at Magny-Cours augured a very close end to the championship between France and Italy in F1.

> On Saturday morning there was a big scare in the Ferrari camp during free practice. Michael came back into his pit with his car's exhaust pipes on fire. It took several seconds to put out the flames; "*It was probably due to an overfilled tank which spilled onto the hot exhausts,*" explained Ross Brawn. "*We had a problem with the on-board extinguishers and we didn't put out the fire as quickly as we should have. But there's no serious damage. The mechanics just have had a little extra work.*"

In brief

At Magny-Cours the Super Aguri team was supposed to sell its second seat to Sakon Yamamoto from Japan for 800 000 euros. It preferred to let Franck Montagny race in his home grand prix to thank him for all the help he had given the team since the start of the season. It was a truly noble gesture.

During qualification the track temperature was 55 degrees and in the shade it was 36 degrees, much higher than forecast and the unexpected heat had repercussions on the tyres. The Bridgestone rubber was able to cope with it much better than the Michelins most of whose drivers opted for the hard compound. Ferrari and Toyota also took advantage of this.

After a fax vote by the members of the World Council several rule changes came into force at Magny-Cours. The third part of qualifying- now called the Super Pole - was reduced from 20 to 15 minutes.

The other two phases of qualifying were also modified. Henceforth a lap begun before the chequered flag fell would be counted – which was not the case up till then.

> Thursday: Like many of his fellow-drivers Ralf Schumacher went to hit a few golf balls on the golf course beside the circuit. The relaxation must have helped as on Saturday he qualified fifth and then finished the race in fourth place.

Starting grid

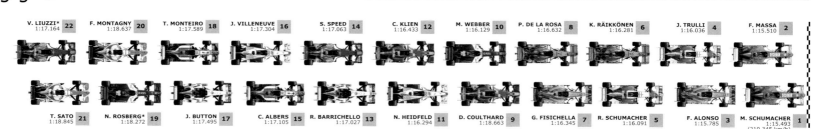

* N. ROSBERG and V. LIUZZI Penalty for an engine change (-10 pos.)

V. LIUZZI* 1:17.164 **22**	F. MONTAGNY 1:18.637 **20**	T. MONTEIRO 1:17.589 **18**	J. VILLENEUVE 1:17.304 **16**	S. SPEED 1:17.063 **14**	C. KLIEN 1:16.433 **12**	M. WEBBER 1:16.129 **10**	P. DE LA ROSA 1:16.632 **8**	K. RÄIKKÖNEN 1:16.281 **6**	J. TRULLI 1:16.036 **4**	F. MASSA 1:15.510 **2**
T. SATO 1:18.845 **21**	N. ROSBERG* 1:18.272 **19**	J. BUTTON 1:17.495 **17**	C. ALBERS 1:17.105 **15**	R. BARRICHELLO 1:17.027 **13**	N. HEIDFELD 1:16.294 **11**	D. COULTHARD 1:18.663 **9**	G. FISICHELLA 1:16.345 **7**	R. SCHUMACHER 1:16.091 **5**	F. ALONSO 1:15.785 **3**	M. SCHUMACHER 1:15.493 (210.345 km/h) **1**

Italy 2 France 0: After the world cup Italy scored another win on French soil!

It was a watershed race. The Ferraris showed their superiority at Magny-Cours, which prefigured the fast circuits that were part of the summer calendar. Fernando Alonso left France with his lead over Schumacher reduced to 17 points.

The Spaniard had dominated the first part of the season totalling 6 victories and 3 second places. When he arrived at Indianapolis he must have felt that he could begin preparing the end-of-year celebrations for his second consecutive title. Two weeks later he probably reckoned that he might have to put them off. In the USA, Michelin opted for caution and brought along tyres that were incapable of matching the pace of the Bridgestones. Alonso finished fifth

It was not too serious. Indianapolis was just a temporary setback in his triumphant march to his second title thanks to the reliability of his R26. When the French team arrived at Magny-Cours on Thursday it was pretty confident. It was back on home territory and things would

go off without a hitch. In addition, the Nevers circuit was similar to the ones on which the season had got off to such a brilliant start for the Renault squad.

Thus, it came as a big surprise to them when the Ferraris proved unbeatable. The Scuderia struck a body blow by putting its cars on the front row and then giving Michael Schumacher an unchallenged victory. "*Indy was special but what's happened here is a lot more worrying,*" grimaced Denis Chevrier, the Renault chief trackside engineer. "*Immediately you think it's the tyres but that's too easy. When you're a bit behind like we were today you have to work in every area. We have to gain a tenth with the engine, a tenth with the brakes, a tenth with the aerodynamics etc. So much the better as it puts us face to face with a technical challenge, a real pleasure for an engineer.*"
Right from the start Alonso was in third place blocked behind Massa while Michael opened up a gap. His car was running like clockwork and he pulled away by several tenths per lap.

Behind him Felipe Massa filled his role to perfection riding shotgun for his team leader and also trying to make sure of hanging on to 2nd place.
Renault evaluated the situation and decided on a change of strategy reducing the number of stops from three to two. It was a stroke of genius. "*When we saw Michael opening up such a gap we knew he'd be impossible to catch so we changed tactics,*" continued Chevrier. " *We had foreseen this possibility but a decision had to be taken before the first round of refuelling stops, as that's when it's necessary to add enough fuel to go far enough to stop just one more time. We changed from three stops to two. It was sure that we'd never catch Michael but we could at least leapfrog Massa.*"
The ploy worked and the Spaniard finished on the second step of the rostrum. It was another proof of his incredible season as in ten out of 11 grands prix he had finished either first or second.

^
Michael Schumacher was as full of beans as if he had just won his first race when he took the Italian flag. It was symbolic as it was the centenary of the first French Grand Prix.

Felipe Massa finished third behind Alonso after qualifying on the front row (below).
∨

> Kimi Raïkkönen and Pedro de la Rosa were team-mates after Montoya's sudden disappearance. The Spaniard was to keep his seat in the McLaren-Mercedes squad until the end of the season.

Ron Dennis: "I'll decide if Montoya races or not."

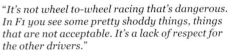

Ron Dennis was very angry. The Ronzer has never been one of the paddock's funny men, but he has rarely been as harsh as on Friday when he evoked the Montoya affair in the paddock.

The sudden departure of the Columbian for NASCAR was not yet settled. Juan Pablo was soon to find out that it was not a wise move to provoke Ron and his band of lawyers. He thought he had left the little world of F1 to its own devices and gone off for a bit of fun on the ovals in the Deep South. He was going to have to think again. "*I'm not going into the details but I can assure you that Juan Pablo is under contract to McLaren until the end of the year,*" thundered Dennis. "*I'll decide whether he'll do more testing or race in grands prix. It's our choice and nobody else's.*"

The British boss went on to explain that he had decided to suspend the Colombian when he learned that the latter had chosen to race in NASCAR in 2007. "*In the team we reckoned that it was better for Juan Pablo to stay calm (!) and do a bit of thinking before continuing for the rest of the season. The drivers are the best paid employees of the company, but they are still employees.*"

Did that mean that the Colombian would be back in F1 before the end of the year? "*Yes, it's more than possible,*" said Dennis. "*In any case I won't allow him to race or test in NASCAR. There would be too many clashes with our sponsors.*"

It was the kind of hard-nosed attitude that would not settle matters between the driver and his team whose relationship had been fairly strained since the start of the season. Juan Pablo had made a couple of major blunders; the first in Canada when he punted off Nico Rosberg and the second

> "Can I help you?" Anything that can bring tourists into this off-the-beaten-track region is good including French charms!
>

at Indianapolis where he caused a general pile up on the Speedway on the first lap. Montoya justified his departure from F1 by the reproaches that had been hurled at him. "*In F1, you're taken for a wild man if you try to pass somebody. That doesn't amuse me any more,*" he declared.

Jacques Villanueva who shared the same racing culture as the Colombian understood his motivation perfectly. For Jacques Montoya-type duels were a hell of a lot more honest than some of the more doubtful methods practised in F 1 – an illusion to the Monaco incident.

"*It's not wheel to wheel racing that's dangerous. In F1 you see some pretty shoddy things, things that are not acceptable. It's a lack of respect for the other drivers.*"

> Magny-Cours is in the centre of France- or in the middle of nowhere if you prefer- so the organisers have to stretch their imagination to bring in the punters. This year they organised a concert with Roger Waters and Nick Mason, two of the former Pink Floyd Group. They sang some of their most famous hits and played the whole of "*Dark Side of the Moon,*" their legendary album.
>
> Roger Waters could not refrain from speaking about politics when he was up on stage evoking the situation in the Lebanon and in Israel. The organisers were not very happy about this. The concert brought in around 20 000 fans and finished at midnight. It was like the F1 paddock on a day's outing as in the lodges were Jacques Villeneuve, Michael Schumacher, Jean Todt and even Max Mosley!

BMW: the "twin towers" worked perfectly!

On Friday, Robert Kubica set the fastest time of the day. "*The track was very hot and the tyres wore out very quickly but we've got the situation under control. In any case, the new aerodynamic devices are working well.*"

The devices in question were a couple of vertical wings on the top of the BMW Saubers' nose. A first in F1! Willy Rampf, the technical director, said that the "twin towers" as the team called them combined with the new appendices on the engine cover created a better air flow to the rear wing and improved grip. The team needed this, as it had been obliged to modify its rear wing said to be flexible – on the request of the FIA. The only fear was that they would interfere with the driver's vision. "*It doesn't hinder my vision of the track and the car seems more stable with them,*" declared Villeneuve.

> In qualifying Jacques Villeneuve was held up by Nico Rosberg and could do no better than sixteenth. Things went a little better in the race. "*I made a good start,*" he explained. "*After that I was blocked behind Scott Speed and Rubens Barrichello and it took me a while to get past them.*" The Canadian was helped to an eleventh-place finish by the retirements of Jarno Trulli and Mark Webber.

Practice

All the time trials

Nº Driver	Nat.	Nº Chassis - Engine [Nbr. GP]	Pos. Free 1 Friday	Laps	Pos. Free 2 Friday	Laps	Pos. Free 3 Saturday	Laps	Pos. Q1 Saturday	Laps	Pos. Q2 Saturday	Laps	Pos. Super Pole Saturday	Laps
1. Fernando Alonso	E	Renault R26 03 [1]	18.	1	2. 1:17.498	14	16. 1:18.447	16	6. 1:16.328	3	4. 1:15.706	3	3. **1:15.785**	12
2. Giancarlo Fisichella	I	Renault R26 05 [2]	17.	1	5. 1:17.916	13	11. 1:17.995	17	12. 1:16.825	3	7. 1:15.901	3	7. **1:16.345**	12
3. Kimi Räikkönen	FIN	McLaren MP4-21 02 - Mercedes [1]	24.	1	15. 1:19.140	9	7. 1:17.556	12	4. 1:16.154	6	5. 1:15.742	3	6. **1:16.281**	11
4. Pedro de la Rosa	E	McLaren MP4-21 07 - Mercedes [1]	19.	1	22. 1:19.809	14	8. 1:17.653	16	10. 1:16.679	5	8. 1:15.902	6	8. **1:16.632**	12
5. Michael Schumacher	D	Ferrari 248 F1 254 [1]			6. 1:17.938	16	14. 1:18.214	5	2. 1:15.865	4	1. 1:15.111	3	1. **1:15.493**	12
6. Felipe Massa	BR	Ferrari 248 F1 252 [1]			13. 1:19.013	20	15. 1:18.396	8	5. 1:16.277	3	3. 1:15.679	3	2. **1:15.510**	12
7. Ralf Schumacher	D	Toyota TF106/09B [1]	4. 1:18.752	6	9. 1:18.274	21	9. 1:17.666	18	3. 1:15.949	6	2. 1:15.625	3	5. **1:16.091**	12
8. Jarno Trulli	I	Toyota TF106/08B [2]	12. 1:19.806	7	11. 1:18.721	23	3. 1:17.056	18	1. 1:15.550	6	6. 1:15.776	3	4. **1:16.036**	12
9. Mark Webber	AUS	Williams FW28 03 - Cosworth [1]			18. 1:19.413	10	5. 1:17.358	12	8. 1:16.531	6	11. **1:16.129**	6		
10. Nico Rosberg	D	Williams FW28 05 - Cosworth [2->1]	10. 1:19.401	6	20. 1:19.692	19	4. 1:17.188	16	9. 1:16.534	6	9. 1:15.926	6	9. **1:18.272**	12
11. Rubens Barrichello	BR	Honda RA106-01 [2]			17. 1:19.259	5	20. 1:18.961	20	15. 1:17.022	6	14. **1:17.027**	6		
12. Jenson Button	GB	Honda RA106-05 [1]	3. 1:18.160	4	12. 1:19.005	18	6. 1:17.476	19	19. **1:17.495**	7				
14. David Coulthard	GB	Red Bull RB2 3 - Ferrari [1]	22.	1	25. 1:20.135	12	10. 1:17.859	19	7. 1:16.350	6	10. 1:15.974	6	10. **1:18.663**	12
15. Christian Klien	A	Red Bull RB2 2 - Ferrari [2]	23.	1	27. 1:20.409	14	19. 1:18.631	17	13. 1:16.921	6	13. **1:16.433**	6		
16. Nick Heidfeld	D	BMW Sauber F1.06-02 [1]			14. 1:19.108	15	2. 1:17.049	16	11. 1:16.686	7	12. **1:16.294**	6		
17. Jacques Villeneuve	CDN	BMW Sauber F1.06-05 [2]	8. 1:19.063	6	26. 1:20.154	11	1. 1:17.005	13	18. **1:17.304**	3				
18. Tiago Monteiro	P	Midland M16-03 - Toyota [1]	13. 1:20.335	7	21. 1:19.701	19	17. 1:18.487	23	20. **1:17.589**	7				
19. Christijan Albers	NL	Midland M16-02 - Toyota [1]	11. 1:19.465	7	16. 1:19.183	21	12. 1:18.059	24	14. 1:16.962	8	16. **1:17.105**	3		
20. Vitantonio Liuzzi	I	Toro Rosso STR01 03 - Cosworth [1->1]	21.	2	19. 1:19.589	14	13. 1:18.199	20	17. **1:17.164**	8				
21. Scott Speed	USA	Toro Rosso STR01 02 - Cosworth [1]	20.	1	24. 1:20.003	12	18. 1:18.545	20	16. 1:17.117	9	15. **1:17.063**	8		
22. Takuma Sato	J	Super Aguri SA05-05 - Honda [1]	15. 1:21.160	10	23. 1:19.996	22	22. 1:21.497	10	22. **1:18.845**	6				
23. Franck Montagny	F	Super Aguri SA05-02 - Honda [1]	14. 1:20.790	11	28. 1:21.132	14	21. 1:19.497	18	21. **1:18.637**	6				
35. Alexander Wurz	A	Williams FW28 04 - Cosworth	7. 1:19.055	17	4. 1:17.859	29								
36. Anthony Davidson	GB	Honda RA106-03	2. 1:17.133	29	3. 1:17.750	37								
37. Robert Doornbos	NL	Red Bull RB2 5 - Ferrari	9. 1:19.311	20	8. 1:18.175	28								
38. Robert Kubica	PL	BMW Sauber F1.06-03	1. 1:16.794	31	1. 1:16.902	33								
39. Adrian Sutil	D	Midland M16-04 - Toyota	5. 1:18.777	32	7. 1:18.049	31								
40. Neel Jani	CH	Toro Rosso STR01 01 - Cosworth	6. 1:18.962	21	10. 1:18.639	32								
41. Sakon Yamamoto	J	Super Aguri SA05-01 - Honda	16. 1:23.891	11	29. 1:21.969	32								

Fastest lap overall
M. Schumacher 1:15.111 (211,415 km/h)

Maximum speed

Nº Driver	S1 Qualifs	Pos.	S1 Race	Pos.	S2 Qualifs	Pos.	S2 Race	Pos.	Finish Qualifs	Pos.	Finish Race	Pos.	Radar Qualifs	Pos.	Radar Race	Pos.
1. F. Alonso	182,9	5	175,1	12	268,7	7	268,0	7	166,5	3	158,1	10	304,4	4	305,7	1
2. G. Fisichella	179,5	11	174,2	15	271,2	4	267,9	8	164,4	7	159,5	6	304,5	3	303,3	4
3. K. Räikkönen	176,2	16	174,1	16	271,9	2	270,0	3	164,5	6	158,8	8	305,0	2	301,9	7
4. P. de la Rosa	172,4	20	174,8	13	268,9	6	269,5	4	166,0	4	161,5	2	299,5	7	302,2	5
5. M. Schumacher	178,8	13	179,3	7	271,9	1	270,1	2	166,6	2	159,9	5	307,4	1	305,6	2
6. F. Massa	179,2	12	180,8	5	271,7	3	270,3	1	164,1	10	161,1	3	303,8	5	303,9	3
7. R. Schumacher	181,9	6	179,7	6	270,8	5	268,1	6	159,1	17	156,5	13	300,5	6	299,5	15
8. J. Trulli	184,3	3	182,3	1	268,3	9	266,4	9	163,5	13	155,2	15	298,9	8	297,1	19
9. M. Webber	180,6	8	182,2	2	266,8	13	265,8	13	161,0	15	154,2	17	293,4	20	301,9	6
10. N. Rosberg	184,9	2	178,5	9	268,4	8	266,0	12	164,3	9	156,3	14	298,3	10	301,0	9
11. R. Barrichello	179,9	10	169,4	20	265,2	19	263,3	19	163,8	12	153,2	19	293,4	19	293,5	22
12. J. Button	180,6	7	179,1	8	266,2	15	266,2	11	160,4	16	159,2	7	297,9	11	299,5	16
14. D. Coulthard	183,9	4	182,0	3	267,8	12	264,2	17	164,3	8	157,1	11	295,2	17	300,8	11
15. C. Klien	176,3	15	174,7	14	266,6	14	266,4	10	166,6	1	160,0	4	295,0	18	300,5	12
16. N. Heidfeld	180,5	9	176,6	10	265,6	18	262,5	20	163,0	14	158,1	9	295,8	16	300,9	10
17. J. Villeneuve	168,1	22	175,6	11	265,6	17	264,6	15	165,1	5	161,7	1	298,3	9	299,0	17
18. T. Monteiro	168,4	21	159,3	21	264,1	21	259,7	21	158,3	20	147,6	21	296,7	14	299,0	18
19. C. Albers	172,9	18	173,7	17	266,0	16	264,3	16	164,0	11	157,1	12	297,1	13	295,9	21
20. V. Liuzzi	184,9	1	172,2	18	268,3	10	269,4	5	157,0	21	153,3	18	296,0	15	301,4	8
21. S. Speed	176,6	14	180,9	4	268,1	11	265,1	14	158,8	18	154,5	16	297,4	12	299,7	14
22. T. Sato	174,3	17	148,2	22	264,9	20			158,8	19			293,0	21	296,0	20
23. F. Montagny	172,6	19	170,9	19	264,0	22	264,1	18	154,9	22	150,3	20	291,8	22	300,3	13

Race

Classification & Retirements

Pos.	Driver	Constructor	Tyres	Laps	Time	Average
1.	M. Schumacher	Ferrari	B	70	1:32:07.803	200,967 km/h
2.	F. Alonso	Renault	M	70	+ 10.131	200,599 km/h
3.	F. Massa	Ferrari	B	70	+ 22.546	200,151 km/h
4.	R. Schumacher	Toyota	B	70	+ 27.212	199,983 km/h
5.	K. Räikkönen	McLaren Mercedes	M	70	+ 33.006	199,774 km/h
6.	G. Fisichella	Renault	M	70	+ 45.265	199,335 km/h
7.	P. de la Rosa	McLaren Mercedes	M	70	+ 49.407	199,187 km/h
8.	N. Heidfeld	BMW	M	69	1 lap	197,626 km/h
9.	D. Coulthard	RBR Ferrari	M	69	1 lap	197,512 km/h
10.	S. Speed	STR Cosworth	M	69	1 lap	196,891 km/h
11.	J. Villeneuve	BMW	M	69	1 lap	196,597 km/h
12.	C. Klien	RBR Ferrari	M	69	1 lap	196,569 km/h
13.	V. Liuzzi	STR Cosworth	M	69	1 lap	196,433 km/h
14.	N. Rosberg	Williams Cosworth	B	68	2 laps	195,205 km/h
15.	C. Albers	MF1 Toyota	B	68	2 laps	195,047 km/h
16.	F. Montagny	Aguri Honda	B	67	3 laps	190,942 km/h

Driver	Constructor	Tyre	Laps	Reason
J. Button	Honda	M	61	Loss of power
M. Webber	Williams Cosworth	B	53	Wheel rim failure, too much damage to continue
J. Trulli	Toyota	B	39	Leak on the braking system
R. Barrichello	Honda	M	18	Engine failure
T. Monteiro	MF1 Toyota	B	11	
T. Sato	Aguri Honda	B	0	Clutch problem

Fastest laps

	Pilote	Temps	Lap	Moyenne
1.	M. Schumacher	1:17.111	46	205,931 km/h
2.	F. Massa	1:17.141	18	205,851 km/h
3.	P. de la Rosa	1:17.625	34	204,568 km/h
4.	K. Räikkönen	1:17.717	30	204,325 km/h
5.	F. Alonso	1:17.770	23	204,186 km/h
6.	R. Schumacher	1:17.809	19	204,084 km/h
7.	J. Villeneuve	1:17.906	56	203,830 km/h
8.	J. Trulli	1:18.036	16	203,490 km/h
9.	G. Fisichella	1:18.057	20	203,435 km/h
10.	V. Liuzzi	1:18.241	54	202,957 km/h
11.	J. Button	1:18.510	47	202,262 km/h
12.	S. Speed	1:18.674	66	201,840 km/h
13.	N. Rosberg	1:18.796	62	201,527 km/h
14.	N. Heidfeld	1:18.809	48	201,494 km/h
15.	M. Webber	1:18.859	34	201,366 km/h
16.	C. Klien	1:18.968	56	201,089 km/h
17.	D. Coulthard	1:18.978	56	201,063 km/h
18.	C. Albers	1:19.356	67	200,105 km/h
19.	R. Barrichello	1:20.094	16	198,262 km/h
20.	F. Montagny	1:20.113	53	198,215 km/h
21.	T. Monteiro	1:21.663	8	194,452 km/h

Pit stops

	Driver	Laps	Duration	Stop	Total
1.	F. Massa	16	20.764	1	20.764
2.	F. Alonso	17	21.412	1	21.412
3.	K. Räikkönen	17	20.651	1	20.651
4.	M. Schumacher	18	20.146	1	20.146
5.	G. Fisichella	18	22.213	1	22.213
6.	P. de la Rosa	18	20.390	1	20.390
7.	M. Webber	19	20.764	1	20.764
8.	F. Montagny	19	20.788	1	20.788
9.	J. Trulli	20	21.254	1	21.254
10.	J. Button	21	22.179	1	22.179
11.	N. Rosberg	21	21.565	1	21.565
12.	R. Schumacher	22	30.654	1	30.654
13.	N. Heidfeld	25	22.434	1	22.434
14.	C. Albers	26	31.955	1	31.955
15.	J. Villeneuve	27	22.434	1	22.434
16.	S. Speed	28	22.746	1	22.746
17.	D. Coulthard	29	21.450	1	21.450
18.	C. Klien	31	21.292	1	21.292
19.	V. Liuzzi	31	21.118	1	21.118
20.	K. Räikkönen	32	24.753	2	45.404
21.	F. Massa	34	20.127	2	40.891
22.	P. de la Rosa	35	20.196	2	40.586
23.	F. Montagny	35	20.483	2	41.271
24.	M. Schumacher	38	19.686	2	39.832
25.	J. Trulli	38	31.856	2	53.110
26.	M. Webber	38	21.584	2	42.348
27.	M. Webber	39	4:36.186	3	5:18.534
28.	F. Alonso	42	23.021	2	44.433
29.	N. Rosberg	44	23.613	2	45.178
30.	G. Fisichella	45	21.616	2	43.829
31.	J. Button	45	21.932	2	44.111
32.	R. Schumacher	46	21.096	2	51.750
33.	N. Heidfeld	46	21.382	2	43.816
34.	C. Albers	48	23.416	2	55.371
35.	P. de la Rosa	50	20.824	3	1:01.410
36.	S. Speed	50	20.565	2	43.311
37.	M. Webber	46	21.383	4	5:39.917
38.	D. Coulthard	52	20.555	2	42.005
39.	F. Massa	53	20.204	3	1:01.095
40.	V. Liuzzi	52	20.399	2	41.517
41.	K. Räikkönen	53	20.415	3	1:05.819
42.	F. Montagny	51	22.090	3	1:03.361
43.	J. Villeneuve	53	20.519	2	42.953
44.	C. Klien	53	22.264	2	43.556
45.	M. Schumacher	55	19.423	3	59.255
46.	N. Rosberg	56	19.951	3	1:05.129

Race leader

Driver	Laps in the lead	Nbr of Laps
M. Schumacher	1 > 18	18
J. Trulli	19 > 20	2
R. Schumacher	21 > 22	2
M. Schumacher	23 > 38	16
F. Alonso	39 > 41	3
M. Schumacher	42 > 70	29

Driver	Nbr of Laps	Kilometers
M. Schumacher	63	277,709 km
F. Alonso	3	13,233 km
J. Trulli	2	8,822 km
R. Schumacher	2	8,822 km

Gaps on the leader board

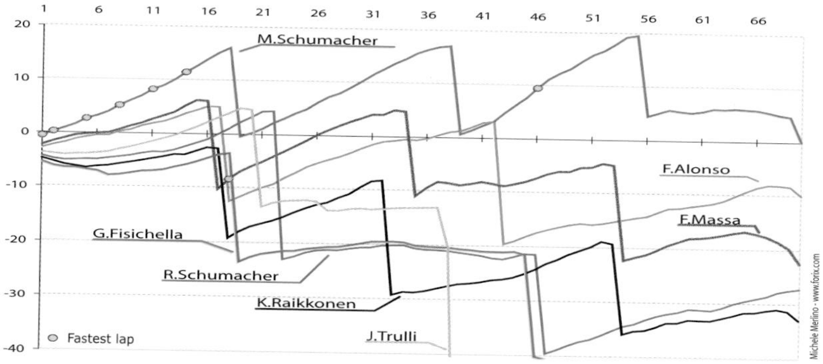

Lap chart

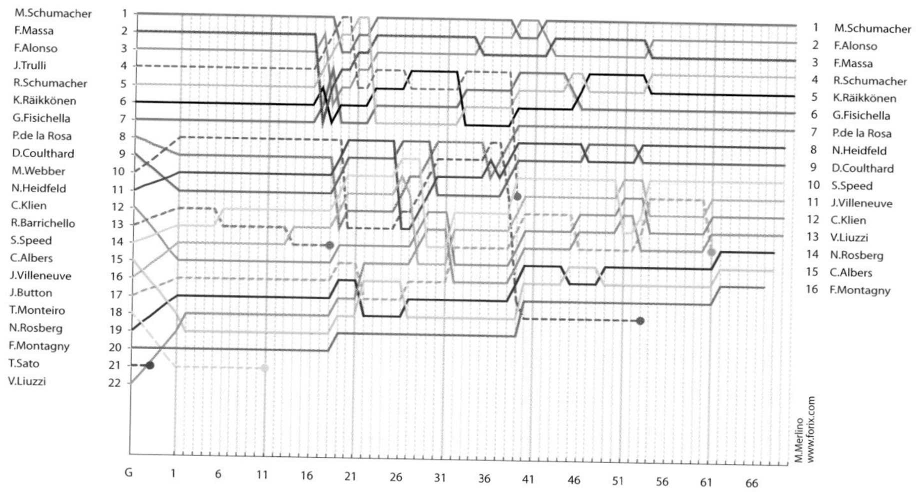

Championships 11/18

Drivers

1. F. Alonso ....Renault ....6 🏆....96
2. M. Schumacher .....Ferrari......................4 🏆....79
3. G. Fisichella..........Renault ....1 🏆....46
4. K. Räikkönen ....McLaren Mercedes 43
5. F. Massa...............Ferrari 42
6. J. Montoya ....McLaren Mercedes..............26
7. J. Button ....Honda 16
8. R. Barrichello........Honda 16
9. R. Schumacher .....Toyota 13
10. N. Heidfeld ....BMW 13
11. D. Coulthard.........RBR Ferrari........................10
12. J. Trulli.................Toyota 8
13. J. Villeneuve ....BMW 7
14. M. Webber............Williams Cosworth................6
15. N. Rosberg ....Williams Cosworth................4
16. P. de la Rosa.........McLaren Mercedes................2
17. V. Liuzzi ....STR Cosworth.......................1
18. C. Klien................RBR Ferrari 1
19. S. Speed ....STR Cosworth.......................0
20. C. Albers..............MF1 Toyota 0
21. T. Monteiro ....MF1 Toyota 0
22. T. Sato.................Aguri Honda 0
23. Y. Ide..................Aguri Honda 0
24. F. Montagny..........Aguri Honda 0

Constructors

1. Mild Seven Renault F1 Team ....7 🏆....142
2. Scuderia Ferrari Marlboro ....4 🏆....121
3. Team McLaren Mercedes 71
4. Lucky Strike Honda Racing F1 Team 32
5. Panasonic Toyota Racing 21
6. BMW Sauber F1 Team...............................20
7. Red Bull Racing 11
8. Williams F1 Team.....................................10
9. Scuderia Toro Rosso...................................1
10. MF1 Racing...0
11. Super Aguri Formula 1 0

The circuit

Name	Magny-Cours, Nevers
Lenght	4411 m
Distance	70 laps, 308,586 km
Date	July 16th 2006

Weather	Cloudy, warm
Air temperature	34-36°c
Track temperature	47-55°c
Humidity	32-31%
Wind speed	1.8 m/s

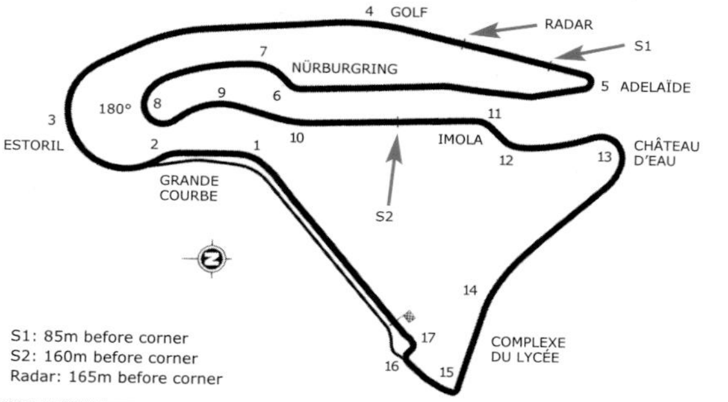

S1: 85m before corner
S2: 160m before corner
Radar: 165m before corner

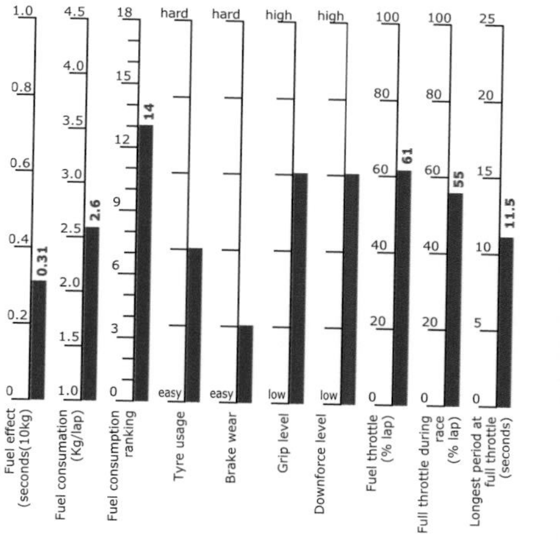

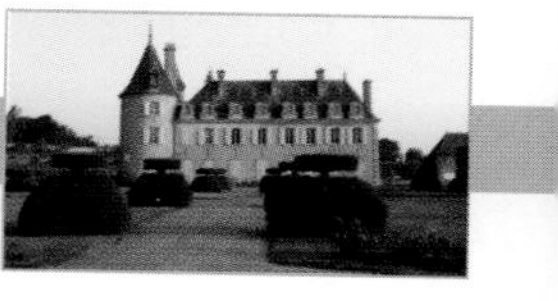

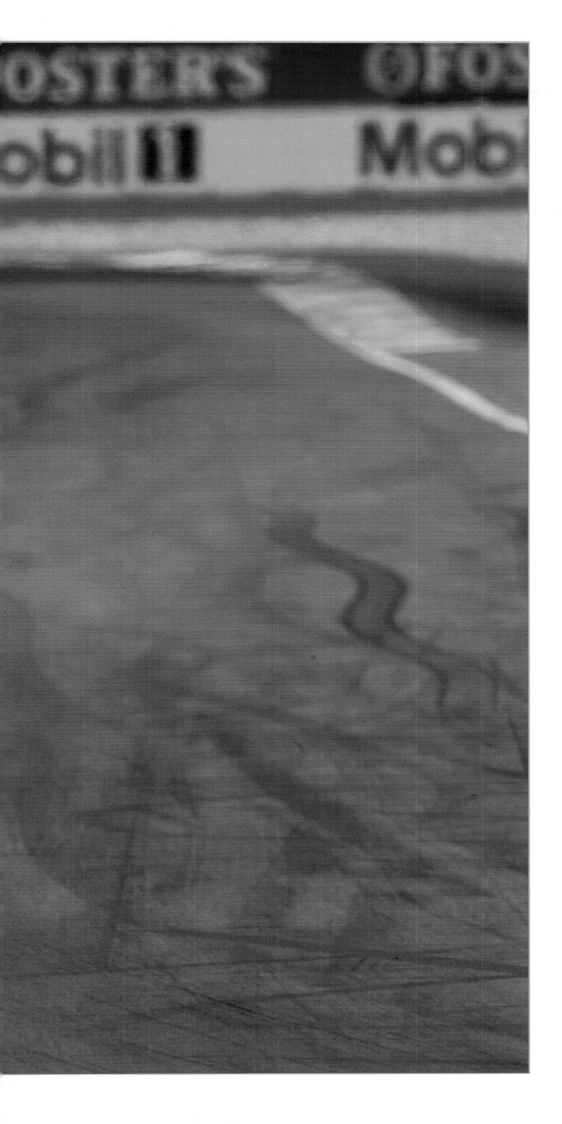

FERRARI WIDENS THE GAP

So far Renault and Ferrari had shared the victories, as there was little to choose between them in terms of performance. But this was not the case at Hockenheim where Michael Schumacher and Felipe Massa crushed their rivals in the German Grand Prix. Renault was in panic mode after the race. The R26s were incapable of matching the pace of the Ferraris and the team didn't really know why.
On the Magny-Cours circuit the gap between the two teams was two or three tenths but at Hockenheim it was around 2 seconds. The Renault people had not seen it coming and they were completely demoralised.

Kimi Raïkkönen on pole. Renault's mass dampers removed. Danger!

> ^
> Kimi Raïkkönen set his first pole of the season at Hockenheim. Was it really as good as it looked or was it just a bit of gamesmanship to please the many Mercedes-Benz guests around the circuit?

Up to Hockenheim the duel between Michael Schumacher and Fernando Alonso had seemed pretty finely balanced but on the German circuit the Spaniard lost a lot of ground to the Ferraris. The problems that hit the Renault varied from the tyres and suspension to the car's nose. The R26 was a full second off the Hockenheim pole time, a gulf in F1 terms.
"We've studied the telemetry read-outs in detail. We can't see anything abnormal. I don't understand it," said a perplexed Denis Chevrier on Saturday evening. The Renault chief engineer was lost in conjecture as to the poor performances of the R26s. The cars had a new aerodynamic kit in Germany that was supposed to improve their efficiency. Contrary to expectations Fernando Alonso qualified down in 7th place, his worst performance of the season. Immediately, the French engineers began to ask themselves if the new aero kit was as good as it was cracked up to be.
The team had received another blow on Friday. The FIA stated that the mass damper system used on the Renaults for almost a year was illegal. The Federation reckoned that it

was nothing other than a moveable aerodynamic device forbidden by the regulations. An appeal had been lodged but while awaiting the outcome the French team decided to remove the device, which represented a loss of several tenths. Finally, tyrewise Renault made the wrong choice for the German Grand Prix. The previous week during private testing after which each team had to choose its compounds for Hockenheim the engineers took a risk concerning the tyre's construction. Alonso did not agree with this decision and he paid the price so the ambience was very morose in the French camp on Saturday evening.
Michael Schumacher was the man who profited from these problems. He qualified on the front row and was out to reduce his 17-point deficit to his rival. "I'm very satisfied," smiled the German on Saturday evening. "I'm well placed and several other drivers are going to cause Fernando problems. The race is looking really good."
Alonso's 7th place on the grid put him in the danger zone: for example an accident in the first corner with Ralf Schumacher beside him

on the 4th row but also the possibility of a bad result because of the advantage enjoyed by his better-placed rivals. In this context the return to form of the McLaren-Mercedes as proved by Raïkkönen's pole that could not have come at a worse moment for the Spaniard. "We've put some new parts on the car including a new front wing that seems to work very well," commented the Finn who risked taking a few precious points off the Spaniard. For Fernando it was a very dicey grand prix.

> >
> Tiago Monteiro was not a happy bunny. The Portuguese was 18th on the grid and was disqualified in the race - like his team-mate Christijan Albers- after finishing 14th when the Midlands' rear wing was declared illegal.

> >
> "Stop doing your big star bit, Sakon. Otherwise you'll finish up like Yuji!" Takuma Sato was giving advice to Ide's replacement in the Super Aguri team. After Franck Montagny's brief interlude the squad was once again 100% Japanese.

Starting grid

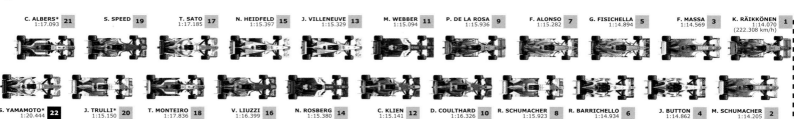

* J. TRULLI et
C. ALBERS
Penalty for an engine change (-10 places).

S. YAMAMOTO
Penalty for an engine change (-10 places).
Start from pit lane.

C. ALBERS* 21 — 1:17.093	S. SPEED 19	T. SATO 17 — 1:17.185	N. HEIDFELD 15 — 1:15.397
J. VILLENEUVE 13 — 1:15.329	M. WEBBER 11 — 1:15.094	P. DE LA ROSA 9 — 1:15.936	F. ALONSO 7 — 1:15.282
G. FISICHELLA 5 — 1:14.894	F. MASSA 3 — 1:14.569	K. RAÏKKÖNEN 1 — 1:14.070 (222.308 km/h)	

S. YAMAMOTO* 22 — 1:20.444	J. TRULLI* 20 — 1:15.150	T. MONTEIRO 18 — 1:17.836	V. LIUZZI 16 — 1:16.399
N. ROSBERG 14 — 1:15.380	C. KLIEN 12 — 1:15.141	D. COULTHARD 10 — 1:16.326	R. SCHUMACHER 8 — 1:15.923
R. BARRICHELLO 6 — 1:14.934	J. BUTTON 4 — 1:14.862	M. SCHUMACHER 2 — 1:14.205	

^
Michael Schumacher drove a faultless race and went into the lead when Kimi Raïkkönen came in for fuel around lap 10 proving that he had started with very light tanks..

Ferrari's crushing double got the paddock in a tizzy at Hockenheim

Apart from the first three grands prix of the season the battle for victory had been fought on almost equal terms between Ferrari and Renault. Since March the duel between Michael Schumacher and Fernando Alonso had been decided by tenths of seconds. Sometimes the German had beaten the Spaniard by a whisker by a better strategy as was the case at Imola and the Nürburgring and on others Alosno defeated the German without too many problems. Since Imola both men had scored the same number of points in the classification and the pundits expected to see a hotly-disputed end of season between the two championship contenders. In this context the Spaniard was hoping to take advantage of his 17-point lead to win his second title. But all that was before the German Grand Prix, which really upset the Renault apple cart. Alonso now had no choice but to go for it. The Ferraris dominated at Hockenheim and

were almost 2 seconds a lap quicker than all their opponents. "*I can't even find the words to describe my car,*" warbled Michael Schumacher. 'It's been fantastic all weekend."

How did the 248 F1s manage to find such a sudden performance hike so quickly? That was the question the Renault people were asking themselves after the finish.

They found a few answers. While all the Michelin-shod teams had prepared for the German Prix on the Jerez circuit in Spain, Ferrari had been the only ones testing at Le Castellet. It looked like the Italian squad had made the right choice, as its tyres at Hockenheim were incredibly quick while the Michelin runners' rubber blistered on most of the cars. "*The compounds that we've brought here were maybe a bit too aggressive,*" said Nick Shorrock, the Michelin F1 boss.

"*My tyres went off after the first few laps and*

I could do nothing about it, otherwise I might have finished on the rostrum," complained Fernando Alonso who saw the flag in 5th place. Ferrari's rivals had little time to react with the Hungarian Grand Prix coming up the following Sunday. Michelin decided to go for broke. The tyres planned for Budapest had already been made. On the evening of the German Grand Prix the French make's engineers decided to throw them out and make new compounds during the night taking into account what had happened at Hockenheim.

Renault held three days of intensive meetings until Wednesday to try and put the R26 back on the winning trail.

This was the price that had to be paid if Fernando Alonso was to stem Ferrari's triumphant advance. In the light of the Hockenheim result it looked a difficult task.

Jean Todt's three favourites on the rostrum

Jean Todt's three favourites on the rostrum Kimi Raïkkönen finished 3rd after starting from pole "*It's not too bad taking into account my problems. A wheel nut blocked during my first stop, then my tyres blistered and finally I had hydraulic glitches,*" complained the Finn. "*The car has made a lot of progress but we're still way off the pace of the Ferraris.*"

After a good start Pedro de la Rosa was forced to retire with brake problems.

However, the strange thing was what Jean Todt said

about Kimi Raïkkönen after the race. "*I'll remember this rostrum for a long time as my three favourite drivers were on it,*" stated the Frenchman more or less confirming the fact that he had taken on Kimi for 2007. Several hours after the race when questioned about that little aside the Scuderia team manager replied that he had always liked Raïkkönen and that no one should read into it that he wanted to hire the Finn. Todt also confirmed that the drivers as well as the new organisation would be announced at Monza a few minutes after the finish of the Italian Grand Prix.

Michael was really delighted with his victory and made it plain for all to see. He always shows a real almost juvenile sense of pleasure each time he wins.
∨

Renault: looking for reasons

The German Grand Prix was the worst of the season from a performance point of view for Renault. What with tyre problems and the removal of the mass damper just about everything went wrong for the French team

> The ambience was a lot better in the Honda camp than of late. After beginning the season in a blaze of glory Jenson Button's team had gone backwards. The Brit qualified on the 2nd row at Hockenheim and finished 4th.

Fernando Alonso's front tyres were not a pretty sight after the race. No wonder the Spaniard had to fight with his car!
∨

Jacques Villeneuve does more damage to his career than to himself.

The BMW Saubers qualified in 14th and 16th places so obviously this was not going to be their race of the year. When Sunday evening came it was certainly their worst! It all began with a collision between the 2 cars, generally enough to send the team bosses ballistic. Jacques Villeneuve made a good start. "*Yeah, the start was OK,*" he explained. "*In the second corner there was a Red Bull in the way which prevented me from slipping through on the inside. Nick (Heidfeld, his team-mate) was on the outside and suddenly he pulled in on top of me and tagged my front wing. It's a pity as it spoiled the race for both of us. Nick acknowledged his mistake. This kind of thing happens.*"

"*Happy birthday, Fernando!*" On Saturday the Spaniard celebrated his 25th birthday and the cake decorated with a replica of a Renault was made before qualifying. While nobody was really in a party mood afterwards Fernando entered into the spirit of things and cut the cake with the help of Flavio Briatore.
>

In fact, little Nick did not acknowledge anything at all and accused the Canadian of having rammed him up the rear. The German was able to continue but then retired on lap 10 while Villeneuve had to come into his pit and have the car's nose changed. He rejoined in last place. "*The wing that they fitted was set up completely differently from the original one. It had a lot more downforce and that upset the rear balance of the car. It was totally undriveable, I was crossed up in all the corners. My engineers saw it on the screen.*"

Jacques Villeneuve's contact with the wall damaged not only his car but also his reputation as he was shown the door by his team, which used this accident as a pretext to fire him
∨

This was an intolerable situation for the "*Quebecois' who managed to keep it between the hedges for around half the race. Then on lap 31 he lost the BMW and slammed into the wall. "I got it all wrong in the second-last corner of the circuit,*" said Villeneuve.

"*I got the car back but I was off line for the last bend. I went straight on and I hit the wall.*" The impact was much heavier than he anticipated. Two hours later he still felt it massaging his neck and grimacing a little. "*My neck hurts. It's the kind of impact that makes you stiff all over.*

Tomorrow I don't think I'll be able to turn my head. The crash was really very violent. I was surprised because I didn't think I'd hit so hard. It's annoying. I don't like bending cars." He did not know it yet but he had done more damage to his career than to his car.

Week end chatter

> On Thursday Frank Williams confirmed that he had signed a 3-year contract with Toyota for a supply of engines for his F1 team from 2007 onwards. Up till then Midland had the right to the Japanese engines so it had to find another solution. It was a very tough blow for Cosworth, which supplied engines only to Williams, and was a poor reward for the real qualities of its V8. Sir Frank had obviously negotiated a better financial deal with the Japanese.

> Michael and Ralf Schumacher do not always get on like brothers. At Hockenheim, Ralf explained in Bild, a kind of German red top, that he did not really consider Michael as his brother. "*There are six-and-a-half years between us and my parents brought me up almost like an only child We've got nothing in common. Michael never helped me. I've got better things to do during my holidays than to go visiting him!*".

> Toyota announced that it had put its trust in Jarno Trulli for another 3 seasons. The Italian resident in Pontresina (in Grisons in Switzerland) would stay with the team until the end of 2009.

Practice

All the time trials

N° Driver	Nat.	N° Chassis - Engine [Nbr. GP]	Pos.	Free 1 Friday	Laps	Pos.	Free 2 Friday	Laps	Pos.	Free 3 Saturday	Laps	Pos.	Q1 Saturday	Laps	Pos.	Q2 Saturday	Laps	Pos.	Super Pole Saturday	Laps
1. Fernando Alonso	E	Renault R26 03 [2]	7.	1:18.328	5	15.	1:18.082	8	11.	1:16.427	15	5.	1:15.518	3	8.	1:14.746	6	7.	**1:15.282**	12
2. Giancarlo Fisichella	I	Renault R26 05 [1]	9.	1:18.664	6	11.	1:17.672	10	6.	1:16.130	16	13.	1:15.916	3	5.	1:14.540	6	5.	**1:14.894**	12
3. Kimi Räikkönen	FIN	McLaren MP4-21 05 - Mercedes [2]	25.		1	4.	1:17.040	9	8.	1:16.218	12	3.	1:15.214	3	4.	1:14.410	6	1.	**1:14.070**	10
4. Pedro de la Rosa	E	McLaren MP4-21 07 - Mercedes [1]	24.		1	8.	1:17.516	10	10.	1:16.322	12	6.	1:15.655	4	10.	1:15.021	6	9.	**1:15.936**	10
5. Michael Schumacher	D	Ferrari 248 F1 254 [2]				2.	1:16.502	14	9.	1:16.307	11	2.	1:14.904	3	1.	1:13.778	3	2.	**1:14.205**	12
6. Felipe Massa	BR	Ferrari 248 F1 252 [2]				5.	1:17.205	11	4.	1:15.977	13	1.	1:14.412	3	2.	1:14.094	3	3.	**1:14.569**	12
7. Ralf Schumacher	D	Toyota TF106/07B [2]	22.		4	13.	1:17.895	14	16.	1:17.419	17	9.	1:15.789	7	7.	1:14.743	7	8.	**1:15.923**	7
8. Jarno Trulli	I	Toyota TF106/08B & 09B [1->1]	21.		4	12.	1:17.844	13	22.		2	4.	1:15.430	8	13.	**1:15.150**	4			
9. Mark Webber	AUS	Williams FW28 03 - Cosworth [2]				7.	1:17.344	6	15.	1:16.834	16	7.	1:15.719	8	11.	**1:15.094**	6			
10. Nico Rosberg	D	Williams FW28 05 - Cosworth [2]	20.	1:34.942	3				14.	1:16.690	20	14.	1:16.183	8	15.	**1:15.380**	6			
11. Rubens Barrichello	BR	Honda RA106-01 [1]	6.	1:18.085	6	9.	1:17.519	13	3.	1:15.963	19	8.	1:15.757	6	6.	1:14.652	6	6.	**1:14.934**	12
12. Jenson Button	GB	Honda RA106-05 [1]	4.	1:17.439	5	10.	1:17.542	13	2.	1:15.651	15	12.	1:15.869	6	3.	1:14.378	5	4.	**1:14.862**	12
14. David Coulthard	GB	Red Bull RB2 3 - Ferrari [2]	10.	1:18.795	5	20.	1:18.616	10	5.	1:16.080	14	11.	1:15.836	7	9.	1:14.826	6	10.	**1:16.326**	12
15. Christian Klien	A	Red Bull RB2 2 - Ferrari [1]	23.		1	17.	1:18.223	13	1.	1:15.628	14	10.	1:15.816	8	12.	**1:15.141**	6			
16. Nick Heidfeld	D	BMW Sauber F1.06-02 [2]	14.	1:19.507	7	21.	1:18.636	10	7.	1:16.167	14	15.	1:16.234	5	16.	**1:15.397**	8			
17. Jacques Villeneuve	CDN	BMW Sauber F1.06-08 [2]	12.	1:18.972	6	24.	1:19.113	9	17.	1:17.740	16	16.	1:16.281	5	14.	**1:15.329**	8			
18. Tiago Monteiro	P	Midland M16-03 - Toyota [2]	17.	1:20.575	7	23.	1:18.991	11	18.	1:17.793	23	20.	**1:17.836**	6						
19. Christijan Albers	NL	Midland M16-02 - Toyota [2->1]	16.	1:20.132	5	22.	1:18.643	11	21.	1:19.254	15	18.	**1:17.093**	5						
20. Vitantonio Liuzzi	I	Toro Rosso STR01 03 - Cosworth [2]	13.	1:19.214	5	18.	1:18.366	13	12.	1:16.532	18	17.	**1:16.399**	9						
21. Scott Speed	USA	Toro Rosso STR01 02 - Cosworth [2]	18.	1:20.950	7	25.	1:19.232	12	13.	1:16.600	17	22.	**DNF**	2						
22. Takuma Sato	J	Super Aguri SA06-03 - Honda [2]	15.	1:20.102	14	26.	1:19.365	8	20.	1:18.668	21	19.	**1:17.185**	5						
23. Sakon Yamamoto	J	Super Aguri SA06-04 - Honda [2]	19.	1:21.218	21	27.		2	19.	1:18.643	19	21.	**1:20.444**	5						
35. Alexander Wurz	A	Williams FW28 06 - Cosworth	1.	1:16.349	26	16.	1:18.164	36												
36. Anthony Davidson	GB	Honda RA106-03	2.	1:16.523	29	6.	1:17.294	26												
37. Robert Doornbos	NL	Red Bull RB2 5 - Ferrari	5.	1:17.835	25	3.	1:16.549	18												
38. Robert Kubica	PL	BMW Sauber F1.06-03	3.	1:17.343	29	1.	1:16.225	18												
39. Markus Winkelhock	D	Midland M16-04 - Toyota	11.	1:18.964	27	14.	1:17.962	20												
40. Neel Jani	CH	Toro Rosso STR01 01 - Cosworth	8.	1:18.539	24	19.	1:18.460	19												

Fastest lap overall
M. Schumacher 1:13.778 (223,188 km/h)

Maximum speed

N° Driver	S1 Qualifs	Pos.	S1 Race	Pos.	S2 Qualifs	Pos.	S2 Race	Pos.	Finish Qualifs	Pos.	Finish Race	Pos.	Radar Qualifs	Pos.	Radar Race	Pos.
1. F. Alonso	214,4	11	210,2	10	262,2	13	258,2	7	266,7	6	263,8	5	309,6	3	310,7	8
2. G. Fisichella	215,9	7	211,6	4	262,9	9	258,6	6	267,1	5	263,9	4	306,9	8	308,4	12
3. K. Räikkönen	216,0	5	212,1	3	263,8	4	260,9	3	267,9	2	264,3	3	305,3	10	308,2	13
4. P. de la Rosa	216,5	3	210,1	11	263,6	5	254,8	16	267,7	3	261,8	8	307,5	6	309,1	11
5. M. Schumacher	216,7	2	211,1	5	266,8	1	261,7	2	266,6	7	263,7	6	308,3	4	313,4	4
6. F. Massa	218,0	1	213,0	1	266,0	2	262,1	1	269,0	1	265,0	1	307,5	5	310,6	9
7. R. Schumacher	212,5	16	210,0	13	261,6	16	256,7	9	264,2	16	261,1	11	311,5	1	312,8	5
8. J. Trulli	211,8	17	210,4	7	264,1	3	260,5	4	265,3	9	263,0	7	311,2	2	317,4	1
9. M. Webber	213,8	13	210,8	6	262,3	12	258,1	8	265,6	8	261,3	10	300,2	19	313,4	3
10. N. Rosberg	212,9	15	159,9	21	262,2	14			264,7	11			303,6	11	311,7	7
11. R. Barrichello	216,0	6	210,4	8	262,1	15	255,3	13	265,2	10	260,8	13	300,8	18	308,1	14
12. J. Button	216,5	4	212,3	2	262,9	8	259,2	5	267,7	4	264,5	2	307,4	7	307,6	15
14. D. Coulthard	215,0	9	210,1	12	262,6	10	256,1	12	264,4	13	260,4	16	299,5	20	310,5	10
15. C. Klien	215,3	8	210,2	9	263,4	6	256,7	10	264,3	15	260,7	15	301,9	16	307,2	16
16. N. Heidfeld	214,9	10	204,3	20	262,4	11	251,1	20	263,9	17	255,9	20	301,3	17	302,6	21
17. J. Villeneuve	213,1	14	206,5	18	262,9	7	253,1	19	264,7	12	259,4	18	302,7	14	306,8	17
18. T. Monteiro	207,7	21	206,2	19	257,6	20	255,0	15	261,0	20	258,4	19	303,1	13	302,8	20
19. C. Albers	211,3	19	207,9	17	258,1	19	255,2	14	262,8	18	260,9	12	306,1	9	306,2	18
20. V. Liuzzi	211,8	18	209,7	14	259,3	18	254,5	18	262,1	19	259,9	17	303,4	12	314,9	2
21. S. Speed	205,5	22	208,2	16	250,0	21	256,4	11	259,0	21	261,6	9	289,2	22	312,6	6
22. T. Sato	214,1	12	208,2	15	259,9	17	254,5	17	264,3	14	260,7	14	302,5	15	305,2	19
23. S. Yamamoto	209,5	20	117,4	22	249,1	22	146,5	21	256,7	22			297,7	21	124,6	22

Race

Classification & Retirements

Pos.	Driver	Constructor	Tyres	Laps	Time	Average
1.	M. Schumacher	Ferrari	B	67	1:27:51.693	209,277 km/h
2.	F. Massa	Ferrari	B	67	+ 0.720	209,249 km/h
3.	K. Räikkönen	McLaren Mercedes	M	67	+ 13.206	208,754 km/h
4.	J. Button	Honda	M	67	+ 18.898	208,530 km/h
5.	F. Alonso	Renault	M	67	+ 23.707	208,340 km/h
6.	G. Fisichella	Renault	M	67	+ 24.814	208,297 km/h
7.	J. Trulli	Toyota	B	67	+ 26.544	208,229 km/h
8.	C. Klien	RBR Ferrari	M	67	+ 48.131	207,384 km/h
9.	R. Schumacher	Toyota	B	67	+ 1:00.351	206,909 km/h
10.	V. Liuzzi	STR Cosworth	M	66	1 lap	206,042 km/h
11.	D. Coulthard	RBR Ferrari	M	66	1 lap	205,864 km/h
12.	S. Speed	STR Cosworth	M	66	1 lap	205,284 km/h

Driver	Constructor	Tyre	Laps	Reason
DQ[13] C. Albers	MF1 Toyota	B	66	1 lap 204,836 km/h Rear wing flexible
DQ[14] T. Monteiro	MF1 Toyota	B	65	2 laps 202,770 km/h Rear wing flexible
M. Webber	Williams Cosworth	B	59	Water pipe between engine & water cooler failure
T. Sato	Aguri Honda	B	38	Gearbox oil leak
J. Villeneuve	BMW	M	30	Crash into the barriers
R. Barrichello	Honda	M	18	Engine failure
N. Heidfeld	BMW	M	9	Rear car damage following incident with Villeneuve
P. de la Rosa	McLaren Mercedes	M	2	Fuel pump failure
S. Yamamoto	Aguri Honda (T-Car)	B	1	Drive shaft failure
N. Rosberg	Williams Cosworth	B	0	Lost the rear of his car, spun

Fastest laps

	Driver	Time	Laps	Average
1.	M. Schumacher	1:16.357	17	215,650 km/h
2.	F. Massa	1:16.392	18	215,551 km/h
3.	K. Räikkönen	1:16.475	4	215,317 km/h
4.	R. Schumacher	1:16.763	64	214,509 km/h
5.	J. Trulli	1:16.807	48	214,386 km/h
6.	M. Webber	1:16.812	43	214,372 km/h
7.	J. Button	1:16.818	14	214,356 km/h
8.	G. Fisichella	1:16.981	18	213,902 km/h
9.	F. Alonso	1:17.256	66	213,140 km/h
10.	V. Liuzzi	1:17.407	51	212,724 km/h
11.	S. Speed	1:17.450	50	212,606 km/h
12.	C. Klien	1:17.719	49	211,870 km/h
13.	D. Coulthard	1:17.811	24	211,620 km/h
14.	R. Barrichello	1:18.029	16	211,029 km/h
15.	C. Albers	1:18.247	35	210,441 km/h
16.	T. Monteiro	1:18.718	46	209,182 km/h
17.	J. Villeneuve	1:18.904	29	208,689 km/h
18.	N. Heidfeld	1:19.264	3	207,741 km/h
19.	T. Sato	1:19.413	26	207,351 km/h
20.	P. de la Rosa	1:19.649	2	206,737 km/h

Pit stops

	Driver	Laps	Duration	Stop	Total
1.	J. Villeneuve	1	28.423	1	28.423
2.	R. Schumacher	1	24.646	1	24.646
3.	N. Heidfeld	1	26.799	1	26.799
4.	K. Räikkönen	10	28.950	1	28.950
5.	J. Button	16	23.413	1	23.413
6.	R. Barrichello	18	24.017	1	24.017
7.	F. Massa	19	22.584	1	22.584
8.	G. Fisichella	19	23.454	1	23.454
9.	M. Schumacher	20	22.934	1	22.934
10.	F. Alonso	20	22.066	1	22.066
11.	D. Coulthard	21	20.915	1	20.915
12.	T. Monteiro	24	22.529	1	22.529
13.	C. Klien	25	22.600	1	22.600
14.	V. Liuzzi	26	22.092	1	22.092
15.	S. Speed	27	21.930	1	21.930
16.	T. Sato	27	22.679	1	22.679
17.	M. Webber	28	22.583	1	22.583
18.	K. Räikkönen	28	21.379	2	50.329
19.	J. Trulli	28	23.653	1	23.653
20.	R. Schumacher	29	21.611	2	46.257
21.	C. Albers	29	22.520	1	22.520
22.	R. Schumacher	•35•	11.126	3	57.383
23.	G. Fisichella	40	21.758	2	45.212
24.	D. Coulthard	40	23.704	2	44.619
25.	J. Button	41	24.035	2	47.448
26.	F. Alonso	43	22.273	2	44.339
27.	F. Massa	44	22.355	2	44.939
28.	T. Monteiro	•43•	11.068	2	33.597
29.	M. Schumacher	45	22.874	2	45.808
30.	T. Monteiro	44	22.717	3	56.314
31.	C. Klien	47	22.314	2	44.914
32.	R. Schumacher	47	20.862	4	1:18.245
33.	M. Webber	48	22.182	2	44.765
34.	C. Albers	48	21.897	2	44.417
35.	S. Speed	48	20.675	2	42.605
36.	V. Liuzzi	49	20.442	2	42.534
37.	J. Trulli	51	20.795	2	44.448
38.	K. Räikkönen	55	20.425	3	1:10.754

•• Drive-through penalty:
> R. Schumacher. Speeding in the Pit lane
> Monteiro. Ignoring waved blue flags

Race leader

Driver	Laps in the lead	Nbr of Laps
K. Räikkönen	1 > 9	9
M. Schumacher	10 > 67	58

Driver	Nbr of Laps	Kilometers
M. Schumacher	58	265,292 km
K. Räikkönen	9	41,166 km

Lap chart

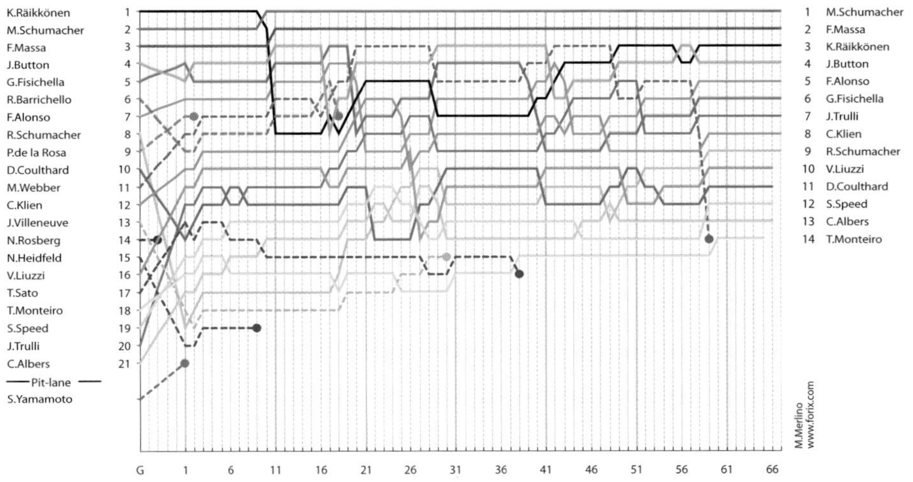

Gaps on the leader board

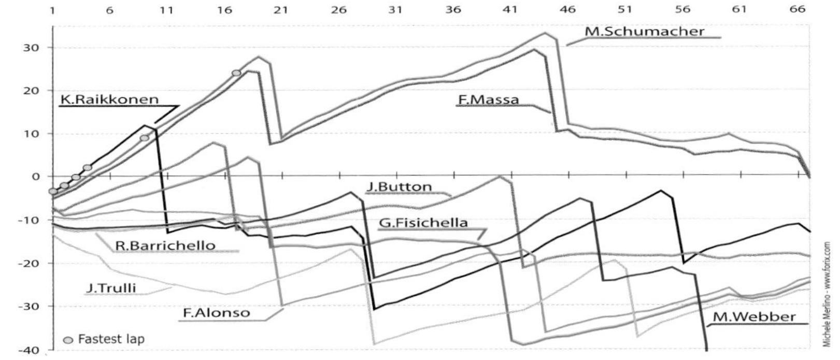

Championships 12/18

Drivers

1. F. Alonso ....Renault ....6 🏆..100
2. M. Schumacher .....Ferrari......................5 🏆...89
3. F. Massa...............Ferrari 50
4. G. Fisichella..........Renault ....1 🏆...49
5. K. Räikkönen ....McLaren Mercedes..............49
6. J. Montoya ....McLaren Mercedes..............26
7. J. Button ....Honda 21
8. R. Barrichello........Honda 16
9. R. Schumacher .....Toyota 13
10. N. Heidfeld ....BMW 13
11. D. Coulthard ....RBR Ferrari........................10
12. J. Trulli.................Toyota 10
13. J. Villeneuve ....BMW 7
14. M. Webber............Williams Cosworth................6
15. N. Rosberg ....Williams Cosworth................4
16. P. de la Rosa ....McLaren Mercedes................2
17. C. Klien................RBR Ferrari 2
18. V. Liuzzi ....STR Cosworth.......................1
19. S. Speed ....STR Cosworth.......................0
20. C. Albers..............MF1 Toyota 0
21. T. Monteiro ....MF1 Toyota 0
22. T. Sato.................Aguri Honda 0
23. Y. Ide...................Aguri Honda 0
24. F. Montagny..........Aguri Honda 0

S. Yamamoto........Aguri Honda ....-

Constructors

1. Mild Seven Renault F1 Team ....7 🏆....149
2. Scuderia Ferrari Marlboro ....5 🏆....139
3. Team McLaren Mercedes 77
4. Lucky Strike Honda Racing F1 Team 37
5. Panasonic Toyota Racing 23
6. BMW Sauber F1 Team.................................20
7. Red Bull Racing 12
8. Williams F1 Team......................................10
9. Scuderia Toro Rosso....................................1
10. MF1 Racing...0
11. Super Aguri Formula 1 0

The circuit

Name	Hockenheimring; Hockenheim	Weather	Cloudy, warm
Lenght	4574 m	Air temperature	32-34°c
Distance	67 laps 306,458 km	Track temperature	51°c
Date	July 30th 2006	Humidity	33%
		Wind speed	0.6 m/s

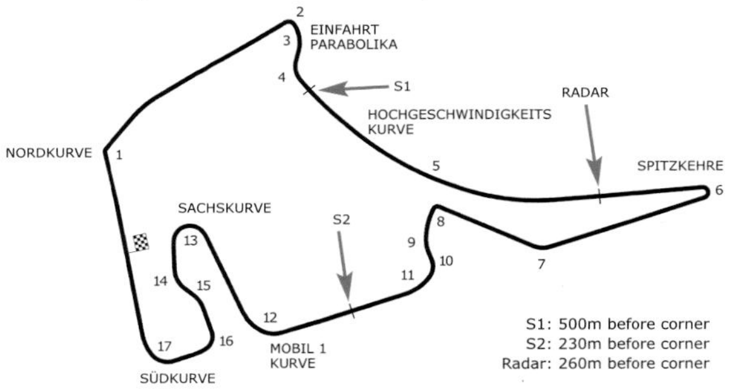

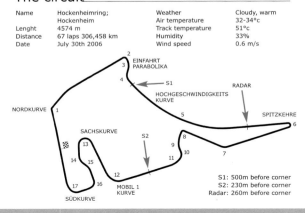

S1: 500m before corner
S2: 230m before corner
Radar: 260m before corner

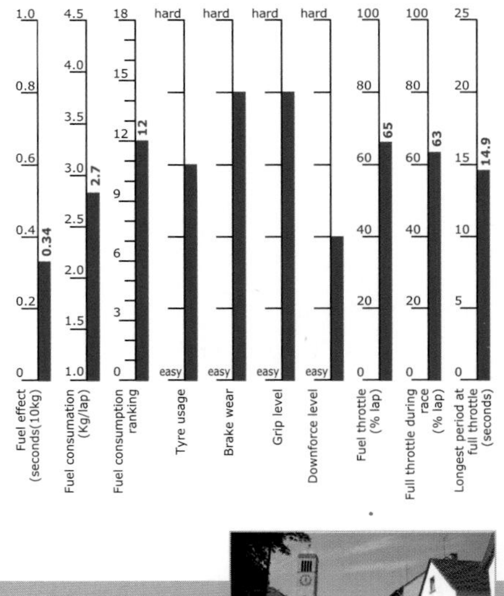

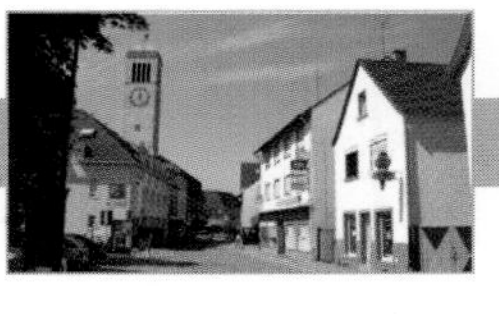

JENSON'S MIND-BOGGLING RACE

Jenson Button started in 14th place on a circuit where overtaking is theoretically impossible and went on to win the Hungarian Grand Prix. It was his first victory and Honda's first since 1967.

The Hungarian Grand Prix was a crazy race. The first half was run in the rain and then the track began to dry. All the favourites fell by the wayside. Alonso did not score any points and Michael Schumacher did not see the flag. Hours after the finish the German was awarded 1 point.

^
"Hello, my name's Kubica. Robert Kubica!" The young Pole Robert Kubica was making his grand prix debut. And a very successful one too as he was quicker than his team-mate Nick Heidfeld. "I first came to Budapest when I was 12-years-old and I was driving karts. If you'd told me that one day I'd be here at the start of a grand prix...!"

Mario Thiessen gets rid of Jacques Villeneuve and replaces him with his protégé

When you cross Mario Thiessen in the paddock you realise that nothing will stop him, an impression underlined by his schoolmaster's air and his impeccable tan. A quick trip back in time. When BMW took over Sauber in 2005 it inherited two drivers including Jacques Villeneuve whose contract ran until the end of the 2006 season.

It was a big thorn in Mario's side. The Bavarian was now the captain of the ship and he alone wanted to decide who his 2006 drivers would be. The problem was that Villeneuve's contract drawn up by Craig Pollock's lawyers was watertight and impossible to break. So he had to make do and accept the man from Quebec, which was a very sore point. Since the start of the season it had been hell for Jacques even if he said that he did not give a damn about his relationship with his boss. In the early part of the summer Villeneuve had had some good results and was hoping to renew his contract. It was a vain wish. Thiessen had not missed an opportunity to criticise the Canadian since

the beginning of the year. All one had to do was to raise the driver's name in conversation for Mario become even more curt than usual. When Villeneuve went off in Canada Thiessen qualified his mistake as a debutante's driving error. In Budapest, he seemed to have achieved his aim of getting rid of the Canadian who was complaining of aching joints that prevented him from driving. Mario promptly replaced him with Robert Kubica. The press release issued on the Tuesday before the race confirmed that "*BMW had not decided who would drive the car for the remaining grands prix or for the following year.*"

Robert quicker than Nick

Robert Kubica's mission that weekend could be summed up in one word: amaze! If he wanted to have the drive for the rest of the year he had to put on an exceptional performance to justify his being kept on in the place of Villeneuve. The Pole put on a stunning show in practice taking into account the fact that he had never

To everybody's amazement and Villeneuve's most of all his seat was up in the air for the rest of the season. "*We wanted to deal with the most urgent things first by naming Robert to replace Jacques,*" explained the BMW Press Service. "*Afterwards we don't know what's going to happen. It'll all depend on Jacques.*"
Finally, Thiessen had managed to get rid of Villeneuve even though the latter had a contract till the end of the season. But by invoking his health problems Mario had got round it, as Villeneuve could not drive. The Bavarian was ruthless.

participated in official qualifying before. He got through the first two elimination phases and made it into the final shootout while his team-mate, pint-sized Nick Heidfeld, did not get beyond phase 2. He ended the session in 10th place and then started from ninth due to Button's engine change.

Starting grid

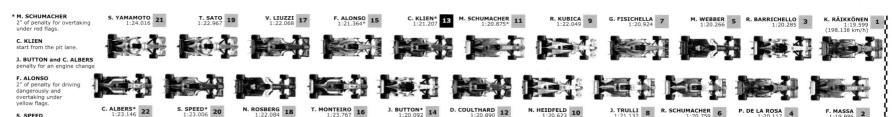

* M. SCHUMACHER
2" of penalty for overtaking under red flags.

C. KLIEN
start from the pit lane.

J. BUTTON and C. ALBERS
penalty for an engine change

F. ALONSO
2" of penalty for driving dangerously and overtaking under yellow flags.

S. SPEED
was relegated for blocking Monteiro. His three fastest times were cancelled.

| S. YAMAMOTO 1:24.016 — 21 | T. SATO 1:22.967 — 19 | V. LIUZZI 1:22.068 — 17 | F. ALONSO 1:21.364* — 15 | C. KLIEN* 1:21.207 — 13 | M. SCHUMACHER 1:20.875* — 11 | R. KUBICA 1:22.049 — 9 | G. FISICHELLA 1:20.924 — 7 | M. WEBBER 1:20.266 — 5 | R. BARRICHELLO 1:20.285 — 3 | K. RÄIKKÖNEN 1:19.599 — 1 (198.138 km/h) |
| C. ALBERS* 1:23.146 — 22 | S. SPEED* 1:23.006 — 20 | N. ROSBERG 1:22.084 — 18 | T. MONTEIRO 1:23.767 — 16 | J. BUTTON* 1:20.092 — 14 | D. COULTHARD 1:20.890 — 12 | N. HEIDFELD 1:20.623 — 10 | J. TRULLI 1:21.132 — 8 | R. SCHUMACHER 1:20.759 — 6 | P. DE LA ROSA 1:20.117 — 4 | F. MASSA 1:19.886 — 2 |

Unbelievable: both Alonso and Schumacher hit by a 2-second penalty!

It was more like a piece of Comedia del'Arte than serious motor racing. First act: on Friday Alonso received a very severe penalty for having brake-tested Robert Doornbos, and then overtaken under yellow flags. Two seconds were added to his qualifying time. It was an F1 first! It caused an uproar in the paddock as this sanction was considered as yet another way of hamstringing the Spaniard and favouring Michael Schumacher. Up until Saturday morning that is when act two unfolded. In free practice the engine in Button's Honda exploded laying down an oil slick on the track. The session was red-flagged to allow mopping up operations to take place. Michael Schumacher passed the spot and then overtook Robert Kubica and Alonso, both of whom had slowed right down, just a few metres before coming into his pit. It was the kind of manoeuvre that the drivers perform every day and was not at all dangerous. But Michael was hit with a 2-second penalty (one for each driver passed) to be added to each of his timed laps in qualifying. Exactly like Fernando Alonso. The Ferrari driver had overtaken under the red flag and had to be punished.

Rarely can the Stewards of the Meeting have made such fools of themselves. Their decision sanctioned a non-existent fault, and threw their capacity for judgement into doubt. On Friday, they probably wanted to allow Schumacher to get as close as possible to Alonso in the championship – to make the rest of the season more exciting. They became prisoners of their own logic and had no choice but to hit the German with the same penalty on Saturday. They were caught in their own trap. The Ferrari driver went ballistic when he heard about his sanction. "*I'd prefer not to talk about what's happened and to try and concentrate on the race,*" he growled. "*I'm going to do my best but it'll be very difficult to make it onto the rostrum. This being said, I refuse to compare my penalty to Alonso's; they're two different things.*" The German ended up eleventh on the grid while his time on Saturday was good enough for pole. The Spaniard thought that Michael's punishment was too severe, just like his own. "*Michael's sanction is a bit odd,*" he acknowledged. "*Like mine there was no accident and nobody was put in danger*" This incident left a bitter taste behind it as it cast doubts on the credibility had a championship in which sanctions were decided according to the person in question? The random decisions taken by the Stewards took the spectators and the hundreds of people employed by the teams for fools. It was an unacceptable way of governing in a sport that pretends to be the most technologically advanced in the world.

The grid: Raïkkönen ahead of Massa

Seven days after setting pole in Germany Kimi Raïkkönen repeated his performance in Hungary after Michael Schumacher was stripped of his fastest time. "*I'm not surprised to be in front because the car's been great so far,*" said the Finn. "*We've taken a few risks with the tyres but I think we've made the right choice.*" The weather was very cool in Budapest all weekend so it was a tricky situation for the tyre manufacturers. "*The temperature is much lower than what we prepared for,*" admitted Nick Shorrock the Michelin F1 boss. "*Our drivers have gone for many different tyres.*" Cool weather makes the rubber more difficult to heat and can lead to rapid degradation.

It was something to be watched closely in the race. The highest-placed Bridgestone runner was Felipe Massa. While Michael Schumacher blitzed his rivals his team-mate did not manage to avenge his no.1 and take pole. The Brazilian put forward the following excuse to justify himself: "*When I went out for my quickest lap a car came out just in front of me in the pit lane. I had to slow down and my tyres cooled so I couldn't get them back up to temperature in the first two corners*".

^
This was the red flag that was behind the unjustified relegation of Michael Schumacher. The session was interrupted and all the cars were going slowly back to their pits. The German overtook two of them and was given a 2-second penalty.

Ralf Schumacher and Pascal Vasselon look a bit worried. The German qualified on the third row in Budapest but the cool weather led to heavy graining on the Bridgestone tyres.
∨

The race began in the rain and Kimi Raïkkönen made the best getaway from Rubens Barrichello. Behind, Massa made a cock-up of his start and finished lap 1 in 7th place. The future winner was in 11th place at the end of this lap.

Kimi Raïkkönen's hopes floundered on the rear of Liuzzi's car. This required the intervention of the safety car: one of many turning points in the race.

Even Mack Sennett couldn't have invented it!

Those who said it was impossible to overtake on the Hungaroring had to eat their words. The 2006 Hungarian Grand Prix was an incredibly exciting race from the first to the last of its 70 laps. Summary:

- There were no incidents in the first corner even though some drivers made blinding starts. From eleventh on the grid Michael Schumacher was up in 4th place at the end of the first lap while Alonso climbed from fifteenth to sixth. It was still raining a little and the track was wet.
- Alonso was on another planet in the opening stages of the race and got past the German on lap 4.
- The very slippery track led to a number of spins and during the first 20 laps Fisichella, Rosberg and Kubica all hit the tyre walls lining the circuit.
- Twenty-fifth time round, Fernando Alonso lapped Michael Schumacher! "*I was very surprised by the lack of speed of our intermediates,*" said the German. "*But you've got to do the best with what you have. It wasn't great at that moment.*" The Bridgestone wets were far too hard for the Hungarian circuit.
- A lap later Kimi Raïkkönen hit Vitantonio Liuzzi who he was lapping. "*I went off on several occasions as my visor was all misted up and*

I couldn't see anything," pleaded the Italian. "*When Kimi caught me I slowed down to let him past and he wasn't expecting it.*" The Finn got past all right but over the top of the Toro Rosso!

- The race was neutralised behind the safety car for 5 laps to get rid of the debris from the 2 cars. Michael Schumacher took advantage of this to put himself back on the same lap as Alonso still in the lead.
- On lap 34, Fernando gave himself a big scare by pressing the wrong button on his steering wheel and stalled but he managed to restart his engine.
- By now the track was almost dry and Michael Schumacher set the fastest time of the race so far. He was lapping 3 seconds quicker than Alonso and was rapidly moving up the classification.
- On lap 52, Alonso came in to put on dry tyres. He went off a few hundred metres after the pit exit due to a defective nut on the left-hand rear wheel.
- Schumacher was now up into 2nd place. However, his rain tyres were deteriorating very quickly and he had to let Pedro de la Rosa past. Then he tried to fend off Nick Heidfeld and hit the German's car. His steering column was broken in the incident and he retired with just 2 laps to go. He finally finished ninth.

- And so Jenson Button who had started from 14th place won the Hungarian race. It was his first victory after 113 grand prix and Honda's first since 1967. Barrichello in the other Honda finished fourth.
- Four hours after the finish Robert Kubica's BMW Sauber was disqualified (2 kilos under the 600 kilos minimum weight because of excessive tyre wear). This let Michael Schumacher into 8th place giving him 1 point.

Thus, the track generally described as the most boring one of the season was the theatre of one of the most exciting races of the last few years. Just at the moment when the powers-that-be were thinking about how to spice up the show the answer was obvious: let the favourites start from the middle of the grid and give the track a good shower! Excitement guaranteed! However, this race showed the importance of the tyres. At the start on a wet track Michael Schumacher was losing 7 seconds a lap to Alonso. As soon as the line dried out the German pulled back 3seconds a lap on the Spaniard. It was a difference of 10 seconds between the quick tyres and the others (the same in the case in question). Today in F1 the compounds cal the shots.

Victory at last. After 70-action-packed laps Jenson Button finally scored his first grand prix win in Hungary.

"It was too good"

Before the season began Jenson Button announced that he would be a serious 2006 championship title contender. Twelve grands prix later it seemed a hollow boast as he was in 7th place overall in the ratings with only a single rostrum finish – third in Malaysia. However, in the weeks before the Hungarian race the Japanese team seemed to be getting its act together. This victory confirmed it. It was the win Jenson Button had been waiting for 6 years. Not for a long time had one seen such a happy driver on the rostrum. "*It's really great to win. Now I've scored a victory and the journalists can't tell me that I've still won nothing,*" said a very elated Brit who did not believe it until the end of the race. "*In the last 10 laps I had a 40-second lead and I really began to see it happening. They were the best laps of my career. I'm was calm with no worries and I was saying to myself that I was going to win. It was fantastic.*"
Up till then the race hadn't been all plain sailing. "*I was fourteenth on the grid and I made a good start. After that I was very quick and I picked off at least one car per lap. By lap 35 I knew that we had a super car. Afterwards...Well, Eh, I don't really remember. I don't remember how many stops I made, what tyres were put on. I don't remember anything!*"

<
He had been waiting for this success for 6 years after making his F1 debut with Williams in 2000. He did not even have time to celebrate that evening as he was taking the plane for China to do a promotional tour for Honda.

<
Pedro de la Rosa came home second in the Hungarian Grand Prix, his first rostrum finish in F1. "*I just tried to go as quickly as possible, keep my head down and avoid problems.*" It was the right tactic.

A 40-year drought

10th September 1967: That was the date of Honda's last victory in F1 and the last time that the Japanese national anthem was heard at a track. Honda withdrew from F1 the following year and did not come back until 1983 as an engine supplier to Spirit, then Williams and McLaren followed by BAR. Not until this season was the make officially entered under its own name.

One of the most striking images of what was a wild grand prix. Fisichella loses his rear wing on the main straight after an off on the previous lap.
∨

A lap too early

When the unfolding of a race is as chaotic as it was in Budapest a driver has to be able to sniff out the right moments. Jarno Trulli's nose let him down! He was hit at the start and was battling with poor grip due to tyre problems. He refuelled a lap too early as he came out just when the safety car appeared. He found himself a lap down until his engine blew. It was a bad hair day for the Italian.

The early stage of the race turned in Fernando Alonso's favour and he looked like he was going to bag the 10 points for victory as Michael Schumacher was down in 8th place. It all went wrong for the Spaniard on lap 52. "*We decided to stop and put on slicks,*" he said. "*I don't know what happened in the pits but when I rejoined I immediately felt that the car was not reacting normally.*" Two corners later he went off. "*This is the quickest we've been all season. Without this problem we'd have had a double. I passed 14 cars in the race. It was fun. And when I saw Michael retiring I said to myself that there was a god after all!*"
While Fernando Alonso and Michael Schumacher provided all the excitement in the grand prix their team-mates did not exactly set the track on fire! Felipe Massa qualified on the front row and finished in an anonymous 7th place. Fisichella crashed out on lap 19 when his rear wing flew off after contact with the guardrail. The Italian was complaining that his car was difficult to drive in the rain!

v

Jacques Villeneuve's supporters' fears were confirmed

As Mario Thiessen had intimated after the European Grand Prix his performances were not good enough to allow him to keep his seat till the end of the season. The Bavarian wanted to push his protégé Robert Kubica into the limelight and used the first pretext to fire the Canadian.
On Monday morning after the Hungarian Grand Prix the BMW Sauber team published a 4-line press release at 11h00 sharp stating that the Canadian would not race for the team for the rest of the season.
Mario Thiessen showed an unexpected sense of ironic humour at this moment by saying that the two parties were separating by common consent. A real thigh-slapper, that! Everybody knew that Villeneuve was hoping to see out the year with the BMW team and stay on in 2007. "*Jacques worked very well with us this season and it was him who scored out first point in Malaysia,*" Thiessen went on. It was easy to imagine his smile as he penned these lines: "*Jacques helped us a lot in the creation of the new BMW Sauber team,*" said the communiqué. "*However, after his Hockenheim accident the team decided to study the various options for 2007 – so it wanted to test Robert Kubica in race conditions, and it had an impact on Jacques' position for the rest of the year. We fully understand that he can no longer maintain his normal level of devotion in such circumstances. We respect his*

position and wish him the best of luck in the future."
All it needed was for Thiessen to push the envelope a little further and say that Villeneuve had resigned! It was time for the Canadian to start looking elsewhere. Despite his cast-iron contract drawn up in 2004 with the help of Craig Pollock's lawyers he was out on his ear. "*Last week BMW told me that I was being replaced in Hungary without giving me any assurance as to my seat after this race,*" Villeneuve revealed on Monday morning. "*So I accepted our separation. It's very disappointing as I was hoping to work with the team on a long-term basis and capitalise on our mutual experience.*"
Of course BMW had to pay damages to its former driver for such a brutal sacking. In the paddock in Hungary the figure of 6 million dollars was being bandied around.
The true amount will probably never be known but it is not sure that it was enough to compensate for the damage caused to Villeneuve. As a BMW driver he could expect to find a seat in 2007 but after being thrown out his chances of finding another drive were virtually nil.

He tried to find another drive in F1 but most of the good ones were already snapped up at this stage of the season. In addition, the Canadian had often said that little teams like Midland or Super Aguri did not interest him.
He thought about going to NASCAR like Juan Pablo Montoya. It had not been at the forefront of his mind but when all the doors in F1 began closing he entered into contact with several teams that very weekend.
"*Jacques will make an announcement about his future next Monday or Tuesday,*" said Ian Lefort, the driver's press officer. It was a very tight deadline which confirmed the NASCAR trail but was not respected.
By the end of the season Jacques had left Switzerland and gone to live in Montreal with his wife Johanna for their child to have Canadian nationality. But at the moment the F1 Yearbook was going to press, he still had not signed anything in NASCAR. He is taking his time to make the right choice.

Mario Thiessen happy with his protégé

With Nick Heidfeld on the rostrum in third and Robert Kubica in 7th place it was party time in the BMW Sauber pit a few minutes after the finish. There was a lot of backslapping, firm handshakes and uproarious laughter as Nick Heidfeld's rostrum finish was equivalent to a victory for the German team. Mario Thiessen was over the moon. He had a beer in his hand, a smile on his lips, hugged the German journalists and shook hands with everybody passing by. "*We've done far better than our objectives; it's been a great race for us. Nick didn't make the slightest mistake,*" laughed the Bavarian. Robert Kubica, Jacques Villeneuve's replacement, scored 2 points on his grand prix debut with a seventh-place finish after a pretty eventful race. "*Robert had a difficult start with a couple of offs and a broken rear wing but he managed to bring the car home in very tricky conditions. It's really great,*" Thiessen went on.

Seen from the exterior the Pole's performance did not seem to justify his replacing Villeneuve for the rest of the season. Mario Thiessen's smiling face said it all. Robert's 7th place seemed enough for the German to convince his bosses. "*I won't take my decision about Jacques until tomorrow morning. All I want to talk about now is today's race,*" grinned the BMW team boss. There was a small incident 4 hours afterwards, which made no difference. Kubica was disqualified as his car weighed 598 kilos, 2 kilos under the minimum weight allowed in F1. In fact, the inexperienced Pole had forgotten to run on the gravel after the chequered flag which enables pebbles to stick to the four tyres and increases the car's weight by around 2 kilos, just the amount that was missing at scrutineering. This did nothing to detract from his talent. Of course, we will never know what Jacques Villeneuve might have achieved in his place.

results

Practice

All the time trials

Nº Driver	Nat.	Nº Châssis - Engine [Nbr. GP]	Pos. Free 1 Friday	Laps	Pos. Free 2 Friday	Laps	Pos. Free 3 Saturday	Laps	Pos. Q1 Saturday	Laps	Pos. Q2 Saturday	Laps	Pos. Super Pole Saturday	Laps
1. Fernando Alonso	E	Renault R26 03 [1]	19.	1	2. 1:23.097	15	5. 1:22.119	25	14. 1:21.792	6	15. **1:21.364**	6		
2. Giancarlo Fisichella	I	Renault R26 05 [2]	22.	1	3. 1:23.189	14	6. 1:22.340	13	10. 1:21.370	4	7. 1.20.154	6	8. **1:20.924**	12
3. Kimi Räikkönen	FIN	McLaren MP4-21 05 - Mercedes [1]	1. 1:21.624	5	25. 1:25.968	11	10. 1:22.599	8	2. 1:20.080	3	2. 1:19.704	3	1. **1:19.599**	11
4. Pedro de la Rosa	E	McLaren MP4-21 06 - Mercedes [2]	4. 1:22.730	6	11. 1:24.252	11	8. 1:22.424	14	8. 1:21.288	3	5. 1:19.991	5	5. **1:20.117**	11
5. Michael Schumacher	D	Ferrari 248 F1 254 [1]	3. 1:22.499	5	8. 1:23.931	19	1. 1:20.795	11	13. 1:21.440	3	12. **1:20.875**	6		
6. Felipe Massa	BR	Ferrari 248 F1 252 [1]			1. 1:21.778	12	2. 1:21.472	11	1. 1:19.742	3	1. 1:19.504	3	2. **1:19.886**	11
7. Ralf Schumacher	D	Toyota TF106/10B [1]	17. 1:30.110	5	6. 1:23.747	19	15. 1:23.963	13	5. 1:21.112	6	9. 1:20.243	6	7. **1:20.759**	11
8. Jarno Trulli	I	Toyota TF106/08B [2]	9. 1:24.620	9	7. 1:23.771	18	19. 1:25.373	16	11. 1:21.434	6	8. 1:20.231	6	9. **1:21.132**	11
9. Mark Webber	AUS	Williams FW28 03 - Cosworth [1]			22. 1:25.393	8	12. 1:22.839	17	9. 1:21.335	6	6. 1:20.047	6	6. **1.20.266**	11
10. Nico Rosberg	D	Williams FW28 05 - Cosworth [1]			18. 1:24.793	12	16. 1:24.381	15	18. **1:22.084**	6				
11. Rubens Barrichello	BR	Honda RA106-01 [1]	6. 1:22.553	6	13. 1:24.445	17	4. 1:21.833	18	6. 1:21.141	6	3. 1:19.783	5	3. **1:20.085**	11
12. Jenson Button	GB	Honda RA106-05 [2->1]	7. 1:23.659	5	14. 1:24.465	15	17. 1:24.731	4	3. 1:20.820	6	4. 1:19.943	5	4. **1:20.092**	11
14. David Coulthard	GB	Red Bull RB2 3 - Ferrari [1]	21.	1	24. 1:25.843	12	11. 1:22.643	14	7. 1:21.163	6	13. **1:20.890**	5		
15. Christian Klien	A	Red Bull RB2 5 - Ferrari [2]	20.	1	23. 1:25.647	14	7. 1:22.362	15	16. 1:22.027	4	14. **1:21.207**	6		
16. Nick Heidfeld	D	BMW Sauber F1.06-02 [1]			9. 1:23.934	11	20. 1:25.597	14	12. 1:21.437	4	11. **1:20.623**	6		
17. Robert Kubica	PL	BMW Sauber F1.06-05 [1]			10. 1:24.106	11	3. 1:21.806	18	4. 1:20.891	3	10. 1:20.256	6	10. **1:22.049**	12
18. Tiago Monteiro	P	Midland M16-03 - Toyota [1]	15. 1:27.321	8	15. 1:24.508	8	13. 1:23.819	12	15. 1:22.009	6	16. **1:23.767**			
19. Christijan Albers	NL	Midland M16-02 - Toyota [2->1]	14. 1:26.680	5	20. 1:25.038	7	21. 1:26.047	12	21. **1:23.146**	6				
20. Vitantonio Liuzzi	I	Toro Rosso STR01 03 - Cosworth [1]	12. 1:25.477	6	26. 1:26.198	16	9. 1:22.560	13	17. **1:22.068**	7				
21. Scott Speed	USA	Toro Rosso STR01 02 - Cosworth [1]	13. 1:26.678	7	21. 1:25.152	16	14. 1:23.858	16	20. **1:23.006**	8				
22. Takuma Sato	J	Super Aguri SA06-03 - Honda [1]	16. 1:29.765	4	17. 1:24.623	23	18. 1:24.847	15	19. **1:22.967**	6				
23. Sakon Yamamoto	J	Super Aguri SA06-04 - Honda [1]	18. 1:30.353	12	27. 1:26.877	20	22. 1:26.260	19	22. **1:24.016**	6				
35. Alexander Wurz	A	Williams FW28 06 - Cosworth	5. 1:22.941	25	16. 1:24.609	31								
36. Anthony Davidson	GB	Honda RA106-03	2. 1:22.396	28	5. 1:23.498	31								
37. Robert Doornbos	NL	Red Bull RB2 1 - Ferrari	8. 1:23.999	27	4. 1:23.195	30								
39. Markus Winkelhock	D	Midland M16-04 - Toyota	10. 1:25.194	26	12. 1:24.381	28								
40. Neel Jani	CH	Toro Rosso STR01 01 - Cosworth	11. 1:25.424	17	19. 1:24.854	33								

Fastest lap overall
F. Massa 1:19.504 (198,374 km/h)
M. Schumacher 1:18.875 + 2sec. penalty = 1:20.875

Maximum speed

Nº Driver	S1 Qualifs	Pos.	S1 Race	Pos.	S2 Qualifs	Pos.	S2 Race	Pos.	Finish Qualifs	Pos.	Finish Race	Pos.	Radar Qualifs	Pos.	Radar Race	Pos.
1. F. Alonso	279,9	11	275,7	8	249,5	3	224,6	12	246,5	10	240,9	10	281,8	11	281,1	14
2. G. Fisichella	283,1	4	261,4	15	248,7	4	214,5	17	247,4	8	240,3	12	281,8	12	287,6	3
3. K. Räikkönen	281,6	7	245,0	19	246,5	9	218,2	16	249,2	4	245,2	3	285,9	3	285,4	8
4. P. de la Rosa	280,0	9	277,9	5	245,5	10	236,8	2	248,9	6	245,3	2	284,7	5	284,6	9
5. M. Schumacher	286,9	1	278,1	3	251,2	1	231,3	7	252,1	1	244,7	4	288,2	2	292,3	1
6. F. Massa	286,0	2	282,5	1	250,4	2	240,5	1	251,5	2	246,8	1	288,6	1	285,5	7
7. R. Schumacher	279,1	14	275,7	9	243,9	13	235,4	3	243,6	18	241,1	9	279,8	17	282,9	12
8. J. Trulli	276,7	22	270,3	13	242,4	16	225,8	11	242,8	19	237,7	18	276,5	21	276,0	20
9. M. Webber	278,6	16	227,2	21	246,9	7			246,4	12	228,0	21	278,3	19	273,4	21
10. N. Rosberg	277,4	20	243,9	20	241,2	19	204,7	20	244,2	16	238,3	15	275,5	22	278,9	16
11. R. Barrichello	284,3	3	279,7	2	247,9	6	234,5	6	249,0	5	244,6	6	285,6	4	285,9	5
12. J. Button	282,7	5	276,4	7	246,9	8	234,9	5	249,3	3	244,6	5	284,5	6	288,0	2
14. D. Coulthard	281,8	6	272,6	12	243,8	14	222,3	15	247,8	7	241,2	8	283,6	7	284,2	10
15. C. Klien	279.8	12	248,7	18	245,2	11	211,4	18	246,5	11	235,1	19	280,8	15	279,5	15
16. N. Heidfeld	280,0	10	278,1	4	245,0	12	234,9	4	247,4	9	243,7	7	281,9	10	285,8	6
17. R. Kubica	280,7	8	275,5	10	247,9	5	226,8	10	246,2	13	239,3	13	281,6	13	286,6	4
18. T. Monteiro	278,2	18	269,1	14	242,0	18	224,5	13	241,1	22	237,9	17	282,2	9	277,2	19
19. C. Albers	277,4	19	273,1	11	240,4	20	230,7	8	241,9	21	238,5	14	277,3	20	277,7	17
20. V. Liuzzi	278,4	17	254,5	17	242,3	17	206,5	19	244,1	17	238,2	16	280,6	16	281,8	13
21. S. Speed	279,6	13	276,7	6	243,7	15	230,5	9	244,6	15	240,3	11	281,3	14	283,1	11
22. T. Sato	278,7	15	259,9	16	236,6	21	223,7	14	245,3	14	234,7	20	283,3	8	277,3	18
23. S. Yamamoto	276,8	21			234,9	22			242,7	20			278,4	18	266,6	22

Race

Classification & Retirements

Pos.	Driver	Constructor	Tyres	Laps	Time	Average	
1.	J. Button	Honda	M	70	1:52:20.941	163,773 km/h	
2.	P. de la Rosa	McLaren Mercedes	M	70	+ 30.837	163,027 km/h	
3.	N. Heidfeld	BMW	M	70	+ 43.822	162,715 km/h	
4.	R. Barrichello	Honda	M	70	+ 45.205	162,682 km/h	
5.	D. Coulthard	RBR Ferrari	M	69	1 tour	160,929 km/h	
6.	R. Schumacher	Toyota	B	69	1 tour	160,377 km/h	
7.	F. Massa	Ferrari	B	69	1 tour	159,921 km/h	
8.	M. Schumacher	Ferrari	B	67	3 tours	161,328 km/h	Transmission shaft broken
9.	T. Monteiro	MF1 Toyota	B	67	3 tours	155,498 km/h	
10.	C. Albers	MF1 Toyota	B	67	3 tours	155,412 km/h	
11.	S. Speed	STR Cosworth	M	66	4 tours	152,787 km/h	
12.	J. Trulli	Toyota	B	65	5 tours	158,811 km/h	Engine failure
13.	T. Sato	Aguri Honda	B	65	5 tours	152,013 km/h	

	Driver	Constructor	Tyres	Laps	Reason
DQ[7]	R. Kubica	BMW	M	69	1 lap 159,931 km/h Weighing not conforms
	F. Alonso	Renault	M	51	Spin and stall
	K. Räikkönen	McLaren Mercedes	M	25	Collision with Liuzzi
	V. Liuzzi	STR Cosworth	M	25	Hit by Räikkönen
	N. Rosberg	Williams Cosworth	B	19	Spin off after an electrical problem
	G. Fisichella	Renault	M	18	Rear wing damaged... new spin off
	C. Klien	RBR Ferrari *(T-Car)*	M	6	Spin off
	M. Webber	Williams Cosworth	B	1	Spin off
	S. Yamamoto	Aguri Honda	B	0	Stall engine after a spin off

Fastest laps

	Driver	Time	Laps	Average
1.	F. Massa	1:23.516	65	188,845 km/h
2.	P. de la Rosa	1:24.315	67	187,055 km/h
3.	R. Barrichello	1:24.678	69	186,253 km/h
4.	J. Button	1:25.143	57	185,236 km/h
5.	R. Schumacher	1:25.247	65	185,010 km/h
6.	J. Trulli	1:25.779	58	183,863 km/h
7.	N. Heidfeld	1:25.801	65	183,816 km/h
8.	C. Albers	1:26.117	67	183,141 km/h
9.	S. Speed	1:26.249	66	182,861 km/h
10.	D. Coulthard	1:27.572	65	180,098 km/h
11.	M. Schumacher	1:27.834	57	179,561 km/h
12.	R. Kubica	1:28.154	55	178,909 km/h
13.	T. Monteiro	1:28.178	66	178,860 km/h
14.	F. Alonso	1:29.408	50	176,400 km/h
15.	T. Sato	1:30.957	53	173,396 km/h
16.	K. Räikkönen	1:33.690	7	168,338 km/h
17.	G. Fisichella	1:35.550	9	165,061 km/h
18.	C. Klien	1:38.702	6	159,790 km/h
19.	V. Liuzzi	1:38.858	8	159,537 km/h
20.	N. Rosberg	1:38.964	9	159,367 km/h

Pit stops

	Driver	Laps	Duration	Stop	Total
1.	R. Barrichello	5	21.446	1	21.446
2.	F. Massa	12	22.713	1	22.713
3.	T. Monteiro	14	22.115	1	22.115
4.	P. de la Rosa	16	26.422	1	26.422
5.	K. Räikkönen	17	26.050	1	26.050
6.	J. Button	17	23.921	1	23.921
7.	M. Schumacher	17	28.578	1	28.578
8.	C. Albers	16	22.658	1	22.658
9.	R. Kubica	18	27.057	1	27.057
10.	R. Schumacher	23	24.869	1	24.869
11.	J. Trulli	24	23.417	1	23.417
12.	P. de la Rosa	26	26.179	2	52.601
13.	R. Barrichello	26	22.256	2	43.702
14.	D. Coulthard	26	26.698	1	26.698
15.	N. Heidfeld	26	23.338	1	23.338
16.	F. Alonso	27	25.760	1	25.760
17.	T. Sato	25	27.018	1	27.018
18.	S. Speed	26	37.044	1	37.044
19.	T. Monteiro	28	27.596	2	49.711
20.	S. Speed	38	23.158	2	1:00.202
21.	F. Massa	41	23.147	2	45.860
22.	S. Speed	41	25.529	3	1:25.731
23.	R. Kubica	44	23.410	2	50.467
24.	J. Button	46	20.480	2	44.401
25.	M. Schumacher	46	22.385	2	50.963
26.	R. Schumacher	47	22.151	2	47.020
27.	C. Albers	46	25.990	2	48.648
28.	J. Trulli	48	23.402	2	46.819
29.	R. Barrichello	50	21.744	3	1:05.446
30.	F. Alonso	51	21.955	2	47.715
31.	P. de la Rosa	51	22.366	3	1:14.967
32.	S. Speed	48	24.980	4	1:50.711
33.	D. Coulthard	53	22.123	2	48.821
34.	J. Button	54	20.869	3	1:05.270
35.	T. Sato	51	22.705	2	49.723
36.	T. Monteiro	52	21.751	3	1:11.462
37.	N. Heidfeld	55	21.065	2	44.403
38.	F. Massa	59	20.686	3	1:06.546

Race leader

Driver	Laps in the lead	Nbr of Laps
K. Räikkönen	1 > 17	17
F. Alonso	18 > 51	34
J. Button	52 > 70	19

Driver	Nbr of Laps	Kilometers
F. Alonso	34	148,954 km
J. Button	19	83,239 km
K. Räikkönen	17	74,470 km

Gaps on the leader board

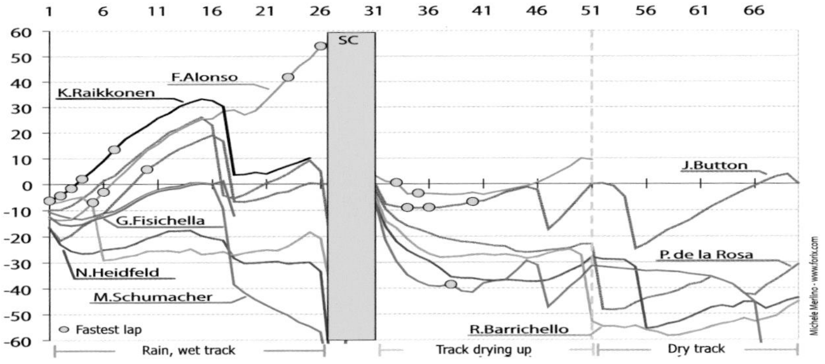

Lap chart

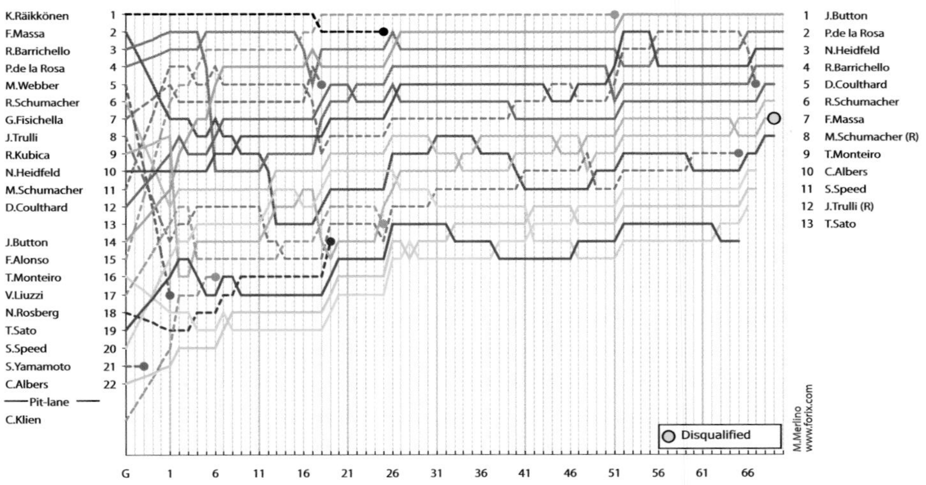

Championships 13/18

Drivers

1. F. Alonso ....Renault ....6 🏆..100
2. M. Schumacher .....Ferrari......................5 🏆....90
3. F. Massa..............Ferrari 52
4. G. Fisichella..........Renault ....1 🏆....49
5. K. Räikkönen ....McLaren Mercedes.............49
6. J. Button ....Honda......................1 🏆....31
7. J. Montoya ....McLaren Mercedes.............26
8. R. Barrichello........Honda 21
9. N. Heidfeld ....BMW 19
10. R. Schumacher .....Toyota 16
11. D. Coulthard ....RBR Ferrari.........................14
12. P. de la Rosa ....McLaren Mercedes.............10
13. J. Trulli.................Toyota 10
14. J. Villeneuve ....BMW 7
15. M. Webber............Williams Cosworth................6
16. N. Rosberg ....Williams Cosworth................4
17. C. Klien................RBR Ferrari 2
18. V. Liuzzi ....STR Cosworth........................1
19. S. Speed ....STR Cosworth........................0
20. T. Monteiro ....MF1 Toyota 0
21. C. Albers ....MF1 Toyota 0
22. T. Sato.................Aguri Honda 0
23. Y. Ide...................Aguri Honda 0
24. F. Montagny..........Aguri Honda 0

S. Yamamoto ....Aguri Honda ....-
R. Kubica ....BMW.....................................-

Constructors

1. Mild Seven Renault F1 Team ....7 🏆...149
2. Scuderia Ferrari Marlboro ....5 🏆...142
3. Team McLaren Mercedes 85
4. Lucky Strike Honda Racing F1 Team...1 🏆 52
5. BMW Sauber F1 Team.................................26
6. Panasonic Toyota Racing 26
7. Red Bull Racing 16
8. Williams F1 Team.....................................10
9. Scuderia Toro Rosso...................................1
10. MF1 Racing...0
11. Super Aguri Formula 1 0

All results :

The circuit

Name	Hungaroring; Budapest	Weather	Overcast
		Air temperature	17-21°c
Lenght	4381 m	Track temperature	19-29°c
Distance	70 laps 306,663 km	Humidity	83%
Date	August 6, 2006	Wind speed	0.6 m/s

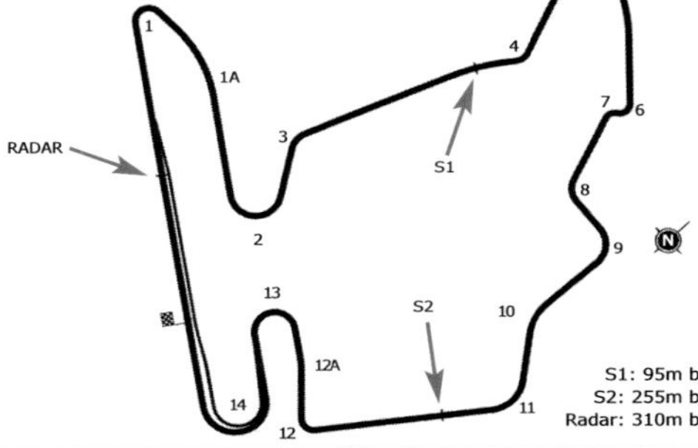

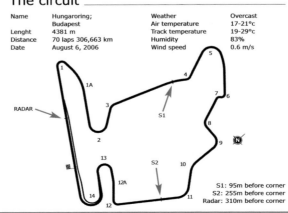

S1: 95m before corner
S2: 255m before corner
Radar: 310m before corner

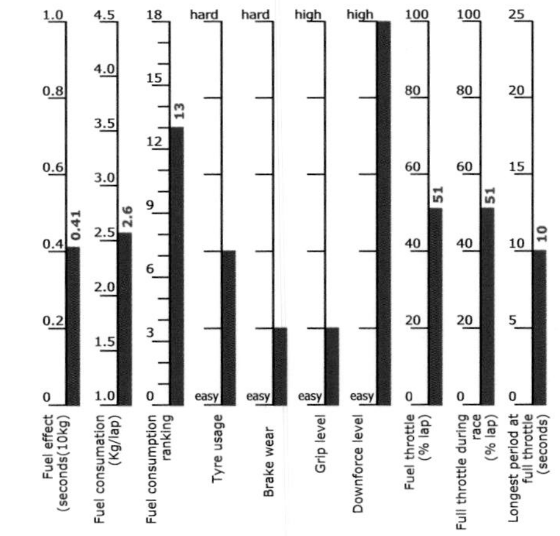

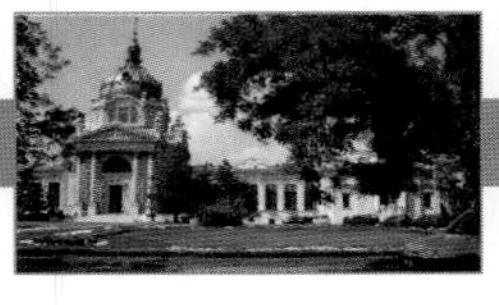

BRAVO FELIPE !

The two Ferraris looked like they were heading for a double until the safety car's intervention upset the Scuderia's plans. In the confusion that followed Michael Schumacher lost 11 seconds and Fernando Alonso overtook him while he was in the pits. The German fought back but despite several passing attempts, he was unable to dislodge the Spaniard from second place losing another 2 points in the championship chase.
Felipe Massa won the first grand prix of his young career and he was deeply moved by his victory bursting into tears after the finish.

Mario Thiessen scores a point with Sebastian Vettel

> The 2 Ferraris monopolised the front row in Istanbul. In corner no.8, the famous triple left-hander which the drivers described as the most difficult bend of the season, they were timed at 269,4 km/h while Alonso's speed was 262,9 km/h. 6,5 km/h that made a world of difference.

"Good luck, my lad!" Bernie Ecclestone proffers some encouragement to Sebastian Vettel under the tender eye of Mario Thiessen.
>∨

Istanbul and its famous water bearers (below). It is a magnificent town bridging Asia and Europe.
∨

The F1 paddock left Sebastian Vettel starry-eyed when he walked down it for the first time.

As the hands of the clock ticked round to 11h00 on Friday morning just before he got into his car Vettel looked like a kid for whom Santa Claus had come early. It was understandable. Up till then he had been racing in the F3 Euroseries in which he was in second place. And suddenly from one day to the next he was thrown into the F1 arena, which, at the age of 19 years and 53 days, made him the youngest driver ever to take part in an F1 grand prix weekend.

But Vettel wanted to show his mettle and at the end of the first day's practice he was quickest overall in front of Michael Schumacher and Fernando Alonso! He did not know the circuit before arriving in Istanbul on Thursday. He did not know his BMW F1 06 chassis very well either having only had a private test session in July.

The young German's exploit was down in part to the team as Mario Thiessen had given orders to do everything possible to enable Vettel to top the time sheets. He went out on an almost empty tank with an engine whose revs were in a range that the other drivers were not allowed to use, and his tyres were changed every time he came in! In the morning he was eighth after 25 laps and then first in the afternoon having covered an additional 29 laps. Once practice was over Sebastian Vettel soon learned what F1 was all about. He had not had much experience with journalists and was a bit lost. "It was great," he mumbled once he was back in the BMW Motorhome. "With those cars the forces in the corners are just simply indescribable."

He had passed his test with flying colours.

He made no mistakes, missed no braking points and did not stray off the straight and narrow. Indeed, it was difficult to know how he managed to find the limits of his car without going beyond them.

But the happiest man in Istanbul was not Vettel; it was Mario Thiessen. Henceforth the Bavarian would always be remembered as the man who discovered Vettel. The latter was to come back and set the fastest time in the Friday session at several grand prix. Mario's eyes were dancing in his head.

Starting grid

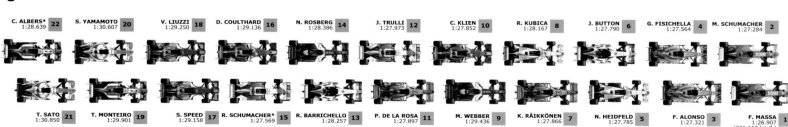

* R. SCHUMACHER et C. ALBERS penalty for an engine change. (-10 positions).

Pos	Driver	Time
22	C. ALBERS*	1:28.639
20	S. YAMAMOTO	1:30.607
18	V. LIUZZI	1:29.250
16	D. COULTHARD	1:29.136
14	N. ROSBERG	1:28.386
12	J. TRULLI	1:27.973
10	C. KLIEN	1:27.852
8	R. KUBICA	1:28.167
6	J. BUTTON	1:27.790
4	G. FISICHELLA	1:27.564
2	M. SCHUMACHER	1:27.284
21	T. SATO	1:30.850
19	T. MONTEIRO	1:29.901
17	S. SPEED	1:29.158
15	R. SCHUMACHER*	1:27.569
13	R. BARRICHELLO	1:28.257
11	P. DE LA ROSA	1:27.897
9	M. WEBBER	1:29.436
7	K. RÄIKKÖNEN	1:27.866
5	N. HEIDFELD	1:27.785
3	F. ALONSO	1:27.321
1	F. MASSA	1:26.907 (221.119 km/h)

Ferrari backs the wrong horse!

Lap 14: the two Ferraris led the dance with Felipe Massa ahead of Michael Schumacher. The latter was catching the Brazilian and the gap was down to 2 seconds. It was obvious that the 7-times world champion would soon take the lead.

Fernando Alonso in 3rd place was already 10 seconds behind and victory looked out of his grasp.

It was then that the unexpected happened and the Scuderia's domination was broken. Vitantonio Liuzzi in his Toro Rosso in 13th place suddenly felt his transmission seize. He spun and stalled right on the line. The two Ferrari drivers who had just begun their 14th lap avoided him by the skin of their teeth. As always race control waited for a few seconds to see if the marshals could remove the stricken Bull. They announced that the safety car was ready to roll, then sent it out and neutralised the race.

As it was almost quarter distance all the leaders dived into the pits to refuel. The two Ferraris finished their lap and came in together with the Brazilian ahead of

the German! Massa was fuelled first while Schumacher waited losing 11 seconds before filling up. This was the turning point in the race as the time lost allowed Alonso to snatch second place.

Michael might have been able to get back in front of the Spaniard during the second round of stops if an off-course excursion had not cost him around 5 seconds. Not until 16 laps from the end was he able to get back on

the Spaniard's tail. The two drivers then waged a no-holds-barred battle that lasted until the flag. Michael tried every trick in the book to get past the Renault but he was unable to force the wily Alonso into making a mistake. Only 81/100s separated them at the finish, the equivalent of a gap of 4,9 metres in a race that lasted for 309 kms!

Michael finished third losing four points as a win looked on the cards for the German.

It was Felipe Massa's first grand prix victory in F1 after 4 years. And it was probably due to an error by the Scuderia.
At the moment when Liuzzi blocked the track why had the Ferrari strategists not asked Felipe to let Michael past just before coming into the pits to refuel?
Once the safety car comes out the drivers must hold position.
Just beforehand, Ferrari had a 30-second window to take action and tell its drivers to swap positions. "*We thought our lead over Fernando was enough for me to stay in front. We were wrong,*" said Schumacher after the race.
Jean Todt, the Scuderia's boss, was scarcely more forthcoming: "*If we'd asked Felipe to let Michael through, he'd have lost all his chances. It wasn't good.*"

Fernando Alonso in second says he could not have won

Alonso was not exactly in the most joyful of moods after the Turkish Grand Prix. He knew that he owed his second place to the intervention of the safety car. "*In one way I'm happy to have finished in front of Michael,*" he stated. "*To be honest we were lucky that the safety car came out when it did as it allowed me to get past him. On the other hand, I'm not all that satisfied with this grand prix. There was no way I could've won. Felipe was uncatchable. I'm all the more disappointed as

I expected a victory here.*"
At the end of the race Alonso came under heavy pressure from Michael Schumacher, which he resisted, to the bitter end finishing 81/1000s in front of the German. "*It wasn't too serious,*" smiled the Spaniard. "*I knew that I could stay in front of him without too many problems. There's only one place where you can overtake here and that's at the end of the straight. All I had to do was to come out of the previous corner quickly and that was

enough. So I played around with the boost button; I lowered the revs everywhere and then I upped them in that corner.*"
The last exit from the corner in question looked pretty hairy. "*No, not really. I closed the door in the last corner of the race to protect myself from a final attack by Michael and that penalised me for the sprint to the flag. I knew I had a little in reserve. It was close as I had only a half-a-length in hand. But it was enough,*" explained the Renault driver.

<
Alonso finished second ahead of Schumacher pulling back 2 points on his rival.

From left to right:
Nick Heidfeld,
Rubens Barrichello and
Vitantonio Liuzzi.
The German was on the
rostrum in Budapest and
had never qualified as
well as in Turkey. He came
home in 14th place after
being hit by Fisichella in
the first corner.
The Brazilian qualified in
13th place and scored 1
point for his eighth-place
finish while the Italian's
spin was the turning point
of the race.

Verdict confirmed. Dampers banned. The R26's balance upset

It was a tough blow for Renault. Its lawyers
thought they had an open and shut case when
they pleaded at the FIA Court of Appeal.
But no. On the Wednesday before the grand prix
the governing body banned the mass dampers,
which used a weight on the springs to stabilise
the car. It was reckoned that they gave
the French car an advantage of around
0.3s per lap, a huge one in F1 terms.
After being allowed for almost a year the mass
damper was now banned. It was a slap in the face
for Renault which was the only top team using
them. What was all the more serious for
the French squad was that its car had been
designed with this system in mind. Among its
rivals Ferrari had also tested mass dampers
during the season but did not manage to make
them work.
This business looked like yet another attempt to
manipulate the outcome of the championship.
According to the paddock bush telegraph the FIA -
warned by Ferrari - had decided to prevent
Alonso from becoming world champion so as
to favour Michael Schumacher. If the German
won his eighth title he would then retire at
the end of the season, which opened the way

for Raïkkönen's transfer to Ferrari.
If not then Michael was going to stay on for
another year and the Scuderia would lose
the Finn to Renault.
So it was to prevent Kimi from escaping his
clutches that Jean Todt had asked the FIA to
intervene which brought out one of its old hobby
horses: rule changes during the season.
"Everybody has his own opinion in this affair,"
growled Alonso. "It's kind of strange that
a system authorised for a year is suddenly
banned. We all know it's legal."

Massa fulfilled all his dreams in one race

Happy was not the right term. Felipe Massa
was not happy when he got out of his car after
winning his first F1 grand prix;
he was delirious with joy, ecstatic, in seventh
heaven.
Compared to the cool exuberance of drivers
like Alonso who is always the same after his
victories, it was a real pleasure to see Massa
smiling, laughing, playing to the cameras,
and jumping for joy. Pole position on Saturday
followed by victory on Sunday, his was
a perfect weekend.
"I've always dreamed of becoming an F1
driver," he laughed after the rostrum.
"I've always dreamed of Ferrari, of winning
grands prix. Today I've fulfilled all my
dreams in one go. It's fantastic. It's very

special, impossible to describe." He was in
tears on the rostrum when he heard the
Brazilian national anthem.
During the post-race press conference he hid
his face in his hands to hide his feelings.
His drive to victory was helped by the safety
car intervention, but that's part and parcel of
F1 and it takes nothing away from his success.

> The Trukish grid girls
were far and away the
most beautiful of the
season. And boy didn't
they know it!

> Both Toyotas finished.
Ralf Schumacher
managed to bag a couple
of points with 7th spot
while Jarno Trulli came
away pointless after his
9th place finish.

results

Practice

All the time trials

N° Driver	Nat.	N° Châssis - Engine [Nbr. GP]	Pos. Free 1	Laps Friday	Pos. Free 2	Laps Friday	Pos. Free 3	Laps Saturday	Pos. Q1	Laps Saturday	Pos. Q2	Laps Saturday	Pos. Super Pole	Laps Saturday
1. Fernando Alonso	E	Renault R26 03 [2]	23.	1	12. 1:29.741	16	2. 1:27.924	16	4. 1:27.861	6	3. 1:26.917	3	3. **1:27.321**	11
2. Giancarlo Fisichella	I	Renault R26 05 [1]	22.	1	18. 1:30.504	16	3. 1:27.963	17	5. 1:28.175	3	8. 1:27.346	5	4. **1:27.564**	11
3. Kimi Räikkönen	FIN	McLaren MP4-21 07 - Mercedes [1]	1. 1:28.315	5	8. 1:29.042	10	9. 1:28.368	11	9. 1:28.236	3	6. 1:27.202	6	8. **1:27.866**	10
4. Pedro de la Rosa	E	McLaren MP4-21 06 - Mercedes [1]	6. 1:29.376	5	9. 1:29.112	10	13. 1:29.034	12	12. 1:28.403	5	12. **1:27.897**	6		
5. Michael Schumacher	D	Ferrari 248 F1 255 [1]	2. 1:28.777	4	6. 1:28.819	13	1. 1:27.203	12	2. 1:27.385	3	1. 1:25.850	3	2. **1:27.284**	11
6. Felipe Massa	BR	Ferrari 248 F1 252 [2]	17. 1:31.904	5	2. 1:28.164	18	7. 1:28.266	14	1. 1:27.306	3	4. 1:27.059	3	1. **1:26.907**	11
7. Ralf Schumacher	D	Toyota TF106/10B [2->1]	20.	5	5. 1:28.614	21	17. 1:29.374	18	3. 1:27.668	6	5. 1:27.062	3	5. **1:27.569**	11
8. Jarno Trulli	I	Toyota TF106/08B [1]	21.	2	15. 1:30.006	18	11. 1:28.861	17	14. 1:28.549	6	13. **1:27.973**	6		
9. Mark Webber	AUS	Williams FW28 03 - Cosworth [1]			21. 1:30.775	13	14. 1:29.069	10	11. 1:28.307	6	1:27.608	6	10. **1:29.436**	10
10. Nico Rosberg	D	Williams FW28 05 - Cosworth [2]			23. 1:31.015	17	15. 1:29.176	13	15. 1:28.889	6	15. **1:28.386**	6		
11. Rubens Barrichello	BR	Honda RA106-01 [2]	11. 1:30.838	5	10. 1:29.214	16	8. 1:28.359	15	13. 1:28.411	6	14. **1:28.257**	6		
12. Jenson Button	GB	Honda RA106-05 [2]	3. 1:28.785	5	3. 1:28.506	10	6. 1:28.190	17	8. 1:28.222	6	2. 1:26.872	6	7. **1:27.790**	11
14. David Coulthard	GB	Red Bull RB2 3 - Ferrari [2]	27.	1	28. 1:31.540	10	16. 1:29.357	12	17. **1:29.136**	7				
15. Christian Klien	A	Red Bull RB2 5 - Ferrari [2]	26.	1	22. 1:30.889	16	10. 1:28.830	9	10. 1:28.271	6	11. **1:27.852**	6		
16. Nick Heidfeld	D	BMW Sauber F1.06-04 [2]	7. 1:29.780	6	27. 1:31.526	10	5. 1:28.151	14	6. 1:28.200	3	7. 1:27.251	6	6. **1:27.785**	11
17. Robert Kubica	PL	BMW Sauber F1.06-05 [2]	25.	1	17. 1:30.502	9	4. 1:27.964	15	7. 1:28.212	3	9. 1:27.405	6	9. **1:28.167**	11
18. Tiago Monteiro	P	Midland M16-03 - Toyota [2]	15. 1:31.566	10	26. 1:31.519	15	21. 1:29.915	17	20. **1:29.901**	8				
19. Christijan Albers	NL	Midland M16-02 - Toyota [2->1]	14. 1:31.475	10	29. 1:32.102	7	19. 1:29.668	19	16. 1:29.021	6	16. **1:28.639**	6		
20. Vitantonio Liuzzi	I	Toro Rosso STR01 03 - Cosworth [2]	19. 1:32.497	6	20. 1:30.551	17	18. 1:29.426	19	19. **1:29.250**	8				
21. Scott Speed	USA	Toro Rosso STR01 02 - Cosworth [2]	13. 1:31.416	5	14. 1:29.890	20	12. 1:28.861	14	18. **1:29.158**	9				
22. Takuma Sato	J	Super Aguri SA06-03 - Honda [2]	24.	1	24. 1:31.091	11	22. 1:30.151	21	22. **1:30.850**	5				
23. Sakon Yamamoto	J	Super Aguri SA06-04 - Honda [2]	18. 1:32.212	11	25. 1:31.316	21	20. 1:29.881	17	21. **1:30.607**	7				
35. Alexander Wurz	A	Williams FW28 04 - Cosworth	4. 1:28.959	24	19. 1:30.509	36								
36. Anthony Davidson	GB	Honda RA106-03	5. 1:29.193	19	4. 1:28.598	31								
37. Robert Doornbos	NL	Red Bull RB2 1 - Ferrari	9. 1:30.391	16	7. 1:28.848	15								
38. Sebastian Vettel	D	BMW Sauber F1.06-08	8. 1:29.964	25	1. 1:28.091	29								
39. Giorgio Mondini	CH	Midland M16-04 - Toyota	12. 1:30.846	28	11. 1:29.719	27								
40. Neel Jani	CH	Toro Rosso STR01 01 - Cosworth	10. 1:30.576	22	13. 1:29.858	30								
41. Franck Montagny	F	Super Aguri SA06-02 - Honda	16. 1:31.814	13	16. 1:30.491	25								

Fastest lap overall
M. Schumacher 1:25.850 (223,841 km/h)

Maximum speed

N° Driver	S1 Qualifs	Pos.	S1 Race	Pos.	S2 Qualifs	Pos.	S2 Race	Pos.	Finish Qualifs	Pos.	Finish Race	Pos.	Radar Qualifs	Pos.	Radar Race	Pos.
1. F. Alonso	280,9	4	280,3	9	285,7	3	284,3	6	238,7	6	239,5	6	314,3	4	310,6	5
2. G. Fisichella	278,9	7	282,3	3	283,9	7	286,4	2	238,4	7	239,8	4	314,4	3	317,8	1
3. K. Räikkönen	278,9	8	176,0	21	284,2	5	152,9	21	240.1	4			308,4	10	138,9	21
4. P. de la Rosa	281,5	3	281,7	5	284,2	6	284,4	5	240,8	3	240,4	3	312,4	6	305,9	11
5. M. Schumacher	282,1	2	283,2	1	287,0	2	286,4	1	241,8	1	243,0	1	315,6	1	313,4	2
6. F. Massa	283,1	1	282,5	2	287,6	1	284,6	4	241,5	2	240,5	2	315,6	2	312,2	3
7. R. Schumacher	278,1	13	276,7	16	283,1	9	281,1	12	236,6	20	235,4	15	310,2	7	310,0	7
8. J. Trulli	278,4	9	280,8	7	283,3	8	281,6	10	236,7	18	235,7	14	312,5	5	310,1	6
9. M. Webber	278,2	12	278,8	11	282,9	11	282,4	9	239,1	5	239,5	7	306,6	12	305,7	12
10. N. Rosberg	277,1	16	277,9	13	281,8	16	280,5	14	238,0	10	237,5	11	305,6	16	306,6	9
11. R. Barrichello	276,3	17	282,2	4	282,2	15	283,8	7	237,7	12	239,6	5	306,3	14	310,7	4
12. J. Button	275,5	19	277,1	14	282,3	13	280,8	13	237,3	14	237,5	10	304,1	17	304,2	14
14. D. Coulthard	279,2	6	280,8	6	282,4	12	281,2	11	238,2	9	236,9	12	306,3	13	306,3	10
15. C. Klien	277,2	15	276,8	15	280,5	17	278,2	16	237,1	15	235,1	16	303,7	19	303,2	17
16. N. Heidfeld	278,4	10	278,5	12	283,0	10	280,2	15	237,5	13	234,9	18	307,5	11	303,7	16
17. R. Kubica	279,7	5	280,7	8	285,1	4	283,3	8	238,0	11	238,0	9	308,9	9	305,6	13
18. T. Monteiro	274,1	21			276,7	22			232,0	22			303,1	20		
19. C. Albers	274,8	20	276,6	17	278,9	21	277,1	19	236,7	17	235,0	17	304,0	18	298,5	19
20. V. Liuzzi	273,5	22	273,6	20	279,3	20	276,0	20	233,8	21	231,6	20	306,2	15	303,7	15
21. S. Speed	278,3	11	280,0	10	282,2	14	285,4	3	237,0	16	238,8	8	309,8	8	309,8	8
22. T. Sato	277,6	14	274,3	19	280,1	18	277,2	18	238,3	8	234,8	19	303,1	21	296,5	20
23. S. Yamamoto	275,7	18	275,5	18	279,3	19	278,0	17	236,6	19	235,9	13	299,1	22	298,6	18

Race

Classification & Retirements

Pos.	Driver	Constructor	Tyres	Laps	Time	Average	
1.	F. Massa	Ferrari	B	58	1:28.51.082	208,930 km/h	
2.	F. Alonso	Renault	M	58	+ 5.575	208,712 km/h	
3.	M. Schumacher	Ferrari	B	58	+ 5.656	208,709 km/h	
4.	J. Button	Honda	M	58	+ 12.334	208,448 km/h	
5.	P. de la Rosa	McLaren Mercedes	M	58	+ 45.908	207,146 km/h	
6.	G. Fisichella	Renault	M	58	+ 46.594	207,120 km/h	
7.	R. Schumacher	Toyota	B	58	+ 59.337	206,630 km/h	
8.	R. Barrichello	Honda	M	58	+ 1:00.034	206,603 km/h	
9.	J. Trulli	Toyota	B	57	1 tour	205,244 km/h	
10.	M. Webber	Williams Cosworth	B	57	1 tour	205,225 km/h	
11.	C. Klien	RBR Ferrari	M	57	1 tour	204,933 km/h	
12.	R. Kubica	BMW	M	57	1 tour	204,625 km/h	
13.	S. Speed	STR Cosworth	M	57	1 tour	204,612 km/h	
14.	N. Heidfeld	BMW	M	56	2 tours	199,245 km/h	
15.	D. Coulthard	RBR Ferrari	M	55	3 tours	204,383 km/h	Gearbox pb.

Driver	Constructor	Tyre	Laps	Reason
C. Albers	MF1 Toyota	B	46	Spun, crash into the barrier
T. Sato	Aguri Honda	B	41	17 laps146,395 km/h Not classified
N. Rosberg	Williams Cosworth	B	25	Failure in water system
S. Yamamoto	Aguri Honda	B	23	Spun... engine stalled
V. Liuzzi	STR Cosworth	M	12	Rear axle locked, spun... engine stalled
K. Räikkönen	McLaren Mercedes	M	1	
T. Monteiro	MF1 Toyota	B	0	Hit by Sato, front suspension broken

Fastest laps

	Driver	Time	Laps	Average
1.	M. Schumacher	1:28.005	55	218,360 km/h
2.	F. Massa	1:28.123	38	218,067 km/h
3.	F. Alonso	1:28.245	38	217,766 km/h
4.	J. Button	1:28.474	58	217,202 km/h
5.	G. Fisichella	1:28.546	29	217,026 km/h
6.	R. Barrichello	1:28.733	26	216,568 km/h
7.	P. de la Rosa	1:28.959	54	216,018 km/h
8.	R. Schumacher	1:29.084	58	215,715 km/h
9.	R. Kubica	1:29.723	34	214,179 km/h
10.	S. Speed	1:29.933	43	213,679 km/h
11.	C. Klien	1:30.025	26	213,460 km/h
12.	D. Coulthard	1:30.026	24	213,458 km/h
13.	J. Trulli	1:30.048	24	213,406 km/h
14.	N. Rosberg	1:30.071	21	213,351 km/h
15.	M. Webber	1:30.088	50	213,311 km/h
16.	N. Heidfeld	1:30.335	56	212,728 km/h
17.	C. Albers	1:30.403	35	212,568 km/h
18.	T. Sato	1:31.814	33	209,301 km/h
19.	V. Liuzzi	1:32.148	12	208,542 km/h
20.	S. Yamamoto	1:32.337	12	208,115 km/h

Pit stops

	Driver	Laps	Duration	Stop	Total
1.	R. Schumacher	1	26.751	1	26.751
2.	G. Fisichella	1	37.855	1	37.855
3.	N. Heidfeld	1	38.856	1	38.856
4.	S. Speed	1	36.449	1	36.449
5.	K. Räikkönen	1	51.901	1	51.901
6.	T. Sato	1	23:56.582	1	23:56.582
7.	F. Massa	14	26.149	1	26.149
8.	M. Schumacher	14	37.947	1	37.947
9.	F. Alonso	14	25.944	1	25.944
10.	J. Button	14	25.369	1	25.369
11.	M. Webber	14	25.003	1	25.003
12.	R. Kubica	14	24.345	1	24.345
13.	C. Albers	14	25.657	1	25.657
14.	S. Yamamoto	14	29.096	1	29.096
15.	J. Trulli	25	24.920	1	24.920
16.	D. Coulthard	25	27.194	1	27.194
17.	C. Klien	26	24.166	1	24.166
18.	N. Heidfeld	25	25.145	2	1:04.001
19.	R. Barrichello	27	24.545	1	24.545
20.	S. Speed	27	24.360	2	1:00.809
21.	P. de la Rosa	30	28.073	1	28.073
22.	G. Fisichella	30	29.001	2	1:06.856
23.	R. Schumacher	32	26.934	2	53.685
24.	R. Kubica	34	26.142	2	50.487
25.	C. Albers	38	35.086	2	1:00.743
26.	F. Massa	39	25.091	2	51.240
27.	F. Alonso	39	25.347	2	51.291
28.	J. Button	39	25.048	2	50.417
29.	M. Webber	39	26.745	2	51.748
30.	M. Schumacher	43	24.602	2	1:02.549
31.	N. Heidfeld	41	33.269	3	1:37.270
32.	C. Klien	43	23.885	2	48.051
33.	S. Speed	43	24.514	3	1:25.323
34.	R. Barrichello	44	23.248	2	47.793
35.	J. Trulli	44	23.864	2	48.784
36.	D. Coulthard	45	23.194	2	50.388
37.	T. Sato	31	29.437	2	24:26.019

Race leader

Driver	Laps in the lead	Nbr of Laps
F. Massa	1 > 39	39
M. Alonso	40 > 43	4
F. Massa	44 > 58	15

Driver	Nbr of Laps	Kilometers
F. Massa	54	288,044 km
F. Alonso	4	21,352 km

Gaps on the leader board

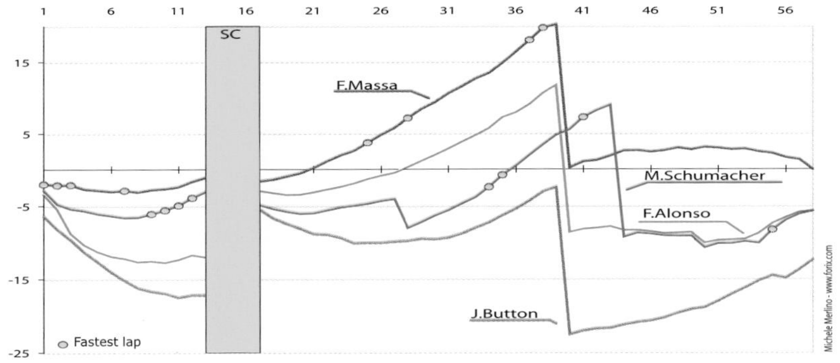

Lap chart

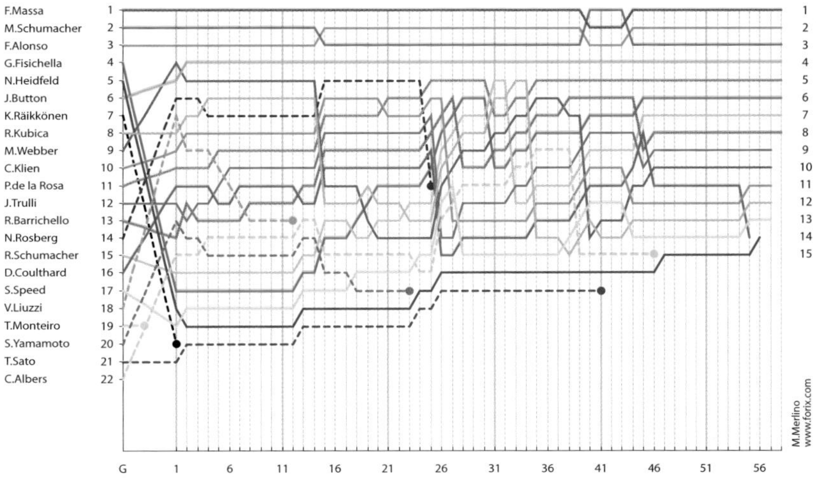

Championships 14/18

Drivers

1. F. Alonso ....Renault ....6 🏆..108
2. M. Schumacher .....Ferrari......................5 🏆....96
3. F. Massa...............Ferrari......................1 🏆....62
4. G. Fisichella..........Renault ....1 🏆....52
5. K. Räikkönen ....McLaren Mercedes..............49
6. J. Button ....Honda.......................1 🏆....36
7. J. Montoya ....McLaren Mercedes..............26
8. R. Barrichello........Honda 22
9. N. Heidfeld ....BMW 19
10. R. Schumacher .....Toyota 18
11. P. de la Rosa.........McLaren Mercedes..............14
12. D. Coulthard ....RBR Ferrari.........................14
13. J. Trulli.................Toyota 10
14. J. Villeneuve ....BMW 7
15. M. Webber............Williams Cosworth................6
16. N. Rosberg ....Williams Cosworth................4
17. C. Klien................RBR Ferrari 2
18. V. Liuzzi ....STR Cosworth.......................1
19. S. Speed ....STR Cosworth.......................0
20. T. Monteiro ....MF1 Toyota 0
21. C. Albers..............MF1 Toyota 0
22. T. Sato.................Aguri Honda 0
23. R. Kubica ....BMW 0
24. Y. Ide...................Aguri Honda 0
25. F. Montagny..........Aguri Honda 0

S. Yamamoto ....Aguri Honda ....-

Constructors

1. Mild Seven Renault F1 Team ....7 🏆...160
2. Scuderia Ferrari Marlboro ....6 🏆...158
3. Team McLaren Mercedes 89
4. Lucky Strike Honda Racing F1 Team...1 🏆 58
5. Panasonic Toyota Racing 28
6. BMW Sauber F1 Team.................................26
7. Red Bull Racing 16
8. Williams F1 Team.......................................10
9. Scuderia Toro Rosso....................................1
10. MF1 Racing...0
11. Super Aguri Formula 1 0

All results :
© 2006 Formula One Administration Ltd,
6 Princes Gate, London, SW7 1QJ, England

The circuit

Name	Istanbul Speed Park; Istanbul	Weather	Sunny and warm
Lenght	5338 m	Air temperature	35-37°c
Distance	58 tours soit 309,396 km	Track temperature	42-53°c
Date	August 27, 2006	Humidity	22%
		Wind speed	1,9 m/s

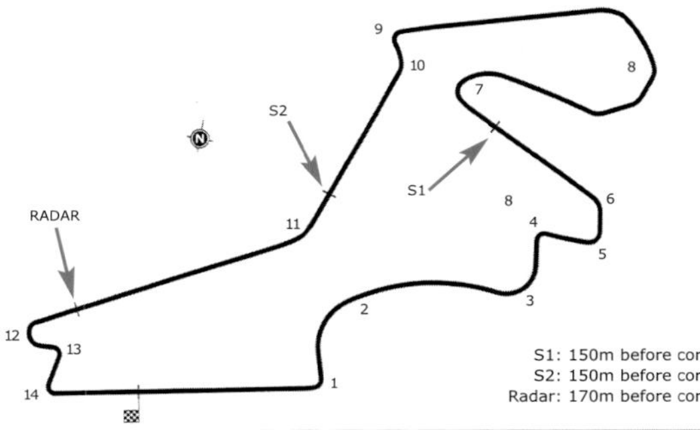

S1: 150m before corner
S2: 150m before corner
Radar: 170m before corner

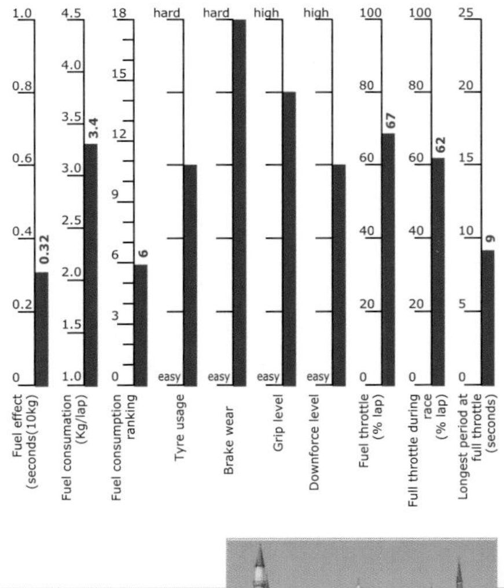

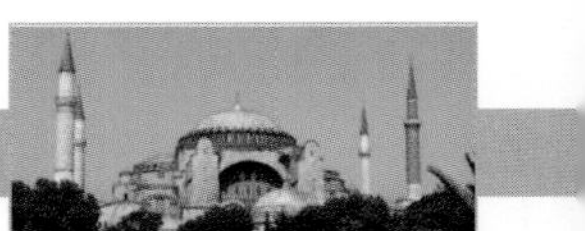

A WEEKEND TO REMEMBER!

The Italian Grand Prix was one of the most highly charged of the season from an emotional point of view. On Saturday, Alonso was the victim of a very odd penalty for having supposedly blocked Massa.
The next day Michael Schumacher won the race cutting his rival's lead in the championship chase to only 2 points. On his slowing-down lap he announced his decision to retire at the end of the year. Kimi Räikkönen will replace him at Ferrari.
Robert Kubica's 3rd place was good news for BMW (photo).
Little Nick Heidfeld in the second Bavarian entry finished the race in 8th place.

The once and future Ferrari drivers on the front row after a scandal – tainted session

Another pole for Kimi Räikkönen, his third and last of the season. It was very close as he was just 2/1000s ahead of Michael Schumacher.

Two thousands of a second were all that separated Kimi Räikkönen on pole and Michael Schumacher after qualifying. The gap corresponded to 14,2 cms over a lap measuring 5,8 kms. However, a question mark hung over the Finn's capacity to maintain a speed capable of keeping him in front of Schumacher until the chequered flag. It was not really too serious for Ferrari as in a manner of speaking it had both drivers on the front row! After the Italian Grand Prix it announced that it had taken on Räikkönen for the 2007 season. Michael Schumacher's only aim was to concentrate on winning the race in which victory was crucial for his chances of an eighth title.

Ah, those Italian charms! On Friday Martini launched its new TV programme concept with the help of four very persuasive arguments!

He received a helping hand on Saturday evening when the Italian Grand Prix Stewards of the Meeting decided to cancel Fernando Alonso's three quickest times demoting the Spaniard from fifth to 10th place on the grid. Race control declared that he had baulked Felipe Massa in his last flying lap breaching Article 116 b of the Formula 1 sporting regulations.

Friday is for peanuts but the test drivers give it their all. Anthony Davidson did not spare his Honda engine, which caught fire.

On Saturday evening the Renault team was dumbfounded as the sanction virtually robbed Alonso of any chance of winning the Italian Grand Prix. In addition, it would help Schumacher to make a big step towards closing the gap in the championship battle. Pat Symonds, the French team's engineering director, came to the pressroom on Saturday to put forward Renault's point of view. He felt that it was an enormous miscarriage of justice: "*This is a very strange decision,*" he stated. "*We've seen the Ferrari drivers do very odd things in Turkey without receiving the slightest penalty.*"

In the Ferrari camp the telemetry readouts were produced to back up its protest showing that Massa had lost a few tenths of a second in the third sector of the circuit because of Fernando Alonso. "*I've seen those readouts,*" added Symonds. "*In my opinion what they show is that Felipe made a driving error in the final corner. He was around 100 metres behind Alonso, which is not a real problem. Five years ago the drivers were hindered by others during all the qualification sessions without anybody getting uptight. F1 has lost its head these days and the current obsession with political correctness is going to kill racing.*" While awaiting that day Alonso had to start the grand prix from the 5th row in the middle of the wild things.

Sebastian Vettel quickest again

BMW continued its show-off policy at Monza. Sebastian Vettel in only his second grand prix weekend again emerged quickest in the Friday session, which, taking the conditions into account, was not really a surprise.
On Saturday, the BMW Sauber team continued to progress. Nick Heidfeld, who had qualified in 5th place in Turkey 2 weeks earlier, got into 3rd spot on the grid. "*I hope I'm not going be involved in another first corner accident,*" said Nick. Robert Kubica in the second BMW qualified in 7th place which then became sixth after Alonso had been demoted. The Swiss-German team had obviously found a few new tweaks.

Starting grid

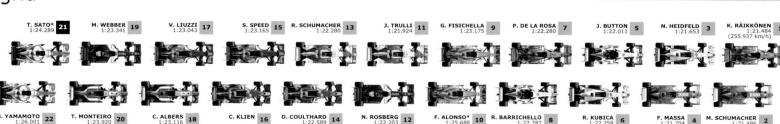

* F. ALONSO
Penalised for having blocked Massa during his quick lap in Q3. His best three laptimes have been deleted.

T. SATO
Starts from pit lane.

Pos	Driver	Time	No
	K. RÄIKKÖNEN	1:21.484 (255.937 km/h)	1
	N. HEIDFELD	1:21.653	3
	J. BUTTON	1:22.011	5
	P. DE LA ROSA	1:22.280	7
	G. FISICHELLA	1:23.175	9
	J. TRULLI	1:21.924	11
	R. SCHUMACHER	1:22.280	13
	S. SPEED	1:23.165	15
	V. LIUZZI	1:23.043	17
	M. WEBBER	1:23.341	19
	T. SATO*	1:24.289	21
	M. SCHUMACHER	1:21.486	2
	F. MASSA	1:21.704	4
	R. KUBICA	1:22.258	6
	R. BARRICHELLO	1:22.787	8
	F. ALONSO*	1:25.688	10
	N. ROSBERG	1:22.203	12
	D. COULTHARD	1:22.589	14
	C. KLIEN	1:22.———	16
	C. ALBERS	1:23.116	18
	T. MONTEIRO	1:23.920	20
	S. YAMAMOTO	1:26.001	22

Were Renault's glory days over?

Flavio Briatore's nefarious past is a subject of speculation. Nobody really knows the story of the Renault team boss. Those who have an inkling keep it to themselves, which says a lot on how he got to where he is today.

Flavio has managed to muddle things and claims that he was born into a modest family of teachers in a little village in Piedmont. He then met up with Luciano Benetton and launched his boutiques in North America after which he was appointed head of Benetton Racing in 1991.

He learned the ropes of F1 very quickly, and also saw its potential. Not only is he the manager of the world championship winning team but he also looks after Fernando Alonso, Mark Webber and Jarno Trulli as well as owning a restaurant in London and a discotheque in Sardinia.

For the flamboyant Italian an F1 team is only a licence to print money. Why not? With arrival at the head of Renault of cost-killer Carlos Ghson the Briatore system seemed doomed to disappear with its creator.

And yet. Flavio is still there and he announced at Monza that he had resigned for another two years, up to the end of 2008 at least. It seems that Ghosn has decided to turn a blind eye to the Italian's very personal way of managing the team. As long as the victories keep rolling in..!

The problem, though, is how long will the winning streak continue? In 2007, the French squad will have to deal with the departure of its star driver, Fernando Alonso, to McLaren as well as changing its long-time tyre supplier Michelin for Bridgestone, as the French manufacturer announced its intention to quit F1 after the Brazilian Grand Prix. It is something that will cause technical problems given the importance assumed by tyres in recent years.

At Monza the team confirmed that it had hired Heikki Kovalainen, its test driver for the past 3 years, to back up Giancarlo Fisichella in 2007. The latter has not been very convincing as Alonso's team-late over the last 2 years but he is called upon to assume the role of team leader with the inexperienced Finn as no.2. The latter at least knows the car well having covered some 28 000 kilometres in testing. What he'll be worth in a race is another kettle of fish!

Flavio hired Ricardo Zonta as test driver to back up the Fisichella/Kovalainen duo. Ricardo has already spent 4 years in this job at Toyota. In addition, the Italian took on young Brazilian

coming man Nelson Piquet Junior who has shown a lot of promise in the GP2 Championship. Thus, a lot of question marks hang over the Renault team in 2007. It is the only one to put its trust in an F1 debutant, Kovalainen, and has to adapt to Bridgestone rubber as well as trying to make up for the huge

loss of Fernando Alonso. All these factors point to the fact that the French team's glory days may be over at the end of the 2006 season. Thus the future looks gloomy for the French squad but that did not seem to spoil Flavio Briatore's good humour. If the team runs into trouble he can always go back to his discotheque!

^
It was to be Christian Klien's last grand prix with Red Bull although the Austrian did not know it yet. He went out quietly after qualifying 16th on the grid, almost his worst performance of the season

<
Hello from Giancarlo Fisichella and Heikki Kovalainen the 2007 Renault driver line-up who don't really look like a championship winning tandem.

<
Sebastian Vettel was again quickest on Friday. He is a quick and hard-working driver.

The crowd went wild below the Monza rostrum with the victory of their idol who had closed the gap in the championship to almost zero.

Schumacher wins and Alonso retires: the gap down to 2 points!

The driver who made the quickest start was pole man Kimi Räikkönen. As many people suspected the Finn did not qualify with as much fuel on board as Michael Schumacher. The Ferrari did 2 laps more than the McLaren in the first stint and emerged from the pits just in front of the silver car. There were no changes between the 2 Ferrari drivers (the 2006 one and his 2007 successor) until the chequered flag.

Finally, Alonso's relegation was of little consequence. He had just made a magnificent comeback to third place when his engine let go in the biggest possible way 10 laps from the finish. Thus, Michael Schumacher's victory reduced the gap between the two drivers to a mere 2 points.

With only 3 races to go till the end of the season the title battle was wide open once again.

"It's a new start," was how Jean Todt analysed

it. "We're going to give our all beginning next week as we've programmed private testing in view of the last three grands prix."

Behind Schumacher and Räikkönen came the amazing Robert Kubica who had replaced Jacques Villeneuve in the BMW Sauber team. In only his third grand prix he finished on the third step of the rostrum. Michael Schumacher is departing the scene and the stars of tomorrow are already arriving.

> A great race by Robert Kubica who finished third

> (right), A delighted Jean Todt falls into the arms of Hisao Suganuma after the finish.

It was a bad day for Alonso. He was on his way to a third-place finish when his engine let go on lap 44.

Michael announces his retirement at the end of the season: a difficult decision

The 53rd and last lap of the Italian Grand Prix and Michael Schumacher crosses the line in his Ferrari 248F1. He has just won the Italian Grand Prix and is now only 2 points behind Fernando Alonso in the drivers' world championship. A dream moment.

Chris Dyer his engineer on the pit wall congratulates Michael on the radio. All the engineers who were listening will never forget his reply. "*Thank you to all the team. It's my last Italian Grand Prix with you. I'm retiring at the end of the season. I'm going to miss you all.*"

The secret had been well kept and the team members only learned the news at that very moment. A wave of emotion seized the whole Scuderia who massed under the rostrum to salute their champion.

The rest of the world soon learned of Michael's decision.

15h37: After coming down from the rostrum, Michael gave a televised press conference with a catch in his throat: "*It's a very special day for me,*" he said. "*It's my last Italian Grand Prix. I've decided to withdraw from racing at the end of the season.*"

His story began in Kerpen, a little town in the Cologne suburbs. Rolf Schumacher built chimneys and Elizabeth served in a little bar. Young Michael was raised in a very humble milieu.

His father put together a kart for him when he was four and then scrimped and saved to enable him to fulfil his passion for karting while he was still a child. The career of the most titled driver of all time was launched.

It finished on 22nd October after the 2006 Brazilian Grand Prix without an eighth world title. A chapter in the history of motor racing was closed. "*I decided to retire during the United States Grand Prix at Indianapolis,*" Michael went on. "*I think that one day I won't have enough energy to do battle at the same level. You have to be enormously motivated and have enormous strength to drive at this standard. I also didn't want to hang on and deprive talented young drivers of having the results they deserve. It's better to bow out when you're battling for the title than to trundle around at the back of the field.*"

In April Ferrari had already taken on Räikkönen for 3 years. Michael Schumacher could have stayed and in that case Felipe Massa would have had to go and look elsewhere. The German preferred to give him his place.

'I've had an exceptional career and I loved all the good times. I have to thank all the guys from Benetton who were with me on my debut and all those at Ferrari. There are so many great people in this team that it wasn't easy to decide not to continue working with them. But of course I have to thank all my family. Without their support I'd never have achieved what I've achieved."

Will Michael Schumacher be remembered as the greatest driver ever? Although it is often asked it is a senseless question. The conditions of the 50s are so different to those of 2006 for example. Michael has always refused to compare himself with the drivers of the past for whom he has expressed the deepest admiration. "*We'll never know if Michael is the greatest ever. One thing, though, is certain he's won the most titles,*" concluded Jean Todt.

The German did not say much about his future. "*The day when I retire I don't think I'll do very much for a while. I'd obviously like to remain a part of the big Ferrari family. We'll see.*"

For Jean Todt it was all cut and dried: "*Michael isn't leaving Ferrari. He'll remain involved with us and the details of his responsibilities will be announced at the end of the season.*" Will he be a kind of roving ambassador or a technical consultant? One thing is sure he will still be seen at the circuits.

15h37: Michael Schumacher announced his retirement during the post-race TV press conference, an intensely emotional moment. At the same time Ferrari published a press release stating that its 2007 drivers would be Kimi Räikkönen and Felipe Massa.
v

On-the-spot reactions in the Monza paddock: the best is leaving

• **Niki Lauda** (3-times F1 World Champion). "*Michael is the greatest driver ever. He's leaving and his decision must be respected. I would like to thank him for all the pleasure he's given me. I don't think he'll come back. I did it once but I took my decision on a sudden impulse. He has thought his through; it can't have been easy.*"

• **Peter Sauber** (former team owner and former boss of Michael Schumacher). "*Michael is a really exceptional driver. F1 is losing someone very important. His departure goes well beyond the context of driving. I think it'll only be in a few months that we'll realise what he represents for motor sport. The figures of what he's accomplished are enough to shut up his detractors.*"

• **Flavio Briatore** (team manager). "*Michael has done a lot for F1 but F1 has done a lot for Michael. He was the first to do so much training to show that winning takes more than just good driving skills. When Senna died I thought F1 was finished. It'll survive Michael too.*"

• **Fernando Alonso** (reigning world champion). "*We're losing a great champion. We're going to miss him on the track. Now that*

we know his decision I hope that the sporting side will be back in its rightful place.*"

• **Ralf Schumacher** (Michael's brother). "*I've always been very happy to race against him and I wish him all the best for the rest of his life.*"

• **Jean Todt** (the Scuderia team boss). "*Michael and I were very close. We were linked by friendship, by affection, by mutual respect. When Ferrari hired Michael it had already had the best set of results. There was "a before Michael" and there'll be "an after Michael".*"

Michael Schumacher starts his last Italian Grand Prix and comes into the first corner just behind Kimi Räikkönen.
v

All flat out in their own way

Whether they are fighting for the world title (Fernando Alonso and Michael Schumacher, centre) or going for points every Sunday (Ralf Schumacher, above) or whether all they're trying to do is finish (Christijan Albers, below), they all go flat out and try to master the wild beast that is an F1 car. The last only give away a few seconds to the first and they all deserve our respect.

> On Sunday morning the Renault team tried to show that Fernando Alonso had not baulked Felipe Massa with back-up videos and figures. The explanation was very convincing and proved that common sense was on the French make's side in this controversy.

>

Flavio Briatore takes a pot shot at the FIA

The guy took a good look around before venturing out of his truck so that he could play the invisible man if necessary. But he got snapped all the same. His mask complete with filter and the fact that he hid himself indicated that his work on the Japanese tyres at Monza was illegal to say the least!

>

The day started with a bang! At 11h00 on Sunday morning Renault held a press conference during which Fernando Alonso, Flavio Briatore and Pat Symonds (the technical director) tried to show that the Spaniard had not blocked Felipe Massa the day before, and that he did not deserve the penalty inflicted on him – a 5-place relegation on the grid.
Fernando Alonso openly criticised the FIA in front of the hundreds of journalists packed like sardines in the team's motorhome. "*I love racing. I love the fans but I no longer consider F1 a sport,*" he said. It was the kind of remark that risked being sanctioned by the FIA as the rules prevent drivers from criticising the championship. Max Mosley, the FIA President, decided to play it cool: "*we know that the*

drivers have a tendency to say whatever comes into their heads," he commented.
On Sunday evening the dispute between the FIA and the Renault team reached new heights. On the Italian RAI channel Flavio Briatore openly accused the Federation of having already decided the outcome of the championship. "*It's all done and dusted. They've decided to give the championship to Schumacher and that's what's going to happen.*"
The FIA was outraged by his words and decided to ask the feisty Italian boss to come and explain himself. Later on the same evening Flavio did a bit of back peddling and claimed that his words had been "*taken out of context.*" He risked being hit with a fine but eventually he escaped any punishment by publishing a press release on Monday in

which he excused himself for his outburst. But Flav also fired off a volley in the direction of Ferrari. "*This time it's war between us,*" he snarled.
"*I'm really sad to see to what level these people have fallen,*" shot back Jean Todt. "*I respect their competitiveness but I don't respect their arrogance and their anti-sporting behaviour. In life you have to learn to lose and respect those who're stronger than you are.*"

Bridgestone suspected of tyre tampering

^
"*Bye, bye, Bib!*" As Michelin had decided to quit F1 at the end of the season the final European Grand Prix saw the last appearance of the Clérmont-Ferrand make's motorhome in the F1 paddock. A leaving party took place on Sunday midday and there were also a number of farewells tinged with nostalgia for those who had looked after Bibendum in F1 for the past 6 years.

The Italian Grand Prix was a hotbed of murky affairs. On Sunday evening the Renault team asked the FIA for clarifications concerning a photo given to its tyre supplier Michelin during the weekend.
This photo (opposite) shows a Bridgestone employee in an impermeable outfit wearing a mask with an air filter. It is the type of protection used when spraying gas on tyre surfaces to improve their grip, something that is completely forbidden by F1

regulations. At Monza Bridgestone came up with the excuse that the man in question was taking the tyre apart to examine its structure! No mask is required for such an operation so the FIA decided to open an investigation as doubt subsisted. Renault, however, said it was satisfied by the explanation put forward by the Japanese manufacturer and that that was the end of the story. The French make was not going to offend its future tyre supplier.

>

A huge crowd massed under the rostrum at Monza. It was an incredibly emotional moment for the Tifosi what with victory, the possibility of more titles and Michael Schumacher's retirement.

results

Practice

All the time trials

N° Driver	Nat.	N° Chassis - Engine [Nbr. GP]	Pos. Free 1 Friday	Laps	Pos. Free 2 Friday	Laps	Pos. Free 3 Saturday	Laps	Pos. Q1 Saturday	Laps	Pos. Q2 Saturday	Laps	Pos. Super Pole Saturday	Laps
1. Fernando Alonso	E	Renault R26 03 [1]			8. 1:24.577	15	5. 1:22.371	15	2. 1:21.747	3	6. 1:21.526	3	10. **1:25.688**	11
2. Giancarlo Fisichella	I	Renault R26 05 [2]			15. 1:25.160	14	6. 1:22.412	15	9. 1:22.486	3	9. 1:21.722	7	9. **1:23.175**	11
3. Kimi Räikkönen	FIN	McLaren MP4-21 07 & 05 - Mercedes [1]	4. 1:24.037	5	6. 1:24.034	11	7. 1:22.682	11	4. 1:21.994	4	3. 1:21.349	3	1. **1:21.484**	11
4. Pedro de la Rosa	E	McLaren MP4-21 06 - Mercedes [2]	14.	1	5. 1:23.970	12	9. 1:22.915	11	7. 1:22.422	5	10. 1:21.878	6	7. **1:22.280**	11
5. Michael Schumacher	D	Ferrari 248 F1 255 [2]			2. 1:23.138	11	3. 1:22.257	14	1. 1:21.711	3	4. 1:21.353	3	2. **1:21.486**	11
6. Felipe Massa	BR	Ferrari 248 F1 252 [1]	15.	1	3. 1:23.182	12	1. 1:21.665	12	5. 1:22.028	3	1. 1:21.225	3	4. **1:21.704**	11
7. Ralf Schumacher	D	Toyota TF106/10B [2]	18.	2	17. 1:25.316	22	11. 1:23.244	17	13. 1:22.622	7	13. **1:22.280**	6		
8. Jarno Trulli	I	Toyota TF106/08B [2]	16.	2	12. 1:25.027	12	14. 1:23.467	15	6. 1:22.093	6	11. **1:21.924**	6		
9. Mark Webber	AUS	Williams FW28 03 - Cosworth [2]	22.	1	20. 1:25.500	11	16. 1:23.599	8	19. **1:23.341**	6				
10. Nico Rosberg	D	Williams FW28 05 - Cosworth [1]	21.	1	13. 1:25.040	9	13. 1:23.334	8	11. 1:22.581	5	12. **1:22.203**	6		
11. Rubens Barrichello	BR	Honda RA106-01 [1]					8. 1:22.835	18	14. 1:22.640	4	8. 1:21.688	6	8. **1:22.787**	11
12. Jenson Button	GB	Honda RA106-05 [1]					12. 1:23.295	15	10. 1:22.512	4	7. 1:21.572	6	5. **1:22.011**	11
14. David Coulthard	GB	Red Bull RB2 3 - Ferrari [1]	24.	1	18. 1:25.318	11	15. 1:23.536	9	12. 1:22.618	6	14. **1:22.589**	8		
15. Christian Klien	A	Red Bull RB2 5 - Ferrari [1]	23.	1	14. 1:25.108	11	10. 1:23.081	11	15. 1:22.898	6	16.			
16. Nick Heidfeld	D	BMW Sauber F1.06-04 [1]	17.	1	7. 1:24.330	9	2. 1:22.052	13	3. 1:21.764	3	5. 1:21.425	6	3. **1:21.653**	11
17. Robert Kubica	PL	BMW Sauber F1.06-05 [1]	2. 1:23.745	5	9. 1:24.813	5	4. 1:22.280	12	8. 1:22.437	4	2. 1:21.270	6	6. **1:22.258**	11
18. Tiago Monteiro	P	Midland M16-03 - Toyota [1]	6. 1:25.413	7	16. 1:25.277	12	20. 1:24.541	14	20. **1:23.920**	5				
19. Christijan Albers	NL	Midland M16-02 - Toyota [1]	8. 1:25.766	7	11. 1:24.985	11	19. 1:24.186	17	18. **1:23.116**	5				
20. Vitantonio Liuzzi	I	Toro Rosso STR01 03 - Cosworth [1]	19.	3	22. 1:25.707	19	18. 1:23.777	20	17. **1:23.043**	9				
21. Scott Speed	USA	Toro Rosso STR01 02 - Cosworth [1]	20.	1	23. 1:25.755	21	17. 1:23.659	20	16. 1:22.943	8	15. **1:23.165**	9		
22. Takuma Sato	J	Super Aguri SA06-03 - Honda [1]	9. 1:26.708	20	26. 1:26.118	21	21. 1:24.549	25	21. **1:24.289**	8				
23. Sakon Yamamoto	J	Super Aguri SA06-04 - Honda [1]	10. 1:27.310	20	27. 1:26.705	14	22. 1:24.717	19	22. **1:26.001**	4				
35. Alexander Wurz	A	Williams FW28 04 - Cosworth	3. 1:23.868	19	4. 1:23.414	26								
36. Anthony Davidson	GB	Honda RA106-03	13.	2	19. 1:25.356	8								
37. Robert Doornbos	NL	Red Bull RB2 1 - Ferrari	7. 1:25.578	19	25. 1:26.058	31								
38. Sebastian Vettel	D	BMW Sauber F1.06-08	1. 1:23.263	22	1. 1:22.631	29								
39. Giorgio Mondini	CH	Midland M16-01 - Toyota	12. 1:28.444	7	21. 1:25.586	29								
40. Neel Jani	CH	Toro Rosso STR01 01 - Cosworth	5. 1:24.196	24	24. 1:25.878	32								
41. Franck Montagny	F	Super Aguri SA06-02 - Honda	11. 1:27.597	7	10. 1:24.943	24								

Fastest lap overall
F. Massa 1:21.225 (256,753 km/h)

Maximum speed

N° Driver	S1 Qualifs	Pos.	S1 Race	Pos.	S2 Qualifs	Pos.	S2 Race	Pos.	Finish Qualifs	Pos.	Finish Race	Pos.	Radar Qualifs	Pos.	Radar Race	Pos.
1. F. Alonso	328,3	6	335,5	1	331,6	6	336,8	2	313,6	9	315,6	2	343,8	7	345,7	4
2. G. Fisichella	327,9	8	328,7	11	330,6	8	332,9	11	314,3	5	311,7	10	346,2	2	342,2	16
3. K. Räikkönen	329,7	5	330,7	7	330,6	9	334,1	8	315,2	3	313,6	5	339,5	16	344,9	8
4. P. de la Rosa	326,9	12	328,4	14	329,5	14	332,9	12	312,8	13	312,8	7	340,0	12	345,6	5
5. M. Schumacher	328,2	7	328,5	13	328,8	16	333,9	9	314,0	7	313,1	6	341,8	9	340,2	19
6. F. Massa	330,3	3	334,0	2	332,6	3	336,3	3	318,6	1	317,5	1	345,9	3	349,9	1
7. R. Schumacher	326,9	11	327,1	17	330,0	12	331,7	13	310,7	19	312,0	8	341,6	10	345,7	3
8. J. Trulli	324,4	17	328,7	12	326,1	21	335,8	4	310,9	18	310,4	18	339,5	15	343,2	14
9. M. Webber	325,3	15	332,3	4	327,5	17	331,5	14	311,8	15	311,0	15	337,3	18	344,0	9
10. N. Rosberg	330,9	2	330,1	9	330,1	10	330,0	18	313,2	10	307,1	21	341,3	11	342,5	15
11. R. Barrichello	323,6	19	325,2	18	326,9	20	327,5	21	312,9	12	311,7	11	335,6	20	338,6	20
12. J. Button	324,0	18	322,2	22	330,1	11	327,1	22	311,3	16	310,3	19	336,6	19	336,7	21
14. D. Coulthard	327,5	9	327,2	16	332,5	4	331,0	16	312,7	14	310,7	17	342,7	8	345,1	7
15. C. Klien	325,5	14	328,3	15	330,8	7	334,3	7	313,6	8	311,5	12	344,2	6	344,0	10
16. N. Heidfeld	332,1	1	331,7	5	334,7	1	334,9	5	317,8	2	315,3	3	348,4	1	349,0	2
17. R. Kubica	329,8	4	331,3	6	333,3	2	336,8	1	314,4	4	314,6	4	344,7	5	343,9	11
18. T. Monteiro	323,5	20	323,9	20	327,4	18	330,6	17	309,8	20	311,7	9	339,9	13	341,3	17
19. C. Albers	326,7	13	330,3	8	329,1	15	331,0	15	310,9	17	311,0	14	339,9	14	345,1	6
20. V. Liuzzi	325,1	16	332,4	3	329,5	13	334,5	6	313,1	11	311,4	13	338,2	17	343,4	13
21. S. Speed	327,0	10	328,9	10	332,4	5	333,0	10	314,1	6	311,0	16	345,1	4	343,6	12
22. T. Sato	322,0	21	324,0	19	326,9	19	327,9	20	308,5	22	309,0	20	334,1	21	340,8	18
23. S. Yamamoto	320,4	22	322,3	21	325,2	22	328,1	19	309,1	21	304,5	22	332,8	22	333,3	22

Race

Classification & Retirements

Pos.	Driver	Constructor	Tyres	Laps	Time	Average
1.	M. Schumacher	Ferrari	B	53	1:14:51.975	245,814 km/h
2.	K. Räikkönen	McLaren Mercedes	M	53	+ 8.046	245,374 km/h
3.	R. Kubica	BMW	M	53	+ 26.414	244,377 km/h
4.	G. Fisichella	Renault	M	53	+ 32.045	244,073 km/h
5.	J. Button	Honda	M	53	+ 32.685	244,038 km/h
6.	R. Barrichello	Honda	M	53	+ 42.409	243,515 km/h
7.	J. Trulli	Toyota	B	53	+ 44.662	243,394 km/h
8.	N. Heidfeld	BMW	M	53	+ 45.309	243,359 km/h
9.	F. Massa	Ferrari	B	53	+ 45.955	243,325 km/h
10.	M. Webber	Williams Cosworth	B	53	+ 1:12.602	241,904 km/h
11.	C. Klien	RBR Ferrari	M	52	1 lap	240,957 km/h
12.	D. Coulthard	RBR Ferrari	M	52	1 lap	240,709 km/h
13.	S. Speed	STR Cosworth	M	52	1 lap	240,650 km/h
14.	V. Liuzzi	STR Cosworth	M	52	1 lap	240,627 km/h
15.	R. Schumacher	Toyota	B	52	1 lap	240,564 km/h
16.	T. Sato	Aguri Honda (T-car)	B	51	2 laps	233,957 km/h
17.	C. Albers	MF1 Toyota	B	51	2 laps	232,885 km/h

Driver	Constructor	Tyre	Lap	Reason
T. Monteiro	MF1 Toyota	B	44	Brakes problem
F. Alonso	Renault	M	43	Engine failure
P. de la Rosa	McLaren Mercedes	M	20	Engine failure
S. Yamamoto	Aguri Honda	B	18	Hydraulic problem
N. Rosberg	Williams Cosworth	B	9	Driveshaft damaged

Fastest laps

	Driver	Time	Laps	Average
1.	K. Räikkönen	1:22.559	13	252,604 km/h
2.	M. Schumacher	1:22.575	14	252,555 km/h
3.	F. Massa	1:23.003	41	251,253 km/h
4.	R. Kubica	1:23.111	21	250,927 km/h
5.	F. Alonso	1:23.121	38	250,896 km/h
6.	N. Heidfeld	1:23.294	20	250,375 km/h
7.	J. Button	1:23.518	51	249,704 km/h
8.	G. Fisichella	1:23.617	25	249,408 km/h
9.	P. de la Rosa	1:23.702	8	249,155 km/h
10.	R. Barrichello	1:23.794	27	248,881 km/h
11.	J. Trulli	1:23.869	25	248,659 km/h
12.	M. Webber	1:24.197	27	247,690 km/h
13.	C. Klien	1:24.571	37	246,595 km/h
14.	V. Liuzzi	1:24.764	52	246,033 km/h
15.	T. Monteiro	1:24.822	27	245,865 km/h
16.	R. Schumacher	1:24.837	41	245,821 km/h
17.	D. Coulthard	1:24.984	51	245,396 km/h
18.	S. Speed	1:25.094	50	245,079 km/h
19.	N. Rosberg	1:25.362	8	244,310 km/h
20.	C. Albers	1:25.494	17	243,932 km/h
21.	T. Sato	1:25.676	15	243,414 km/h
22.	S. Yamamoto	1:26.548	15	240,962 km/h

Pit stops

	Driver	Laps	Duration	Stop	Total
1.	P. de la Rosa	14	28.482	1	28.482
2.	K. Räikkönen	15	27.063	1	27.063
3.	M. Schumacher	17	28.176	1	28.176
4.	F. Massa	19	27.595	1	27.595
5.	F. Alonso	19	26.546	1	26.546
6.	C. Albers	19	1:00.102	1	1:00.102
7.	J. Button	20	27.305	1	27.305
8.	N. Heidfeld	21	27.437	1	27.437
9.	R. Kubica	22	26.013	1	26.013
10.	N. Heidfeld	••25••	15.122	2	42.559
11.	T. Sato	25	30.490	1	30.490
12.	G. Fisichella	26	27.649	1	27.649
13.	R. Schumacher	28	26.903	1	26.903
14.	T. Monteiro	28	29.333	1	29.333
15.	J. Trulli	29	27.336	1	27.336
16.	S. Speed	29	27.732	1	27.732
17.	R. Barrichello	30	28.148	1	28.148
18.	M. Webber	30	28.706	1	28.706
19.	V. Liuzzi	30	27.401	1	27.401
20.	D. Coulthard	32	27.378	1	27.378
21.	C. Klien	35	25.503	1	25.503
22.	K. Räikkönen	38	25.702	2	52.765
23.	M. Schumacher	39	25.678	2	53.854
24.	F. Massa	39	26.953	2	54.548
25.	N. Heidfeld	40	24.406	3	1:06.965
26.	R. Kubica	41	24.616	2	50.629
27.	F. Alonso	41	24.273	2	50.819
28.	J. Button	41	24.865	2	52.170
29.	T. Monteiro	40	44.807	2	1:14.140
30.	F. Massa	44	25.115	3	1:19.663
31.	T. Monteiro	43	33.890	3	1:48.030

••Drive-through penalty: Heidfeld Speeding in pit lane

Race leader

Driver	Laps in the lead	Nbr of Laps
K. Räikkönen	1 > 14	14
M. Schumacher	15 > 17	3
R. Kubica	18 > 22	5
M. Schumacher	23 > 53	31

Driver	Nbr of Laps	Kilometers
M. Schumacher	34	196,962 km
K. Räikkönen	14	80,793 km
R. Kubica	5	28,965 km

Lap chart

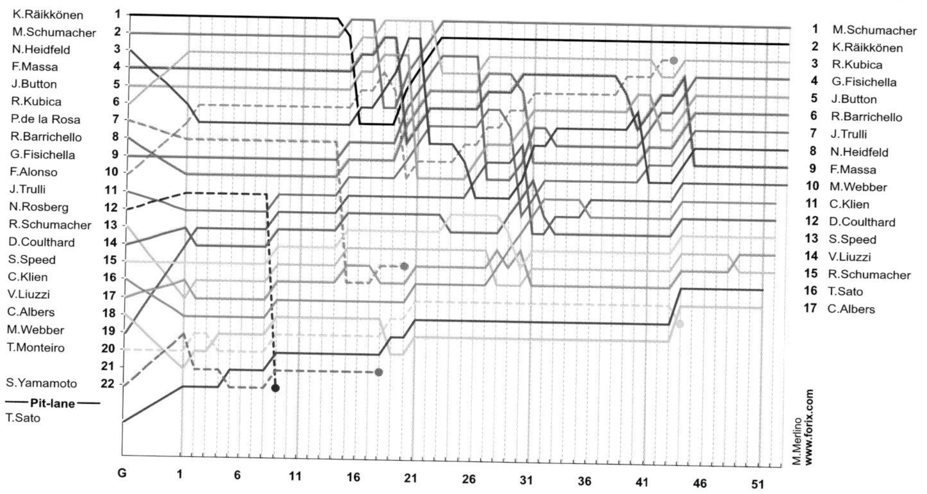

Gaps on the leader board

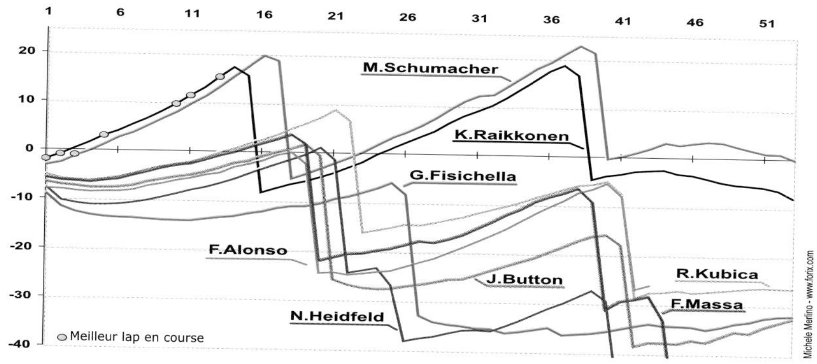

Championships 15/18

Drivers

1. F. Alonso ....Renault ....6 🏆..108
2. M. Schumacher.....Ferrari......................6 🏆..106
3. F. Massa...............Ferrari......................1 🏆....62
4. G. Fisichella..........Renault ....1 🏆....57
5. K. Räikkönen ....McLaren Mercedes.............57
6. J. Button ....Honda.......................1 🏆....40
7. J. Montoya ....McLaren Mercedes.............26
8. R. Barrichello........Honda 25
9. N. Heidfeld ....BMW 20
10. R. Schumacher .....Toyota 18
11. P. de la Rosa.........McLaren Mercedes.............14
12. D. Coulthard.........RBR Ferrari........................14
13. J. Trulli.................Toyota 12
14. J. Villeneuve ....BMW 7
15. R. Kubica ....BMW 6
16. M. Webber............Williams Cosworth...............6
17. N. Rosberg ....Williams Cosworth...............4
18. C. Klien................RBR Ferrari 2
19. V. Liuzzi ....STR Cosworth.......................1
20. S. Speed ....STR Cosworth.......................0
21. T. Monteiro ....MF1 Toyota 0
22. C. Albers..............MF1 Toyota 0
23. T. Sato.................Aguri Honda 0
24. Y. Ide...................Aguri Honda 0
25. F. Montagny..........Aguri Honda 0
S. Yamamoto.........Aguri Honda ....-

Constructors

1. Scuderia Ferrari Marlboro ....7 🏆...168
2. Mild Seven Renault F1 Team ....7 🏆...165
3. Team McLaren Mercedes 97
4. Lucky Strike Honda Racing F1 Team...1 🏆 65
5. BMW Sauber F1 Team..................................33
6. Panasonic Toyota Racing 30
7. Red Bull Racing 16
8. Williams F1 Team.......................................10
9. Scuderia Toro Rosso....................................1
10. MF1 Racing...0
11. Super Aguri Formula 1 0

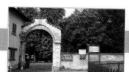

All results : © 2006 Formula One Administration Ltd, 6 Princes Gate, London, SW7 1QJ, England

The circuit

Name	Autodromo Nazionale di Monza; Monza	Weather	Cloudy, warm
Lenght	5793 m	Air temperature	28-30°c
Distance	53 laps 306,720 km	Track temperature	35-41°c
Date	September 10, 2006	Humidity	36%
		Wind speed	0.6 m/s

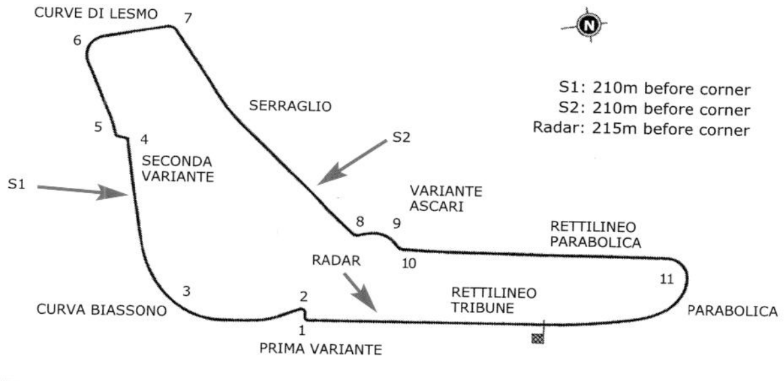

S1: 210m before corner
S2: 210m before corner
Radar: 215m before corner

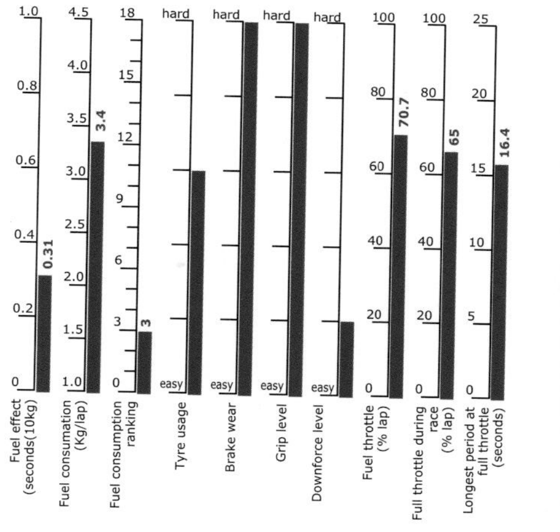

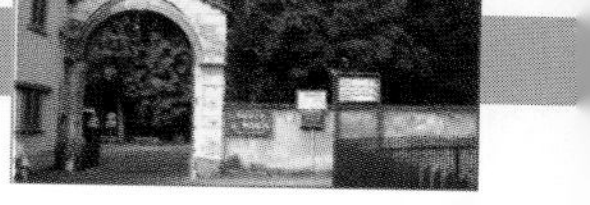

IT WAS ALMOST TOO GOOD TO BE TRUE

Michael Schumacher should never have won the Chinese Grand Prix on the Shanghaï circuit and Fernando Alonso never should have lost it. On lap 14 the Spaniard was already 25 seconds in front of the German. His tyres made the all difference in the rain. Then Fernando made the mistake of changing them and Michael ate into his lead, passed him and went on to score one of the most unexpected wins of his career. Thus, the two rivals left Shanghai on level pegging with 116 points each and 2 races still to go. For Schumacher and his team it was almost too good to be true.

> The rain that flooded the track was a help to Fernando Alonso and the Spaniard banged in his sixth pole of the season and his first since Canada in June.

It was all change in the Midland team that had been renamed Spyker and was in the hands of a Dutch group. Alexandre Prémat was selected as the third driver.
∨

Bridgestone in the doldrums in Shanghais

The Bridgestone tyres had already shown that they were unable to cope with a damp track in the Hungarian Grand Prix part of which was run in wet conditions. At the start of the race Michael Schumacher in a car shod with Japanese rubber was giving away 7 seconds a lap to Fernando Alonso. It was the pits for a driver famous for his wet-weather driving skills.

On the Shanghaï circuit Michael used this talent to hoist himself up onto sixth place on the starting grid. The next Bridgestone user, Webber's Williams, was down in fourteenth place. "*It's what's called a damage limitation exercise,*" said the German after practice.

There were glum faces in the Bridgestone camp. "*We have to admit that our performances in the rain are not good,*" confessed Hisao Suganuma,

the firm's technical director. What was even more discouraging for the Bridgestone runners was that the weather forecast was more rain for the race.

This looked like a godsend to the 2 Renault drivers qualified on the front row. It was all roses and sunshine (despite the murky conditions) for Fernando Alonso who had racked up his sixth pole of the season. The Spaniard had even shaved off his beard and moustache keeping only a tiny goatee as a good luck charm. "*We're very confident,*" he smiled. Of course, you have to finish the race but it's looking good. Today, I was really surprised by the car's performance. I set the quickest times in all phases of qualifying and it was easy as the R26 was so pleasant to drive.*"

In the Renault camp on Saturday the more the rain fell the more the morale rose! The 3 weeks that had elapsed since the Italian Grand Prix had been used to get the cars fully prepared for the last 3 grands prix of the year. "*I hope we're going to win the last three races,*" Alonso went on. "*We were very unlucky in both Hungary and Italy with the loss of a wheel and a blown engine. Without that I'd have had a lead of almost 20 points in the championship and it would have been done and dusted.*"

Whatever the case the Spaniard could not be crowned before the following week's Japanese Grand Prix at the earliest. A race in the rain would be a big help to him even if he refused to admit it: "*Rain is always a lottery. I prefer a grand prix in the dry.*" The outcome was now up to the Chinese Gods!

Alonso continues to fire warning shots across the FIA's bows

On Friday during the drivers' briefing Ralf Schumacher, Mark Webber and Fernando Alonso were elected directors of the GPDA, the Grand Prix Drivers' Association, replacing the outgoing board of Michael Schumacher, David Coulthard and Jarno Trulli.
>∨

When the Spaniard arrived in Shanghaï on Thursday with his moustache and impeccably trimmed beard his face did not betray the slightest doubt despite an increasingly precarious situation. In the space of 6 grands prix his lead over Michael Schumacher had melted from 25 to 2 points. According to him it did not change his approach. "*There's no such thing as a cushion. I tackle each race with the same aim: victory always victory, nothing but victory!*"

At Monza the Renault team had been all

shook up by his relegation. Alonso played down the incident: "*I've banished it from my mind until after the season's over to concentrate on the title. But it'll be part of my memories all my life. I'll never forget Monza.*"

There was not much love lost between the Renault driver and the FIA. On Monday the Federation published a kind of pseudo poll carried out on the Internet about the drivers'

popularity. Michael Schumacher came out on top while Alonso was down in fourth place. He laughed it off: "*I said that F1 is no longer a sport and I stick to that. It's a bit of everything. It's a big show and there's a lot of money at stake what with TV, sponsors etc. The driver is only a cog in the wheel. Things happen in F1 that you don't see in other sports.*"

One in the teeth for the FIA!

Starting grid

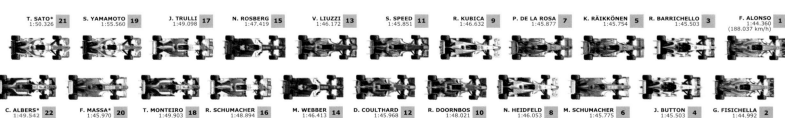

* F. MASSA et T. SATO penalty for an engine exchange (-10 pos.).

C. ALBERS relegated to the back of the grid for having by-passed the weight-in. All his times were cancelled

| T. SATO* 1:50.326 21 | S. YAMAMOTO 1:55.560 19 | J. TRULLI 1:49.098 17 | N. ROSBERG 1:47.419 15 | V. LIUZZI 1:46.172 13 | S. SPEED 1:45.851 11 | R. KUBICA 1:46.632 9 | P. DE LA ROSA 1:45.877 7 | K. RÄIKKÖNEN 1:45.754 5 | R. BARRICHELLO 1:45.503 3 | F. ALONSO 1:44.360 (188.037 km/h) 1 |

| C. ALBERS* 1:49.542 22 | F. MASSA* 1:45.970 20 | T. MONTEIRO 1:49.903 18 | R. SCHUMACHER 1:48.894 16 | M. WEBBER 1:46.413 14 | D. COULTHARD 1:45.968 12 | R. DOORNBOS 1:48.021 10 | N. HEIDFELD 1:46.053 8 | M. SCHUMACHER 1:45.775 6 | J. BUTTON 1:45.503 4 | G. FISICHELLA 1:44.992 2 |

Michael whips up a storm

After the Chinese Grand Prix both drivers had 116 points and Michael Schumacher was in the championship lead for the first time in the 2006 season by virtue of his greater number of victories – seven as against Alonso's six. In Shanghaï the German chances of beating the Spaniard looked very slim as his Bridgestone tyres were unable to cope with the weather conditions. The rainstorm that hit the circuit 2 hours before the start left him little hope of achieving anything other than a damage limitation exercise.

In fact, his result went way beyond his wildest expectations. *"At the start of the race I was surprised to see that I could match the pace of those in front of me. The track was still very wet. Then it began to dry and things began to turn in my favour,"* he stated afterwards. On lap 8 Michael nipped past his former team-mate Rubens Barrichello into fifth but Alonso was already 20 seconds up the road.

He pressed on picking off those in front of him up to his first refuelling stop. This was the crunch moment. *"We had to decide whether I'd keep the same tyres or not,"* he continued. *"When driving I had problems seeing if they were worn but the telemetry showed that I was going quicker and quicker.*

So we took a calculated risk and I kept them on. And it worked!"*

But to win he still had to get past Fisichella. Which he did with a superb overtaking manoeuvre on lap 42 just when the Italian rejoined after his second pit stop having put on dry tyres. *"It was the most delicate part of the race,"* grinned the Ferrari driver. *"I had slid coming out of the pits because we were on a very wet zone. I knew I could overtake him in this spot. I pushed gently but I was still a bit too quick. I slid and I had to drive on the grass but I got through. I really loved that moment!"* That win, the ninety-first and last of his career, was one of his best. The enthusiasm that he showed after his Shanghaï victory made the fact that he was retiring at the end of the season all the more difficult to believe.

^
Victory! In Shanghaï Michael Schumacher racked up the last win of his fabulous career. It was all the sweeter as 2 hours earlier it looked like he hadn't a snowball's chance in hell.

By opting for safety Renault took a risk that cost it a lot

On lap 19, Alonso was 19.4s ahead of everybody, a huge gap in such a short space of time. When he came in for his first pit stop he was full of confidence. Everything went off normally according the strategy decided by the team. The main question was whether or not to change the rain tyres fitted at the start. Normally, the wheels are changed at every refuelling stop but it is a different matter with wet-weather tyres, which are more difficult to heat up and also have grooves that are too deep for a drying track. *"We had to decide what we were going to do together with Fernando and the Michelin engineers,"* confided a member of the team. *"We were so far in front that we didn't think it would cost us too much. So we decided to change the tyres for safety reasons".*

The Spanish driver had pushed so hard at the start of the race that his tyres were very worn. *"I didn't think they'd last until the next stop,"* Alonso admitted; *"Normally, when you put on new rain tyres they take around four or five laps to become smooth. This time they suffered from graining for eight or nine laps."*

These laps were hell for the world champion. He was 4 or 5 seconds slower than his team-mate Fisichella and more importantly Michael Schumacher and had to let them past. He put on slicks during his second refuelling stop and then he flew setting fastest lap after fastest lap and repassing Fisichella into second place (the latter did not put up much of a fight!). But it was too late. Renault and Fernando Alonso had made a small tactical error that was to have serious consequences as it allowed Schumacher to overtake the Spaniard in the championship ratings. Opting for safety Renault had taken a risk: namely, changing only the front tyres. A lap earlier Michael had kept his on. Tactically speaking not taking a risk would have meant basing Alonso's strategy on Schumacher's (whether it was good or bad).

<
22nd lap: Fernando Alonso's first refuelling stop. Unlike Michael Schumacher a lap earlier the Spaniard decided to change his front tyres. It was the crunch moment of the race.

Alonso opened up a gap right from the start. At the end of lap 1 he was already 3 seconds ahead of his team-mate.
v<

Nick Heidfeld in his own version of "3 wheels on my wagon!" Rubens Barrichello hit him up the rear on the last lap and he limped home as best he could. Up until the Brazilian's unexpected puck Nick was heading for fourth place.
v

Back from the void!

Races in the rain provide superb images.
In Shanaghaï, Pedro de la Rosa finished fifth.
He was eighth at the start of the final lap until
Rubens Barrichello decided to play bumper cars.

As Michael Ammermüller took his place Neel Jani opted for the USA

Once again the GP2 championship fulfilled its mission: namely, to allow young drivers to get into the top formula. The 2006 champion, Lewis Hamilton, will probably be the first coloured driver to race in F1- he tested an F1 McLaren 15 days before China- while Nelsinho Piquet Junior, son of the triple world champion was already a member of the Renault team. The week of the Chinese Grand Prix 20-year-old Michael Ammermüller signed a contract as Red Bull's third driver and made his debut on Friday. It was a big disappointment for

Neel Jani, the Toro Rosso team's third driver, who was after the seat filled by Ammermüller. The Swiss was very calm and never showed the slightest emotion throughout the season even if he was never really able to demonstrate his talent as he was running in the conditions dictated by his engineers – with full tanks and worn rubber - contrary to the other drivers who practised on Friday with nearly empty tanks and new tyres. It was a frustrating season for the young Swiss as he was never really able to show what he could do. A young driver

cannot allow his career to stagnate so Jani chose to race in the 2007 Cart Championship, the American equivalent of F1, at the wheel of a car financed by his sponsor Red Bull. "*I think it's easier to shine in Champ Car and come back to F1 rather than vegetate at Toro Ross and be thrown out at the end of the year,*" he argued. "*So not to stagnate I had no choice. And maybe I'll finally earn a little money for a change.*"
Neel said he did not want the third seat at Red Bull taken by Michael Ammermüler: "*I could have been Red Bull's third driver but next year the third drivers will not run on the Friday any more and testing is limited to 30 000 kilometres par year and per team. The race drivers will do everything. It was the wrong choice.*"
Jani admitted that he knew nothing about Champ Car. "*I watched a race on TV for the first time...last week! I've never been there but I know that the cars push out around 750 bhp and that they've got no driver aids. The races are long so it should be good practice.*"
What is important is not to stay there like Sébastien Bourdais. "*Sébastien did not win straight away, only in his second year. I have to win in my first one. If I manage I'll have every possibility of coming back into F1. It's risky but you have to take risks in your life.*"

Week end chatter

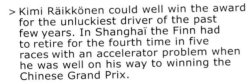

> Kimi Räikkönen could well win the award for the unluckiest driver of the past few years. In Shanghaï the Finn had to retire for the fourth time in five races with an accelerator problem when he was well on his way to winning the Chinese Grand Prix.

> It was Nico Rosberg's first visit to China and like most Westerners he was fascinated by the Wild West aspect of the country, the abruptness of the contacts with its inhabitants plus the incredible economic progress in some cities. On Wednesday he drove his

Williams in the streets of Guangzou, not far from Shanghaï: "*I think it's one of the quickest developing towns in the world,*" he said. His demonstration took place behind closed doors, as spectators were not allowed to attend. At the track the tickets were also reserved for the elite; they cost 400 dollars, 20 times the salary in rural areas!

> Ferrari announced that it had signed a contract to supply engines to the new Spyker team (ex-Midland, ex-Jordan) from 2007 onwards.

Practice

All the time trials

N° Driver	Nat.	N° Chassis - Engine [Nbr. GP]	Pos. Free 1 Friday	Laps	Pos. Free 2 Friday	Laps	Pos. Free 3 Saturday	Laps	Pos. Q1 Saturday	Laps	Pos. Q2 Saturday	Laps	Pos. Super Pole Saturday	Laps
1. Fernando Alonso	E	Renault R26 04 [1]			6. 1:36.739	10	2. 1:40.365	7	1. 1:44.128	5	1. 1:43.951	6	1. **1:44.360**	10
2. Giancarlo Fisichella	I	Renault R26 06 [1]			10. 1:37.718	12	8. 1:41.691	6	2. 1:44.378	4	2. 1:44.336	6	2. **1:44.992**	9
3. Kimi Räikkönen	FIN	McLaren MP4-21 05 - Mercedes [2]	18. 1:45.890	4	21. 1:39.179	4	22.	2	4. 1:44.909	7	8. 1:45.622	6	5. **1:45.754**	9
4. Pedro de la Rosa	E	McLaren MP4-21 06 - Mercedes [1]			12. 1:38.022	9	9. 1:41.823	7	3. 1:44.808	6	5. 1:45.095	8	7. **1:45.877**	9
5. Michael Schumacher	D	Ferrari 248 F1 255 [1]	4. 1:37.712	4	5. 1:36.641	12	1. 1:40.193	8	14. 1:47.366	6	9. 1:45.660	9	6. **1:45.775**	9
6. Felipe Massa	BR	Ferrari 248 F1 256 [2->1]			4. 1:36.599	8	15. 1:43.500	10	13. 1:47.231	6	13. **1:45.970**	9		
7. Ralf Schumacher	D	Toyota TF106/10B [1]	21.	2	17. 1:38.888	14	19. 1:46.023	12	17. **1:48.894**	9				
8. Jarno Trulli	I	Toyota TF106/08B [1]	20.	2	18. 1:38.959	11	17. 1:44.027	14	18. **1:49.098**	9				
9. Mark Webber	AUS	Williams FW28 03 - Cosworth [1]			13. 1:38.045	6	6. 1:41.287	10	16. 1:48.560	9	15. **1:46.413**	9		
10. Nico Rosberg	D	Williams FW28 05 - Cosworth [2]			23. 1:39.522	15	11. 1:42.588	11	15. 1:47.535	9	16. **1:47.419**	9		
11. Rubens Barrichello	BR	Honda RA106-01 [2]	12. 1:39.217	4	16. 1:38.276	16	14. 1:43.448	9	12. 1:47.072	9	6. 1:45.288	8	3. **1:45.503**	9
12. Jenson Button	GB	Honda RA106-05 [2]	3. 1:37.291	4	11. 1:37.861	10	3. 1:40.590	12	6. 1:45.809	9	3. 1:44.662	9	4. **1:45.503**	9
914. David Coulthard	GB	Red Bull RB2 3 - Ferrari [2]	22.	1	26. 1:40.155	15	10. 1:41.836	18	7. 1:45.931	8	12. **1:45.968**	7		
15. Robert Doornbos	NL	Red Bull RB2 5 - Ferrari [2]	23.	2	27. 1:40.214	15	18. 1:45.434	12	11. 1:46.387	7	10. 1:45.747	8	10. **1:48.021**	9
16. Nick Heidfeld	D	BMW Sauber F1.06-04 [2]	19.	1	14. 1:38.062	11	13. 1:43.216	5	10. 1:46.249	8	4. 1:45.055	9	8. **1:46.053**	10
17. Robert Kubica	PL	BMW Sauber F1.06-09 [2]	8. 1:38.062	6	22. 1:39.217	5	21.	1	8. 1:46.049	8	7. 1:45.576	9	9. **1:46.632**	9
18. Tiago Monteiro	P	Spyker Midland M16-03 - Toyota [2]	16. 1:39.947	7	9. 1:37.698	13	12. 1:42.612	14	20. **1:49.903**	6				
19. Christijan Albers	NL	Spyker Midland M16-02 - Toyota [2]	14. 1:39.494	6	28. 1:40.319	14	7. 1:41.463	11	19. **1:49.542**	8				
20. Vitantonio Liuzzi	I	Toro Rosso STR01 03 - Cosworth [2]	11. 1:39.000	6	24. 1:39.570	20	4. 1:40.795	9	5. 1:45.564	6	14. **1:46.172**	9		
21. Scott Speed	USA	Toro Rosso STR01 02 - Cosworth [2]	13. 1:39.428	7	19. 1:39.080	18	5. 1:41.150	11	9. 1:46.222	8	11. **1:45.851**	7		
22. Takuma Sato	J	Super Aguri SA06-03 - Honda [2->1]	15. 1:39.887	8	29. 1:41.315	9	16. 1:43.722	12	21. **1:50.326**	6				
23. Sakon Yamamoto	J	Super Aguri SA06-04 - Honda [2]	17. 1:41.415	10	25. 1:39.636	22	20. 1:46.850	10	22. **1:55.560**	7				
35. Alexander Wurz	A	Williams FW28 04 - Cosworth	1. 1:35.574	21	1. 1:35.539	26								
36. Anthony Davidson	GB	Honda RA106-03	2. 1:35.591	26	3. 1:35.714	30								
37. Michael Ammermuller	D	Red Bull RB2 1 - Ferrari	9. 1:38.460	18	8. 1:37.678	26								
38. Sebastian Vettel	D	BMW Sauber F1.06-08	7. 1:37.913	24	2. 1:35.579	23								
39. Alexandre Premat	F	Spyker Midland M16-01 - Toyota	6. 1:37.787	24	15. 1:38.098	26								
40. Neel Jani	CH	Toro Rosso STR01 01 - Cosworth	5. 1:37.734	21	20. 1:39.118	28								
41. Franck Montagny	F	Super Aguri SA06-02 - Honda	10. 1:38.464	19	7. 1:37.278	26								

Fastest lap overall
F. Alonso 1:43.951 (188,777 km/h)

Maximum speed

N° Driver	S1 Qualifs	Pos.	S1 Race	Pos.	S2 Qualifs	Pos.	S2 Race	Pos.	Finish Qualifs	Pos.	Finish Race	Pos.	Radar Qualifs	Pos.	Radar Race	Pos.
1. F. Alonso	275,2	2	278,8	4	264,2	5	270,9	4	251,0	3	253,4	5	311,5	2	313,2	8
2. G. Fisichella	275,2	1	278,9	3	265,4	2	271,7	2	250,5	5	254,9	3	311,9	1	317,1	3
3. K. Räikkönen	273,0	4	277,4	5	263,6	7	265,8	14	251,5	1	251,0	10	306,0	6	310,3	12
4. P. de la Rosa	273,6	3	276,7	6	263,9	6	270,8	5	251,5	2	254,7	4	309,7	3	315,6	4
5. M. Schumacher	272,4	5	279,8	1	265,8	1	271,6	3	250,6	4	256,2	1	306,9	4	320,4	2
6. F. Massa	272,1	6	279,7	2	265,0	3	273,6	1	246,9	13	255,0	2	305,5	8	324,4	1
7. R. Schumacher	264,8	21	274,7	7	256,8	17	267,9	7	244,1	19	249,5	15	294,8	18	311,2	11
8. J. Trulli	266,5	18	272,1	15	256,6	19	261,5	21	244,5	18	245,6	20	294,3	19	308,8	18
9. M. Webber	267,8	15	270,4	18	258,8	15	265,8	13	247,4	8	251,6	9	298,5	16	305,4	22
10. N. Rosberg	266,9	17	272,3	14	259,2	14	265,7	15	246,8	14	251,6	8	294,0	20	309,4	15
11. R. Barrichello	265,6	19	270,4	19	258,0	16	263,8	17	246,3	15	248,7	17	298,5	15	307,5	19
12. J. Button	267,0	16	271,0	16	260,6	9	266,6	10	246,0	16	250,2	14	302,0	12	313,2	9
14. D. Coulthard	270,7	8	273,1	11	259,6	12	267,1	9	248,2	7	250,4	12	302,0	13	314,5	7
15. R. Doornbos	270,6	9	274,5	8	260,4	10	268,5	6	249,0	6	251,6	7	305,8	7	315,0	5
16. N. Heidfeld	270,4	10	272,4	13	263,2	8	265,4	16	247,3	9	251,0	11	303,3	10	309,1	17
17. R. Kubica	270,8	7	274,5	9	265,0	4	266,0	12	247,0	12	250,4	13	306,3	5	314,7	6
18. T. Monteiro	265,2	20	270,1	20	253,5	22	261,1	22	240,8	21	243,4	22	292,8	22	306,6	21
19. C. Albers	264,1	22	269,3	22	254,4	21	262,7	19	240,0	22	244,7	21	293,3	21	307,4	20
20. V. Liuzzi	268,9	12	270,8	17	259,6	13	262,5	20	247,3	10	246,9	19	305,1	9	310,2	13
21. S. Speed	268,5	13	269,6	21	259,6	11	263,0	18	247,1	11	248,0	18	301,5	14	313,0	10
22. T. Sato	268,1	14	273,0	12	256,5	20	267,4	8	244,6	17	253,0	6	295,6	17	309,2	16
23. S. Yamamoto	269,1	11	273,2	10	256,7	18	266,5	11	243,4	20	249,4	16	302,7	11	309,5	14

Race

Classification & Retirements

Pos.	Driver	Constructor	Tyres	Laps	Time	Average	
1.	M. Schumacher	Ferrari	B	56	1:37:32.747	187,644 km/h	
2.	F. Alonso	Renault	M	56	+ 3.121	187,544 km/h	
3.	G. Fisichella	Renault	M	56	+ 44.197	186,238 km/h	
4.	J. Button	Honda	M	56	+ 1:12.056	185,362 km/h	
5.	P. de la Rosa	McLaren Mercedes	M	56	+ 1:17.137	185,203 km/h	
6.	R. Barrichello	Honda	M	56	+ 1:19.131	185,141 km/h	
7.	N. Heidfeld	BMW	M	56	+ 1:31.979	184,741 km/h	
8.	M. Webber	Williams Cosworth	B	56	+ 1:43.588	184,381 km/h	
9.	D. Coulthard	RBR Ferrari	M	56	+ 1:43.796	184,374 km/h	
10.	V. Liuzzi	STR Cosworth	M	55	1 lap	183,052 km/h	
11.	N. Rosberg	Williams Cosworth	B	55	1 lap	183,017 km/h	
12.	R. Doornbos	RBR Ferrari	M	55	1 lap	182,677 km/h	
13.	R. Kubica	BMW	M	55	1 lap	182,253 km/h	
14.	S. Speed	STR Cosworth	M	55	1 lap	181,177 km/h	
15.	C. Albers	MF1 Toyota	B	53	3 laps	174,535 km/h	○ +25.0 penalty
16.	S. Yamamoto	Aguri Honda	B	52	4 laps	174,047 km/h	

	Driver	Constructor	Tyres	Laps	Reason
DQ[14]	T. Sato	Aguri Honda	B	55	1 lap disqualified
	R. Schumacher	Toyota	B	49	Oil pressure
	F. Massa	Ferrari	B	44	Collision with Coulthard
	J. Trulli	Toyota	B	38	Tyre pressure
	T. Monteiro	MF1 Toyota	B	37	Spin and stall
	K. Räikkönen	McLaren Mercedes	M	18	Throttle failure

Fastest laps

	Driver	Time	Laps	Average
1.	F. Alonso	1:37.586	49	201,090 km/h
2.	M. Schumacher	1:38.553	50	199,117 km/h
3.	P. de la Rosa	1:39.149	45	197,920 km/h
4.	N. Heidfeld	1:39.164	53	197,890 km/h
5.	J. Button	1:39.206	51	197,806 km/h
6.	G. Fisichella	1:39.332	53	197,555 km/h
7.	F. Massa	1:39.397	42	197,426 km/h
8.	S. Speed	1:39.681	49	196,863 km/h
9.	R. Barrichello	1:39.749	52	196,729 km/h
10.	R. Doornbos	1:39.801	52	196,627 km/h
11.	R. Schumacher	1:39.823	47	196,583 km/h
12.	M. Webber	1:39.907	44	196,418 km/h
13.	R. Kubica	1:40.193	51	195,857 km/h
14.	N. Rosberg	1:40.471	52	195,316 km/h
15.	D. Coulthard	1:40.549	52	195,164 km/h
16.	T. Sato	1:40.856	48	194,570 km/h
17.	C. Albers	1:41.483	50	193,368 km/h
18.	V. Liuzzi	1:41.710	53	192,936 km/h
19.	S. Yamamoto	1:41.847	42	192,677 km/h
20.	K. Räikkönen	1:44.094	14	188,518 km/h
21.	J. Trulli	1:44.787	24	187,271 km/h
22.	T. Monteiro	1:45.356	35	186,259 km/h

Pit stops

	Driver	Laps	Duration	Stop	Total
1.	R. Doornbos	1	30.705	1	30.705
2.	J. Button	15	24.936	1	24.936
3.	K. Räikkönen	16	26.323	1	26.323
4.	R. Barrichello	17	26.032	1	26.032
5.	P. de la Rosa	17	25.173	1	25.173
6.	S. Yamamoto	18	30.392	1	30.392
7.	N. Rosberg	20	25.905	1	25.905
8.	M. Schumacher	21	24.313	1	24.313
9.	M. Webber	21	24.043	1	24.043
10.	S. Yamamoto	20	27.722	2	58.114
11.	F. Alonso	22	25.654	1	25.654
12.	G. Fisichella	23	23.759	1	23.759
13.	T. Monteiro	23	25.848	1	25.848
14.	R. Kubica	24	23.936	1	23.936
15.	S. Speed	24	25.436	1	25.436
16.	R. Schumacher	24	28.846	1	28.846
17.	N. Heidfeld	25	23.287	1	23.287
18.	J. Trulli	25	28.473	1	28.473
19.	T. Sato	25	24.359	1	24.359
20.	R. Kubica	25	28.954	2	52.890
21.	C. Albers	25	26.680	1	26.680
22.	C. Albers	26	33.183	2	59.863
23.	R. Doornbos	28	26.110	2	56.815
24.	F. Massa	29	27.862	1	27.862
25.	D. Coulthard	29	27.941	1	27.941
26.	V. Liuzzi	31	26.707	1	26.707
27.	S. Yamamoto	30	15.131	3	1:13.245
28.	N. Rosberg	32	26.596	2	52.501
29.	S. Speed	33	25.390	2	50.826
30.	J. Button	34	26.570	2	51.506
31.	M. Webber	34	27.585	2	51.628
32.	F. Massa	34	24.893	2	52.755
33.	F. Alonso	35	35.892	2	1:01.546
34.	S. Yamamoto	33	26.945	4	1:40.190
35.	P. de la Rosa	36	26.896	2	52.069
36.	R. Barrichello	37	26.176	2	52.208
37.	R. Doornbos	37	23.975	3	1:20.790
38.	T. Monteiro	37	27.644	2	53.492
39.	T. Sato	38	25.291	2	49.650
40.	C. Albers	37	27.108	3	1:26.971
41.	D. Coulthard	39	24.347	2	52.288
42.	M. Schumacher	40	24.570	2	48.883
43.	N. Heidfeld	40	24.271	2	47.558
44.	G. Fisichella	41	23.403	2	47.162
45.	R. Kubica	40	23.625	3	1:16.515

Race leader

Driver	Laps in the lead	Nbr of Laps
F. Alonso	1 > 22	22
G. Fisichella	23	1
F. Alonso	24 > 29	6
G. Fisichella	30 > 41	12
M. Schumacher	42 > 56	15

Driver	Nbr of Laps	Kilometers
F. Alonso	28	152,438 km
M. Schumacher	15	81,765 km
G. Fisichella	13	70,863 km

Gaps on the leader board

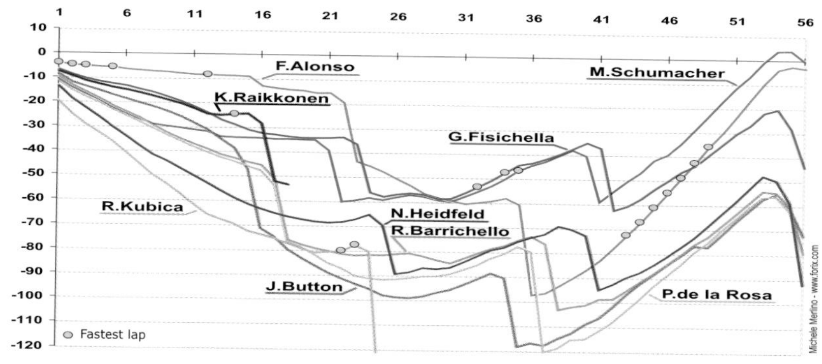

1 6 11 16 21 26 31 36 41 46 51 56
10 0 -10 -20 -30 -40 -50 -60 -70 -80 -90 -100 -110 -120
F.Alonso
M.Schumacher
K.Raikkonen
G.Fisichella
R.Kubica
N.Heidfeld
R.Barrichello
J.Button
P.de la Rosa
Fastest lap
Michele Merlino - www.forix.com

Lap chart

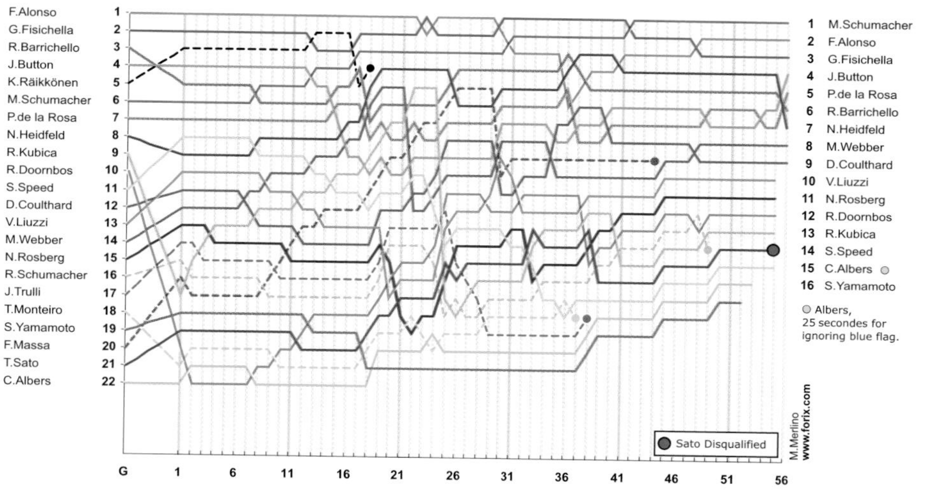

F.Alonso 1
G.Fisichella 2
R.Barrichello 3
J.Button 4
K.Räikkönen 5
M.Schumacher 6
P.de la Rosa 7
N.Heidfeld 8
R.Kubica 9
R.Doornbos 10
S.Speed 11
D.Coulthard 12
V.Liuzzi 13
M.Webber 14
N.Rosberg 15
R.Schumacher 16
J.Trulli 17
T.Monteiro 18
S.Yamamoto 19
F.Massa 20
T.Sato 21
C.Albers 22
1 M.Schumacher
2 F.Alonso
3 G.Fisichella
4 J.Button
5 P.de la Rosa
6 R.Barrichello
7 N.Heidfeld
8 M.Webber
9 D.Coulthard
10 V.Liuzzi
11 N.Rosberg
12 R.Doornbos
13 R.Kubica
14 S.Speed
15 C.Albers
16 S.Yamamoto
Albers, 25 secondes for ignoring blue flag.
Sato Disqualified
G 1 6 11 16 21 26 31 36 41 46 51 56
M.Merlino www.forix.com

Championships 16/18

Drivers

1. M. Schumacher ..... Ferrari .... 7 🏆 .. 116
2. F. Alonso .... Renault .... 6 🏆 .. 116
3. G. Fisichella .... Renault .... 1 🏆 63
4. F. Massa .... Ferrari .... 1 🏆 62
5. K. Räikkönen .... McLaren Mercedes 57
6. J. Button .... Honda .... 1 🏆 45
7. R. Barrichello .... Honda 28
8. J. Montoya .... McLaren Mercedes 26
9. N. Heidfeld .... BMW 22
10. P. de la Rosa .... McLaren Mercedes 18
11. R. Schumacher ..... Toyota 18
12. D. Coulthard .... RBR Ferrari 14
13. J. Trulli .... Toyota 12
14. M. Webber .... Williams Cosworth 7
15. J. Villeneuve .... BMW 7
16. R. Kubica .... BMW 6
17. N. Rosberg .... Williams Cosworth 4
18. C. Klien .... RBR Ferrari 2
19. V. Liuzzi .... STR Cosworth 1
20. S. Speed .... STR Cosworth 0
21. T. Monteiro .... MF1 Toyota 0
22. C. Albers .... MF1 Toyota 0
23. T. Sato .... Aguri Honda 0
24. R. Doornbos .... RBR Ferrari 0
25. Y. Ide .... Aguri Honda 0
26. F. Montagny .... Aguri Honda 0
27. S. Yamamoto .... Aguri Honda 0

Constructors

1. Mild Seven Renault F1 Team .... 7 🏆 ... 179
2. Scuderia Ferrari Marlboro .... 8 🏆 ... 178
3. Team McLaren Mercedes 101
4. Lucky Strike Honda Racing F1 Team ... 1 🏆 73
5. BMW Sauber F1 Team 35
6. Panasonic Toyota Racing 30
7. Red Bull Racing 16
8. Williams F1 Team 11
9. Scuderia Toro Rosso 1
10. Spyker M F1 Team 0
11. Super Aguri Formula 1 0

The circuit

Name	Shanghai International Circuit; Shanghai	Weather	Cloudy, warm
		Air temperature	22-23°c
Lenght	5451 m	Track temperature	22-24°c
Distance	56 laps, 305,066 km	Humidity	88%
Date	October 1, 2006	Wind speed	0.2 m/s

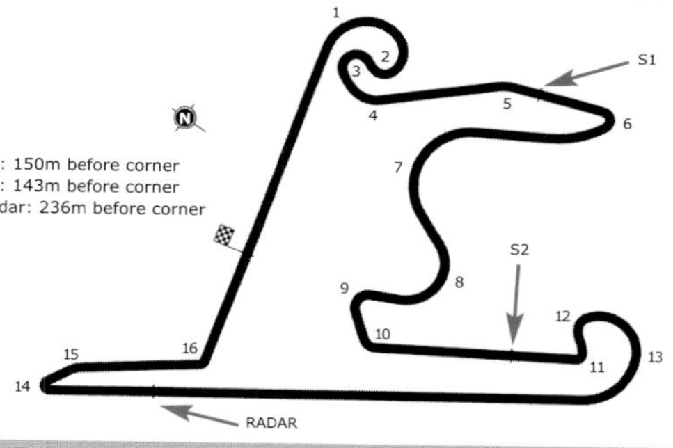

1 2 3 4 5 6 7 8 9 10 11 12 13 14 15 16
S1
S2
RADAR

S1: 150m before corner
S2: 143m before corner
Radar: 236m before corner

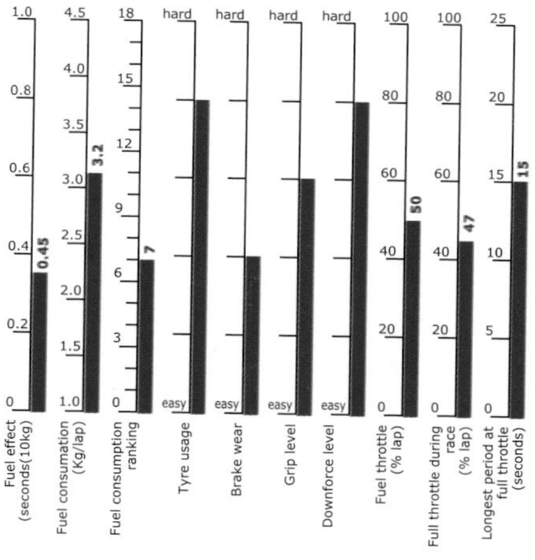

Fuel effect (seconds/10kg) 0.45
Fuel consumption (Kg/lap) 3.2
Fuel consumption ranking 7
Tyre usage
Brake wear
Grip level
Downforce level
Fuel throttle (% lap) 80
Full throttle during race (% lap) 47
Longest period at full throttle (seconds) 15
hard
easy

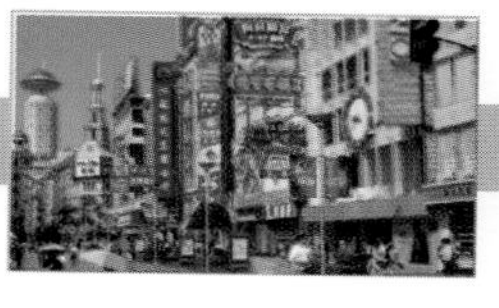

ALMOST ALL OVER BAR THE SHOUTING!

The 2 Ferraris monopolised the front row for the Japanese Grand Prix and another victory for Michael Schumacher looked on the cards.
With only 16 laps to go to the chequered flag his engine exploded in a cloud of white smoke.
And so against all expectations Fernando Alonso won the race giving him a ten-point lead over his rival. It was almost all over bar the shouting. On the rostrum the Spaniard jumped for joy just like Michael would have done.

^
It was Felipe's second pole of the season after Turkey.

The Suzuka circuit is one of the greatest. Everybody was sorry to leave it and its fun fair and environment as well as its unique layout.
v

Massa on pole. Briatore ballistic

The 2 Ferraris set the 2 quickest times in practice locking out the front row for the fifth time in the 2006 season. Felipe was on pole but he did not hide the fact that he would let Michael Schumacher pass him. *"I'm here to help Ferrari win the two titles,"* he acknowledged.

In qualifying the Bridgestone tyres were far superior to the Michelins as proved by the presence of the 2 Toyotas on the second row. The Renaults of Alonso and Fisichella were on row 3. Flavio Briatore was very unhappy with his cars' poor qualifying performance and took out his ire on Massa after practice. The on-board cameras showed that Massa did his best to slow Alonso in the opening minutes of the session. Flavio said that it was almost the same situation that had led to Alonso being penalised at Monza when accused of baulking the Brazilian. However, the similarity stopped there.

The Ferrari driver only hindered Fernando at the very start of the session long before the drivers start going for a time. In Italy, on the other hand, the Spaniard was supposed to have baulked Massa on his last and quickest lap. These differences did not matter to Flag. *"Massa is just a kid nothing more,"* he roared. *"He's a little guy in every sense of the word. He was in front of Fernando and braked to slow him down."*

Fernando was furious and yelled in his helmet. *"They'll speak about it in race control and they'll do nothing. You'll see. We already know what the reply is."* It being understood that race control would never sanction a Ferrari driver.

A packed house at Suzuka for the final grand prix

For the first time since 1994 the Japanese Grand Prix was a sell-out! All 120 000 tickets were purchased in advance. The 2006 race was the last F1 event to be held on the Suzuka circuit as in 2007 Fuji will host the grand prix so the spectators grabbed the last opportunity to see F1 cars on the famous Japanese track. Michel Schumacher's retirement and the uncertainty surrounding the championship also contributed to the sell-out.

Most of the drivers were sorry about not coming back to Suzuka with the exception of Kimi Raïkkönen even though he won the race in 2005. The Finn said it was perfectly all right with him if he never came back to this circuit. Ron Dennis was also happy to leave Suzuka: *"When I arrived in my hotel room it smelled of damp and was not aired. It hadn't been used since the previous year. While circuits like Silverstone and Hockenheim are fighting to keep their grand prix Suzuka has never done anything with this in mind. It's normal that the event has gone to people who are more motivated."*

Starting grid

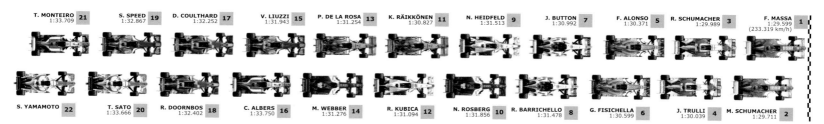

T. MONTEIRO 21 1:33.709	S. SPEED 19 1:32.867	D. COULTHARD 17 1:32.252	V. LIUZZI 15 1:31.943	P. DE LA ROSA 13 1:31.254	K. RÄIKKÖNEN 11 1:30.827	N. HEIDFELD 9 1:31.513	J. BUTTON 7 1:30.992	F. ALONSO 5 1:30.371	R. SCHUMACHER 3 1:29.989	F. MASSA 1 1:29.599 (233.319 km/h)
S. YAMAMOTO 22 1:33.666	T. SATO 20 1:32.402	R. DOORNBOS 18	C. ALBERS 16 1:33.750	M. WEBBER 14 1:31.276	R. KUBICA 12 1:31.094	N. ROSBERG 10 1:31.856	R. BARRICHELLO 8 1:31.478	G. FISICHELLA 6 1:30.599	J. TRULLI 4 1:30.039	M. SCHUMACHER 2 1:29.711

Fernando Alonso only a point away from happiness. He exploded with joy in his helmet

The first 36 laps of the Japanese Grand saw a breath-taking battle between Michael Schumacher and Fernando Alonso. 5.4 seconds separated them at the end of lap 13 when the Spaniard managed to get past Ralf Schuùmacher who had been holding him up. On lap 31 before the second round of refuelling stops the gap was exactly the same!

Michael Schumacher's race and title hopes went up in a cloud of white smoke just after his second stop. His Ferrari's engine let go without warning. It was a body blow to the whole Italian team that had been working flat out over the previous months. "*It was a huge disappointment,*" admitted Jean Todt. "*Up till then the race was panning out perfectly and we well well-placed to win both world titles. But the engine went and we've only ourselves to blame.*"

Michael Schumacher did not blame anyone. He came to his pit on foot and hugged all his mechanics one after another. "*That's racing. I don't feel sad,*" he commented. "*Sometimes you win, sometimes you lose. That's what makes life exciting. We shouldn't be disappointed. Instead we should feel proud of ourselves. After the Canadian Grand Prix we were 25 points behind Alonso and nobody believed that we'd still got a chance. We've managed to keep the championship alive up to here and that's a victory in itself.*"

The euphoria in the Renault camp after the race was beyond description. Flavio Briatore was so overcome that he was unable to get up onto the rostrum. Fernando Alonso let out a scream

of joy on lap 37 when he passed the stricken Ferrari. "*When I saw the smoke, I thought it was a Spyker,*" laughed the Spaniard. "*I was trying not to slide on the oil when I suddenly realised it was a Ferrari. I screamed. This win is a fantastic surprise.*"

After that Alonso lifted off and concentrated on making it to the chequered flag. He had the 2006 title in his pocket (almost). All he needed was one point from the Brazilian race.

^
With 16 laps to go to the finish Michael Schumacher and Ferrari were in front in both championships. When the chequered flag fell it was Fernando Alonso who had a 10-point lead.

Michael Schumacher reckoned it was all over

They started with the same number of points. When Fernando Alonso crossed the finishing line 53 laps later his victory gave him a 10-point lead over Michael Schumacher.

To pull back 10 points in a single race was verging on the miraculous. To do so Michael had to win the Brazilian Grand Prix and Alonso had to finish outside the first eight. The German adopted a realistic outlook: "*I don't want to go to Brazil hoping to win the title. That would mean that Fernando would have to retire and*

it's not very nice to want a rival to retire. That's not how I want to win."

In the battle for the constructors' title Ferrari was only 9 points behind Renault. "*Nine points is not impossible. We're going to do everything we can to win,*" he stated. "*Brazil will be the last race of my career and I'm going to try and keep as many memories from it as possible. Whatever the outcome I'll come away happy.*" A bit of wisdom there!

That evening Jean Todt saw things in a realistic

light. "*To win the world championship, we need a good car, good tyres, good drivers, and good reliability, which is what we lacked. It's been our weak point this season and we've had to change engines on too many occasions which has cost us 10 places on the grid.*"

Michael was unlucky at Suzuka. It was the first time he had suffered engine failure since France 2000! Fate had caught up with him two races from the end of his career.

A glimmer of hope

Takuma Sato and the Super Aguri team were racing on home turf at Suzuka owned by Honda. The Japanese driver started from twentieth on the grid and finished fifteenth. His team-mate Sakon Yamamoto saw the flag in 17th place giving the Aguri squad its best result of the season.

Mathematics catch up with Michael Schumacher

Early on in the race after Michael went into the lead lap 3 with Alonso behind him and the gap between the two drivers varied between 5 or 6 seconds despite their efforts to increase or reduce it.

They were locked in a ruthless battle in which they were flat out without any compromise or thought for their cars. The tenths gained or lost here and there when lapping a tail-ender assumed enormous proportions. In the Ferrari and Renault pits all nails were chewed down to the quick.

The crunch point came on lap 37. In a fraction of a second the whole face of the race changed. Without warning Michael Schumacher's Ferrari's engine let go in a cloud of white smoke. A wave of despondency gripped the whole of the Ferrari pit. The efforts of many months hard work had just vanished like the last notes of the V8.

So what could have happened in the block of the no.5 Ferrari? Why should an F1 engine fail? *"You must remember that Formula is are prototypes,' said Schumacher. "This kind of thing can occur, it's racing."*

Denis Chevrier the Renault trackside engineer gave a slightly more scientific explanation. *"Suzuka is a very hard circuit on engines, especially this year with the V8s. Here the accelerator pedal is flat to the floor on over 65% of the total length. The engines have very little time to breathe."*

Thus, the engineers have to reduce the revs to avoid going into the red zone. *"We define a rev limit that we stick to on each circuit"*, Chevrier went on. *"I think that like us Ferrari were at the limit of their engine's potential but I'm sure they didn't take any risks. They must have been within their rev range when, the engine went."*

The driver can reduce or increase his engine power when it under full load to overtake a rival or he can lift off and nurse it when there is no longer any danger. In the Renault the drivers have a switch with 5 positions. When the standard position, for example, is no.2 they can use no.5 briefly to pass another car. When the engine is running a computer records around 30 parameters in a black box, which enables the engine failure to be retraced, and also to see it coming in practice. Before being fitted into a chassis the V8 covers thousands of kilometres on a test bed to simulate complete grands prix. But engines still fail. "Several things can cause the break-down," said the Renault engineer. *"It can come from the valves, pistons, connecting rods and crankshafts." "If the distribution fails everything is bust. If the connecting rods breach the sump, everything is broken. If the valves go through the pistons, they cause mayhem. Each time the pieces rip through the sleeves out comes the oil."* Hence the typical, much-feared white clouds of smoke.

When the engine blows completely there is not much to be learned from examining it. All that remains is the black box. *"With each breakage we survey all the parameters measured. We trace all their deviations just before the explosion, and we can generally determine the origin."* This is to correct the causes for the next grand prix. When Fernando Alonso's V8 went at Monza the Renault test team got down to the job of tracing the failure and managed to find it. *"We calculate a risk factor for each part in the engine (over 3000) and when we assemble one we have a kind of global reliability envelope limited to the least reliable part"*. When we modify the engine we define the new rev range that it can tolerate, an extra 250 rpm for example. These calculations are somewhat empirical. You have to have experience. Above all when you increase the revs the stresses on the parts increase in an exponential manner.

The last time a Ferrari engine went in a race on Michael Schumacher's car was in the French Grand Prix in the year 2000. Overall the engine failures were down to his team-mates Rubens Barrichello and Felipe Massa, which ended up by being a real challenge to the laws of probability.

Thus, the failure on lap 37 demonstrated that even Schumacher could not beat statistics even if he was only 2 races way from retirement.

Albers – Massa: spectacular breakage and a slow puncture

Both Toyotas qualified on
the second row, their best
performance of the
season and they went on
to finish in the points.
Another 2006 first.

On lap 21 Christijan Albers' Spyker was the victim of a spectacular incident on the straight. He lost his rear wing, half the rear drive train and the right-hand rear wheel. The team was not really able to explain what had happened. *"We're going to have to study the incident,"* said Dominic Harlow, the technical director.

Felipe Massa suffered a slow puncture and the team was forced to call him in on lap 13, three earlier than planned. This prevented Michael's team-mate from staying in front of Alonso. The Brazilian rejoined behind Nick Heidfeld and remained stuck behind the German while the Spaniard got past him in the pits. *"That puncture cost me victory,"* he groaned after the race.

On lap 21 Christijan
Albers' rear drive train
exploded. An F1 first.

results

Practice

All the time trials

N° Driver	Nat.	N° Chassis - Engine [Nbr. GP]	Pos. Free 1 Friday	Laps	Pos. Free 2 Friday	Laps	Pos. Free 3 Saturday	Laps	Pos. Q1 Saturday	Laps	Pos. Q2 Saturday	Laps	Pos. Super Pole Saturday	Laps
1. Fernando Alonso	E	Renault R26 04 [2]	19.	1	4. 1:34.863	5	5. 1:32.555	14	6. 1:30.976	3	8. 1:30.357	3	5. **1:30.371**	10
2. Giancarlo Fisichella	I	Renault R26 06 [2]	21.	1	1. 1:34.337	8	4. 1:32.527	13	11. 1:31.696	4	6. 1:30.306	3	6. **1:30.599**	10
3. Kimi Räikkönen	FIN	McLaren MP4-21 05 - Mercedes [1]	14.	1	10. 1:35.367	5	8. 1:32.730	12	15. 1:32.080	3	11. **1:30.827**	6		
4. Pedro de la Rosa	E	McLaren MP4-21 06 - Mercedes [2]	23.	1	8. 1:35.064	6	12. 1:33.163	12	9. 1:31.581	6	13. **1:31.254**	6		
5. Michael Schumacher	D	Ferrari 248 F1 255 [2]			3. 1:34.565	10	1. 1:30.653	13	8. 1:31.279	3	1. 1:28.954	3	2. **1:29.711**	11
6. Felipe Massa	BR	Ferrari 248 F1 256 [2]			2. 1:34.408	10	10. 1:32.790	15	1. 1:30.112	3	2. 1:29.830	3	1. **1:29.599**	10
7. Ralf Schumacher	D	Toyota TF106/10B [1]	26.	1	11. 1:35.375	12	2. 1:31.863	15	4. 1:30.595	6	5. 1:30.299	3	3. **1:29.989**	10
8. Jarno Trulli	I	Toyota TF106/08B [1]	25.	1	9. 1:35.343	12	20. 1:34.118	15	2. 1:30.420	6	3. 1:30.204	3	4. **1:30.039**	10
9. Mark Webber	AUS	Williams FW28 03 - Cosworth [2]	12.	1	14. 1:35.866	5	15. 1:33.339	17	10. 1:31.647	6	14. **1:31.276**	5		
10. Nico Rosberg	D	Williams FW28 05 - Cosworth [1]	13.	1	15. 1:36.176	10	7. 1:32.730	18	3. 1:30.585	6	7. 1:30.321	6	10. **1:31.856**	10
11. Rubens Barrichello	BR	Honda RA106-01 [1]	24.	1	13. 1:35.528	10	18. 1:33.748	16	14. 1:31.972	5	10. 1:30.598	6	8. **1:31.478**	10
12. Jenson Button	GB	Honda RA106-05 [1]	27.	1	7. 1:35.002	6	3. 1:32.310	12	5. 1:30.847	6	4. 1:30.268	6	7. **1:30.992**	10
14. David Coulthard	GB	Red Bull RB2 3 - Ferrari [1]	18.	1	22. 1:37.596	6	16. 1:33.451	16	17. **1:32.252**	6				
15. Robert Doornbos	NL	Red Bull RB2 5 - Ferrari [1]	16.	1	25. 1:37.788	9	17. 1:33.663	12	18. **1:32.402**	7				
16. Nick Heidfeld	D	BMW Sauber F1.06-04 [1]	20.	1	27. 1:38.779	5	6. 1:32.590	15	13. 1:31.811	3	9. 1:30.470	5	9. **1:31.513**	10
17. Robert Kubica	PL	BMW Sauber F1.06-09 [1]	17.	1	18. 1:36.299	5	9. 1:32.787	17	7. 1:31.204	3	12. **1:31.094**	5		
18. Tiago Monteiro	P	Spyker Midland M16-03 - Toyota [1]	22.	4	23. 1:37.702	9	19. 1:33.824	19	21. **1:33.709**	3				
19. Christijan Albers	NL	Spyker Midland M16-02 - Toyota [1]	7. 1:47.838	6	16. 1:36.180	4	14. 1:33.270	23	16. 1:32.221	7	16. **1:33.750**	6		
20. Vitantonio Liuzzi	I	Toro Rosso STR01 03 - Cosworth [1]	15.	2	20. 1:37.441	15	11. 1:32.977	20	12. 1:31.741	7	15. **1:31.943**	7		
21. Scott Speed	USA	Toro Rosso STR01 02 - Cosworth [1]	6. 1:47.814	7	21. 1:37.501	16	13. 1:33.213	20	19. **1:32.867**	7				
22. Takuma Sato	J	Super Aguri SA06-03 - Honda [2]	10. 1:48.042	11	26. 1:38.533	18	22. 1:34.727	20	20. **1:33.666**	6				
23. Sakon Yamamoto	J	Super Aguri SA06-04 - Honda [1]	11. 1:50.479	9	28. 1:38.955	14	21. 1:34.646	10	22. **DNF**	2				
35. Alexander Wurz	A	Williams FW28 04 - Cosworth	9. 1:47.919	19	17. 1:36.234	25								
36. Anthony Davidson	GB	Honda RA106-03	1. 1:45.349	18	5. 1:34.906	23								
37. Michael Ammermuller	D	Red Bull RB2 1 - Ferrari	4. 1:47.162	21	12. 1:35.433	25								
38. Sebastian Vettel	D	BMW Sauber F1.06-06	3. 1:46.585	20	6. 1:34.912	30								
39. Adrian Sutil	D	Spyker Midland M16-01 - Toyota	5. 1:47.773	21	29. 1:43.914	14								
40. Neel Jani	CH	Toro Rosso STR01 01 - Cosworth	2. 1:46.138	21	24. 1:37.741	26								
41. Franck Montagny	F	Super Aguri SA06-02 - Honda	8. 1:47.918	13	19. 1:37.354	20								

Fastest lap overall
M. Schumacher 1:28.954 (235,011 km/h)

Maximum speed

N° Driver	S1 Qualifs	Pos.	S1 Race	Pos.	S2 Qualifs	Pos.	S2 Race	Pos.	Finish Qualifs	Pos.	Finish Race	Pos.	Radar Qualifs	Pos.	Radar Race	Pos.
1. F. Alonso	283,3	4	283,8	2	306,2	4	306,2	6	285,8	8	287,1	3	309,8	3	309,8	3
2. G. Fisichella	284,5	3	283,3	3	306,7	3	308,6	2	286,0	6	287,7	2	309,8	4	310,8	2
3. K. Räikkönen	280,6	12	280,4	8	304,1	6	307,5	3	286,8	4	284,6	9	305,5	9	307,6	6
4. P. de la Rosa	279,5	13	280,2	9	302,7	11	304,7	11	285,8	9	286,8	4	301,0	17	304,6	10
5. M. Schumacher	286,7	1	284,7	1	307,2	2	306,8	5	289,4	1	286,5	5	312,7	1	311,0	1
6. F. Massa	285,3	2	283,0	4	308,3	1	308,8	1	288,4	2	286,4	6	309,9	2	308,9	4
7. R. Schumacher	283,2	6	281,2	7	304,1	5	302,6	18	285,9	7	283,0	13	307,3	5	307,2	7
8. J. Trulli	283,2	5	281,9	5	302,0	14	302,6	17	284,3	12	284,0	10	304,1	12	303,7	13
9. M. Webber	277,6	16	277,4	17	297,2	20	307,0	4	282,6	17	280,9	17	295,9	21	296,0	21
10. N. Rosberg	281,1	11	277,2	18	302,6	12	302,9	14	284,1	14	288,3	1	303,5	14	300,1	17
11. R. Barrichello	283,1	7	281,7	6	303,2	10	305,9	8	287,1	3	282,8	14	304,9	10	307,1	8
12. J. Button	281,5	10	279,6	12	303,2	9	303,3	13	286,2	5	283,3	12	304,1	11	306,6	9
14. D. Coulthard	276,9	17	279,4	13	300,1	17	301,7	19	283,0	16	285,6	7	302,7	15	304,4	11
15. R. Doornbos	276,0	18	280,1	10	300,4	16	306,0	7	281,8	18	284,9	8	301,4	16	303,0	16
16. N. Heidfeld	283,0	8	277,9	15	303,2	8	302,7	16	285,1	10	280,2	18	306,7	6	304,3	12
17. R. Kubica	282,5	9	280,0	11	303,9	7	305,6	9	285,1	11	281,7	16	306,6	7	307,9	5
18. T. Monteiro	272,5	21	274,0	21	298,8	18	302,8	15	280,3	19	277,7	22	299,4	18	297,0	20
19. C. Albers	274,1	19	274,6	19	298,5	19	298,0	20	279,5	20	279,2	20	299,0	19	295,4	22
20. V. Liuzzi	279,4	15	277,4	16	302,0	13	304,2	12	283,6	15	281,7	15	306,2	8	303,7	14
21. S. Speed	279,4	14	278,1	14	300,4	15	305,3	10	284,2	13	283,9	11	304,0	13	303,2	15
22. T. Sato	272,4	22	274,3	20	293,2	22	296,6	22	278,0	22	279,4	19	294,7	22	297,6	19
23. S. Yamamoto	273,4	20	273,4	22	294,7	21	296,8	21	278,2	21	278,9	21	298,1	20	297,7	18

Race

Classification & Retirements

Pos.	Driver	Constructor	Tyres	Laps	Time	Average	
1.	F. Alonso	Renault	M	53	1:23:53.413	219,982 km/h	
2.	F. Massa	Ferrari	B	53	+ 16.151	219,278 km/h	
3.	G. Fisichella	Renault	M	53	+ 23.953	218,940 km/h	
4.	J. Button	Honda	M	53	+ 34.101	218,502 km/h	
5.	K. Räikkönen	McLaren Mercedes	M	53	+ 43.596	218,093 km/h	
6.	J. Trulli	Toyota	B	53	+ 46.717	217,959 km/h	
7.	R. Schumacher	Toyota	B	53	+ 48.869	217,867 km/h	
8.	N. Heidfeld	BMW	M	53	+ 1:16.095	216,706 km/h	
9.	R. Kubica	BMW	M	53	+ 1:16.932	216,670 km/h	
10.	N. Rosberg	Williams Cosworth	B	52	1 lap	215,491 km/h	
11.	P. de la Rosa	McLaren Mercedes	M	52	1 lap	215,287 km/h	
12.	R. Barrichello	Honda	M	52	1 lap	214,204 km/h	
13.	R. Doornbos	RBR Ferrari	M	52	1 lap	213,272 km/h	
14.	V. Liuzzi	STR Cosworth	M	52	1 lap	212,680 km/h	
15.	T. Sato	Aguri Honda	B	52	1 lap	212,212 km/h	
16.	T. Monteiro	MF1 Toyota	B	51	2 laps	211,316 km/h	
17.	S. Yamamoto	Aguri Honda	B	50	3 laps	206,439 km/h	
18.	S. Speed	STR Cosworth	M	48	5 laps	210,977 km/h	Power steering failure

Driver	Constructor	Tyre	Lap	Reason
M. Webber	Williams Cosworth	B	39	Spun out at the last corner
M. Schumacher	Ferrari	B	36	Engine failure
D. Coulthard	RBR Ferrari	M	35	Gearbox failure
C. Albers	MF1 Toyota	B	20	Rear right suspension failure

Fastest laps

	Driver	Time	Laps	Average
1.	F. Alonso	1:32.676	14	225,572 km/h
2.	M. Schumacher	1:32.792	32	225,290 km/h
3.	F. Massa	1:33.296	37	224,073 km/h
4.	K. Räikkönen	1:33.344	24	223,958 km/h
5.	J. Button	1:33.451	35	223,702 km/h
6.	R. Kubica	1:33.509	39	223,563 km/h
7.	G. Fisichella	1:33.564	13	223,432 km/h
8.	R. Schumacher	1:33.607	2	223,329 km/h
9.	J. Trulli	1:33.866	2	222,713 km/h
10.	R. Barrichello	1:34.071	40	222,227 km/h
11.	P. de la Rosa	1:34.120	22	222,112 km/h
12.	V. Liuzzi	1:34.131	22	222,086 km/h
13.	N. Heidfeld	1:34.525	31	221,160 km/h
14.	S. Speed	1:34.560	37	221,078 km/h
15.	N. Rosberg	1:34.802	33	220,514 km/h
16.	D. Coulthard	1:35.052	20	219,934 km/h
17.	T. Sato	1:35.082	26	219,864 km/h
18.	M. Webber	1:35.092	19	219,841 km/h
19.	R. Doornbos	1:35.099	37	219,825 km/h
20.	T. Monteiro	1:35.260	27	219,454 km/h
21.	S. Yamamoto	1:35.594	22	218,687 km/h
22.	C. Albers	1:36.036	19	217,680 km/h

Pit stops

	Driver	Laps	Duration	Stop	Total
1.	R. Barrichello	2	24.846	1	24.846
2.	J. Trulli	12	21.454	1	21.454
3.	F. Massa	13	23.037	1	23.037
4.	R. Schumacher	13	21.262	1	21.262
5.	G. Fisichella	14	22.266	1	22.266
6.	F. Alonso	15	22.909	1	22.909
7.	N. Rosberg	15	22.918	1	22.918
8.	J. Button	16	23.742	1	23.742
9.	M. Schumacher	18	23.656	1	23.656
10.	N. Heidfeld	18	22.107	1	22.107
11.	D. Coulthard	18	21.636	1	21.636
12.	R. Kubica	20	22.389	1	22.389
13.	M. Webber	20	22.788	1	22.788
14.	P. de la Rosa	20	24.302	1	24.302
15.	V. Liuzzi	20	22.124	1	22.124
16.	S. Yamamoto	20	22.236	1	22.236
17.	R. Doornbos	21	20.754	1	20.754
18.	K. Räikkönen	22	23.143	1	23.143
19.	R. Barrichello	22	22.917	2	47.763
20.	S. Speed	23	21.787	1	21.787
21.	T. Sato	23	22.203	1	22.203
22.	T. Monteiro	25	25.497	1	25.497
23.	J. Trulli	29	23.607	2	45.061
24.	R. Schumacher	30	23.255	2	44.517
25.	G. Fisichella	33	23.008	2	45.274
26.	N. Rosberg	34	24.090	2	47.008
27.	S. Yamamoto	33	32.641	2	54.877
28.	F. Alonso	35	21.824	2	44.733
29.	F. Massa	35	22.459	2	45.496
30.	D. Coulthard	34	23.028	2	44.664
31.	V. Liuzzi	34	22.125	2	44.249
32.	M. Schumacher	36	21.984	2	45.640
33.	S. Yamamoto	34	23.513	3	1:18.390
34.	R. Doornbos	35	22.775	2	43.529
35.	S. Speed	35	23.101	2	44.888
36.	N. Heidfeld	36	21.679	2	43.786
37.	J. Button	37	21.763	2	45.505
38.	R. Kubica	37	23.299	2	45.688
39.	M. Webber	38	21.990	2	44.778
40.	T. Sato	38	22.060	2	44.263
41.	T. Monteiro	39	23.524	2	49.021
42.	P. de la Rosa	40	21.161	2	45.463
43.	K. Räikkönen	41	19.897	2	43.040
44.	R. Barrichello	41	21.478	3	1:09.241

Race leader

Driver	Laps in the lead	Nbr of Laps
F. Massa	1 > 2	2
M. Schumacher	3 > 36	34
F. Alonso	37 > 53	17

Driver	Nbr of Laps	Kilometers
M. Schumacher	34	197,438 km
F. Alonso	17	98,719 km
F. Massa	2	11,416 km

Gaps on the leader board

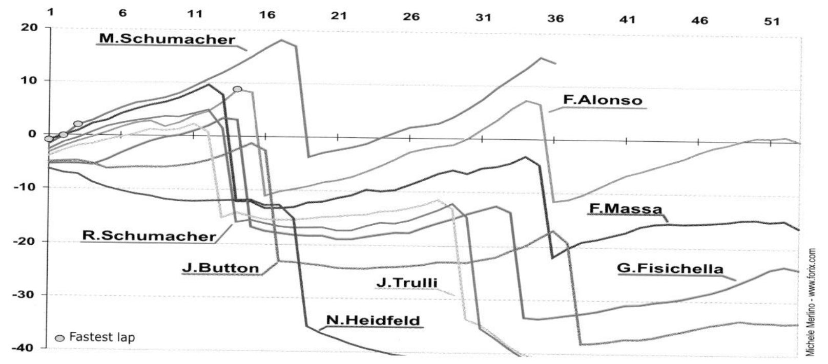

Lap chart

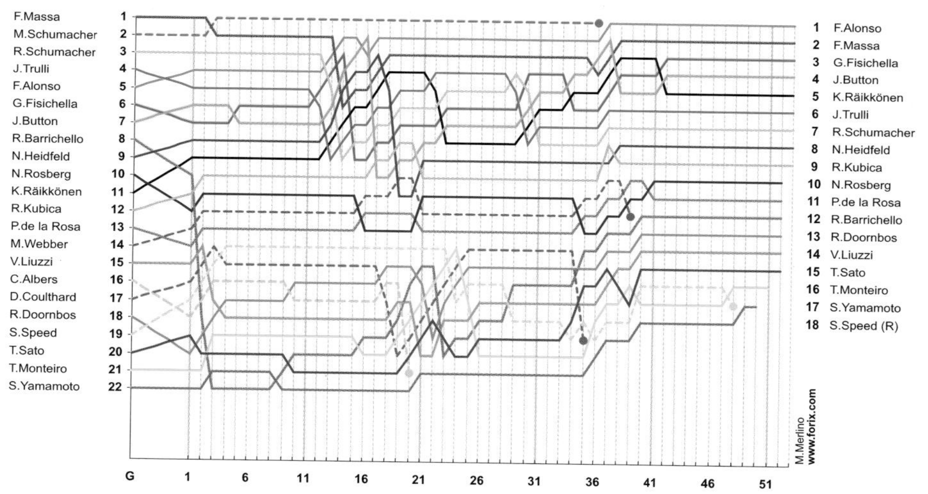

Championships 17/18

Drivers

1. F. Alonso ....Renault ....7 🏆..126
2. M. Schumacher .....Ferrari......................7 🏆..116
3. F. Massa..............Ferrari......................1 🏆....70
4. G. Fisichella.........Renault ....1 🏆....69
5. K. Räikkönen ....McLaren Mercedes.............61
6. J. Button ....Honda......................1 🏆....50
7. R. Barrichello........Honda 28
8. J. Montoya ....McLaren Mercedes.............26
9. N. Heidfeld ....BMW 23
10. R. Schumacher .....Toyota 20
11. P. de la Rosa.........McLaren Mercedes.............18
12. J. Trulli.................Toyota 15
13. D. Coulthard ....RBR Ferrari.......................14
14. M. Webber............Williams Cosworth...............7
15. J. Villeneuve ....BMW 7
16. R. Kubica ....BMW 6
17. N. Rosberg ....Williams Cosworth...............4
18. C. Klien................RBR Ferrari 2
19. V. Liuzzi ....STR Cosworth.......................1
20. S. Speed ....STR Cosworth.......................0
21. T. Monteiro ....MF1 Toyota 0
22. C. Albers ....MF1 Toyota 0
23. T. Sato.................Aguri Honda 0
24. R. Doornbos ....RBR Ferrari 0
25. Y. Ide...................Aguri Honda 0
26. F. Montagny..........Aguri Honda 0
27. S. Yamamoto ....Aguri Honda 0

Constructors

1. Mild Seven Renault F1 Team ....8 🏆...195
2. Scuderia Ferrari Marlboro ....8 🏆...186
3. Team McLaren Mercedes 105
4. Lucky Strike Honda Racing F1 Team...1 🏆 78
5. BMW Sauber F1 Team..............................36
6. Panasonic Toyota Racing 35
7. Red Bull Racing 16
8. Williams F1 Team.....................................11
9. Scuderia Toro Rosso...................................1
10. Spyker M F1 Team 0
11. Super Aguri Formula 1 0

All results :
© 2006 Formula One Administration Ltd,
6 Princes Gate, London, SW7 1QJ, England

The circuit

Name	Suzuka Circuit International; Suzuka	Weather	Cloudy, warm
Lenght	5807 m	Air temperature	25-23°c
Distance	53 laps 307,573 km	Track temperature	29-21°c
Date	Octobre 8, 2006	Humidity	36%
		Wind speed	2.5 m/s

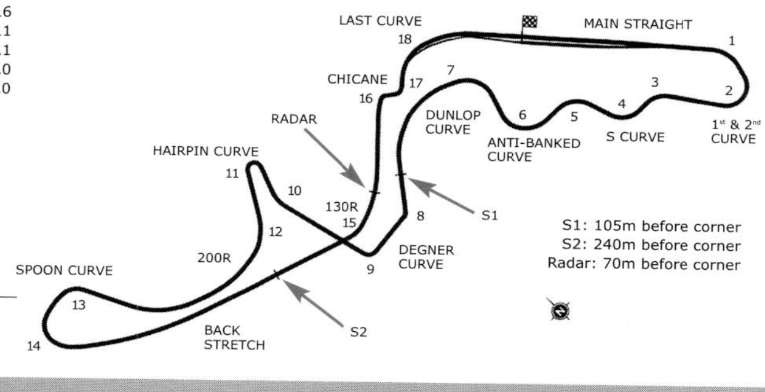

S1: 105m before corner
S2: 240m before corner
Radar: 70m before corner

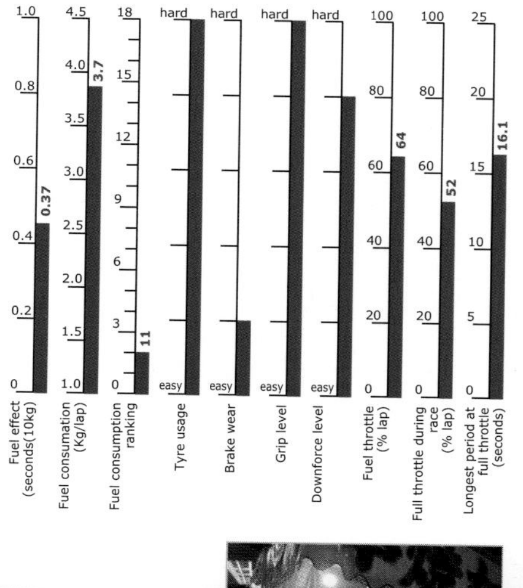

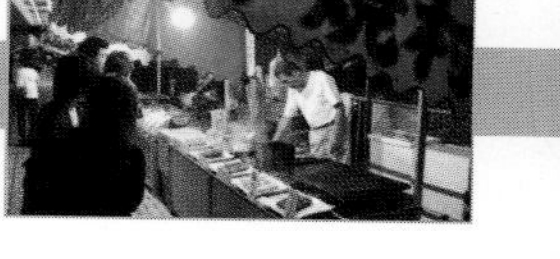

CHAMPAGNE!

A crazy weekend. A fantastic race full of twists.
An extraordinary ambience. The Brazilian Grand Prix was one that will be talked about for years to come.
The world title was at stake and Michael Schumacher in tenth place on the grid knew the game was over. He fought like a lion and drove one of the greatest races of his career. His team-mate Felipe Massa won the grand prix. Alonso won his second F1 World Championhip while Schumacher won everybody's admiration. At the finish all three were winners in their own way. For Fernando Alonso it was the culmination of what had been a very difficult, very tense season full of complications with moments when all seemed lost until he finally came out on top. Champagne!

A body blow for Michael Schumacher

The Ferraris were on another planet at Interlagos. On Saturday during the second phase of the qualifying session Michael Schumacher stunned everybody with a lap in 1m 10.313s, a time that nobody would get near for the rest of the weekend. It showed the incredible potential of the 248 F1. And then it all started to go south for the German and the Scuderia. Just when the cars were going out for the Super Pole shootout Michael realised that something was not right with his car. But it was too late. Reversing in the pits is forbidden and he had to do a full lap of the circuit at low speed before coming in. A fuel feed problem linked to the pump was diagnosed. It could not be repaired in time and he was not able to fight for pole, and had to start the race from tenth place on the grid. Meanwhile Massa confirmed the red cars' potential by setting pole in front of his home crowd. A cautious Fernando Alonso qualified in fourth place. He did not really need to do much better as eighth place in the race was good enough to win him the championship. In fact, the Spaniard emerged victorious from the qualifying session as Michael Schumacher's tenth position presented him with a very tough challenge if he wanted to win the title. But he could still do it, as Interlagos is one of the easier circuits on which to overtake. All the more so as it was when faced with the most difficult situations that he showed just how great driver he was.

> The Toyotas suddenly found a new lease of life at the end of the season. After monopolising the second row in Japan 2 weeks previously Jarno Trulli again qualified third at Interlagos. The race was a lot less brilliant. There was a bitter struggle for fifth place in the constructors' championship between BMW Sauber and Toyota. Only 1 point separated them before the Brazilian Grand Prix and it was the German team that grabbed that much-coveted fifth place after both Japanese cars retired on laps 10 and 11 respectively with the same problem: rear suspension failure.

Family, friends, BMW: Their goodbyes to their champion

Denis Chevrier sits on his perch on the pit wall just before the formation lap. The Renault team was in a state of high anxiety at Interlagos. All Alonso had to do was to finish to win the drivers' title but paradoxically it was on his shoulders that there was the most pressure. Michael Schumacher was after victory and really had nothing to lose.

They were all there. Rolf, his father who had put him in a kart at the age of four. Corinna, his faithful wife since 1995, their two children Mick and Gina Maria who did not leave the hotel to avoid being hassled by the photographers. Also present were his childhood friends from his karting days and from his home town, Kerpen. They had all come to say goodbye to their champion whether he was their son, husband, father or friend, to support him and tell how much they appreciated him. And, of course, to be with him on Sunday evening at Ferrari's party (with or without titles) to express the Scuderia's gratitude to the 7-times world champion.

They were not alone. All the weekend photographers were jostling each other around the Ferrari pit. They were all trying to record on film the slightest twitch of the greatest driver in history for posterity. Michael Schumacher had written all his victories on his helmet and the presence of his "tribe" plus the incredible media feeding frenzy caused by his retirement did not make his work any easier. "Of course, I know it's my last grand prix," he commented. "But once I'm sitting in my car, I don't feel any different. It's like the other races. The fact that my family and friends are here makes me happy and I'd like the thank the BMW team for its nice gesture."

In brief

> Hisao Suganuma, the Bridgestone technical director, quit his F1 post after the Brazilian Grand Prix.

> The Williams team's results had not been very good in 2006, a bit like its cash flow. However, change was in the air and Frank Williams announced the signing of a big contract with AT & T, the American Telecommunications giant that was to become the English squad's title sponsor in 2007.

> The FIA met in Barcelona to clarify a few opaque points of the 2007 regulations. Among the decisions taken was one allowing Ferrari to sell its V8 engines to 2 teams, and the Scuderia duly announced deals with Toro Rosso and Spyker.

> The last grand prix of the 2006 season was the scene of a record number of parties. Honda celebrated the departure of Lucky Strike, the team's sponsor since 1998. Red Bull did things in its usual extravagant style by hiring the Morumbi football stadium and laying on the biggest churrascaria in Brazil for the space of a night!

Starting grid

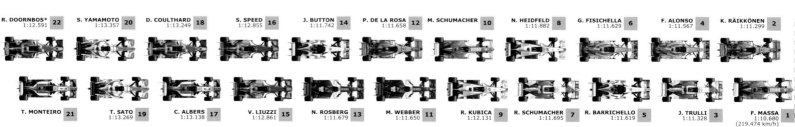

| * R. DOORNBOS penalty for an engine exchange (-10 pos.). | R. DOORNBOS* 22 1:12.591 | S. YAMAMOTO 20 1:13.357 | D. COULTHARD 18 1:13.249 | S. SPEED 16 1:12.855 | J. BUTTON 14 1:11.742 | P. DE LA ROSA 12 1:11.658 | M. SCHUMACHER 10 | N. HEIDFELD 8 1:11.882 | G. FISICHELLA 6 1:11.629 | F. ALONSO 4 1:11.567 | K. RÄIKKÖNEN 2 1:11.299 |
| T. MONTEIRO 21 | T. SATO 19 1:13.269 | C. ALBERS 17 1:13.138 | V. LIUZZI 15 1:12.861 | N. ROSBERG 13 1:11.679 | M. WEBBER 11 1:11.650 | R. KUBICA 9 1:12.131 | R. SCHUMACHER 7 1:11.695 | R. BARRICHELLO 5 1:11.619 | J. TRULLI 3 1:11.328 | F. MASSA 1 1:10.680 (219.474 km/h) |

Celebrations for Felipe: the title for Alonso

The race looked like being one of the most emotionally charged of the past few years. The drivers' title was at stake between Alonso and Schumacher and the constrictors' between Renault and Ferrari.
Michael qualified in tenth spot so the challenge was equal to the man's talent. It fulfilled its promises.
First time round the German was up into sixth place before the safety car came out following Nico Rosberg's accident. The race was neutralised for 5 laps.
On the restart Michael tried to overtake Giancarlo Fisichella and the cars brushed each other. The result was a puncture on the Ferrari's left-hand rear tyre. He pitted after covering a full lap at low speed and then rejoined in nineteenth and last place.
Up front Felipe Massa was in complete control and when the safety car pulled off the little Brazilian opened up a gap of 2 seconds in a single lap over his immediate pursuer, Kimi Raïkkönen. It was all over bar the shouting and he was never again threatened by his rivals. No Brazilian had won at Interlagos since Ayrton Senna's victory in 1993 and the spectators went wild. "*It was crazy,*" smiled Massa after the race. "*Winning here is my life's dream and it's come true. The car was just perfect. It was the easiest race of my career except at the end. I tried to remain concentrated but I couldn't stop looking at the stands in which the spectators were already celebrating my victory. When I crossed the line I yelled in my helmet.*" Massa said he remembered Senna's victory 13 years ago: "*And how! I was twelve at the time and I watched the race at home on TV. I remember it well; it was crazy. People ran onto the track exactly like they did today.*" There were a lot of different emotions under the Brazilian Grand Prix rostrum after the finish. Felipe was ecstatic to have won his home grand prix. Felipe Alonso in second place was over the moon as he had won the world title for the second time. The Renault team under the rostrum was delighted at having won the constructors' title once again. And the Michelin squad was torn between joy and tears at having added another 2 F1 titles to its laurels. They surrounded their mascot a Bibendum dancing for joy in what was to be their last grand prix. The race was not one of the most difficult of the season for Fernando Alonso.

The Spaniard started off in fourth place and soon saw that his main rival Michael Schumacher was hit by a puncture. From then on it was easier for him. "*Barely 3 laps after the safety car pulled off the team asked me to reduce the engine revs by modifying the power switch. It seemed a bit strange so early on but they didn't tell me what had happened. Not until three laps later did they inform me that Michael Schumacher had had a puncture and that he was down in eighteenth place. From then on my sole aim was to finish. All I needed was to see the flag in eighth place so I lifted off. Above all I had to stay concentrated, not make any mistakes and finish.*"
Michael Schumacher finally saw the flag in fourth place after a fantastic comeback drive. "*It's a pity that I couldn't have finished on the rostrum to have been able to congratulate Felipe,*" he said. He drove a perfect race. "*I did the best I could but after the puncture things were compromised. Finishing my career is a very special moment for me. I'm proud to have met so many incredible people over all these years. I've so much to say that it's not easy to find the right words.*"
A memorable grand prix was over as was an awesomely exciting season. "*I was delighted to have fought against Michael,*" summed up Alonso on Sunday evening. "*I've been very lucky to have won the last two championships in which he's raced. That gives my titles even more value. I wish him a great future with his family.*"

^
Felipe was overjoyed to have won his home grand prix in front of his family and friends. His driving suit in Brazilian colours brought him luck.

"Racing forever," was written on the Hondas' side pods. It was Lucky Strike's last F1 grand prix and it ended in a rostrum finish for Jenson Button who saw the flag in third place.
<

Nico Rosberg did not manage to complete a lap of the race. He hit his team-mate Mark Webber and lost his front wing, which sent him off into the wall on the main straight. It was a heavy impact but the young German got out unhurt.
<<

Michael Schumacher goes back out after changing his punctured tyre. At that moment he was nineteenth and last. He had a long way to go to his fourth-place finish.
∨

Soo Happy!

It is not always easy for everybody to grasp the emotion felt by a driver who has just won the world title especially after such a tough battle as in 2006.

These images are more evocative than a long discourse to glimpse the joy felt by Fernando Alonso on climbing up onto the rostrum for his second world crown. Soo happy!

Michael Schumacher retires after one of the best races of his career

Michael knew that his chances of winning an eighth world title were extremely slim, especially since Saturday when a fuel pump problem dropped him back to tenth place on the grid. He knew that only a miracle would save him.

Throughout his career the German had always been labelled a lucky driver – in addition to his enormous talent – and now destiny had caught up with him in the last 2 weeks as if it wanted to balance the scales before his retirement.

His engine exploded in Japan, his fuel pump went on the blink on Saturday and the third stroke of misfortune to hit him came in the race when he suffered a puncture overtaking Giancarlo Fisichella and the left-hand tyre pressure immediately dropped. The Ferrari driver went for broke and failed. He pitted and rejoined in 19th and last place. He picked off those in front of him one by one in an awesome drive that he knew was not going to bring him the ultimate reward.

He pulled some marvellous overtaking manoeuvres before the flag especially the one on Kimi Raïkkönen towards the very end of the grand prix. It was a fitting end to his 249-grand prix career and when the race was over he did not give a damn about that eighth title that had escaped him. In any case his awesome drive more than eclipsed his setback. The German hugged his mechanics, friends and family and managed to restrain his tears. This was not the case for several members of the Scuderia most of whom were in tears as they wept for their hero, their champion who had now retired.

And what a champion! Eleven seasons with Ferrari, 7 world titles, 91 victories, 68 pole positions, 75 fastest laps, 5069 kms in the lead. After Michael Schumacher Formula 1 will look like a field that's been trampled by the hordes of Attila! It will take a long time for the grass to grow, a long time for such records to be beaten by another driver.

Alonso bring the number 1 to McLaren

It was party time in the Renault pit after the race. The French team had just won its second world title on the trot by the skin of its teeth. Had Michael Schumacher not had a puncture the Ferraris would have scored a double, which would have given it the constructors' prize. As night fell the mechanics from Viry-Châtillon gave their V8 full voice as it interpreted the Marseillaise, God save he Queen and the Spanish National Anthem in its own particular fashion. On Sunday evening the whole team met up in the "Café de la Musique" to celebrate its worldwide success.

The ambience was good but it did not hide the fact that a certain disquiet reigned in the Renault camp some of whose directors did not forgive Alonso his departure to McLaren. It deprived the French team of the number 1 that it deserved to carry in 2007. Alonso did not give a damn; he deserved his world title. "It's been an unbelievable day," he laughed. "I'd never have been able to imagine what's happened today even in my wildest dreams. A fantastic race. Me world champion for the second time and I'm only twenty-five. It's just unbelievable."

results

Practice

All the time trials

N° Driver	Nat.	N° Chassis - Engine [Nbr. GP]	Pos. Free 1 Friday	Laps	Pos. Free 2 Friday	Laps	Pos. Free 3 Saturday	Laps	Pos. Q1 Saturday	Laps	Pos. Q2 Saturday	Laps	Pos. Super Pole Saturday	Laps
1. Fernando Alonso	E	Renault R26 04 [1]	25.	1	10. 1:13.820	16	7. 1:12.721	14	4. 1:11.791	3	3. 1:11.148	3	4. **1:11.567**	13
2. Giancarlo Fisichella	I	Renault R26 06 [1]	24.	1	12. 1:14.053	17	5. 1:12.567	15	12. 1:12.042	3	6. 1:11.461	6	6. **1:11.629**	13
3. Kimi Räikkönen	FIN	McLaren MP4-21 05 - Mercedes [2]	1. 1:13.764	5	9. 1:13.803	8	8. 1:12.723	12	10. 1:12.035	3	5. 1:11.386	6	2. **1:11.299**	12
4. Pedro de la Rosa	E	McLaren MP4-21 04 - Mercedes [1]	5. 1:14.237	5	11. 1:13.926	16	9. 1:12.780	15	5. 1:11.825	6	12. **1:11.658**	6		
5. Michael Schumacher	D	Ferrari 248 F1 255 [1]			6. 1:13.713	15	2. 1:11.631	15	2. 1:11.565	3	1. 1:10.313	3	10.	1
6. Felipe Massa	BR	Ferrari 248 F1 256 [1]			17. 1:14.561	15	1. 1:11.443	17	1. 1:10.643	3	2. 1:10.775	3	1. **1:10.680**	13
7. Ralf Schumacher	D	Toyota TF106/10B [2]	11. 1:16.168	6	7. 1:13.765	22	16. 1:13.642	20	3. 1:11.713	8	7. 1:11.550	6	7. **1:11.695**	13
8. Jarno Trulli	I	Toyota TF106/08B [2]	7. 1:14.888	8	4. 1:13.483	21	20. 1:14.051	19	6. 1:11.885	8	4. 1:11.343	5	3. **1:11.328**	13
9. Mark Webber	AUS	Williams FW28 03 - Cosworth [1]			19. 1:14.839	15	11. 1:13.205	16	7. 1:11.973	6	11. **1:11.650**	5		
10. Nico Rosberg	D	Williams FW28 05 - Cosworth [2]			23. 1:15.124	14	12. 1:13.380	13	8. 1:11.974	6	13. **1:11.679**	6		
11. Rubens Barrichello	BR	Honda RA106-01 [2]	9. 1:15.661	6	13. 1:14.434	17	6. 1:12.697	18	9. 1:12.017	7	8. 1:11.578	7	5. **1:11.619**	12
12. Jenson Button	GB	Honda RA106-05 [2]	6. 1:14.487	4	5. 1:13.485	13	3. 1:12.306	15	13. 1:12.085	6	14. **1:11.742**	4		
14. David Coulthard	GB	Red Bull RB2 3 - Ferrari [1]	22.	1	24. 1:15.214	21	19. 1:13.944	20	19. **1:13.249**	7				
15. Robert Doornbos	NL	Red Bull RB2 5 - Ferrari [2>1]	23.	1	28. 1:16.251	8	15. 1:13.564	21	15. 1:12.530	7	15. **1:12.591**	3		
16. Nick Heidfeld	D	BMW Sauber F1.06-04 [2]	18.	1	18. 1:14.793	13	10. 1:13.037	15	14. 1:12.307	4	10. 1:11.648	6	8. **1:11.882**	13
17. Robert Kubica	PL	BMW Sauber F1.06-09 [2]	19.	1	16. 1:14.510	15	4. 1:12.535	20	11. 1:12.040	3	9. 1:11.589	6	9. **1:12.131**	13
18. Tiago Monteiro	P	Spyker Midland M16-03 - Toyota [2]	21.	1	15. 1:14.468	18	18. 1:13.832	15	22.	2				
19. Christijan Albers	NL	Spyker Midland M16-02 - Toyota [2]	20.	1	22. 1:15.086	21	21. 1:14.108	19	18. **1:13.138**	7				
20. Vitantonio Liuzzi	I	Toro Rosso STR01 03 - Cosworth [2]	15. 1:17.311	8	25. 1:15.737	22	14. 1:13.530	20	16. 1:12.855	8	16. **1:12.861**	7		
21. Scott Speed	USA	Toro Rosso STR01 02 - Cosworth [1]	14. 1:17.047	14	26. 1:15.855	28	13. 1:13.455	18	17. **1:12.856**	8				
22. Takuma Sato	J	Super Aguri SA06-03 - Honda [1]	12. 1:16.534	16	21. 1:15.023	27	17. 1:13.814	21	20. **1:13.269**	7				
23. Sakon Yamamoto	J	Super Aguri SA06-04 - Honda [2]	16. 1:17.388	14	29. 1:18.321	9	22. 1:14.875	21	21. **1:13.357**	10				
35. Alexander Wurz	A	Williams FW28 04 - Cosworth	3. 1:13.922	25	1. 1:12.547	33								
36. Anthony Davidson	GB	Honda RA106-03	2. 1:13.902	32	2. 1:12.653	37								
37. Michael Ammermuller	D	Red Bull RB2 1 - Ferrari	10. 1:15.711	22	14. 1:14.436	31								
38. Sebastian Vettel	D	BMW Sauber F1.06-08	4. 1:14.204	29	3. 1:12.870	33								
39. Ernesto Viso	YV	Spyker Midland M16-01 - Toyota	13. 1:16.737	32	20. 1:14.972	26								
40. Neel Jani	CH	Toro Rosso STR01 01 - Cosworth	8. 1:15.159	25	27. 1:15.868	22								
41. Franck Montagny	F	Super Aguri SA06-02 - Honda	17. 1:17.744	6	8. 1:13.792	20								

Fastest lap overall
M. Schumacher 1:10.313 (220,619 km/h)

Maximum speed

N° Driver	S1 Qualifs	Pos.	S1 Race	Pos.	S2 Qualifs	Pos.	S2 Race	Pos.	Finish Qualifs	Pos.	Finish Race	Pos.	Radar Qualifs	Pos.	Radar Race	Pos.
1. F. Alonso	306,6	5	305,9	7	260,9	5	257,0	7	308,0	3	309,3	4	309,1	2	309,8	3
2. G. Fisichella	307,4	3	308,8	2	260,1	6	258,0	2	309,2	1	312,0	2	309,4	1	312,1	2
3. K. Räikkönen	304,3	6	307,1	4	261,7	3	258,0	3	302,4	9	308,2	6	303,5	7	307,7	5
4. P. de la Rosa	306,6	4	306,2	5	262,9	2	256,5	8	307,4	6	308,6	5	307,7	4	307,6	6
5. M. Schumacher	307,8	1	313,5	1	263,5	1	261,8	1	307,6	5	316,4	1	308,4	3	318,0	1
6. F. Massa	307,5	2	307,6	3	261,6	4	257,5	4	308,9	2	309,9	3	307,4	5	308,6	4
7. R. Schumacher	300,8	15	300,4	16	259,4	10	246,1	20	307,7	4	298,0	18	303,2	8	298,4	17
8. J. Trulli	301,2	10	300,6	15	258,8	15	247,0	19	303,3	7	299,1	15	306,4	6	301,2	13
9. M. Webber	301,9	9	297,7	19	259,2	12	212,8	22	298,7	16			301,1	13	222,8	22
10. N. Rosberg	299,8	16	306,2	6	259,1	13	218,5	21	301,2	10			301,1	12	229,6	21
11. R. Barrichello	302,6	7	303,6	10	259,1	14	255,6	10	302,8	8	301,5	11	300,8	14	302,3	10
12. J. Button	300,9	13	304,9	8	259,4	9	257,2	5	298,8	15	305,4	8	299,9	16	305,1	8
14. D. Coulthard	299,7	17	297,6	20	257,7	16	248,2	18	297,8	18	297,8	19	299,5	18	299,6	16
15. R. Doornbos	301,9	8	304,2	9	259,9	7	257,2	6	301,0	11	306,9	7	301,3	11	305,6	7
16. N. Heidfeld	299,2	18	303,3	11	259,4	11	254,5	13	298,0	17	303,9	9	300,1	15	304,7	9
17. R. Kubica	300,8	14	302,4	12	259,9	8	255,9	9	298,9	14	301,1	12	299,6	17	301,0	14
18. T. Monteiro	292,2	22	295,7	22	239,7	22	251,8	17	288,8	22	296,7	20	289,9	22	297,7	20
19. C. Albers	294,3	21	297,0	21	253,5	21	254,1	16	292,1	20	298,2	17	293,7	20	297,7	19
20. V. Liuzzi	301,0	11	302,2	13	257,3	19	254,5	14	300,3	13	302,0	10	301,5	10	302,3	11
21. S. Speed	301,0	12	301,7	14	257,5	17	254,4	15	300,4	12	299,8	14	301,8	9	300,6	15
22. T. Sato	295,0	20	299,2	18	255,2	20	255,5	11	291,9	21	299,0	16	293,0	21	298,4	18
23. S. Yamamoto	297,5	19	299,3	17	257,5	18	255,5	12	296,7	19	300,3	13	297,7	19	302,0	12

Race

Classification & Retirements

Pos.	Driver	Constructor	Tyres	Laps	Time	Average	
1.	F. Massa	Ferrari	B	71	1:31:53.751	199,731 km/h	
2.	F. Alonso	Renault	M	71	+ 18.658	199,058 km/h	
3.	J. Button	Honda	M	71	+ 19.394	199,031 km/h	
4.	M. Schumacher	Ferrari	B	71	+ 24.094	198,862 km/h	
5.	K. Räikkönen	McLaren Mercedes	M	71	+ 28.503	198,704 km/h	
6.	G. Fisichella	Renault	M	71	+ 30.287	198,640 km/h	
7.	R. Barrichello	Honda	M	71	+ 40.294	198,282 km/h	
8.	P. de la Rosa	McLaren Mercedes	M	71	+ 52.068	197,863 km/h	
9.	R. Kubica	BMW	M	71	+ 1:07.642	197,311 km/h	
10.	T. Sato	Aguri Honda	B	70	1 lap	196,883 km/h	
11.	S. Speed	STR Cosworth	M	70	1 lap	196,068 km/h	
12.	R. Doornbos	RBR Ferrari	M	70	1 lap	195,982 km/h	
13.	V. Liuzzi	STR Cosworth	M	70	1 lap	195,587 km/h	
14.	C. Albers	MF1 Toyota	B	70	1 lap	195,005 km/h	
15.	T. Monteiro	MF1 Toyota	B	69	2 laps	194,003 km/h	
16.	S. Yamamoto	Aguri Honda	B	69	2 laps	193,784 km/h	
17.	N. Heidfeld	BMW	M	63	8 laps	195,196 km/h	Spin off

Driver	Constructor	Tyres	Laps	Reason
D. Coulthard	RBR Ferrari	M	14	Gearbox
J. Trulli	Toyota	B	10	Rear suspension brocken
R. Schumacher	Toyota	B	9	Rear suspension brocken
M. Webber	Williams Cosworth	B	1	Collision with Rosberg, damaged car
N. Rosberg	Williams Cosworth	B	0	Collision with Webber, wing brocken, spin off

Fastest laps

	Driver	Time	Laps	Average
1.	M. Schumacher	1:12.162	70	214,966 km/h
2.	F. Massa	1:12.877	23	212,857 km/h
3.	F. Alonso	1:12.961	70	212,612 km/h
4.	J. Button	1:13.053	71	212,344 km/h
5.	G. Fisichella	1:13.121	70	212,146 km/h
6.	K. Räikkönen	1:13.281	58	211,683 km/h
7.	S. Yamamoto	1:13.379	67	211,401 km/h
8.	R. Barrichello	1:13.391	48	211,366 km/h
9.	T. Sato	1:13.401	47	211,337 km/h
10.	V. Liuzzi	1:13.687	69	210,517 km/h
11.	R. Doornbos	1:13.700	62	210,480 km/h
12.	P. de la Rosa	1:13.817	63	210,146 km/h
13.	S. Speed	1:13.862	69	210,018 km/h
14.	R. Kubica	1:14.117	25	209,296 km/h
15.	N. Heidfeld	1:14.163	18	209,166 km/h
16.	T. Monteiro	1:14.410	38	208,471 km/h
17.	C. Albers	1:14.591	61	207,966 km/h
18.	J. Trulli	1:14.882	9	207,157 km/h
19.	D. Coulthard	1:16.045	12	203,989 km/h
20.	R. Schumacher	1:16.835	8	201,892 km/h

Pit stops

	Driver	Laps	Duration	Stop	Total
1.	M. Schumacher	9	29.476	1	29.476
2.	K. Räikkönen	21	25.482	1	25.482
3.	G. Fisichella	21	26.612	1	26.612
4.	R. Barrichello	21	25.601	1	25.601
5.	F. Massa	24	25.916	1	25.916
6.	J. Button	25	24.903	1	24.903
7.	F. Alonso	26	25.969	1	25.969
8.	C. Albers	26	24.995	1	24.995
9.	R. Kubica	27	25.746	1	25.746
10.	S. Yamamoto	27	24.638	1	24.638
11.	N. Heidfeld	28	23.763	1	23.763
12.	T. Sato	28	24.116	1	24.116
13.	V. Liuzzi	32	26.744	1	26.744
14.	S. Speed	33	24.507	1	24.507
15.	P. de la Rosa	35	27.841	1	27.841
16.	R. Doornbos	35	25.160	1	25.160
17.	N. Heidfeld	38	27.887	2	51.650
18.	T. Monteiro	39	27.683	1	27.683
19.	R. Barrichello	46	25.514	2	51.115
20.	S. Yamamoto	46	25.361	2	49.999
21.	M. Schumacher	47	24.624	2	54.100
22.	T. Sato	48	24.866	2	48.982
23.	C. Albers	48	26.239	2	51.234
24.	G. Fisichella	49	23.891	2	50.503
25.	R. Kubica	49	24.582	2	50.328
26.	J. Button	50	24.432	2	49.335
27.	K. Räikkönen	51	23.872	2	49.354
28.	F. Massa	52	24.395	2	50.311
29.	V. Liuzzi	53	24.432	2	51.176
30.	F. Alonso	54	24.101	2	50.070
31.	S. Speed	54	23.832	2	48.339
32.	R. Doornbos	59	23.266	2	48.426
33.	S. Yamamoto	63	22.886	3	1:12.885

Race leader

Driver	Laps in the lead	Nbr of Laps
F. Massa	1 > 24	24
F. Alonso	25 > 26	2
F. Massa	27 > 71	45

Driver	Nbr of Laps	Kilometers
F. Massa	69	297,291 km
F. Alonso	2	8,618 km

Lap chart

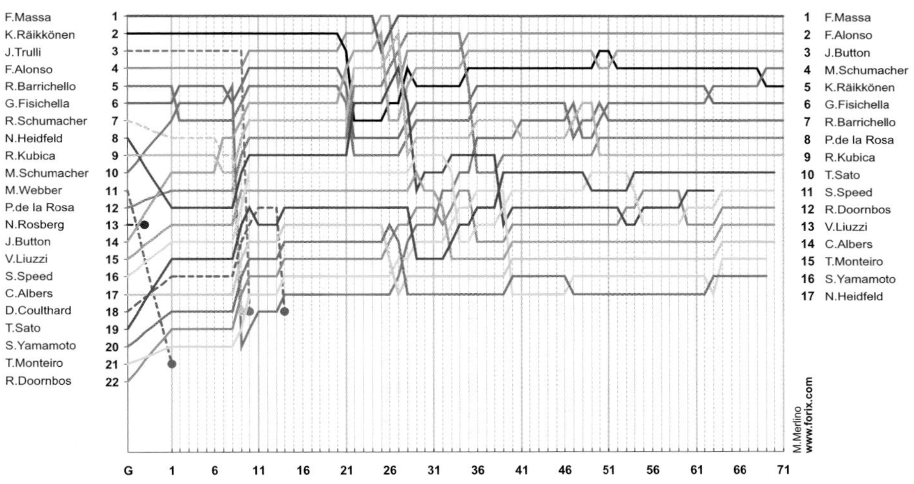

Gaps on the leader board

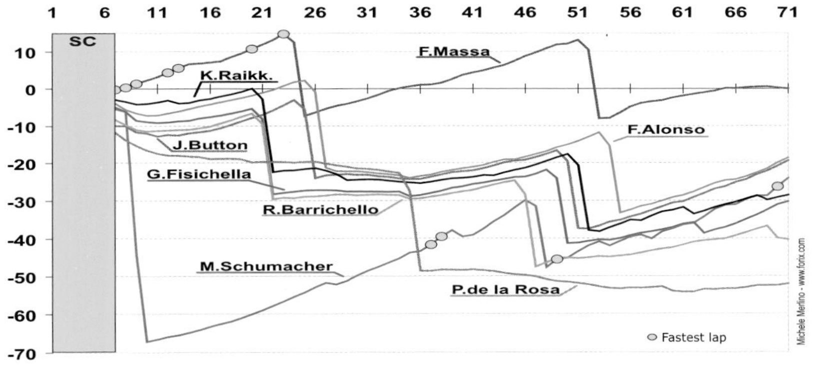

Championships 18/18

Drivers

1. **F. Alonso** .... Renault .... 7 🏆 .. 134
2. M. Schumacher .... Ferrari .... 7 🏆 .. 121
3. F. Massa .... Ferrari .... 2 🏆 ... 80
4. G. Fisichella .... Renault .... 1 🏆 ... 72
5. K. Räikkönen .... McLaren Mercedes 65
6. J. Button .... Honda .... 1 🏆 ... 56
7. R. Barrichello .... Honda 30
8. J. Montoya .... McLaren Mercedes 26
9. N. Heidfeld .... BMW 23
10. R. Schumacher .... Toyota 20
11. P. de la Rosa .... McLaren Mercedes 19
12. J. Trulli .... Toyota 15
13. D. Coulthard .... RBR Ferrari 14
14. M. Webber .... Williams Cosworth 7
15. J. Villeneuve .... BMW 7
16. R. Kubica .... BMW 6
17. N. Rosberg .... Williams Cosworth 4
18. C. Klien .... RBR Ferrari 2
19. V. Liuzzi .... STR Cosworth 1
20. S. Speed .... STR Cosworth 0
21. T. Monteiro .... MF1 Toyota 0
22. C. Albers .... MF1 Toyota 0
23. T. Sato .... Aguri Honda 0
24. R. Doornbos .... RBR Ferrari 0
25. Y. Ide .... Aguri Honda 0
26. S. Yamamoto .... Aguri Honda 0
27. F. Montagny .... Aguri Honda 0

Constructors

1. **Mild Seven Renault F1 Team** ..... 8 🏆 ... 206
2. Scuderia Ferrari Marlboro .... 9 🏆 ... 201
3. Team McLaren Mercedes 110
4. Lucky Strike Honda Racing F1 Team ... 1 🏆 86
5. BMW Sauber F1 Team 36
6. Panasonic Toyota Racing 35
7. Red Bull Racing 16
8. Williams F1 Team 11
9. Scuderia Toro Rosso 1
10. Spyker M F1 Team 0
11. Super Aguri Formula 1 0

All results :
© 2006 Formula One Administration Ltd,
6 Princes Gate, London, SW7 1QJ, England

The circuit

Name	Autódromo José Carlos Pace; São Paulo	Weather	Cloudy, warm
Lenght	4309 m	Air temperature	24-23°c
Distance	71 laps 305,909 km	Track temperature	45-32°c
Date	Octobre 22, 2006	Humidity	56%
		Wind speed	2.5 m/s

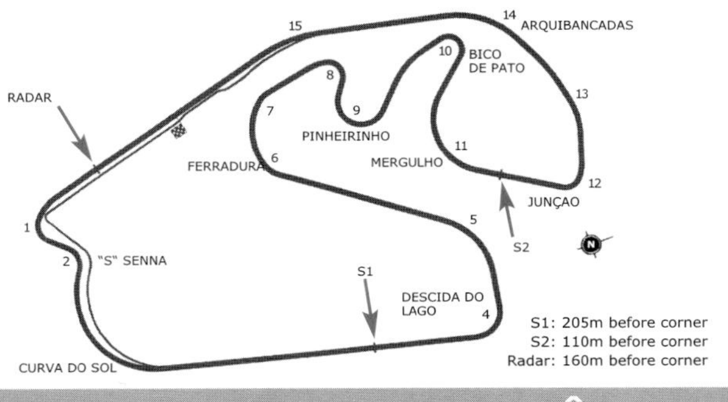

S1: 205m before corner
S2: 110m before corner
Radar: 160m before corner

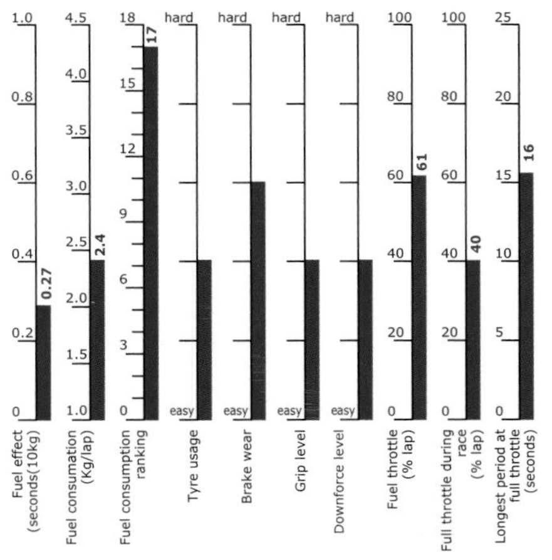

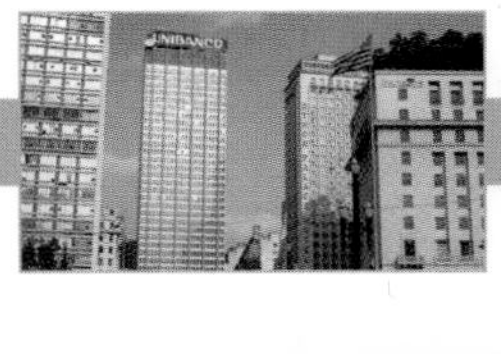

In F1 time goes quicker and quicker. 2007 is already here!

What will the Hockenheim stands be like next year without Michael Schumacher. Empty is the answer as the German Grand Prix will not be held on the Hockenheim circuit in 2007, and will be off the calendar for the first time since 1985. Hockenheim's disappearance is not the most important of the changes that will intervene next season Michael Schumacher's retirement will leave a big hole even if he will have a role as a kind of super consultant at

Ferrari, and will attend all the races alongside Jean Todt as his assistant. Thus, there will be only one world champion on the grid in 2007: Fernando Alonso.
He is leaving Renault for McLaren bring the number 1 with him. It is a nice little gift for the English team but has left a bad taste behind at Renault whose cars will carry the numbers 4 and 5. The name of Alonso's team-mate in the Woking squad has not yet been announced but it could well be Lewis Hamilton, the young coming man who has just won the GP 2 Championship. Together with the arrival of Kubica, Rosberg, Vettel and Kovalianen, Formula 1 has been rejuvenated.

Alonso will replace Raïkkönen gone to Ferrari to fill Schumacher's vacant seat. He is the hot favourite for the 2007 title, which, many pundits reckon will fall into Ferrari's hands.
The 2007 technical regulations limit revs to 19 000 rpm as against over 20 000 rpm in 2006. The engines' characteristics will remain frozen until 2011, which may see the arrival of green/hybrid engines (electricity/petrol as well as recycling the energy generated under braking) whose regulations have not yet been defined. These measures, the FIA hopes, will incite manufacturers to work on engines that will power the touring cars of the future.
The FIA has also tried to make cuts in an

> Fernando Alonso in his blue and yellow work clothes. It will be all change next year and he will wear the new red and white McLaren colours of its new ≠sponsors Emirates and Vodaphone. A red and white McLaren, a hungry champion; now doesn't that remind you of the good old days?

> Vitantonio Liuzzi had an eventful season at Toro Rosso but still managed to score a point at Indianapolis.

area that was partially responsible for the huge budget explosions. From 2008 onwards, the electronic engine management systems will be standardised. It will no longer be possible to adapt the engine mapping systems to each corner, as is the case today.

The main cause of the engineers' sleeplessness nights will be the tyres. Michelin's withdrawal after the Brazilian Grand Prix has given Bridgestone a monopoly? The Japanese company has been asked by the FIA to produce slower tyres with the aim of increasing times by a couple of seconds per lap in 2007. The tyres will probably be new, difficult to exploit and difficult to heat up. It will no longer be possible to pit when the safety car comes out to avoid traffic jams in the pit lane. On Fridays the teams will be able to practice for 3 instead of 2 hours and it will not count concerning the number of engines. These will still have to last for 2 grand prix weekends but Friday will not be included in this definition. Economically speaking several major sponsors quit F1 for good after the Brazilian Grand Prix including cigarette manufacturers Lucky Strike and Mild Seven. Cosworth also bowed out, as nobody wanted its V8s. Ferrari will supply Toro Rosso and Spyker. 17 grands prix were initially down on the 2007 calendar with both Imola and Hockenheim disappearing. Back will be a rejuvenated Spa-Francorchamps with a new pit complex. You can read all about the ups and downs of the coming season in 2007 Formula 1 Yearbook.

^
Nico Rosberg will continue with the Williams-Toyota team next year. It will lose RBS but has managed to snatch another big sponsor and its millions from under the noses of its rivals: AT & T.

<
Giancarlo Fisichella and Heikki Kovalainen will defend the world championship-winning team's colours next season.

<
Ferrari is the hot favourite for 2007 because of its familiarity with the Bridgestone tyres. Kimi Raïkkönen will replace Michael Schumacher alongside Felipe Massa. It remains to be seen how Iceman will integrate himself into the Scuderia.

A recap of the 2006 season

Driver	Nationality	Team	Number of points	BAH 12/03 1	MAL 19/03 2	AUS 02/04 3	RSM 23/04 4	EUR 07/05 5	ESP 14/05 6	MON 28/05 7	GBR 11/06 8	CAN 25/06 9	USA 02/07 10	FRA 16/07 11	ALL 30/07 12	HON 06/08 13	TUR 27/08 14	ITA 10/09 15	CHI 01/10 16	JAP 08/10 17	BRE 22/10 18	Number of pole positions	Number of victories	Number of fastest laps	Number of podiums	Number of GP in the lead	Number of laps in the lead	Number of km in the lead
1. Fernando ALONSO	E	Renault	134	10 1	8 2	10 1	8 2	8 2	10 1	10 1	10 1	10 1	4 5	8 2	10 1	6 3	10 1	10 1	NC	5 4	6 3	6	7	5	14	15	463	2171,232
2. Michael SCHUMACHER	D	Ferrari	121	8 2	3 6	NC	10 1	10 1	8 2	4 5	8 2	4 5	10 1	10 1	8 2	1 8	7 3	10 1	9	8 2	8 2	4	7	7	12	11	366	1803,313
3. Felipe MASSA	BR	Ferrari	80	NC	10 1	4 5	5 4	6 3	5 4	9	5 4	8 2	4 5	6 3	8 2	7 3	10 1	9	8 2	8 2	10 1	3	2	2	7	4	154	718,319
4. Giancarlo FISICHELLA	I	Renault	72	NC	10 1	4 5	1 8	3 6	6 3	3 6	5 4	5 4	6 3	3 6	3 6	NC	3 6	5 4	6 3	6 3	3 6	1	1	-	5	4	57	313,437
5. Kimi RÄIKKÖNEN	FIN	McLaren Mercedes	65	6 3	NC	8 2	4 5	5 4	4 5	NC	6 3	6 3	NC	NC	NC	4 5	NC	8 2	5 4	6 3	3 6	3	-	3	6	6	54	264,721
6. Jenson BUTTON	GB	Honda	56	5 4	6 3	10	2 7	NC	3 6	11	NC	NC	NC	5 4	10 1	5 4	4 5	5 4	5 4	3 6	6 3	1	1	-	3	4	25	115,646
7. Rubens BARRICHELLO	BR	Honda	30	15	10	2 7	9	4 5	2 7	6 3	NC	3 6	NC	5 4	1 8	3 6	3 6	3 6	12	2 7		-	-	-	2	2	6	31,566
8. Juan Pablo MONTOYA	CO	McLaren Mercedes	26	4 5	5 4	NC	6 3	NC	NC	8 2	3 6	NC										-	-	-	1	-	-	-
9. Nick HEIDFELD	D	BMW	23	12	NC	5 4	13	10	1 8	2 7	2 7	2 7	NC	1 8	NC	6 3	14	1 8	2 7	1 8	17	-	-	-	1	1	2	8,822
10. Ralf SCHUMACHER	D	Toyota	20	14	1 8	6 3	NC	NC	1 8	NC	NC	NC	5 4	9	3 6	2 7	2 7	NC	2 7	NC		-	-	-	1	-	-	-
11. Pedro DE LA ROSA	E	McLaren Mercedes	19										2 7		8 2	4 5	5 4	NC	4 5	5 4	1 8	-	-	-	1	1	2	8,822
12. Jarno TRULLI	I	Toyota	15	16	NC	NC	9	10	17	11	3 6	5 4	NC	2 7	NC	NC	2 7	NC	3 6	NC	NC	-	-	-	1	-	-	-
13. David COULTHARD	GB	RBR Ferrari	14	10	NC	1 8	NC	8 2	NC	5 4	9	11	2 7	9	11	NC	12	NC	10	10	1 8	NC	NC	-	-	-	2	3	13,946
14. Mark WEBBER	AUS	Williams Cosworth	7	3 6	NC	3 6	NC	3 6	NC	NC	9	NC	1 8	1 8	NC	12	1 8	NC	11	NC		-	-	-	-	-	-	-
15. Jacques VILLENEUVE	CDN	BMW	7	NC	2 7	3 6	12	1 8	NC	14	8 2		DQ (7)		6 3	9	9	9		-	-	-	-	1	5	28,965
16. Robert KUBICA	PL	BMW	6														9	14	NC	11		-	1	-	-	-	-	-
17. Nico ROSBERG	D	Williams Cosworth	4	2 7	NC	NC	11	2 7	11	NC	NC	14	11	NC	1 8	NC	14	11	11			-	-	-	-	-	-	-
18. Christian KLIEN	A	RBR Ferrari	2	1 8	NC	NC	NC	14	NC	11	NC	8	1 8	NC	14	NC	14	10	14	13		-	-	-	-	-	-	-
19. Vitantonio LIUZZI	I	STR Cosworth	1	11	11	NC	9	15	14	NC	10	10	NC	10	11	13	13	14	18	11		-	-	-	-	-	-	-
20. Scott SPEED	USA	STR Cosworth	0	13	11	NC	15	14	9	5	NC	14	NC	NC	13	10	NC	16	16	9		-	-	-	-	-	-	-
21. Tiago MONTEIRO	P	Spyker MF1 Toyota	0	17	13	NC	16	12	NC	12	NC	14	NC	NC	DQ (14)	9	NC	16	15	10		-	-	-	-	-	-	-
22. Christijan ALBERS	NL	Spyker MF1 Toyota	0	NC	12	11	NC	13	12	NC	17	15	DQ (13)	10	NC	17	DQ (14)	15	10			-	-	-	-	-	-	-
23. Takuma SATO	J	Super Aguri Honda	0	18	14	12	NC	17	NC	17	NC	17	NC	13	NC	16	12	NC	14			-	-	-	-	-	-	-
24. Robert DOORNBOS	NL	RBR Ferrari	0															12	13	12		-	-	-	-	-	-	-
25. Yuji IDE	J	Super Aguri Honda	0										NC	NC	NC	16	17	16				-	-	-	-	-	-	-
26. Sakon YAMAMOTO	J	Super Aguri Honda	0				NC	NC	16	18	NC	16										-	-	-	-	-	-	-
27. Franck MONTAGNY	F	Super Aguri Honda	0																			-	-	-	-	-	-	-

			Number of points	1	2	3	4	5	6	7	8	9	10	11	12	13	14	15	16	17	18	pole	vict	fast	pod	GP lead	laps	km
1. Renault	F		206	10	18	14	9	11	16	13	15	15	10	11	7		11	5	14	16	11	7	8	5	19	15	520	2484,669
2. Ferrari	I		201	8	7		15	16	13	4	12	12	18	16	18	3	16	10	10	8	15	7	9	9	19	12	520	2521,632
3. McLaren Mercedes	GB		110	10	5	8	10	5	4	8	9	6		6	6	8	4	8	4	4	5	3	-	3	9	8	60	296,287
4. Honda	J		86	5	6	2	2	4	5	5		3		5	15	6	7	8	5	8	8	1	1	-	3	4	25	115,646
5. BMW	D		36		2	8		1	2	3	2		1		6		7	2	1			-	-	-	1	1	5	28,965
6. Toyota	J		35		1	6					3	5	5	2	3	2	2	2		5		-	-	-	1	-	-	-
7. RBR Ferrari	A		16	1		1			6		1	2		1	4					1		-	-	1	-	2	3	13,946
8. Williams Cosworth	GB		11	5		3	2															-	-	-	-	-	-	-
9. STR Cosworth	GB		1										1									-	-	-	-	-	-	-
10. Spyker MF1 Toyota	NL		0																			-	-	-	-	-	-	-
11. Super Aguri Honda	J		0																			-	-	-	-	-	-	-

Erratum: p. 179, in the chart «Race Leader», read *M. Schumacher* instead of *F. Alonso* on both cases.

Family picture of the 2006 World Championship.
From left to right: Vitantonio Liuzzi, Scott Speed, Takuma Sato, Sakon Yamamoto, Christijan Albers, Tiago Monteiro, Ralf Schumacher & Jarno Trulli.
In the middle: David Coulthard, Robert Doornbos, Mark Webber, Nico Rosberg, Kimi Räikkönen & Pedro de la Rosa.
Sitting: Rubens Barrichello, Jenson Button, Giancarlo Fisichella, Fernando Alonso, Michael Schumacher, Felipe Massa, Nick Heidfeld & Robert Kubica.

Number of kms and laps raced in 2006

	Maximum 5478,789 km	Maximum 1137 tours	GP finished	GP classified	GP raced
1. Alonso	5337,620	1108	16	16	18
2. M. Schumacher	5234,352	1092	15	16	18
3. Massa	5103,385	1066	16	16	18
4. Fisichella	5056,145	1049	16	16	18
5. Heidfeld	4785,731	981	14	15	18
6. Barrichello	4741,462	972	15	15	18
7. Button	4700,578	971	13	14	18
8. Speed	4598,741	951	13	14	18
9. R. Schumacher	4544,620	938	11	11	18
10. Liuzzi	4539,507	949	13	14	18
11. Coulthard	4447,209	932	12	13	18
12. Trulli	4318,632	895	11	13	18
13. Monteiro	4261,910	883	12	11	18
14. Sato	4234,547	857	11	10	18
15. Räikkönen	4060,296	840	12	12	18
16. Albers	3979,370	831	10	9	18
17. Webber	3293,124	669	7	7	18
18. Rosberg	3212,536	662	9	9	18
19. Klien	3149,507	655	8	8	18
20. Villeneuve	3042,378	646	8	8	12
21. Montoya	2141,585	441	5	5	10
22. de la Rosa	1962,085	399	6	6	8
23. Kubica	1826,157	358	6	5	6
24. Yamamoto	1101,810	213	3	3	7
25. Montagny	1042,926	240	3	3	7
26. Doornbos	902,981	177	3	3	3
27. Ide	772,275	145	1	1	4

	Max. 10957,578	Max. 2274			
1. Renault	10393,765	2157	32	32	36
2. Ferrari	10337,737	2158	31	32	36
3. BMW	9654,266	1985	28	28	36
4. Honda	9442,040	1943	28	29	36
5. STR Cosworth	9138,248	1900	26	28	36
6. Toyota	8863,252	1833	22	24	36
7. RBR Ferrari	8499,697	1764	23	24	36
8. Midland Toyota	8241,280	1714	22	20	36
9. McLaren Mercedes	8163,966	1680	23	23	36
10. Super Aguri Honda	7151,558	1455	18	17	36
11. Williams Cosworth	6505,660	1331	16	16	36

Drivers: GP raced

PATRESE Riccardo	256	PACE Carlos	72	Da MATTA Cristiano	28
SCHUMACHER Michael	249	De La ROSA Pedro	72	TAYLOR Trevor	27
BARRICHELLO Rubens	233	PIRONI Didier	70	COURAGE Piers	27
COULTHARD David	211	MODENA Stefano	70	ROSSET Ricardo	27
BERGER Gerhard	210	MASSA Felipe	70	GONZALEZ Jose-Froilan	26
De CESARIS Andrea	208	GIACOMELLI Bruno	69	Von TRIPS Wolfgang	26
PIQUET Nelson	204	SATO Takuma	69	GODIN de BEAUFORT Carel	26
ALESI Jean	201	VILLENEUVE Gilles	67	PEREZ-SALA Luis	26
PROST Alain	199	MORBIDELLI Gianni	67	MAGGS Tony	25
ALBORETO Michele	194	MOSS Stirling	66	ANDERSON Bob	25
MANSELL Nigel	187	FABI Teo	64	KEEGAN Rupert	25
FISICHELLA Giancarlo	177	SUZUKI Aguri	64	ROTHENGATTER Huub	25
LAFFITE Jacques	176	LEHTO JJ	62	MAGNUSSEN Jan	25
HILL Graham	175	BLUNDELL Mark	61	SALAZAR Eliseo	24
LAUDA Niki	171	RINDT Jochen	60	BRABHAM David	24
TRULLI Jarno	164	COMAS Erik	59	MARQUES Tarso	24
BOUTSEN Thierry	163	MERZARIO Arturo	57	CLAES Johnny	23
VILLENEUVE Jacques	163	PESCAROLO Henri	56	MUSSO Luigi	23
SCHUMACHER Ralf	163	CAFFI Alex	56	BOESEL Raul	23
SENNA Ayrton	161	SCHELL Harry	55	LAMMERS Jan	23
HERBERT Johnny	161	RODRIGUEZ Pedro	54	DALMAS Yannick	23
HAKKINEN Mika	161	BEHRA Jean	53	De GRAFFENRIED E.	22
BRUNDLE Martin	158	STOMMELEN Rolf	53	WISELL Reine	22
PANIS Olivier	157	STREIFF Philippe	53	LIUZZI Vitantonio	22
FRENTZEN Heinz-Harald	156	WURZ Alexander	53	BAGHETTI Giancarlo	21
WATSON John	152	GINTHER Richie	52	GUERRERO Roberto	21
ARNOUX René	149	FANGIO Juan-Manuel	51	MAZZACANE Gaston	21
REUTEMANN Carlos	146	IRELAND Innes	50	BELLOF Stefan	20
WARWICK Derek	146	HAILWOOD Mike	50	MONTERMINI Andrea	20
IRVINE Eddie	146	OLIVER Jackie	49	BAUMGARTNER Zsolt	20
FITTIPALDI Emerson	144	JABOUILLE Jean-Pierre	49	PIZZONIA Antonio	20
JARIER Jean-Pierre	134	DALY Derek	49	BIRA Prince	19
REGAZZONI Clay	132	LARINI Nicola	49	ERTL Harald	19
CHEEVER Eddie	132	BADOER Luca	49	HENTON Brian	19
ANDRETTI Mario	128	HILL Phil	47	HESNAULT François	19
BRABHAM Jack	123	WINKELHOCK Manfred	47	KARTHIKEYAN Narain	19
PETERSON Ronnie	123	GACHOT Bertrand	47	TARUFFI Piero	18
MARTINI Pierluigi	118	SALVADORI Roy	46	SCHECKTER Ian	18
BUTTON Jenson	118	CEVERT François	46	SERRA Chico	18
JONES Alan	116	KLIEN Christian	46	CECOTTO Johnny	18
HILL Damon	115	HAWTHORN Mike	45	INOUE Taki	18
HEIDFELD Nick	115	BERNARD Eric	45	BRUNI Gimmi	18
ICKX Jacky	114	BANDINI Lorenzo	42	ROSBERG Nico	18
ROSBERG Keke	114	PRYCE Tom	42	SPEED Scott	18
TAMBAY Patrick	114	MORENO Roberto	42	MIERES Roberto	17
HULME Denny	112	REBAQUE Hector	41	HERRMANN Hans	17
SCHECKTER Jody	112	GROUILLARD Olivier	41	BIANCHI Lucien	17
SURTEES John	111	WENDLINGER Karl	41	GALLI Nanni	17
SALO Mika	110	ZANARDI Alessandro	41	CAMPOS Adrian	17
ALLIOT Philippe	109	FITTIPALDI Christian	40	ALLISON Cliff	16
De ANGELIS Elio	108	ROSIER Louis	38	ATTWOOD Dick	16
VERSTAPPEN Jos	107	BROOKS Tony	38	TUERO Esteban	16
MASS Jochen	105	GREGORY Masten	38	McNISH Allan	16
RAIKKONEN Kimi	104	TARQUINI Gabriele	38	WILSON Justin	16
BONNIER Jo	103	PIRRO Emanuele	37	BONETTO Felice	15
STEWART Jackie	99	ZONTA Ricardo	37	CHIRON Louis	15
McLAREN Bruce	98	MONTEIRO Tiago	37	WHARTON Ken	15
DINIZ Pedro	98	ALBERS Christijan	37	BURGESS Ian	15
SIFFERT Jo	96	SPENCE Mike	36	SULLIVAN Danny	15
AMON Chris	96	BALDI Mauro	36	DUMFRIES Johnny	15
DEPAILLER Patrick	95	DANNER Christian	36	BURTI Luciano	15
KATAYAMA Ukyo	95	GENE Marc	36	CASTELLOTTI Eugenio	14
MONTOYA Juan-Pablo	94	GANLEY Howden	35	GOULD Horace	14
CAPELLI Ivan	93	FITTIPALDI Wilson	35	LEWIS-EVANS Stuart	14
HUNT James	92	SCHENKEN Tim	34	GENDEBIEN Olivier	14
ALONSO Fernando	87	LUNGER Brett	34	DONOHUE Mark	14
GURNEY Dan	86	FARINA Giuseppe	33	YOONG Alex	14
WEBBER Mark	86	NAKANO Shinji	33	FIRMAN Ralph	14
BELTOISE Jean-Pierre	85	ASCARI Alberto	32	PANTANO Giorgio	14
PALMER Jonathan	83	COLLINS Peter	32	...	
SURER Marc	82	LAMY Pedro	32		
TRINTIGNANT Maurice	81	TAKAGI Tora	32		
JOHANSSON Stefan	79	VILLORESI Luigi	31		
GHINZANI Piercarlo	76	NILSSON Gunnar	31		
NANNINI Alessandro	76	De ADAMICH Andrea	30	DOORNBOS Robert	11
STUCK Hans Joachim	74	REVSON Peter	30	MONTAGNY Franck	7
BRAMBILLA Vittorio	74	GETHIN Peter	30	YAMAMOTO Sakon	7
NAKAJIMA Satoru	74	MANZON Robert	28	KUBICA Robert	6
GUGELMIN Mauricio	74	BEUTTLER Mike	28	IDE Yuji	4
CLARK Jim	72	BERNOLDI Enrique	28		

Drivers: GP in the lead

SCHUMACHER Michael	141	GONZALEZ Jose-Froilan	9	MASS Jochen	2
SENNA Ayrton	86	TAMBAY Patrick	9	De CESARIS Andrea	2
PROST Alain	84	GINTHER Richie	8	JOHANSSON Stefan	2
COULTHARD David	60	IRVINE Eddie	8	WARWICK Derek	2
PIQUET Nelson	59	COLLINS Peter	7	CAPELLI Ivan	2
MANSELL Nigel	55	BEHRA Jean	7	SALO Mika	2
STEWART Jackie	51	BANDINI Lorenzo	7	HOLLAND Bill	1
HAKKINEN Mika	48	RODRIGUEZ Pedro	7	ROSE Mauri	1
HILL Damon	45	AMON Chris	7	SOMMER Raymond	1
BARRICHELLO Rubens	44	PACE Carlos	7	WALLARD Lee	1
CLARK Jim	43	JABOUILLE Jean-Pierre	7	DAVIES Jimmy	1
LAUDA Niki	41	BROOKS Tony	6	GREEN Cecil	1
ALONSO Fernando	39	DEPAILLER Patrick	6	VILLORESI Luigi	1
FANGIO Juan-Manuel	38	RATHMANN Jim	5	BONETTO Felice	1
RAIKKONEN Kimi	34	McLAREN Bruce	5	TARUFFI Piero	1
BERGER Gerhard	33	SIFFERT Jo	5	AGABASHIAN Fred	1
HILL Graham	32	CEVERT François	5	DAYWALT Jimmy	1
MONTOYA Juan-Pablo	32	BOUTSEN Thierry	5	MIERES Roberto	1
MOSS Stirling	31	MASSA Felipe	5	SWEIKERT Bob	1
PATRESE Riccardo	29	VUKOVICH Bill	4	MENDITEGUY Carlos	1
BRABHAM Jack	28	McGRATH Jack	4	LEWIS-EVANS Stuart	1
PETERSON Ronnie	27	BONNIER Jo	4	BETTENHAUSEN Tony	1
ARNOUX René	25	Von TRIPS Wolfgang	4	AMICK George	1
HUNT James	24	BELTOISE Jean-Pierre	4	BOYD Johnny	1
JONES Alan	24	BRAMBILLA Vittorio	4	GENDEBIEN Olivier	1
SCHECKTER Jody	23	De ANGELIS Elio	4	BAGHETTI Giancarlo	1
ANDRETTI Mario	22	HERBERT Johnny	4	TAYLOR Trevor	1
ASCARI Alberto	21	FAGIOLI Luigi	3	MAIRESSE Willy	1
SCHUMACHER Ralf	21	KLING Karl	3	SCARFIOTTI Ludovico	1
REGAZZONI Clay	20	SCHELL Harry	3	PARKES Mike	1
ROSBERG Keke	20	CASTELLOTTI Eugenio	3	LOVE John	1
VILLENEUVE Jacques	20	HANKS Sam	3	SERVOZ-GAVIN Johnny	1
ICKX Jacky	19	MUSSO Luigi	3	COURAGE Piers	1
REUTEMANN Carlos	19	TRINTIGNANT Maurice	3	HAILWOOD Mike	1
ALESI Jean	19	BRYAN Jimmy	3	GETHIN Peter	1
HULME Denny	18	THOMSON Johnny	3	STOMMELEN Rolf	1
FITTIPALDI Emerson	18	RUTTMAN Troy	3	PRYCE Tom	1
VILLENEUVE Gilles	18	OLIVER Jackie	3	NILSSON Gunnar	1
SURTEES John	17	JARIER Jean-Pierre	3	STUCK Hans Joachim	1
GURNEY Dan	16	NANNINI Alessandro	3	GIACOMELLI Bruno	1
FARINA Giuseppe	14	WEBBER Mark	3	MARTINI Pierluigi	1
LAFFITE Jacques	14	CROSS Art	2	LARINI Nicola	1
FRENTZEN Heinz-Harald	13	PARSONS Johnnie	2	PANIS Olivier	1
BUTTON Jenson	13	FREELAND Don	2	Da MATTA Cristiano	1
FISICHELLA Giancarlo	13	O'CONNOR Pat	2	SATO Takuma	1
HAWTHORN Mike	12	RUSSO Paul	2	PIZZONIA Antonio	1
RINDT Jochen	12	FLAHERTY Pat	2	HEIDFELD Nick	1
HILL Phil	10	GREGORY Masten	2	KUBICA Robert	1
PIRONI Didier	10	SACHS Eddie	2		
WATSON John	10	WARD Rodger	2		
ALBORETO Michele	10	IRELAND Innes	2		
TRULLI Jarno	10	REVSON Peter	2		

Drivers: laps in the lead

SCHUMACHER Michael	5 096	ALESI Jean	265	CAPELLI Ivan	46
SENNA Ayrton	2 931	HAWTHORN Mike	225	HERBERT Johnny	44
PROST Alain	2 683	ALBORETO Michele	218	IRELAND Innes	43
MANSELL Nigel	2 058	BRYAN Jimmy	216	McLAREN Bruce	41
CLARK Jim	1 940	FISICHELLA Giancarlo	209	MENDITEGUY Carlos	39
STEWART Jackie	1 921	GURNEY Dan	203	OLIVER Jackie	36
PIQUET Nelson	1 633	AMBAY Patrick	197	RUSSO Paul	35
8LAUDA Niki	1 590	WARD Rodger	188	CROSS Art	32
HAKKINEN Mika	1 489	AMON Chris	183	BRAMBILLA Vittorio	32
HILL Damon	1 358	JABOUILLE Jean-Pierre	179	De CESARIS Andrea	32
FANGIO Juan-Manuel	1 347	HILL Phil	172	GIACOMELLI Bruno	31
MOSS Stirling	1 181	WALLARD Lee	165	De ANGELIS Elio	28
HILL Graham	1 102	DEPAILLER Patrick	164	BETTENHAUSEN Tony	24
ALONSO Fernando	956	BOUTSEN Thierry	164	SACHS Eddie	22
ASCARI Alberto	927	Von TRIPS Wolfgang	156	CASTELLOTTI Eugenio	21
COULTHARD David	896	IRVINE Eddie	156	NILSSON Gunnar	21
BRABHAM Jack	825	MASSA Felipe	156	NANNINI Alessandro	21
ANDRETTI Mario	799	FRENTZEN Heinz-Harald	150	DAVIES Jimmy	18
BERGER Gerhard	754	RATHMANN Jim	147	KLING Karl	18
BARRICHELLO Rubens	722	TRULLI Jarno	147	BOYD Johnny	18
PETERSON Ronnie	694	BANDINI Lorenzo	143	AMICK George	18
SCHECKTER Jody	674	HANKS Sam	140	Da MATTA Cristiano	17
HUNT James	666	BONNIER Jo	139	WARWICK Derek	16
REUTEMANN Carlos	650	FLAHERTY Pat	138	PANIS Olivier	16
25RAIKKONEN Kimi	638	BROOKS Tony	133	ROSE Mauri	15
VILLENEUVE Jacques	633	PARSONS Johnnie	131	SCHELL Harry	14
MONTOYA Juan-Pablo	605	CEVERT François	129	STUCK Hans Joachim	14
JONES Alan	589	COLLINS Peter	127	GREGORY Masten	13
PATRESE Riccardo	565	GINTHER Richie	116	LOVE John	13
VILLENEUVE Gilles	534	BEHRA Jean	107	HOLLAND Bill	8
ICKX Jacky	528	BUTTON Jenson	104	FAGIOLI Luigi	8
ROSBERG Keke	512	BELTOISE Jean-Pierre	101	DAYWALT Jimmy	8
3ARNOUX René	507	SIFFERT Jo	99	STOMMELEN Rolf	8
VUKOVICH Bill	485	SWEIKERT Bob	86	FREELAND Don	7
FITTIPALDI Emerson	478	RODRIGUEZ Pedro	86	BAGHETTI Giancarlo	7
HULME Denny	448	JARIER Jean-Pierre	79	PARKES Mike	7
SCHUMACHER Ralf	401	TRINTIGNANT Maurice	78	MUSSO Luigi	6
RINDT Jochen	387	McGRATH Jack	71	MER Raymond	5
REGAZZONI Clay	360	REVSON Peter	63	GREEN Cecil	5
FARINA Giuseppe	336	RUTTMAN Troy	59	LEWIS-EVANS Stuart	5
SURTEES John	308	THOMSON Johnny	55	WEBBER Mark	5
PIRONI Didier	295	SCARFIOTTI Ludovico	55	KUBICA Robert	5
WATSON John	287	PACE Carlos	50	SATO Takuma	2
LAFFITE Jacques	283	TARUFFI Piero	46	HEIDFELD Nick	1
GONZALEZ Jose-Froilan	272	O'CONNOR Pat	46		

Drivers: points

SCHUMACHER Michael	1 369	VUKOVICH Bill	19
PROST Alain	798	SALVADORI Roy	19
SENNA Ayrton	614	PRYCE Tom	19
BARRICHELLO Rubens	519	ROSIER Louis	18
COULTHARD David	513	BRYAN Jimmy	18
PIQUET Nelson	485	GENDEBIEN Olivier	18
MANSELL Nigel	482	MARTINI Pierluigi	18
LAUDA Niki	420	BONETTO Felice	17
HAKKINEN Mika	420	KLING Karl	17
BERGER Gerhard	385	SCARFIOTTI Ludovico	17
ALONSO Fernando	381	SURER Marc	17
STEWART Jackie	360	MODENA Stefano	17
HILL Damon	360	VERSTAPPEN Jos	17
RAIKKONEN Kimi	346	MANZON Robert	16
SCHUMACHER Ralf	324	LEWIS-EVANS Stuart	16
REUTEMANN Carlos	310	NAKAJIMA Satoru	16
MONTOYA Juan-Pablo	307	BRAMBILLA Vittorio	15
HILL Graham	289	DALY Derek	15
FITTIPALDI Emerson	281	MORENO Roberto	15
PATRESE Riccardo	281	WARD Rodger	14
FANGIO Juan-Manuel	277	PARKES Mike	14
CLARK Jim	274	BAGHETTI Giancarlo	14
BRABHAM Jack	261	STOMMELEN Rolf	14
SCHECKTER Jody	255	PALMER Jonathan	14
HULME Denny	248	GIACOMELLI Bruno	14
FISICHELLA Giancarlo	246	WENDLINGER Karl	14
ALESI Jean	241	KLIEN Christian	14
VILLENEUVE Jacques	235	MIERES Roberto	13
LAFFITE Jacques	228	WISELL Reine	13
BUTTON Jenson	223	OLIVER Jackie	13
REGAZZONI Clay	212	REBAQUE Hector	13
PETERSON Ronnie	206	Da MATTA Cristiano	13
JONES Alan	206	PARSONS Johnnie	12
McLAREN Bruce	196	ARUNDELL Peter	12
IRVINE Eddie	191	PESCAROLO Henri	12
MOSS Stirling	186	FITTIPALDI Christian	12
ALBORETO Michele	186	FRERE Paul	11
ICKX Jacky	181	BETTENHAUSEN Tony	11
ARNOUX René	181	ALLISON Cliff	11
SURTEES John	180	ATTWOOD Dick	11
ANDRETTI Mario	180	GETHIN Peter	11
HUNT James	179	MERZARIO Arturo	11
TRULLI Jarno	175	STREIFF Philippe	11
FRENTZEN Heinz-Harald	174	FISCHER Rudi	10
WATSON John	169	THOMSON Johnny	10
ROSBERG Keke	159	HERRMANN Hans	10
DEPAILLER Patrick	141	GANLEY Howden	10
ASCARI Alberto	140	GUGELMIN Mauricio	10
GURNEY Dan	133	BERNARD Eric	10
BOUTSEN Thierry	132	LEHTO JJ	10
HAWTHORN Mike	127	DINIZ Pedro	10
FARINA Giuseppe	127De	RUTTMAN Troy	9
ANGELIS Elio	122	WALLARD Lee	9
RINDT Jochen	109	PARNELL Reg	9
GINTHER Richie	107	McGRATH Jack	9
VILLENEUVE Gilles	107	De GRAFFENRIED Emmanuel	9
MASSA Felipe	107	MENDITEGUY Carlos	9
TAMBAY Patrick	103	SERVOZ-GAVIN Johnny	9
PIRONI Didier	101	RUSSO Paul	8
HILL Phil	98	MORBIDELLI Gianni	8
BRUNDLE Martin	98	MARIMON Onofre	8
HERBERT Johnny	98	NAZARUK Mike	8
CEVERT François	89	CROSS Art	8
JOHANSSON Stefan	88	BIRA Prince	8
AMON Chris	83	SWEIKERT Bob	8
HEIDFELD Nick	79	FLAHERTY Pat	8
GONZALEZ Jose-Froilan	77	ANDERSON Bob	8
BELTOISE Jean-Pierre	77	TAYLOR Trevor	8
PANIS Olivier	76	ELFORD Vic	8
BROOKS Tony	75	REDMAN Brian	8
TRINTIGNANT Maurice	72	DONOHUE Mark	8
RODRIGUEZ Pedro	71	SUZUKI Aguri	8
MASS Jochen	71	PIZZONIA Antonio	8
WARWICK Derek	71	MAIRESSE Willy	7
CHEEVER Eddie	70	SCHENKEN Tim	7
WEBBER Mark	69	ANDRETTI Michael	7
SIFFERT Jo	68	ALLIOT Philippe	7
NANNINI Alessandro	65	COMAS Erik	7
REVSON Peter	61	LARINI Nicola	7
De CESARIS Andrea	59	MONTEIRO Tiago	7
BANDINI Lorenzo	58	CARTER Duane	6
PACE Carlos	58	HOLLAND Bill	6
Von TRIPS Wolfgang	56	AMICK George	6
BEHRA Jean	51	GODIA-SALES Chico	6
VILLORESI Luigi	49	GOLDSMITH Paul	6
COLLINS Peter	47	BIANCHI Lucien	6
IRELAND Innes	47	LOVE John	6
MUSSO Luigi	44	De ADAMICH Andrea	6
TARUFFI Piero	41	CAFFI Alex	6
SATO Takuma	40	KUBICA Robert	6
BONNIER Jo	39		
SALO Mika	33		
FAGIOLI Luigi	32		
SCHELL Harry	32		
BLUNDELL Mark	32		
WURZ Alexander	32		
JARIER Jean-Pierre	31		
NILSSON Gunnar	31		
CAPELLI Ivan	31		
RATHMANN Jim	29		
HAILWOOD Mike	29		
STUCK Hans Joachim	29		
De la ROSA Pedro	29		
SPENCE Mike	27		
MAGGS Tony	26		
FABI Teo	23		
GREGORY Masten	21		
JABOUILLE Jean-Pierre	21	...	
HANKS Sam	20	ROSBERG Nico	4
COURAGE Piers	20	ALBERS Christijan	4
CASTELLOTTI Eugenio	19	LIUZZI Vitantonio	2

Drivers: kilometers in the lead

SCHUMACHER Michael	24 070	ICKX Jacky	3 119	ALESI Jean	1 285	RODRIGUEZ Pedro	587
SENNA Ayrton	13 430	RAIKKONEN Kimi	3 059	BROOKS Tony	1 268	HANKS Sam	563
PROST Alain	12 474	MONTOYA Juan-Pablo	2 966	PIRONI Didier	1 240	CEVERT François	560
CLARK Jim	10 110	VILLENEUVE Jacques	2 965	WATSON John	1 238	FLAHERTY Pat	555
MANSELL Nigel	9 503	SCHECKTER Jody	2 851	FISICHELLA Giancarlo	1 088	BONNIER Jo	547
FANGIO Juan-Manuel	9 316	JONES Alan	2 847	TAMBAY Patrick	970	PARSONS Johnnie	527
STEWART Jackie	9 191	FARINA Giuseppe	2 651	COLLINS Peter	946	BUTTON Jenson	522
PIQUET Nelson	7 756	ARNOUX René	2 571	JABOUILLE Jean-Pierre	942	SIFFERT Jo	521
HAKKINEN Mika	7 194	PATRESE Riccardo	2 553	ALBORETO Michele	932	JARIER Jean-Pierre	453
LAUDA Niki	7 056	VILLENEUVE Gilles	2 251	BRYAN Jimmy	869	BEHRA Jean	439
MOSS Stirling	6 369	FITTIPALDI Emerson	2 235	AMON Chris	852	BELTOISE Jean-Pierre	378
HILL Damon	6 310	ROSBERG Keke	2 165	IRVINE Eddie	838	SWEIKERT Bob	346
ASCARI Alberto	5 902	SURTEES John	2 123	Von TRIPS Wolfgang	788	TARUFFI Piero	335
HILL Graham	4 747	HULME Denny	1 966	WARD Rodger	756	CARFIOTTI Ludovico	316
ALONSO Fernando	4 585	VUKOVICH Bill	1 951	FRENTZEN Heinz-Harald	751	PACE Carlos	294
BRABHAM Jack	4 540	SCHUMACHER Ralf	1 937	GINTHER Richie	737	McGRATH Jack	286
COULTHARD David	4 206	RINDT Jochen	1 898	MASSA Felipe	727	REVSON Peter	271
BERGER Gerhard	3 718	REGAZZONI Clay	1 851	WALLARD Lee	664	TRINTIGNANT Maurice	261
ANDRETTI Mario	3 577	HAWTHORN Mike	1 635	BOUTSEN Thierry	662	...	
BARRICHELLO Rubens	3 487	GURNEY Dan	1 606	BANDINI Lorenzo	640	KUBICA Robert	29
HUNT James	3 363	HILL Phil	1 532	DEPAILLER Patrick	614	WEBBER Mark	22
REUTEMANN Carlos	3 314	GONZALEZ Jose-Froilan	1 525	TRULLI Jarno	605	SATO Takuma	10
PETERSON Ronnie	3 262	LAFFITE Jacques	1 519	RATHMANN Jim	591	HEIDFELD Nick	5

Drivers: pole positions

SCHUMACHER Michael	68	HILL Phil	6	FAULKNER Walt	1
SENNA Ayrton	65	FITTIPALDI Emerson	6	NALON Duke	1
CLARK Jim	33	JABOUILLE Jean-Pierre	6	AGABASHIAN Fred	1
PROST Alain	33	JONES Alan	6	VUKOVICH Bill	1
MANSELL Nigel	32	REUTEMANN Carlos	6	McGRATH Jack	1
FANGIO Juan-Manuel	29	SCHUMACHER Ralf	6	HOYT Jerry	1
HAKKINEN Mika	26	FARINA Giuseppe	5	CASTELLOTTI Eugenio	1
LAUDA Niki	24	AMON Chris	5	FLAHERTY Pat	1
PIQUET Nelson	24	REGAZZONI Clay	5	O'CONNOR Pat	1
HILL Damon	20	TAMBAY Patrick	5	RATHMANN Dick	1
ANDRETTI Mario	18	ROSBERG Keke	5	THOMSON Johnny	1
ARNOUX René	18	HAWTHORN Mike	4	BONNIER Jo	1
STEWART Jackie	17	PIRONI Didier	4	SACHS Eddie	1
MOSS Stirling	16	GONZALEZ Jose-Froilan	3	Von TRIPS Wolfgang	1
ALONSO Fernando	15	BROOKS Tony	3	BANDINI Lorenzo	1
ASCARI Alberto	14	GURNEY Dan	3	PARKES Mike	1
HUNT James	14	JARIER Jean-Pierre	3	REVSON Peter	1
PETERSON Ronnie	14	CHECKTER Jody	3	HULME Denny	1
HILL Graham	13	De ANGELIS Elio	3	DEPAILLER Patrick	1
BRABHAM Jack	13	FABI Teo	3	PACE Carlos	1
ICKX Jacky	13	TRULLI Jarno	3	BRAMBILLA Vittorio	1
VILLENEUVE Jacques	13	FISICHELLA Giancarlo	3	PRYCE Tom	1
BARRICHELLO Rubens	13	BUTTON Jenson	3	GIACOMELLI Bruno	1
MONTOYA Juan-Pablo	13	MASSA Felipe	3	De CESARIS Andrea	1
BERGER Gerhard	12	LEWIS-EVANS Stuart	2	BOUTSEN Thierry	1
COULTHARD David	12	SIFFERT Jo	2	HEIDFELD Nick	1
RAIKKONEN Kimi	11	WATSON John	2		
RINDT Jochen	10	VILLENEUVE Gilles	2		
SURTEES John	8	ALBORETO Michele	2		
PATRESE Riccardo	8	ALESI Jean	2		
LAFFITE Jacques	7	FRENTZEN Heinz-Harald	2		

Drivers: fastest laps

SCHUMACHER Michael	76	GURNEY Dan	6	McGRATH Jack	1
PROST Alain	41	FITTIPALDI Emerson	6	HERRMANN Hans	1
MANSELL Nigel	30	REUTEMANN Carlos	6	MARIMON Onofre	1
CLARK Jim	28	LAFFITE Jacques	6	BEHRA Jean	1
HAKKINEN Mika	25	FRENTZEN Heinz-Harald	6	KLING Karl	1
LAUDA Niki	24	FARINA Giuseppe	5	MIERES Roberto	1
FANGIO Juan-Manuel	23	PACE Carlos	5	RUSSO Paul	1
PIQUET Nelson	23	SCHECKTER Jody	5	MUSSO Luigi	1
BERGER Gerhard	21	PIRONI Didier	5	BETTENHAUSEN Tony	1
MOSS Stirling	19	WATSON John	5	THOMSON Johnny	1
SENNA Ayrton	19	ALBORETO Michele	5	TRINTIGNANT Maurice	1
HILL Damon	19	SIFFERT Jo	4	IRELAND Innes	1
RAIKKONEN Kimi	19	BELTOISE Jean-Pierre	4	BAGHETTI Giancarlo	1
COULTHARD David	18	DEPAILLER Patrick	4	SCARFIOTTI Ludovico	1
STEWART Jackie	15	ALESI Jean	4	ATTWOOD Dick	1
REGAZZONI Clay	15	VUKOVICH Bill	3	RODRIGUEZ Pedro	1
BARRICHELLO Rubens	15	BROOKS Tony	3	OLIVER Jackie	1
ICKX Jacky	14	McLAREN Bruce	3	PESCAROLO Henri	1
JONES Alan	13	GINTHER Richie	3	HAILWOOD Mike	1
PATRESE Riccardo	13	RINDT Jochen	3	BRAMBILLA Vittorio	1
ASCARI Alberto	12	AMON Chris	3	HASEMI Masahiro	1
BRABHAM Jack	12	JARIER Jean-Pierre	3	NILSSON Gunnar	1
ARNOUX René	12	ROSBERG Keke	3	SURER Marc	1
MONTOYA Juan-Pablo	12	RATHMANN Jim	2	HENTON Brian	1
SURTEES John	11	BANDINI Lorenzo	2	De CESARIS Andrea	1
HILL Graham	10	CEVERT François	2	PALMER Jonathan	1
ANDRETTI Mario	10	MASS Jochen	2	GUGELMIN Mauricio	1
HULME Denny	9	TAMBAY Patrick	2	NAKAJIMA Satoru	1
PETERSON Ronnie	9	WARWICK Derek	2	BOUTSEN Thierry	1
VILLENEUVE Jacques	9	FABI Teo	2	GACHOT Bertrand	1
HUNT James	8	NANNINI Alessandro	2	MORENO Roberto	1
VILLENEUVE Gilles	8	FISICHELLA Giancarlo	2	WURZ Alexander	1
SCHUMACHER Ralf	8	MASSA Felipe	2	IRVINE Eddie	1
ALONSO Fernando	8	PARSONS Johnnie	1	DE LA ROSA Pedro	1
GONZALEZ Jose-Froilan	6	WALLARD Lee	1	ROSBERG Nico	1
HAWTHORN Mike	6	TARUFFI Piero	1		
HILL Phil	6	VILLORESI Luigi	1		

Number of Constructors' Championships

(since 1958)

14: Ferrari
1961 - 64 - 75 - 76 - 77 - 79 - 82 - 83 - 99 - 2000 - 01 - 02 - 03 - 04

9: Williams
1980 - 81 - 86 - 87 - 92 - 93 - 94 - 96 - 97

8: McLaren
1974 - 84 - 85 - 88 - 89 - 90 - 91- 98

7: Lotus
1963 - 65 - 68 - 70 - 72 - 73 - 78

2: Cooper 1959 - 60
Brabham 1966 - 67
Renault 2005 - 06

1: Vanwall 1958
BRM 1962
Matra 1969
Tyrrell 1971
Benetton 1995

Constructors: victories

Ferrari	192	Alfa Romeo	10	Wolf	3
McLaren	148	Mercedes	9	Honda	3
Williams	113	Maserati	9	Epperly	2
Lotus	79	Vanwall	9	Kuzma	1
Brabham	35	Matra	9	Porsche	1
Renault	33	Ligier	9	Eagle	1
Benetton	27	Kurtis	5	Hesketh	1
Tyrrell	23	Jordan	4	Penske	1
BRM	17	Watson	3	Shadow	1
Cooper	16	March	3	Stewart	1

Constructors: pole positions

Ferrari	186	Ligier	9	Honda	2
Williams	125	Mercedes	8	Stevens	1
McLaren	125	Vanwall	7	Lesovsky	1
Lotus	107	Kurtis	6	Ewing	1
Renault	50	March	5	Lola	1
Brabham	39	Matra	4	Porsche	1
Benetton	15	Shadow	3	Wolf	1
Tyrrell	14	Lancia	2	Arrows	1
Alfa Romeo	12	Watson	2	Toleman	1
Cooper	11	Jordan	2	Stewart	1
BRM	11	BAR	2		
Maserati	10	Toyota	2		

Constructors: Grands Prix

Ferrari	741	Spirit	23	Trevis	4
McLaren	613	Forti	23	Emeryson	4
Williams	494	Pacific	22	Martini	4
Lotus	491	Simtek	21	Deidt	3
Tyrrell	430	Rial	20	Pawl	3
Brabham	394	Fondmetal	19	Moore	3
Minardi	340	Super Aguri	18	Dunn	3
Ligier	326	Toro Rosso	18	Gilby	3
Arrows	291	Midland	18	Token	3
Benetton	260	BMW Sauber	18	LEC	3
Jordan	250	Connaught	17	RAM March	3
Sauber	215	Parnelli	16	Marchese	2
Renault	210	Onyx	16	Sherman	2
BRM	197	Venturi	16	Aston	2
March	197	Simca Gordini	14	BMW	2
Lola	149	HWM	14	Nichels	2
Osella	132	Eurobrun	14	Pankratz	2
Cooper	129	Talbot Lago	13	Ewing	2
Surtees	118	BRP	13	Christensen	2
BAR	117	Coloni	13	Scarab	2
Alfa Romeo	110	Mercedes	12	Alfa Special	2
Shadow	104	Kurtis	12	Bellasi	2
Ensign	99	Tecno	11	Kojima	2
Footwork	91	Kuzma	10	Olson	1
ATS	89	De Tomaso	10	Langley	1
Toyota	87	Hill	10	Rae	1
Jaguar	85	Merzario	10	Wetteroth	1
Prost	83	Lesovsky	9	Snowberger	1
Dallara	78	Watson	9	Adams	1
Copersucar	71	Eifelland March	8	Hall	1
Maserati	70	ERA	7	Del Roy	1
Matra	62	Phillips	7	Turner	1
Toleman	57	Veritas	6	EMW	1
Zakspeed	53	Stevens	6	Klenk	1
Honda	53	A-T-S	6	Bugatti	1
Hesketh	52	Trojan	6	Elder	1
Stewart	49	Boro	6	Sutton	1
Wolf	47	Lamborghini	6	Tec Mec	1
AGS	47	Alta	5	Meskowski	1
Penske	40	Epperly	5	Ferguson	1
Red Bull	36	Aston Martin	5	ENB	1
Theodore	34	JBW	5	Stebro	1
Gordini	33	Scirocco	5	Shannon	1
Porsche	33	LDS	5	Protos	1
Fittipaldi	32	Maserati Milano	4	Politoys	1
Larrousse	32	Frazer Nash	4	Connew	1
Iso-Marlboro	30	OSCA	4	Amon	1
Leyton House	30	AFM	4	Lyncar	1
Vanwall	28	Bromme	4	Rebaque	1
RAM	28	Schroeder	4	Monteverdi	1
Eagle	25	Lancia	4	Andrea Moda	1

Constructors: fastest laps

Ferrari	193	Matra	12	Toleman	2
Williams	129	Mercedes	9	Jordan	2
McLaren	129	Ligier	9	Gordini	1
Lotus	71	Kurtis	7	Lancia	1
Brabham	41	March	7	Lesovsky	1
Benetton	36	Vanwall	6	Watson	1
Renault	27	Surtees	3	Hesketh	1
Tyrrell	20	Epperly	2	Parnelli	1
Maserati	15	Eagle	2	Kojima	1
BRM	15	Honda	2	Ensign	1
Cooper	14	Shadow	2	Toyota	1
Alfa Romeo	14	Wolf	2		

Constructors: points

Ferrari	3647	Shadow	67	Fittipaldi	12
McLaren	3159	Vanwall	57	BRP	11
Williams	2506	Surtees	53	Leyton House	8
Lotus	1368	Alfa Romeo	50	ATS	7
Renault	925	Red Bull	50	Maserati	6
Brabham	864	Jaguar	49	Iso-Marlboro	6
Benetton	851	Porsche	48	Parnelli	6
Tyrrell	621	Hesketh	48	Rial	6
BRM	433	Stewart	47	Onyx	6
Ligier	388	Lola	43	Osella	5
Cooper	342	Minardi	38	Larrousse	5
Jordan	291	BMW Sauber	36	Hill	3
BAR	227	Prost	35	Theodore	2
Sauber	195	Copersucar	32	Zakspeed	2
March	173	Toleman	26	AGS	2
Matra	163	Footwork	25	Tecno	1
Toyota	150	Penske	23	Venturi	1
Arrows	142	Ensign	19	Toro Rosso	1
Honda	134	Eagle	17		
Wolf	79	Dallara	15		

Constructors: 1-2

Ferrari	72	Mercedes	5	Renault	2
McLaren	40	BRM	5	Benetton	2
Williams	33	Alfa Romeo	4	Maserati	1
Lotus	8	Kurtis	2	Ligier	1
Brabham	8	Epperly	2	Jordan	1
Tyrrell	8	Watson	2		
Cooper	6	Matra	2		

217 STATISTICS

The 768 winners

	GB	MC	INDY 500	CH	B	F	I	D	E	NL	RA	PESCARA	P	MA	USA	ZA	MEX
1950	Farina	Fangio	Parsons	Farina	Fangio	Fangio	Farina										
1951	Gonzalez		Wallard	Fangio	Farina	Fagioli/Fangio	Ascari	Ascari	Fangio								
1952	Ascari		Ruttman	Taruffi	Ascari	Ascari	Ascari	Ascari		Ascari							
1953	Ascari		Vukovich	Ascari	Ascari	Hawthorn	Fangio	Farina		Ascari	Ascari						
1954	Gonzalez		Vukovich	Fangio	Fangio	Fangio	Fangio	Fangio	Hawthorn		Fangio						
1955	Moss	Trintignant	Sweikert		Fangio		Fangio			Fangio	Fangio						
1956	Fangio	Moss	Flaherty		Collins	Collins	Moss	Fangio			Musso/Fangio						
1957	Brooks/Moss	Fangio	Hanks			Fangio	Moss	Fangio			Fangio	Moss					
1958	Collins	Trintignant	Bryan		Brooks	Hawthorn	Brooks	Brooks		Moss	Moss		Moss	Moss			
1959	Brabham	Brabham	Ward			Brooks	Moss	Brooks		Bonnier			Moss		McLaren		
1960	Brabham	Moss	Rathmann		Brabham	Brabham	P. Hill			Brabham	McLaren		Brabham		Moss		
1961	Von Trips	Moss			P. Hill	Baghetti	P. Hill	Moss		Von Trips					Ireland		
1962	Clark	McLaren			Clark	Gurney	G. Hill	G. Hill		G. Hill					Clark	G. Hill	
1963	Clark	G. Hill			Clark	Clark	Clark	Surtees		Clark					G. Hill	Clark	Clark
1964	Clark	G. Hill			Clark	Gurney	Surtees	Surtees		Clark					G. Hill		Gurney
1965	Clark	G. Hill			Clark	Clark	Stewart	Clark		Clark					G. Hill	Clark	Ginther
1966	Brabham	Stewart			Surtees	Brabham	Scarfiotti	Brabham		Brabham					Clark		Surtees
1967	Clark	Hulme			Gurney	Brabham	Surtees	Hulme		Clark					Clark	Rodriguez	Clark
1968	Siffert	G. Hill			McLaren	Ickx	Hulme	Stewart	G. Hill	Stewart					Stewart	Clark	G. Hill
1969	Stewart	G. Hill				Stewart	Stewart	Ickx	Stewart	Stewart					Rindt	Stewart	Hulme
1970	Rindt	Rindt			Rodriguez	Rindt	Regazzoni	Rindt	Stewart	Rindt					Fittipaldi	Brabham	Ickx
1971	Stewart	Stewart				Stewart	Gethin	Stewart	Stewart	Ickx					Cevert	Andretti	
1972	Fittipaldi	Beltoise			Fittipaldi	Stewart	Fittipaldi	Ickx	Fittipaldi		Stewart				Stewart	Hulme	
1973	Revson	Stewart			Stewart	Peterson	Peterson	Stewart	Fittipaldi	Stewart	Fittipaldi				Peterson	Stewart	
1974	Scheckter	Peterson			Fittipaldi	Peterson	Peterson	Regazzoni	Lauda	Lauda	Hulme				Reutemann	Reutemann	
1975	Fittipaldi	Lauda			Lauda	Lauda	Regazzoni	Reutemann	Mass	Hunt	Fittipaldi				Lauda	Scheckter	
1976	Lauda	Lauda			Lauda	Hunt	Peterson	Hunt	Hunt	Hunt					Lauda		
1977	Hunt	Scheckter			Nilsson	Andretti	Andretti	Lauda	Andretti	Lauda	Scheckter				Lauda		
1978	Reutemann	Depailler			Andretti	Andretti	Lauda	Andretti	Andretti	Andretti	Andretti					Peterson	
1979	Regazzoni	Scheckter			Scheckter	Jabouille	Scheckter	Jones	Depailler	Jones	Laffite					G. Villeneuve	
1980	Jones	Reutemann			Pironi	Jones	Piquet	Laffite		Piquet	Jones					Arnoux	
1981	Watson	G. Villeneuve			Reutemann	Prost	Prost	Piquet	G. Villeneuve	Prost	Piquet						
1982	Lauda	Patrese		Rosberg	Watson	Arnoux	Arnoux	Tambay		Pironi						Prost	
1983	Prost	Rosberg			Prost	Prost	Piquet	Arnoux		Arnoux						Patrese	
1984	Lauda	Prost			Alboreto	Lauda	Lauda	Prost		Prost	Lauda		Prost		Rosberg		
1985	Prost	Prost			Senna	Piquet	Prost	Alboreto		Lauda			Senna		Rosberg	Mansell	
1986	Mansell	Prost			Mansell	Mansell	Piquet	Piquet	Senna				Mansell		Senna		Berger
1987	Mansell	Senna			Prost	Mansell	Piquet	Piquet	Mansell				Prost		Senna		Mansell
1988	Senna	Prost			Senna	Prost	Berger	Senna	Prost				Prost		Senna		Prost
1989	Prost	Senna			Senna	Prost	Prost	Senna	Senna				Berger		Prost		Senna
1990	Prost	Senna			Senna	Prost	Senna	Senna	Prost				Mansell		Senna		Prost
1991	Mansell	Senna			Senna	Mansell	Mansell	Mansell	Mansell				Patrese		Senna		Patrese
1992	Mansell	Senna			M.Schumacher	Mansell	Senna	Mansell	Mansell				Mansell			Mansell	Mansell
1993	Prost	Senna			D. Hill	Prost	D. Hill	Prost	Prost				M.Schumacher			Prost	
1994	D. Hill	M.Schumacher			D. Hill	M.Schumacher	D. Hill	Berger	D. Hill				D. Hill				
1995	Herbert	M.Schumacher			M.Schumacher	M.Schumacher	Herbert	M.Schumacher	M.Schumacher		D. Hill		Coulthard				
1996	J. Villeneuve	Panis			M.Schumacher	D. Hill	M.Schumacher	D. Hill	M.Schumacher		D. Hill		J. Villeneuve				
1997	J. Villeneuve	M.Schumacher			M.Schumacher	M.Schumacher	Coulthard	Berger	J. Villeneuve		J. Villeneuve						
1998	M.Schumacher	Häkkinen			D. Hill	M.Schumacher	M.Schumacher	Häkkinen	Häkkinen		M.Schumacher						
1999	Coulthard	M.Schumacher			Coulthard	Frentzen	Frentzen	Irvine	Häkkinen								
2000	Coulthard	Coulthard			Häkkinen	Coulthard	M.Schumacher	Barrichello	Häkkinen						M.Schumacher		
2001	Häkkinen	M.Schumacher			M.Schumacher	M.Schumacher	Montoya	R.Schumacher	M.Schumacher						Häkkinen		
2002	M.Schumacher	Coulthard			M.Schumacher	M.Schumacher	Barrichello	M.Schumacher	M.Schumacher						Barrichello		
2003	Barrichello	Montoya				R.Schumacher	M.Schumacher	Montoya	M.Schumacher						M.Schumacher		
2004	M.Schumacher	Trulli			Räikkönen	M.Schumacher	Barrichello	M.Schumacher	M.Schumacher						M.Schumacher		
2005	Montoya	Räikkönen			Räikkönen	Alonso	Montoya	Alonso	Räikkönen						M.Schumacher		
2006	Alonso	Alonso				M.Schumacher	M.Schumacher	M.Schumacher	Alonso						M.Schumacher		

Grand Prix circuits (country codes)

A | CDN | BR | S | USA-W | USA-E | J | RSM | LAS-VEGAS | EUR | AUS | H | PACIFIC | L | MAL | BRN | PRC | TR

The 57 World Champions

Year	Driver	Nationality	Team	Number of GPs	Number of poles	Number of victories	Number of fastest laps
1950	Giuseppe Farina	I	Alfa Roméo	7	2	3	3
1951	Juan Manuel Fangio	RA	Alfa Roméo	8	4	3	5
1952	Alberto Ascari	I	Ferrari	8	5	6	5
1953	Alberto Ascari	I	Ferrari	9	6	5	4
1954	Juan Manuel Fangio	RA	Mercedes/Maserati	9	5	6	3
1955	Juan Manuel Fangio	RA	Mercedes	7	3	4	3
1956	Juan Manuel Fangio	RA	Lancia/Ferrari	8	5	3	3
1957	Juan Manuel Fangio	RA	Maserati	8	4	4	2
1958	Mike Hawthorn	GB	Ferrari	11	4	1	5
1959	Jack Brabham	AUS	Cooper Climax	9	1	2	1
1960	Jack Brabham	AUS	Cooper Climax	10	3	5	3
1961	Phil Hill	USA	Ferrari	8	5	2	2
1962	Graham Hill	GB	BRM	9	1	4	3
1963	Jim Clark	GB	Lotus Climax	10	7	7	6
1964	John Surtees	GB	Ferrari	10	2	2	2
1965	Jim Clark	GB	Lotus Climax	10	6	6	6
1966	Jack Brabham	AUS	Brabham Repco	9	3	4	1
1967	Denny Hulme	NZ	Brabham Repco	11	0	2	2
1968	Graham Hill	GB	Lotus Ford	12	2	3	0
1969	Jackie Stewart	GB	Matra Ford	11	2	6	5
1970	Jochen Rindt	A	Lotus Ford	13	3	5	1
1971	Jackie Stewart	GB	Tyrrell Ford	11	6	6	3
1972	Emerson Fittipaldi	BR	Lotus Ford	12	3	5	0
1973	Jackie Stewart	GB	Tyrrell Ford	15	3	5	1
1974	Emerson Fittipaldi	BR	McLaren Ford	15	2	3	0
1975	Niki Lauda	A	Ferrari	14	9	5	2
1976	James Hunt	GB	McLaren Ford	16	8	6	2
1977	Niki Lauda	A	Ferrari	17	2	3	3
1978	Mario Andretti	USA	Lotus Ford	16	8	6	3
1979	Jody Scheckter	ZA	Ferrari	15	1	3	1
1980	Alan Jones	AUS	Williams Ford	14	3	5	5
1981	Nelson Piquet	BR	Brabham Ford	15	4	3	1
1982	Keke Rosberg	FIN	Williams Ford	16	1	1	0
1983	Nelson Piquet	BR	Brabham BMW Turbo	15	1	3	4
1984	Niki Lauda	A	McLaren TAG Porsche Turbo	16	0	5	5
1985	Alain Prost	F	McLaren TAG Porsche Turbo	16	2	5	5
1986	Alain Prost	F	McLaren TAG Porsche Turbo	16	1	4	2
1987	Nelson Piquet	BR	Williams Honda Turbo	16	4	3	4
1988	Ayrton Senna	BR	McLaren Honda Turbo	16	13	8	3
1989	Alain Prost	F	McLaren Honda	16	2	4	5
1990	Ayrton Senna	BR	McLaren Honda	16	10	6	2
1991	Ayrton Senna	BR	McLaren Honda	16	8	7	2
1992	Nigel Mansell	GB	Williams Renault	16	14	9	8
1993	Alain Prost	F	Williams Renault	16	13	7	6
1994	Michael Schumacher	D	Benetton Ford	14	6	8	9
1995	Michael Schumacher	D	Benetton Renault	17	4	9	7
1996	Damon Hill	GB	Williams Renault	16	9	8	5
1997	Jacques Villeneuve	CDN	Williams Renault	17	10	7	3
1998	Mika Häkkinen	FIN	McLaren Mercedes	16	9	8	6
1999	Mika Häkkinen	FIN	McLaren Mercedes	16	11	5	6
2000	Michael Schumacher	D	Ferrari	17	9	9	2
2001	Michael Schumacher	D	Ferrari	17	11	9	3
2002	Michael Schumacher	D	Ferrari	17	7	11	7
2003	Michael Schumacher	D	Ferrari	16	5	6	5
2004	Michael Schumacher	D	Ferrari	18	8	13	10
2005	Fernando Alonso	E	Renault	19	6	7	2
2006	Fernando Alonso	E	Renault	18	6	7	5

Grand Prix winners by circuit and year

A	CDN	BR	S	USA-W	USA-E	J	RSM	LAS-VEGAS	EUR	AUS	H	PACIFIC	L	MAL	BRN	PRC	TR	Year
																		1950
																		1951
																		1952
																		1953
																		1954
																		1955
																		1956
																		1957
																		1958
																		1959
																		1960
																		1961
																		1962
																		1963
Bandini																		1964
																		1965
																		1966
	Brabham																	1967
	Hulme																	1968
	Ickx																	1969
Ickx	Ickx																	1970
Siffert	Stewart																	1971
Fittipaldi	Stewart																	1972
Peterson	Revson	Fittipaldi	Hulme															1973
Reutemann	Fittipaldi	Fittipaldi	Scheckter															1974
Brambilla		Pace	Lauda															1975
Watson	Hunt	Lauda	Scheckter	Regazzoni	Hunt	Andretti												1976
Jones	Scheckter	Reutemann	Laffite	Andretti	Hunt	Hunt												1977
Peterson	G. Villeneuve	Reutemann	Lauda	Reutemann	Reutemann													1978
Jones	Jones	Laffite		G. Villeneuve	G. Villeneuve													1979
Jabouille	Jones	Arnoux		Piquet	Jones													1980
Laffite	Laffite	Reutemann		Jones			Piquet	Jones										1981
De Angelis	Piquet	Prost		Lauda	Watson		Pironi	Alboreto										1982
Prost	Arnoux	Piquet		Watson	Alboreto		Tambay		Piquet									1983
Lauda	Piquet	Prost			Piquet		Prost		Prost									1984
Prost	Alboreto	Prost			Rosberg		De Angelis		Mansell	Rosberg								1985
Prost	Mansell	Piquet			Senna		Prost			Prost	Piquet							1986
Mansell		Prost			Senna	Berger	Mansell			Berger	Piquet							1987
	Senna	Prost			Senna	Senna	Senna			Prost	Senna							1988
	Boutsen	Mansell				Nannini	Senna			Boutsen	Mansell							1989
	Senna	Prost				Piquet	Patrese			Piquet	Boutsen							1990
	Piquet	Senna				Berger	Senna			Senna	Senna							1991
	Berger	Mansell				Patrese	Mansell			Berger	Senna							1992
	Prost	Senna				Senna	Prost		Senna	Senna	D. Hill							1993
	M.Schumacher	M.Schumacher				D. Hill	M.Schumacher		M.Schumacher	Mansell	M.Schumacher	M.Schumacher						1994
	Alesi	M.Schumacher				M.Schumacher	D. Hill		M.Schumacher	D. Hill	D. Hill	M.Schumacher						1995
	D. Hill	D. Hill				D. Hill	D. Hill		J. Villeneuve	D. Hill	J. Villeneuve							1996
J. Villeneuve	M.Schumacher	J. Villeneuve				M.Schumacher	Frentzen		Häkkinen	Coulthard	J. Villeneuve		J. Villeneuve					1997
Häkkinen	M.Schumacher	Häkkinen				Häkkinen	Coulthard			Häkkinen	M.Schumacher		Häkkinen					1998
Irvine	Häkkinen	Häkkinen				Häkkinen	M.Schumacher		Herbert	Irvine	Häkkinen			Irvine				1999
Häkkinen	M.Schumacher	M.Schumacher				M.Schumacher	M.Schumacher		M.Schumacher	M.Schumacher	Häkkinen			M.Schumacher				2000
Coulthard	R.Schumacher	Coulthard				M.Schumacher	R.Schumacher		M.Schumacher	M.Schumacher	M.Schumacher			M.Schumacher				2001
M.Schumacher	M.Schumacher	M.Schumacher				M.Schumacher	M.Schumacher		Barrichello	M.Schumacher	Barrichello			R.Schumacher				2002
M.Schumacher	M.Schumacher	Fisichella				Barrichello	M.Schumacher		R.Schumacher	Coulthard	Alonso			Räikkönen				2003
	M.Schumacher	Montoya				M.Schumacher	M.Schumacher		M.Schumacher	M.Schumacher	M.Schumacher			M.Schumacher	M.Schumacher	Barrichello		2004
	Räikkönen	Montoya				Räikkönen	Alonso		Alonso	Fisichella	Räikkönen			Alonso	Alonso	Alonso	Räikkönen	2005
	Alonso	Massa				Alonso	M.Schumacher		M.Schumacher	Alonso	Button			Fisichella	Alonso	M.Schumacher	Massa	2006

Sporting regulations

The FIA will organise the FIA Formula One World Championship (the Championship) which is the property ofthe FIA and comprises two titles of World Champion, one for drivers and one for constructors. It consists of the Formula One Grand Prix races which are included in the Formula One calendar and in respect of which the ASNs and organisers have signed the organisation agreement provided for in the 1998 Concorde Agreement (Events). All the participating parties (FIA, ASNs, organisers, competitors and circuits) undertake to apply as well as observe the rules governing the Championship and must hold FIA Super Licences which are issued to drivers, competitors, officials, organisers and circuits.

REGULATIONS

1. The final text of these Sporting Regulations shall be the English version which will be used should any dispute arise as to their interpretation. Headings in this document are for ease of reference only and do not form part of these Sporting Regulations.

2. These Sporting Regulations were first published on 30 October 2005 and came into force on 1 January 2006. They were subsequently amended on 8 March 2006 with the unanimous agreement of all competing teams and replace all previous FIA Formula One World Championship Sporting Regulations.

GENERAL UNDERTAKING

3. All drivers, competitors and officials participating in the Championship undertake, on behalf of themselves, their employees and agents, to observe all the provisions as supplemented or amended of the International Sporting Code (the Code), the Formula One Technical Regulations (the Technical Regulations) and the present Sporting Regulations together with all the provisions of the 1998 Concorde Agreement (the Agreement) of which they have had due notice.

4. The Championship is governed by the Agreement and its schedules.

5.Any special national regulations must be submitted to the FIA with the original application for inclusion of an Event on the international calendar. Only with the approval of the FIA can such special regulations come into force for an Event. The FIA will ensure that all applicant competitors are informed of such special regulations before entries close under Article 41.

GENERAL CONDITIONS

6. It is the competitor's responsibility to ensure that all persons concerned by his entry observe all the requirements of the Agreement, the Code, the Technical Regulations and the Sporting Regulations. If a competitor is unable to be present in person at the Event he must nominate his representative in writing.
The person having charge of an entered car during any part of an Event is responsible jointly and severally with the competitor for ensuring that the requirements are observed.

7. Competitors must ensure that their cars comply with the conditions of eligibility and safety throughout practice and the race.

8. TThe presentation of a car for scrutineering will be deemed an implicit statement of conformity.

9. All persons concerned in any way with an entered car or present in any other capacity whatsoever in the paddock, pit lane, or track must wear an appropriate pass at all times.

LICENCES

10. All drivers, competitors and officials participating in the Championship must hold a FIA Super Licence. Applications for Super Licences must be made to the FIA through the applicant's ASN. The driver's name will remain on the list for Super Licences for one year.

CHAMPIONSHIP EVENTS

11. Events are reserved for Formula One cars as defined in the Technical Regulations.

12. Each Event will have the status of an international restricted competition.

13. With the exception of Monaco, the distance of all races, from the start signal referred to in Article 139 to the chequered flag, shall be equal to the least number of complete laps which exceed a distance of 305 km. However, should two hours elapse before the scheduled race distance is completed, the leader will be shown the chequered flag when he crosses the control line (the Line) at the end of the lap during which the two hour period ended. However, should the race be suspended (see Article 150) the length of the suspension will be added to this period.
The Line is a single line which crosses both the track and the pit lane.

14. The maximum number of Events in the Championship is 17, the minimum is 8.

15. The final list of Events is published by the FIA before 1st January each year.

16. An Event which is cancelled with less than three months written notice to the FIA will not be considered for inclusion in the following year's Championship unless the FIA judges the cancellation to have been due to force majeure.

17. An Event may be cancelled if fewer than 12 cars are available for it.

WORLD CHAMPIONSHIP

18. The Formula One World Championship driver's title will be awarded to the driver who has scored the highest number of points, taking into consideration all the results obtained during the Events which have actually taken place.

19. The title of Formula One World Champion Constructor will be awarded to the make which has scored the highest number of points, results from both cars being taken into account.

20. The constructor of an engine or rolling chassis is the person (including any corporate or unincorporated body) which owns the intellectual property rights to such engine or chassis. The make of an engine or chassis is the name attributed to it by its constructor. If the make of the chassis is not the same as that of the engine, the title will be awarded to the former which shall always precede the latter in the name of the car.

21. Points for both titles will be awarded at each Event according to the following scale: 1st: 10 points,
2nd: 8 points, 3rd: 6 points, 4th: 5 points, 5th: 4 points, 6th: 3 points, 7th: 2 points, 8th: 1 point

22. If a race is suspended under Article 150, and cannot be resumed, no points will be awarded if the leader has completed less than two laps, half points will be awarded if the leader has completed more than two laps but less than 75% of the original race distance and full points will be awarded if the leader has completed more than 75% of the original race distance.

23. The drivers finishing first, second and third in the Championship must be present at the annual FIA Prize Giving ceremony.

DEAD HEAT

24. Prizes and points awarded for all the positions of competitors who tie, will be added together and shared equally.

25. If two or more constructors or drivers finish the season with the same number of points, the higher place in the Championship (in either case) shall be awarded to:
a) the holder of the greatest number of first places,
b) if the number of first places is the same, the holder of the greatest number of second places,
c) if the number of second places is the same, the holder of the greatest number of third places and so on until a winner emerges.
d) if this procedure fails to produce a result, the FIA will nominate the winner according to such criteria as it thinks fit.

COMPETITORS APPLICATIONS

41. Applications to compete in the Championship may be submitted to the FIA at any time between 1 March two years prior to the Championship in which the applicant wishes to compete and 15 November immediately preceding such Championship, on an entry form as set out in Appendix 2 hereto accompanied by the entry fee provided for in the Agreement, together with the deposit provided for in Article 44 where applicable. Applications from Teams not already competing in the Championship will only be considered where a place is available, taking into account all the Teams who are entitled to compete under the Agreement. Entry forms will be made available by FIA who will notify the applicant of the result of the application within thirty days of its receipt. Successful applicants are automatically entered in all Events of the Championship and will be the only competitors at Events.

42. Applications shall include:
a) confirmation that the applicant has read and understood the Agreement (including its schedules), the Code, the Technical Regulations and the Sporting Regulations and agrees, on its own behalf and on behalf of everyone associated with its participation in the Championship, to observe them,
b) the name of the team (which must include the name of the chassis),
c) the make of the competing car,
d) the make of the engine,
e) the names of the drivers. A driver may be nominated subsequent to the application upon payment of a fee fixed by the FIA,
f) an undertaking by the applicant to participate in every Event with the number of cars and drivers entered.
g) an undertaking that the car does not make use of any component, system, software or device which has been (or might reasonably be suspected to have been) designed, supplied or constructed by or with the help of anyone who has been involved on behalf of the FIA with checking Formula One electronic systems during the 24 months immediately preceding the application.

43. A competitor may change the make and/or type of engine at any time during the Championship. All points scored with an engine of different make to that which was first entered in the Championship will count (and will be aggregated) for the assessment of Benefits, however such points will not count towards (nor be aggregated for) the FIA Formula One Constructors Championship.

44. With the exception of those whose cars have scored points in the Championship of the previous year, applicants must supply information about the size of their company, their financial position and their ability to meet their prescribed obligations. Any applicant which did not take part in the Championship for the previous year must also deposit US$48,000,000 (forty-eight million United States dollars) with the FIA when submitting its application. This sum will be returned to it forthwith if its application is refused or in twelve equal monthly instalments (including interest) commencing immediately after the first Event in which it competes, provided it has met and continues to meet all the requirements of the Agreement and its schedules. If the applicant fails to appear for the Championship for which it has entered, its deposit will be forfeit save only that the applicant may delay its participation by one year, in which case US$12,000,000 (twelve million United States dollars) will be forfeit and the balance repaid as set out above.

45. All applications will be studied by the FIA which will publish the list of cars and drivers accepted together with their race numbers on 1 December (or the following Monday if 1 December falls on a week-end), having first notified unsuccessful applicants as set out in Article 41.

46. No more than 24 cars will be admitted to the Championship, two being entered by each competitor.

47. If in the opinion of the Formula One Commission a competitor fails to operate his team in a manner compatible with the standards of the Championship or in any way brings the Championship into disrepute, the FIA may exclude such competitor from the Championship forthwith.

PASSES

48. No pass may be issued except in accordance with the Agreement. A pass may be used only by the person and for the purpose for which it was issued.

INSTRUCTIONS AND COMMUNICATIONS TO COMPETITORS

49. In exceptional circumstances, the stewards may give instructions to competitors by means of special circulars in accordance with the Code. These circulars will be distributed to all competitors who must acknowledge receipt.

50. All classifications and results of practice and the race, as well as all decisions issued by the officials, will be posted on the official notice board.

51. Any decision or communication concerning a particular competitor must be given to him within twenty five minutes of such decision and receipt must be acknowledged.

INCIDENTS

52. Incident means any occurrence or series of occurrences involving one or more drivers, or any action by any driver, which is reported to the stewards by the race director (or noted by the stewards and referred to the race director for investigation) which:
- necessitated the stopping of a race under Article 150;
- constituted a breach of these Sporting Regulations or the Code;
- caused a false start by one or more cars;
- caused a collision;
- forced a driver off the track;
- illegitimately prevented a legitimate overtaking manoeuvre by a driver;
- illegitimately impeded another driver during overtaking.

Unless it was completely clear that a driver was in breach of any of the above, any incidents involving more than one car will normally be investigated after the race.

53. a) It shall be at the discretion of the stewards to decide, upon a report or a request by the race director, if a driver or drivers involved in an incident shall be penalised.
b) If an incident is under investigation by the stewards a message informing all teams which driver or drivers are involved will be displayed on the timing monitors.
Provided that such a message is displayed no later than five minutes after the race has finished the driver or drivers concerned may not leave the circuit without the consent of the stewards.

54. The stewards may impose any one of three penalties on any driver involved in an Incident:
a) A drive-through penalty. The driver must enter the pit lane and re-join the race without stopping;
b) A ten second time penalty. The driver must enter the pit lane, stop at his pit for at least ten seconds and then re-join the race.
c) a drop of ten grid positions at the driver's next Event.
However, should either of the penalties under a) and b) above be imposed during the last five laps, or after the end of a race, Article 55b) below will not apply and 25 seconds will be added to the elapsed race time of the driver concerned.

55. Should the stewards decide to impose either of the penalties under Article 54a) or b), the following procedure will be followed:
a) TThe stewards will give written notification of the penalty which has been imposed to an official of the team concerned and will ensure that this information is also displayed on the timing monitors.
b) From the time the stewards' decision is notified on the timing monitors the relevant driver may cover no more than three complete laps before entering the pit lane and, in the case of a penalty under Article 54b), proceeding to his garage where he shall remain for the period of the time penalty.
However, unless the driver was already in the pit entry for the purpose of serving his penalty, he may not carry out the penalty after the Safety Car has been deployed. Any laps carried out behind the Safety Car will be added to the three lap maximum.
Whilst a car is stationary in the pit lane as a result of incurring a time penalty it may not be worked on. However, if the engine stops it may be started after the time penalty period has elapsed.
c) When the time penalty period has elapsed the driver may rejoin the race.
d) Any breach or failure to comply with Articles 55b) or 55c) may result in the car being excluded.

PROTESTS

56. Protests shall be made in accordance with the Code and accompanied by a fee of 2000 US Dollars.

SANCTIONS

57. The stewards may inflict the penalties specifically set out in these Sporting Regulations in addition to or instead of any other penalties available to them under the Code.

CHANGES OF DRIVER

58. a) During a season, each team will be permitted to use four drivers (excluding any third driver taking part in either of the free practice sessions on the first day of practice). Changes may be made at any time before the start of the qualifying practice session provided any change proposed after 16.00 on the day of scrutineering receives the consent of the stewards.
Additional changes for reasons of force majeure will be considered separately.
Any new driver may score points in the Championship.
b) In addition to the above all teams, other than those who finished in the top four positions of the previous year's World Chmapionship for Constructors, will be permitted to run a third driver during both free sessions on the first day of practice provided:
- he is not one of the team's nominated drivers for the Event in question;
- he is in possession of a Super Licence;

If one of the team's nominated drivers is unable to drive at some stage after the end of initial scrutineering, and the stewards consent to a change of driver, the third driver may take part in the remainder of the Event. Under such circumstances the driver concerned must use the engine and tyres which were allocated to the original driver (see Articles 75 and 87).

DRIVING

59. The driver must drive the car alone and unaided.

CAR LIVERY

60. The provisions of the Code relating to national colours shall not apply to the Championship.
Both cars entered by a competitor must be presented in substantially the same livery at each Event, any change to this livery during a Championship season may only be made with the agreement of the Formula One Commission. These requirements do not apply to any car being run under Article 58(b).
In order that the cars of each team may be easily distinguished from one another whilst they are on the track, the on board camera located above the principle roll structure of the first car must be predominantly fluorescent red, the same camera on the second car must remain as supplied to the team and any third car fluorescent yellow.

61. Each car will carry the race number of its driver (or his replacement) as published by the FIA at the beginning of the season. This number must be clearly visible from the front of the car.

62. The name or the emblem of the make of the car must appear on the front of the nose of the car and in either case be at least 25mm in its largest dimension. The name of the driver must also appear on the bodywork, on the outside of the cockpit, or on the driver's helmet and be clearly legible.

TESTING

63. a) No testing is permitted at sites which are not currently approved for use by Formula 1 cars. In order to ensure that venue licence conditions are respected at all times during testing, Competitors are required to inform the FIA of their test schedule in order that an observer may be appointed if deemed necessary.
b) During all Formula One testing :
- red flag procedures must be respected ;
- no other type of vehicle is permitted on the track ;
- every reasonable effort should be made to ensure that the recommendations concerning emergency services detailed in Article 16 of Appendix H to the Code are followed.

PIT LANE

64. a) For the avoidance of doubt and for description purposes, the pit lane shall be divided into two lanes. The lane closest to the pit wall is designated the "fast lane", and the lane closest to the garages is designated the "inner lane". Other than when cars are at the end of the pit lane under Articles 136, the inner lane is the only area where any work can be carried out on a car.
b) The FIA will designate an area in the pit lane where each team may work and one place where pit stops may be carried out.
c) Except during the five minutes preceding Q3, unless a car is pushed from the grid at any time during the start procedure, cars may only be driven from the team's designated garage area to the end of the pit lane.
d) Any driver intending to start the race from the pit lane may not drive his car from his team's designated garage area until the 15 minute signal has been given and must stop in a line in the fast lane. Under these circumstances working in the fast lane will be permitted but any such work is restricted to :
- starting the engine and any directly associated preparation ;
- the fitting or removal of cooling and heating devices ;
- changing wheels.

When cars are permitted to leave the pit lane they must do so in the order they arrived at the end of the pit lane unless another car is unduly delayed. At all times drivers must follow the directions of the marshals.
e) Other than drying, sweeping or any tyre rubber left when cars leave their pit stop position, Competitors may not attempt to enhance the grip of the surface in the pit lane unless a problem has been clearly identified and a solution agreed by the FIA safety delegate.
f) Competitors must not paint lines on any part of the pit lane.
g) Other than under c) above no equipment may be left in the fast lane.
h) Team personnel are only allowed in the pit lane immediately before they are required to work on a car and must withdraw as soon as the work is complete.

SCRUTINEERING

65. Between 10.00 and 16.00 three days before the race (four days in Monaco) initial scrutineering of all cars will take place in the garage assigned to each team.

66. Unless a waiver is granted by the stewards, competitors who do not keep to these time limits will not be allowed to take part in the Event.

67. No car may take part in the Event until it has been passed by the scrutineers.

68. The scrutineers may:
a) check the eligibility of a car or of a competitor at any time during an Event,
b) require a car to be dismantled by the competitor to make sure that the conditions of eligibility or conformity are fully satisfied,
c) require a competitor to pay the reasonable expenses which exercise of the powers mentioned in this Article may entail,
d) require a competitor to supply them with such parts or samples as they may deem necessary.

69. Any car which, after being passed by the scrutineers, is dismantled or modified in a way which might affect its safety or call into question its eligibility, or which is involved in an accident with similar consequences, must be re-presented for scrutineering approval.

70. The race director or the clerk of the course may require that any car involved in an accident be stopped and checked.

71. Checks and scrutineering shall be carried out by duly appointed officials who shall also be responsible for the operation of the parc fermé and who alone are authorised to give instructions to the competitors.

72. The stewards will publish the findings of the scrutineers each time cars are checked during the Event. These results will not include any specific figure except when a car is found to be in breach of the Technical Regulations.

SUPPLY OF TYRES IN THE CHAMPIONSHIP AND TYRE LIMITATION DURING THE EVENT

73. Supply of tyres:
a) Any tyre company wishing to supply tyres to Formula One teams must notify the FIA of its intention to do so no later than 1 January preceding the year during which such tyres will be supplied.
Any tyre company wishing to cease the supply of tyres to Formula One Teams must notify the FIA of its intention to do so no later than 1 January of the year preceding that in which such tyres were to be supplied.
b) No tyre may be used in the Championship unless the company supplying such tyre accepts and adheres to the following conditions :
- one tyre supplier present in the Championship: this company must equip 100% of the entered teams on ordinary commercial terms;
- two tyre suppliers present: each of them must, if called upon to do so, be prepared to equip up to 60% of the entered teams on ordinary commercial terms;
- three or more tyre suppliers present: each of them must, if called upon to do so, be prepared to equip up to 40% of the entered teams on ordinary commercial terms;
- each tyre supplier must undertake to provide no more than two specifications of dry-weather tyre to each team at each Event, each of which must be of one homogenous compound. Any modification or treatment, other than heating, carried out to a tyre or tyres will be considered a change of specification ;
- each tyre supplier must undertake to provide no more than two specifications of dry-weather tyre to each team at each Event, each of which must be of one homogenous compound. Any modification or treatment, other than heating, carried out to a tyre or tyres will be considered a change of specification ;
- each tyre supplier must undertake to provide no more than one specification of wet-weather tyre at each Event which must be of one homogenous compound ;
- each tyre supplier must undertake to provide no more than one specification of extreme-weather tyre at each Event which must be of one homogenous compound ;
- if, in the interests of maintaining current levels of circuit safety, the FIA deems it necessary to reduce tyre grip, it shall introduce such rules as the tyre suppliers may advise or, in the absence of advice which achieves the FIA's objectives, specify the maximum permissible contact areas for front and rear tyres.

74. Type of tyres :
a) All dry-weather tyres must incorporate circumferential grooves square to the wheel axis and around the entire circumference of the contact surface of each tyre.
b) Each front dry-weather tyre, when new, must incorporate 4 grooves which are :
- arranged symmetrically about the centre of the tyre tread ;
- at least 14mm wide at the contact surface and which taper uniformly to a minimum of 10mm at the lower surface;
- at least 2.5mm deep across the whole lower surface ;
- 50mm (+/- 1.0mm) between centres.

Furthermore, the tread width of the front tyres must not exceed 270mm.
c) Each rear dry-weather tyre, when new, must incorporate 4 grooves which are:
- arranged symmetrically about the centre of the tyre tread ;
- at least 14mm wide at the contact surface and which taper uniformly to a minimum of 10mm at the lower surface ;
- at least 2.5mm deep across the whole lower surface ;
- 50mm (+/- 1.0mm) between centres.

The measurements referred to in b) and c) above will be taken when the tyre is fitted to a wheel and inflated to 1.4 bar.
d) A wet-weather tyre is one which has been designed for use on a wet or damp track.
All wet-weather tyres must, when new, have a contact area which does not exceed 280cm2 when fitted to the front of the car and 440cm2 when fitted to the rear. Contact areas will be measured over any square section of the tyre which is normal to and symmetrical about the tyre centre line and which measures 200mm x 200mm when fitted to the front of the car and 250mm x 250mm when fitted to the rear. For the purposes of establishing conformity, void areas which are less than 2.5mm in depth will be deemed to be contact areas.
Prior to use at an Event, each tyre manufacturer must provide the technical delegate with a full scale drawing of each type of wet-weather tyre intended for use.
e)An extreme-weather tyre is one which has been designed for use on a wet track.
All extreme-weather tyres must, when new, have a contact area which does not exceed 240cm2 when fitted to the front of the car and 375cm2 when fitted to the rear. Contact areas will be measured over any square section of the tyre which is normal to and symmetrical about the tyre centre line and which measures 200mm x 200mm when fitted to the front of the car and 250mm x 250mm when fitted to the rear. For the purposes of establishing conformity, void areas which are less than 5.0mm in depth will be deemed to be contact areas.
Prior to use at an Event, each tyre manufacturer must provide the technical delegate with a full scale drawing of each type of extreme-weather tyre intended for use.
f) Tyre specifications will be determined by the FIA no later than 1 September of the previous season. Once determined in this way, the specification of the tyres will not be changed during the Championship season without the agreement of the Formula One Commission.

75. Quantity of tyres:
a) During the Event no driver may use more than seven sets of dry-weather tyres, four sets of wetweather tyres and three sets of extreme-weather tyres. A set of tyres will be deemed to comprise two front and two rear tyres all of which must be of the same specification.
If a driver change is made during an Event the tyres allocated to the original driver must be used by the new driver. If the new driver is a third driver entered under Article 58(b), any tyres used on the first day of practice will not count towards his total number of sets.

76. Control of tyres :
a) The outer sidewall of all tyres which are to be used at an Event must be marked with a unique identification.
b) Other than in cases of force majeure (accepted as such by the stewards of the meeting), all tyres intended for use at an Event must be presented to the FIA technical delegate for allocation prior to the end of initial scrutineering.
c) At any time during an Event, and at his absolute discretion, the FIA technical delegate may select alternative dry-weather tyres to be used by any team or driver from among the relevant stock of tyres which such team's designated supplier has present at the Event.
d) A competitor wishing to replace one unused tyre by another identical unused one must present both tyres to the FIA technical delegate.
e) The use of tyres without appropriate identification may result in deletion of the relevant driver's qualifying time or exclusion from the race.
f) The only permitted type of tyre heating devices are blankets which use resistive heating elements.

77. Use of tyres :
a) No driver may use more than one specification of dry-weather tyre after the start of the qualifying practice session.
b) Prior to the start of the qualifying practice session wet and extreme-weather tyres may only be used after the track has been declared wet by the race director, following which extreme, wet or dryweather tyres may be used for the remainder of the session.

78. Wear of tyres :
The Championship will be contested on grooved tyres. The FIA reserve the right to introduce at any time a method of measuring remaining groove depth if performance appears to be enhanced by high wear or by the use of tyres which are worn so that the grooves are no longer visible.

WEIGHING

79. (a) During the qualifying practice session cars will be weighed as follows:
1) the FIA will install weighing equipment in the first pit garage (the FIA garage) which will be used for the weighing procedure;
2) all cars which complete a flying lap will undergo the weighing procedure ;
3) the driver will proceed directly to the FIA garage and stop his engine ;
4) the car will then be weighed with driver (and without driver if necessary) and the result given to the driver in writing ;
5) if the car is unable to reach the FIA garage under its own power it will be placed under the exclusive control of the marshals who will take the car to be weighed;
6) a car or driver may not leave the FIA garage without the consent of the FIA technical delegate;
7) if a car stops on the circuit and the driver leaves the car, he must go to the FIA garage immediately on his return to the pit lane in order for his weight to be established.
b) After the race every classifed car will be weighed. If a driver wishes to leave his car before it is weighed he must ask the technical delegate to weigh him in order that this weight may be added to that of the car.
c) The relevant car may be excluded should its weight be less than that specified in Article 4.1 of the Technical Regulations when weighed under a) or b) above, save where the deficiency in weight results from the accidental loss of a component of the car.
d) No substance may be added to, placed on, or removed from a car after it has been selected for weighing or has finished the race or during the weighing procedure. (Except by a scrutineer when acting in his official capacity).
e) No oneother than scrutineers and officials may enter or remain in the FIA garage without the the specific permission of the FIA technical delegate.

80. Any breach of these provisions for the weighing of cars may result in the delegation of the relevant driver's qualifying time or exclusion from the race.

GENERAL CAR REQUIREMENTS

81. Electromagnetic radiation between 2.0 and 2.7GHz is forbidden save with the written consent of the FIA.

82. Accident data recording :
a) Each car must be fitted with an FIA accident data recorder during each Event and during all tests which are attended by more than one team. Teams must use their best endeavours to ensure that the recorder is in working order at all times. The only purpose of these units is to monitor, record or control one or more of the following :
- data relevant to an accident or incident ;
- a deceleration warning light on board the car ;
- a lap trigger ;
- the driver input signal used to initiate the propulsion of the car at the start of a race.

b) At any time following an accident or incident competitors must make the data recorder available and accessible to the FIA.
A representative of the team concerned may be present when data relevant to an accident or incident is being uploaded from the recorder. A copy of the data will be made available to the team.
c) Any conclusions as to the cause of an accident, or any data relevant to an accident, may only be published in the form of a report which has been agreed between the team concerned and the FIA.

83. During the entire Event, no screen, cover or other obstruction which in any way obscures any part of a car will be allowed at any time in the paddock, garages, pit lane or grid, unless it is clear any such covers are needed solely for mechanical reasons, which could, for example, include protecting against fire.
In addition to the above the following are specifically not permitted :
- engine, gearbox or radiator covers whilst engines are being changed or moved around the garage ;
- covers over spare wings when they are on a stand in the pit lane not being used ;
- parts such as (but not limited to) spare floors, fuel rigs or tool trolleys may not be used as an obstruction.

The following are permitted :
- covers which are placed over damaged cars or components ;
- a transparent tool tray, no more than 50mm deep, placed on top of the rear wing ;
- warming or heat retaining covers for the engine and gearbox on the grid ;
- a rear wing cover designed specifically to protect a mechanic starting the car from fire ;
- tyre heating blankets ;
- covers over the tyre manufacturer's code numbers (not the FIA bar code numbers) ;
- a cover over the car in the parc ferme overnight ;
- a cover over the car in the pit lane or grid if it is raining.

SPARE CARS AND ENGINES

84. Subject to the requirements of Article 87, a competitor may use several cars for practice and the race provided that :
a) he has no more than three cars available for use at any one time ;
b) he uses no more than two cars for each practice session (other than when a third driver is used under Article 58). A car will be deemed to have been used once the timing transponder has shown that it has left the pit lane ;
c) they are all of the same make and were entered in the Championship by the same competitor,
d) they have been scrutineered in accordance with these Sporting Regulations,
e)each car carries its driver's race number.

85. Any driver who decides to use another race car or a spare car following the qualifying practice session, must start the race from the pit lane following the procedures detailed in Article 136. Under these circumstances no restrictions on fuel load will be applied.

86. No change of car is permitted after the start of the race.
A change of car will be deemed to have taken place once a driver is seated in his new car and such change may only take place in the team's designated garage area.

87. a) Each driver may use no more than one engine for two consecutive Events in which his team competes. Should a driver use a replacement engine before the end of the qualifying practice session he will drop ten places on the starting grid at that Event each time a further engine is used. Unless the driver fails to finish the race (see below) the engine fitted to the car at the end of the Event must remain in it until the end of the next. Any driver who failed to finish the race at the first of the two Events for reasons beyond the control of the team or driver, may start the second with a different engine without a penalty being incurred.
b) If a driver is replaced after the first of a two Event period, having finished the first Event, the replacement driver must use the engine which was used for the first Event.
c) Should a driver use a replacement engine after the qualifying practice session at either of the two Events, he will be required to start the relevant race from the back of the starting grid in accordance with Article 130.
d) After consultation with the relevant engine supplier the FIA will attach seals to each engine in order to ensure that no significant moving parts can be rebuilt or replaced.
Following the first of the two Events, and within two hours of the end of the post race parc fermé, further seals will be applied in order to ensure that the engine cannot be run until the second Event. These seals will be removed at 09.00 on the day of initial scrutineering at the second Event.
e) Other than the straightforward replacement of one engine unit with another, a change will also be deemed to have taken place if any of the FIA seals are damaged or removed from the original engine after it has been used for the first time.

REFUELLING

88. a) Refuelling is only permitted in the team's designated garage area or the FIA garage.
b) Fuel may not be added to nor removed from any car eligible to take part in Q3 during that period. Fuel used during Q3 may be replaced immediately after the cars are released from parc ferme on the day of the race, this will be carried out in grid order.
c) Other than a fuel breather and an external fuel pressurising device for starting the engine (in which case only fuel on board the car may be used for running the engine), no connection may be made to the fuel system of any car eligible to take part in Q3 during that period.
d) Other than a fuel breather and an external fuel pressurising device for starting the engine (in which case only fuel on board the car may be used for running the engine), or when race fuel is being added, no connection may be made to the fuel system of any car between the end of qualifying practice and the start of the race.
e) If a race is suspended refuelling is forbidden unless a car is already in the pit entry or pit lane when the signal to stop is given.

89. The driver may remain in his car throughout refuelling but, unless an FIA approved race refuelling system is used, the engine must be stopped.
Race refuelling systems may only be used in the pit lane but may not be used during, or immediately after, any free practice session. Whilst being used during the qualifying practice session or the race all team personnel working on the car must wear clothing which will protect all parts of their body from fire. Each competitor must ensure that an assistant equipped with a suitable fire extinguisher of adequate capacity is beside the car throughout all refuelling operations.

GENERAL SAFETY

90. Official instructions will be given to drivers by means of the signals laid out in the Code. Competitors must not use flags similar to these.

91. Drivers are strictly forbidden to drive their car in the opposite direction to the race unless this is absolutely necessary in order to move the car from a dangerous position.

92. Any driver intending to leave the track should signal his intention to do so in good time making sure that he can do this without danger.

93. a) During practice and the race, drivers may use only the track and must at all times observe the provisions of the Code relating to driving behaviour on circuits.
b) Other than by driving on the track, Competitors are not permitted to attempt to alter the grip of any part of the track surface.

94. A driver who abandons a car must leave it in neutral or with the clutch disengaged and with the steering wheel in place.

95. The organiser must make at least two fire extinguishers of 5kg capacity available to each competitor and ensure that they work properly.

96. Save as specifically authorised by the Code or these Sporting Regulations, no one except the driver may touch a stopped car unless it is in the paddock, the team's designated garage area, the pit lane or on the starting grid.

97. At no time may a car be reversed in the pit lane under its own power.

98. During the period commencing 15 minutes prior to and ending 5 minutes after every practice session and the period between the commencement of the formation lap which immediately precedes the race and the time when the last car enters the parc fermé, no one is allowed on the track, the pit entry or the pit exit with the exception of :
a) marshals or other authorised personnel in the execution of their duty ;
b) drivers when driving or on foot, having first received permission to do so from a marshal ;
c) team personnel when either pushing a car or clearing equipment from the grid after all cars able to do so have left the grid on the formation lap;

99. During a race, the engine may only be started with the starter except :
a) iin the pit lane or the team's designated garage area where the use of an external starting device is allowed, or ;
b) under Article 142(b).

100. Drivers taking part in practice and the race must always wear the clothes, helmets and head and neck supports specified in the Code.
101. A speed limit of 60km/h will be imposed in the pit lane during all free practice sessions, this will be raised to 100km/h for the remainder of the Event. Under exceptional circumstances the Permanent Bureau of the Formula One Commission may amend these limits.
Except in the race, any driver who exceeds the limit will be fined US$250 for each km/h above the limit (this may be increased in the case of a second offence in the same Championship season).
During the race, the stewards may impose either of the penalties under Article 54a) or b) on any driver who exceeds the limit.
102. If a driver has serious mechanical difficulties during practice or the race he must leave the track as soon as it is safe to do so.
103. The car's rear light must be illuminated at all times when it is running on wet-weather tyres. It shall be at the discretion of the race director to decide if a driver should be stopped because his rear light is not working. Should a car be stopped in this way it may re-join when the fault has been remedied.
104. Only six team members per participating car (all of whom shall have been issued with and wearing special identification) are allowed in the signalling area during practice and the race. People under 16 years of age are not allowed in the pit lane.
105. Animals, except those which may have been expressly authorised by the FIA for use by security services, are forbidden on the track, in the pit lane, in the paddock or in any spectator area.
106. The race director, the clerk of the course or the FIA medical delegate can require a driver to have a medical examination at any time during an Event.

PRACTICE SESSIONS

107. Save where these Sporting Regulations require otherwise, pit lane and track discipline and safety measures will be the same for all practice sessions as for the race.
108. No driver may start in the race without taking part in at least one practice session on the second day of practice.
109. During all practices there will be a green and a red light at the end of the pit lane. Cars may only leave the pit lane when the green light is on. Additionally, a blue flag and/or a flashing blue light will be shown at the pit exit to warn drivers leaving the pits if cars are approaching on the track.
110. Unless written permission has been given by the FIA to do otherwise, the circuit may only be used for purposes other than the Event after the last practice session on each day of practice and on the day of the race no less than one hour before the pit lane is opened to allow cars to cover a reconnaissance lap.
111. The interval between the fourth free practice session and the qualifying practice session may never be less than two hours.
112. In the event of a driving infringement during practice the Stewards may delete the relevant driver's qualifying time. In this case, a team will not be able to appeal against the steward's decision.
113. The clerk of the course may interrupt practice as often and for as long as he thinks necessary to clear the track or to allow the recovery of a car. In the case of free practice only, the clerk of the course with the agreement of the stewards may decline to prolong the practice period after an interruption of this kind.
Should one or more sessions be thus interrupted, no protest can be accepted as to the possible effects of the interruption on the qualification of drivers admitted to start.

FREE PRACTICE

114. Free practice sessions will take place :
a) The day after initial scrutineering from 11.00 to 12.00 and from 14.00 to 15.00.
b) The day before the race from 11.00 to 12.00.

QUALIFYING PRACTICE

115. The qualifying practice session will take place on the day before the race from 14.00 to 15.00.
The session will be run as follows :
a) From 14.00 to 14.15 (Q1) all cars will be permitted on the track and at the end of this period the slowest five cars will be prohibited from taking any further part in the session.
Lap times achieved by the fifteen remaining cars will then be deleted.
b) From 14.22 to 14.37 (Q2) the fifteen remaining cars will be permitted on the track and at the end of this period the slowest five cars will be prohibited from taking any further part in the session.
Lap times achieved by the ten remaining cars will then be deleted.
c) From 14.45 to 15.00 (Q3) the ten remaining cars will be permitted on the track.
The above procedure is based upon a Championship entry of 20 cars. If 22 are entered six cars will be excluded after Q1 and Q2 and, if 24 are entered, six cars will be excluded after Q1 and Q2 leaving 12 cars eligible for Q3.
116. a) Any driver whose car stops on the circuit during the qualifying session will not be permitted to take any further part in the session. Any car which stops on the circuit during the qualifying session, and which is returned to the pits before the end of the session, will be held in parc ferme until the end of the session.
b) If, in the opinion of the stewards, a driver deliberately stops on the circuit or impedes another driver in any way during the qualifying practice session his times will be cancelled.

POST QUALIFYING PARC FERMÉ

117. Each car will be deemed to be in parc fermé from the time at which it leaves the pit lane for the first time during qualifying practice until the green lights are illuminated at the start of the formation lap which immediately precedes the start of the race.
Between these times, other than when cars are returned to the parc fermé overnight, the following work may be carried out :
- engines may be started ;
- subject to the requirements of Article 88 fuel may be added or removed and a fuel breather fitted ;
- wheels and tyres may be removed, changed or rebalanced and tyre pressures checked ;
- spark plugs may be removed in order to carry out an internal engine inspection and cylinder compression checks ;
- heating or cooling devices may be fitted ;
- a jump battery may be connected and on board electrical units may be freely accessed via a physical connection to the car ;
- the main electrical battery and radio batteries may be changed ;
- the brake system may be bled ;
- engine oil may be drained ;
- compressed gases may be drained or added ;
- fluids used for replenishment must conform to the same specification as the original fluid. Fluids with a specific gravity less than 1.1 may be drained and / or replenished, however, no replenishment may take place less than one hour and 30 minutes before the start of the formation lap unless specific approval has been given by the FIA. In order to ensure that fluids are not being used as ballast the FIA reserves the right to weigh cars which took part in Q3 at random during the one hour period commencing one hour and 30 minutes before the start of the formation lap. When a car is weighed in this way, and taking into account any fuel added under Article 88(b), its weight must be within 3kg of its weight at the completion of its final qualifying run, if not, fluids other than fuel may be replenished or drained under FIA supervision ;
- the aerodynamic set up of the front wing may be adjusted using the existing parts. No parts may be added, removed or replaced ;
- if the FIA technical delegate is satisfied that changes in climatic conditions necessitate alterations to the specification of a car changes may be made to the brake cooling and radiator ducts. These changes may be made at any time after the message "CHANGE IN CLIMATIC CONDITIONS" is shown on the timing monitors, from this point the choice of brake cooling and radiator ducts is free.
- bodywork (excluding radiators) may be removed and / or cleaned ;
- cosmetic changes may be made to the bodywork and tape may be added ;
- any part of the car may be cleaned ;
- on board cameras, timing transponders and any associated equipment may be removed, refitted or checked ;
- any work required by the FIA technical delegate ;
- changes to improve the drivers comfort. In this context anything other than addition or removal of padding (or similar material) and adjustment of mirrors, seat belts and pedals may only be carried out with the specific permission of the FIA technical delegate ;
- repair of genuine accident damage ;
- any parts which are removed from the car in order to carry out any work specifically permitted above,
or any parts removed to carry out essential safety checks, must remain close to it and, at all times, be visible to the scrutineer assigned to the relevant car.
Any work not listed above may only be undertaken with the approval of the FIA technical delegate following a written request from the team concerned. It must be clear that any replacement part a team wishes to fit is similar in mass, inertia and function to the original. Any parts removed will be retained by the FIA.
118. Every car which took part in the qualifying practice session, or was intended for use during the session (in the event of a driver failing to leave the pit lane), will be required in parc fermé. Any car which failed to leave the pit lane during the second part of the session must be taken by the team to the parc fermé immediately. If a car is damaged during the second part of the session the FIA technical delegate may make alternative arrangements according to the level of damage and any other circumstances he deems relevant.
Each car will be deemed to be in parc fermé from the time at which the light at the end of the pit lane turns green for the start of its qualifying run in the second part of the session until the green lights are illuminated at the start of the formation lap which immediately precedes the first start of the race.
Between these times, other than when cars are returned to the parc fermé overnight, the following work may be carried out :
- cooling devices may be fitted ;
- changes to improve the drivers comfort. In this context anything other than addition or removal of padding (or similar material) and adjustment of mirrors and pedals may only be carried out with the specific permission of the FIA technical delegate ;
- a fuel breather may be fitted ;
- bodywork (excluding radiators) may be removed and / or cleaned ;
- cosmetic changes may be made to the bodywork ;
- any part of the car may be cleaned ;
- any parts which are removed from the car in order to carry out any work specifically permitted below must remain close to it and, at all times, be visible to the scrutineer assigned to the relevant car ;
- fluids used for replenishment must conform to the same specification as the original fluid ;
- on board cameras, timing transponders and any associated equipment may be removed, refitted or checked.
117. After weighing during the qualifying practice session all cars will be detained in the parc fermé for further checks. Whilst the cars are being detained there three appropriate members from each team will be permitted in the parc fermé at any one time for the purpose of:
- checking tyre pressures ;
- connecting a jump battery under the supervision of the FIA ;
- downloading data by physical connection to the car under the supervision of the FIA ;
- fitting water heaters ;
- engine oil may be drained ;
- changing tyres before the car is pushed back to the team's garage. These, or any other tyres, may be used when the car is returned to the parc fermé the same evening and back to the team's garage on Sunday morning. The wheels and tyres used for qualifying will be marked and / or sealed by the scrutineers before being released to the team ;
- carrying out any work required by the FIA technical delegate.
Once any such work has been carried out the team personnel must leave the parc fermé immediately.
No other work of any kind will be permitted at this time unless deemed absolutely necessary by the FIA technical delegate.
118. At the end of the qualifying practice at least six cars will be chosen at random to undergo further checks, once informed their car has been selected the team concerned must take the car to the parc fermé immediately.
119. At some time before 18.30 all cars used during the qualifying practice session (or which were intended for use but failed to leave the pit lane) must be taken to the parc fermé, where they will remain secure until the following day. Whilst cars are in the parc fermé they may be covered and fitted with devices to keep them warm, no team personnel will be permitted there unless specifically authorised by the FIA technical delegate.
120. At 08.30 on the day of the race, or at other times if the relevant Event timetable makes this necessary, teams will be permitted to take their cars back to their garages where, again, they will remain under parc fermé conditions until the green lights are illuminated at the start of the formation lap which immediately precedes the first start of the race.
121. If a competitor modifies any part on the car or makes changes to the set up of the suspension whilst the car is being held under parc fermé conditions the relevant driver must start the race from the pit lane and follow the procedures laid out in Article 136.
122. One scrutineer will be allocated to each car for the purpose of ensuring that no unauthorised work is carried out whilst cars are being held under parc fermé conditions.
123. IA list of parts replaced with the specific agreement of the FIA technical delegate whilst cars are being held under parc fermé conditions will be published and distributed to all teams prior to the race.
124. In order that the scrutineers may be completely satisfied that no alterations have been made to the suspension systems or aerodynamic configuration of the car (with the exception of the front wing) whilst in post-qualifying parc fermé, it must be clear from physical inspection that changes cannot be made without the use of tools.

STOPPING THE PRACTICE

125 Should it become necessary to stop the practice because the circuit is blocked by an accident or because weather or other conditions make it dangerous to continue, the clerk of the course will order red flags to be shown at all marshal posts and the abort lights to be shown at the Line.
When the signal is given to stop, all cars shall immediately reduce speed and proceed slowly back to the pit lane, and all cars abandoned on the track will be removed to a safe place.
At the end of each practice session no driver may cross the Line more than once.

PRESS CONFERENCES AND DRIVERS PARADE

126. The FIA press delegate will choose a maximum of five drivers who must attend a press conference in the media centre for a period of one hour at 15.00 on the day before first practice. At Events taking place in North or South America this press conference will take place at 11.00. These drivers' teams will be notified no less than 48 hours before the conference. In addition, a maximum of two team personalities may be chosen by the FIA press delegate to attend this press conference.
On the first day of practice, a minimum of three and a maximum of six drivers and/or team personalities, (other than those who attended the press conference on the previous day and subject to the consent of the team principal) will be chosen by ballot or rota by the FIA press delegate during the Event and must make themselves available to the media for a press conference in the media centre for a period of one hour at 16.00.
No driver may enter into a contract which restricts his right to talk to any representative of the media during an Event. It shall be the duty of each team to ensure that their drivers do not unreasonably refuse to speak to any representative of the media during the Event.
127. Immediately after the qualifying practice session the first three drivers in the session will be required to make themselves available for television interviews in the unilateral room and then attend a press conference in the media centre for a maximum period of 30 minutes.
128. One and a half hours before the race all drivers must attend a drivers parade, Competitors will be given details of the parade by the press delegate.

THE GRID

129. At the end of qualifying practice the times achieved by each driver will be officially published.
130. a) The grid will be drawn up as follows :
I. The last five positions will be occupied by the cars eliminated during Q1, the fastest in 16th position.
II. The next five positions will be occupied by the cars eliminated during Q2, the fastest in 11th position.
III. The top ten positions will be occupied by the cars which took part in Q3, the fastest from the position on the grid which was the pole position in the previous year or, on a new circuit, has been designated as such by the FIA safety delegate.
If two or more drivers set identical times during Q1, Q2 or Q3 priority will be given to the one who set it first.
If more than 20 cars are entered in the Championship appropriate amendments will be made to the above in accordance with Article 115.
b) If more than one driver fails to set a time during Q1, Q2 or Q3 they will be arranged in the following order :
I. any driver who attempted to set a qualifying time by starting a flying lap ;
II. any driver who failed to start a flying lap ;
III. any driver who failed to leave the pits during the period.
c) Any driver who incurs a penalty under Article 87(a), and as a result is placed behind the last car from Q1, will take precedence over any driver who incurs a penalty under Article 87(c). Both of the above will take precedence over any driver whose qualifying times have been deleted for any reason.
In all the above cases if more than one driver falls into a single category they will be arranged on the grid in numerical order.
131. The starting grid will be published four hours before the race. Any competitor whose car(s) is (are) unable to start for any reason whatsoever (or who has good reason to believe that their car(s) will not be ready to start) must inform the stewards accordingly at the earliest opportunity and, in any event, no later than one hour before the start of the race. If one or more cars are withdrawn the grid will be closed up accordingly. The final starting grid will be published one hour before the start of the race.
132. The grid will be in a staggered 1 x 1 formation and the rows on the grid will be separated by 16 metres.

MEETINGS

133. Meetings, chaired by the race director, will take place at 16.00 on the day before first practice and 17.00 on the first day of practice. The first must be attended by all team managers and the second by all drivers.
Should the race director consider another meeting necessary it will take place three hours before the race, Competitors will be informed no later than three hours after the end of the qualifying practice session. All drivers and team managers must attend.

STARTING PROCEDURE

134. 30 minutes before the start of the formation lap the cars will leave the pit lane to cover a reconnaissance lap. At the end of this lap they will stop on the grid in starting order with their engines stopped.
Should they wish to cover more than one reconnaissance lap, this must be done by driving down the pit lane at greatly reduced speed between each of the laps.
135. Any car which has not taken up its position on the grid by the time the five minute signal is shown will not be permitted to do so and must start from the pit lane in accordance with Article 136.
136. 17 minutes before the start of the formation lap, a warning signal will be given indicating that the end of the pit lane will be closed in two minutes.
15 minutes before the start of the formation lap the end of the pit lane will be closed and a second warning signal will be given. Any car which is still in the pit lane can start from the end of the pit lane provided it got there under its own power. If more than one car is affected they must line up in the order in which they reached the end of the pit lane. These cars may then join the race once the whole field has passed the end of the pit lane for the first time after the start.
137. The approach of the start will be announced by signals shown ten minutes, five minutes, three minutes, one minute and fifteen seconds before the start of the formation lap, each of which will be accompanied by an audible warning.
When the ten minute signal is shown, everybody except drivers, officials and team technical staff must leave the grid. When the three minute signal is shown all cars must have their wheels fitted, after this signal wheels may only be removed in the pit lane or on the grid during a race suspension.
Any car which does not have all its wheels fully fitted at the three minute signal must start the race from the back of the grid or the pit lane. Under these circumstances a marshal holding a yellow flag will prevent the car (or cars) from leaving the grid until all cars able to do so have left to start the formation lap.
When the one minute signal is shown, engines should be started and all team personnel must leave the grid by the time the 15 second signal is given taking all equipment with them. If any driver needs assistance after the 15 second signal he must raise his arm and, when the remainder of the cars able to do so have left the grid, marshals will be instructed to push the car into the pit lane. In this case, marshals with yellow flags will stand beside any car (or cars) concerned to warn drivers behind.
When the green lights are illuminated, the cars will begin the formation lap with the pole position driver leading.
When leaving the grid all drivers must proceed at a greatly reduced speed until clear of any team personnel standing beside the track. Marshals will be instructed to push any car (or cars) which remain on the grid into the pit lane by the fastest route immediately after cars able to do so have left the grid. If the driver is able to re-start the car whilst it is being pushed he may rejoin the formation lap.
During the formation lap practice starts are forbidden and the formation must be kept as tight as possible.
Overtaking during the formation lap is only permitted if a car is delayed when leaving its grid position and cars behind cannot avoid passing it without unduly delaying the remainder of the field. In this case, drivers may only overtake to re-establish the original starting order.
Any driver who is delayed leaving the grid may not overtake another moving car if he was stationary after the remainder of the cars had crossed the Line, and must start the race from the back of the grid. If more than one driver is affected, they must form up at the back of the grid in the order they left to complete the formation lap. If the Line is not situated in front of pole position, and for the purposes of this Article as well as 138 and 149(m), it will be deemed to be a white line one metre in front of pole position.
Either of the penalties under Article 54a) or b) will be imposed on any driver who, in the opinion of the Stewards, unnecessarily overtook another car during the formation lap.
138. Any driver who is unable to start the formation lap must raise his arm and, after the remainder of the cars have crossed the Line, of the cars have crossed the Line, the car will be pushed into the pit lane by the fastest route.
139. When the cars come back to the grid at the end of the formation lap, they will stop on their respective grid positions, keeping their engines running.
There will be a standing start, the signal being given by means of lights activated by the permanent starter.
Once all the cars have come to a halt the five second light will appear followed by the four, three, two and one second lights. At any time after the one second light appears, the race will be started by extinguishing all red lights.
140. Unless specifically authorised by the FIA, during the start of a race the pit wall must be kept free of all persons with the exception of officials and fire marshals.
141. Any car which is unable to maintain starting order during the entire formation lap or is moving when the one second light comes on must enter the pit lane and start from the end of the pit lane as specified in Article 136.
This will not apply to any car which is temporarily delayed during the lap and which is able to regain its position, without endangering itself or any other car, before the leading car has taken up its position on the grid.
142. If, after returning to the starting grid at the end of the formation lap a problem arises, the following procedures shall apply :
a) If a car develops a problem that could endanger the start the driver must immediately raise his hands above his head and the marshal responsible for that row must immediately wave a yellow flag. If the race director decides the start should be delayed the green lights will be illuminated two seconds after the abort lights, a board saying "EXTRA FORMATION LAP" will be displayed and all cars able to do so must complete a further formation lap whilst the car which developed the problem is moved into the pit lane.
The team may then attempt to rectify the problem and, if successful, the car may then start from the end of the pit lane.
Should there be more than one car involved their starting order will be determined by the order in which they reached the end of the pit lane.
Every time this happens the race will be shortened by one lap.
b) If any other type of problem arises, and if the race director decides the start should be delayed, the following procedures shall apply :
1) If the race has not been started, the abort lights will be switched on, a board saying "DELAYED START" will be displayed, all engines will be stopped and the new formation lap will start 5 minutes later with the race distance reduced by one lap. The next signal will be the three minute signal.
Every time this happens the race will be shortened by one lap.
2) If the race has been started the marshals alongside the grid will wave their yellow flags to inform the drivers that a car is stationary on the grid.
3) If, after the start, a car is immobilised on the starting grid, it shall be the duty of the marshals to push it into the pit lane by the fastest route. If the driver is able to re-start the car whilst it is being pushed he may rejoin the race.
4) If the driver is unable to start the car whilst it is being pushed his mechanics may attempt to start it in the pit lane. If the car then starts it may rejoin the race. The driver and mechanics must follow the instructions of the track marshals at all times during such a procedure.
143. Should Article 142 apply, the race will nevertheless count for the Championship no matter how often the procedure is repeated, or how much the race is shortened as a result.
144. Either of the penalties under Article 54a) or b) will be imposed for a false start judged using an FIA supplied transponder which must be fitted to the car as specified.
145. Only in the following cases will any variation in the start procedure be allowed:
a) If it starts to rain after the three minute signal but before the race is started and, in the opinion of the race director teams should be given the opportunity to change tyres, the abort lights will be shown on the Line and the starting procedure will begin again at the ten minute point. If necessary the procedure set out in Article 137 will be followed.
b) If the start of the race is imminent and, in the opinion of the race director, the volume of water on the track is such that it cannot be negotiated safely even on wet-weather tyres, the abort lights will be shown on the Line and information concerning the likely delay will be displayed on the timing monitors. Once the start time is known at least ten minutes warning will be given.
c) If the race is started behind the safety car, Article 149(m) will apply.
146. The stewards may use any video or electronic means to assist them in reaching a decision. The stewards may overrule judges of fact. A breach of the provisions of the Code or these Sporting Regulations relating to starting procedure, may result in the exclusion of the car and driver concerned from the Event.

THE RACE

147. Team orders which interfere with a race result are prohibited.
148. During the race, drivers leaving the pit lane may only do so when the light at the end of the pit lane is green and on their own responsibility, a marshal with a blue flag, or a flashing blue light, will also warn the driver if cars are approaching on the track.

SAFETY CAR

149. (a) The FIA safety car will be driven by an experienced circuit driver. It will carry an FIA observer capable of recognising all the competing cars, who is in permanent radio contact with race control.
b) 30 minutes before the race start time the safety car will take up position at the front of the grid and remain there until the five minute signal is given. At this point (except under m) below) it will cover a whole lap of the circuit and enter the pit lane.
c) The safety car may be brought into operation to neutralise a race upon the decision of the clerk of the course.
It will be used only if competitors or officials are in immediate physical danger but the circumstances are not such as to necessitate stopping the race.
d) When the order is given to deploy the safety car, all observer's posts will display waved yellow flags and a board "SC" which shall be maintained until the intervention is over.
e) The safety car will start from the pit lane with its orange lights illuminated and will join the track regardless of where the race leader is.
From this time any car being driven unnecessarily slowly, and which is deemed potentially dangerous to other drivers, will be reported to the stewards. This will apply whether any such car is being driven on the track, the pit entry or the pit lane.
f) All competing cars must then form up in line behind the safety car no more than 5 car lengths apart and overtaking, with the following exceptions, is forbidden until the cars reach the Line after the safety car has returned to the pits. Overtaking will be permitted under the following circumstances :
- if a car is signalled to do so from the safety car ;
- under m) below ;
- any car entering the pits may pass another car or the safety car after it has crossed the first safety car line ;
- when the safety car is returning to the pits it may be overtaken by cars on the track once it has crossed the first safety car line ;
- if any car slows with an obvious problem.
g) When ordered to do so by the clerk of the course the observer in the car will use a green light to signal to any cars between it and the race leader that they should pass. These cars will continue at reduced speed and without overtaking until they reach the line of cars behind the safety car.
h) The safety car shall be used at least until the leader is behind it and all remaining cars are lined up behind him.
Once behind the safety car, the race leader must keep within 5 car lengths of it (except under j) below) and all remaining cars must keep the formation as tight as possible.
i) While the safety car is in operation, competing cars may enter the pit lane, but may only rejoin the track when the green light at the end of the pit lane is on. It will be on at all times except when the safety car and the line of cars following it are about to pass or are passing the pit exit. A car rejoining the track must proceed at reduced speed until it reaches the end of the line of cars behind the safety car.
Under certain circumstances the clerk of the course may ask the safety car to use the pit lane. In these cases, and provided it's orange lights remain illuminated, all cars must follow it into the pit lane without overtaking. Any car entering the pit lane under these circumstances may stop at its designated garage area.
j) When the clerk of the course calls in the safety car, it must extinguish its orange lights, this will be the signal to the drivers that it will be entering the pit lane at the end of that lap.
At this point the first car in line behind the safety car may dictate the pace and, if necessary, fall more than five car lengths behind it.
As the safety car is approaching the pit entry the yellow flags and SC boards at the observer's posts will be withdrawn and waved green flags will be displayed for no more than one lap.
k) Each lap completed while the safety car is deployed will be counted as a race lap.
l) If the race ends whilst the safety car is deployed it will enter the pit lane at the end of the last lap and the cars will take the chequered flag as normal without overtaking.
m) In exceptional circumstances the race may be started behind the safety car. In this case, at any time before the one minute signal its orange lights will be turned on. This is the signal to the drivers that the race will be started behind the safety car. When the green lights are illuminated the safety car will leave the grid with all cars following in grid order no more than 5 car lengths apart. There will be no formation lap and race will start when the green lights are illuminated.
Overtaking, during the first lap only, is permitted if a car is delayed when leaving its grid position and cars behind cannot avoid passing it without unduly delaying the remainder of the field. In this case, drivers may only overtake to re-establish the original starting order.
Any driver who is delayed leaving the grid may not overtake another moving car if he was stationary after the remainder of the cars had crossed the Line, and must form up at the back of the line of cars behind the safety car. If more than one driver is affected, they must form up at the back of the field in the order they left the grid.
Either of the penalties under Article 54a) or b) will be imposed on any driver who, in the opinion of the Stewards, unnecessarily overtook another car during the first lap.

SUSPENDING A RACE

150. Should it become necessary to suspend the race because the circuit is blocked by an accident or because weather or other conditions make it dangerous to continue, the clerk of the course will order red flags to be shown at all marshal posts and the abort lights to be shown at the Line.
When the signal is given overtaking is forbidden, the pit exit will be closed and all cars must proceed slowly to the red flag line where they must stop in staggered formation. If the leading car on the track is not at the front of the line any cars between it and the red flag line will be waved off to complete another lap one minute before the race is resumed.
If any cars are unable to return to the grid as a result of the track being blocked they will be brought back when the track is cleared and will be arranged in the order they occupied before the race was suspended. Any such cars will then be permitted to resume the race.
The Safety Car will then be driven to the front of the line of cars behind the red flag line.
Whilst the race is suspended :
- neither the race nor the timekeeping system will stop ;
- cars may be worked on once they have stopped behind the red flag line or entered the pits but any such work must not impede the resumption of the race ;
- refuelling is forbidden unless a car was already in the pit entry or pit lane when the signal to suspend the race was given ;
- only team members and officials will be permitted on the grid.
Cars may enter the pit lane when the race is suspended but a drive through penalty (see Article 54) will be imposed on any driver who enters the pit lane or whose car is pushed from the grid to the pit lane after the race has been suspended. Any car which was in the pit entry or pit lane when the race was suspended will not incur a penalty.
All cars in the pit lane will be permitted to leave the pits once the race has been resumed but any which were in the pit entry or pit lane when the race was suspended will be released before any others. Subject to the above, any car intending to resume the race from the pit exit may do so in the order they got there under their own power, unless another car was unduly delayed. Under these circumstances working in the fast lane will be permitted but any such work will be restricted to:
- starting the engine and any directly associated preparation ;
- the fitting or removal of cooling and heating devices ;
- changing wheels.
At all times drivers must follow the directions of the marshals.

RESUMING A RACE

151. The delay will be kept as short as possible and as soon as a resumption time is known teams will be informed via the timing monitors, in all cases at least ten minutes warning will be given.
Signals will be shown ten minutes, five minutes, three minutes, one minute and fifteen seconds before the resumption and each of these will be accompanied by an audible warning.
When the three minute signal is shown all cars must have their wheels fitted, after this signal wheels may only be removed in the pit lane or on the grid during a further race suspension. Any car which does not have all its wheels fully fitted at the three minute signal must start the race from the back of the grid or the pit lane. Under these circumstances a marshal holding a yellow flag will prevent the car (or cars) from leaving the grid until all cars able to do so have crossed the red flag line.
When the one minute signal is shown, engines should be started and all team personnel must leave the grid by the time the 15 second signal is given taking all equipment with them. If any driver needs assistance after the 15 second signal he must raise his arm and, when the remainder of the cars able to do so have left the grid, marshals will be instructed to push the car into the pit lane. In this case, marshals with yellow flags will stand beside any car (or cars) concerned to warn drivers behind.
The race will be resumed behind the safety car when the green lights are illuminated. The safety car will enter the pits after one lap unless team personnel are still clearing the grid or a further incident occurs necessitating another intervention.
When the green lights are illuminated the safety car will leave the grid with all cars following, in the order they stopped behind the red flag line, no more than 5 car lengths apart. Soon after the last car in line behind the safety car passes the end of the pit lane the pit exit light will be turned green, any car in the pit lane may then enter the track and join the line of cars behind the safety car.
Overtaking during the lap is permitted only if a car is delayed when leaving the red flag line and cars behind cannot avoid passing it without unduly delaying the remainder of the field. In this case, drivers may only overtake to re-establish the order before the race was suspended.
Any driver who is delayed leaving the red flag line may not overtake another moving car if he was stationary after the remainder of the cars had crossed the Line, and must form up at the back of the line of cars behind the safety car. If more than one driver is affected, they must form up at the back of the field in the order they left the grid.
Either of the penalties under Article 54a) or b) will be imposed on any driver who, in the opinion of the Stewards, unnecessarily overtook another car during the lap.
During this lap Articles 149 j), k) l) and m) will apply.
If the race cannot be resumed the results will be taken at the end of the penultimate lap before the lap
during which the signal to suspend the race was given.

FINISH

152. The end-of-race signal will be given at the Line as soon as the leading car has covered the full race distance in accordance with Article 13.
153. Should for any reason the end-of-race signal be given before the leading car completes the scheduled number of laps, or the prescribed time has been completed, the race will be deemed to have finished when the leading car last crossed the Line before the signal was given.
Should the end-of- race signal be delayed for any reason, the race will be deemed to have finished when it should have finished.
154. After receiving the end-of-race signal all cars must proceed on the circuit directly to the post race parc fermé without stopping, without overtaking (unless clearly necessary), without receiving any object whatsoever and without any assistance (except that of the marshals if necessary).
Any classified car which cannot reach the post race parc fermé under its own power will be placed under the exclusive control of the marshals who will take the car to the parc fermé.

POST RACE PARC FERME

155. Only those officials charged with supervision may enter the post race parc fermé. No intervention of any kind is allowed there unless authorised by such officials.
156. When the parc fermé is in use, parc fermé regulations will apply in the area between the Line and the parc fermé entrance.
157. The parc fermé shall be secured such that no unauthorised persons can gain access to it.

CLASSIFICATION

158. The car placed first will be the one having covered the scheduled distance in the shortest time, or, where appropriate, passed the Line in the lead at the end of two hours (or more if the race is suspended, see Article 13). All cars will be classified taking into account the number of complete laps they have covered, and for those which have completed the same number of laps, the order in which they crossed the Line.
159. Cars having covered less than 90% of the number of laps covered by the winner (rounded down to the nearest whole number of laps), will not be classified.
160. The official classification will be published after the race. It will be the only valid result subject to any amendments which may be made under the Code and these Sporting Regulations.

PODIUM CEREMONY

161. The drivers finishing the race in 1st, 2nd and 3rd positions and a representative of the winning constructor must attend the prize-giving ceremony on the podium and abide by the podium procedure set out in Appendix 3 (except Monaco); and immediately thereafter make themselves available for a period of one hour and 30 minutes for the purpose of television unilateral interviews and the press conference in the media centre.

Meaning of the flags

- White flag: service vehicule on track.
- Blue flag: (immobile): a car is close behind you. (waving): a car is about to overtake you.
- Yellow flag: (immobile): overtaking is prohibited, danger. (waving) immediate danger, slow down.
- Red flag: (by marshals and the Clerk of the race): stopping of the race on the Line.
- Green flag: end of danger, free track.
- Yellow with red stripes flag: danger, slippery surface.
- Black flag: (with car number): stop on the next lap.
- Black with yellow circle flag: your car is in danger.
- Black and white flag: non-sporting behaviour, warning.
- Chequered flag: end of the race or the practice.